THE TRICYCLE:
COLLECTED TRIBUNAL PLAYS 1994-2012

Victoria Brittain, Nicolas Kent
Richard Norton-Taylor, Gillian Slovo

THE TRICYCLE: COLLECTED TRIBUNAL PLAYS 1994-2012

OBERON BOOKS
LONDON

WWW.OBERONBOOKS.COM

This collection first published in 2014 by Oberon Books Ltd
521 Caledonian Road, London N7 9RH
Tel: +44 (0) 20 7607 3637 / Fax: +44 (0) 20 7607 3629
e-mail: info@oberonbooks.com
www.oberonbooks.com

Introduction copyright © Michael Billington, 2014, Verbatim Theatre © Richard Norton-Taylor, Nicolas Kent, Gillian Slovo, David Edgar 2014, *Half the Picture* copyright © Richard Norton-Taylor, 1994, *Nuremberg* copyright © Richard Norton-Taylor, Date, *Srebrenica* copyright © Nicolas Kent, 1996, *The Colour of Justice* copyright © Richard Norton-Taylor, 1999, *Justifying War* copyright © Richard Norton-Taylor, 2003, *Guantanamo* copyright © Gillian Slovo & Victoria Brittain, 2004, *Bloody Sunday* copyright © Richard Norton-Taylor, 2005, *Called to Account* copyright © Richard Norton-Taylor & Nicolas Kent, 2007, *Tactical Questioning* copyright © Richard Norton-Taylor, 2011, *The Riots* copyright © Gillian Slovo, 2011

Half the Picture first published in *Truth is a Difficult Concept: Inside the Scott Inquiry*, 4th Estate/Guardian Books 1995.

Nuremberg reprinted by permission of Nick Hern Books.

Reprinted in 2015

Richard Norton-Taylor, Nicolas Kent, Gillian Slovo and Victoria Brittain are hereby identified as authors of these plays in accordance with section 77 of the Copyright, Designs and Patents Act 1988. The authors has asserted their moral rights.

All rights whatsoever in this play are strictly reserved and application for performance etc. should be made before commencement of rehearsal to Oberon Books. No performance may be given unless a licence has been obtained, and no alterations may be made in the title or the text of the play without the author's prior written consent.

You may not copy, store, distribute, transmit, reproduce or otherwise make available this publication (or any part of it) in any form, or binding or by any means (print, electronic, digital, optical, mechanical, photocopying, recording or otherwise), without the prior written permission of the publisher. Any person who does any unauthorized act in relation to this publication may be liable to criminal prosecution and civil claims for damages.

A catalogue record for this book is available from the British Library.

PB ISBN: 978-1-78319-068-3
E ISBN: 978-1-78319-567-1

Cover design by James Illman

Printed, bound and converted by CPI Group (UK) Ltd, Croydon, CR0 4YY.

Contents

Introduction
Michael Billington 1

Verbatim Theatre (Verbatim) 4

Half the Picture 41
Richard Norton-Taylor

Nuremberg 113
Richard Norton-Taylor

Srebrenica 195
Nicolas Kent

The Colour of Justice 291
Richard Norton-Taylor

Justifying War 417
Richard Norton-Taylor

Guantanamo 511
Gillian Slovo & Victoria Brittain

Bloody Sunday 569
Richard Norton-Taylor

Called to Account 663
Richard Norton-Taylor & Nicolas Kent

Tactical Questioning 771
Richard Norton-Taylor

The Riots 855
Gillian Slovo

Introduction

'We read non-fiction as well as fiction. On the radio we listen as attentively to feature programmes as to plays. On screens of all sizes we watch documentaries. Why, then, should we not have documentary plays?'

That was the question posed by Kenneth Tynan in 1958 in *The Observer* in a review of a play by Robert Ardrey, *Shadow of Heroes*, about the Hungarian uprising of 1956. Since then Tynan's question has been decisively answered. In the 1960s and 70s there was a whole series of documentary dramas loosely grouped under the heading Theatre of Fact. One outstanding example was Peter Weiss's *The Investigation* (1965) which used transcripts from the West German enquiry into war crimes at Auschwitz and which was given a late-night public reading, staged by Peter Brook and David Jones, at the Aldwych in October, 1965. In a similar vein Eric Bentley's *Are You Now Or Have You Ever Been?* (1972) put on stage an edited version of the McCarthyite hearings of the 1950s in which prominent public figures, including Lillian Hellman, Elia Kazan and Jerome Robbins, were asked to name names of suspected communists in the entertainment industry. But, while these were important landmarks, it was a sequence of productions at the Tricycle Theatre, starting with *Half the Picture* in 1993 and climaxing in *The Riots* in 2011, that showed there was a huge public appetite for what we now call Verbatim Theatre. And, before investigating the form, it is worth asking ourselves why this happened.

One obvious answer is that Nicolas Kent, as director of the Tricycle, not only believed that the theatre had a moral duty to address public issues: he also had the terrier-like tenacity to pursue his vision. And it helped that he was able to rely on the services of a journalist like Richard Norton-Taylor who shared his convictions and was prepared to sift through a mass of material from public enquiries to shape a play. Later Gillian Slovo and Victoria Brittain performed a similar function with oral evidence from Guantanamo detainees and Slovo in *The Riots* examined both the events and possible causes of the street riots that shook London in August 2011. But the resurgence of verbatim drama also springs, I believe, from a profound popular disillusion with both politics and the media. For a start, there is the fact that so much British life is still shrouded in secrecy. No cameras, for instance, were allowed into the Macpherson enquiry into the Metropolitan Police's handling of the killing of Stephen Lawrence. And, although the enquiry was spasmodically reported, it was only through *The Colour of Justice* that its shocking revelations made a strong, sensory impact. The ultimate irony is that it was the theatrical success of Norton-Taylor's stage play that prompted BBC Two to televise the Tricycle production and thereby finally give the public access to explosive material.

If Verbatim Theatre opens hitherto closed doors, it also strikes me as a reaction against the loaded nature of public debate in Britain today. We live in what is laughably known as the Information Society; yet rarely have we been so ill-informed. Politicians regularly lie with impunity and the discussion of important issues is often confined to soundbites. TV, with a few notable exceptions such as Channel 4's *Dispatches*, is often either partial or pusillanimous. And, although there are still some serious newspapers left and my own employer, *The Guardian*, has done a remarkable job both over the Wikileaks exposures and the Snowden revelations, in many cases serious debate is undermined by proprietorial bias. If the referendum on Europe ever does take place, it's difficult to imagine the issues being presented with any objective clarity. That, for me, is one reason why Verbatim Theatre has proved so popular: it provides us with the data that enables us to make up our own minds on a particular subject. Looking at the plays in this volume, another thought strikes me: Verbatim Theatre is at its best when it fulfils the conditions of art. David Hare wrote of *The Colour of Justice* that 'in the act of editing he (Norton-Taylor) laid before a live audience all the subtleties and intricacies of British racism, all its forms and gradations, with a clarity which I had never seen emulated by television, documentary or newspaper.' Quite true. But equally impressive was the structure which revealed, in a form reminiscent of Sophocles or Ibsen, the way racial prejudice was embedded in the Metropolitan Police from the lowest level to the highest. I'm not equating the play with *Oedipus Rex* or *Ghosts*: I'm simply saying it used the same tactic of peeling off the layers of deception.

But each of the plays in this volume works in a different way. *Bloody Sunday* operates more through a process of accretion as we gradually learn the enormity of what happened on that day in Derry in 1972 when 13 civil-rights marchers were killed. In *Guantanamo* the action moves outwards from the specific cases of individual detainees to the general principle of the violation of international law. And in *The Riots* the first half is made up of eye-witness accounts of the events in Tottenham on the night of August 6. Only in the second half do we hear MPs, social workers and police officers speculating on the underlying causes. Verbatim Theatre, it is clear, can take many different forms. It can be re-active, as with the staging of public enquiries. It can also be pro-active as in the case of *Called to Account* which asked whether Tony Blair should be indicted for crimes of aggression against Iraq. Verbatim Theatre can work through the classic tight-knit structure of forensic investigation, as with *The Colour of Justice*. It can also mix reportage and opinion as in the case of *The Riots*. But what the plays in this volume make clear is that Verbatim Theatre is now accepted as a valid theatrical form and that, although it flourished during Nicolas Kent's tenure of The Tricycle, it is far too deeply rooted to disappear. 'Why should we not have documentary drama?' asked Tynan in 1958. The short answer is that we need it because it both enriches our theatre and enhances our understanding of the world we live in.

Michael Billington, 2014

VERBATIM THEATRE (VERBATIM)
This conversation took place on 17/06/2014. Present were: Nicolas Kent, Richard Norton-Taylor, Gillian Slovo and David Edgar.

EDGAR: Here we are gathered, and I think we should say who we are. I'm David Edgar, I'm a playwright, I've never written verbatim drama but I'm very interested in it, and fascinated to talk to three practitioners of different kinds of verbatim drama here today. They are:

NORTON-TAYLOR: Richard Norton-Taylor, a journalist, principally a journalist on the *Guardian* but also a compiler, or a playwright, the editor, of the tribunal plays.

KENT: Nicolas Kent, who was the artistic director of the Tricycle from 1984 to 2012, and first collaborated with Richard on verbatim theatre, and that led me, later on, to teaming up with Gillian Slovo, and to a number of different forms of verbatim which we did at the Tricycle.

SLOVO: And I'm Gillian Slovo, and I'm a novelist, who'd been lucky enough to be asked by Nick to do two of the verbatim plays in a slightly different way, because I did the interviews that made up the material that became the plays.

EDGAR: One thing that Rembrandt's Self-Portraits, Shakespeare's History Plays and Beethoven's Symphonies and the Tricycle Verbatim Dramas have in common is that none of them were conceived as a series, or certainly they weren't conceived as a series with the number that they ended up being. I'm right, presumably, that *Half the Picture*, which was the first verbatim play in 1994 about the Scott Inquiry, was originally conceived as a one-off?

KENT: Yes. Absolutely as a stand-alone.

EDGAR: And what inspired you to do it?

KENT: Well, I suppose, going back quite a long way I'd always been interested in verbatim theatre, or certainly big public inquiries or trials, I'd been terribly impressed as a student with *Are You Now Or Have You Ever Been?* by Eric Bentley about the McCarthy Hearings (on Un-American Activities) and also I'd been enormously impressed too by the Steve Biko trial reconstruction. So that was in the dim distant past. Then I'd had a foray myself into this, when I was working at the Oxford Playhouse, when Howard Brenton's *The Romans in Britain* happened, the *Romans in Britain* trial happened, and I conceived of the idea that we should try and put that onstage, contemporaneously with the hearings, because it was about a theatre event, and I didn't quite understand why it should only be in the newspapers. I commissioned Guy Hibbert, who has now become a well-known writer, to go down to the Inquiry, and we got a number of stenographers to be present at the trial, and to do a verbatim report. Then they came back on the train to Oxford when the trial hearing ended each day at 4 o'clock, and they edited the verbatim material. We performed it at 11 o'clock that night and we had a whole group of actors standing by, because we didn't quite know how many witnesses or how many people there would be. We were warned by the court that we could be in contempt, and we should be very careful about what we did. Luckily on that first night of doing it, the BBC broadcast it on *Newsnight*, with a quarter of an hour delay for legal reasons, but the court was closed the next morning and there were representations made by the prosecution and Mary Whitehouse's lot that we were in contempt. The Judge said that he was a little worried about the BBC but most jury people went to bed by 11 o'clock so they wouldn't have seen it, and Oxford was rather outside the ambit of most jury members who might go to the theatre so we were sort of allowed to get away with it. But it was made quite clear to us that if any actor inflected any line or anyone laughed, or if anyone made any reaction in the audience they would be in contempt. Therefore the actual performance gave a feeling of danger like walking a tightrope. So I suppose that experience, actually, got me interested in this method of doing things.

EDGAR: And particularly why the Scott Inquiry? It was the arms to Iraq trial... it was very complicated and rather arcane.

KENT: Well it was a very long process. At that time I played tennis with Richard Norton-Taylor (who was following it for the *The Guardian*) on a regular basis on Sundays and we used to get a distillation every Sunday of what had gone on in the past week and who the major witnesses had been, and there were obviously people like Margaret Thatcher and Alan Clark and Michael Heseltine appearing as witnesses, so these little anecdotes each Sunday of how they'd appeared and what they'd done, were mesmerising. Then one summer Sunday I went home, having had an accumulation of about twenty weeks of this, and I went home and looked at my *Observer* and *Sunday Times*, and both of them in their leading articles said that the Scott Inquiry was going to be the most important constitutional document of the latter half of the twentieth century, which seemed a big claim. At that point I rang up Richard and said 'What about writing, you know, bringing this together these transcripts as a play', and Richard said he was busy doing a book, he was on *The Guardian* so didn't have time to do this, but he would think about it, I said he'd find it very interesting working with actors and there was some decent money in it, and he'd have a good time. Then I rang up David Aukin who was Administrative Director at the National at the time, I was just curious about his reaction as a mate, and said what he did think of the idea? He said he thought it was a very good idea, and then I rang John McGrath who was gung-ho for doing it.

EDGAR: Obviously I want to talk about the way the form developed, and one thing that's different about *Half the Picture* from any of the others is that you've got pieces of original imaginative writing, though I imagine also based partially on interviews, so just talk a little bit about the theory of that.

KENT: Well the theory of that was I think we thought it would be too dry just to present the transcripts by themselves.

EDGAR: And what you had was a whistleblower, you had the Head of Matrix Churchill who was one of the people accused of illegally selling arms to Iraq, and you had a Kurd and a Palestinian who were on either side of the argument.

KENT: It just seemed like a good idea to allow someone imaginatively to put something perhaps a little more dramatic into what we thought wouldn't necessarily *be* that dramatic. When I told the Tricycle Box Office that I was doing the Scott Inquiry they all said 'well that'll be a good time for our holidays, two men and a dog are going to come and see this show'. John, because of his politics and talents would keep us on the straight and narrow and be a very good sounding board for the two of us. He was very supportive and incredibly helpful. I think he helped us map it out a bit and to tell the story and it also gave us, gave the audience I think, a little more background to why Saddam Hussein's regime was like it was. I mean Iraq was not the biggest of issues at that time in the news, I mean for the past twenty-five years it's dominated, but at that time it wasn't dominating it to that extent. There was obviously the Iran/Iraq war but it was very much a side issue and not in the mainstream of British politics. So it seemed interesting to deal with the Matrix Churchill arms contract, how it had impacted on one man's life, also to deal with a Kurd, how it had affected him, the gassing of the Kurds. The whole issue of Halabja was in the news but people didn't know as much about it as they know now. Also the internet was in its infancy at that time.

EDGAR: And why did you *(To RNT.)* say yes to doing it, what was it that appealed to you about it?

NORTON-TAYLOR: Well I said yes because I, well I didn't say yes immediately as Nick suggested, because I was frustrated actually, any journalist is frustrated because you're writing, trying to cover a long Inquiry and you know it's going to be long, and it wasn't even halfway through when Nick suggested editing a play based on it, and you get 500 words one day, and maybe a thousand words if you're lucky one weekend, and it's a long story, news editors on papers and broadcasting media too they have very short attention spans, butterfly minds by definition I think, it's an occupational hazard. So there I am a frustrated journalist, and Nick may have told you about during a rehearsal I thought 'My god this is not going to work, how can this possibly work?'. But then we gradually got to editing it, distilling things really, and realising that you could explain something in two or three hours that most people out there didn't really get, you'd get dribs and drabs, that goes for other tribunal plays as well for that matter, there was humour, you say it was dry, there's actually unintended humour, you get a civil servant or a cabinet secretary, the title of the thing, *Half the Picture*, 'half the picture can be true', says Robin Butler, who was then the Cabinet Secretary, and you know most of the time [Civil Servants] they're talking in private amongst themselves, or in clubs on Pall Mall, you know here they're very exposed, and there was a lot of humour there, and there were quite well-known people, you know Thatcher, Alan Clark. There was almost a postmodern moment when at one point one person came out, saying to his mother: 'Wasn't I wonderful Mummy?'

KENT: That was Gore-Booth.

EDGAR: After *Half the Picture* the next one was *Nuremberg*, and of course the Nuremberg trials have been dramatised on film, they've been dramatised on television, they've been doubtless dramatised on radio, what was it that made you want to revisit them?

KENT: I should go back for one second if I may. One of the main reasons to do the Scott Inquiry was that when Richard told us these stories I always said 'How many people were in the room watching this Inquiry, and it always turned out there were six or seven, or at the most there were thirty, you know the day Thatcher was there I think there was enough room for eighty or ninety people to be in the room, two thirds of them were journalists, maybe a hundred people, so you had a public inquiry, that was actually not seen by the public, because it wasn't televised, it wasn't on the net, and it was only reported in segments that the journalist chose to write about and the editor chose to sub-edit into his newspaper. So you had a very censored version of this inquiry as it went on and progressed over long periods, Bloody Sunday was six years, the Scott Inquiry I think was a year and a half, the Lawrence was about nine months wasn't it? So they're all different lengths but they are all very long periods, and very dry. By doing this on stage you can get an overview. Now when you come to the Nuremberg War Crimes trial, obviously that had been ventilated, and there had been bits on newsreel, but again there was not an overview on what was considered to be 'victor's justice'. You could read about it, but you couldn't actually see the whole thing play out. In 1996 it was the 50th anniversary of the Nuremberg War Crimes trial, so Richard suggested it. It seemed a very appropriate time to do it, because there was for the first time since Nuremberg, an international war crimes tribunal in The Hague, but it was only in respect of ex-Yugoslavia and Rwanda, only two countries, it was the first time there had been an international justice process since Nuremberg. Then there was a very good speech by Richard Goldstone about this fact, we didn't know at the time that there was going to be such a speech but we incorporated it later as a curtain raiser to *Nuremberg*, saying how necessary it was that there should be an international criminal court of justice. It shows, I think, how quickly a zeitgeist or an idea can be fleshed out in world politics: in that, in 1996 there was not an international criminal court, apart for from ex-Yugoslavia and Rwanda, and by 2001 there was one, and that had been unthinkable in 1996. I suppose both of us thought this would be a very good campaigning play to do, to look at a form of justice, which had pronounced on genocide and that's why I wanted Richard to write it, it was Richard's idea, not mine, but I was encouraging, because I thought it was a wonderful idea.

EDGAR: And then you added *Srebrenica* to that which was based on the Srebrenica hearings at The Hague which were as I understand it, basically indicting Karadžić and Mladić.

KENT: It's under the Rule 61 Hearings – the victims' charter, having a hearing on whether, in absentia, an accused person had a case to answer so that an international arrest warrant could then be issued.

EDGAR: Which ultimately was successful.

KENT: Ultimately the criteria for an international arrest warrant was fulfilled, and it wouldn't have been had the Rule 61 hearings not allowed the court to issue it. But it was a year after *Nuremberg* that we did *Srebrenica*. Because Richard Goldstone came to see *Nuremberg*, he came to see his own speech being portrayed by an actor, and he watched *Nuremberg*, and afterwards he said to me: 'You *have* to come to The Hague to watch the international court in The Hague, to watch the Rule 61 Hearings.' And I said I know nothing about the Rule 61 Hearings, and he explained what they were to me, and he said: 'Tickets will be like gold dust, everyone will be there, and I will get you two tickets.' I turned up in The Hague and there were seven people in the courtroom, and five were journalists, and there were two others besides me. The proceedings were being reported nightly on Dutch television, as the Dutch had been the garrison at Srebrenica. But it was *absolutely* not reported in the British Press, at all, during that week, it was reported once on the BBC World Service, it was mentioned once on *The World Tonight*, and there was a very small paragraph about it in *The Financial Times* on the Saturday after the five days of the hearings concluded. I was so angry at this neglect I thought this just has to be put on stage.

EDGAR: And am I right you revived *Nuremberg* so that they were next door to each other?

KENT: Yes.

EDGAR: So were they in rep, as it were?

KENT: No, it was alongside it. When we did *Nuremberg* originally we did *Ex-Yu* as a curtain-raiser, in a way we took the John McGrath idea, we commissioned three pieces about world trouble spots which would be imaginary responses to those trouble spots. So Goran Stefanovski wrote *Ex-Yu* which was a companion piece, and they went on as Curtain-Raisers, so they were half an hour, and then *Nuremberg* was played straight through for an hour fifty-nine. So there was a half hour, then a break, then *Nuremberg*. Then there was *Haiti* by Keith Reddin or there was *Reel Rwanda* by Femi Osofisan. And then we ditched those plays when we revived it and played *Srebrenica* instead. So then we played it effectively in rep.

EDGAR: *(To RNT.)* And what was the interest in Nuremberg? What had fascinated you about that?

NORTON-TAYLOR: Well, I think partly because I thought the theatre was a great platform to do something else, edit from a previous Inquiry or trial in this case and also you realise talking to people younger than me, how ignorant they are actually of big events. Now the The Tricycle Theatre in Kilburn, the audience was I suppose of all ages, but it did actually strike a chord. This woman came out whose relations had been in Auschwitz and when Goering was doing his bit defending himself, speaking very confidently and cockily as he did, she got up, stood up and said 'You liar, you liar! Don't listen to him, he's a liar!'

KENT: And then she realised where she was...

NORTON-TAYLOR: And this is what I'd hoped, as I did from *Half the Picture*, the theatre can be a tremendous platform to explain and to provoke an audience – David Hare said there's a special scrutiny the theatre brings, I think he used that phrase once.

KENT: I remember you said to me, *(NK turns to the others)* I think Richard was very interested in the philosophy underpinning Nazism, he'd already studied Nuremberg, and he was interested in (Alfred) Rosenberg, the anti-Semitic philosopher and the way he underpins his philosophy and what his thought process is, and also the head (of the) army Keitel and the whole idea of Lebensraum and the way the army was looking at Nazism and the way they were using it. The way they were distancing themselves from some Nazism philosophy whilst using other portions of it, and I remember you talking about all of that and what *interesting* material there was here.

NORTON-TAYLOR: How these evil people defended themselves, how they could defend themselves, when you're Rosenberg, a kind of Nazi Philosopher as it were, or a General, a German General, in their different ways. The commandant of Auschwitz, and the way he talked in a very cold way about a chemical called Zyklon B, so it wasn't just ranting or people defending themselves, in the courtroom, but people describing particular detailed instances. And this is something I learned from Nick actually because earlier on as a journalist I would think 'Oh this is just a fairly inconsequential anecdote, episodes like this, but it doesn't tell you anything which when you're writing a piece of journalism, a short piece, every word's got to be, probably overblown, but telling the reader emphatically, probably too stridently, that something's important and you've got to read it whereas actually in two or three hours, you can explain, getting into the mind of the people you're hearing.

SLOVO: Can I ask a question? You're dealing with things that went on for a very long time, huge texts – how did you decide what to select?

NORTON-TAYLOR: It differed slightly on the different plays, the different enquires we were doing, for example Bloody Sunday was ten years in the making as we know, many millions of words, and I didn't see much of what was happening at the beginning, in Northern Ireland itself, although the soldiers were here in London, giving evidence, so I had one or two helpers, and advisors, you know people who were covering it for the Irish papers say in the Bloody Sunday case, but also you have instinctive things as a journalist, you think although this Inquiry is going on for a long time and many millions of words are being spoken, and the text is there, the transcripts are there, actually they're only talking about one thing, they're talking about one incident, whether it's the killing of Stephen Lawrence in *The Colour of Justice*, or whether it's an Inquiry about selling arms to Saddam Hussein in *Half the Picture*. *Nuremberg* was slightly more discursive really, but I suppose when you've been a journalist for a long time you get a sixth sense for what's significant.

KENT: You're slightly helped by the narrative aren't you, inquiries are always set out in a narrative, they don't go haphazardly, they look at what happened and how it happened. We made a rule that we would never ever jump the chronology. We'd always take witnesses in the order in which they appeared in the Inquiry.

EDGAR: I understand that, but in *Half the Picture* the major government witnesses were asked about incidents that went through the whole story. In other words, you didn't, as Gillian was able to do in her interview-based plays, you weren't able to bring people back and jump between them. It seems to me you get to a point after *Srebrenica* where you've kind of purified the form as it were and you've dropped the other material that was before *Nuremberg*, you've reproduced as accurately as possible the courtroom, you have a feel that things are not chosen for their dramatic value, you don't have anything as vulgar as a curtain-call, you have people doing things that are done in court, people going in and out, stenographers changing and so on, clearly not for dramatic effect, or seemingly not for dramatic effect, you've made it very very pure, which means that certain things suddenly pop up, like the black bags in the Macpherson Inquiry that the killers took out of the house, which was a crucial piece of evidence that was missed, so in a way, in the audience you are experiencing what the people sitting in the courtroom experienced. It becomes very strong as an aesthetic, I think, very powerful to watch in different ways, but was it frustrating that you weren't able, as you were in *Half the Picture*, occasionally to editorialise and give people a bit of help?

NORTON-TAYLOR: In the beginning it was, but actually not, because I thought the words and the people expressed themselves so well, as I quite soon discovered through the words. The characters showed themselves in their different ways, whether it's a completely arrogant Foreign Office guy called Gore-Booth, or Thatcher doing her bit, or Major doing it, but they're almost a caricature of themselves these people actually, and you took out the essence, being as objective as possible.

EDGAR: Well I was going to ask, because Gillian's point obviously is *how* you compress and what decision you make in order to compress, and you've confessed the first part of it is the entertainment value of some of the witnesses, but was part of that thematic? It does seem to me that *The Colour of Justice*, what's so compelling about it is that you're actually saying the same thing happened however many... ten times, you're seeing a policeman standing up having prepared a story, and watching it falling apart, and in a way, the same thing was happening ten times, against all dramatic instincts of what one should do, but I imagine it was selected on the basis of drawing that truth out.

KENT: Well some of it's pragmatic, because you've only got the two hours' traffic of the stage. You don't want to spend too little time with one witness, because somehow if you only have a quick interchange and then they go, you've got to swear them in and then they go away and it's not long enough for the audience to begin to understand where this witness is coming from, so in a way you're never going to have more than eight or nine witnesses. Plus you've got the economics of how many people you can afford to employ. I remember when Richard first gave *The Colour of Justice* to me, it had about twenty-five witnesses or twenty witnesses I think, and we had to synthesize it down. He'd already synthesized it down greatly as to who was the most important, but they become emblematic to some extent in that you're only going to take inevitably one of the suspects because otherwise you're going to do all those scenes four or five times. So you've got to find the best one and the one that then encapsulates the best story.

EDGAR: By doing it in such a pure way, you don't change location, you have no domestic scenes, no soliloquies, none of the things by which playwrights traditionally ring the changes, but it does seem to me that actually when you do get something that's dramatic and surprising, it actually becomes more powerful, and I'd like to give one example which I may have completely mis-spotted but that involved Gillian as well. Obviously one of the things the playwright has at their command is What You Do Last, and it seems to me that in *Justifying War*, and also in *The Riots*, you end with a speech that actually goes slightly against what you've heard before, in other words you end these rather arcane sophisticated politicians talking about the death of David Kelly with his widow, so you get a sudden feeling of the human cost of it. At the end of *Bloody Sunday*, which is a very convincing case for the army having unjustifiably fired on innocent civilians, you get the coup that the official IRA admitted that they had indeed fired on troops, and then at the end of *The Riots*, which I think is an attempt largely to understand the rioters, you get a speech by a Muslim man whose house has burned down. Now was that intentional, or was the intention just to take the audience in one direction and say, 'Hang on a minute,' at the end?

KENT: I think it was intentional, yes. I think we've always tried to be as unbiased and objective as possible. So we've always tried to give both sides of the story, but also we've looked for the human side of the story. For me, the one that doesn't reverse your attitude or turn your ideas upside down is the Shawcross speech. (It) is the most human and most dramatic. It was at the end of *Nuremberg*, and is about the engineer Graber watching a man with a child in his arms and pointing up to Heaven, just before he's being shot with a whole group of 200-300 Jews being shot and falling into a pit. He's just shown the child there's some hope. Like Mrs Kelly, there are those moments that make the whole thing enormously human, like the interview that Gillian did with the Muslim shop-keeper.

EDGAR: And can I ask Gillian, what was the thinking behind ending with that very powerful speech?

SLOVO: Because I think a lot of the play was about how this happened, why it happened, and what it meant. That speech was about trying to remind people that human beings were involved, and there was a cost. I'm not sure it's in complete contradiction to the play, because I think that particular person was quite amazing in the sense that he was an immigrant to this country who had all his memories in that flat, they were completely burned out, so that he lost his past as well, because he lost the pictures of his original family back home, and yet he was completely without rage. He was talking honestly about something that had happened to him that was really terrible, but he wasn't a hanger and flogger, he wasn't trying to say you have to do this, you have to do that. It was consistent with what the play was trying to do which was to understand what happened. Also it brought the audience together. The play started with an explosion, and it brought the audience to understand that this explosion had a human cost and that somebody who had not done anything had been the victim of what happened. He was a great interviewee as well, and he managed to express something that I think we needed to know and we needed to hear.

I'm quite interested in asking you two *(To NK & RNT.)* a question, which is about your deliberate decision not to mess with the chronology; because of course I had a completely different experience. I messed with chronology and that messing with the chronology is that the man who was burned out on the first day ended the play. Your not messing with the chronology seems to me to be something where it's anti-editorial; you are leaving the audience to make the editorial because they have to make the connections. Why did you do that?

NORTON-TAYLOR: In one particular play, *Bloody Sunday*, because chronologically we have the guy at the end, the official IRA fellow, who was actually quite an interesting fellow, a British person from the Royal Navy, and he goes against everything by admitting there were some guns there, official IRA and so on. Chronologically, he spoke at the end. We had to have him, because that was rather important evidence. That was chronological, but I would have loved it to have been earlier on actually, because it ends like that - which I thought jarred a bit.

KENT: The reason we did it I think is very clear. We were setting out to present a public inquiry on stage. We always did the plays before the public inquiry reported, after the hearings and before the report. So we wanted to be objective, to say to an audience 'This is what the public inquiry heard, here is the evidence, here's the order in which they heard it. It isn't all of it, but it's as much as we can encapsulate to tell the story, we don't want to mess with the chronology, but we want *you* to say, before the report is published, what you think the conclusions of the report should be.'

NORTON-TAYLOR: And on this occasion, *Bloody Sunday* in particular, if we hadn't mentioned this crucial evidence, everyone would say, this is a defensive point, 'You've missed that out.'

EDGAR: But I thought it was interesting precisely because it was a sort-of anti-editorial line, saying absolutely we're not putting a case.

KENT: One quick caveat if I may. The only time we did mess with the chronology was in the Hutton Inquiry with Mrs Kelly, because she wasn't present in any of the argument, all that was happening to her was happening to her emotionally. She gave evidence possibly about the state of mind of her husband, but not about any of the facts that were laid out at the inquiry, so we put her at the end because it just seemed very odd to do it before, and we felt it would be a human story, a catharsis, about the emotional implications of an individual's death at the end of a dry inquiry.

EDGAR: Remind me of the *mise-en-scene* of that: there was a picture of her, and then she was speaking somewhere else; that really happened.

KENT: Yes, there was a still photograph of her and she spoke in another room exactly as had happened at the inquiry.

EDGAR: And of course that was very dramatic because they'd reproduced that. Was the picture a picture of her, or a picture of the actor?

KENT: It was a picture of her, because you never saw the actor.

EDGAR: Indeed. And I want to talk a little bit about one of things that's quite enticing, which is that there are two companies, because you have a number of lawyers, particularly Michael Mansfield, who pop up from time to time and you also have a company of actors, and indeed Jeremy Clyde of course played Michael Mansfield who I think is the most frequent appearer, several times.

KENT: And Thomas Wheatley has been in them all.

EDGAR: Indeed, [in] I think about half a dozen. (NK: Except *The Riots*.) Now, did people go to meet their originals, did they go to the tribunals?

KENT: I only managed to get one or two people to the tribunals, because I never knew I was going to do them until too late really, but for *Tactical Questioning* we got some actors down there because we knew fairly early on we were going to do that one. For the Hutton I got one or two down there because I went to every single day of the hearings of the Hutton. I went to a few of the Bloody Sunday hearings in Derry, and I managed to get one or two people to Bloody Sunday when it came to London, but it was going on for so long that on the whole we didn't manage to get the actors there as we were never sure which witnesses we were going to include in the play. A few of the actors went to some of the inquiries, but once we were in rehearsals we did get the actors to meet their people whenever possible.

EDGAR: Talk a little bit about mimicry, because you've got a large number of well-known public figures: Margaret Thatcher, Michael Heseltine, in *Half the Picture* you've got Alastair

Campbell and a number of others in *Justifying War*. Did you talk to the actors, did you discourage them from doing certain things, did you encourage them to do certain things in terms of the obvious problems as well as the delights of mimicry?

KENT: Yes we always said less is more. We tried to get to the essence of what the scene was about, what they were arguing in the scene and the point of view, so that Mrs Thatcher for instance in *Half the Picture*, goes on about guidelines…

EDGAR: She was played by…

KENT: … Sylvia Syms. She keeps on repeating 'They were guidelines', that was her mantra, her defence, 'They were guidelines, they were guidelines': the imperious nature of her defence was very much her essence. When you're playing a well-known figure like that, it is more difficult to deal with than playing someone who is less well known. On the whole I tried to get actors to meet the people they were playing, watch the people and find their essence, and capture an essence, but I mean actors did find wonderful things, often with hands, in that…

EDGAR: I remember Sylvia Syms's shoulder, somehow, Thatcher pushing her shoulder forward.

KENT: Yeah she did do that, but Bill Hoyland (in *Half the Picture*) discovered that John Major's hands never worked in sync, he would say 'The papers that sometimes came across my desk,' and he would do the hand gesture just after the word 'across'. There was something just a little bit awkward about his hand gestures, and we also discovered, and this was something the actor Thomas Wheatley invented when he played William Waldegrave in *Half the Picture*, he'd watched Waldegrave a lot, and he'd sort of discovered that Waldegrave had a gesture whereby he sort of washed his hands, like a doctor does, as he spoke, and he did that in the play. I remember two journalists came up to me and said 'Oh, so you were at the inquiry on the Waldegrave day?' And I said, 'No,' and they said 'Well that's what he did all the way through,' he was like Pontius Pilate washing his hands of this evidence, so actors intuitively somehow do understand these things.

SLOVO: What I was really struck with in *Guantanamo* is actors understand words, they understand what's *behind* words, that's why they're actors, that's why they're good at it. The one who struck me in this way was Paul Bhattacharjee. He played Moazamm Begg who was in Guantanamo the whole time that our play was on and being made. All we had was his letters, and access to his father actually. But Paul played Moazamm Begg in a particular way, that when I met Moazamm Begg I thought 'That's Paul'. He understood from the words that Moazamm Begg had used in his letters, who this man was and what his being was, and that was pretty amazing.

KENT: That happened time and time again.

EDGAR: Well there is the classic one – John Major in *Half the Picture* when he says 'You're presuming that because I was Chancellor, because I was Foreign Secretary, because I was Prime Minister, I knew what was going on,' and I think *Half the Picture*'s an interesting one because there's a lot of those. It did strike me that by concentrating those you did get a picture of how things happened and how that occurred and particularly with Alan Clark when he was saying 'We were creating fiction', that you kind of saw linguistically that fiction being created.

NORTON-TAYLOR: The language of Whitehall is fascinating, actually…the euphemisms and when Major was saying on that point, 'Just because I was Prime Minister etc' he was actually not taking the mickey out of himself, that's actually what happens, all these papers get shoved and people *do* misinterpret. He said 'I get 33,000 things from GCHQ every day, how can I possibly…?' You know, these are topical points actually, ministers do not know, cannot know everything. The permanent government knows things, and the permanent government wants to shield themselves by language. Civil servants never say 'I lied,' they'll say, 'It wasn't a *direct* lie,' or 'I misled myself,' – all that stuff.

EDGAR: Again, on what comes out of that compression, I was thinking 'Is there an overall arching theme?', is there an overall theme about cover-ups, and an overall theme about lying and so on, but it's interesting that, particularly in *Colour of Justice, Bloody Sunday,* and *Tactical Questioning,* the one about the killing of an Iraqi prisoner by British servicemen, that there is an awful lot about blaming your inferiors – what's that BBC line, 'Deputy Heads Will Roll'? *(Chuckling.)* – that towards the end of those three you get the more senior people, and all of them are being very gracious and apologising a great deal and saying 'I knew absolutely nothing about it'. Again, is that kind of thing one of the things that informs your selection, or is it like the Michelangelo statue, that you discover it by the process of chipping away?

NORTON-TAYLOR: It's *there*, it's almost there on a plate, you don't have to chisel terribly hard actually, and people know it's there, they come up and say 'Yeah', the audience I mean, they say they knew it was pretty bad, they didn't know it was *that* bad, because they're not paying attention, they're not reading the news stories, they hear a clip on the radio or half a minute on television, you don't get all this stuff, and I think they understand a bit more; that this is how they defend themselves, they blame others.

KENT: It's like the Irish thing of being asked for directions and saying 'I wouldn't start from here…' The mere fact you're starting from where you are means you're involved in a public inquiry and often you're in deep doo-doo, that's already the starting point, therefore it's incumbent upon you as someone responsible to pass the shit down the line as fast as you can.

EDGAR: But there is a remarkable thing in *The Colour of Justice,* the number of notes that are lost, and the number of people who then say 'Yes I'm very sorry, it would have been very useful if I'd had them.'

KENT: Yes, exactly.

NORTON-TAYLOR: And at one point we did Inspector Groves in *Colour of Justice,* and he's not playing it for laughs, he says, 'I'm not sure there's a bit of paper; but I have the clipboard.' *(Laughter.)*

EDGAR: One of the nice things, and it happens a little bit in Gillian's interviews, you get a lot of these little detailed moments about the process itself, stuff about leaning into the microphone, speaking up a bit, and explaining – I don't know quite how the Saville courtroom was constructed, but Saville keeps saying 'I'm over here', this is the person you look at…

KENT: But there were so many people: in the Guildhall in London/Derry, there were probably about a hundred people, lawyers, researchers who were working on legal teams, there were so many people, and there were the four judges who were placed at the side. And the acoustic was so disembodied in this huge place, that the witness never knew where Saville was really; I mean if you'd come suddenly into the witness box, he wasn't facing you, he was suddenly on the right hand side of you, it was weird.

EDGAR: Why did you seek to reproduce the courtrooms to the level of accuracy that you did? Was there an intention to make it accurate?

KENT: Yes, and to leave the house lights on, and to deal with the detail, so that you felt this was some form of machine that was going on over a very long process, over in some cases years, and this was like the establishment in a way, so you were portraying the establishment searching for a truth, and so it seemed important to me that you didn't play around with the environment in which that search was taking place.

SLOVO: Not to be rude about the theatre, but I think the Tricycle helped in that way –

KENT: Oh it did, enormously.

SLOVO: – Because the Tricycle does look very workaday, like it could be a tribunal. One of the things that struck me when Guantanamo moved to the West End and we kept the house lights on as we had before it was seriously distracting, because there were all these theatrical 'curlies' around which the Tricycle doesn't have. And so it really did help for the audience to feel that they were in the room in the Tribunal plays because they were in a similar kind of (place).

KENT: There was one other thing which helped too, which was mic-ing the actors, because that actually meant that the level of performance was never histrionic. No one had to project, everyone could mumble. If you'd made a set for it then that would have been a false thing to do – to mic the actors – and it would have moved away from something that was uber-naturalistic, but actually useful because you're dealing in detail.

EDGAR: And the screens? In the early ones you didn't use screens.

KENT: We didn't have screens, there was technology but the inquiries were not paperless like today.

EDGAR: But towards the end you were using screens. Now were you using screens just to see what the people would have been looking at on the stage or were you using it to give covert helpful information?

KENT: Both, because what happened was we, as a nation, adopted a paperless court gradually, and were becoming more and more paperless, so the evidence was coming up as documents on screen, as maps, and people were moving pointers around and you needed the audience to share in the same things the witness was getting. When you go into an inquiry room, some of the screens are set up for *you*, as an audience in the inquiry room, and you do get to see what's going on.

EDGAR: One final thing about the actors and their relationship with the people they played. Did people come to see themselves?

KENT: Yes, almost always.

EDGAR: Well, presumably not Mrs. Thatcher.

KENT: Alan Clark did, and Clare Short did. Richard Perle did.

NORTON-TAYLOR: Scott came.

KENT: Scott came incognito, Macpherson sent someone, Robin Butler came, Chris Clarke who was the lead attorney on Bloody Sunday came. Bernadette Devlin came.

EDGAR: And did anybody object?

NORTON-TAYLOR: Nobody objected to me, they had the opportunity to object to me but they didn't.

KENT: No one objected.

EDGAR: And why do you think that was, do you think the people who came were the people who came out of it well, or do you think people were just flattered to be portrayed?

KENT: I think people are always flattered to be portrayed, I was always amazed that two cabinet ministers at the beginning of the Coalition Government and the height of the post-Riots chaos, were prepared to give Gillian an hour and a half of their time for a play in a small North-West London theatre, to ask a few questions that might be seen by an audience of two hundred a night.

EDGAR: And that was Iain Duncan Smith and Michael Gove. So tell us about your people: how many of your people came to *The Riots*?

SLOVO: I don't think the major politicians came.

KENT: Some of the other politicians did come though.

SLOVO: Some of the others did come; in the two plays that I did, there were two people who didn't like the portrayal of themselves, and I think that was about the way they came across as people. I think it was the way that the actor interpreted their words physically that they found difficult. But I think mostly people like to see themselves on a stage.

EDGAR: Talking about that, Alecky Blythe who wrote *Come Out Eli* and a series of very strict verbatim dramas, so strict that people actually have an ear-piece so that they don't 'actor' it up; how much were you concerned about the accuracy?

KENT: We had no references, so I could only get people's impressions, like I would talk to Michael Mansfield and say 'How did so-and-so come over?' And he would say 'Oh, immensely arrogant and cocky,' for instance, and I'd say

'Well in what way?' He'd say, 'He'd be a smart-aleck, he'd try and answer the question before you'd even finished it.' So you tended to find those things out and I tended to snoop around a lot in the Inquiry and ask a lot of people who'd been there, seen people, Richard has a whole cadre of journalists from the *Independent* or… I mean, for the whole of the Hutton Inquiry I sat next to Anne McElvoy (who was reporting it for the *Evening Standard*) every single day, we'd pal up so I would ask her sometimes for her impressions of those I'd seen to get another objective view, but I didn't for instance go to the Macpherson Inquiry at all, so I needed to ask everyone I could find who'd been there.

EDGAR: And Gillian, did your actors listen to the taped interviews?

SLOVO: Yeah, the actors had both the transcripts and the taped interviews. I think that was tremendously helpful because I had edited down quite a lot, and they were able to hear the whole thing so they were able to hear the meaning. Even so there were occasions when I would say to Nick, 'I don't think that's the way to say that line', and that was a question of understanding what was really being said, and even though they had the tapes, because they were so heavily edited, they could use the right inflections from the tapes but say the wrong thing, by not putting the emphasis on the right bit of what the sentence is. It didn't happen very often, but it did happen.

KENT: She'd been there obviously for the interviews, and I hadn't been there for most of the interviews, I had been for one or two, but on the whole 90% of them I hadn't been, so for instance Scott – what was his name? The main guy in –

SLOVO: Stafford Scott.

KENT: Stafford. Gillian was very unhappy to begin with, with his portrayal because she thought it was too angry I think, and we had to calm it back and make it more arrogant rather than angry. Not arrogant: confident, really. I think I'd made him come over as a little too angry and fiery, and in another way he was someone who was slightly above the fray and had tremendous charisma, and we found that charisma eventually, but that was thanks to Gillian. And the same with Richard; all these plays have been totally collaborative.

EDGAR: We've been talking about how truthful everything is and how it really happened and how important it was and how that makes it different from a play with invented characters. There's obviously one play we haven't talked about at all, which is the play that departed from that most dramatically which is *Called To Account*, which was an imaginary trial of Tony Blair for war crimes. I'd like first of all for you to talk about how, why you did that, and then talk a little bit about how you put it together.

KENT: Well I think it came about partly through Philippe Sands.

NORTON-TAYLOR: Philippe Sands, a lawyer (NK: An international lawyer who was often on the radio talking about bringing Blair to justice.) … Would it have happened without him?

KENT: Probably not. Somehow we got into a conversation and he said 'Well, you could stage a trial,' and then we got him and one of his counterparts Julian Knowles, doing the defence, but we made the great mistake of trying to do the whole thing in Matrix Chambers without letting Cherie Blair know that we were doing it there. She suddenly found out that there was a trial of her husband going on in her own chambers! And we'd already had Quinlan who was a very high-up Civil Servant in the Ministry of Defence giving evidence, for three hours in Matrix Chambers, and we decamped pretty quickly to a merchant bank who shall remain nameless, who gave us offices to work in and we worked from there.

EDGAR: You interviewed about twelve people?

KENT: Fifteen.

EDGAR: You didn't use everybody.

KENT: We did an interview, they were cross-examined, they gave evidence as though they were in court, so the camera was set up on them, and they were told that we expected them to tell the Truth, the whole Truth and nothing but the Truth, and then the prosecution would lead their witness, or the defence would lead if they were theirs.

EDGAR: And a couple were telephone calls?

KENT: Yes, the Chilean ambassador to the United Nations was a telephone call.

EDGAR: And then there were eight people who declined to be interviewed.

KENT: Yes, can't remember who they were, but there were a few.

SLOVO: Tony himself, presumably.

KENT: We didn't ask Tony, but there were others.

EDGAR: Presumably at the end of that, you had material which is very similar to the material that you normally work with.

KENT: We had almost the same material that Chilcott is currently working on.

EDGAR: And then did you do it to the same rules? Was it in order?

KENT: We did it in any order we wanted to.

NORTON-TAYLOR: And there were two lawyers, one for defence and one for prosecution.

KENT: They had a very antagonistic relationship.

NORTON-TAYLOR: Personally they did, afterwards.

KENT: They took it terribly seriously…

NORTON-TAYLOR: They made a real trial of it.

KENT: … One accused the other of acting in bad faith, of not giving full disclosure of who he was going to call.

EDGAR: And it does strike me that only Michael Mates, and only just, broke the frame, and implied that we're playing a game. Everybody else seemed to take it terribly seriously. What was the *mise-en-scene* in which you set it?

KENT: We just did it around a table, effectively.

EDGAR: So you didn't intend it as a courtroom.

KENT: No, we did it on stage as we'd done it, we'd had a big table, each lawyer had a junior, both of whom are pretty well-known lawyers now, there was no judge, and there was just the witness at the head of the table being cross-examined from both sides of the table effectively.

EDGAR: Did you ever worry that it might devalue the others? I mean, did you ever worry that having created a fictional trial you might call in to question the power of the ones that were real?

KENT: The one thing I think Richard's been absolutely brilliant at doing, or one of the many things, is being totally objective, trying to present it as objectively as possible, trying to put the arguments for both sides, so I think everyone knew this was an exercise, but no one thought it was a bit of *Guardian* agit-prop. I don't think we proved that he was guilty of the crime of aggression.

NORTON-TAYLOR: Which is what would happen actually in real life, because of the rules of the International Criminal Court. But I take your point, I think we were slightly uncomfortable about that. But it was saved I think by various people, Sir Michael Quinlan, I think, and Richard Perle came out with a very interesting description of Bush. Clare Short said, and this is relevant now, even today, Blair charms his way through- he didn't see it as lies but I'm afraid it was lies. I think things came out which were quite credible - in a way that they weren't sort of putting the boot in to this 'evil man'. Michael Quinlan was the most senior official in the Ministry of Defence, a great defender of the nuclear deterrent and all that stuff, but he really opposed the invasion of Iraq because he disapproved of the way the whole theory, concept, of deterrence, was being undermined.

KENT: It was all about a 'Just' war too wasn't it.

EDGAR: But it's interesting of course that all of these, they are things recollected in tranquillity, or relative tranquillity. They're all about violent incidents – *Bloody Sunday*, extremely violent incidents, suicide, war, selling arms which led to deaths and so on, but all of them are within a courtroom now, they're deliberately calm, which is why trials to me are so fascinating. Now moving over to *Guantanamo* and particularly *The Riots*, if we can talk about it the wrong way round, in that play there was much more of an attempt, it seems to me, to reproduce and communicate what it felt like to be involved, either as a rioter or as a victim. Is that right?

SLOVO: Well, what it felt like to be involved in it, but also why it happened, because I think what happened in real life was that a riot started for one reason then turned into something else, but because it happened so fast, what we got on our news was just rioting, pictures of rioting everywhere with no explanation of why it had happened. So the first act of *The Riots* was an attempt to reconstruct what had happened, to look at exactly how this broke out, and in fact the play *The Riots* might have been called the play *The Riot*, because it actually mostly looked at what happened in Tottenham. It referred to the riots in Manchester, it referred to the spread throughout the country, and it certainly tried to address why and what does this mean for us, but the bulk of the action was about what happened in Tottenham.

EDGAR: I recollect finding that narrative particularly persuasive and followable, I think there were visuals which helped.

KENT: There was a whole mapping exercise about the policing in Tottenham at the beginning of the riot, but I thought Gillian carved an extraordinary story out of it because the first act, effectively, was telling you what happened and how it happened, and then the second act actually tried to deal with the societal forces that had caused this to happen. Yet both had a narrative in their own way, they were completely different.

SLOVO: Of course, for the first act it was relatively easy to have narrative drive, because a riot is intrinsically dramatic. It goes from a small beginning to a massive something-or-other, so it was quite easy to put drama into that. The second, more philosophical, understanding of *what* this means for our society and what various people say to it was I think a more difficult thing. But I actually think that after you had seen a riot you needed to know, and therefore the audience was probably ready to have a little more speaking about it, to have a little more listening and have a little more understanding.

EDGAR: And that very clear game of two halves in the play, was that something that you decided on after you'd done the interviews, or was that something that you went out to get?

SLOVO: No, for both the plays I went out in a naïve state of not knowing what the play was going to be. Partly because in the first one in *Guantanamo* I had never written a play before. The only reason I did it was because Nick asked me if I was interested and I was and the reason I found the courage to do it was when I said to him, '– you've got a slot in the theatre – what happens if I spend three weeks interviewing and then can't make a play out of it?' He said 'Well then it won't be very good, will it?' And I am a great believer that that is what creating art is about. You have to take a risk, and sometimes it works and sometimes it doesn't work, and you have to be allowed to take that risk. Something which I think is increasingly not allowed to playwrights and novelists these days. So the risk I took with both of them was they were subjects I was really interested in, that I had read the newspapers about, but as Richard said, journalists know a lot more than they can put in their articles and therefore as a reader what you're getting is just the tip of what that knowledge is. And this was an opportunity to go and ask the questions. I mean the riots – I was in Scotland in a country house in the middle of nowhere when the riots were happening, and I think very many people in Britain were looking at the television screen and thinking what on earth is going on, this is incomprehensible, so I went out to do *The*

Riots to try and understand for myself. The same thing with *Guantanamo*; I went out to try and understand what is going on. I had to have the faith that by the time I'd finished the interviews and sat down with the transcripts, I would have that In that way I think my verbatim plays are very different from yours *(RNT)* because I think there clearly *is* an editorial in the ones that I did and clearly the editorial – not that I wanted to tell people what to think because I don't believe in that, and I don't want to lay out – but that clearly there was a journey of mine in both of those plays, a journey of *mine* to understand.

EDGAR: You face obviously the same problem that Richard faced, which is that you got a lot more material than you could use and therefore you're selecting it, and therefore you're concentrating. In *Guantanamo*, which doesn't have as obviously strong a narrative as *The Riots*, did you develop a kind of 'I'm editing in order to find a particular thing'? Do you think there's an organizing principle for how you selected the material?

SLOVO: I think that again is divided into two, and the first half is about trying to tell the story of what it's like to be, an ordinary person in Tipton, the father of a young man who may or may not have done something crazy, to have a knock on the door and have the British police say 'I've just come to tell you, your son's in a place that you never knew existed.' So the first act is really about what happened to those people, how they began to understand what had happened, and also we used the letters from people in Guantanamo. While we were preparing *Guantanamo* the first of the British prisoners came out, and so we were then able to actually interview somebody who had been there. This was the first time we had an eyewitness account of what it was like, and his account is also threaded in. But the rest is done from letters and interviews with the relatives. The journey in the first act was really again *my* journey as I tried to understand what happened to these people, and who they are, and for me that journey contained a tremendous number of surprises. Just, for example, to go to Tipton and to see it so poverty-stricken, where racism is rife because everybody is desperate, because communities don't have enough. And to meet these families of these boys who were isolated even in their own communities, whose mosque did not want to have anything to do with them because there was such an anti-Muslim feeling at the time, they didn't want to be identified with anybody who might have been a terrorist, who might have done 9/11. And also for me it was a journey into asking: what does it mean to have a system where all the normal rules of how one conducts, decides whether somebody is guilty or innocent, are bypassed?

KENT: Because you *don't* decide.

SLOVO: When *Guantanamo* was on there were people who came up to me afterwards and asked the question, 'Are you saying these people are innocent or guilty? Are you saying they're all innocent?' And the only answer I could give after having done all this is, 'Innocent of what? Guilty of what? They were not charged.' That was what I discovered in meeting the incomprehension of these families.

EDGAR: It does seem to me you've got a mechanism which Richard and Nick didn't have on the Tribunal plays, you have a number of different ways of speaking: you've got letters, you've got a chilling press conference with Donald Rumsfeld, you've got interviews, you've got speeches, and you're not dealing with chronology. But again like the Tribunal, one of the striking things is, you've got these odd little surprising details is, one of them writes home with 'Will you see that my motorbike insurance is renewed?' I think for me the most important line in the play is when Gareth Pierce says 'These were just ordinary British guys who ended up in situations of Hell, of medieval horror.' That's interesting of course because people want to accuse Muslims of taking things back to situations of medieval horror. That did seem to me to be a very strong organizing principle, that you were constantly saying: these are actually much more complicated and culturally interesting and specific people than you think them to be.

SLOVO: And that's what you get when you meet their relatives and see where they live and see how they are. When I first started doing this with Victoria, I hadn't actually even met a lot of Muslims, and I expected that along my way I might meet a lot of men who would not want to shake my hand, for example. It didn't happen, not one. And what *Guantanamo* helped people see, was that these were people very much like us, in many circumstances for a London audience less well-off than us, who are just struggling through their lives and who got caught up in this impossible situation from which there is no escape.

EDGAR: One of the things that playwrights love is to have something that they can use and then re-use and then re-use again and gets more freight as it goes on, and sometimes it's a property, sometimes it's a line which gets quoted again and again. If you're doing the interviews of course, you can set up that very brilliantly, as it seems to me you do in *The Riots*: you ask everybody to sum up the rioters in three words.

SLOVO: And it was totally telling, once we hit on that.

EDGAR: And it gives you the end of the first act, *and* the end of the second act. And indeed the guy at the end who's the guy whose house has burned down, ends up with 'just bloody angry': his three words. But were you thinking when you were doing the interviews of how I can ask questions that are going to provide me with dramatic material?

SLOVO: The three words was deliberate. I have to say was the idea of my researcher, Cressida Brown. She came to quite a few of the interviews. She came from the straight theatre, and was more worried than me that I wasn't going to be able to pull a narrative (together). Because my way of doing these interviews was to follow where my interest went, so although I'd go in with a set of questions in case I dried or they dried, but after the first question I would follow my interest. Mostly I was just talking to people about their experiences, and what I had discovered about *Guantanamo* is that if I listened hard enough I can find out things out of my own interest that will interest other people, I would allow myself to be an idiot, and ask the kind of questions that were really trying to work out what was going on. And Cressida worried that I'd never find a play out of this because I was all over the place, and she suggested the three words, and a very good suggestion it turned out to be. Nick also pre-pepped the interviews and we would discuss the kind of questions that I might ask, so although he wasn't actually there for a lot of them he played a role. Then after a while once I've done a few of them, each interview helps the next interview if somebody tells you something interesting and then the next interview you try and find out if somebody else can add to that. And so as a result those plays, although they were done on individual interviews, are a kind of a conversation edited by me but happening between them. And without the tyranny of the chronology this allowed me to have a bit of interaction on the stage.

KENT: You had a bit of tyranny that you inherited from Richard, in that we wouldn't allow you to change any words.

SLOVO: Yeah that was tyranny, but that's what makes the power.

EDGAR: And the other thing is juxtaposition, that you don't have.

KENT: It was very interesting, because here I am working with two people, neither of whom started as playwrights. And their one common ingredient is that they absolutely stuck to deadlines more than any playwrights I know, which for him as a journalist and she as a novelist writing for deadlines, the publishers absolutely expect it, which is great, so I knew deadlines weren't going to be a problem. The other thing is that Richard can sub-edit and make a story very brief, very concise and absolutely wonderful, and something that's terribly complex he can render into something that's very simple, in prose, in a short article in *The Guardian*, and suddenly I understand it. And Gillian has this brilliant thing about narrative, because she's done thrillers, and she knew the telling power of narrative all the way through. It was great, I was very lucky, I found two people who were not playwrights, who are consummate playwrights, in a rather wonderful way.

EDGAR: And can I ask about your work with Victoria Brittain?

SLOVO: We did all the interviews together and we did some of the research together, she found some of the people, Nick found some of the people, we did all the interviews together.

KENT: Corin Redgrave helped us greatly.

SLOVO: Yeah, and Corin Redgrave helped us because people trusted him, so they talked to us because we were his friends. Without him we wouldn't have been able to do what we did because some of these families had been tortured by the Press and were very suspicious about outsiders coming in and asking questions. Corin made us not outsiders. Victoria and I did all the interviews together and then when it came to making the play I had to sit on my own with all the material and I had to make it into a shape that made sense to me. And once I had done that we had meetings with Victoria and Nick and Sacha Wares who co-directed *Guantanamo*, to talk about how to make the second draft, and then I would go and do it. In the end what I did discover is I am a lone writer. When I'm plotting something which is what I was doing, the tick of a plot is very important to me, So while I'm plotting I need to be in my own head. When I had done [that] we then talked about what was missing, how I had structured it, where it was dragging, where it was needing more, and I'd go again and do it again.

KENT: Sacha Wares brought a lot to the party too. It's the only play I co-directed, all the others I did with an assistant, but with Sacha it was an equal process. Although it had been my idea, I got Gillian and Victoria on board, Sacha brought an aesthetic to the piece which was incredibly useful, and the thing she did which I'm certain I would not have managed to do, she brought an ethos of being in Guantanamo, of doing the five times prayer, and being a Muslim, so that somehow she brought that whole feeling to it, which helped in the structure enormously, she was very clever on structure.

SLOVO: I just have to say one thing: when he says we kept to deadlines, both with *Guantanamo* and *The Riots* there was absolutely no choice but to keep to deadlines because Nick said 'This play will go on on this day, and I have to find out how many actors I need to get by this day, then you've got a little bit of time while they're rehearsing to finalise it, and it has to happen,' and that's why I stuck to deadlines!

KENT: We did both *The Riots* and *Guantanamo* in twelve weeks from the moment of deciding to do them, to actually having them on stage in front of the Press.

SLOVO: That's what I actually think helped make them alive. Because in that situation you cannot go on forever, you have to be very directed about who you can talk to and how much you can do. I think it's quite interesting – I'm proud of both of them, but particularly *The Riots*. We had very little time, we talked to relatively little people, and *The Guardian* did a much greater project that went on for much longer, they had many more staff involved, and we both came to the same conclusion about what had happened. It shows what you can do if you really don't have a lot of time but you find the right people, and listen properly to them: you can then create something that a lot more research will eventually back up.

EDGAR: Who had the brilliant idea to advertise in prison newspapers?

KENT: I think I thought of that. It's interesting how all of this is so coincidental; I went to a party and I met someone who was an editor of *Inside Time*, and I then said 'Can we put an article in there,' they said 'Yes'. And then when we did *Guantanamo*, there was a guy who used to come in to our bar every day and have coffee in the Tricycle. He was a lawyer, worked in legal aid, and he was suddenly interviewed by Gillian and became a character in *Guantanamo* because he represented the Tipton Three, and his office was literally fifty yards across the road in the Kilburn High Road. It's always those coincidences…

SLOVO: He was very good as well.

KENT: He was wonderful.

EDGAR: I mention the prison because one of the great dramatic coups is when the woman who was shopped by her mother writes in from prison and her complaint is that it's been assumed that she's a low-life from an estate, but 'she's not that at all'. But the two men who are referred to, Man 1 and Man 2, who were clearly rioters, what was their provenance?

KENT: Well again, a wonderful coincidence: someone we'd had in our youth theatre, had been working in Youth Theatres for quite some time and he'd got into an underground film company and I'd heard a little about him. Then I went to a dinner party, and there at the dinner party was (Margaret Hodge), and she said 'My son is working with this guy, so and so...' and I said, 'Oh what are they doing?' and they said, 'They're doing guerrilla filming!' Margaret Hodge's son was doing this as well, was doing something where they were interviewing rioters anonymously and making a movie. We couldn't get rioters because they could have gone to jail, if we'd interviewed them the police could have come to us and said -

SLOVO: We did actually have a phone line asking rioters to ring in anonymously and nobody rung in anonymously.

KENT: One person did.

SLOVO: A woman phoned in to complain about the riots. But they had been filming during the riots, when rioters were prepared to talk about what they were doing. As soon as the riots were over, which was when we started work on the play, the punitive nature of the justice system meant that nobody involved was going to talk about it. But the material we got is because that's people who weren't watching themselves, they were in the middle of rioting.

KENT: And we bought the footage, I mean we actually had to pay for the footage, it cost quite a lot of money. But it allowed some young film makers to progress their career, so that was worth doing.

SLOVO: Nick's dinner parties were very helpful throughout this: he was continually picking people up at them.

KENT: Well partly through Richard, he had great connections, through *The Guardian*.

EDGAR: I want to ask you all the big question that comes out of this, which is that there have been interview plays before, there have been Tribunal plays before, there have been trial plays before. The first play we have, *The Persians* by Aeschylus, is a fact-based drama – but clearly since 9/11 it's been the predominant way that political theatre has existed. You were obviously there earlier because the first four plays were done in the 90s. But why do you think the normal way of making political theatre, which is to embed characters in fictional settings which are representative of social and political issues, seems to have been found wanting over the last fifteen or twenty years. Why is it that fact-based drama has become so potent?

KENT: Well I've just gone the other way around actually, in many ways, because *The Bomb* and *The Great Game: Afghanistan* have been going towards fiction, taking a group of playwrights writing on a common theme. But I think that the reason that we came to these plays, which are now being *called* Tribunal plays, was because I think justice was not restorative in the way that Archbishop Tutu has talked about. These public inquiries have been about where something has gone very wrong with our society, that's why they've been set up, and in a way *The Riots* and *Guantanamo* were our own public inquiries. There's been a necessity, I think, to use the facts that those plays have thrown up and to expose those facts to a very wide public, and to allow people to engage with those issues because they are facts and they are true. And do something about purging society in some way.

EDGAR: So it's not just that it's very effective, and it's very dramatic and immediate.

KENT: No, there's been a mission. For me, there's been a mission.

SLOVO: Can I answer: I do think that there are a number of reasons for it. One of them *is* the Tribunal plays. What Nick and Richard did at the Tricycle has partly been why there have been more of these plays: people took and ran with the idea. I think it's something to do with what's happened to television, that there are no documentaries any more. There used to be long feature documentaries on television that would do some of what was done here. I think the nature of newspapers has also changed so that people can't get the whole story going on. And then I suspect it's something about the way people think about politics. Those kind of plays were left-wing political plays and it's no longer so. You know, the last twenty years have not been so great for left-wing politics but this is a way of talking politics without seeming to come from a particular point.

NORTON-TAYLOR: I think it's absolutely right, because there are a lack of heavy, good documentaries like *Dispatches* used to be but also because people don't trust what they read because of spinning – after Blair and all that, Alastair Campbell, and so on. It is happening all the time now of course, and it doesn't have to be Labour, it can be all parties. People trust what they heard, it seems to me, in the theatre whether it's *Guantanamo, The Riots* or our Tribunal plays.

EDGAR: One of the things about all of these plays is that they wear their research on their sleeve, don't they? They're actually saying, you could write a play about the riots or a film about the riots in which you didn't have to quote from the interviews at all, but based on those interviews. But I think to a certain extent we've lost faith in what we receive, and one of the things we've lost faith in is fiction. Which is why a lot of novelists are now writing fact-based novels. The idea that novelists create a completely imagined world full of complete characters that they have created and know everything about, is now deeply unfashionable, even among novelists.

SLOVO: But actually if you think about David Hare's *Stuff Happens*: that was a combination of fact and fiction that he had made up, and to my mind the fiction was more successful than the fact, it seemed more real to me than the fact.

EDGAR: Well it's interesting that there's a note in the published version of David Hare's *Gethsemane,* which is that the three fact-based plays that he had done which were *Permanent Way*, which was an interview-based play about the privatisation of the railways, and then *Stuff Happens* which was about the build-up to the Iraq War, and then *Gethsemane* which is a fictionalised version of New Labour that had become progressively less fact-based. I get the feeling that people are now moving away from fact-based drama, that fact-based drama has, as it were, done its job. And it may be that part of that job has been to put theatre back at the centre of political life.

***

HALF THE PICTURE

Adapted and redacted by
Richard Norton-Taylor

with additional material
by John McGrath

First performed at the Tricycle Theatre on 14 June, 1994.
Directed by Nicolas Kent.

starring

Margaret Thatcher and John Major

with

Sir Nicholas Lyell
Michael Heseltine
William Waldegrave
Alan Clark

and introducing

Presiley Baxendale QC

With the exception of a very few phrases added only to clarify points of fact and identify individuals, the words are those exchanged between Lord Justice Scott and Presiley Baxendale QC and the witnesses.

Act One

SCENE I

Enter a 56-year-old woman, smart, attractive: COLETTE, who worked in the office at Matrix Churchill. She faces audience.

COLETTE: I worked in the office at Matrix Churchill, Coventry. I saw what was going on. The machine tools Matrix Churchill were selling to Iraq were undoubtedly designed for making artillery shells and mortar-bombs. So when I wrote to Geoffrey Howe, the Foreign Secretary, telling him this, they said I was just being menopausal. I swallowed the insult to women in general, and thought quietly about the tens of thousands of women and their babies being killed among the Kurds and the Marsh Arabs in Iraq. I felt a great sense of identification with them. So I wrote to the Foreign Secretary, so he would know, and couldn't say he didn't, about what we were being asked to do. But, of course, he was a man. I believe he sent copies of my letter to other men, in the Ministry of Defence, in the Department of Trade and Industry, and in MI6. What I didn't realise was that, of course, they all knew. Mr Henderson had been telling MI6 all along. They all denied they knew, but my letter I suppose they couldn't avoid. Anyway, when Mr Henderson was arrested and put on trial, the judge eventually had to admit they knew. God bless him. He must have been a bit...menopausal. He dismissed the case against Mr Henderson, but now what I wonder is: does this mean it's all right to sell machine tools for horrible weapons to people like Saddam Hussein as long as you tell the Secret Service? Or as long as we ordinary people don't find out? The Government said it *wasn't* doing what it was doing and it helped to kill all those people. Why? We're all out of work now anyway... Does this mean I shouldn't have written to Geoffrey Howe? I've got three children, all boys, growing up. I wonder what I should be teaching them. What they're learning.

(She goes off, thoughtful.)

SCENE II

Evidence of John Major.

BAX: 10th November 1992. You are answering this question in Parliament, a question from Mr John Smith: 'Does the Prime Minister recall assuring the House in January 1991 that 'For some considerable time, we have not supplied arms of Iraq'? How does the Prime Minister reconcile the assurance with the revelation in the government documents produced at the Matrix Churchill trial, that as late as 27th July, 1990, only six days before the invasion of Kuwait, machine tools, known to be intended to make fuses for missiles and artillery shells, were supplied to Iraq?' Then your answer: 'The Right Honourable and learned Gentleman knows that from 1985 until the Iraqi invasion of Kuwait, the Government operated under guidelines first set out by then Foreign Secretary.' And then you refer to the full embargo since the invasion.

MAJOR: The question I was specifically asked, of course, was about supplying arms to Iraq, and, of course, arms are self-evidently lethal. I was responding to the fact that those arms were banned, and that the embargo was clear-cut.

SCOTT: One of the problems is not only in questions, but also sometimes in answers, the expression 'arms' is used in its correct sense.

MAJOR: I agree.

SCOTT: And sometimes in a broad sense, including also just defence-related equipment. It is often not quite clear in what sense it should be read.

MAJOR: I agree. Here, there was no doubt, I think, in terms of the question, that it was referring to arms. I responded to it entirely accurately.

BAX: You are saying that the original question was: 'We have not supplied arms to Iraq', and so, although –

SCOTT: The original question was talking about machine tools.

MAJOR: The question here is: 'Does the Prime Minister recall assuring the House in January 1991 that "For some considerable time we have not supplied arms to Iraq"?'

SCOTT: It goes on to refer to machine tools. He – John Smith – wants to know whether that assurance is consistent with what he says has been happening in regard to machine tools.

MAJOR: If it is thought that machine tools were likely to be used for lethal weapons, and that is, of course, why we have the guidelines. One of the points you have to consider, of course, is whether there was a change in 1988. I had no knowledge of any discussion of the change in 1988. It was on that basis I replied to the question in the House.

SCOTT: Did you regard your answer as dealing with arms strictly, or with arms and things like machine tools?

MAJOR: In the heat of the Prime Minister's question time, it is difficult to recall at this distance, but, by that, you mean did I think I was making a clever and cunning distinction between the two in order to hide something that I knew and did not want to reveal, the answer is no.

SCOTT: I did not meant that. I wondered… I wondered were you interpreting the question as being directed strictly to arms?

MAJOR: I was responding to the fact that, in my judgement, and on the basis of the information available to me, we, that is to say the Government, had followed the guidelines strictly, from their inception and thereafter.

BAX: I would like to go on, we can now carry on with the chronology. Three days later, on 13th November, 1992, you received a minute from your private secretary, Stephen Wall, saying: 'The Cabinet Office and other departments will be working through the weekend to produce as comprehensive a chronology as possible on the Matrix Churchill issue. There are a lot of simple questions, but very few simple answers. It emerges, for example, that the Howe guidelines of 1985 were amended by ministers in December 1988, but the amendment was never announced in Parliament.' I see a cross against the bit about the amendment. Is that your cross? Is that not your writing at the top of the page?

MAJOR: Yes, it is my cross because Mr Wall's note of 13th November 1992 was the first I knew about it.

BAX: There is a tick against documents that you had seen, the bit about 'there is no evidence'?

MAJOR: I have ticked the sentence here which says: 'There is no evidence that, as Foreign Secretary, you saw the documents.' In retrospect, one can never be certain of those things. I asked to check what I had actually known in the welter of papers that crossed the ministers' desks, and there is the response from the Civil Service that I had not seen the documents.

BAX: If we go over the page, there are suggestions about the accusations that could be made against you.

MAJOR: That is correct. One of the charges at the time, of course, was that, in some way, I must have known, because I had been the Chancellor, because I had been Foreign Secretary, because I had been Prime Minister – that, therefore, I must have known what was going on… I was asking precisely what I had known and I asked for all the documentation to be checked. What you have read is the response that came back checking over again what I knew.

BAX: Going back to the beginning of this document, you have marked the bit about the amendment was never announced to Parliament. It is only a very short time after the answer to Mr Smith in the House of Commons. In the light of the evidence you have been giving us, did you consider at this stage, 'Gosh, perhaps I should be clarifying that answer and saying, "The guidelines *were* amended"?'

MAJOR: I did – you will see why I did not – you can recall the atmosphere at the time. There was a great deal of high-profile publicity. It was a very interesting few days. I asked for further inquiries to be made.

BAX: Some days later, on 23rd November, 1992, Mr Heseltine made a speech in the House of Commons. He said. 'A change in the wording of the guidelines was obviously necessary to reflect the fact that there had been a ceasefire in the Iran-Iraq war.' So at this stage, Mr Heseltine was saying there *was* a change.

MAJOR: He thought there was. Two days later further research suggested that there was not.

BAX: Do you have the document sent to your private secretary – copied to Sir Robin Butler, the Cabinet Secretary, from Miss Neville-Jones, on 25th November, 1992?

MAJOR: Yes.

BAX: Wonderful, good. If we could go through it. She refers to a further element 'that has come to light since I last minuted you. Further research in files obtained from the Foreign Office show that a group of junior ministers which considered a change in the guidelines subsequently decided not to do so. There was, therefore, no cause for a statement in the House of Commons and it is absolutely true to say that the guidelines were not changed, and, therefore the House was not misled'. Your cross is against that part of it?

MAJOR: That is correct. There was a great deal of uncertainty over what had actually happened...we were in a very frenetic atmosphere.

BAX: Then a few days later, we get a comment from Mr Heseltine: 'Mr. Heseltine accepts the Cabinet Office conclusion that the guidelines themselves were never formally changed, and that it was in their interpretation that the ceasefire was reflected.' He goes on to say: 'It seems clear that ministers involved at the time intended the change of approach to represent a more liberal policy towards defence exports to Iraq... It would be extremely disingenuous for us now to say that there had been no change. It underlines the unstable nature of the ground beneath ministers' feet.'

MAJOR: I agree with the conclusion of Mr Heseltine's letter. I have to say I did not necessarily accept all his phraseology. What Mr Heseltine was seeking to do in that letter, and sensibly seeking to do, was the same point I referred to a moment ago: to look for a way to avoid misleading or confusing people. At that stage, of course, Mr Heseltine had not seen all the documentation, which has subsequently been submitted to this inquiry.

BAX: I am now going back a month to October 1992, just before the Matrix Churchill trial. It is a minute from the Foreign Secretary's office to 10 Downing Street. 'The trial may be embarrassing for the Government because it will involve the disclosure of documents which reveal discussions between ministers and officials. The press may use the disclosures in an unhelpful sense to suggest that ministers knowingly broke their own guidelines.'

MAJOR: I do not remember this specifically, but clearly did not agree to drop the prosecution.

SCOTT: Prime Minister, that, I am sure you will be glad to hear, brings to an end the questions which we wanted your help about. If you want to make any additions or corrections, of course we will be very glad if you would.

MAJOR: Sir Richard, thank you very much indeed.

SCENE III

Evidence of Mark Higson.

BAX: Mr Higson, please can I confirm that from 23rd March, 1989 until January 1990, you were desk for Iraq at the Foreign Office?

HIGSON: Yes. Under David Gore-Booth who was the assistant under-secretary responsible for Middle Eastern affairs, it involved input into other departments' work with Iraq, and political input. That could be anything from answering letters to an awful lot of work on political hostages or prisoners (depending on what you want to call them) and lobbying or drafting lobbying papers for ministers and senior officials.

SCOTT: Lobbying papers? What sort of lobbying papers?

HIGSON: Lobbying other possible intermediaries for the release of the likes of Mrs Parish and Ian Richter.

BAX: Were you the person who was principally responsible for drafting the letters that were directly related to Iraq? How did it work?

HIGSON: How it worked was that a particular room in the Middle East Department had two sides and both had flags up at either end, one which was Iranian and one which was Iraqi.

BAX: So you would remember which side you were on?

HIGSON: Yes, I certainly do. I was very partisan.

BAX: I want to go to a Foreign Office document dated 6th October 1989. There is some handwriting on the left-hand side of it. Rather than squint and try to work out what it says, if you turn over the page, you have a transcription of it. That is a handwritten note by Mr Waldegrave, is it not?

HIGSON: Yes.

BAX: Could we just look at it for a minute? 'I doubt if there is any future market of such a scale anywhere where the UK is potentially so well placed if we play our diplomatic hand correctly, nor can I think of any major market where the importance of diplomacy is so great on our commercial position. We must not allow it to go to the French, Germans, Japanese, Koreans etcetera... The priority of Iraq in our policy should be very high: in commercial terms, comparable to South Africa in my view... A few more Bazofts or another bout of internal repression would make this more difficult.' What I wanted to ask you about was did those comments of Mr Waldegrave sum up, so far as you were aware, the Foreign Office view of Iraq at the time?

HIGSON: Yes.

BAX: It was seen that it was a very important commercial market?

HIGSON: The Iraqi market, after the end of the Iran-Iraq war, was summed up as being 'the big prize'. However distasteful we found the Iraqi regime, we could not afford to be left behind in developing trade links, and we were in prime position, to use a motor racing phrase.

SCOTT: Everybody recognised the big prize, but the Foreign Office was not prepared to go as far as other ministries to try to achieve it and to try to capture it?

HIGSON: We needed – this my opinion, which you have asked for – to sort out other problems as well. The fact that we were the Ministry tasked with all the other questions, such as gassing of Kurds, removal of the marsh Arabs, etcetera, from the south of the country, to the execution of Bazoft, etcetera, meant that, yes, we took a slightly more reserved position.

BAX: In your statement, you say you were aware of changes to the guidelines through the discussions between Mr Waldegrave, Lord Trefgarne, and Alan Clark in 1988. There was a relaxation, was there not?

HIGSON: Yes, and it was not announced – we continued to churn out the same old line.

BAX: On 7th February, 1989, there was a letter from Mr Waldegrave's private secretary to Alan Clark's private secretary, where he says: 'Mr Waldegrave is content for us to implement a more liberal policy on defence sales without any public announcement.' Did you know why at that stage it was preferable not to have to announce publically any change in the guidelines?

HIGSON: To be quite honest, I was simply advised that it was preferable not to make any public announcement, so I continued to use the old guidelines in response to members of the public and to MPs.

BAX: Did anyone tell you why it was preferable not to announce them? What was the reason? What was the Foreign Office's view about it?

HIGSON: I am very much ex-Foreign Office. It was an issue at the time that we officially kept a position of neutrality officially between the two countries. There was obviously a swing towards Iraq. Iran was still being seen as a complete pariah, and we wanted to allow greater flexibility towards Iraq which was going to be potentially very lucrative indeed.

BAX: No one wanted to announce this?

HIGSON: You will have to ask ministers about that.

BAX: I just wondered what –

HIGSON: I just did what I was told... Can I just come back to that last point, when I listed what I was told? The answer is obviously that public perceptions of both regimes would have been that they were as vile as each other and we had particular problems with both. Yet the potential for Britain in relation to trade was with Iraq, but this would have been seen as unacceptable.

SCOTT: You mean the public would not stand for it?

HIGSON: We were getting, you know, tens and tens of letters about gassing of the Kurds and political prisoners or hostages and whatever. It would have been unacceptable to have announced the fact that we were relaxing a policy in favour of Iraq.

SCOTT: Unacceptable because of the public reaction?

HIGSON: Public and parliamentary reaction.

BAX: Unacceptable to members of the public and Members of Parliament?

HIGSON: Yes.

BAX: Would there have been a lot of trouble?

HIGSON: There would have been a lot of unanswered letters sitting around. There would have been trouble from the public and Members of Parliament if we had announced publicly that there was a relaxation in favour of Iraq.

BAX: You have been saying you have been giving your view. What I want to know is: at the time, is that the reason you understood why it was not being announced publicly?

HIGSON: We were doing a juggling act. There was a lot to gain and there was also a lot to lose. As Mr Waldegrave said in his letter to Mr Clark, he was satisfied with going along that line provided that, if it came out into the public domain, the Department of Trade would take the responsibility, the onus.

BAX: I want to make quite sure about this. Are you saying that the position was that Parliament was not to know, because otherwise Members of Parliament would have disagreed and wanted to discuss it?

HIGSON: Personal view – yes.

BAX: Members of the House of Lords did not leave it there. They picked it up. The answer you have drafted: 'British arms supplies to both Iraq and Iran continued to be governed by very strict guidelines', does not set out the true position, does it?

HIGSON: No.

SCOTT: If one was looking for an adjective to describe the answer as compared to the the then current practice, what one would you choose?

HIGSON: I am not allowed to swear, am I?

SCOTT: Without swearing, how would you react to the adjective, 'misleading'?

HIGSON: It was certainly misleading.

BAX: This was not telling the truth, was it?

HIGSON: It was one of the contributory reasons for why I actually left the Foreign Office.

BAX: Had you at any time been told, when you were at the Foreign Office, whether it was important to tell truthful answers to the House of Lords or the House of Commons.

HIGSON: Well, any civil servant's job is going to be, to quote somebody else, 'economical with the truth'. Sometimes, for reasons which obviously were not in the public domain, we had to sort of give only 75 per cent of the story and not 100 per cent.

BAX: Less than 75 per cent?

HIGSON: Fifty.

SCOTT: There is a distinction between a half truth and an untruth. Your 75 per cent is not a half, it is a three-quarter truth. Then there is an untruth, which is just not true. It is not a question of just being true to a point.

HIGSON: I will have to think about this one.

SCOTT: Just tell me… If someone in the Foreign Office asks for information from another department, either he gets answered or he is told to go and mind his own business.

HIGSON: The moment you enter a ministry, you are indoctrinated with 'need-to-know'. I find it as risible and unacceptable as I think you both do… We were lying to each other.

SCENE IV

Evidence of David Gore-Booth.

SCOTT: Mr Gore-Booth, good morning. Thank you very much for sending us your statement which we have of course, read with great interest. Miss Baxendale, on my left, will mainly be asking you some questions arising from it, and I may ask some myself.

BAX: Can I ask you about asking questions in Parliament? If there is a question, it should be fully answered, should it not? The answer should be sufficiently full to give a true meaning?

G-BOOTH: Questions should be answered so as to give the maximum degree of satisfaction possible to the questioner.

BAX: I am not sure you really mean that, because that is rather like people just giving you the answer you want to hear, I think is what you have just said. I do not think you quite mean that.

G-BOOTH: No, it might be the answer you do not want to hear.

BAX: That does not give you much satisfaction. Should the answer be accurate?

G-BOOTH: Of course.

BAX: And they should not be half the picture?

G-BOOTH: They might be half the picture. You said, should they be accurate and I said yes, they should.

SCOTT: On a more broad approach to answering questions, there would be nothing the matter with an approach which proceeded on the footing that you would in every case be as forthcoming as you could?

G-BOOTH: Correct. But there are often cases in which you cannot be so forthcoming, for reasons of what are called foreign policy.

SCOTT: It is a question of where you start from. If you start from the view that you are going to be as forthcoming as you can, you will have a very good reason for holding something back.

SCOTT: It is very much for a minister to decide how to answer a parliamentary question and then the civil servants draft it. So the extent to which an answer should be full, half-full, or empty, is very much a ministerial decision.

BAX: Lord Glenarthur's answer in the House of Lords on 20th April, 1989, does not really set out the full picture, does it, with the sentence: 'British arms supplies to both Iran and Iraq continue to be governed by very strict guidelines preventing the supply of lethal equipment to either side'?

G-BOOTH: That is a correct statement.

SCOTT: Notwithstanding the decision to be more liberal in the approach for applications for exports for Iraq?

G-BOOTH: I think the statement as made by Lord Glenarthur is absolutely correct. Given that it had been decided that there would be no announcement of the modification of the guidelines, that seems to me to be an entirely appropriate response.

BAX: You say that the original guideline 3 is still in place?

G-BOOTH: It is kept under constant review and applied on a case by case basis in the light of the prevailing circumstances, including the ceasefire.

BAX: That is completely ridiculous, is it not, in the light of the fact that it has been amended for Iraq, to completely different words?

G-BOOTH: I do not think so at all. We come back to the point of whether you think the British public and parliament are so dumb as to realise that there has not been a ceasefire.

SCOTT: They certainly cannot have known what the revised wording was.

G-BOOTH: Indeed not, but it had been decided not to make a public announcement.

BAX: It is not completely misleading?

G-BOOTH: I do not think so at all.

BAX: Can I ask you about something? It is a document put out by the Ministry of Defence. It is about guidance on answering parliamentary questions: 'Ministries generally prefer to give parliamentary answers that are factual and straightforward. Answers must be meticulously accurate and worded in clear and unambiguous terms. An error of fact or an answer that misleads the House can be dreadfully embarrassing to the minister.' Do you think that what we have just seen in relation to Lord Glenarthur would have complied with the Ministry of Defence guidelines that we have just been looking at?

G-BOOTH: Yes.

BAX: In your view, is it factual, straightforward, meticulously accurate and in clear unambiguous terms?

G-BOOTH: Yes.

BAX: Can I suggest that, in fact, for various policy reasons, there was a view that the House of Lords should not be told that a more relaxed attitude had been adopted in respect of Iraq?

G-BOOTH: Yes, it had been agreed that there should be no public announcement ... and that is what happened.

SCOTT: Why should that have not been announced?

G-BOOTH: Because there are all sorts of reasons why Iraqis were not very popular, even though they were slightly more popular than the Iranians.

SCOTT: There would have been domestic upset because of the chemical warfare.

G-BOOTH: Kurds, chemical warfare and so on, on the other hand; and also that we were trying, rather unsuccessfully

I admit, to establish and maintain a relationship with Iran. Of course, one of the factors that would have complicated that would be the Iranians knowing that we were giving the Iraqis a slightly better treatment than the Iranians were getting. There was a myriad of foreign policy reasons tucked away.

BAX: Rather like you were saying that the British public are not idiots; presumably neither are the Iranians…

G-BOOTH: That is a very hazardous statement.

BAX: I would have not thought so. If they had just issued a *fatwa* against Salman Rushdie, there is enormous political upset going on about it. Would they not be surprised to discover that maybe the British Government was favouring to some extent the Iraqi government?

G-BOOTH: The Iranians are not people who think in very logical terms. They thought the *fatwa* was perfectly justified and we should not have reacted to it at all.

BAX: I am now going to the consideration of the Matrix Churchill export licence applications at the beginning of 1989. What you need is MoD 24, Volume 1. It is page 72A. This document sets out the view of Defence Intelligence. Then the document refers to Hutteen, described as the main ammunition manufacturing plant in Iraq, and to Nassr, capable of producing 500,000 artillery rounds of assorted calibres annually. Defence Intelligence says that if this information had been available originally, the export licences would not have been granted. Do you think it would have been useful to have known about this intelligence?

G-BOOTH: When I was discussing my travel plans with a doctor in Riyadh before coming, he referred me to something called a retrospectrascope, which you stick into people and it enables you to look backwards. You are drawing me down the track of trying to look backwards in the light of information which we now have and which we did not have at the time. I am reluctant to get drawn too far down that track.

SCOTT: I think you have a rely on me to make a fair use of your answers. Of course, I understand you are being asked to look back. Can you answer the question?

G-BOOTH: If we had known then what we know about Iraqi arms procurement programmes now, and if we had known then that Saddam was intending to invade Kuwait, I dare say the decision would have gone differently. Of course, my own view at the time was that it should have gone differently.

BAX: I was going to move…you'll be delighted to hear we're moving on to another section. We are whizzing through sections now. We are going on to FCO 230, page 48. A Foreign Office official wrote a note saying: 'We need to know if Matrix Churchill cheat, by not returning to the UK the equipment on display at the Baghdad Trade Fair.' Then it refers to a letter from DTI to FO, Middle East Department, about a request from Matrix Churchill to have made permanent a temporary export licence issued for two lathes, taken to the Baghdad Trade Fair last year: 'The company now has a firm order from Iraq for these lathes, but the end user was known to be the Iraqi missile programme.' Do you think you should have known about it?

G-BOOTH: If I had not seen it, how do I know if it existed?

SCOTT: You are seeing it now and you are being asked now whether you think this ought to be brought to your attention.

G-BOOTH: Again this is not the line of questioning that I think is appropriate, the retrospectrascopic line of questioning.

BAX: I would now like to ask you about a parliamentary question. It is directed to DT1 Ministers, sent to the Foreign Office for clearance. It is MoD 40/3, page 293, 7th November 1989: 'To ask the Secretary of State for

Trade and Industry what investigations his department has undertaken into the Matrix Churchill company and the possibility that the company is supplying parts to Iraq which could be used in ballistic missile production.' The answer given is: 'I have no reason to believe that the company has contravened UK export controls.' The response is not an answer to the question, is it?

G-BOOTH: I thought you were going to ask me whether this was an accurate and sufficient answer to the question to which I say, 'Yes', in the light of information available at the time.

BAX: Give yourself a chance to think before you say something like that. Look carefully at the question. The answer: 'I have no reason to believe that the company has contravened UK export controls', is not an answer to the question, is it?

G-BOOTH: I think you must put these questions to those more concerned.

SCOTT: It is not an answer to the question, is it? It is an evasion of the question, and the answer to the question would have been an extremely embarrassing one?

G-BOOTH: It must eventually be for ministers to decided the terms in which they answer parliamentary questions.

SCENE V

Enter Mustafa, a Kurd, in Kurdish costume. He sits and talks to the audience.

MUSTAFA: To be a Kurd is to be at war. Our country and our people live up in one big mass of mountains, but foreigners have drawn lines, have divided the home of the Kurds between Turkey, Syria, Iran, Russia, and Iraq. Our legend says the Prophet called all the princes of the world to embrace Islam. Oguz Khan, the Prince of Turkestan, sent a Kurd to represent him. When the Prophet saw this giant, with his piercing eyes, and learnt he was a Kurd,

Mohammed prayed to God that such a terrifying people will never unite as a single nation. So far, his prayer has been answered. Sometimes it seems every nation in the world take it in turn to try to destroy us. This is maybe lucky – when they stop for a week, we try to destroy each other. There was a time when we came to realise that whenever Turks fought Persian, Iraqi fought Turk, it was always Kurdish blood that was split. We tried to stop fighting each other, and to stop fighting as mercenaries in other people's wars. We began to unite, to behave like a nation. What we needed was to have some self-government in Iraq. In 1968, Saddam Hussein came to our mountains to promise exactly that. But he was, of course, lying, playing games with us. Then the Shah of Persia, and the CIA, said they would support us if we fought against Saddam. We did. But after three years, no more. They were playing games with us. When Saddam went to war with the Ayatollah, of course we fought against Saddam again. We were not prepared for what came next. Perhaps we are aggressive, perhaps we trust no one but ourselves, we have no reason. We do not deserve genocide. From 1985, Saddam tried to wipe us out. In Suleimaniyeh, 300 Children were rounded up and tortured, 23 people shot, eight buried alive. We demonstrated: 200 more were shot. In 1987, Saddam sent his cousin, Majid, the one he later sent to govern Kuwait. He was to 'Arabize' Kurdistan. Four thousand villages were demolished, half a million Kurds sent to protected camps, many out of our country, whole areas were prohibited, emptied, any person or animal in them was shot, artillery, helicopter gun-ships, jet planes were used against us. Then Majid ordered chemical warfare against us – sulphur mustard gas, and nerve gas, the worst of all. Men, women and children are left with a film over their eyes, out of their nose and mouth comes a horrible slime, their skin peels, it bubbles up. On 16 March, 1988, Iraqi planes flew over Halabja. They dropped cyanide, mustard, nerve gas. Five thousand people died this horrible death. Nearly all of them were civilians. They died because they were born Kurdish. Your Government knew about this. Yet your Government allowed your countrymen to help these unspeakable people to make the shells they fired, even the bombs they dropped the chemicals in. They found out, as we found out, what a friend they had in Saddam after he defeated Ayatollah's people. He turned on us with even more cruelty. Then he turned on you: he took Kuwait. And you may think you have won. But he is still there. We know he is still there. And we are still there. *(He goes.)*

SCENE VI

Evidence of William Waldegrave.

BAX: Mr Waldegrave, please can I confirm that you were Minister of State at the Foreign Office from July 1988 until November 1990?

WALDE: That is right.

BAX: You say in your statement to us that: 'It was important that the policy of restraint in defence sales to Iran and Iraq, and indeed other countries in the region, was understood and, if there had been a change in policy, Parliament should normally be told.' Did you think it was important that Parliament, and through it, the public, should know about the guidelines?

WALDE: Yes.

SCOTT: There had been, for very many years, within the Foreign Office internal guidelines as to the manner in which export applications relating to defence equipment should be dealt with, indicating the importance to be given to the human rights record of the country concerned, the military capability of the country and so on. What was the difference that prompted the 1985 guidelines?

WALDE: I guess – I am now out of my period – but I think the Iran-Iraq was turning out to be a really major war. It was not just an incursion. Persians and Arabs had been squabbling with each other for 8,000 years, but this was turning out to be a very major war with hundreds of thousands of people killed. Though it is notable that there is not much debate. There is understandable concern when there is an atrocity on one side or the other. But I think Parliament took the realistic view there was not actually much we could do about it. In terms of, I remember, parliamentary interest, there were far more debates, for example, about Cambodia and there was not much we could do about that either.

SCOTT: There were quite a number of questions arising out of the atrocities?

WALDE: I am not saying there was no interest. When there was some frightful horror, like gassing of Kurds, like a variety of horrors that went back beyond my time, actually in the conduct of the war and in the awful things that happened immediately after the war, there was indeed interest.

BAX: That is one of the reasons why Parliament should be told. If MPs do not agree with policy, it can be discussed, it can be debated in Parliament.

WALDE: I guess so.

BAX: There was a paper prepared by the Foreign Office, the intention was it should go to the Prime Minister. Subject: 'Implications of a ceasefire for defence sales to Iran and Iraq.'

SCOTT: This seems to me contemplating relaxing restrictions, letting through things that would have otherwise been refused.

WALDE: The Foreign Secretary, Sir Geoffrey Howe, says, 'We do not want to have a great shaboozal in public, which is then going to cause a bad signal to Iraq, which has been behaving extremely badly.'

BAX: If we go to the Foreign Secretary's comments on defence sales – he says he is 'reluctant to put this paper forward'. He feels it would look 'very cynical if so soon after expressing outrage over Iraqi treatment of the Kurds, we were to adopt a more flexible approach on arms sales'. It is clear the Foreign Secretary did not think the paper should be circulated.

WALDE: Right.

BAX: Then there is a letter of 4th November from Mr Clark to you. It says: 'Concerned about a large number of licence applications, for exports of dual use equipment for Iraq and Iran.' He refers to the harm that is being done to British Industry. Then he says: 'I recognise, of course, that whatever is agreed between us will require the Prime Minister's approval.'

WALDE: Yes.

BAX: All this correspondence between you and Alan Clark is copied to the Prime Minister, is it not? That is presumably because of an earlier comment from her private secretary saying that the Prime Minister wanted to be kept closely in touch with it?

WALDE: Sorry, I do not expect you to understand this extremely well, but silence is an important event when you are circulating things to other ministers, and I think that the lack of comfort from on high means something too.

SCOTT: I am not quite sure what that means. If ministers' correspondence goes to the Prime Minister and there is silence, it does not mean anything at all?

WALDE: All that it can be taken as meaning is that the argument will continue.

SCOTT: The point remains open?

WALDE: The point remains open.

BAX: Are you saying the new wording covering exports to Iraq was never used, or are you saying, because it never went to the Foreign Secretary and the Prime Minister and it was not announced, the guidelines were never changed?

WALDE: It is perfectly clear the guidelines were never changed.

SCOTT: There is a problem about this, which has been keeping me awake at night. The proposition that seems to come from your paper to the inquiry is that the guidelines were announced in 1985. The guidelines could not be changed without the proposal going to senior ministers, the Prime Minister, and being announced in Parliament. None of these things ever happened. Ergo, the guidelines were never changed.

WALDE: To accept that is the only argument, you have to believe that Whitehall is basically honest, which I do believe.

BAX: Surely the most important thing is what they are doing?

WALDE: Absolutely.

BAX: The policy you are operating is not what you say, it is what you do.

WALDE: We kept saying to each other, 'You cannot agree these revised guidelines until they have gone to Number 10 and goodness knows what.'

BAX: What happens next is the *fatwa* on 14th February 1989.

SCOTT: There was a tilt in favour of Iraq as a result of the *fatwa*.

WALDE: There was, indeed, but not derived from any change in British policy about the neutrality that we had in the Iran-Iraq conflict.

SCOTT: That conflict, of course, at this stage being at an end?

WALDE: Being at an end, but still fragile. I do not know whether I can just say a word about the extraordinary capacity of people in the Middle East to believe peculiar things about Britain. There is a story which I believe is true that the Iranians say that if you lift up the beard of the Ayatollah, you find 'Made in England' written underneath because we had clearly put the Ayatollah there because we wanted to get rid of the Shah, because that Shah was too pro-America. It is quite difficult to redress that kind of public opinion.

SCOTT: It is something you should try?

WALDE: I think the Foreign Office came to the conclusion it was doomed sometimes.

BAX: You said that, after the *fatwa*, I think you said no one referred to the revised wording of the guidelines again.

WALDE: You have clearly shown me from the documents that this is wrong. If you, Sir Richard, have been worrying about this at night, you can imagine that I have, because it is jolly important to me, and I have come to the conclusion that we did not do wrong.

BAX: There was a Ministry of Defence paper from Mr Barrett saying: 'Mr Waldegrave is content for us to implement a more liberal Policy on defence sales without an public announcement on the subject.'

WALDE: It is not the most brilliantly drafted note.

BAX: It fits very nicely. I do not understand any problems with it.

WALDE: The letter should have said something like: 'Mr Waldegrave is content for us to implement the more liberal *interpretation* of the *existing* guidelines.'

SCOTT: Why can you not tell Parliament what [formula] is being used [even] on a trial basis?

WALDE: We did not want to stir up a hornet's nest. I will say again, when Sir Richard said he had sleepless nights worrying about this and I subsequently said I had sleepless nights too. After the collapse of the Matrix Churchill trial and all this comes right to the fore. I looked at this and I remember talking to Sir Robin Butler, the Cabinet Secretary, about it at the time saying I do not remember changing the guidelines. Into the papers we dived and find actually that it is not what happened.

BAX: You dive into the papers and you find it is not what happened. We have dived into the papers and we have seen that in practice that *is* what happened. I was now going to move on to what was said publicly. Lord Glenarthur says, 'We should continue to scrutinise rigorously all applications for export licences for the supply of defence equipment to Iraq and Iran.'

SCOTT: Why is not the right answer to say there is the flexible interpretation, the flexible policy, call it what you like, in relation to Iraq?

WALDE: Because it was judged that there were overriding reasons for giving misleading information about tilts to one side or another, to put British citizens at risk, and all the rest of it.

SCOTT: It is not a very healthy feature of a mature democracy that serious issues of this sort can be debated.

WALDE: But it is also, Sir Richard, a definition of what a mature democracy means. I think, that it knows from time to time, in relation to foreign affairs, it is going to be necessary not for everything to be said in detail. There is in this country a certain ambivalence. We are, after France, the free world's second trader in arms-related goods. People want the jobs they do not always want to think about. Whenever Mrs Thatcher or Mr Major comes back, having batted for Britain and won a great deal, everyone says, 'Hooray!' They are heroes on the front page.

SCENE VII

Enter a distinguished North American economist: KENNETH GALBRAITH. *He reads from his own book to the audience.*

GALBRAITH: Because it is so visible, there has been some error of emphasis in identifying the true locus of the military power. In the seemingly sophisticated tradition that associates power with industrial enterprise – in reality, a holdover of Marxist thought and the dominant critical attitudes of that last century – military power is extensively assumed to be associated with the defence industries. The military industrialists are the deus ex-machina; they both procure and profit from the military budget. There is no doubt that the power thus exercised is great: the submission of scientists, engineers, executives is great: the submission of scientists, engineers, executives, workers, and the defence-dependent communities is won thereby. Of this power legislators are made acutely conscious, and the campaign contributions from the corporations involved add to their awareness. But the defence industries are only an extension of a larger structure, the heart of which lies in the autonomous processes of government.

SCENE VIII

Evidence of Alan Barrett.

BAX: Mr Barrett, you were in post at the Defence Export Services Secretariat from June 1987 to September 1990. A Treasury official reported that the Ministry of Defence's defence export services organisation was gung-ho to support sales of military equipment to Iraq and almost anywhere.

BARR: I think that is totally unjustified.

BAX: Also, Colonel Glazebrook of the Ministry of Defence had written to you commenting that Alan Clark was 'gung-ho for defence sales!' You agree you may have said something that implied that meaning, is that right?

BARR: Yes, I do not dispute that at all. I cannot remember using those precise words. What does 'gung-ho' mean?

SCOTT: I would take it as meaning very, very enthusiastic – perhaps double the 'verys' – very, very, enthusiastic?

BARR: Yes, very enthusiastic.

BAX: What I would like to do now is to come to your briefing for the ministerial meeting of 23rd December, 1988.

'The Prime Minister agreed that, in order to protect the intelligence source, the licences already granted should not be revoked.' The point is picked up again at Page 45. 'More disturbing intelligence coming to light. Press for a separate submission to go to the Prime Minister, as she was involved last time.' At that time, you clearly thought the Prime Minister had been involved in the initial consideration of the Matrix Churchill lathes?

BARR: That is what I wrote at that time, yes. I would like, at this stage, to read what I have actually written in my present submission to you: 'I cannot now find any papers to corroborate the statement in the aide memoire I drafted then. I can only assume now that I was mistaken.'

BAX: In the 1988 aide memoire, you have referred to the Prime Minister twice in one paragraph. This is no casual dropping of the name in. I cannot imagine you would casually drop the Prime Minister's name in. It seems to me that would have been a rather peculiar thing to do?

BARR: I certainly did not make it up.

SC IX

Evidence of Alan Clark (1).

SCOTT: Mr Clark, thank you very much for coming here today, and thank you for your extremely helpful statement that you provided us with. Presiley Baxendale on my left asks most of the questions, but I may ask a few myself arising out of it.

BAX: Mr Clark, we asked you to provide a general statement describing your role as a minister at the Department of Trade and Industry and the Ministry of Defence. You say: 'My general understanding, coloured possibly by some personal prejudice, is that it was my duty to promote, facilitate and give impetus to British exports and the industries from which they emanated.' Can I then move on the guidelines? You compare them to a

Cheshire Cat, and then you go on to say: 'They were high-sounding, combining, it seemed, both moral and practical considerations, and yet imprecise enough to be overridden in exceptional circumstances.'

CLARK: Yes. I would argue they illustrate the – and this is the kind of thing you could say about them – the constructive tension between positivism and ambiguity, a doctoral thesis of Professor Ayer. The whole of guideline 3 is magnificent – 'We should not in future sanction any new orders which, in our view, would significantly enhance the capability of either side to prolong or exacerbate the conflict.' It is a brilliant piece of drafting, because it is far from being restrictive. It is open to argument in respect of practically every one of its elements. I regarded the guidelines as being so imprecise and so obviously drafted with the objective of flexibility in either direction – elasticity, shall I say – as to make them fair game. It denies the ordinary meaning of the English language to say that the guidelines were not changed.

BAX: You say [in your statement]: 'It must be understood that the guidelines were an extremely useful adjunct to foreign policy, offering a form of words elusive of definition. There was an understandable reluctance in Whitehall to stir up Parliament.'

CLARK: Yes. The House of Commons is a very volatile place and you get rows and scenes and 'ooh-err' on tape, and ministers have an aversion to this unless they are exhibitionists and like participating. Can I just add a small postscript? You must not ever lie to the House of Commons. If you do lie, what I find is, normally, your registration should follow immediately.

BAX: You say, 'It is a matter of record' that guidelines 3 remained, I am not quite sure what you are saying.

CLARK: One is back now to the slightly Alice in Wonderland suggestion, where I remember my former colleague, Mr Waldegrave, said, 'Because something was not announced, it had not happened.' He was arguing that because it had not been announced, it could not have happened, a sort of Berkeleyan philosophy.

BAX: Can I go to your statement. You say: 'The Prime Minister most certainly was informed of the new approach and indeed it included it in her parliamentary answer to Harry Cohen MP.'

CLARK: She must have had something, because otherwise we would not have tagged onto the answer: 'and in the light of developments in the peace negotiations with Iran.' That indicates a loosening, you see, that was the agreed form of words. The trail was laid.

SCENE X

Evidence of Lady Thatcher.

BAX: Lady Thatcher, I should like to start with the establishment of the guidelines in December 1984... The document is Lord Howe's minute to you of 4th December, 1984.

THATCH: I have it.

BAX: Some of the witnesses we have had have described these guidelines as a framework, within which they had to work, or as a hurdle which exporters had to cross in addition to other existing constraints on exports. Does that fit in with how you saw the guidelines?

THATCH: They are exactly what they say, guidelines, they are not law. They are guidelines.

BAX: Did they have to be followed?

THATCH: I beg your pardon?

BAX: Did they have to be followed?

THATCH: Of course they have to be followed, but they are not strict law. That is why they are guidelines and not law and, of course, they have to be applied according to the relevant circumstances.

BAX: They are expected to be followed?

THATCH: Of course, they need to be followed. They need to be followed for what they are, guidelines.

BAX: The Ministry of Defence Working Group assesses…and decides that the equipment would significantly enhance the capability of either Iran or Iraq to wage a war. In those circumstances, can the equipment be granted a licence for other factors, for example, encouraging exports?

THATCH: We would not, I think – I say, 'We would not' – I was not involved in the actual application of these guidelines. I was involved in the policy… The precise question was, Miss Baxendale? I am sorry, you are more familiar with this. I have seen so much paper that I have never seen before. I was concerned with the policy not with the administration.

BAX: What I was asking you about was, if you have the Ministry of Defence Working Group saying, 'This equipment will significantly enhance the capability of either side', can other factors, such as employment in the United Kingdom override guideline 3?

THATCH: I do not believe you would ignore the guidelines solely for exports.

BAX: If there was going to be exceptional overriding, would you expect that to go up to ministers and maybe the Cabinet and perhaps even to yourself?

THATCH: If there was an exceptional case. And the only one that came to me that I recall was the question of the export of the Hawk trainer, which was a big order, a big issue. The big things have come up… Only one came up, as I recall or have been able to identify in that way. That was the possibility of supplying the Hawk trainer to Iraq.

BAX: If you go to page 49, this is a memo from the Secretary of State for Defence.

THATCH: I think it is to the Foreign Secretary. I do not think I saw this document at the time. It has not got my initials on it anywhere.

BAX: Would it not go to you if it says: 'I am sending copies to other members of the Cabinet's Overseas and Defence Committee, then the Cabinet Secretary'?

THATCH: Miss Baxendale, if I had seen every copy of every minute that was sent in Government, I would have been in a snowstorm.

BAX: If we could go to 'Questions of Procedures for Ministers'. I think it is attached to the letter we sent you yesterday. I am sure you know the document anyway.

THATCH: All ministers are very familiar with their accountability to Parliament.

BAX: I would like you to look at the Cabinet Secretary's minute. It starts: 'The Government believes that Ministers are well aware of the principles that should govern their duties and responsibilities in relation to Parliament and in relation to civil servants. They include the duty to give Parliament and the public as full information as possible about the policy decisions and actions of the Government and not to deceive or mislead Parliament or the public.' Yes?

THATCH: Indeed. I would not quarrel with a word of that.

BAX: I was presuming that would be the basis on which you and your Government, the Ministers, were working?

THATCH: Yes, indeed, but the advice to me, and I think there is a document about it, is it is quite unusual to reveal guidelines.

BAX: If we go to the comments of officials concerned at the time the originals guidelines were published.

THATCH: Is there more paper? I've never seen so much paper.

BAX: That is only part of it. There is much more.

THATCH: The majority of it I have never seen as Prime Minister. I find a lot very interesting now that I never knew before.

BAX: Can we go to another bundle? If we go to FCO, 13/1 Page 29. This is a document of the 4th July, 1986 written in the context of the licensing of small boats.

THATCH: Miss Baxendale, I did not see this document at the time. I have no knowledge of it. It is the comment of an official to a minister on how the policy should be administered. I was concerned with the policy. The administration was by officials under another cabinet minister. I could not possibly have got involved in these things. I could never have done my job as Prime Minister on policy if I got involved in all of these things.

SCOTT: The purpose of putting some of these notes and minutes to you is because you were held of the administration at the time. You have an almost unparalleled experience in government. I do not think Miss Baxendale has actually asked the question. Could we leave her to ask it, and then see whether you would be able to help with an answer to it?

BAX: I was going to ask you about a comment from a senior official in the Foreign Office. He says, 'The guidelines should be regarded primarily as a set of criteria for use in defending against public and parliamentary criticism, whatever decision we take on grounds of commercial and political interest.' So you take the decision on the basis of commercial and political interest, and you use the guidelines as a defence against public and parliamentary criticism?

THATCH: Does your export policy override the guidelines? The answer is no, it does not.

BAX: I would like to move on to 1988/9. It is page 6 of the questionnaire. Where we are now is there has been the Iranian acceptance of the UN Security Council Resolution, and the Foreign Secretary minuted you with this paper, 'The Economic Consequences of Peace in the Gulf'. It refers to relaxing control. Then your advisor, Mr Powell's response to the Foreign Office: 'The general strategy will obviously require decision on a number of difficult and sensitive issues, such as the guidelines for defence sales to Iran and Iraq. The Prime Minister will wish to be kept very closely in touch at every stage and consulted on all relevant decisions.'

THATCH: Policy changes, I think, would have to come to me. It seems to me abundantly clear that, when ministers proposed this change, they did not regard it as a change of policy, but a change of circumstance. That would explain why certainly it may well be that I was just told there had been a change without a different policy.

SCOTT: What is your view? Plainly, there was a change of circumstance. Plainly, the original guidelines 3 was formulated to deal with the then continuing war, so there was a change in circumstance and a new formulation was needed. Is this the sort of thing you would have expected to have been referred to you?

THATCH: If they regarded this as a change in policy, yes, it should have come to me. It may have been mentioned to me by one of my secretaries. I have no recollection if it was.

BAX: There is a letter from Mr Clark to the two other ministers, suggesting there should be a revision to the guidelines.

SCOTT: This is a proposal for a change of policy. Would that not come to you?

THATCH: I just cannot keep tabs on all this. It just has to be delegated.

BAX: 10th January, 1989. Mr Clark to Mr. Waldegrave: 'The recent telegram from Washington implies their acceptance of the proposed revision... With so many conflicting interests, any change would be likely to upset someone. We would, therefore, favour the implementation of a more liberal policy, without any public announcement.'

THATCH: These were not submitted to me formally. Whether they were just mentioned to me, I have no recollection.

BAX: Mr Waldegrave was seeing this as implementing a more liberal policy?

THATCH: On a trial basis. And I do not like the use of the word 'liberal'.

SCOTT: Lady Thatcher, what I do think you can help me with is giving me an indication as we go through these letters, of whether you think the point had arrived at which you ought to have been informed.

THATCH: If there is a material change in policy, I would have preferred to have been informed. And if I am informed, I must be informed in a letter to me. Of course it would have been easier if I had been informed of any change. I assume that the reason that they did not inform me was that they thought there was not a change of policy, but a change of circumstances to which the policy applied.

SCOTT: References to a more liberal policy does not fit easily with the concept of there being no change in substance.

THATCH: 'Liberal' is not a word I would have adopted.

BAX: I would like to go to an answer that you gave to a parliamentary question from Harry Cohen on 21st April, 1989. 'To ask the Prime Minister whether Her Majesty's Government propose to change their current policy of prohibiting the export to Iraq of any weapon which could enhance its offensive capability or will agree to granting export exhibitors at the Baghdad fair and if she will make a statement'. Your reply was: 'The Government have not changed their policy on defence sales to Iraq.' Do you not think this answer is correct?

THATCH: It is a mixed question, is it not?

SCOTT: It is a mixed answer.

THATCH: Yes, indeed. It was a mixed question and it may require a mixed answer.

SCOTT: It is the shift from 'weapons' in the question, to 'defence sales' in the answer. That is the problem.

THATCH: It would, I am afraid my Lord, come back to the same point we have been concerned about for quite a long time – was it a change of policy, to which my advisers would say no. It was a change in circumstance.

BAX: Do you think that the fact that a different wording [in the guidelines] is being used should have been announced to Parliament?

THATCH: They did not think it was a change of substance.

BAX: What I do not understand is why you say ministers thought that it should not be announced because it was just a technical matter, because the documents that we have looked at show they thought it should not be announced because it was going to cause trouble.

SCOTT: It seems to come across that, if a policy of a more relaxed approach to Iraq had been publicly announced, there would have been some degree of public outcry against it because of revulsion at what Iraq was doing to the Kurds. Is that a matter which could properly play any part in a decision whether or not to make an announcement to Parliament?

THATCH: Anything to do with the gassing of the Kurds – as you see what happened when the Hawk decision came up – what decided us not to do it, was we simple could not supply *that* kind of weapon, the Hawk trainer, to a government that did the gassing of the Kurds.

BAX: What I would like to do, Lady Thatcher, is to move on to Matrix Churchill. Mr Barrett, an official in the Defence Export Services Secretariat, is dealing with specific cases: 'Intelligence sources indicated that the lathes were to be used for making shells and missiles. The Prime Minister agreed that, in order to protect the intelligence source, the licenses already should not be revoked.' Do you have any idea at all why Mr Barrett should have thought you were involved?

THATCH: No. I understand that he retracted afterwards.

SCOTT: He did not quite. He could not recall why he had thought you were involved, but he just thought there might have been a reason.

THATCH: I have no recollection, which is why I asked for minutes to see if there was something which I had not recalled.

BAX: I wanted to ask you briefly about the use of diversionary routes for to Iraq. We know that after the invasion of Kuwait, you were personally involved in discussions with the King of Jordan, but I want to ask you about the period before the invasion of Kuwait and the period before sanctions.

THATCH: When I saw the king there were many matters to discuss with him, the one being that he appeared to be on the side of Iraq, which was horrific. Jordan always had a destabilising danger. I had visited PLO camps in Jordan. There was a possibility that this rather remarkable country and this very, very courageous king, who never flinched from personal danger, might be stabilised. That would not have done British interests any good at all. To destabilise Jordan would have been a very, very serious matter indeed. So we took the course of doing as much as we could and seeking what for the king was unusual to give a personal assurance. I hope, therefore, that I have explained what was in our minds. Life is a question of alternatives.

Possibly with the alternatives that you face, neither of them are very palatable.

SCOTT: I am very grateful for you coming. There will be a transcript prepared of everything that has been said in the course of today, which we will supply to you as soon as we can, and, if you have time to read it, and if it occurs to you that there is anything that you wish you could add or that you would wish to correct, then we would be very grateful if you would do that.

THATCH: I fear there will be much grammar to be corrected.

SCOTT: Never mind grammar, that is the least of the problems.

Act Two

SCENE I

Enter Paul Henderson.

HEND: Sometimes, on very rare occasions, I think about myself, and I suppose on one or two occasions, I don't quite know what to feel about myself, but really *(Laughs.)* can a salesman afford to gaze at his navel, does the Pope shit in the woods? As MD of Matrix Churchill I had a job to do. If we went under, who was to blame? Paul Henderson was to blame. I can't afford the luxury of a conscience. Look, I inhabit a wicked, sinful, and highly competitive world, and I deal on a daily basis with hard, hard men, and I will do whatever I can to succeed. That doesn't mean I'm immoral, or do anything immoral. I do what I do, I sell what I sell for excellent reasons. I'm not one of your public school, Oxbridge types creeping into business not knowing anything about the work, the people on the shop floor, the engineering, how it all comes about. I went in at 15, did my apprenticeship, did my engineering, my City and Guilds. I worked the lathes, and I know the people on the shopfloor – I was one of them. And I've seen what happens to those people when a plant closes. I've seen too much of that in Coventry! I've seen what can happen – did happen – at Alfred Herbert's to the livelihood of hundreds of skilled, dedicated toolmakers. That's why I go all over the world to get orders for our machine tools, and why I'll sell them to whoever wants to buy them even if they are going to use them to make armaments, and why when the moment came, I went along with the Iraqis buying into Matrix, to stop some competitor buying us in order to close us down. Sentimental? Not exactly. As I say, you simply don't think too hard about the morality of it all, you're in business, and business is business, competition is competition, and success is success. And if I succeed, I expect a reward – a personal reward of course, but above all, the reward of seeing my company busy, growing and profitable. There's no way I will apologise for that. After the mess of the Seventies, that's what the Eighties was all about. The self-interest of the managers harnessed to bring about the well-being of the workforce. That's what Thatcher was all about: real jobs, they called them. If there had to be rules to their 'game' of selling what I was selling, if there had to be prohibitions on who I could sell to, what I could sell, I certainly wasn't going to make them up: it's hard enough beating off the French, the Germans and the Japanese without tying one hand behind your back. If there was to be regulation, that was the Government's job, not mine. Fortunately, they didn't want to close Matrix Churchill down any more than I did. And if ancient regulations inhibited my chances against the French, then as Lord Nelson said, putting his blind eye to a telescope, I see no Iraqi arms factories. This Government are all business men – they understand business – business is business. Besides, they owed me a one. For years I'd been travelling behind the Iron Curtain, gaining the confidence, the friendship of the arms makers. And for years, I'd been filling in our Secret Intelligence Service on exactly where I'd been and what I'd seen. Risky, but interesting. Then, when it came to my dealings with Iraq in the Eighties, they came back to me, 'Spy for us.' Saddam Hussein has the most efficient and ruthless counter-intelligence people in the world. I was supposed to go into Baghdad, off into arms plants, highly-sensitive Iraqi military installations, and spy for Britain, the hated imperialist power. And I did. Not out of self-interest, nor for reward, certainly not. I happen to believe in my country. Sentimental? Yes, but I did my bit. For Britain. I reported every single thing I saw, and did. They knew exactly what I was doing. It was a touch dicey at times. But I did it. What thanks did I get? A VC? I'm afraid not. They humiliated me. They arrested me, put me behind bars like a common criminal. Of course the trial collapsed. But by then, my business was ruined, my plant closed down, and 600 hundred more jobs went in Coventry – good jobs, good people. What was wrong was that they let this prosecution go ahead. And when it did, they tried to say they knew nothing about it, that it all came as a complete shock to them and what a wicked person I was to give comfort to the enemy. I am going back into business now. Those 600 engineers aren't. That's what annoys me. And my pride, of course.

SCENE II

Evidence of Alan Clark (2).

BAX: Mr Clark, I would like to go now to the note of your meeting with the Machine Tools Technologies Association in January 1988: 'Choosing his words carefully and noting that the Iraqis would be using the current orders for general engineering purposes, Mr Clark stressed it was important for the UK companies to agree to a specification with the customer, in advance, which highlighted the peaceful – i.e. non-military – use to which the machine tools would be put.'

CLARK: Yes.

BAX: The members from the Machine Tools Technologies Association knew there was a concern that the machine tools are going to be used for military purposes?

CLARK: Yes.

SCOTT: You refer to 'general engineering' purposes. But given that the meeting had been called because of a known concern that the actual use was going to be military, does not the use of that phrase carry the implication that, provided the 'general engineering' heading can be relied on, the Government will not mind about the exports?

CLARK: Yes, that was the impression I wanted to give, certainly. If you like, I had to indulge in a fiction, and invite them to participate in a fiction.

BAX: The way of communicating that you were using at the time was you were entering into a fiction, and you were choosing your words carefully, you were deliberately using neutral words, which could encompass both military manufacture and civil manufacture?

CLARK: Yes.

BAX: I think now we ought to look at your witness statement for the prosecution at the trial. 'At the same meeting I was advised that the machine tools were intended for general engineering purposes.' Is that right?

CLARK: There was an implied invitation to them to participate in a fiction.

BAX: Were you concerned, though, when you were signing this witness statement for the trial that it did not actually set out what happened at the meeting?

CLARK: It set out what happened at the meeting. It omits my knowledge.

BAX: That is right. It omits government knowledge, does it not?

CLARK: Yes. I suppose I should have insisted that I – I do not know what...

BAX: You met officers from Customs and Excise. You say, 'Their principle objective seemed to be to persuade me that the defendants had been grossly misleading in the description which they had tendered [in the licence application].' Was there any in-depth discussion or any discussion at all with you about evidential matters that you might know about, rather than officials giving their reasons why they wanted to run the prosecution?

CLARK: No. The whole thing was so dotty really. I do not see why it should be followed by this whole paraphernalia of a prosecution, unless real damage had taken place over a long period. If it did, it seems to me the prime responsibility for that lies with those charged with the duty of scrutinising and inspecting machines.

BAX: Did Customs and Excise tell you that it was thought likely that the defence would be that the Government had known at the time that the licences were what the likely use would be.

CLARK: No.

SCOTT: The proposition is that you, as the relevant minister, were being misled, because you thought these things were going to be used for civil application and, hey presto – they are not, they are being used for military purposes. The minister was deceived, so were all his officials deceived.

CLARK: There may be an element of sleight of hand in it, I suppose. The trouble about this situation is, I am defending a position, defending conduct, which I am satisfied is defensible, but because the sails are right over and almost touching the water at times, if you understand the analogy, I have to choose my words carefully. My attitude, I am satisfied can be defended, but I recognise that it has involved periodically a certain amount of dissimulation.

BAX: If we look at page 6 of your reply to our questionnaire. You say, 'I was still doubtful about the wisdom of prosecuting them' – and that was without, at the time, knowing Mr Henderson was an intelligence source – 'and I suppose this irritation or scepticism may have shown'.

CLARK: Yes, but the Customs and Excise investigator has not recorded that. He has not recorded my scepticism.

SCOTT: Is it possible that you made your opinion clear, that the prosecution was not one which you thought was very sensible?

CLARK: Not very sensible, yes, certainly.

BAX: I would like to go to the trial itself. Can we go to page 82 of the transcript of your evidence. At page 82, between D and E, Mr Robertson, counsel for Mr Henderson, puts to you: 'The writer of the minute of the meeting of the Machine Tools Technologies Association is attributing to you a statement that the Iraqis will be using the current order for general engineering purpose. That statement cannot be correct to your knowledge.' Your reply: 'Well, it is our old friend, being economical, is it not?'

CLARK: Because you are not extending it into the other potential.

BAX: That is what you then referred to, in the next bit of evidence?

CLARK: Yes. All I did not say was 'and for making munitions'.

BAX: Yes, exactly. Then it is suggested to you by the defence: 'So the signal you are sending to these people is: 'I am a Minister. I will help you through these orders and follow-ups through the rather loose guidelines and the rather Byzantine ways of Whitehall. Help me by keeping your mouth firmly shut about military use.' Your answer: 'That is too imaginative an interpretation. I think it was more at arm's length than that. I do not think I said "nothing military".' The defence's question: 'They got it by implication'? Your answer: 'Yes, "by implication" is different. By implication they got it.' That sound as though you were accepting that the implication, from what you said, that the exporters would receive was: 'Do not say anything about military use'?

CLARK: Yes.

SCOTT: Mr Clark, that finishes all the questions we wanted to ask you.

CLARK: Sir Richard, thank you very much, and I have enjoyed it and found it enlightening.

SCENE III

Enter noisily, through the audience a Palestinian Arab. He is angry.

SIDDIQI: Long life to Gamal abd al-Nasir. Long life to Saddam Hussein. My name is Abdul Siddiqi. I am an Arab. My home is in Palestine. In Saffed, what the Israelis call Zfat. My beautiful house is still there, looking out from

Saffed to the peaceful mountains of Lebanon. But I live in a camp, with ten thousand others, outside Beirut. In my beautiful house, the son of a bank manager from Hendon. If I had a knife I would kill him, or any Israeli, or you. In Arabic, we do not use words from the West. But there are four foreign words we have not avoided: a car – tumubil; telephones – tilifun; television – tilivisiun; and democracy – demokratiyyah. We embrace: cars, telephones, television. Democracy we spit on. What does it mean? America. Germans. Japanese. They say – democracy needs a free market with open borders; and who has the capital to dominate these free markets? America. Germans. Japanese. In fact we do not mind buying their cars, their computers, their technology. It is everything else that comes with them that we hate: American imperialism, German efficiency, Japanese brainwashing of their workers. Look at eastern Europe. Look at yourselves. We live in our world. There are many things wrong with the Arab way of doing things, but it is our way, and it us for us to make better. We will not sell it to the imperialist for a taste of democracy, because it is precisely what real democracy stands for – the right to control our own destiny – that imperialist democracy takes away. In the name of a Christianity you did not practice, you tried to take my Palestine, for centuries we fought you. Now in the name of a democracy that you do not practise, you are trying to conquer the Arabs again, we will fight you. Why so many fundamentalists? Because so many Arabs are afraid. Afraid to lose our world, and to be swallowed up into your world. And how can we fight you? My uncles and my grandmother hijacked aeroplanes, shot Israeli schoolchildren, drove you English out of Iran, Iraq, Jordan, Egypt, Libya, the French out of Algeria, the Lebanon. They got rid of King Farouk, the Shah, all the crooked, cruel men you kept in power to look after your interests. We found ways to win those fights. Nasser was our hero. Long life Gamal abd al-Nasir. But still you tell us we are weak, we cannot win, you have aeroplanes, tanks, rockets, you have nuclear bombs to wipe us out. America has everything, of this and more, bombs that can find a house, find a chimney pot, go down the chimney and explode in the fireplace! How can we hold up our heads, how can we even talk to you at the same table, without these things? Israel is our enemy, the Israelis took my house, my country, by force, they keep them because they have these terrible things, and we don't. Gadaffi in Libya can't get them. Mubarak in Egypt is becoming the new Farouk, he doesn't need them. Hussein in Jordan, no way. No, my friends, it is Saddam Hussein in Iraq who has shown the Arabs what to do now, today. He bought your technology, with money from oil: from France, from Germany, from Austria, from England. He even bought banks to finance it all, he bought the people, he bought Matrix Churchill in Coventry. Who is our hero? Saddam. You may say, 'Ah, but he is cruel.' To be a leader, one must be cruel, ruthless, even criminal. We Arabs have always suffered. There was a time when mothers had to bury their girl-children alive, so they would not have to suffer. But that is not the point. The Kurds are not the point. Chemical warfare is not the point. The point is for an Arab to have power in the world – the point above all is what he will do with his power. Will he make himself rich, with places of gold – or will he fight for his brother Arabs, stand against the evil forces of imperialist democracy, and give us our own lives, and our own voice in the world? That is what Saddam has done. That is why when he defied the imperial powers and took back Kuwait, taken from Iraq by the trick of a British diplomat, there was rejoicing all over the Arab world. That is why when he fired Scud missiles into Tel Aviv, we Palestinians rejoiced because we had at last an ally with power to attack Israel. In our minds we can see what you can see, but in our spirits we need Saddam. I know you don't listen to your spirit very much in England, so there we are different. Saddam is what our spirit is looking for. Long live Gamal abd al-Nasir. Long life to Saddam Hussein. *(He goes.)*

SCENE IV

Evidence of Tony Steadman.

BAX: Mr Steadman, you drafted briefing papers before the meeting on the 20th January, 1988 of the Machine Tools Technologies Association with Alan Clark, who supported sales of machine tools to Iraq?

STEAD: Yes.

BAX: You see on the first page of the association's record of the meeting, it is quite hard to read, but you see in the middle of it: 'There was no doubt, by persons attending this meeting, that we were being advised to cloud the truth.' Did you see that reference?

STEAD: Yes, I would have done.

BAX: Then, you say: 'Difficulty for DTI witnesses if he was asked at the trial when we first knew the exports could be for arms manufacture. Then there was an accusation that the Department of Trade and Industry encourage the company to falsify and end use.'

STEAD: Yes.

BAX: Then paragraph 8 reads: 'In December 1988, MoD, DTI, and FO ministers met to agree a revised but unpublished interpretation to the Iran/Iraq guidelines.'

STEAD: Yes.

BAX: I would like now to go to your prosecution witness statement for the trial. I want to look at the deletions. That sentence: 'This was a result of information received. There was, however, no hard evidence as far as I am aware' – has been crossed out.

STEAD: Yes.

BAX: Were you concerned that after the deletion, it now did not refer to the knowledge or the information that the Government had received?

STEAD: I assumed there was good reason why that had to be deleted.

BAX: Were you not concerned that it did not accurately reflect what had occurred?

STEAD: I do not think I was concerned, because I had been advised that it should be deleted. So there must have been good reason for that.

BAX: At the time, did you read it and think, 'This is not representing the truth'?

STEAD: It is not that it was untrue, but it did not go as far as obviously the previous witness statement had.

BAX: It is more than that, is it not? You knew those licences were going to make munitions?

STEAD: Yes.

SCOTT: To say: 'We accepted their assurances' is more than not accurate. It is just not true.

STEAD: Yes.

SCOTT: Is that not right?

STEAD: Yes.

SCOTT: Why did you let it stand like this?

STEAD: I had legal advice, and I assumed that the legal advice was correct.

SCOTT: It is you who has to sign things to swear it is true.

BAX: I am looking at your witness statement for the trial. We had noted that your references to briefing ministers have also gone.

STEAD: Yes.

BAX: I am now looking at page 16 of your witness statement. You knew, did you not, that the defendants were likely to run a defence that the Government knew?

STEAD: Yes.

BAX: And were encouraging them?

STEAD: Yes.

BAX: From what you have told us and what you have written, you could see that the company could have drawn the wrong conclusions from the Machine Tools Technologies Association meeting with Alan Clark?

STEAD: They could have done, yes.

BAX: You could see their point? Is that a good way of putting it?

STEAD: It was a point of view.

SCOTT: I think you said it was a 'reasonable' point of view?

STEAD: It was a reasonable point of view, yes.

BAX: There is no suggestion of anything like that in your witness statement, is there?

STEAD: No.

BAX: There is no reference to intelligence information, is there?

STEAD: Did it worry you a bit that things were being taken in and out of your witness statement at will?

STEAD: I assumed that people were acting in good faith.

SCENE V

Evidence of Andrew Leithead.

SCOTT: Mr Leithead, thank you very much for coming this morning, and thank you for your statements. You have obviously very carefully prepared them. Most of the questions Miss Baxendale will be asking. I may be asking some myself.

BAX: I am going to TSD27, TS1, page 3. Mr Steadman's witness statement for the trial. Mr Steadman was saying: 'I recall there was concern by ourselves and departments involved in advising on licence applications as to whether these machine tools might actually be used by the Iraqis for military production.' Then he had written: 'There was no evidence as far as I am aware to support these suspicions.' You had crossed that out?

LEIT: Yes.

BAX: Why did you suggest that deletion?

LEIT: It did not seem a sensible course – there must have been some evidence, if there were some suspicions. You know, it is precisely the sort of thing a witness gets caught out on when being cross-examined in a witness box.

BAX: Then on page 12, where he said: 'The background briefing that I gave to the minister was on the basis that, despite our concerns, these machine tools could have dual-use civil/military.' Right?

LEIT: Yes.

BAX: You have crossed out both these bits.

LEIT: Yes.

BAX: Then: 'I was aware of suspicions; but in the face of assurances from Matrix Churchill, we relied on statements in the licence applications.' Do you think, looking back at it, that it might have been sensible to discover what Mr Steadman could say about what he was relying on in the assurances he had had?

LEIT: I am sorry. I have the greatest difficulty remembering what happened.

SCOTT: The point is a broad one. It is what are the officials doing, including the lawyers of whom you were one, in drafting what Mr Steadman is going to say in his witness statement? What business have officials got to be drafting something like that?

LEIT: Well, it is merely suggesting to Mr Steadman what the correct position would be.

SCOTT: Suggesting what?

LEIT: Suggesting to Mr Steadman what the correct position would be.

SCOTT: His evidence in a criminal case, or perhaps a civil case too for that matter, is evidence as to the truth as known by the witnesses, is it not?

LEIT: Yes.

BAX: Do you remember, there would be two strands of defence?

LEIT: Yes.

BAX: Firstly, that the DTI turned a blind eye to the military possibilities and, secondly, that since Mr Henderson of Matrix Churchill had been involved with the security service, the Government were in any event aware of the full facts?

LEIT: Yes.

BAX: You know that those were possible or likely defences. Did you still consider that you were going to suggest that all the documents were irrelevant? I am going to the Public Interest Immunity certificate.

LEIT: When one is dealing with PII claims, one tends to take a rather generous sort of view of the –

SCOTT: Take what sort of view?

LEIT: A generous view.

SCOTT: Generous to whom?

LEIT: Generous to the government departments. Anything that involves advice to ministers is considered to be within that class. That is why PII tends to work.

SCOTT: The way Government tends to work PII?

LEIT: Yes, that is right.

SCOTT: Who regards it as damaging to the public interest that any of this decision-making process should be exposed? Who?

LEIT: I think it is a general view of people who deal with this subject.

BAX: I did not hear, I am sorry.

LEIT: It is a general view of people who deal with this subject.

BAX: The Government?

LEIT: Yes.

BAX: Not necessarily the ministers concerned?

LEIT: No.

BAX: It is not the minister's view, is it? We are going to come to one case where it certainly was not the view of the minister concerned.

SCOTT: Is this approach bred of a desire for convenient administration?

LEIT: I think so, yes. We go back to the point that the policy and advice is worthy of the protection... It is this whole process of confidentiality.

SCOTT: Confidentiality has never been the basis of Public Interest Immunity certificates alone. What has been required is damage to the public interest.

LEIT: What damages the public interest is the disclosure of a whole process as regards to ministers.

SCOTT: Regardless of the contents?

LEIT: Yes.

SCOTT: That is a very difficult proposition to justify, is it not?

LEIT: These certificates by no means are final. If the judge considers the documents ought to be disclosed, then he will order them to be disclosed.

BAX: The judge is meant to receive assistance from the minister, is he not?

LEIT: Yes.

BAX: And if the judge is told that this is a case where it is in the public interest that these discussions, once revealed, would be injurious to the public good, the judge is likely to believe that?

LEIT: Yes.

BAX: He has no yardstick to know that, in fact, these discussions between the officials really would not injure a flea, and it is just because it is inconvenient?

LEIT: That is right.

SCOTT: Would not every certificate have this in common – that it constitutes a representation to the judge by the person making the certificate, usually a minister, that material will be damaging to the public interest?

LEIT: Yes.

SCOTT: Is it an unfair impression that there was a desire to keep the knowledge of the existence of these documents from the defence?

LEIT: Well, the prosecution obviously thought so.

BAX: What the minister has to do, is it not, is make a judgement on the facts? Is that not what he is meant to be doing?

LEIT: He has to make a judgement as to whether the document is within the class or not.

SCOTT: Why does he not have to make a judgement as to whether disclosure is going to be contrary to the public interest?

LEIT: Well –

SCOTT: Why is that not the point?

LEIT: The point is that any disclosure of documents within this class is going to be contrary to the public interest.

BAX: You are saying that.

SCOTT: Who says so Mr Leithead? The minister may say so, but if the minister does not say so, then who is it to correct him?

LEIT: It is open to challenge in court, of course.

SCOTT: Mr Leithead, it is not the Attorney-General's job, let alone that of prosecuting counsel, to decide whether disclosure of a particular document would be contrary to the public interest. That is for the minister, is it not?

LEIT: Yes, I suppose it is. But on the other hand, the minister is constrained by what has happened in past cases –

BAX: Why?

LEIT: Because of the policy.

SCOTT: Do you have draft Public Interest Immunity certificates in your department on the word processor?

LEIT: No. We use the Xerox machine quite a bit. The minister either agrees or is brought to agree with the policy and he has formed a view.

BAX: He either agrees or is brought to agree, he is told he jolly well has to.

LEIT: We, he is advised, as ministers are.

BAX: He is told he has no choice.

LEIT: Not really.

BAX: Let us take the background documents of the meeting of the Machine Tools Technologies Association. I think we should actually look at them. They are briefings for the meeting with Alan Clark.

LEIT: Yes.

BAX: It is Mr Steadman's note. I entirely understand there may be parts of this that one would not want disclosed, but what I cannot immediately see is why is this document not relevant to the case?

LEIT: It does not exactly say what happened at the meeting.

BAX: It is before the meeting. It is saying what the Government's knowledge is.

LEIT: Yes.

BAX: Why would that not be relevant, remembering what you know about defence?

LEIT: That is certainly what the prosecution counsel thought, otherwise he would have not settled the certificate.

BAX: He did not settle it. You settled it. You approved it. Who wrote those words? Who thought up, saying: 'It is improbable that such documents can have any significant relevance'? Or was it just put on the Xerox copy?

LEIT: Certainly not.

SCOTT: Do you, sitting there now, regard it as a document of no significant relevance?

LEIT: Yes, I do not, no. I think that is probably wrong.

SCOTT: I am sorry, what is your present view?

LEIT: My present view is that it is relevant, but that it is with the benefit of hindsight.

BAX: A minister is entitled to have a view that disclosure would not be injurious?

LEIT: Well, I am not sure about that.

SCOTT: Your stance, as I understand it, is that once it is established that the documents fall within the requisite class, the minister has no discretion?

LEIT: In effect, yes. As I say, it is damaging to the public interest to have the decision-making process exposed.

SCENE VI

Scene between Alan Moses and Geoffrey Robertson. An argument between Alan Moses QC, counsel for the prosecution, and Geoffrey Robertson QC, counsel for Henderson, before the trial judge, his honour Judge Smedley QC, at the Old Bailey on 30 September, 1992.

MOSES: My lord, the issue before the court today is whether documents, in respect of which public interest immunity is claimed, should be disclosed to the defence. My Lord, there are before the court a number of certificates from different ministers. In the green bundle, your Lordship sees the certificate from the Foreign Office Minister of State, Mr Garel-Jones. In the red bundle, your Lordship will find a certificate from Mr Rifkind, Secretary of State for Defence. In the purple bundle, a certificate from Mr Heseltine, president for the Board of Trade. And my Lord, finally, there are certificates from Kenneth Clarke, the Secretary of State for the Home Department. They concern – your Lordship will be able to read them for yourself – consideration and application of policy relating to the export of machine tools to Iraq; the state of mind of those considering the policy; and consideration of whether to forbid export of the machines. I have read those documents, so has my learned junior. We do not consider they assist the defence in relation to any foreseeable issue, still less assist the defence in relation to whether the Department of Trade and Industry connived at concealment by the defendants of the true purpose for which the machines were to be used. The documents do not in any sense help the defence.

ROBERT: In looking at the certificates, to begin with the certificate of Mr Garel-Jones, he notes that these documents relate to the formation of policy of Her Majesty's Government, in particular with regard to relations with, and the export of, military and quasi-military products. Mr Garel-Jones forms an opinion that the requirements of witnesses to give oral evidence as to meetings, discussions, and deliberations would be injurious to the public interest. We do not know what meetings he is talking about, because we have not seen the documents, but we have a most disquieting note sounding there that this minister seems to think that he can limit the scope of evidence. His reasoning is: all these documents fall into a class of documents relating to the formation of government policy and the internal dealings of government departments. Well, the answer to that is that ministers are being called by the prosecution in this case and it is fundamental that they are going to give a version of policy which may be contested by the defence as not being the true or correct policy. The defence must be entitled to know what the real policy was.

(Reads.) 'It would be against the public interest if Category B documents revealed the process of providing ministers with honest and candid advice.' This is, of course, a long way from the position today where ministers within a couple of years of leaving public office publish their memoirs or diaries. Indeed, a central prosecution witness, Mr Alan Clark – the publication of his diaries is about to happen. So then we come to the documents in category C – that the security and intelligence services require secrecy. Here we have the central claim which needs care and scrutiny.

(Reads.) 'Evidence about the identity of members of the security and intelligence services could put their lives at risk and substantially impair their capability to perform the tasks assigned to them.' The first point to be made about that is that the only person whose life is at risk is Mr Paul Henderson, who has assisted the security and intelligence services in relation to matters with which he is charged.

SCENE VII

Evidence of Tristan Garel-Jones.

SCOTT: Good morning, Mr Garel-Jones.

G-JONES: Good morning.

BAX: Mr Garel-Jones, you were Minister of State at the Foreign Office From 1990 to 1993 and I would like to ask you about Public Interest Immunity certificates you signed in that capacity. Can we go to FCO 114/2, page 186. It is a submission to you of September 3, 1992 from Mr Nixon that went through Mr Gore-Booth. What you need out is the questionnaire, your statement and the bundle.

G-JONES: I have them.

BAX: It says: 'Problem: Should the minister sign the attached PII certificate?' It was recommended you should sign it 'today'. 'Background: Customs and Excise are prosecuting three British directors of Matrix Churchill in respect of illegal export of equipment to Iraq in 1988 to 1990. At the time, Matrix Churchill was a largely Iraqi-owned British company. Leading counsel for the prosecution has examined Foreign Office files relating to Matrix Churchill licence applications, and has identified those papers likely to be relevant and potentially disclosable to the defence. They are all of a type which it would be normal for the Government to refuse to disclose. They fall into three categories: Category A, which is the informant category; Category B, which includes the minutes, notes and letters between ministers and/or officials. All these documents relate to the formulation of policy of the Government, in particular with regard to relations with and the export of military and quasi-military equipment to foreign countries. And Category C has documents which include material relating to secret intelligence. Then paragraph 4 continues: 'The Crown can seek to prevent the disclosure of documents in legal proceedings on the basis that disclosure would not be in the public interest. A certificate to this effect has to be given by a minister, but it is not conclusive. Whether PII can be claimed is a matter for the court to decide.' Prior to receiving this submission, had you been concerned at all about signing a PII certificate?

G-JONES: No.

BAX: Were you satisfied that the classes referred to need to be protected from disclosure?

G-JONES: I have no doubts about that. Curiously enough, I had a letter two weeks ago, a friendly letter on another matter, from a constituent, who clearly believes that arms exports to Iraq were agreed by the Government in secret, deceiving Parliament and so on. I believe that to be wholly unfounded.

BAX: The public disquiet is because the public perceives that the PII claims were too broad.

SCOTT: The minister signs a PII certificate. But there are degrees of damage. If the degree of damage is going to be trivial, it is almost inevitable that the judge is going to come down in favour of disclosure.

G-JONES: As he did in this case.

SCOTT: The minister has to certify that the documents, if disclosed, will cause significant public damage.

G-JONES: 'Unquantifiable' – is that not the word?

SCOTT: 'Unquantifiable' was the word you used. The question that troubles me is whether the nature of that damage to the public interest, which is no more than a fear that the Government might be exposed to what has been described as 'captious and ill-informed criticism' is enough to justify non-disclosure?

G-JONES: You say, 'No more' dismissively. I regard that as quite important. I regard all advice to ministers as being, in principle, confidential. The trial judge took the view that the interests of justice override. If I may add this. The general view is that, because these documents were made public, the trial collapsed. The trial collapsed because Mr Alan Clark changed his evidence, not because of anything to do with these documents.

SCOTT: That is a point of view. It is not the only point of view.

G-JONES: What is the other point of view?

SCOTT: It has also been argued that the disclosure of the documents made it inevitable that the prosecution would fail.

G-JONES: I see.

SCOTT: I did not want you to take it as axiomatic that everybody agreed that the prosecution collapsed because of Mr Clark's evidence.

BAX: I would like to go to a document to the Foreign Secretary copied to your private secretary, page 249 of the bundle. It refers to the fact that documents were going to be redacted, and that there might be other documents that would have to be disclosed; and they were considering whether there needed to be further PII certificates. In fact, when the trial judge ordered that the Category C documents with the redactions should be revealed to the defendants, did you suggest that the national interest still required that the documents should not be disclosed, even if this led to the case being dropped?

G-JONES: No.

BAX: Did you ever consider doing that?

G-JONES: No.

BAX: Do you think that it is surprising in the light of the strong language in your PII certificate?

G-JONES: No.

BAX: Why not?

G-JONES: Because I think the word 'unquantifiable' can mean unquantifiably large or unquantifiably small.

SCOTT: So when the text of your certificates reads: 'The disclosure of any sources or alleged sources of intelligence information would cause unquantifiable damage to the functions of security and intelligence in relation to the United Kingdom and abroad', the trial judge should have read that as covering both unquantifiably great and also *miniscule*?

HALF THE PICTURE: ACT TWO

G-JONES: Yes.

BAX: I am sorry to depress you, but can we look at one or two documents. It is the comments of the Foreign Secretary on November 16th, 1992: 'PII certificates. The Secretary of State is not at all happy about the procedure which has affected Mr Garel-Jones and finds the role which is expected of ministers to be baffling.'

G-JONES: I think I made it clear I was irked at being given an important decision of this kind at such short notice. I felt it rather strongly that I should have it in my weekend box.

SCOTT: The Foreign Secretary is not, here, talking about the time constraints that may apply to ministers, is he?

G-JONES: I think it could be directed to a whole range of things. In principle, it is baffling that quite an important decision – I said earlier on, although it meets with derision amongst the press – that no minister in a democracy would regard it as a light thing to withhold information from the public.

SCOTT: This is not withholding from the public. This is withholding it from defence.

JONES: Or indeed from a court. Therefore it is 'baffling' that a decision of this kind turns up in my box at 2.00 in the morning and I have to spit out an answer by 9.00 the next day. That is one aspect of the case that is baffling.

SCOTT: Apart from whatever time constraints there may be, do you not find the role of ministers in the PII procedure baffling at all?

JONES: No.

SC VIII

Evidence of Michael Heseltine.

SCOTT: Mr Heseltine, good morning. Thank you very much indeed for coming here this morning to help us, and thank you for sending us the statement in answer to the questionnaire, which we have carefully read.

BAX: I would like to move to the question of Public Interest Immunity. It's page 10 of your statement to the inquiry. I would like to pick it up on September 2nd, 1992, when you received a submission from Mr Meadway, one of your officials. There are comments in the top-right hand corner: 'This is potentially troublesome. In the short-term, it appears we have no choice but to claim immunity but, it if comes to court, the press will have a field day.' Was that you?

HESEL: No, that was Peter Smith, who is my private secretary. All the hieroglyphics on this document are me.

BAX: Then in paragraph 11 it refers to the involvement of Mr Henderson and how he was providing information to the Security Service. Then in paragraph 12, it refers to an informant letter from a Matrix Churchill employee, and the fact that no action has been taken following that letter. Against that paragraph you have put lots of lines, you have put five lines. Were you very concerned about what paragraph 12 said?

HESEL: Miss Baxendale has actually rightly gone through the rolling sense of concern and the way in which I recorded it at the time, not very articulately but nevertheless graphically. I had come across paragraph 10 where it says: 'The involvement of the security services...the case against the defendants is not that the goods were used for manufacturing military equipment, but that they had lied as to whether the machines were specially designed.' So my question was, if the real crime was the export of this equipment, why were they not being prosecuted for that as opposed to just the fact that they filled in a form inaccurately? We then went on to the two question marks which are here: 'The case for the prosecution is a good one, but unfortunately it may appear to the uninformed reader that the Government did not and does not care that Matrix Churchill was selling equipment for manufacturing weapons of war, and only that lies were told.' That is exactly what people would say. We then go on: 'It is also true that, when the security services man called upon Matrix Churchill, the defendant had told the reception that the visitor was from the Department of Trade and Industry, and so the cover was maintained. Parliamentary questions were tabled at the time this information became public, but were given a suitably uncommunicative blocking answer.' Here we have a line and a question mark, because what this was telling me was that the security services at that time were in touch with Matrix Churchill. If they were in touch with Matrix Churchill, and we were prosecuting them for lying about forms and not for the manufacture, I began to be preoccupied that we knew more than the superficialities of this official submission would indicate. Then we go to paragraph 12. This is where it really became rather serious: 'A further consideration is that in 1988, a Matrix Churchill employee wrote to Sir Geoffrey Howe telling him that Matrix Churchill were making machine tools to produce mortar shells.' That got three lines under it, because we knew, apparently. It then goes on: 'No action appears to have been taken on this letter by the Ministry of Defence, to whom it was sent, or by the DTI's export licensing branch, or the Security Service, who also received a copy.' By that time you have two or three lines, because it told me that *everybody* knew. Then it goes on: 'Assuming the writer retains his public-spirited interest, it may well be that, as the details of the case get into public domain, he may well feel moved to write again, but possibly to the press.' This attracted five lines, and the reason it attracted five lines is because it became apparent to me that I would have to go and try and indulge in the process of – what is the word – 'uncommunicative' answers, and I was not prepared to do that. So that was where we were when I first read the submission. I said: 'Up with this, I will not put.'

SCOTT: How would you describe the 'this'?

HESEL: That I was being asked to sign a document which would deny these documents to the proper trial. The upshot was I said I would not sign the PII certificate that was put in front of me. I simply said, 'I am not signing it.' It could not be right to suggest that the documents were not relevant to the defence.

BAX: Did you consider that the timescale that you had been given, which was from 3rd September to 4th September, was too short to consider what you were meant to be doing?

HESEL: Yes, but I think that about most of the documents on my desk.

BAX: So you see it as inevitable –

HESEL: I happen to know the figures. Five hundred documents come into my private office a day. One hundred of them come through to me. There is always a foot of paper waiting to be dealt with, and it is always urgent. The whole psychology of Whitehall is at 6 o'clock they close their desk, send it to me, asking for a reply by first thing tomorrow morning. That is the way the system works.

BAX: In a note, a lawyer in your department says: 'The papers Mr Heseltine had seen suggested that Whitehall departments had been well aware of the intended military use, yet the defendants seemed to be being prosecuted for concealing it... It would look as though Mr Heseltine had been engaged in a cover-up. You were concerned that you thought these documents should be disclosed and if you put in a certificate 'seeking to support public interest immunity' it would look as though you had not thought that?

HESEL: My interest was not whether the case proceeded. My interest was whether I could in any way do anything to damage the defence prospects. That was my interest in the matter. My view was that the documents should be released. If there was injury to the public interest, for the reasons that would flow from the class category of documents that, in my view, should be overwhelmed by the justice argument. The Attorney-General's letter to me of September 7th, 1992, makes clear his understanding of my concern. I was reassured by the following passage in his letter. It says: 'The drafting of the certificate is unusual, and the judge and defendants will be alert to its limited scope which can, if necessary, be emphasised by counsel for the Crown orally.' It was on that basis that I signed the certificate. I defend absolutely the system of public interest immunity. I believe that it is a system which has been justified but it is a special privilege, of course it is.

BAX: Kenneth Clarke, the Home Secretary, Tristan Garel-Jones at the Foreign Office, and Malcolm Rifkind, the Defence Secretary, also signed PII certificates. Did they know you had signed a different certificate?

HESEL: They did... I just did not want them to be in a position where they discovered I had done this without being told.

BAX: I want to pick up a point. It is a DTI document, page 16742. The second page says: 'Mr Heseltine said that in the Matrix Churchill case, no rational person who had looked at the files could have said that the documents should not have been disclosed. It would have been terrible if a defendant had gone to jail as a result of non-disclosure.' Right?

HESEL: That was the whole basis of what I was doing.

BAX: I would like to look at another prosecution involving the DTI in November 1992, shortly after the collapse of the Matrix Churchill trial, where the question of PII certificates also arose. Your private secretary says in a letter to Miss Wheldon of the Attorney-General's office: 'Mr Heseltine commented that he found this incredible. In the Matrix Churchill case, he was told he had a duty to sign a PII certificate. Now, however, he was told that the prosecuting counsel had a discretion denied to ministers.' Pausing here, did you find it strange that the discretion could lie with prosecution counsel and not with yourself?

HESEL: Yes.

BAX: Then it was decided the best thing was to have a meeting between yourself and the Attorney-General. We find a note of that at page 16742 – 'Mr Heseltine said that no one had explained to him in the context of Matrix Churchill that there was a discretion as to whether PII should be claimed or not. He was told he had a duty.' Then: 'Mr Heseltine queried whether Mr Moses, the leading prosecuting counsel, had, in fact, been aware of the difference in position between ministers on their PII certificates on the Matrix Churchill case.' He quoted from the notes which Mr Moses had subsequently prepared, in which he said that neither he, nor the judge, understood that other ministers were taking a different line to that taken by Mr Heseltine.

HESEL: There is a note by Mr Moses.

BAX: That is right. It says: 'In the event, I argued, and the judge accepted, that all minister were adopting the same stance, and were not intending to make any comments as to how the balancing exercise should be carried out. I was never instructed to the contrary.'

HESEL: Here you have counsel for the prosecution saying that he did not understand it and neither did the judge, that there was any difference between what I had done and other ministers.

BAX: Having now looked at the passages we have drawn to your attention to in the submissions that were made to the judge, do you think a clear message of the kind you were intending was sent to the judge?

HESEL: No, and it should have been.

BAX: Does that concern you?

HESEL: Of course. I thought I had done all I properly could to indicate to the judge what I thought the position to be and I find it difficult to explain the way in which events worked out.

SCENE IX

Evidence of Sir Nicholas Lyell.

BAX: Sir Nicholas, what I would like to do is to come to what happened to Mr Heseltine.

SCOTT: The courts have made it clear on many, many occasions, that the judge of what the public interest requires, and what is going to damage the public interest, is primarily the minister. If Mr Heseltine is running his eye down the list of documents and he concludes it is clear that these documents must be disclosed, he does not sign the certificate?

LYELL: His view deserves respect.

SCOTT: It is more than that. He conscientiously thinks it is clear that these documents must be disclosed, and it is a sort of instinct for justice...knowing the purpose for which the documents are wanted... He has had advice and he still thinks it is a clear case. He happens not to agree with the advice he has had. In such a situation, the conscientious refusal would apply, would it not?

LYELL: It could do.

BAX: I would like to go to Mr Kenneth Clarke's certificate for a moment. On what basis do you understand Mr Clarke authorised the giving of prosecution evidence by members of the security and intelligence services?

LYELL: You have suggested he is exercising his discretion to allow disclosure of information normally covered by PII certificates. I do not think it is correct. A minister does not have discretion.

SCOTT: It was said Kenneth Clarke had to conclude that evidence from the security and intelligence services was necessary for the prosecution?

LYELL: Yes.

SCOTT: You must of course accept that the other side of that coin is that if other information is necessary for the defence, they should also be disclosed? In the Matrix Churchill case, you do not think that the material about civil servants advice to ministers was just as necessary to the defence as this evidence about the security services was necessary to the prosecution?

LYELL: No, I do not. And I could not have exercised a personal judgement in the Matrix Churchill case because I had never seen the documents.

SCOTT: I have to look at your personal involvement, and there are questions about that. I also have to look at the case overall and about whether the overall conduct of it was fair to the defence. The prosecution does not seem bound by the PII rigours in the same way as the defence does?

LYELL: Not necessarily so.

BAX: Were you aware that Mr Henderson had been in contact with the intelligence agencies?

LYELL: I do not believe that I learnt anything about Mr Henderson being an agent until the trial.

BAX: Is it not strange that a minister – and it is particularly a minister because of his knowledge of the public interest – is not allowed to say in the certificate: 'In my view, these documents should be disclosed'?

SCOTT: I suppose this was probably not considered, but it would not have been the clearest way of pointing out Mr Heseltine's views to add a sentence to the certificate to say: 'I wish to raise no argument against disclosure of these documents'?

LYELL: Yes.

BAX: The letter was not copied to Mr Moses, counsel for the Crown?

LYELL: No, but I certainly expected Mr Moses to see it. I am very surprised that it was not shown to him through the Treasury solicitors.

BAX: Did you expect Mr Moses to see it via the Treasury solicitors?

LYELL: Yes.

BAX: Did you take steps to make sure that Mr Moses did know about what you said?

LYELL: I did not take extra steps and I was not aware until certainly long after the trial had collapsed that he had not seen it.

BAX: Was it not reasonable of Mr Heseltine to take the view, having seen the correspondence passing between the two of you, that Mr Moses, the prosecution counsel, was going to be instructed as to Mr Heseltine's view?

LYELL: The way that his view was going to be conveyed was by the points made in those letters. There was no other way that his view was going to be conveyed.

BAX: There could have been, could there not? You could have rung up, lots of things could have happened?

LYELL: Miss Baxendale, masses of things *could* have happened.

SCOTT: Sir Nicholas, to what extent do you think you have a responsibility for this lack of instructions to Mr Moses?

LYELL: I am a minister of the Crown. The Treasury Solicitor's Department as to how they were to approach the briefing of counsel in regard to the PII matter?

LYELL: No.

SCOTT: Do you think you should have done?

LYELL: No.

SCOTT: Is there any more to be said than just 'no'.

SCENE X

Leithead, Higson, Thatcher, Clark, Heseltine, Gore-Booth, Garel-Jones, Major and Waldegrave reappear:

LEIT: It is damaging to the public interest to have decision-making process exposed.

HIG: The Iraqi market, after the end of the Iran-Iraq war, was summed up as being the 'big prize'.

THATCH: They are exactly what they say – guidelines – they are not law. They are guidelines.

BAX: Do they have to be followed?

THATCH: I beg your pardon?

CLARK: There was an implied invitation to them to participate in a fiction.

HESEL: The upshot was I said I would not sign the PII certificate that was put in front of me. I simply said, 'I'm not signing it.'

THATCH: Remember, they are guidelines. It is not like interpreting law... They are guidelines.

G-BOOTH: Questions should be answered so as to give the maximum degree of satisfaction.

LEIT: When one is dealing with PII claims, one tends to take a rather generous view of the –

SCOTT: Take what sort of view?

LEIT: Generous.

SCOTT: Generous to whom?

G-JONES: I think the word 'unquantifiable' can mean unquantifiably large or unquantifiably small.

LEIT: Yes, I do not, no. I think that is probably wrong.

HESEL: I thought I had done all I properly could to indicate to the judge what I thought the position to be and I find it difficult to explain the way in which events worked out.

CLARK: My former colleague, Mr Waldegrave, said, 'Because something was not announced, it had not happened.' He was arguing that because it had not been announced, it could not have happened, a sort of Berkeleyan philosophy.

MAJOR: One of the charges at the time, of course, was that, in some way, I must of known, because I had been the Chancellor, because I had been Foreign Secretary, because I had been Prime Minister, that, therefore, I must have known what was going on... I was asking precisely what I had known.

LYELL: Miss Baxendale, masses of things could have happened.

WALDE: You have to believe that Whitehall is basically honest, which is what I believe.

SCOTT: Is there any more to be said than just 'no'?

THATCH: I fear there will be much grammar to be corrected.

The End.

NUREMBERG

Edited by
Richard Norton-Taylor

Introduction

THE LEGACY OF NUREMBURG

The core crimes were genocide and crimes against humanity. Rudolf Hoess, first commandant of Auschwitz – who appeared as a witness for Kaltenbrunner whose counsel hoped his client's role would look relatively mild in comparison – with apparent insouciance described in detail the search for ever more efficient measures of gassing its inmates. (Hoess was hanged in April 1947 in the grounds of Auschwitz. He said after his capture in 1946 that he believed three million people had died in the camp. Though he later lowered his estimate to 1.13 million, US prosecutors at Nuremberg used the figure of three to four million.)

But the transcripts of the trial show how relatively little time was devoted to these atrocities which raised uncomfortable questions. As Aslain Destexhe says in his book, *Rwanda and Genocide in the Twentieth Century* (Pluto Press): 'During the Second World War, at no time did the Allies modify their military objectives in order to save Jews, even after 1944 when there was no longer any possible doubt as to what was happening. Half a million Jews were murdered in Auschwitz between March and November 1944, when the last gassings took place, yet the railway lines leading to the death camps were never targeted.'

The Nuremberg Trials became bogged down in lengthy arguments about Counts One and Two, whose problems were compounded by Jackson's ineffective cross-examinations, in particular of Goering, who showed himself to be a clever and confident defendant. Counts One and Two caused difficulties for the Allies. As E.L. Woodward, historical adviser to the Foreign Office, told Whitehall: 'Up to September 1st, 1939, His Majesty's Government was prepared to condone everything Germany had done to secure her position in Europe.' And while the West laid itself open to the charge of appeasement – as it has done since, in response to atrocities elsewhere, most recently in the former Yugoslavia – the Soviet Union was also culpable. It had attacked Poland, Finland and the Baltic States at the beginning of the War. It took Moscow fifty years to admit responsibility for the massacre – for at Nuremberg it blamed the Nazis – of nearly 15,000 Polish officers, including those killed in the Katyn Forest in Byelorussia. And there were Stalin's gulags…

Nuremberg prosecutors laid themselves open to the charge that they were indulging in victors' justice. The Allies were vulnerable to the 'dirty hands' defence – that they were conveniently ignoring their own actions. Lord Shawcross confesses in his recent memoirs *Life Sentence* (Constable) to be worried by the 'historical view that by their own conduct of the war, the Allies had lost the moral authority to conduct the trial. I have always felt it was difficult to defend our saturation bombing of Dresden and Hamburg at a time when Germany was already collapsing. I have felt a similar difficulty about the atom bombing of Hiroshima and Nagasaki – especially if, as is now believed by some, this horrific demonstration was intended not so much to bring an early end to the war with Japan as to warn the Soviet Union of the power available to the West.'

The very title of the Tribunal – of German Major War Criminals – gave away its limitations. The world had to wait, notably for the Eichmann trial, for a fuller, more complete picture. It showed, as Destexhe puts it, 'how the overall plan to exterminate the Jews was part of a huge bureaucratic process, a mosaic of minuscule fragments, each one individually very ordinary and commonplace… Only a tiny percentage of those who participated in the genocide actually shot a Jew or turned on the gas. It was the bureaucrats who helped to destroy the Jewish people, often whilst remaining at their desks. Gassing rather than shooting was an ingenious system which avoided any one person being directly responsible for an actual killing.' Of the tens of thousands estimated by Lord Shawcross as having committed crimes which, he says, 'cried out for punishment', a few hundred were sentences to death by the four victorious powers.

In Britain, The War Crimes Act of 1991 is an admission of Whitehall's failure or reluctance to vet those implicated from coming to Britain. Anthony Glees, historian and adviser to the inquiry that led to the Act, estimates that there are about 100 'serious suspects' still alive in Britain.

Shawcross confidently predicted at Nuremberg that the Tribunal would 'provide a contemporary touchstone and an authoritative and impartial record to which future historians may turn for truth, and future politicians for warning.' Fifty years later, these words have a hollow ring in the light of war crimes perpetuated by the Nuremberg victors – the bombing of Cambodia during the Vietnam War, for example, or the treatment of Algerians fighting for independence. (The US writer Noam Chomsky, has said: 'If the Nuremberg laws were applied, then every post-war American President would have been hanged.')

Yet even those who accept that the Nuremberg Trial was flawed insist that nevertheless it remains deeply significant. 'For the first time,' says David Cesarani, Professor of Modern Jewish Studies at Manchester University, 'individuals were put on trial for sending their people to war and ordering them to commit atrocities...it was no longer enough to say: "We were just obeying orders."'

Now, for the first time since Nuremberg, the UN has set up war crimes tribunals – for the former Yugoslavia and Rwanda. Richard Goldstone, the South African judge and first chief prosecutor at both of the tribunals, has described them as 'a major step ushering in a new era in the history of international law and especially international humanitarian law.' Like Shawcross, he is pressing for a permanent international war crimes tribunal.

Richard Norton-Taylor

The Nuremberg War Crimes Trial, 1946

The Nuremberg Trial of German Major War Criminals opened amid great fanfare and rhetoric on 29 November 1945. More than ten months later, on 1 October 1946, of the twenty-two defendants, twelve were sentenced to death by hanging – Martin Bormann in absentia – three were sentenced to life imprisonment, four were sentenced to prison terms ranging from ten to twenty years, and three were acquitted. Goering committed suicide by swallowing a cyanide capsule shortly before he was due to be hanged.

There were four judges with one alternate from each of the victorious powers, with Britain's Lord Justice Lawrence serving as President: the Russian member of the Tribunal, General Nikitchenko, gave a dissenting opinion against the acquittal of three of the defendants, the refusal to sentence Rudolf Hess (not to be confused with Hoess) to death, and against the majority decision to acquit the Reich Cabinet and the General Staff and High Command of the German armed forces of being criminal organisations.

The Tribunal was established by Britain, the US, France and the Soviet Union (with the support of Governments-in-exile whose countries were occupied by Germany) under a Charter indicting both individuals and organisations, not only for war crimes and crimes against humanity, but also for crimes against peace and for conspiring in a common plan.

Count One charged the defendants, over a ten-year period up to May 1945, with participating in a common plan or conspiracy to commit crimes against peace, war crimes and crimes against humanity as defined in the Charter.

Count Two charged them over the same period with crimes against peace – participating in the planning, preparation, initiating, and waging wars of aggression.

Count Three charged the defendants with committing war crimes between September 1939 and 8 May 1945, including the murder and ill-treatment of civilian populations of occupied territories, murder and ill-treatment of prisoners of war, killing of hostages, plunder of public and private property, exacting collective penalties, wanton destruction not justified by military necessity, conscription of civil labour and 'Germanisation' of occupied territories.

Count Four charged the defendants with the commission of crimes against humanity in Austria, Czechoslovakia and in Germany itself prior to May 1945 and in all countries occupied by German armed forces after 1 September 1939. The crimes cited included murder, extermination, enslavement, deportation and persecution of political, racial and religious groups.

The prosecuting countries divided up the counts between them: the US was given responsibility for Count One – the conspiracy charge; Britain for Count Two; and the French and Russians dealt with the Third and Fourth Counts in, respectively, Western and Eastern Europe.

All the defendants, who could choose their own counsel, pleaded not guilty. A not guilty plea was entered for Martin Bormann in his absence. Robert Ley, Director of the Labour Front, hanged himself in his cell shortly before the trial started. Ernst Kaltenbrunner, Chief of the Reich Security Department, who was in hospital at the start of the trail after a stroke, later made a personal plea of not guilty. Gustav Krupp, the industrialist, was too ill to face a trial. Hitler – the Führer, Himmler – of Propaganda, had all committed suicide before the trial. The proceedings were simultaneously translated into four languages – English, Russian, French and German. The official transcript runs to about six million words. The prosecution called 33 witnesses, the defendants called 61. Over 50 million pages of documents were produced at the trial.

THE DEFENDANTS

Karl Doenitz
Commander of the German Navy, appointed Chancellor in May 1945 after Hitler's death

Hans Frank
Governor-General of Poland

Wilhelm Frick
Reich Minister of the Interior and Protector of Bohemia and Moravia

Hans Fritzsche
A Reich Ministry of Propaganda official

Walther Funk
President of the Reichbank

Hermann Goering
Hitler's successor-designate in September 1939, Chairman of the Reich Council for National Defence and Commander of the Luftwaffe

Rudolf Hess
Hitler's former deputy who flew to Britain in 1941 with a peace offer, apparently on his own accord

Alfred Jodl
Chief of the Wehrmacht Operations Staff

Ernst Kaltenbrunner
Chief of the Reich Security Department

Wilhelm Keitel
Chief of Staff of the Wehrmacht

Constantin von Neurath
Former Protector of Bohemia and Moravia and Minister without Portfolio

Franz von Papen
Former Chancellor of Germany

Erich Raeder
Former Commander-in-Chief of the German Navy

Joachim von Ribbentrop
Foreign Minister

Alfred Rosenberg
Minister for the Occupied Eastern Territories and the Nazi Party's official 'philosopher' – his book *The Myth of the Twentieth Century* was a best-seller – and the propagator of crude anti-Semitism

Fritz Sauckel
Plenipotentiary for labour Mobilisation

Hjalmar Schacht
Former Minister of Economics and President of the Reichbank

Baldur von Schirach
Reich Youth Leader

Arthur Seyss-Inquart
Reich Commissioner in the Netherlands

Albert Speer
Minister of Armaments and War Production

Julius Streicher
Former Gauleiter of Franconia and founding editor of *Der Stümer*, a rabidly anti-Semitic newspaper.

Martin Bormann
Head of the Nazi Party Chancellery – tried in absentia.

CONVICTIONS AND SENTENCES

All the defendants pleaded not guilty

Defendant	Count One	Count Two
Martin Bormann	Not guilty	Not charged
Karl Doenitz	Not guilty	Guilty
Hans Frank	Not guilty	Not guilty
Wilhelm Frick	Not guilty	Guilty
Hans Fritzsche	Not guilty	Not charged
Walther Funk	Not guilty	Guilty
Hermann Goering	Guilty	Guilty
Rudolf Hess	Guilty	Guilty
Alfred Jodl	Guilty	Guilty
Ernst Kaltenbrunner	Not guilty	Not charged
Wilhelm Keitel	Guilty	Guilty
Erich Raeder	Guilty	Guilty
Joachim von Ribbentrop	Guilty	Guilty
Alfred Rosenberg	Guilty	Guilty
Fritz Sauckel	Not guilty	Not guilty
Hjalmar Schacht	Not guilty	Not guilty
Arthur Seyss-Inquart	Not guilty	Guilty
Albert Speer	Not guilty	Not guilty
Julius Streicher	Not guilty	Not charged
Constantin von Neurath	Guilty	Guilty
Franz von Papen	Not guilty	Not guilty
Baldur von Schirach	Not guilty	Not charged

Count Three	Count Four	Sentence
Guilty	Guilty	Death
Guilty	Not charged	Ten years
Guilty	Guilty	Death
Guilty	Guilty	Death
Not guilty	Not guilty	Acquitted
Guilty	Guilty	Life imprisonment
Guilty	Guilty	Death
Not guilty	Not guilty	Life imprisonment
Guilty	Guilty	Death
Guilty	Guilty	Death
Guilty	Guilty	Death
Guilty	Not charged	Life imprisonment
Guilty	Guilty	Death
Guilty	Guilty	Death
Guilty	Guilty	Death
Not charged	Not charged	Acquitted
Guilty	Guilty	Death
Guilty	Guilty	Twenty years
Not charged	Guilty	Death
Guilty	Guilty	Fifteen years
Not charged	Not charged	Acquitted
Not charged	Guilty	Twenty years

Nuremberg was first presented on stage together with *Ex-Yu* by Goran Stefanovski, *Haiti* by Keith Reddin and *Reel Rwanda* by Femi Osofisan, at the Tricycle Theatre, London, on 10 May 1996, with the following cast:

Mr Justice Ribert H.Jackson *Chief Prosecutor for the US*	Colin Bruce
Sir Hartley Shawcross, H. M. Attorney General *Chief Prosecutor for the UK*	Richard Heffer
General R.A. Rudenko *Chief Prosecutor for the USSR*	Mark Powley
Lord Justice Lawrence *President of the Tribunal*	David Webb
Reichsmarschall Hermann Goering *Commander of the Luftwaffe* *and Hitler's designated successor*	Michael Cochrane
Dr Stahmer *Counsel for Goering*	Hugh Simon
Sir David Maxwell-Fyfe *Deputy Chief Prosecutor for the UK*	Mark Penfold
Field-Marshal Wilhelm Keitel *Chief of the Staff of the Wehrmacht*	William Hoyland
Dr Otto Nelte *Counsel for Keitel*	Raad Rawi
Rudolf Hoess *Commandant of Auschwitz*	Thomas Wheatley
Dr Kurt Kauffmann *Counsel for Kaltenbrunner*	James Woolley
Alfred Rosenberg *Reich Minister for Eastern* *Occupied Territories*	Jeremy Clyde
Dr Thomas *Counsel for Rosenberg*	Mark Penfold

Mr Thomas Dodd *US Assistant Prosecutor*	Raad Rawi
Albert Speer *Minister of Armaments and* *War Production*	Michael Culver
Dr Hans Flaechsner *Counsel for Speer*	Hugh Simon

Director, Nicolas Kent

Set Designer, Saul Radomsky

Costume Designer, Jacqueline Abrahams

Lighting Designer, Simon Opie

The production was revived with the same cast in September – October 1996, together with *Srebrenica*, edited by Nicolas Kent, which was an account of the Rule 61 hearings against Dr Karadžić and General Mladić at the International War Crimes Tribunal in The Hague.

In the Tricycle production, the words used by Francis Biddle were spoken by the President of the Tribunal.

Nuremberg was commissioned from an idea by Nicolas Kent for the Tricycle Theatre in 1995.

The court pioneered the use of a simultaneous translation system. A red light on the prosecutors' and witnesses' boxes stopped proceedings and a yellow light signalled the speakers to slow down.

MR JUSTICE ROBERT H. JACKSON *(Chief Prosecutor for the United States of America)*: The privilege of opening the first trial in history for crimes against the peace of the world imposes a grave responsibility. The wrongs which we seek to condemn and punish have been so calculated, so malignant, and so devastating, that civilisation cannot tolerate their being ignored, because it cannot survive their being repeated.

That four great nations, flushed with victory and stung with injury, stay the hands of vengeance and voluntarily submit their captive enemies to the judgement of the law, is one of the most significant tributes that Power ever has paid to Reason.

We must never forget the record on which we judge these defendants today is the record on which history will judge us tomorrow. To pass these defendants a poisoned chalice is to put our lips to it as well.

We would also make clear that we have no purpose to incriminate the whole German people. We know that the Nazi Party was not put in power by a majority of German vote.

These defendants were men of a station and rank which does not soil its own hands with blood. They were men who knew how to use lesser folk as tools.

The most savage and numerous crimes committed by the Nazis were those against the Jews.

Of the nine million, six hundred thousand Jews who lived in Nazi-dominated Europe, 60 percent are authoritatively estimated to have perished. History does not record a crime ever perpetrated against so many victims nor one ever carried out with such calculated cruelty.

'Undesirables' were exterminated by the injection of drugs into the bloodstream, by asphyxiation in gas chambers. They were shot with poison bullets, to study the effects.

I am one who received, during the war, most atrocity tales with suspicion and scepticism. But the proof here will be so overwhelming that I venture to predict that not one word I have spoken will be denied. These defendants will only deny personal responsibility or knowledge.

The Third Count of the Indictment is based on the definition of War Crimes contained in the Charter. It will appear, for example, that the defendant Keitel was informed by official legal advisers that the orders to brand Russian prisoners of war, to shackle British prisoners of war, and to execute Commando prisoners were clear violations of International Law. Nevertheless, these orders were put into effect.

The Fourth Count of the Indictment is based on Crimes against Humanity. Chief among these are mass killings of countless human beings in cold blood. Does it take these men by surprise that murder is treated as a crime?

The First and Second Counts of the Indictment add to these crimes the crime of plotting and waging wars of aggression. The idea that a State, any more than a corporation, commits crimes, is a fiction. Crimes always are committed only by persons.

The Charter recognises that one who has committed criminal acts may not take refuge in superior orders nor in the doctrine that his crimes were acts of State.

PRESIDENT: I will now call upon the Chief Prosecutor for the United Kingdom of Great Britain and Northern Ireland.

HM ATTORNEY-GENERAL, SIR HARTLEY SHAWCROSS *(Chief Prosecutor for the United Kingdom of Great Britain and Northern Ireland)*: By agreement between the chief Prosecutors, it is my task – on behalf of the British Government, and of the other States associated in this prosecution to present the case on Count Two of the Indictment and to show how these defendants, in conspiracy with each other and with persons not now before this Tribunal, planned and waged a war of aggression in breach of the Treaty obligations by which, under International Law, Germany, as other States, had sought to make such wars impossible.

Under the General Treaty for the Renunciation of War of 27th August, 1928, practically the whole civilised world abolished war as a legally permissible means of enforcing the law or changing it. The right of war was no longer of the essence of sovereignty.

Let us see how these defendants, Ministers and High Officers of the Nazi Government, individually and collectively, comported themselves in these matters.

On 1st September, 1939, in the early hours of the morning, under manufactured and, in any event, inadequate pretexts, the armed forces of the German Reich invaded Poland along the whole length for her frontiers and thus launched the war which was to bring down so many of the pillars of our civilisation.

As early as August 1938, steps were being made to utilise the Low Countries as defence bases for decisive action in the West in the event of France and England opposing Germany in the aggressive plan on foot against Czechoslovakia.

On the 10th May, 1940, at about 0500 hours in the morning, the German invasion of Belgium, Holland and Luxemburg began. The only fault of these unhappy countries was that they stood in the path of the German invader in his designs against England and France. But that was enough.

On the 6th of April, 1941, German forces invaded Greece and Yugoslavia.

On the 22nd of June, 1941, the German armed forces invaded Russia, without warning, without declaration of war. The Nazi armies were flung against the power with which Hitler had so recently sworn friendship, and Germany embarked upon that last act of aggression in Europe which, after long and bitter fighting, was eventually to result in Germany's own collapse.

It is indeed true, as Great Britain fully accepts, that immediately as State accepts international obligations it limits its sovereignty. In that way, and that way alone, lies the future peace of the world.

The government of a totalitarian country may be carried on without representatives of the people, but it cannot be carried on without any assistance at all. It is no use having a leader unless there are also people willing and ready to serve their personal greed and ambition by helping and following him.

It is no excuse for the common thief to say, 'I stole because I was told to steal', for the murderer to plead, 'I killed because I was asked to kill.' And these men are in no different position. Political loyalty, military obedience, are excellent things, but they neither require nor do they justify the commission of patently wicked acts. There comes a point where a man must refuse to answer to his leader if he is also to answer to his conscience. Even the common soldier, serving in the ranks of his army, is not called upon to obey illegal orders.

If these crimes were in one sense the crimes of Nazi Germany, they also are guilty as the individuals who aided, abetted, counselled, procured and made possible the commission of what was done.

GENERAL R.A. RUDENKO *(Chief Prosecutor for the Union of Soviet Socialist Republics)*: Having prepared and carried out the perfidious assault against the freedom-loving nations, fascist Germany turned the war into a system of militarised banditry.

The murder of war prisoners, extermination of civilian populations, plunder of occupied territories and other war crimes were committed as part of a totalitarian lightning war programme – 'Blitzkrieg' – projected by the fascists. In particular, the terrorism practised by the fascists on the temporarily-occupied Soviet territories reached fabulous proportions and was carried out with fiendish cruelty.

'We must', said Hitler, 'pursue a policy of systematic depopulation. If you ask me what I mean by the term "depopulation", I would tell you that I understand it to be the complete removal of whole racial groups. And that is what I am going to do; such, roughly, is my purpose.'

The names have already been mentioned here of the concentration camps, with their gas chambers. The Germans also carried out mass shootings of Soviet citizens. The mass murders, this arbitrary regime of terror, was fully approved by the defendant Rosenberg in a speech in November 1942:

'If we are to subjugate all these peoples (i.e. peoples inhabiting the territory of the USSR) then arbitrary rule and tyranny will be an extremely suitable form of Government.'

In April, 1942, a top secret circular, 'Programme of the General-Plenipotentiary for the Employment of Labour,' was sent. It noted that 'it is extremely necessary fully to utilise the human reserves available in occupied Soviet territories.' 400,000 to 500, 000 'selected, healthy and strong girls' were ordered to be brought to Germany from the eastern Territories 'in order that the burden on the overworked German peasant woman should be noticeably lightened.'

The German fascist invaders completely or partially destroyed or burnt 1,170 cities and more than 70,000 villages and hamlets; they burnt or destroyed over 6 million buildings and rendered some 25 million persons homeless.

Himmler mentioned that it was necessary to cut down the number of Slavs by 30 million.

Now, when as a result of the heroic struggle of the Red Army and the Allied Forces, Hitlerite Germany is broken and overwhelmed, we have no right to forget the victims who have suffered.

May justice be done!

THE PRESIDENT: Will you give your name please?

GOERING *(Commander in Chief of the Air Force and successor-designate to Hitler)*: Hermann Goering.

THE PRESIDENT: Will you repeat this oath after me: I swear by God the Almighty and Omniscient that I will speak the pure truth and will withhold and add nothing.

The witness repeated the oath.

THE PRESIDENT: You may sit down if you wish. Dr Stahmer do you wish to examine the defendant?

DR STAHMER: When were you born and where?

GOERING: I was born on 12th January, 1893, in Rosenheim Bavaria.

STAHMER: Give the Tribunal a short account of your life up to the outbreak of the First World War, but briefly, please.

GOERING: Normal education, first tutored at home; then cadet corps, then an active officer. A few points which are significant with relation to my later development: the position of my father as first Governor of South-West Africa, his connections at that time, especially with two British statesmen, Cecil Rhodes and the elder Chamberlain…

STAHMER: Tell the Tribunal when and under what circumstances you came to know Hitler?

GOERING: After the collapse in the First World War, I settled down in the neighbourhood of Munich… I found out I could hear Hitler speak, as he held a meeting every Monday evening. Finally, I saw a man here who had a clear and definite aim.

He gave me for the first time a very wonderful and profound explanation of the concept of National Socialism; the uniting of the concept of Nationalism on the one hand and Socialism on the other, which could prove itself the absolute bearer of Socialism as well as Nationalism, the Nationalism, if I may say so, of the bourgeois world and the Socialism of the Marxist world.

In the middle of 1932, after numerous elections had taken place, we became the strongest Party, and I was elected President of the Reichstag, and thereby took over a definite political task.

Then in January, 1933, there were further elections. One must not forget that at this moment Germany had arrived at the lowest point of her downward development, 8 million unemployed; all programmes had failed; no more confidence in the Parties; a very strong rise on the part of the revolutionary Leftist side; and political insecurity.

In the end, we were the strongest Party with 232 seats.

At 11 o'clock in the morning of 22nd January 1933, the Cabinet was formed and Hitler appointed Reich Chancellor.

STAHMER: What measures were taken to strengthen Hitler's power?

GOERING: The Führer told me that the simplest thing to do would be to take as example the United States of America, where the Head of State is at the same time the Head of the Government. That he thereby automatically became also the Commander-in-Chief of the German Armed Forces followed as a matter of course, according to the Constitution.

STAHMER: Did you create the Gestapo, and the concentration camps?

GOERING: For the consolidation of power, the first prerequisite was to create along new lines that instrument which at all times and in all nations is always the inner political instrument of power, namely the police. There was no Reich police. In order to make clear from the outset that the task of this police was to make the State secure, I called it the Secret State Police.

STAHMER: The concentration camps?

GOERING: When the need for creating order, first of all, and removing the most dangerous element of disorder directed against us now became evident, I reached the decision to have the Communist functionaries and leaders arrested all at once.

STAHMER: The Party Programme included two points dealing with the question of the Jews. What was your basic attitude towards the question?

GOERING: The Nuremberg Laws were intended to be about a clear separation of races and, in particular, to do away with the concept of a person of mixed blood in the future…

STAHMER: You said you had been considered the Führer's successor. Were you in this capacity included in all political problems by Hitler?

GOERING: Of course, he informed me of all important political and military problems.

PRESIDENT: Do the Chief Prosecutors wish to cross-examine?

MR JUSTICE JACKSON: You are perhaps aware that you are the only living man who can expound to us the true purposes of the Nazi Party and the inner workings of its leadership?

GOERING: I am perfectly aware of that.

JACKSON: You, from the very beginning, together with those who were associated with you, intended to overthrow, and later did overthrow, the Weimar Republic?

GOERING: That was, as far as I am concerned, my firm intention.

JACKSON: And, upon coming to power, you immediately abolished parliamentary government in Germany?

GOERING: We found it to be no longer necessary. Also I should like to emphasise the fact that we were, moreover, the strongest. Parliamentary procedure was done away with because the various parties were disbanded and forbidden.

The people were merely to acknowledge the authority of the Führer. Thus, not the individual persons were to be selected according to the will of the people, but solely the leadership itself.

JACKSON: After you came to power, you regarded it necessary, in order to maintain power, to suppress all opposition parties?

GOERING: We found it necessary not to permit any more opposition, yes.

JACKSON: And you also held it necessary that you should suppress all individual opposition lest it should develop into a Party of Opposition?

GOERING: In so far as opposition seriously hampered our work of building up, this opposition of individual persons was, of course, not tolerated.

JACKSON: Now, in order to make sure that you suppressed the parties, and individuals also, you found it necessary to have a secret political police to detect opposition?

GOERING: I have already stated that I considered that necessary, similar to the former political police, but on a firmer basis and larger scale.

JACKSON: And upon coming to power you also considered it immediately necessary to establish concentration camps to take care of your incorrigible opponents?

GOERING: The reason for the concentration camps was not because it could be said, 'Here are a number of people who are opposed to us and they must be taken into protective custody.' Rather they were set up as an emergency measure against the functionaries of the Communist Party who were attacking us in their thousands and who, since they were taken into protective custody, were not put in prison.

JACKSON: But you are explaining, as the high authority of this system, to men who do not understand it very well. And I want to know what was necessary to run the kind of system that you set up in Germany. The concentration camp was one of the things you found immediately necessary upon coming into power, was it not? And you set them up as a matter of necessity, as you saw it?

GOERING: That was faultily translated – it went too fast. But I believe I understood the sense of your remarks. You asked me if I considered it necessary to establish concentration camps immediately in order to eliminate opposition. Is that correct?

JACKSON: Your answer is, 'Yes', I take it?

GOERING: Yes.

JACKSON: Protective custody meant that you were taking people into custody who had not committed any crime but who, you thought, might possibly commit a crime?

GOERING: Yes. People were arrested and taken into protective custody who had not yet committed any crime, but who could be expected to do so if they remained free, just as similar protective measures are being taken in Germany today on a tremendous scale

JACKSON: Now, it is also a necessity, in the kind of State that you had, that you have some kind of organisation to carry propaganda down to the people and to get their reaction and inform the leadership of it, is it not?

GOERING: The last part of that question has not been intelligibly translated.

JACKSON: Well, you had to have organisations to carry out orders and to carry your propaganda in that kind of State, did you not?

GOERING: The Leadership Corps was there, of course, partly to spread our ideas among the people. Secondly, its purpose was to lead and organise the people.

JACKSON: When it was State necessity to kill somebody, you had to have somebody to do it, did you not?

GOERING: Yes, just as in other States; whether it is called Secret Service or something else, I do not know.

JACKSON: And the SS, organisations of that kind, were the organisations that carried out the orders and dealt with people on a physical level, were they not?

GOERING: The SS never received an order to kill anybody, not in my time. Anyhow I had no influence on it... I know that orders were given for executions, and these were carried out by the police, that is by a State organ.

JACKSON: What police?

GOERING: As far as I can recall, through the Gestapo. At any rate, that was the organisation that received the order. You see, it was a fight against enemies of the State.

JACKSON: The SS carried out all the functions of the camps, did they not?

GOERING: If an SS unit was guarding a camp and an SS leader happened to be the camp commander, then this unit carried out all the functions.

JACKSON: As to organisation, everybody knew what the Gestapo was, did they not?

GOERING: Yes, everyone knew what the Gestapo was.

JACKSON: And what its programme was, in general, not in detail?

GOERING: I explained that programme clearly. At the very beginning, I described that publicly, and I also spoke publicly of the tasks of the Gestapo, and I even wrote about it for foreign countries.

JACKSON: And there was nothing secret about the establishment of a Gestapo as a political police, about the fact that people were taken into protective custody, about the fact that there were concentration camps? Nothing secret about those things, was there?

GOERING: There was at first nothing secret about it at all.

JACKSON: As a matter of fact, part of the effectiveness of a secret police and part of the effectiveness of concentration camp penalties is that the people do know that there are such agencies, is it not?

GOERING: It is true that everyone knows that if he acts against the State he will end up in a concentration camp, or will be accused of high treason before a court, according to the degree of his crime. But the original reason for creating the concentration camps was to keep there those people whom we rightfully considered enemies of the State.

JACKSON: Now, is that type of government – the government which we have just been describing – the only type of government which you think is necessary to govern Germany?

GOERING: I should not like to say that the basic characteristic of this government and its most essential feature was the immediate setting up of the Gestapo and the concentration camps in order to take care of our opponents. Over and above that we had set down as our government programme a great many, much more important, things, and those other things were not the basic principles of our government.

JACKSON: But all those things were necessary things, as I understood you, for purposes of protection?

GOERING: Yes, these things were necessary because of the opponents that existed.

JACKSON: And I assume that that is the only kind of government that you think can function in Germany under present conditions?

GOERING: Under the conditions existing at that time, it was, in my opinion, the only possible form, and it also demonstrated that Germany could be raised in a short time from the depths of misery, poverty and unemployment to relative prosperity.

JACKSON: Now, all this authority of the State was concentrated? Perhaps I am taking up another subject...

You have related to us the manner in which you and others co-operated in concentrating all authority in the German State in the hands of the Führer; is that right?

GOERING: I was speaking about myself and to what extent I had a part in it.

JACKSON: Is there any defendant in the box you know of, who did not co-operate toward that end so far as was possible?

GOERING: That none of the defendants here opposed or obstructed the Führer in the beginning is clear.

JACKSON: By January 1945...there was no way to prevent the war going on as long as Hitler was the head of the German Government, was there?

GOERING: As long as Hitler was the Führer of the German people, he alone decided whether the war was to go on. As long as my enemy threatens me and demands absolutely unconditional surrender, and held out those terrible conditions which had been intimated, I would have continued fighting whatever the circumstances.

SIR DAVID MAXWELL FYFE *(Deputy Chief Prosecutor for the UK)*: Will you look at the document, Document D-728, Exhibit GB 282. Witness, I want you to deal with the sentence in paragraph 6, 'the administration, enlargement, installations and deterrent tasks in the concentration camps must be destroyed at all costs. Also the extermination of some families etc. These files must under no circumstances fall into the hands of the enemy, since they are, after all, secret orders by the Führer.'

Now this paragraph is certainly directed to all administrative levels, down to the country leaders of the Nazi Party, and it assumes they knew all about the running of concentration camps. Are you telling the tribunal that you, who up to 1943 were the second man in the Reich, knew nothing about the concentration camps?

GOERING: First of all, I want to say that I do not accept this document and that its whole wording is unknown to me and that this paragraph seems unusual to me. I did not know anything about what took place and the methods used in the concentration camps until later, when I was no longer in charge.

FYFE: Let me remind you of the evidence that has been given before this Court, that as far as Auschwitz alone is concerned, 4 million people were exterminated. Do you remember that? Are you telling this tribunal that a minister with your power in the Reich could remain ignorant that that was going on?

GOERING: These things were kept secret from me. I might add that, in my opinion, not even the Führer knew the extent of what was going on.

FYFE: But, witness, had you not access to the foreign Press, the Press Department in your ministry, to foreign broadcasts? You see, there is evidence that altogether, when you take the Jews and other people, something like 10 million people have been put to death in cold blood, apart from those killed in battle. Something like 10 million people. Do you say that you never saw or heard from the foreign Press, in broadcast, that this was going on?

GOERING: First of all, the figure 10 million is not established in any way. Secondly, throughout the war I did not read the foreign Press because I considered it nothing but propaganda. Thirdly, though I had the right to listen to foreign broadcast, I never did so, simply because I did not want to listen to propaganda. Neither did I listen to home propaganda.

FYFE: The Führer, at any rate, must have had full knowledge of what was happening with regard to concentration camps, the treatment of the Jews, and the treatment of the workers, must he not?

GOERING: The Führer did not know about the details in concentration camps, about atrocities. In so far as I know him, I do not believe he was informed.

FYFE: I am not asking about details; I am asking about the murder of 4 or 5 million people. Are you suggesting that nobody in power in Germany, except Himmler and perhaps Kaltenbrunner, knew about that?

GOERING: I am still of the opinion that the Führer did not know about these figures.

FYFE: Now, Witness, you said that Hitler, in your opinion, did not know about or was ignorant about the question of concentration camps and the Jews. I would like you to look at document USSR 170.

Now this is a conference which you had with a number of people. Lohse, who was at the conference, says: 'There are only a few Jews left alive. Tens of thousands have been disposed of.' Do you still say, in the face of the documents, that neither Hitler nor yourself knew that the Jews were being exterminated?

GOERING: This should be understood. From this you cannot conclude that they have been killed. It is not my remark. The Jews were only left in smaller numbers. From this remark you cannot conclude that they were killed. It could also mean that they were removed.

FYFE: I suggest that you make it clear what is meant by 'there are only a few Jews left alive, whereas tens of thousands have been disposed of.'

GOERING: They were still living there. That is how you should understand that.

FYFE: You heard what I read to you about Hitler. Hitler said the Jews must either work or be shot. That was in April 1943. Do you still say that neither Hitler nor you knew of this policy to exterminate the Jews?

GOERING: For the correction of the document –

FYFE: Will you please answer the question? Do you still say that neither Hitler nor you knew of the policy to exterminate the Jews?

GOERING: As far as Hitler is concerned, I have said I do not believe it. As far as I am concerned, I have said that I did not know, even approximately, to what degree this thing took place.

FYFE: You did not know to what degree, but you knew there was a policy that aimed at the extermination of the Jews?

GOERING: No, a policy for emigration, not liquidation, of the Jews. I only knew that there had been isolated cases of such perpetrations.

FYFE: Thank you.

GENERAL RUDENKO *(Chief Prosecutor for the USSR)*: If I understand you, defendant Goering, you said that all the basic decisions concerning foreign, political and military matters were taken by Hitler alone? Do I understand you rightly?

GOERING: Yes, certainly. After all, he was the Führer.

RUDENKO: Am I to understand that Hitler took these decisions without listening to the opinions of the experts who studied the questions, and the intelligence reports on those matters?

GOERING: It depends upon the circumstances. In certain cases, he would ask for data to be submitted to him, without the experts knowing the exact reason.

RUDENKO: 16th September, 1941, is the date of this document. Paragraph B of the document. It states that as a general rule the death of one German solider must be paid for by the lives of 50 to 100 Communists. I am interested in whether this document was unknown to you.

GOERING: Yes, it was. It was not directed to me either. Here again it merely went to some administrative office. The Air Force had very little to do with such matters.

RUDENKO: Please tell me, do you know about Himmler's directives given in 1941 about the extermination of 30 million Slavs?

GOERING: Yes. This was not an order, but a speech. In all speeches Himmler made to assistant leaders, he insisted on the strictest secrecy.

Consequently, I have no knowledge of this nonsense.

RUDENKO: You did not know about it. Very well. Tell me, in the German totalitarian State was there not a governing centre, which meant Hitler and his immediate entourage, in which you acted as deputy? Could Himmler of his own volition have issued directives for the extermination of 30 million Slavs without being empowered by Hitler or by you?

GOERING: Himmler gave no order for the extermination of 30 million Slavs. Had Himmler issued such an order de facto, then he would have had to ask the Führer, not me, but the Führer, and the latter would probably have told him at once that it was impossible.

RUDENKO: I have a few concluding questions to put to you. First of all, regarding the so-called theory of the Master Race. Were you in accord with this principle of the Master Race and education of the German people in the spirit of it or were you not in accord with it?

GOERING: I have never expressed my agreement with the theory that one race should be considered as a Master

Race superior to the others, but I have emphasised the difference between the races.

RUDENKO: You can answer this question; apparently you do not consider it right?

GOERING: I personally do not consider it right.

RUDENKO: The next question: You have stated here at the Tribunal that you did not agree with Hitler regarding the question of annexation of Czechoslovakia, the Jewish Question, the question of war with the Soviet Union, the value of the theory of the Master Race, and the question of the shooting of the British airmen who were prisoners of war. How would you explain that, having such serious differences, you still thought it possible to collaborate with Hitler and to carry out his policy?

GOERING: All right. I may have had a different opinion from that of my supreme leader, and I may have also expressed my opinion clearly. If the supreme leader insists on his opinion and I have sworn allegiance to him, then the discussion comes to an end, just as is the case elsewhere. I do not think I need to elaborate that point.

RUDENKO: In other words, you thought it possible, even in spite of these differences, to collaborate with Hitler?

GOERING: I have emphasised it and I maintain that it is true. My oath does not only hold good in good times but also in bad times, although the Führer never threatened me and never told me that he was afraid for my health.

RUDENKO: If you thought it possible to co-operate with Hitler, do you recognise that, as the second man in Germany, you are responsible for the organising, on a national scale, of the murders of millions of innocent people, independently of whether you knew about those facts or not? Tell me briefly: yes or no.

GOERING: No, because I did not know anything about them and did not cause them... If I actually did not know about them, I cannot be held responsible for them.

RUDENKO: It was your duty to know about these facts.

GOERING: In what way my duty? Either I know the fact, or I do not know it. You can only ask me if I was negligent in failing to obtain knowledge.

RUDENKO: You ought to know yourself better. Millions of Germans knew about the crimes which were being perpetrated, and you did not know about them?

GOERING: Neither did millions of Germans know about them. That is a statement which has in no way been proved.

RUDENKO: You stated to the Tribunal that Hitler's Government brought great prosperity to Germany. Are you still sure that that is so?

GOERING: Definitely until the beginning of the war. The collapse was only due to war being lost.

RUDENKO: I have no more questions.

PRESIDENT: Dr Stahmer, do you wish to re-examine the witness?

DR STAHMER: During your examination, you stated, regarding certain accusations, that you want to assume responsibility for them.

GOERING: I acknowledge my responsibility for having done everything to carry out the preparations for the seizure of power, and to have made the power firm in order to make Germany free and great. I did everything to avoid this war. But after it started, it was my duty to do everything to win it.

PRESIDENT: Will you state your full name?

KEITEL (*Chief of the High Command of the Armed Forces*): Wilhelm Keitel.

PRESIDENT: Will you repeat this oath after me: I swear by God the Almighty and Omniscient, that I will speak the pure truth, and will withhold and add nothing.

The Witness repeats the oath

You may sit down if you wish. Dr Nelte, do you wish to examine the witness?

DR NELTE: Do you have any sons?

KEITEL: I had three sons, all of whom served at the front as officers during the war. The youngest one died in battle in Russia in 1941. The second was a major in Russia and has been missing in action, and the eldest son, who was a major, is a prisoner of war.

NELTE: Field Marshal Keitel, to begin with essential matters, I would like to put the following basic questions to you:

What basic attitude did you as a soldier, an officer, and a general have toward the problems with which you came in contact in your profession?

KEITEL: I can say that I was a soldier by inclination and conviction. For more than 44 years without interruption I served my country and my people as a soldier, and I tried to do my best in the service of my profession. I did this with the same devotion under the Kaiser, under President Ebert, under Field Marshal von Hindenburg, and under the Führer, Adolf Hitler.

NELTE: What is your attitude today?

KEITEL: As a German officer, I naturally consider it my duty to admit what I have done, even if it should have been wrong. I am grateful that I am being given the opportunity to give an account here and before the German people of what I was and my participation in the events which have taken place. It will not always be possible to differentiate clearly whether it was guilt or circumstances.

I am convinced that the large mass of our brave soldiers were basically decent, and that where even they overstepped the bounds of acceptable behaviour, our soldiers acted in good faith, believing in the military necessity, and the orders which they received.

NELTE: Will you please tell us something about the co-operation between you and Hitler? Much will depend upon discovering in what manner your work with Hitler can be estimated, particularly to what extent you could be considered his collaborator or adviser. Will you tell me whether Hitler discussed his plans with you in the manner which is customary in close collaboration?

KEITEL: In general I must answer no. It was not in any way in keeping with Hitler's peculiar disposition and personality to have advisers of that kind. One had to assist by procuring documents, but concerning the main point, the decision itself, he did not brook any influence. Therefore, strange as it may sound, the final answer always was: 'This is my decision and it is unalterable.' That was the announcement of his decision.

NELTE: I would like to know whether the expression 'intimate', which is contained in the Indictment, is correct in order to describe the relations between you and Hitler, privately or officially?

KEITEL: I found the word 'intimate' in the Indictment and I asked myself the question, 'Where did this conception originate?' To be quite frank, I can only answer that no one knew the constant difficulties that I had. I kept quiet about them. Intimate relations are, according to my definition of 'intimate' – I do not know if the English translation 'intimate' expresses the same thing which we call 'intim' – mean relations where there is confidence and frank discussions and these did not exist. Intimacy was not Hitler's attitude towards the older generals to whose circle I also belonged.

NELTE: I come to the question of re-armament, and the various cases of Austria, Czechoslovakia, etc. I would like to ask you about the accusation of the prosecution, that you participated in the planning and preparation of wars of aggression. Will you tell us your views on that subject?

KEITEL: As a soldier, I must say that the term, war of aggression, as used here is meaningless as far as I am concerned; we learned how to conduct aggressive warfare, defensive actions, and actions of retreat. However, according to my own personal feeling as a military man, the concept 'war of aggression' is a purely political concept and not a military one. I mean that if the Wermacht and the soldier are a tool of the politicians, they are not qualified in my opinion to decide or to judge whether these military operations did or did not constitute a war of aggression. These decisions are not the task of the soldier, but solely that of the statesman.

NELTE: But you are not only a soldier, you are also an individual with a life of your own. When facts brought to your notice in your professional capacity revealed that a projected operation was unjust, did you not have private and personal doubts?

KEITEL: I believe I can truthfully say that throughout the whole of my military career I was brought up, so to speak, in the old tradition, which never concerned itself in this question. Naturally, one has one's opinion and a life of one's own, but in the exercise of professional functions as a soldier and officer this life has been given away, yielded up.

RUDENKO: Defendant Keitel, I am asking you about the directive concerning the so-called Communist insurrectionary movement in the occupied territories. It is dated September 14, 1941. It states: One must bear in mind that human life in the countries affected has absolutely no value, and that intimidation is only possible through the application of extraordinarily harsh measures.' You remember this basic idea of the order, that human life is absolutely valueless. Do you remember this statement, the basic statement of the order, that 'human life has absolutely no value'? Do you remember this sentence?

KEITEL: Yes.

RUDENKO: You signed the order containing this statement?

KEITEL: Yes.

RUDENKO: Do you consider that necessity demanded this extremely evil order?

KEITEL: These instructions were addressed in the first place to the Supreme Commander of the Wehrmacht offices in the south-east; that is, in the Balkan regions where extensive partisan guerrilla warfare and a war between the leaders had assumed enormous proportions, and secondly, because the same phenomena had been observed and established on the same or similar scale in certain defined areas of the occupied Soviet territory.

THE PRESIDENT: The Tribunal considers that you are not answering the question. The question was perfectly capable of an answer 'yes' or 'no' and an explanation afterwards.

RUDENKO: I ask you once more, do you consider this order, this particular order – and I emphasise – in which it is stated that 'human life has absolutely no value.' Do you consider this order correct?

KEITEL: It does not contain these words, but I knew from years of experience that in the south-eastern territories and in certain parts of the Soviet territory human life was not highly valued.

RUDENKO: You say that these words do not figure in the order?

KEITEL: Those exact words do not appear to my knowledge; but it says that human life has very little value in these territories. I remember something like that.

RUDENKO: These are documents 389-PS and R-98. Defendant Keitel, have you familiarised yourself with the documents?

KEITEL: Yes. The text in the German language says that 'human life in the countries affected frequently has no value.'

RUDENKO: And further?

KEITEL: '...and they can be intimidated by extreme harshness as atonement for the life of a German soldier.'

RUDENKO: Quite clear. And in this same order in this same sub-paragraph 'b' it is stated that: 'To atone for the death of one German soldier, 50 to 100 Communists must, as a rule, be sentenced to death. The method of execution should strengthen the intimidation measure.' Is that correct?

KEITEL: The German text is slightly different. It says: Generally speaking, 50 to 100 persons must be sentenced to death in such cases.'

That is the German wording.

RUDENKO: For one German soldier?

KEITEL: Yes. I know that and I see it here.

RUDENKO: That is what I was asking you about. So now I ask you once more...

KEITEL: Do you want an explanation of that or am I not to say any more?

RUDENKO: I shall now interrogate you on this matter. I ask you whether, when signing this order, you thereby expressed your personal opinion on these cruel measures? In other words, were you in agreement with Hitler?

KEITEL: I signed the order, but the figures contained in it are alterations made personally in the order by Hitler himself.

RUDENKO: And what figures did you present to Hitler?

KEITEL: The figures in the original were 5 to 10.

RUDENKO: In other words, the divergence between you and Hitler consisted merely in the figures and not in the spirit of the document?

KEITEL: The idea was that the only way of intimidating them was to demand several sacrifices for the life of one soldier, as is stated here.

RUDENKO: But you…

THE PRESIDENT: That was not an answer to the question. The question was whether the only difference between you and Hitler on this document was a question of figures. That admits of the answer, Yes or No. Was the only difference between you and Hitler a question of figures?

KEITEL: Then I must say that with reference to the underlying principle there was a difference of opinion, the final results of which I no longer feel myself in a position to justify, since I added my signature on behalf of my department.

RUDENKO: You consider yourself a member of the Nazi Party?

KEITEL: I have always thought of myself as a soldier; not as a political soldier or politician.

RUDENKO: Should we not conclude, after all that has been said here, that you were a 'Hitler' General, not because duty called you but on account of your own convictions?

KEITEL: I have stated here that I was a true and obedient soldier of my Führer. I do not think that there are generals in Russia who do not give Marshal Stalin implicit obedience.

RUDENKO: I have no further questions.

MAXWELL FYFE: Just look at page 110(a) of the document book which you have. This is quite an early order of the 1st October, 1941:

'Attacks committed lately on members of the armed forces in the occupied territories necessitate emphasising that it is advisable that military commanders always have at their disposal a number of hostages of different political tendencies: namely:
1. Nationalists
2. Democratic-bourgeois, and
3. Communists.

It is important that these should include well-known, leading personalities or members of their families whose names are to be made public. Hostages belonging to the same group as the culprit are to be shot in case of attacks. It is asked that commanders be instructed accordingly.

(Signed) Keitel.'

Why were you so particular that, if you happened to arrest a democratic-bourgeois, your commanders should have a sufficient bag of democratic-bourgeois as hostages to shoot? I thought you were not a politician.

KEITEL: I was not at all particular and the idea did not originate with me; but it is in accordance with the instructions – the official regulations – regarding hostages which state that those held as hostages must come from the circles responsible for the attacks.

MAXWELL FYFE: I am asking you a perfectly simple question, defendant. Did you or did you not approve of a number of democratic-bourgeois being taken as hostages for one democratic-bourgeois who happened to be –

KEITEL: It does not say so in the document; it only says that hostages must be taken. It says nothing about shooting them.

MAXWELL FYFE: Would you mind looking at it since you correct me emphatically – depending upon the membership of the culprits, that is, whether they are nationalists, or democratic-bourgeois or communists, 'hostages of the corresponding group are to be shot in case of attacks.'

KEITEL: I personally had different views on the hostage system; but I signed it, because I had been ordered to do so.

PRESIDENT: Dr Nelte: do you wish to re-examine?

DR NELTE: How was it possible and how do you explain that orders and instructions were carried out and passed on by you and how is it that no effective resistance was met with?

KEITEL: To find an explanation for this, I must say that you had to know the Führer, that you had to know what atmosphere I worked in day and night for years.

The Führer would advance arguments which to him appeared decisive in his own forceful and convincing way, stating the military and political necessities and making felt his concern for the welfare of his soldiers and their safety as well as his concern about the future of our people.

So I would transmit the orders that were given, and promulgated them without letting myself be deterred by any possible effect they might have.

But never did it enter my mind to revolt against the Head of the State and Supreme Commander of the Armed Forces or refuse him obedience. As far as I'm concerned as a soldier, loyalty is sacred to me. I may be accused of having made mistakes, and also of having shown weakness in face of the Führer, Adolf Hitler. But never can it be said that I was cowardly, dishonourable or faithless.

PRESIDENT: Now, Dr Kauffman.

KAUFFMANN: With the agreement of the tribunal I now call the witness Hoess.

PRESIDENT: Will you state your name.

HOESS: Rudolf Franz Ferdinand Hoess.

PRESIDENT: Will you repeat this oath after me: I swear by God, the Almighty and omniscient, that I will speak the pure truth and will withhold and add nothing?

The witness repeated the oath.

Will you sit down?

DR KURT KAUFFMANN *(Counsel for Kaltenbrunner)*: Witness, your statements will have far-reaching significance. You are perhaps the only one who can throw some light upon certain hidden aspects, and who can tell what people gave the order for the destruction of European Jewry, and can further state how this order was carried out and to what degree the execution was kept a secret.

PRESIDENT: Dr Kauffman, will you kindly put questions to the witness?

KAUFFMANN: Yes. From 1940 to 1943, you were the commandant of the camp at Auschwitz. Is that true?

HOESS: Yes.

KAUFFMANN: Is it true that you, yourself, have made no exact notes regarding the figures of the number of those victims because you were forbidden to make them?

HOESS: Yes, that is correct.

KAUFFMANN: Is it furthermore correct that only one man, by the name of Eichmann, recorded the figure, the man who had the task of organising and assembling these people?

HOESS: Yes.

KAUFFMANN: Is it furthermore true that Eichmann stated to you that in Auschwitz a sum total of more than 2 million Jews had been destroyed?

HOESS: Yes.

KAUFFMANN: Men, women, and children?

HOESS: Yes.

KAUFFMANN: You were a participant in the (First) World War?

HOESS: Yes.

KAUFFMANN: And then, in 1922, you entered the Party?

HOESS: Yes.

KAUFFMANN: Were you a member of the SS?

HOESS: Since 1934.

KAUFFMANN: And then at the end of 1934, you went to the concentration camp in Dachau?

HOESS: Yes.

KAUFFMANN: When were you commander in Auschwitz?

HOESS: I was commandant at Auschwitz from May 1940 until 1ˢᵗ December, 1943.

KAUFFMANN: What was the highest number of internees ever held at one time at Auschwitz?

HOESS: The highest number of internees held at one time at Auschwitz was about 140,000 men and women.

KAUFFMANN: Is it true that in 1941, you were ordered to Berlin to see Himmler? Please, state briefly what was discussed.

HOESS: Yes. In the summer of 1941, I was summoned to Berlin to Reichsführer SS Himmler to receive personal orders. He told me something to the effect – I don't remember the exact words – that the Führer had given the order for a definite solution of the Jewish question. We, the SS, must carry out that order. If it was not carried out now then the Jews would later on destroy the German people. We had chosen Auschwitz because of its easy access by rail and also because the extensive site could readily be isolated.

KAUFFMANN: During that conference, did Himmler tell you that this planned action had to be treated as a 'Secret Reich Matter' *(Geheime Reichssache)*.

HOESS: Yes. He stressed the point. He told me not to say anything about it to my immediate superior, Gruppenführer Glucks. This conference only concerned the two of us and I was to observe the strictest secrecy.

KAUFFMANN: Does the expression, 'Secret Reich Matter' mean that no one was permitted to make even the slightest allusion to outsiders without endangering his own life?

HOESS: Yes, 'Secret Reich Matter' means that no one was allowed to speak about such matter with any person and that everyone promised upon his life to observe the utmost secrecy.

KAUFFMANN: Did you break that promise?

HOESS: No, not until the end of 1942.

KAUFFMANN: Why did you mention that date? Did you talk to outsiders after that date?

HOESS: At the end of 1942 my wife's curiosity was aroused by remarks made by the then Gauleiter of Upper Silesia regarding happenings in my camp. She asked me whether this was the truth and I admitted that it was. Otherwise, I have never talked about it to anybody else.

KAUFFMANN: Will you briefly tell whether it is correct that the camp at Auschwitz was completely isolated, and describe the measures taken to ensure the secrecy of the carrying out of the task given to you?

HOESS: The camp Auschwitz as such was about 3 kilometres from the town. About 20,000 acres of the surrounding country has been cleared of all inhabitants, and the entire area could be entered by SS men or civilian employees who had special passes. The actual compound called 'Birkenau', where later on the extermination camp was constructed, was situated 2 kilometres from the Auschwitz camp. The camp installations themselves, that is to say the provisional installations used at first, were deep in the woods and could from nowhere be detected by the eye. In addition to that, this area had been declared a prohibited area and not even members of the SS who did not have a special pass could enter it. Thus it was impossible, as far as one could judge, for anyone, except authorised persons, to enter the area.

KAUFFMANN: Were there any signs that might indicate to an outsider, who saw railway transports arrive, that people were being destroyed or was that possibility so small because there was in Auschwitz an unusually large number of incoming transports consisting of shipments of material and so forth?

HOESS: Yes, an observer who did not make notes exclusively for that purpose could obtain no idea about that... The trains themselves were closed, that is to say, the doors of the freight cars were closed so that it was not possible, from the outside, to see the people being transported.

KAUFFMANN: And after the arrival of the transports did the victims have to dispose of everything they had? Did they have to undress completely; did they have to surrender their valuables? Is that true?

HOESS: Yes.

KAUFFMANN: And then they immediately went to their death?

HOESS: Yes.

KAUFFMANN: I asked you, according to your knowledge, did these people know what was in store for them?

HOESS: The majority of them did not, for steps were taken to keep them in doubt about it so that the suspicion would not arise that they were to go to their death. For instance, all doors and all walls bore inscriptions to the effect that they were to undergo a delousing operation or take a shower. This was proclaimed in several languages to the detainees by other detainees who had come in earlier transport and who were being used as auxiliary crews during the whole action.

KAUFFMANN: And then, you told me the other day, that death from gassing occurred within a period of 3 to 15 minutes. Is that correct?

HOESS: Yes.

KAUFFMANN: You also told me that even before death definitely set in the victims fell into a state of unconsciousness?

HOESS: Yes. From what I was able to find out myself or from what was told me by medical officers, the time necessary for the arrival of unconsciousness or death varied according to the temperature and the number of people present in the chambers. Loss of consciousness took place after a few seconds or minutes.

KAUFFMANN: Did you yourself ever sympathise with the victims, thinking of your own family and children?

HOESS: Yes.

KAUFFMANN: How was it possible then for you to carry out these actions?

HOESS: In spite of all the doubts which I had, the only one and decisive argument was the strict order and the reason given for it by the SS Reichsführer Himmler.

KAUFFMANN: I ask you whether Himmler inspected the camp and convinced himself that the order for annihilation was being carried out?

HOESS: Yes. Himmler visited the camp in 1942 and he watched in detail one processing from beginning to end.

KAUFFMANN: Does the same apply to Eichmann?

HOESS: Eichmann came repeatedly to Auschwitz and knew precisely what was being done there.

KAUFFMANN: I ask you whether you have any knowledge regarding the treatment of detainees, whether certain methods became known to you according to which detainees were tortured and cruelly treated?

HOESS: The main reason why detainees towards the end of the war were in such a bad condition, why so many thousands of them were found sick and emaciated in the camps, was that every detainee had to be employed in the armament industry to the extreme limit of his physical power.

KAUFFMANN: Therefore, there can be no doubt that the longer the war lasted, the larger became the number of the ill-treated and also tortured inmates. Didn't you ever, when you inspected the concentration camps, learn something of this state of affairs through complaints etc, or do you consider that the conditions which have been described are more or less due to sporadic excesses of individual officials?

HOESS: These so-called ill-treated and torturing in concentration camps, stories of which were spread everywhere amongst the people, and particularly by detainees who were liberated by the occupying armies were not, as assumed, inflicted methodically, but by individual leaders, sub-leaders and men who laid violent hands on them.

KAUFFMANN: To what do you attribute the particularly bad and shameful conditions which were found on invasion by allied troops, and which to an extent were photographed and filmed?

HOESS: The catastrophic situation at the end of the war was due to the fact that, as a result of the destruction of the railways and of the continuous bombing of the industrial works, it was no longer possible to properly care for these masses, for example Auschwitz with its 140,000 detainees.

DR THOMA *(Rosenberg's counsel)*: Herr Rosenberg, please give the tribunal your biographical data.

ROSENBERG: I was born on 12th January 1893, in Revel, Estonia. When the German-Russian front lines approached in 1915, the Institute of Technology was evacuated to Moscow and there I continued my studies. To the Baltic Germans, notwithstanding their loyalty toward the Russian State, the Homeland of German culture was their intellectual home and the experience I had in Russia strengthened my decision to do everything within my power to help to prevent the political movement in Germany from backsliding into Bolshevism.

THOMA: You mentioned Germany as your intellectual home. Will you tell the Tribunal through which studies and by which scientists you were influenced in favour of Germany?

ROSENBERG: In addition to my immediate interest in architecture and painting, I had since childhood pursued historical and philosophical studies and thus, of course, I felt compelled to read Goethe, Herder and Fichte in order to develop intellectually along these lines. At the same time, I was influenced by the social ideas of Charles Dickens, Carlyle and Emerson.

THE PRESIDENT: The Tribunal wants you to confine yourself to your own philosophical subjects at all times.

THOMA: How did you come to the National Socialist party and to Hitler in Munich?

ROSENBERG: In May 1919, the publisher of a journal was visited by a man by the name of Anton Drexler, who introduced himself as the chairman of the newly founded German Labour Party. There, in the autumn of 1919, I also met Hitler.

THOMA: When did you join Hitler?

ROSENBERG: Well, at the time I had a serious conversation with Hitler, and on that occasion I noticed his broad view of the entire European situation. He said that, in his opinion, Europe was at that time going through a social and political crisis.

I would like to add that the name 'National Socialism', I believe, originated in the Sudetenland, and there the small German Labour Party was founded under the name of 'National Socialist German Labour Party'. We considered that the representation of national interests should not be based on privileges of certain classes but, on the contrary, on a national basis; the demand for national unity and dignified representation on the part of the people was the right attitude. This resulted for Hitler in the device…

THE PRESIDENT *(Interposing)*: Dr Thoma, would you try to confine the witness to the charges which are against him?

THOMA: In my opinion, we have to devote some time to Rosenberg's train of thought to determine the motives for his actions, but I will now ask him this: Why did you fight against democracy, as a matter of international struggle?

MR DODD *(Executive trial counsel)*: Mr President, I should like to say that no one in the prosecution has made any charge against this defendant for what he has thought. I think we are all, as a matter of principle, opposed to prosecuting any man for what he thinks.

THOMA: To my knowledge, the defendant is also accused of fighting democracy, and that is why I believe I should put this question to him.

THE PRESIDENT: What is the question?

THOMA: Why he was fighting democracy, why National Socialism and he himself fought democracy.

THE PRESIDENT: I don't think that has got anything to do with the case. The only question is whether he used National Socialism for the purpose of conducting international offences.

THOMA: To my knowledge, the charge of waging a war of aggression was preferred because it was a war against democracy based on nationalism and militarism.

PRESIDENT *(interposing)*: Democracy outside Germany, not in Germany.

THOMA: Then, I would like to ask the defendant how he will answer the charge that National Socialism preached a master-race.

ROSENBERG: I have never heard the word master-race *(Herrenrasse)* as often as in this court-room. To my knowledge I did not mention or use it at all in my writing. I spoke of a master-race as mentioned by Homer only once, and I found a quotation from a British author who, in writing about the life of Lord Kitchener, said the Englishman who had conquered the world had proved himself as a creative superman *(Herrenmensch)*.

THOMA: Now, I would like to ask the following question: you believed that the so-called Jewish problem in Europe could only be solved by removing the Jews from the European continent. How and why did you arrive at that opinion? I mean to say, how in your opinion would the departure of the last Jew from Europe solve the problem?

ROSENBERG: It seemed to me that after an epoch of generous emancipation in the course of national movements of the nineteenth century, an essential part of the Jewish nation also remembered its own tradition and its own character and more and more consciously segregated itself from other nations.

But my attitude in the political sphere to the Jewish question was due partly to my observations and experience of Jews in Russia and later to my experience of them in Germany, which especially seemed to confirm their strangeness.

THOMA: Herr Rosenberg, what do you have to say to the fact that in the First World War 12,000 Jewish soldiers died at the front?

ROSENBERG: Of course, I was always conscious of the fact that many Jewish-German citizens were assimilated into the German environment. But on the whole this did not involve the entire social and political movement… Prominent Jewish people and the chairman of the Democratic party suggested three times quite openly that in view of the increase in unemployment Germans should be deported to Africa and Asia.

THOMA: Herr Rosenberg, you were the official appointed by the Führer for the supervision of the entire Spiritual and Ideological Education in the National Socialist party. Did you exert any influence on national law-making in that capacity?

ROSENBERG: The Party Chancellery occasionally asked me to define my position with regard to this or that question but was not obliged to take my view into consideration.

THOMA: Witness, did you know anything about concentration camps?

ROSENBERG: Yes. This question, of course, has been put to everybody, and the fact that concentration camps existed became known to me in 1933. But I must state that I knew by name only two concentration camps, Oranienburg and Dachau.

THOMA: Did you participate in the evacuation of Jews from Germany?

ROSENBERG: I should perhaps add one thing: I visited no real concentration camp, neither Dachau nor any other one. I once questioned Himmler – it was in 1938 – about the concentration camps and told him that one saw in the foreign Press all sorts of reports of alleged atrocities which were being committed in them. Himmler said to me: 'Why don't you come to Dachau and take a look at the things for yourself? We have a swimming pool there, we have sanitary installations – irreproachable – no objections can be raised.'

I did not visit the camp because if something improper had been going on, Himmler would probably not have shown it to me. On the other hand, for reasons of good taste I did not want to go simply to observe people who had been deprived of their liberty.

An American chaplain has very kindly given me in my cell a church paper from Colombus. I gather from that the United States, too, arrested Jehovah's Witnesses during the war and that until December 1945, 11,000 of them were still detained in camps.

I presume that under such conditions, every state would take similar actions against nationals who refused to do war service in some form or another; and that was my attitude too; I could not consider Himmler wrong in this connection.

DODD: Yesterday, you stated before the Tribunal that you did have a discussion with Heinrich Himmler, the SS Reichsführer, about concentration camps, and if I remember correctly, you said that that was some time in 1938; is that so?

ROSENBERG: Yes. I testified that I discussed the concentration camps with him once, but I cannot say with certainty that it was in 1938, as I did not make a note of it.

DODD: Very good. He suggested you should go through one or the other of these camps, Dachau or some other camp; is that so?

ROSENBERG: Yes, he then told me that I should take a look at the Dachau camp.

DODD: And you declined the invitation?

ROSENBERG: Right.

DODD: And if I recollect correctly, I understood you to say that you declined because you were quite sure that he would not show you the unfavourable things that were in that camp?

ROSENBERG: Yes, I assumed more of less that if there really were unfavourable things, I certainly would not see them anyway.

DODD: You mean that you simply assumed that there were unfavourable things; that you didn't know there were unfavourable things?

ROSENBERG: I heard this through the foreign Press and it is about...

DODD: When did you first hear that through the foreign Press?

ROSENBERG: That was in the months of 1933.

DODD: And did you continuously read the foreign Press about the concentration camps in Germany from 1933 to 1938?

ROSENBERG: I did not read the foreign Press at all for unfortunately I do not speak English. I only received some excerpts from it from time to time, and in the German Press there were occasional references to the allegations in the foreign Press, and it was emphatically denied that there was any truth in these allegations. I can still remember a statement by Goering in which he said that it was beyond his comprehension that anything like that could be written.

DODD: Did you ever talk about the extermination of the Jews?

ROSENBERG: I have not in general spoken about the extermination of the Jews in the sense of this term. One has to consider the words. The term 'extermination' has been used by the British Prime Minister…

DODD: You will refer to the words. You just tell me now whether you ever said it or not. You said that you did not?

ROSENBERG: Not in a single speech in that sense.

DODD: I understand the sense. Did you ever talk about it with anybody as a matter of State policy or Party policy, about the extermination of the Jews?

ROSENBERG: In a conference with the Führer there was once an open discussion on this question apropos of an intended speech which was not delivered.

DODD: When was it you were going to deliver that speech? Approximately what was the date?

ROSENBERG: In December, 1941.

DODD: Then you had written into your speech remarks about the extermination of Jews, hadn't you? Answer that yes or no.

ROSENBERG: I have said already that that word does not have the sense which you attribute to it.

DODD: I will come to the word and the meaning of it. I am asking you, did you use the word or the term, extermination of the Jews, in the speech which you prepared to make in the Sportpalast in December of 1941? Now, you can answer that pretty simply.

ROSENBERG: That may be, but I do not remember. I myself did not prepare the phrasing of the draft. In which form it was expressed I can no longer say.

DODD: Well then, perhaps we can help you on that. I will ask you to be shown Document 1517-PS. It becomes Exhibit USA-824.

Witness handed document.

Now this is a memorandum of yours, written by you, about a discussion you had with Hitler on 14 December 1941… If you will look at the second paragraph, you will find these words:

'I took the standpoint not to speak of the extermination *(Ausrottung)* of the Jews. The Führer affirmed this and said that they had thrust the war upon us and that they had brought the destruction; it is no wonder if the results would strike them first.'

Now, you have indicated that you have some difficulty with the meaning of that word and I am going to ask you be shown – you are familiar with the Standard German-English dictionary, Cassell's, I suppose, are you? Do you know this work, ever heard of it?

ROSENBERG: No.

DODD: This is something you will be interested in. Will you look up and read out to the Tribunal what the definition of *'Ausrottung'* is?

ROSENBERG: I do not need a foreign dictionary in order to explain what various meanings in the German language the word *'Ausrottung'* may have. One can exterminate an idea, an economic system, a social order and, as a final consequence, also a group of human beings, certainly. Those are many possibilities which are contained in that word. For that I do not need an English-German dictionary. Translations from German into English are so often wrong. For example, in that last document you have submitted to me, I heard again the translation of *'Herrenrasse'*.

DODD: Alright, I am not interested in that. Let us deal on this term of *'Ausrottung'*. I take it then that you agree it does mean to wipe out or to kill off, as it is understood, and that you did use the term in speaking to Hitler.

ROSENBERG: Here again, I hear a different translation, which again used new German words, so I cannot determine what you wanted to express in English.

DODD: Are you very serious in pressing this apparent inability of yours to agree with me about this word or are you trying to kill time? Don't you know that there are plenty of people in this court room who speak German and who agree that that word does mean to wipe out, to extirpate?

ROSENBERG: It means to overcome in one sense and then it is used not with respect to individuals but rather to judicial entities, to certain historical traditions. In another sense, the word had been used with respect to the German people and we have not believed that it meant that 60 million Germans would be shot.

DODD: I want to remind you that this speech of yours in which you use the term *'Ausrottung'* was about six months after Himmler told Hoess, whom you heard on this witness stand, to start exterminating Jews. That is a fact, is it not?

ROSENBERG: Then, may I perhaps say something about the use of the words here? We are speaking here of extermination of Jewry; there is also still a difference between Jewry and individual Jews.

DR HANS FLAECHSNER *(Speer's counsel)*: Herr Speer, will you please tell the Tribunal about your life up until the time you were appointed minister?

SPEER: I was born on 19th March, 1905. My grandfather and my father were successful architects. At first I wanted to study mathematics and physics but studied architecture, more because of tradition than inclination. In 1934 Hitler noticed me for the first time. Hitler was quite fanatical on the subject of architecture and I received many important constructional contracts from him.

FLAECHSNER: How did your activity as a minister start?

SPEER: In 1942, my predecessor was killed in an aeroplane crash... Immediately upon assuming office, it was plain that not building but armament production was to be my main task.

FLAECHSNER: The prosecution makes the charge that you shared the responsibility for the recruitment of foreign workers and prisoners of war and took manpower from concentration camps. What do you say to this?

SPEER: In this connection, neither I nor the ministry were responsible for this. The ministry was a new establishment, which had a technical problem to deal with. It took no competence in any field away from an existing authority.

FLAECHSNER: Herr Speer, in the year 1943, you visited the concentration camp at Mauthausen?

SPEER: The camp, or the small part of the camp which I saw, appeared to me to be very clean. But I did not see any of the workers, any of the camp inmates, since at the time they were all engaged in work.

FLAECHSNER: Did you learn, on your visit to Mauthausen or on another occasion, about the cruelties which took place at this concentration camp and at other concentration camps?

SPEER: No.

FLAECHSNER: Herr Speer, according to this document – Document RF 24, Exhibit USA 179 – you proposed that factories should be staffed entirely with internees from concentration camps. Did you carry that out?

SPEER: No.

FLAECHNER: As far as you remember, did you ever make statements regarding ideology, anti-Semitism, etc?

SPEER: No, I assume that otherwise the prosecution would be in a position to produce some evidence of such statements.

FLAECHSNER: Were you able to carry on political discussions with Hitler?

SPEER: No, he regarded me as a purely technical Minister. Attempts to discuss political or personal problems with him always failed because of the fact that he was unapproachable. Hitler knew how to confine every man to his own speciality. He himself was therefore the only co-ordinating factor. This was far beyond his strength and also his capacity.

FLAECHSNER: Then, as an expert Minister, do you wish to limit your responsibility to your sphere of work?

SPEER: No, I should like to say something of fundamental importance here. This war has brought inconceivable catastrophe to the German people and has started a world catastrophe. Therefore, it is my unquestionable duty to assume my share of responsibly for this misfortune before the German people... In so far as Hitler gave me orders and I carried them out, I assume the responsibility for them. I did not, of course, carry out all the orders which he gave me.

FLAECHSNER: In January, 1945, Speer sent a memorandum to Hitler: 'The material superiority of the enemy can no longer be counter-balanced, even by the bravery of our soldiers.' Herr Speer, what did you mean by the sentence I quoted?

SPEER: During this period, Hitler attributed the outcome of the war in an increasing degree to the failure of the German people: but he never blamed himself.

FLAECHSNER: Was no unified action taken by some of Hitler's closer advisers in this hopeless situation to demand the termination of war?

SPEER: No. No unified action was taken by the leading men in Hitler's circle. A step like this was quite impossible, for these men considered themselves either as pure specialists, or else as people whose job it was to receive orders, or merely resigned themselves to the situation.

FLAECHSNER: You have described how much you did to preserve industrial plants and other economic installations. Did you also act on behalf of the foreign workers?

SPEER: My responsibility was the industrial sector. I felt it my duty, therefore, to hand over my sector undamaged. As regards the foreign workers in Germany, several of my actions were in their favour…for example, through the steps which I had taken to secure the food situation.

FLAECHSNER: Herr Speer, during the last phase of the war you were opposed to Hitler and his policies. Why did you not resign?

SPEER: I thought it was my duty to remain at my post.

FLAECHSNER: I have one last question. Was it possible for you to reconcile your actions during the last phase of the war with your oath and your conception of loyalty to Adolf Hitler?

SPEER: There is one loyalty which everyone must always keep and that is loyalty towards one's own people. That duty comes before everything. If I am in a leading position and if I see that acts are being committed against the interests of the nation, I must oppose them. That Hitler had broken faith with the nation must have been clear to every intelligent member of his circle, certainly at the latest in January or February, 1945. Hitler had been given his mission by the people; but he had no right to gamble away the destiny of the people with his own. Therefore, I fulfilled my natural duty as a German. I did not succeed in every way, but I am proud today that with my achievements I was able to render one more service to the workers in Germany and the Occupied Territories.

MR JUSTICE JACKSON: It was known throughout Germany, was it not, that the concentration camps were pretty rough places in which to be put?

SPEER: Yes, but not to the extent which has been revealed during this trial.

JACKSON: And the bad reputation of the concentration camps, as a matter of fact, was useful in making people afraid of being sent there, was it not?

SPEER: No doubt concentration camps were a means, a menace used to keep order.

JACKSON: And to keep people at work?

SPEER: I would not like to put it that way. I would say that a great number of the foreign workers in our country did their work quite voluntarily once they had come to Germany.

JACKSON: You knew the policy of the Nazi Party and the policy of the Government towards the Jews, did you not?

SPEER: I knew that the National Socialist policy was anti-Semitic, and I knew that the Jews were being evacuated from Germany.

JACKSON: In fact, you participated in that evacuation, did you not?

SPEER: No… It is clear that if the Jews who were evacuated had been allowed to work for me, it would have been a considerable advantage to me.

JACKSON: As I understand it, you knew about the deportation of 100,000 Jews from Hungary for subterranean aeroplane factories and that you made no objection to it. That is true, is it not?

SPEER: That is true, yes.

JACKSON: And whether legal or illegal means were used to obtain workers did not worry you?

SPEER: I consider that in the light of the whole war situation and of our views in general on this question it was justified.

JACKSON: Yes, it was in accordance with the policy of the Government, and that satisfied you at the time, did it not?

SPEER: Yes. I am of the opinion that at the time I took over my office, in February 1942, all the violations of International Law, which later...which are now brought up against me, had already been committed.

JACKSON: Later, where you differed with the people who wanted to continue the war to the bitter end was that you wanted to see Germany have a chance to restore her life. Is that not a fact? Whereas Hitler took the position that, if he could not survive, he did not care whether Germany survived or not?

SPEER: That is true... The letter which I wrote to Hitler on the 29th of March, 1945, shows that he said so himself.

The unreasonable people who were still left only amounted perhaps to a few dozens. The remaining 80 millions were perfectly sensible as soon as they knew what the situation really was.

JACKSON: Perhaps you had a sense of responsibility for having put the 80 millions completely in the power of the Führer principle. Did that occur to you, or does it now as you look back on it?

SPEER: May I have the question repeated, because I didn't understand its sense.

JACKSON: You have 80 million sane and sensible people facing destruction; you have a dozen people driving them on to destruction and they, the 80 million, are unable to stop it. And I ask if you have a feeling of responsibility for having established the Führer principle, which Goering has so well described to us, in Germany?

SPEER: I, personally, when I became minister in February, 1942, placed myself at the disposal of the Führer principle. But I admit that in my organisation I soon saw that the Führer principle was in many ways defective and so I tried to weaken its effect. The tremendous danger of the totalitarian system, however, only became really clear at the moment when we were approaching the end. It was then that one could see what the principle really meant, namely, that every order should be carried out without criticism. The combination of Hitler and this system has brought about these tremendous catastrophes in the world.

JACKSON: I want to ask you some questions about your efforts to produce essential goods, and the conditions that this regime was imposing upon labour. I think you can give some information about this. You were frequently at the Krupp plant, were you not?

SPEER: I was at the Krupp plant five or six times.

JACKSON: Very well. I will ask to have you shown Document 230-D which is an inter-office record of the steel switches, and the steel switches which have been found in the camp will be shown to you, 80 of them, distributed according to the reports.

SPEER: Those are nothing but replacements for rubber truncheons. We had no rubber; and, for that reason, the guards probably had something like this. *(Indicating.)*

JACKSON: That is the same inference that I drew from the document.

SPEER: Yes, but the guards did not immediately use these steel switches any more than your police use their rubber truncheons. But they had to have something in their hands. It is the same thing, all over the world.

JACKSON: In a statement some time ago, you said you had a certain responsibility as a minister of the Government for the condition of foreign and German workers... You refer to common responsibility. What do you mean by your common responsibility, along with others?

SPEER: Oh, yes. In my opinion, a State functionary has two types of responsibility. One is the responsibility for his own sector and for that, of course, he is fully responsible. But above that, I think that in decisive matters there is and must be, among the leaders, a joint responsibility, for who is to take responsibility for general developments if not the close associates of the Head of State?

PRESIDENT: Dr Flaechsner would you like to re-examine the witness?

FLAECHSNER: Herr Speer, I refer to the answer which you gave to Justice Jackson at the end of the cross-examination, and to clarify that answer I would like to ask you this: in assuming a common responsibility, did you want to acknowledge measurable guilt or co-responsibility under the penal law, or did you want to record an historical responsibility before your own people?

SPEER: That question is very difficult to answer; it is actually one which the Tribunal will decide its verdict. I only wanted to say that even in an authoritarian system the leaders must accept a common, united responsibility, and that it is impossible after the catastrophe to avoid this responsibility. If the war had been won the leaders would presumably have laid claim to full responsibility. But to what extent that is punishable or immoral, that I cannot decide and it is not for me to decide.

FRANCIS BIDDLE *(US tribunal member)*: You said the concentration camps had a bad reputation, remember? Is that right?

SPEER: Yes.

BIDDLE: What did you mean by 'bad reputation'? What sort of reputation, for what?

SPEER: That is hard to define. It was known in Germany that a stay in a concentration camp was an unpleasant experience. I knew that, but I did not know any details.

BIDDLE: Well, even if you did not know any details, is not 'unpleasant' putting it a little mildly? Wasn't the reputation that violence and physical punishment were used in the camps? Was not that the reputation that you meant? Is it not fair to say that, really?

SPEER: No, that is going a little too far, on the basis of what we knew. I assumed that there was ill-treatment in individual cases, but I did not assume that it was the rule. I did not know that... I must explain that during the time I was a Minister, strange as it may sound, I became less disturbed about the fate of concentration camp inmates than I had been before I became a Minister, because while I was in office I heard only good and reassuring reports about the concentration camps from official sources. It was said that the food was being improved, and so on and so forth...

Closing speech of ROBERT JACKSON.

JACKSON: It is common to think of our own time as standing at the apex of civilisation, from which the deficiencies of preceding ages may patronisingly be viewed in the light of what is assumed to be 'progress'. The reality is that in the long perspective of history the present century will not hold an admirable position, unless its second half is to redeem its first. No half-century ever witnessed slaughter on such a scale, such cruelties and inhumanities, such wholesale deportations of people into slavery, such annihilations of minorities.

Crimes in the conduct of warfare were planned with thoroughness as a means of ensuring the victory of German arms. I admit that Hitler was the chief villain. But for the defendants to put all blame on him is neither manly nor true. We know that even the head of a State has the same limits to his senses and to the hours of his day as have lesser men. He must rely on others to be his eyes and ears for most that goes on in a great empire. Other legs must run his errands; other hands must execute his plans.

On whom did Hitler rely for such things more than upon these men in the dock? Who led him to believe he had an invincible air armada if not Goering? Who fed his illusion of German invincibility if not Keitel? Who kept his hatred of the Jew inflamed more than Rosenberg?

These men had access to Hitler. They were the Praetorian Guard, and while they were under Caesar's orders, Caesar was always in their hands.

These defendants now ask this Tribunal to say that they are not guilty of planning, executing, or conspiring to commit this long list of crimes and wrongs.

They stand before the record of this trial as bloodstained Gloucester stood by the body of his slain king. He begged of his widow, as they beg of you: 'Say I slew them not'. And the Queen replied: 'Then say they were not slain. But dead they are…'. If you were to say of these men that they are not guilty, it would be as true to say there has been no war, there are no slain, there has been no crime.

PRESIDENT: I call upon the Chief Prosecutor for the United Kingdom and Northern Ireland.

Closing speech by SHAWCROSS.

SIR HARTLEY SHAWCROSS: That these defendants participated in and are morally guilty of crimes so frightful that the imagination staggers and reels back at their very contemplation is not in doubt.

In their graves, crying out not for vengeance but that this shall not happen again, are 10 million who might be living in peace and happiness at this hour, soldiers, sailors, airmen and civilians killed in battles that ought never to have been.

Nor was that the only or greatest crime. Not in battle, not in passion, but in the cold, calculated, deliberate attempt to destroy nations and races, to disintegrate the traditions, the institutions and the very existence of free and ancient States.

Two-thirds of the Jews in Europe exterminated, more than 6 million of them on the killers' own figures.

For such crimes these men might well have been proceeded against by summary executive action, and had the treatment which they had been parties to meting out against so many millions of innocent people been meted out to them, they could hardly have complained. But this Tribunal is to adjudge their guilt not on any moral or ethical basis alone, but according to law.

Let them now, accused murderers as they are, attempt to belittle the power and influence they exercised how they will. We have only to recall their ranting, as they strutted across the stage of Europe dressed in their brief authority, to see the part they played. They did not then tell the German people of the world that they were merely the ignorant, powerless puppets of their Führer. The defendant Speer has said: 'Even in a totalitarian system there must be total responsibility…it is impossible after the catastrophe to evade this total responsibility. If the war had been won, the leaders would also have assumed total responsibility.'

Almost immediately after the war had started the organised extermination of the Jewish race began. Hoess describes the improvements that he made at Auschwitz.

He introduced the new gas, Zyklon B, which 'took from three to fifteen minutes to kill the people in the death chamber, dependent on climatic conditions. We knew the people were dead because their screaming stopped…'

Let the engineer Graebe speak of the massacre at Dubno:

'On 5th October 1942, my foreman told me that Jews from Dubno had been shot in 3 large pits, each about 30 metres long and 3 metres deep. About 1,500 persons had been killed daily. All of the 5,000 Jews who had been living in Dubno before the pogrom were to be liquidated.

I drove to the site and went directly to the pits. The people who had gotten off the trucks – men, women, and children of all ages – had to undress upon orders of an SS man, who carried a riding or dog whip.

They had to put down their clothes in fixed places, sorted according to shoes, top clothing and underclothing. I saw a heap of shoes of about 800 to 1,000 pairs, great piles of underlinen and clothing. Without screaming or weeping these people undressed, stood around in family groups, kissed each other, said farewells, and waited for a sign from another SS man, who stood near the pit, also with a whip in his hand.

During the 15 minutes that I stood near I heard no complaint or plea for mercy. I watched a family of about 8 persons, a man and a woman both about 50 with their children of about 1, 8 and 10, and two grown-up daughters of about 20 to 24.

An old woman with snow-white hair was holding the one-year-old child in her arms and singing to it and tickling it. The child was cooing with delight. The couple were looking on with tears in their eyes.

The father was holding the hand of the boy about ten years old and speaking to him softly; the boy was fighting his tears. The father pointed to the sky, stroked his head and seemed to explain something to him.

At that moment the SS man at the pit shouted something to his comrade. The latter counted off about 20 persons and instructed them to go behind the earth mound. Among them was the family which I have mentioned.

I well remember a girl, slim and with black hair who, as she passed close to me, pointed to herself and said, 'twenty-three'. I walked around the mound and found myself confronted by a tremendous grave. People were closely wedged together and lying on top of each other so that only their heads were visible. Nearly all had blood running over their shoulders from their heads. Some of the people shot were still moving. Some were lifting their arms and turning their heads to show that they were still alive. The pit was already two-thirds full. I estimated that it already contained about 1,000 people.

I looked for the man who did the shooting. He was an SS man, who sat at the edge of the narrow end of the pit, his feet dangling into the pit. He had a tommy gun on his knees and was smoking a cigarette.

The people, completely naked, went down some steps which were cut in the clay wall of the pit and clambered over the heads of the people lying there, to the place to which the SS man directed them. They laid down in front of the dead or injured people; some caressed those who were still alive and spoke to them in a low voice. Then I heard a series of shots. I looked into the pit and saw that the bodies were twitching or heads lying motionless on top of the bodies which lay before them. Blood was running away from the necks.

I was surprised I was not ordered away... On the morning of the next day, when I again visited the site, I saw about 30 naked people lying near the pit – about 30 to 50 metres away from it. Some of them were still alive; they looked straight in front of them with a fixed stare and seemed to notice neither the chilliness of the morning nor the workers of my firm who stood around. A girl of about 20 spoke to me and asked me to give her clothes and help her escape. At that moment we heard a fast car approach and I noticed that it was an SS detail. I moved away to my site. Ten minutes later we heard shots from the vicinity of the pit. The Jews still alive had been ordered to throw the corpses into the pit; then they had themselves to lie down in this to be shot in the neck.'

The proposition you are asked to accept is that a man who was either a minister or a leading executive in a State which, within the space of 6 years, transported in horrible conditions some 7 million men, women, and children for labour, exterminated 275,000 of its own aged and mentally infirm, and annihilated in gas chambers or by shooting what must at the lowest computation be 12 million people, remained ignorant of or irresponsible for these crimes.

You are asked to accept that the horrors of the transports, of the conditions of this slave labour, deployed as it was in labour camps throughout the country, the smell of the burning bodies, all of which were known to the world, were not known to these 21 men, by whose orders such things were done.

In one way the fate of these men means little; their personal power for evil lies forever broken; they have convicted and discredited each other and finally destroyed the legend they created round the figure of their leader.

This trial must form a milestone in the history of civilisation, not only bringing retribution to these guilty men, but also that the ordinary people of the world (and I make no distinction between friend or foe) are now determined that the individual must transcend the State.

You will remember when you come to give your decision the story of Dubno, but not in vengeance – in a determination that these things shall not occur again.

'The father' – do you remember – 'pointed to the sky, and seemed to say something to his boy.'

THE PRESIDENT: Article 24 (j) provides that each defendant may make a statement to the Tribunal. I therefore now call upon the defendants who wish – whether they wish to make statements. Defendant Hermann Wilhelm Goering.

GOERING: The prosecution uses the fact that I was the second man of the State as proof that I must have known everything that happened. But it does not present any documentary or other convincing proof in cases where I have denied under oath that I knew about certain things, or even desired them.

Repeatedly we have heard here how the worst crimes were veiled with the utmost secrecy. I wish to state expressly that I condemn utterly these terrible mass murders and so that there shall be no misunderstanding in this connection, I wish to state emphatically and quite clearly once more before the High Tribunal that I have never decreed the murder of a single individual at any time nor decreed any other atrocities nor tolerated them while I had the power and the knowledge to prevent them.

I stand behind the things that I have done, but I deny most emphatically that my actions were dictated by the desire to subjugate foreign peoples, or to commit atrocities or crimes. The only motive which guided me was my ardent love for my people, and my desire for their happiness and freedom. And for this I call on the Almighty and my German people as witness.

THE PRESIDENT: I call on the defendant Wilhelm Keitel.

KEITEL: It is far from my intention to minimise my part in what took place. At the end of this Trial, I want to present frankly the avowal and confession I have to make today. In the course of the Trial my defence counsel submitted two fundamental questions to me:

'In case of victory would you have refused to participate in any part of the success?' I answered: 'No, I should certainly have been proud of it'.

The second question was: 'How would you act if you were in the same position again?' My answer: 'Then I would rather choose death than allow myself to be drawn into the net of such pernicious methods'.

I believed, I erred, and I was not in a position to prevent what should have been prevented. That is my guilt.

It is tragic to have to realise that the best I had to give as a soldier, obedience and loyalty, was exploited for purposes which could not be recognised at the time, and that I did not see that there is a limit set even for a soldier's performance of his duty. That is my fate.

THE PRESIDENT: I call on the defendant Alfred Rosenberg.

ROSENBERG: Besides repeating the old accusations, the prosecution claims that we all attended secret conferences in order to plan a war of aggression. Besides that, we are supposed to have ordered the alleged murder of 12 million people. These accusations are described as 'genocide' – the murder of peoples. In this connection, I wish to summarise as follows. I know my conscience to be completely free from any such guilt. I attempted to improve the physical and spiritual conditions of their existence; instead of destroying their personal security and human dignity.

The thought of a physical annihilation of Slavs and Jews, that is to say the actual murder of entire peoples, has never entered my mind. I was of the opinion that the existing Jewish question would have to be solved by the creation of a minority right, emigration, or by settling Jews in a national territory. The White Paper of the British Government of 24th July, 1946, shows how historical developments can bring about measures which were never previously planned.

I understood my struggle, just as it was understood by many thousands of my comrades, to be one conducted for the noblest idea, an idea which had been fought for under flying banners for over a hundred years.

THE PRESIDENT: I call on the defendant Albert Speer.

SPEER: Mr President, may it please the Tribunal: Hitler and the collapse of his system have brought a time of tremendous suffering upon the German people. The useless continuation of the war and the unnecessary destruction make the work of reconstruction more difficult. Privation and misery have come to the German people. After this trial, the German people will despise and condemn Hitler as the proved author of its misfortune. But the word will learn from these happenings not only to hate dictatorship as a form of government, but to fear it.

Hitler's dictatorship differed in one fundamental point from all its predecessors in history. His was the first dictatorship in the present period of modern technical development, a dictatorship which made a complete use of all technical means in a perfect manner for the domination of its own country.

Through technical devices like the radio and the loudspeaker, 80 million people were deprived of independent thought. It was thereby possible to subject them to the will of one man. The telephone, teletype and radio made it possible, for instance, that orders from the highest sources could be transmitted directly to the lowest ranking units by whom, because of the high authority, they were carried out without criticism. Therefore, the more technical the world becomes, the more necessary is the promotion of individual freedom and the individual's awareness of himself as a counterbalance.

In 5 to 10 years, the technique of warfare will make it possible to fire rockets from continent to continent with uncanny precision. By atomic fission it can destroy one million people in the centre of New York in a matter of seconds. Science is able to spread pestilence among human beings and animals and to destroy crops by insect warfare. Chemistry has developed terrible weapons with which it can inflict unspeakable suffering upon helpless human beings.

This Trial must contribute towards preventing such degenerate wars in the future and towards establishing rules whereby human beings can live together.

Of what importance is my own fate after everything that has happened in comparison with the high goal?

It is not war alone which shapes the history of humanity, but also, in a higher sense, the cultural achievements which one day will become the common property of all humanity. But a nation which believes in its future will never perish. May God protect Germany and the culture of the West.

Sir Hartley Shawcross: After Nuremberg...

We have since failed to establish a tribunal to deal with such crimes if they occur. This could have been done long ago, either by establishing an International Court of Criminal Justice akin to the existing Court of International Justice at The Hague, or by giving a criminal jurisdiction to that court. So far – although I have tried to persuade the UK Government and others – the international community has failed to agree on an institution but to its individual member states. For the Assembly of the UN did indeed on my motion in 1948 vote in favour of such a tribunal. At the time of the Gulf War, much lip service was given to International Law. I cannot help feeling, however, that law or no law, the United States and ourselves would have felt compelled by our political and economic interests in the Middle East to go to the assistance of Kuwait.

What is particularly to be regretted is that Saddam Hussein's surrender for trial by an international tribunal was not insisted upon as a term of the armistice with Iraq. And that no effort has since been made to set up a permanent International Criminal Jurisdiction. Mrs Thatcher has at an early stage expressly stated that Saddam Hussein would be brought to trial 'as the Nazi leaders were at Nuremberg'. But when the armistice became possible the Americans were so anxious to get 'their boys' back home that they did not make the further two days' march to Bagdad, with the result that Saddam saved a large part of his crack regiment and still holds fast to leadership. Since the end of the Gulf War I have made several public statements urging the establishment of an international court and have written more than once to the Prime Minister – only to receive charming but wholly non-committal replies. International law will never gain its full impact until an international court is established. Nor would the establishment of such a court present any great difficulty whether financially or politically.

From 'Nuremberg and the Nazi War Criminals'
By Sir Hartley Shawcross

Justice Richard Goldstone: Address

The judgement of the International Military Tribunal at Nuremberg was delivered on Monday, 30th September 1946. That Tribunal was given the power by the victorious nations after the Second World War to try and punish persons who had committed Crimes against Peace, War Crimes and Crimes against Humanity as defined in its Charter.

Virtually the whole of humankind was of the view that crimes of the magnitude and bestiality of those committed by the Nazi regime would never be repeated. It was the view of most observers that the crimes were unique and a horrible deviation on the road of civilisation. That view proved not to be correct.

Crimes against peace, war crimes and crimes against humanity, including genocide, mass rape, torture, disappearances, forced removals and many other human rights violations have occurred repeatedly, on four continents, in the years since that judgement was delivered in this city. The hope of 'Never Again' has become the reality of 'Again and Again'. People in every country have to ask themselves and their leaders why this century has witnessed the death of 160 million people in wars – a ghastly statistic. What went wrong and is the 21st century to be a repeat?

One of the few beacons to shine out of the 20th Century is the Trial of the Major War Criminals at Nuremberg. The trails of Nuremberg – and at Tokyo – served a number of important ends. They ensured that guilt was personalised – when one looks at the emotive photographs of the accused in the dock at Nuremberg one sees a group of criminals. One does not see a group representative of the German people – the people who produced Goethe or Heine or Beethoven. The Nuremberg Trials were a meaningful instrument for avoiding the guilt of the Nazis being ascribed to the whole German people. They were important not only in the immediate context of the

Nazi regime. They had a much broader significance for humanity. This was the first time that a multinational court was established in order to apply international law. The concept of crimes against humanity made it easier for the international community to become within the borders of sovereign states.

Why did the UN Security Council act with regard to the former Yugoslavia and thereafter Rwanda? After all, it had failed to take a similar step in other egregious cases such as Cambodia and Iraq, to mention only two obvious cases. In my view, the reasons are not hard to find. In the first place, the conduct which galvanised the Security Council in respect of the former Yugoslavia was reminiscent of the Holocaust – ethnic cleansing and photographs which could have been taken in Nazi concentration camps. It was happening in Europe and that had become inconceivable in the post-Nuremberg era. Then the international media was present and able to witness, report and film the events in question. They were seen by hundreds of millions of people all over the world.

The case of Rwanda was easier. In the first place the precedent had been created. Secondly, Rwanda was a member of the Security Council and the Government which had been instrumental in bringing the massacres to an end had itself requested the establishment of the Tribunal.

To date, the Tribunal for the former Yugoslavia has issued indictments in which over 50 alleged war criminals have been named. They include Radovan Karadžić, the President of the Bosnian Serb administration in Pale, Ratko Mladić, the commander of the army of the Bosnian Serb administration, and Milan Martić, the president of the former Croatian Serb administration in Knin.

There are 16 counts against Karadžić and Mladić. They include Genocide and Crimes against Humanity, and other war crimes. The counts relate to events which occurred between April 1992 and May 1995. They include the persecution of many hundreds of thousands of Bosnian- Croat civilians. This includes unlawful confinement, murder, rape, sexual assault, torture, beating and robbery. They include the unlawful deportation and transfer of civilians, the unlawful shelling of civilians and, especially over a period of years in the city of Sarajevo, the destruction of places of worship.

On television and radio stations, in universities and schools in tens of countries, because of the tribunals, people are talking about war crimes.

The prosecution of war crimes in the former Yugoslavia and Rwanda, I hope, will be seen with hindsight to have been the beginning of a new era of enforcement of international humanitarian law.

The success of these tribunals will, to a large extent, determine if and when a permanent international criminal court will be established by the international community.

From the address by Judge R.J. Goldstone,
Prosecutor at The UN War Crimes Tribunals
For the former Yugoslavia and Rwanda,
At the conference on
'Human Rights Crimes Before the Law'.
Nuremberg, September, 1995.

APPENDIX

NOTES ON THE DEFENDANTS

Hermann Goering

Goering's surrender was typical. He arrived laden with jewellery, joy and a trunkful of paracodeine pills – the entire German stock of the drug; and since the drug was unknown outside Germany, that means the entire world supply of paracodeine. He greeted his captors jovially, accepted the Army's contention that he was a prisoner of war, and gladly surrendered his valuable baton, the symbol of his marshalship...

... He carried gold cigar and cigarette cases, gold pens and pencils, and four jewelled watches and travelling clocks in his baggage. Everything he had was of the finest quality – and most of it had come from the occupied countries...

... In his final suicide, Goering carried out his ideals to the very end. He had faced the International Tribunal with courage but denied its right to judge or sentence him. In his last moments of life, he took matters into his own hands and, once again the dominant figure, cheated the hangman of the Allied Nations.

> From 'Twenty-Two Cells in Nuremberg' by Douglas M. Kelly
> (American psychologist at Nuremberg)
> Published by W. H. Allen, 1947

On 20 May 1945, in the sky-blue uniform of the Luftwaffe, Hermann Goering, the Number Two in the German hierarchy, swaggered in. He was brought to my office perspiring profusely. With the blubber of high living wobbling under his jacket, he presented a massive figure. He was weighed and the scales registered 264 1b.

The accused were seated meticulously in the order in which they appeared in the indictment. In the first few minutes Goering began the extroverted, flamboyant play-acting that was to go on throughout the trial. He lounged with one fat arm spread out behind his thin neighbour, Hess, the other elbow hanging over the edge of the dock. Then he would loll forward, elbows on the barrier of the wooden dock in front...

From 'The Infamous of Nuremberg's, by Colonel Burton Andrus, Commandant of Nuremberg Prison during the trial

Goering looks like the Queen in Alice.

Francis Biddle, US Judge of the Tribunal

Goering I remember even more vividly. He never lost his arrogance and his willingness to defend the Nazi regime. He was very skilful with words; he was a natural born lawyer. He understood English, I think, although he worked through interpreters.

*Bernard Meltzer, Lawyer,
From 'Eyewitness at Nuremberg', by Hilary Gaskin, Arms and Armour Press, 1990*

Wilhelm Keitel

Keitel was undoubtedly an ideal assistant to Hitler; his conditioning to unquestioned obedience was absolute. For him there was no such thing as objecting to an order of the Commander-in-Chief. When I asked him how officers and gentlemen could have carried out the outrageous orders of Hitler, he said again and again, 'We can only receive orders and obey. It is hard for Americans to understand the Prussian code of discipline.'

In jail he worked hard at trying to understand the non-Prussian code; and by the time the trial ended, he said in open court: 'I did not see the limit which is set for a soldier's performance of his duty.'

Keitel attributed the atrocities to the SS, and the disgrace of the Army to its connection with the fanatical elite corps which Hitler set up outside the regular organisation. He maintained that he, personally, knew nothing of any atrocities and that, if he had learned of them, he would have left the Party. Hitler, he said, had limited his knowledge to what needed to be known for the planning of military action.

From 'Twenty-two Cells in Nuremberg's by Douglas M. Kelly

Keitel gave the impression to all of us that he would make a fine First Sergeant. He would obey anything his commander said... He sees the honour of the German military profession disgraced by the trial, feels let down by the Führer to whom he gave unquestioning obedience. His ramrod appearance conceals a weak, dependent character.

Leslie Frewin, 1969

Keitel told the psychologist Colonel Dunn about the responsibilities of a soldier – to accept orders and obey, as well as to accept the fate of his men.

'The Infamous of Nuremberg', by Colonel Burton Andrus

Alfred Rosenberg

Alfred Rosenberg, the Nazi Party philosopher, was a tall, slender, flaccid, womanish creature whose appearance belied his fanaticism and cruelty.

...Ordinarily Rosenberg's face wore a somewhat mild and somnolent expression; but it came awake, alive, and flushed with excitement, when he discussed his theories or his major work, *Myth of the Twentieth Century.* This opus was the foundation of his prestige, a basic book of the Nazi Party, and the authority on all racial problems. In it he had delineated his theories, but in unbelievably obscure and hazy fashion...

... Rosenberg explained that he had always held the idea that the Jews should be transported, and he suggested Madagascar – a French possession, incidentally – as a likely resettlement area for American Jews. He excused the

Germans for not transporting their Jews by saying this was made impossible by outside pressure, so they simply had to exterminate them.

From 'Twenty-two Cells in Nuremberg', by Douglas M. Kelly

Albert Speer

Speer certainly seemed a man of courage, of moral discrimination, when contrasted with most of his fellow defendants. This image was not tarnished for some people even by the evidence against him. Lady Maxwell-Fyfe, for instance, responded with admiration to his character and intelligence. She commented to Mervyn Griffith-Jones that Speer was surely the sort of man Germany would need in the future. Griffith-Jones replied by producing a length of bloodstained telephone wire, about ten feet long, which had been picked up at Krupp's and had been used to flog workers. The admirers of Speer, then and now, must always ask by what means Speer had accomplished an industrial miracle between 1942 and the end of the War.

From 'The Nuremberg Trial' by Ann and John Tusa
BBC Books, 1983

The Lawyers

All the defendants were represented by German lawyers, many of whom were distinguished, and they all put up an adequate defence. That is not to say that the German team was as good as those for the prosecution. The most eminent Nazi lawyers were conspicuous by their absence. Some of the German lawyers were ex-Nazis, some were not. They were severely handicapped by the lack of professional staff and assistants to help them in research and other work preparatory to the trial. And, I am afraid, the prosecuting team hardly treated them as professional equals: the no-fraternisation policy was strictly adhered to. They tended to become rather second-class citizens and their position was not enviable.

Some were genuinely shocked by the terrible things brought out in evidence. Yet although some of the German advocates were better than others, I do not think any prisoner suffered through inadequacy of defence. I have met some of those advocates in happier circumstances since; one of them, Naval Judge Kranzbuehler, a most able man who would have reached distinction in any society, took part in a programme on German television with me in the 1980s: we met as equals with courtesy.

From 'Life Sentence: the Memoirs of Lord Shawcross', published by Constable, 1996

NOTES ON THE EVIDENCE

Rudolf Hoess

Commandant of Auschwitz, defence witness

One of the ill-considered moved by the defence was the calling as a witness of Rudolf Hoess, who had been Commandant of the notorious Auschwitz concentration camp. Hoess was called in a half-hearted attempt to counter the charge of conspiracy by showing that the defendants did not know what happened in the concentration camps. Hoess did testify that the killings had been carried out in secret and that they were not part of a general conspiracy. His evidence was given to a court that became hushed with horror, for he described coldly and unemotionally the mass suffering and deaths, but at the same time the efficiency with which he personally had supervised the deaths of a million and a half innocent human beings.

From 'Life Sentence: the Memoirs of Lord Shawcross', Published by Constable, 1996

Hoess made his confession, not in philosophical justification of what he had done, but simply as the explanation of a loyal member of the Party – a follower of Hitler and of Himmler. In 1941 he was called to Berlin to confer with Himmler. Himmler told him that a decision of the greatest importance had been reached at the highest level. That decision was to exterminate European Jewry...

... Devoid of moral principle, he reacted to the order to slaughter human beings as he would have to an order to fell trees. It was his 'war task'. And it was sufficient to him that someone higher in authority in the Party had given him 'the order'. As Hoess testified: 'In view of all these doubts which I had, the only one and decisive argument was the strict order and the reason given for it by the Reichsführer Himmler.'

From 'Crimes Against Humanity'

Rudolf Hoess was hanged on April 16, 1947 in the grounds of Auschwitz, sentenced for the 'mass murder of 4 million prisoners in the camp'.

The Hossbach Memorandum

One document, vital to the prosecution case...was known as the Hossbach Memorandum, the notes made by Hitler's adjutant Colonel Hossbach, of a conference held in the Reich Chancellery in Berlin on 5 November 1937. This conference was a crucial element in the prosecution argument that Nazi leaders had conspired to wage aggressive war. Present at the meeting were the Minister for War (Blomberg), the commanders of the Army, Navy and Air Force (Fritsch, Raeder and Goering), and the Minister for Foreign Affairs (Neurath). From 4.15pm to 8:30pm they were harangued by Hitler with his views on foreign policy – a statement which he said should be viewed as his last will and testament. According to Colonel Hossbach's notes Hitler defined the main problem of Germany, a nation of 85 million people, as one of 'living space' or *'lesbensraum'*. To prevent 'sterility', 'tension' and above all to gain enough food, Germany must secure a 'greater living space'. 'It is not a case of conquering people, but of conquering agriculturally useful space' – and in Europe.

From 'The Nuremberg Trial' by John and Ann Tusa

As early as November 5 1937, the Führer addressed his commanders-in-chief and Foreign Minister at the Reich Chancellry in Berlin. This, according to one of his military adjutants named Hossbach, is what he said:

'The Führer stated initially that the subject-matter of today's conference was of such high importance that its detailed discussion *in other states* would certainly take place before the Cabinet, in full session. However, he, the Führer, had decided *not* to discuss this matter in the larger circle of the Reich Cabinet, because of its importance. His subsequent statements were the result of detailed deliberations and of the experience of his four and a half years in Government; he desired to explain to those present his fundamental ideas on the possibilities and necessities of expanding our foreign policy and in the interests of a far-sighted policy he requested that his statements be looked upon in the case of his death as his last will and testament.'

He went on: 'The aim of the German policy is the security and the preservation of the nation and its propagation. This is consequently a problem of space.'

'The German nation comprises 85 million people, who, because of the number of individuals and the compactness of habitation, form a homogeneous European racial body the like of which cannot be found in any other country. On the other hand it justifies the demand for larger living space more than for any other nation.'

From 'The Nuremberg Trial', by R.W Cooper,
Penguin Books, 1947

Mme Valliant Couturier,
A prisoner in Auschwitz, prosecution witness

The Block 25, which was the anteroom of the gas chamber, if one may so call it, is well known to me because at that time we had been transferred to Block 26 and our windows opened on the yard of Block 25. One saw stacks of corpses piled up in the courtyard, and from time to time a hand or head would stir amongst the bodies trying to free itself; it was a dying woman attempting to get free and live…

… The Jewish women, when they arrived in the first months of pregnancy, were subjected to abortion. When their pregnancy was near the end, after confinement, the babies were drowned in a bucket of water…

… We saw the unsealing of the coaches and the soldiers letting men, women and children out of them. We then witnessed heart-rending scenes, old couples forced to part from each other, mothers made to abandon their young daughters, since the latter were sent to the camp whereas mothers and children were sent to the gas chambers. All these people were unaware of the fate awaiting them. They were merely upset at being separated but they did not know that they were going to their death. To render their welcome more pleasant at this time – June, July 1944 – an orchestra composed of internees – all young and pretty girls, dressed in little white blouses and navy blue skirts – played, during the selection on the arrival of the trains, gay tunes such as *The Merry Widow*, the *Bacarolle* from *The Tales of Hoffman*, etc.

They were then informed that this was a labour camp, and since they were not brought into the camp they only saw the small platform surrounded by flowering plants. Naturally, they could not realise what was in store for them.

From the transcripts of the Nuremberg Trials

SREBRENICA

Contents

Introduction by Nicolas Kent, 200

'After Nuremberg': Remarks by Sir Hartley Shawcross and Justice R J Goldstone, 201

THE BACKGROUND TO SREBRENICA, 203

United Nations War Crimes Tribunal, 204

Rule 61: The Voice of the victims, 205

Ex-Yugoslavia: The Facts, 207

Ex-Yugoslavia: The People and organisations, 209

Judges and Prosecution, July 1996: Biographical notes, 211

SREBRENICA, 213

Appendix: From the evidence of Witness A, 260

THE REACTIONS TO SREBRENICA, 265

Robert D Kaplan: A 'Parish-pump holocaust', 266

Report: Two eye-witness accounts of mass graves, 267

Martin Bell: A Conflict of interest, 269

Ed Vulliamy: Who cares as judgement falls on Serb hell camp?, 273

Amnesty International report: 'To bury my brothers' bones', 278

Report: Bosnia war crimes judge condemns half-hearted West, 281

Report: The sentencing of Drazen Erdemovic, 283

Geoffrey Robertson: The Srebrenica question, 285

Report: Bosnian Serb panel links 17,000 to roles in Srebrenica massacre, 291

Introduction

In May 1996 when the Tricycle Theatre mounted *Nuremberg* we used as a prologue a speech by Judge Richard Goldstone to mark the fiftieth anniversary of the Nazi War Crimes Tribunal. Richard Goldstone, an eminent South African judge, had just been appointed Chief Prosecutor to the UN War Crimes Tribunal for the Former Yugoslavia in The Hague. His speech was a passionate plea for a comprehensive International War Crimes Court that would cover more cases than just the two – Former Yugoslavia and Rwanda – it was assigned.

His was a lonely voice at the time. It still seems incredible that the international mood changed so rapidly that such an International Criminal Court was established by the Rome Treaty only four years later, though the US Government has still, in 2005, to ratify it.

Richard Goldstone came to see our production of *Nuremberg*, with his speech re-enacted. After the play he urged me to go to The Hague for the Rule 61 Hearings. He told me that tickets would be like 'gold dust' but he would arrange seats for me. In the event, I was one of only about twenty people in the public and press galleries who attended the hearings.

I was so upset that this testimony to the worst massacre in Europe since World War II was receiving so little public and media attention that the editing of this material into a play for the theatre became a necessity.

Nicolas Kent

After Nuremberg...

'WE HAVE SINCE failed to establish a tribunal to deal with such crimes if they occur. This could have been done long ago either by establishing an International Court of Criminal Justice akin to the existing Court of International Justice at The Hague, or by giving a criminal jurisdiction to that court. So far – although I have tried to persuade the UK Government and others – the international community has failed to agree on such a policy. And here I refer not to the United Nations as an institution but to its individual member states. For the Assembly of the UN did indeed on my motion in 1948 vote in favour of such a tribunal. At the time of the Gulf War, much lip service was given to International Law. I cannot help feeling, however, that law or no law, the United States and ourselves would have felt compelled by our political and economic interests in the Middle East to go to the assistance of Kuwait.

What is particularly to be regretted is that Saddam Hussein's surrender for trial by an international tribunal was not insisted upon as a term of the armistice with Iraq. And that no effort has since been made to set up a permanent International Criminal Jurisdiction. Mrs Thatcher had at an early stage expressly stated that Saddam Hussein would be brought to trial 'as the Nazi leaders were at Nuremberg'. But when the armistice became possible the Americans were so anxious to get 'their boys' back home that they did not make the further two days' march to Baghdad, with the result that Saddam saved a large part of his crack regiment and still holds fast to the leadership. Since the end of the Gulf War I have made several public statements urging the establishment of an international court and have written more than once to the Prime Minister – only to receive charming but wholly non-committal replies.

International Law will never gain its full impact until an international court is established. Nor would the establishment of such a court present any great difficulty whether financially or politically.'

from Nuremberg and the Nazi War Criminals
by Sir Hartley Shawcross

'THE BEST POSSIBLE LAWS will have no effect in preventing or even curbing criminal conduct if there are no means of enforcing them, that is, apprehending, trying and punishing persons who transgress those laws. Criminal conduct can be curbed not only by passing laws, but also by instilling at least a fear of apprehension and punishment. That is certainly true in respect of national states. In my opinion, it is no less true in respect of the international community.'

from the address by Justice R J Goldstone
to the Conference of Commonwealth Chief Justices
and International Appellate Judges in Ottawa
on Thursday 28 September 1995

THE BACKGROUND TO SREBRENICA

United Nations War Crimes Tribunal at The Hague July 1996

ON 11 JULY 1996 the court issued international warrants of arrest for Radovan Karadzic and Ratko Mladic and ordered that they 'shall be transmitted to all states and if necessary, to the Implementation Force (IFOR). It also noted that the failure to effect personal service of the indictment can be ascribed to the refusal to co-operate with the Tribunal by the Federal Republic of Yugoslavia (Serbia and Montenegro), and by tbe Bosnian Serb administration in Pale which has become Republika Srpska, and entrusts responsibilily of so informing the Security Council to the President of the Tribunal, pursuant to Rule 61 (E).'

The evidence that you are hearing on stage has been transcribed from audio recordings of the proceedings in The Hague. The United Nations court has not yet issued the transcripts of the proceedings and there is some doubt as to whether transcripts will ever be released in English.

Rule 61 : The Voice of the victims
BACKGROUND COMMENTARY

RULE 61 of the Tribunal's Rules of Procedure and Evidence addresses the case where a warrant of arrest has not been executed and where, as a result, the indictment has not been served on the accused. This may be due to several causes: the accused has voluntarily eluded justice; the authorities of the territory concerned have not succeeded in locating him; or those same authorities have refused to co-operate with the Tribunal.

The provisions of Rule 61 foresee the convening of a Trial Chamber and a hearing in open court during which the Prosecutor submits the evidence on which the indictment was initially founded and may also call witnesses to testify.

If the Judges consider that there are reasonable grounds for believing that the accused has committed the crimes with which he is charged, they endorse the indictment and issue an international warrant of arrest in respect of the accused.

In addition, the Judges may determine that there has been a lack or refusal of co-operation on the part of the authorities who were to serve the indictment on the accused, with a view to the President of the Tribunal informing the Security Council thereof.

The Rule 61 procedure is not a trial *in absentia*, which is not provided for by the Tribunal's Statute, under which every accused has the right to attend his trial. Moreover, Rule 61 does not allow for a determination of the accused's guilt. It follows that the Trial Chamber cannot pronounce any sentence.

That said, the practical implications of this rule should not be underestimated:

1. Rule 61 safeguards the Tribunal against the obstruction of Justice in the event an initial warrant of arrest is not executed. The first effect of its application is to prevent the judicial process from being defeated simply by the non-appearance of the accused.

   Rule 61 allows the procedure to continue by the issue of an international warrant of arrest, and allows a trial to take place after the warrant has been executed.

2. The issuance of an international warrant of arrest entails, secondly, a series of very definite consequences:
   - the responsibility for arresting the accused no longer rests with the authorities which received the initial warrant: it is upgraded and becomes an international obligation resting on all States;
   - the accused is publicly branded an 'international fugitive', and the country within which he shelters becomes an 'open-air prison';
   - the accused becomes a hostage to any political changes which may take place in his country of refuge: any protection he enjoys today may transpire to be only temporary.

In conclusion, Rule 61 affords a formal means of redress for the victims of the absent accused's alleged crimes by giving them an opportunity to have their testimony recorded for posterity either directly if they are invited to testify or indirectly when the Prosecutor speaks on their behalf. Thus the accused cannot escape from international justice simply by staying away from the Tribunal, and the Tribunal will create an historical record against him. The disclosure of this public record could create a climate inviting political leaders to adopt a more robust policy with regard to the effective arrest of the accused.

Ex-Yugoslavia: The Facts

April 1992	Serb campaign of systematic ethnic 'cleansing' begins in north and east Bosnia, expelling Muslim population to create a pure Serb corridor linking Serb areas of western Bosnia with Serbia.
Early May 1992	'Cleansing' of Muslims and Croats from Brcko begins, and systematic killing at Luka and other facilities starts, resulting in some 3,000 dead.
August 1992	Existence of Serb-run concentration camps disclosed.
September 1992	UN envoy Tadeusz Mozwiecki reports to the UN Human Rights Commission in Geneva that Serbs are responsible for most crimes in Bosnia.
January 1993	America's Secretary of State, Lawrence Eagleburger, a former United States ambassador to Yugoslavia, names 10 Serb leaders who might be prosecuted for war crimes. Serbia's President Slobodan Milosevic tops the list.
February 1993	UN Security Council votes to create War Crimes tribunal.
May 1993	War Crimes Tribunal for the Former Yugoslavia established at The Hague.
May 1993	UN proposes establishing six protected 'safe areas' which include Sarajevo, Srebrenica and Zepa.
February 1994	Possible Serb mortar attack on Sarajevo market. Mortar blast in Sarajevo kills 43, and prompts NATO air strikes against Bosnian Serb military positions.
October 1994	Tribunal begins to hear first case, of Serb Dragan Nikolic, charged with murder

	and torture at a Serb-run prison camp in Bosnia.
July 1995	Bosnian Serb forces take over Srebrenica, a UN-protected 'haven'. After the Serb capture of the enclave, an estimated 6,000–8,000 Bosnian Muslims go missing, most of whom are still unaccounted for to date. Thousands of arbitrary killings by the Bosnian Serb Army of civilians attempting to flee. The atrocities are considered comparable to those of the Second World War.
21 July 1995	Dutch United Nations battalion leave Srebrenica enclave.
August 1995	General Rupert Smith, the new Commander of the United Nations forces in Bosnia, having ensured there are no more potential hostages in Serb areas, strikes, paralysing the Serbs. Within months a ceasefire is in place.
November 1995	Bosnian-wide peace accord agreed in Dayton, Ohio, requiring all parties in the former Yugoslavia to co-operate with the tribunal.
July 1996	Rule 61 Hearings against alleged war criminals Radovan Karadzic and Ratko Mladic at the United Nations International War Crimes Tribunal for the Former Yugoslavia in the Hague.

Source: Seasons in Hell: Understanding Bosnia's War
by *Ed Vulliamy (St Martin's Press, 1994)*

Ex-Yugoslavia: The People and organisations

THE PRESIDENTS
Slobodan Milosevic, President of Serbia
Franjo Tudjman, President of Croatia
Alija Izetbegovic, President of Bosnia-Herzegovina
Milan Panic & **Dobrica Cosic**, Presidents of the rump Yugoslavia (Serbia and Montenegro)

BREAKAWAY PRESIDENTS WITHIN BOSNIA
Radovan Karadzic, President of the Serbian Republic of Bosnia-Herzegovina
Mate Boban, President of the Croatian Union of Herzeg-Bosnia

OTHERS
General Ratko Mladic, Commander, Bosnian-Serbian forces
General Sefer Halilovic, Commander, Army of Bosnia-Herzegovina
Ejup Ganic, Deputy President of Bosnia-Herzegovina
Stjepan Kljuic, Ousted Croatian member of the Bosnian presidency, loyal to the government

ORGANISATIONS

MILITARY
HVO army of the Bosnian Croats
HV army of Croatia proper
Armija (mixed, mainly Muslim) Government Army of the Republic of Bosnia-Herzegovina
MOS Muslim Armed Forces or 7th Muslim Brigade (Fundamentalist Brigade in the Armija)
HOS Croatian Defence Association (Fascist Croat Militia)

POLITICAL
SDS Serbian Democratic Party (Serbs in Bosnia)
SDA Democratic Action Party (Muslims in Bosnia)
HDZ Croatian Democratic Union

(Croats in Croatia proper and in Bosnia)
INTERNATIONAL
EC European Community
NATO North Atlantic Treaty Organisation
WEU Western European Union
UN United Nations
UNHCR United Nations High Commission for Refugees
UNPROFOR United Nations Protection Force

Source: Seasons in Hell: Understanding Bosnia's War
by Ed Vulliamy (St Martin's Press, 1994)

Biographical notes (as at July 1996)

MEMBERS OF TRIAL CHAMBER I

Claude Jorda, *France – Presiding Judge*

Judge Jorda (born in 1938) was appointed to the Tribunal in early 1994 to replace the previous French Judge, Judge Le Foyer de Costil, who resigned due to ill-health. Judge Jorda brings with him considerable experience as a prosecutor, having been Procureur Général at the Court of Appeal in Bordeaux from 1985 to 1992, and then Procureur Général of the Court of Appeal in Paris. Prior to that time, he was Director of Judicial Services at the Ministry of Justice and also taught for six years at the *École Nationale de la Magistrature*.

Elizabeth Odio-Benito, *Costa Rica*

One of the two female Judges at the Tribunal, Judge Odio-Benito (born in 1939) was twice Minister of Justice for Costa Rica (1978–82 and 1990–94). She is also a Professor of Law at the University of Costa Rica, with a long-term private practice as an attorney. In addition, since 1980, Judge Odio-Benito has been involved in Human Rights Task Forces at the United Nations, including appointment as Special Rapporteur on Intolerance and Discrimination on grounds of Religion or Belief, and is the Latin American representative on the Board of Trustees of the United Nations Voluntary Fund for Victims of Torture.

Fouad Riad, *Egypt*

Appointed on 2 October 1995, Judge Riad (born in 1928) has a long career as Professor of Law at Cairo University, and he has also taught in New York, Paris and The Hague. Judge Riad has published a number of books and articles in Arabic, English and French. He has equally been active as Arbitrator and International Legal Consultant. In 1977 and 1978, he chaired the Plenary Committee of the UN Conference on State Succession to Treaties. Judge Riad is a member of the *Institut de droit international,* and served from 1993 to 1995 as Vice-President. He is the President of the Egyptian Society of International Law since 1990.

MEMBERS OF THE PROSECUTION BENCH

Mr Mark Harmon, 51, an assistant trial attorney, is an attorney with Office of the Prosecutor. Born in the United States, he was a career federal prosecutor at the US Department of Justice, prosecuting criminal civil rights and environmental cases. He received the Attorney General's Distinguished Service Award for his participation in the Exxon Valdez prosecution.

Mr Terree Bowers, 41, an assistant trial attorney, has been seconded to the ICTY from the US Department of Justice. Born in the United States, he served from September 1992 until January 1994 as the US Attorney in Los Angeles. He also served as Assistant US Attorney, prosecuting cases involving terrorism, narcotics organisations, and insurance, computer, and telemarketing fraud. He received the Attorney General's Distinguished Service Award for prosecuting fraud cases arising from the massive bank failures of the 1980s.

SREBRENICA

I owe an enormous debt to Judge Richard Goldstone who was the inspiration for this play, to Richard Norton-Taylor who collaborated with me on all the other Tricycle Tribunal plays, and to all the actors and all those working at the Tricycle who have made such a commitment to the success of these plays – particularly to Mary Lauder without whose steadfast support none of this would have happened.

Nicolas Kent

Characters

Un Press Officer
Judge Jorda, Presiding Judge
Judge Riad
Judge Benito
Mark Harmon, Deputy Prosecutor
Terree Bowers, Assistant Prosecutor
Jean RenÉ Ruez, Chief Investigating Officer
Colonel Karremans, Commanding Officer,
Dutch Peace-Keeping Force in Srebrenica
Corporal Groenewegen, Member of the
Dutch Forces in Srebrenica
Drazen Erdemovic, Former member of the
Bosnian Serb Army

The Hague, 3–5 July 1996.

The Rule 61 Hearings against Dr Karadzic and General Mladic lasted for approximately ten days and more than a dozen witnesses were called, and evidence was given in Dutch, English, French and Serbo-Croatian. The evidence presented on stage relates solely to the events surrounding the fall of Srebrenica – the court also heard evidence about the hostage-taking of UN Forces in Bosnia-Herzegovina and the blockade and shelling of Sarajevo.

Srebrenica was first performed at the Tricycle Theatre on 10 October 1996, with the following cast:

UN PRESS OFFICER, Richard Heffer
JUDGE JORDA, Hugh Simon
JUDGE RIAD, Mark Penfold
JUDGE BENITO, Moira Govan
DEPUTY PROSECUTOR HARMON, James Woolley
ASSISTANT PROSECUTOR BOWERS,
    Thomas Wheatley
JEAN RENÉ RUEZ, Colin Bruce
COLONEL KARREMANS, William Hoyland
CORPORAL GROENEWEGEN, Mark Powley
DRAZEN ERDEMOVIC, Jay Simpson

Directed by Nicolas Kent
Set designed by Saul Radomsky
Costumes designed by Patricia Fortini
Lighting designed by Simon Opie
Production Manager, Richard Long
Casting, Suzanne Crowley and Gilly Poole

Srebrenica subsequently transferred to the Royal National Theatre on 10 November 1997 and then to the Waterfront Theatre for the Belfast International Festival on 21–30 November 1997.

RUEZ

HARMON: Good morning, your Honours: we will first be calling Jean René Ruez.

JORDA: Good morning, sir. First if you would be so good as to read the declaration. Can you hear me?

RUEZ: Yes.

I solemnly declare to tell the truth, the whole truth, and nothing but the truth.

JORDA: Please be seated.

HARMON: Please state your name.

RUEZ: My name is Jean René Ruez.

HARMON: Can you inform the Court of what you did?

RUEZ: I worked in the judicial police in France. I worked in Paris and Marseilles, and I was in charge of a unit in Nice – that was my last position.

HARMON: How long have you been employed at the Office of the Prosecutor?

RUEZ: I have been working for the Office of the Prosecutor since April 1995.

JORDA: You are having translation problems. Can you hear the presiding judge? Are you sure you can hear the witness, Mr Harmon?

Please go ahead, Mr Harmon.

HARMON: Mr Ruez, when did you start your investigations into the events of Srebrenica?

RUEZ: The investigations began in Tuzla on the 25th of July 1995. Now the first possibility to go into Republic Srpska was on the 25th of January 1996, and since then several missions have been carried out.

HARMON: I would like to ask you some questions about the background events that led to Srebrenica becoming a UN safe area. Can you please describe those events, Mr Ruez?

RUEZ: Towards mid-'92 the people in the surrounding villages, given the aggression that was being carried out against them, had to flee, and they gathered around the enclave. Late '92, early '93, the Bosnian-Serb Army launched an offensive on these refugees in the enclave. The humanitarian conditions were awful there, and there were airlifts to supply the people there. When the offensive was going full-scale General Maurillon took action there, and the offensive was stopped temporarily until April 1993, when resolution 819 was adopted by the Security Council.

HARMON: When did the Dutch battalion go into the enclave, Mr Ruez?

RUEZ: In February 1994 a Dutch battalion replaced the Canadian battalion that was stationed within the enclave.

HARMON: Before the actual invasion of the enclave was there a Bosnian-Serb blockade of it?

RUEZ: Yes. The offensive started with a blockade: the convoys were no longer allowed to enter into the enclave, which gave rise to big problems when it came to humanitarian aid supplies. By way of an example, a kilo of coffee cost 80 Deutschmarks at the time.

HARMON: Could you please explain when the invasion began and describe what happened in the initial phases of it?

RUEZ: The invasion as such began on the 5th of July 1995. In the night of the 5th/6th of July some Bosnian-Serb soldiers entered the enclave. With more and more pressure on the enclave the observation posts that had been set up by the Dutch battalion were under fire. A number of posts, they were falling one after the other. The people there were caught in the cross-fire. The Bosnian Army also used the observation posts in response to the firing from the

Bosnian-Serb Army. The hostages – Dutch hostages – were taken to assembly points. Their equipment was taken from them.

The environs were being bombed more and more regularly, more and more intensely. The people there had to flee, and they moved into Srebrenica. And they are gathering there, awaiting an intervention on the part of NATO forces.

HARMON: Mr Ruez, could you please describe for the Court the significant events that occurred in the enclave on July the 10th?

RUEZ: The day before, that is to say the 9th of July, the UN sent an ultimatum to the Bosnian-Serb troops calling for withdrawal of their troops from the enclave by 8am the next morning, otherwise there would be air strikes.

HARMON: What was the reaction of General Mladic to the UN ultimatum?

RUEZ: The reaction of General Mladic to that ultimatum was in turn an ultimatum. The Bosnian Army was given 24 hours to surrender. Also the Dutch battalion was given an ultimatum not to allow any refugees within the UN compound.

HARMON: What happened to the refugees who had been in the enclave?

RUEZ: On the 11th of July, subsequent to the ultimatum from Mladic, the crowd gathered at Srebrenica at the Dutch compound. People gathered there right from the morning waiting for the air raids that were supposed to take place. There were some 15,000 people at Srebrenica at the time, gathered there in front of the compound: the crowd tried to get inside – managed to get inside, and then the ultimatum from the day before goes into effect, and three shells land within the compound among the people. We don't know how many people were hurt, or killed, because there is an outbreak of panic amongst the crowd, and people are running towards Potocari. The evacuation of the hospital takes place around 11 o'clock that morning. The people there are fleeing from the bombs. The road is being bombed all along its way – that's some four kilometres from Srebrenica to Potocari. Once they got to Potocari, the people are then gathered around the Dutch compound. People are let within it, but quite quickly the situation becomes unbearable. There is not enough room to let everyone in. The people are directed towards other empty factories in the neighbourhood. This is an industrial area you have round Potocari. The firing goes on; there are several shells that land around the compound, and people have to seek shelter within the factories there.

HARMON: Did air strikes occur on that date?

RUEZ: Yes. There were air strikes late in the morning while the people were fleeing towards Potocari. The soldiers – the Muslim soldiers who were there, seeing that the strikes were not what they had hoped for, that the result was not such that would make the Bosnian-Serb Army retreat, the military leaders decided to evacuate the army, the Muslim Army from Srebrenica. So people took two different directions: women, elderly, children fled towards Potocari; men – the fit-to-serve men who didn't want to fall into the hands of the Bosnian-Serb Army – head for the woods.

HARMON: I would like to focus your attention on Potocari, the UN compound there, particularly on the morning of July the 12th. Can you describe to the Court what was occurring at that compound?

RUEZ: Yes. On the 12th of July, the night had been quiet – people had gathered in the factories. Everyone was very concerned about what was going to be happening the following day. Now in the morning, the first troops entered the city, and immediately asked the Blue Helmets to hand over their equipment. They take away the bullet-proof vests; they take away their helmets. They mix with the people. The refugees talk to these people and realise that they are not Dutch, that they are Serbian, and they realise what a terrible situation is developing. The soldiers starting handing out candy to children, and ask them questions about the Army – where the Army is; where have the men gone? The meeting that's taking place at that time at Potocari between General Mladic and the Dutch Commander is not yet over, and there is already a large number of trucks showing up in Potocari. Now shortly after the trucks arrived, General Mladic turns up at Potocari, and he talks to the crowd; he explains to the people that they are going to be evacuated, that nobody is going to harm them.

HARMON: Mr Ruez, can you describe to the Court what happened at Potocari after the arrival of General Mladic of the Bosnian-Serb Army?

RUEZ: The deportation evacuations happened almost immediately. The people went to the buses. The Dutch soldiers tried to have some order, and instil the order in the crowd. General Mladic also was in charge, or controlled the evacuation, and explained to everybody before they got into the bus that the men would follow on. The men tried to get on the bus. A murder was done by two soldiers of General Mladic of a man who tried to get on to the bus. There was another group of soldiers who were hiding behind a house – two of their colleagues went towards the crowd that was gathering just in front of the factory, and pointed out the men, and put them in small groups behind the factory. An opening was created so that the people could pass and go a bit to the side, away from the crowd. Men arrived in small groups of 10. About 20 soldiers were waiting for them, and killed them with knives one after the other. There was no movement of revolt that was felt or seen. This lasted for several hours. The bodies piled up. Prisoners were ordered to put them in order; a truck arrived, and they were loaded onto the truck. Those who had to do the work were then executed. The trucks came about five times to collect the bodies, and took them to an unknown destination.

HARMON: Mr Ruez, what happened that night?

RUEZ: People sought refuge in the factories, but also outside the factories, because the factories were crammed. During the night soldier groups continued to monitor them. They went amongst the people with electric torches, and selected this or that man. They had to get up and follow the soldiers. Women were shouting when their husbands or children were taken. No-one really knew what was going on. Everyone was panicking. At the end of the evening, in one of those factories, soldiers who were going into the crowd separated the men out: they selected a family with three children; they separated the children from the mother, who fell unconscious because she was so frightened. The three young men – about 11, 17 and 18 – fell behind the factory, and then there was a group of women who appeared who wanted some news about what was happening behind the factory which wasn't lit and therefore no-one wanted to go there. And they saw the three bodies of those young men who had been slit – their throats had been slit just behind the factory. The procedure continued throughout the night.

HARMON: Did the evacuation process begin again on the 13th July?

RUEZ: Yes. General Mladic said that the deportation would take place at 7 o'clock and in fact that did take place; quite a few buses arrived. Then again murder was committed. One soldier approached a woman in the middle of the crowd who was trying to get onto a bus. Her child was crying; the soldier asked why the child was crying, and she explained that he was hungry. The soldier made a comment saying, 'Oh well, the child won't be hungry anymore,' and slit the child's throat in front of everybody.

HARMON: Mr Ruez, could you please describe what happened to the column of men that went into the woods?

RUEZ: The night of the 12th/13th was very very difficult for the population who were fleeing into the woods. During the night these groups became more dispersed and tried to escape the ambushes waiting for them, but many were captured.

During that time other groups, who no longer knew what direction to take, heard the Bosnian-Serbian Army – who were along the strategic route – promising through loudspeakers that they would help them, that they had the Red Cross, that nothing would happen to them, that the United Nations soldiers were there, present. And they also saw Blue Helmets along the road side, but they weren't really Blue Helmets, they were Bosnian-Serbian soldiers who were using stolen material in fact. A large group of prisoners which was surrounded were taken into a field which is in San Dici. They were asked to stay there, and wait until further instructions. One person expressed his dissatisfaction, and he was immediately beaten by the soldiers, and was killed. After some hours on that site in the field, the prisoners were taken on foot in the direction of Kraviza which is very close by. At Kraviza that entire group – there were about five hundred to a thousand individuals – were forced to enter into a hangar. The people were forced to sit down. When the last one entered into the hangar there wasn't enough place for him to sit down. The soldiers ordered him to sit down, and because he didn't fast enough he was beaten, and immediately the soldiers who were around the hangar fired into all the openings of the hangar. Grenades were thrown into the hangar. Those who tried to escape by the openings were beaten by the soldiers at the outside of the hangar.

HARMON: Mr Ruez, have you visited that hangar?

RUEZ: Yes.

HARMON: I would like to show you exhibits 4, 5, 6 and 7 and ask you to describe the significance of each of those to the court.

RUEZ: This is the hangar at Kraviza. This is a photo taken inside the hangar near a window: grenades had been thrown through the windows and all these spots you see here on the wall are blood. There was some sampling done on the 21st January of this year and it was human blood. On this following photograph you can see human debris, if you will, that has been splashed onto the wall, and this is what you will see throughout the hangar on the inside – all these human remains that have been splashed against the walls. Next photo: this is the ceiling, and you can see the blood on the ceiling that is some three metres high.

HARMON: Mr Ruez, would you please continue with your description of what happened to the people in the column who fled Srebrenica?

RUEZ: There's a man who is accompanied by his young son and a soldier comes up to him, makes some comment about the fact that his father's in the process of killing off Serbian children. He takes the old man, puts the knife through his hand, fixes it to the tree, and then cuts open the stomach of the little boy and then on the tip of the knife he has a bit of an organ from the inside of the child's stomach, and then he forces the man to eat that part of the child's innards. A child is separated from its mother who's fighting with two soldiers to try to get her son back. Her son is brought up and is hit with by an axe before being beaten once he hits the ground. And this process goes on the *whole* afternoon. The soldiers are taking their time – they are going around picking up one or another and executing them in front of everyone else. There is a lot of suicides that are committed. Seeing what happens to people who are being detained, some people would rather commit suicide than fall into the hands of their enemy. A lot of people go mad.

HARMON: Do you have an estimate on how many people are missing from Srebrenica?

RUEZ: There are several figures that have been put forward. The highest estimate, which was one from the civilian authorities, gives a figure of missing at about 10,300 people, but this estimate has not yet been totally confirmed.

Also it should also be pointed out that the process of prisoner exchange according to the Dayton agreement has been concluded now for approximately three months.

HARMON: Mr Ruez, have you and other investigators from the Office of the Prosecutor travelled to Bosnia and Herzegovina, and conducted preliminary investigations of execution sites and mass grave sites?

RUEZ: Yes. The first missions on site took place on the 21st January of this year, and there were other trips that took place since then.

HARMON: Now I turn, Mr Ruez, your attention to a map that is underneath the large white map that is on the board to your left.

Mr Ruez, I am going to ask you to explain what is on that map.

RUEZ: Now on this map you can see that we have different colours here. Green areas was a concentration of prisoners sites. And red you have the mass graves and blue is the mass graves that have been identified in connection with our investigations.

HARMON: Did General Mladic see any of these locations?

RUEZ: Yes. General Mladic was seen at several of these sites.

HARMON: Would you mark on the map the particular locations where he was seen?

RUEZ: Now for practical reasons I am going to have to put some labels – black labels – these black stickers will indicate where Mladic went to over those several days. Now the first site where Mladic was seen was at Srebrenica.

And moving on we already know what General Mladic had to say on that occasion.

Second site is at Potocari, and Mladic was there the following day, that is to say July 12th, and he had a little bit of a conference with the journalists, talked to the crowds, but he was also seen with the men who had separated from the other refugees and put in the houses awaiting transfer towards Bratunac, and he tells them that they are going to be exchanged subsequently.

Now still the 12th, General Mladic was seen at Bratunac. He visits the detainees who were being held in a hangar at Bratunac, and he tells them as well that they will subsequently be exchanged.

In the course of the 13th, General Mladic goes to the field where a lot of prisoners are concentrated at San Dici, and the prisoners have been there for five hours. He talked to the prisoners and he tells them again that they will be exchanged. Fifteen minutes after General Mladic leaves, all of these prisoners are taken and taken in their hundreds to Kraviza where they are all executed.

That same day, on the 13th that is, General Mladic was seen speaking to a crowd of prisoners before they were transferred to the Nova Karvasa football stadium, and he tells the crowd that they will be exchanged later on as well. He participates personally in the separation of a group of some 30 men from these prisoners without telling them why they are being separated from the others.

The following day, 14th of July, General Mladic is seen at the Korvachi School. He speaks to the prisoners, he explains to them that there is some technical difficulties involved in their exchange, but that the situation should be improving. And shortly after his departure the prisoners are given a glass of water, are blindfolded and are taken to the execution site nearby.

In the evening General Mladic is seen at that execution site while the executions are taking place.

HARMON: Now I am going to change the subject, and ask you: since the takeover of Srebrenica has Dr Karadzic or representatives of the Republic of Srpska made public statements about the events that occurred in Srebrenica?

RUEZ: Yes.

HARMON: Inform the Court what they said.

RUEZ: On Banjaluca Serbian Television on the 24th January 1996, questioned as to the acts Radovan Karadzic said: 'Our Army did not commit war crimes. Our Army followed orders from the General Staff and the General Staff Commander, therefore our Army and our Police did not commit crimes.'

HARMON: Could you read the last sentence as well? Just continue with that one sentence more.

RUEZ: 'The propaganda against us will turn to our advantage one day.'

HARMON: Please continue.

RUEZ: 12th February 1996. In the course of an interview to *The Times* Radovan Karadzic said in connection with so-called massacres of Muslims in Srebrenica – 'There was no order to kill them. Nobody under my command would dare kill those who were arrested or captured as Prisoners of War. I am absolutely fully involved. Everything concerning the Serb Republic is in my hands.'

KARREMANS

JORDA: Colonel Karremans. Good morning, you can hear me?

KARREMANS: Fine.

JORDA: So we shall resume with your testimony.

HARMON: Colonel Karremans, yesterday you described the Bosnian-Serb Army blockade that so enstrangled the enclave as 'convoy terror'. What effect did this have on the occupants in the enclave?

KARREMANS: I would like to stipulate some things which I have said yesterday, concerning the circumstances. I must say the miserable circumstances in April, May and June which were caused by a total blockade. That meant for the population for instance that their situation was poorer than poor. There was starvation for refugees, some died by starvation. There was no medical treatment at all for the population. No doctors, no dentists, no medicines. We couldn't do anything about infrastructure to support the local authorities, like housing, like generators, power and electricity, water supplies for the population. And it ended up for instance that hundreds of inhabitants of the enclave lived literally on the garbage collection point. On the other side, for the battalion, I would like to describe that a little bit too, if I may. Because of the lack of diesel we had to patrol by foot with all the consequences of the mines all over the area. There was no possibility of resupplying my observation posts, I had a lack of personnel because they couldn't enter the enclave as of 26th April. They got no mail from home. There was no freedom of movement; you couldn't leave the enclave; you couldn't enter the enclave. We were not able to support the population within the enclave. One of the other parameters was the psychological effect on the soldiers, but also on the population. And that ended up with the 25th of May that I informed in a long report to all the higher echelons that I was not able to fulfil my mission any longer, and that meant end of the mission –

period. And then we started with making all improvisations; using those improvisations we could handle the mission more or less till the 6th of July.

HARMON: Colonel Karremans, based on the Bosnian-Serb blockade and its effects, as well as the capture of 55 of your soldiers by the Bosnian-Serb Army, did you feel that you had the means to finish your mission?

KARREMANS: Not at the end. In the beginning I could fulfil the mission based on the mandate, based on what I had: personnel, equipment, the incoming convoys; but at the end of my stay over there, the answer is no.

HARMON: Now I would like to turn your attention to the actual invasion itself. What was the effect on the civilian population once the invasion started?

KARREMANS: As you know, your Honours, the invasion started on the 6th of July. It started with heavy fights in the southern part of the enclave in the direct vicinity of O[bservation] P[ost] Foxtrot, and by shelling the city of Srebrenica itself. As soon as the attacks started in the southern part, [3,000] refugees fled in a northern direction towards the city of Srebrenica. You can imagine there was panic, chaos in those days, what I explained before there was no food, and no way to give them houses in Srebrenica itself. Panic I must say.

HARMON: Did they flee to the UN compound in Srebrenica?

KARREMANS: Not in the beginning. That was I think, on the 10th, on the Monday and of course, on the last day, on Tuesday the 11th.

HARMON: How many refugees were in or around the UN compound in Srebrenica?

KARREMANS: I do not know exactly, but there must be hundreds at the compound, and maybe thousands around it. All guarded together.

HARMON: Colonel Karremans, some of the BSA [Bosnian Serb Army] artillery shells landed in and around the UN compound itself in Srebrenica. Is that correct?

KARREMANS: That's correct, sir.

HARMON: And did that cost civilian casualties?

KARREMANS: That cost civilian casualties.

HARMON: As a result of the attacks on the city of Srebrenica itself there was a large exodus of civilians that fled to Potocari. Is that correct?

KARREMANS: That's correct.

HARMON: Approximately how many people gathered in and around the UN compound in Potocari?

KARREMANS: It's just an estimation of course, but we were forced to split up the group of refugees because they were so many thousands, and we put, or invited, that's a better word, 4 to 5,000 refugees within our own compound at Potocari. Then we were completely full with refugees and own personnel. And then we had another 15 to 20,000 persons still outside of the compound of Potocari, and we used two or three shelled factories just in the vicinity of the compound at Potocari.

HARMON: Could you please describe the general conditions that were present in and around the compound?

KARREMANS: Yes I can. It was poorer than poor. They hadn't food and water supplies during the six days' war over there. They were in very bad condition, and we had no means to supply them, only by the water we had left into our own compound. And some food, and some medicines left, but the general condition of the people was miserable – more than miserable.

HARMON: And in amongst those 25,000 refugees, were there some pregnant women who were delivering their babies?

KARREMANS: There were, I heard later on, five pregnant women who delivered babies. What I heard were that one man hung himself during the stay over there, and life was, let's say, going on during the two days that we had all those refugees around us.

HARMON: I would like to turn your attention to air strikes. Can you please describe those air strikes to the Court?

KARREMANS: Yes, I can. As everybody knows, I have asked several times for air strikes. As soon as attacks started on the 6th, I asked for close air support because one of the OPs [observation posts] was attacked. The UN troops were attacked, the city of Srebrenica had been shelled. There was no close air support available on the days that I asked for that, except at the last day, on the 11th, on Tuesday, I have asked that very early in the morning. I expected that at 6 o'clock. That didn't come. It didn't show up. After noon, about 2 o'clock the air strikes started. It had no effect on the population; it had no effect on the mission of the battalion, because everybody knows that the air strikes, or close air support, was too late and too little. It had effect on the way General Mladic reacted.

HARMON: Was it your understanding when you were the commanding officer of the Dutch battalion unit in Srebrenica that air support was supposed to be a significant part of the protection measures available to you and to the population of Srebrenica. Is that correct?

KARREMANS: That's correct. It was.

HARMON: Okay. What effect did those air strikes have on General Mladic?

KARREMANS: The effect was that through the hijacked soldiers, about 30, in Bratunac, Mladic or one of his officers used the communications equipment of the vehicles over there and ordered me to stop immediately using air support. And if that was not the case, if I wasn't able to stop that immediately, he should use all his weaponry to shell, that's what he told, to shell the compound of Potocari; to shell the refugees within and around the compound and kill the 30 hijacked soldiers.

HARMON: Did General Mladic have the ability to deliver on those threats?

KARREMANS: He could, he had the ability because he had guarded a lot of weaponry around the compound on top of all the hills. He could use that.

HARMON: In fact he had already used that on the UN compound in Srebrenica?

KARREMANS: Yes he did.

HARMON: On 13th July, what time did the first transports arrive to take the refugees away from the compound?

KARREMANS: At 3 o'clock.

HARMON: What type of transport arrived?

KARREMANS: A lot of buses – I think 20 or 30 vans; big lorries and small military vehicles. I think the first evacuation was about between 40 and 50 vehicles.

HARMON: So as a result of the number of vehicles you realised that you did not have enough troops to put on one soldier per vehicle to accompany the convoys. Is that correct?

KARREMANS: That's correct, sir.

HARMON: So did you formulate another solution?

KARREMANS: We formulated indeed another solution.

HARMON: Describe that solution please.

KARREMANS: That solution was that, we should escort each convoy by two vehicles, two jeeps. In every jeep one officer, or a non-commissioned officer, and a driver with communications up to Kladine, and then they should return and pick up, let's say, the next evacuation.

HARMON: What happened to those escort vehicles?

KARREMANS: In the first escort – in the first evacuation – I put my personnel officer, a captain and one of the liaison officers and they managed to go with all those persons in that convoy to cross the border in the area of Kladine.

HARMON: Did any of your other escort vehicles make it to Kladine?

KARREMANS: Some of them in beginning, but they didn't return.

HARMON: Okay, so what happened to those vehicles?

KARREMANS: They were hijacked, stolen.

HARMON: And what happened to the equipment that was used by the soldiers who participated in those escorts?

KARREMANS: The same weaponry – their personal weapons were stolen. Helmets, flak jackets, private belongings were stolen.

HARMON: By the end of the 13th of July had all the refugees been deported from Potocari compound area?

KARREMANS: Yes sir. I'll have a look at my notebook. At 16.00 on the Thursday the last refugee was gone outside the compound, and then they started with the evacuation of the 4 to 5,000 refugees which were able to stay within the compound. They started at 16.00 and they finished about 7 o'clock. That was in three hours.

HARMON: At the end of that at 7 o'clock there were no further refugees in and around Potocari?

KARREMANS: No. There were no refugees in and around Srebrenica – I mean the compound Potocari.

HARMON: When was the next time you saw General Mladic?

KARREMANS: The next time when I saw General Mladic was on the date of our departure on the 21st of July. It was on a Friday morning. The day after the evacuation. All of a sudden a convoy with food – a lot of food – a lot of diesel was accepted, and came to the Potocari area. So from that day we had food enough, diesel enough, medicines and we had eight days to recover from what happened in the weeks before. When I saw General Mladic on the Friday he invited me with my liaison officer to that same hotel in Bratunac where I had my three meetings.

HARMON: What happened?

KARREMANS: We drove to that hotel with one vehicle with my liaison officers. There was General Mladic with a crowd of officers. Most of them I knew already from the meetings. They offered us a breakfast and we had some talks over a couple of things about weaponry. Asking again what happened with my weaponry and that I would like to have it back. I knew already that we should leave at noon towards the Serbian territory, and then the way up to Zagreb. Again I asked where are all my vehicles, I would like to have them back with me. Then he said after some general things, but I have forgotten those, that he would like to visit the compound, but that was not possible in the time frame. It was not possible, so I told General Mladic that it wasn't such a good idea talking to soldiers, not such a good idea visiting the compound. But he insisted, and he said okay I won't be there at 11 o'clock, I will be there escorted by the Chief of Staff of the BH command at 11.30. So I left the hotel, went back to the compound of Potocari. I asked my deputy, are we able to start at noon? He said yes, and I told him General Mladic would come. He said okay, so I ran back to the gate, and he was already there before half past 11. He was held up by the Commander of the Guard. A very broad sergeant. You couldn't go around that sergeant. We were held up, General Mladic had a quick talk with him, and then it was half past 11. I took him with me to my own briefing room within the compound.

Had a quick talk for I think twenty minutes about some general things, and then I asked him two specific questions. One question was, 'What will happen with my equipment?', and I told him what equipment I lost during the last two weeks. This was the first question.

HARMON: What was his response?

KARREMANS: His response was that he should sort that out. He was in contact with his Ministry of Internal Affairs.

My second question which I can remember asking him was just a general one, asking him what should happen, or should have happened if during the stay of United Nations troops in the safe areas, Goradze, Jeppa and especially of course Srebrenica, what happened if the Bosnian-Army soldiers were disarmed totally? Completely demilitarised. If they shouldn't have executed raids outside the enclave. If both civilian and military authorities should live according the 1993 cease fire regulations? Then he answered that he, at least that was his answer, that he wouldn't have thought about attacking the enclave. But he said it with a smile more or less and that was more or less the end of our discussion there in the briefing room.

HARMON: Colonel Karremans, thank you very much. I have no further questions. Your Honours, I have concluded my examination of Colonel Karremans.

JORDA: Thank you very much, Mr Harmon. Let me look at fellow judges. Judge Odio-Benito, I do believe that you have some questions. Please proceed.

BENITO: I am going to ask for your personal opinion, Colonel. Looking back would you say that the United Nations and NATO did its best to help people to save their lives?

KARREMANS: On one hand, yes. They should have had a freedom of movement which was one of the points of the NATO / United Nation resolutions of 1993, and we could travel forth and back to the safe areas in general and to Srebrenica in particular – not just for my battalion, but also the International Red Cross and the other non-governmental organisations like the Médecins Sans Frontières, the UNHR – and we were able to assist, help the refugees, I think the answer's yes. But because of the strangulation, and because of the isolation not having had no support at all, then the answer's no.

BENITO: Strangulation and isolation ordered by General Mladic?

KARREMANS: Yes, your Honour.

GROENEWEGEN

BOWERS: At this time the Prosecution would call Corporal Groenewegen to the stand please.

Good afternoon Corporal Groenewegen. Would you start by stating your full name, please.

GROENEWEGEN: My name is Groenewegen.

BOWERS: You currently serve in the Dutch Army. Is that correct?

GROENEWEGEN: That is correct.

BOWERS: Corporal, have you served in Bosnia-Herzegovina?

GROENEWEGEN: That is correct.

BOWERS: Would you tell the Court the period of your tour of duty?

GROENEWEGEN: January 1995 to July 1995.

BOWERS: Who was your commanding officer at that time?

GROENEWEGEN: Colonel Karremans.

BOWERS: On the 11th of July it was your turn as far as the rotation of duty to return to the Potocari area. Is that correct?

GROENEWEGEN: That's correct.

BOWERS: When you returned to the Potocari compound, at some point refugees started arriving from the Srebrenica compound. Is that correct?

GROENEWEGEN: On July 11th, in the morning.

BOWERS: Now did you have any responsibilities with regard to receiving this exodus of refugees from the Srebrenica area?

GROENEWEGEN: I was requested to form a line from the compound to receive the people as best as possible.

BOWERS: How many soldiers were stationed outside the compound in this receiving line?

GROENEWEGEN: Approximately 30 to 50 men.

BOWERS: Now once you were assigned to this receiving line, did you stay out amongst the refugees?

GROENEWEGEN: *Few refugees* that arrived at our side of the river, indeed we received them.

BOWERS: And in fact over the next several days you slept outside the compound?

GROENEWEGEN: That is correct.

BOWERS: Could you just briefly describe what you saw on July 11th when the refugees arrived.

GROENEWEGEN: Our responsibility was to see to refugees that arrived, they had to be led towards the compound but it became clear very quickly that we couldn't have everybody go there, so the rest of the people had to remain outside. As much as possible we placed them in the factories, in the buildings in the vicinity. It was very chaotic.

BOWERS: Did the wounded get some sort of priority as far as being allowed into the compound?

GROENEWEGEN: That is correct. Women and children as far as possible were helped first, and then men.

BOWERS: Now while you were on this receiving line, did you see someone inflict an injury upon himself in an attempt to get into the compound?

GROENEWEGEN: That's correct.

BOWERS: Were you on the receiving line when the first soldiers arrived into Potocari?

GROENEWEGEN: That's correct.

BOWERS: About what time did these first soldiers arrive?

GROENEWEGEN: Noon.

BOWERS: And that was on July 12th?

GROENEWEGEN: Yes.

BOWERS: Can you describe for the Court what type of soldiers these were that first arrived?

GROENEWEGEN: Those were soldiers who didn't wear the regular clothing. All kinds of camouflage clothing, and headwear.

BOWERS: How were they armed?

GROENEWEGEN: Heavily.

BOWERS: Did the evacuations begin the next day on July 13th?

GROENEWEGEN: That's correct.

BOWERS: Now at this point in time on the morning of July 13th, did you start seeing any type of separation effort?

GROENEWEGEN: That's correct. As from that point in time the men were separated from the women.

BOWERS: And who was doing this separation?

GROENEWEGEN: It was all the Serbs that were there in the vicinity.

BOWERS: And you watched this process at a fairly close range?

GROENEWEGEN: Yes. We were walking around in between.

BOWERS: Would you describe for the Court how the Serb soldiers would separate a man from the crowd?

GROENEWEGEN: Mostly groups of three to four men – a maximum of two men were taken away.

BOWERS: Was it always a situation where the armed Serb soldiers outnumbered the men that they were taking out of the crowd or the group of men that they were removing from the crowd?

GROENEWEGEN: That's correct.

BOWERS: Did you see what happened to the men that were separated out of the crowd?

GROENEWEGEN: The men were taken to a house that was nearby until that floor was full of people, and then they were deported.

BOWERS: Could you see into this particular house where the men were collected?

GROENEWEGEN: That's correct.

BOWERS: Is that because part of the front wall was missing?

GROENEWEGEN: That's correct.

BOWERS: Now did you observe this house throughout the day?

GROENEWEGEN: I was there all day, but I didn't constantly concentrate on the house.

BOWERS: During the course of the day did you see men brought to the house and then taken away from the house on a fairly regular basis?

GROENEWEGEN: That's correct. As soon as the house was almost full if you looked after some time you saw that it was empty again.

BOWERS: Now on the afternoon of July 13th, did you witness a killing?

GROENEWEGEN: That's correct.

BOWERS: Approximately what time of day was that?

GROENEWEGEN: 4 o'clock.

BOWERS: What did you see that day? What happened?

GROENEWEGEN: From my position, the line where I was to keep people out who wanted to move towards the buses. I saw that a group of Serb soldiers from the crowd took one man and then I didn't take any notice of that anymore, and then later on I heard shouting. I responded, and it appeared to be the same group with a man that they had taken along.

BOWERS: How many men took the individual out of the crowd?

GROENEWEGEN: Four.

BOWERS: And were they soldiers? Armed soldiers?

GROENEWEGEN: All four of them were armed. Yes.

BOWERS: The man taken from the crowd, was he armed?

GROENEWEGEN: No.

BOWERS: Did he resist in any way?

GROENEWEGEN: No. He probably knew what was going to happen.

BOWERS: Continue and tell the Court what you saw after he was taken from the crowd.

GROENEWEGEN: He was taken from the crowd. I no longer took any notice of them. Later on when I heard the shouting I looked towards them, and I saw the same group, Serbs, with the man they had taken along, and afterwards round the corner he was shot dead.

BOWERS: Now when he was taken behind the house did you hear shouting from that area?

GROENEWEGEN: Not really loud shouting but noise, a lot of noise.

BOWERS: And when you heard the noise you turned and what did you see when you first looked behind the house?

GROENEWEGEN: From the position where I was standing I saw that the men gestured to the man that they'd captured to face the wall. Soldiers themselves looked at one another for a second that they were asking each other who's going to do it, and one stepped out and he was a few metres behind the man and shot him with an AK.

BOWERS: Could you tell from that distance where the bullet impacted?

GROENEWEGEN: Some of them walking around said they could see it. Yes.

BOWERS: How many also were behind the house in addition to the men that were responsible for extracting the individual from the crowd and shooting him?

GROENEWEGEN: At the time of the murder two at that moment.

BOWERS: Now from where you are standing across the way, you could hear the gunshot? Is that correct?

GROENEWEGEN: That's correct.

BOWERS: Did the two soldiers standing behind the house react when the men were shot?

GROENEWEGEN: They looked up in that direction, but then they resumed their own work quite quickly.

BOWERS: After the man was shot what did the soldiers responsible for the shooting do?

GROENEWEGEN: Men disappeared behind some bushes very nearby.

BOWERS: Do you know what happened to the body?

GROENEWEGEN: Negative.

BOWERS: Did the soldier use a single round to shoot this individual?

GROENEWEGEN: Yes, a single round.

BOWERS: Now during the rest of the day on July 13th, did you continue to hear these single shots throughout the day?

GROENEWEGEN: That's correct.

BOWERS: Would you please tell the Court how often during the course of July 13th you heard these single isolated shots?

GROENEWEGEN: Approximately 20 to 30 an hour.

BOWERS: Could you determine approximately what area these shots originated?

GROENEWEGEN: Mainly from the house – the area with the houses.

BOWERS: And would that be up away from where the crowd of refugees was being kept?

GROENEWEGEN: That is correct. A lot further in the hills.

BOWERS: In your opinion were these single rounds being fired in any type of combat situation?

GROENEWEGEN: Single shots.

BOWERS: So that doesn't indicate any type of combat occurring in your opinion?

GROENEWEGEN: Negative.

BOWERS: Now at the time you were hearing these single shots I assume there were Serb soldiers in the area?

GROENEWEGEN: Correct.

BOWERS: And did they exhibit any concern when these single shots would occur?

GROENEWEGEN: Negative.

BOWERS: Did you see General Mladic in Potocari? Could you tell the Court some of the things that he was doing during the course of the day?

GROENEWEGEN: Speaking to his own people and our own people.

BOWERS: Did he appear to be in charge of the situation?

GROENEWEGEN: That's correct.

BOWERS: Now the day July 13th that you saw General Mladic in Potocari, is that the same day that you saw the Serb soldiers begin separating the fighting age men out from the crowd?

GROENEWEGEN: That's correct.

BOWERS: And the day you saw General Mladic is also the same day that you saw the execution of the man behind the house. Is that correct?

GROENEWEGEN: That's correct.

BOWERS: And it's also the same day that you heard the continuous repetition of single shots being fired in the area beyond the refugees?

GROENEWEGEN: That's correct.

BOWERS: We have no further questions, your Honour.

JORDA: Thank you Prosecutor. Do you have any questions?

RIAD: Corporal, you mentioned that you heard single shots repeatedly till nightfall, did you or did your battalion enquire what it was about?

GROENEWEGEN: We all had our own ideas about it. But nothing was done.

RIAD: Nothing was done. You mean that there was no protest or objection or contact with the Serbs to ask them what it was about?

GROENEWEGEN: If we asked we didn't get any reaction, so we didn't get answers from them.

RIAD: And when this execution was undertaken, at your side was there any objection to it, or to the Serbians, or did you draw your attention to what they were doing?

GROENEWEGEN: At that moment it was so chaotic that we were all very busy, and we couldn't act as we would normally act.

DRAZEN ERDEMOVIC

HARMON: As our next witness we would call Drazen Erdemovic.

JORDA: Mr Prosecutor, would you like to remind us of what Drazen Erdemovic's present situation is in respect of the Tribunal?

HARMON: Mr Erdemovic has entered a guilty plea on proceedings relating to the indictment that was confirmed against him. He has been scheduled for a sentencing hearing; and the sentencing hearing has been continued to a further date yet to be decided.

JORDA: If Mr Erdemovic could be given a headset? Do you hear me, Mr Erdemovic? Can you hear me? Can you hear me? Can you hear me, Mr Erdemovic?

ERDEMOVIC: I can't hear you.

JORDA: If we can straighten out these headphones. Can you hear me?

ERDEMOVIC: Yes.

JORDA: Can you hear me in Serbo-Croatian?

ERDEMOVIC: Yes.

JORDA: Please read the declaration.

ERDEMOVIC: I do solemnly declare that I will speak the truth, the whole truth, and nothing but the truth.

JORDA: Please be seated.

Please proceed, Counsel.

HARMON: Yes, your Honour. Thank you very much. Mr Erdemovic, can you hear me?

ERDEMOVIC: Yes.

HARMON: Would you please state your name?

ERDEMOVIC: My name is Drazen Erdemovic. I was born on the 25th November 1971 in Tuzla and I am Croat by origin.

HARMON: Mr Erdemovic, before joining the Bosnian-Serb Army, were you a member of the JNA [Yugoslavian National Army]?

ERDEMOVIC: Yes.

HARMON: How long did you serve in the JNA?

ERDEMOVIC: For a year that was my regular service, and four months on the reserve.

HARMON: Mr Erdemovic, if you could move just a little closer to the microphone? Thank you.

What were your duties and responsibilities in the JNA?

ERDEMOVIC: I was with the Military Police.

HARMON: When did you leave the JNA?

ERDEMOVIC: In March 1992.

HARMON: And you eventually joined the Bosnian-Serb Army, is that correct?

ERDEMOVIC: No.

HARMON: Please explain your sequence of events that led you to join ultimately the Bosnian-Serb Army.

ERDEMOVIC: In July I was called up and I went to join the Army of Bosnia-Herzegovina. In the Army of Bosnia-Herzegovina I spent some three months. After that in Tuzla the Croat Defence Council was formed and I received a summons and I went to join the Croat Defence Council and I was assigned to a police station in a place near Tuzla. On the 3rd November 1993 I moved from Tuzla to the Republic of Serbska. Since I had moved from Tuzla with my wife I needed a status of some kind since I was a Croat in the Republic of Serbska so as to qualify for some accommodation, I had to join to the Army of the Republic of Serbska.

HARMON: As I understand it, Mr Erdemovic, your particular sabotage unit was directly reporting to the main staff of the Bosnian-Serb Army. Is that correct?

ERDEMOVIC: Yes it is. Yes.

HARMON: Mr Erdemovic. On the 10th July did your unit receive orders to participate in the Bosnian-Serb operation against the enclave of Srebrenica?

ERDEMOVIC: Yes.

HARMON: And did you follow those orders?

ERDEMOVIC: Yes.

HARMON: And when you entered into the town of Srebrenica did you encounter any resistance?

ERDEMOVIC: No.

HARMON: Were there any civilians in Srebrenica when you entered?

ERDEMOVIC: Yes. There were civilians, most of them of an advanced age.

HARMON: Approximately how many civilians did your unit encounter when you came into the town of Srebrenica?

ERDEMOVIC: Not very many. Not very many civilians. I would not know exactly but not many.

HARMON: Did you also run into a young man who was approximately 30 years old?

ERDEMOVIC: Yes.

HARMON: And, let me back-track for one moment, had you received any orders with regard to what you were supposed to do with civilians that you encountered in the city of Srebrenica?

ERDEMOVIC: Yes. We had been told not to touch them. Explicitly told.

HARMON: Who told you that?

ERDEMOVIC: Ilarick Pelamic.

HARMON: Were those orders followed in respect to this young man who was about 30 years old?

ERDEMOVIC: The Lieutenant Ilarick Pelamic ordered again another man to kill that man.

HARMON: To whom did he issue that order?

ERDEMOVIC: I know only his first name and his name is Zoron. I don't know his family name.

HARMON: Did Zoron obey Lieutenant Pelamic's order?

ERDEMOVIC: Yes.

HARMON: What did he do to the young man?

ERDEMOVIC: He slit his throat.

HARMON: Now this was a deviation from the general orders that you had received previously from Lieutenant Pelamic. Is that correct?

ERDEMOVIC: Yes.

HARMON: Was this man who was killed by Zoron the only civilian male of military age that you encountered in Srebrenica?

ERDEMOVIC: Yes.

HARMON: Where in the town of Srebrenica did that killing take place?

ERDEMOVIC: I think it was in the centre of the town but I don't know exactly because that was the first time that I had entered Srebrenica, so I wouldn't know exactly.

HARMON: Was the body left in plain view in the town of Srebrenica?

ERDEMOVIC: Yes.

HARMON: But later that same morning, Mr Erdemovic, did you have an opportunity to see General Mladic in Srebrenica?

ERDEMOVIC: Yes. I was ordered by my commander to return to the entrance to the town where we had come in, and to wait near to more friends and when we would see General Mladic arrive to let Lieutenant Pelamic know about that, and I did that when General Mladic passed by.

HARMON: When did your unit leave Srebrenica and return to Vlasnic?

ERDEMOVIC: Around noon. Sometime around noon.

HARMON: Mr Erdemovic. For your comfort there is a water pitcher and a glass of water next to you if you feel that you might just need a glass of water. Are you prepared to proceed?

ERDEMOVIC: Just a moment please. Just a moment. Just to calm down. (*Pours water.*)

HARMON: Mr Erdemovic, I would now like to turn your attention to the 16th July and ask you whether on that day you and other soldiers in your unit received orders to participate in a special detail?

ERDEMOVIC: Yes.

HARMON: Now in response to the orders that you received on the 16th July, Mr Erdemovic, where did you go next?

ERDEMOVIC: We went to Zvornik, and Brano Goykovic, the driver, reported to a Lieutenant Colonel whose name I don't know.

HARMON: Was the Lieutenant Colonel with anyone else?

ERDEMOVIC: Yes. He was accompanied by two military policemen.

HARMON: What happened next?

ERDEMOVIC: We went from Zvornik in the direction of Bijeljina and on the road we stopped at a farm that was at a place that was called Pilicza.

HARMON: After you arrived, after you arrived at that farm Mr Erdemovic, did you receive additional orders from your superiors?

ERDEMOVIC: I personally did not, but I heard when Brano and the Lieutenant Colonel were talking saying that buses would be coming to that farm.

HARMON: And in relation to those buses did you receive any additional information?

ERDEMOVIC: Afterwards when the Lieutenant Colonel left Brano said that buses would be coming with Muslims from Srebrenica.

HARMON: And did he say what you and the members of your unit were supposed to do regarding these Muslims from Srebrenica?

ERDEMOVIC: Yes.

HARMON: What did he say?

ERDEMOVIC: That we had to execute those people – to shoot them.

HARMON: When you say he told you you had to shoot them, for the record, who was that? You can identify him by name?

ERDEMOVIC: Brano Goykovic.

HARMON: Now you mentioned that members of your unit were present. Can you identify the other members of your unit who were present?

ERDEMOVIC: I can. Cos Franz was present;
> Goran Isoran;
> Savanovic Stanko;
> Svetnovic Alexander;
> Bosnic Marco;
> Goylan Blaskivir;
> Goykovic Brano.

HARMON: Approximately at what time did the first buses arrive?

ERDEMOVIC: I do not know exactly but I think it was between 9.30 and 10 in the morning – am.

HARMON: When the first buses arrived – or when the first bus arrived – Mr Erdemovic, was it filled with men?

ERDEMOVIC: I don't know exactly whether it was full but there were men and they were wearing civilian clothes.

HARMON: Can you provide to the Court the range of ages of these men?

ERDEMOVIC: I don't know exactly but maybe between 17 and 60 or 70 years of age.

HARMON: Now on each of these buses carrying these civilians were there armed escorts?

ERDEMOVIC: Yes. Each bus I think, I don't know exactly, but there were two military policemen belonging to the Drina Corps.

HARMON: Did these buses arrive one at a time at the farm, or did they arrive in large convoys?

ERDEMOVIC: One at a time.

HARMON: What happened once the bus arrived at the farm? Could you describe what happened, please.

ERDEMOVIC: When the bus arrived at the farm, as I said the commander of the group Brano Goykovic would tell us how to stand as an execution squad and two military policemen would bring out ten people of Muslim nationality from Srebrenica at a time, and Brano Goykovic and Goylan Blaskivir would bring them to the execution squad.

HARMON: Once the civilians arrived and were taken off the buses, Mr Erdemovic, where did they go?

ERDEMOVIC: They went to the meadow next to the farm.

HARMON: And where were you in relation, where were you and other members of your squad in relation to where the prisoners were brought?

ERDEMOVIC: We were I think about 50 or 100 metres from the buses in the field.

HARMON: And when the men were brought in your presence how far away were they from you when they stopped?

ERDEMOVIC: I think about 20 metres.

HARMON: Were they facing you, or facing away from you?

ERDEMOVIC: They were turned with their backs to me.

HARMON: What happened to those civilians?

ERDEMOVIC: We were given orders to fire at those civilians. That is to execute them.

HARMON: Did you follow that order?

ERDEMOVIC: Yes. But at first I resisted, and Brano Goykovic told me that if I was sorry for those people that I should line up with them, and I knew that this was not just a mere threat, but that it could happen because in our unit the situation had become such that the commander of the group has the right to execute on the spot any individual if he threatens the security of the group, or if in any other way he opposes the commander of group.

HARMON: Do you know how many buses were brought to Pilicza Farm on July 16th?

ERDEMOVIC: I don't know exactly, but I think between 15 and 20 buses.

HARMON: And did the same thing that you described just a moment ago happen to each one of those bus loads of civilian persons who came off the buses? In other words were they executed at Pilicza Farm?

ERDEMOVIC: Yes.

HARMON: What time, Mr Erdemovic, did the last bus arrive at the Pilicza Farm?

ERDEMOVIC: I really don't know exactly what time it was that the last bus arrived, but I know that before the last bus came a group of about 10 soldiers from Bratunac came to the farm, so I cannot know exactly. I don't know what time it was, but maybe around 15.30 or 16 hours.

HARMON: You say a group of soldiers from Bratunac also joined your unit at Pilicza Farm. Did they act in a way that was different to the civilians, and members of your unit acted?

ERDEMOVIC: Yes. They beat the civilians with bars. They said all kinds of things to them. They forced them to kneel and to pray in the Muslim manner. To bow their heads.

HARMON: Did it appear to you, Mr Erdemovic, that they were attempting to humiliate some of these victims before they killed them?

ERDEMOVIC: Yes. I think even that some of them from Bratunac knew some of those from Srebrenica.

HARMON: You mentioned, Mr Erdemovic, that once the bus arrived groups of prisoners – approximately 10 – were moved from the buses, taken to a field and executed. Is that correct?

ERDEMOVIC: Yes.

HARMON: Mr Erdemovic, in the course your time spent at Pilicza Farm on July 16th, did you have an opportunity to talk to one of the victims that day?

ERDEMOVIC: Yes. It was an elderly man. I think between 50 and 60, and when he was coming out of the bus he started immediately to complain. He said that he had saved Serbs from Srebrenica who were now in the Federal Republic of Yugoslavia and that he had the telephone numbers of those people, and he begged to be allowed to live.

HARMON: After listening to him what did you do, Mr Erdemovic?

ERDEMOVIC: I said to Brano Goykovic to let him live. I wanted to save that man. I was sorry for those people simply. I had no reason to shoot at those people. They had done nothing to me.

HARMON: What response did you get from Brano Goykovic?

ERDEMOVIC: That he didn't want to have any witnesses of that crime.

HARMON: And did he then lead that man away to the field?

ERDEMOVIC: Not he, but Goylan Blaskivir did. I quarrelled with them but there was nothing I could do.

HARMON: Were there some members of your unit who boasted about how many they had killed on July 16th?

ERDEMOVIC: There were.

HARMON: Could you expand on that, please.

ERDEMOVIC: There was a man who alleged, or so he said, that the Bosnian Muslims had killed his brother who was 17, and he said that he wanted his revenge, and that on that day he had killed 250 Muslims from Srebrenica.

HARMON: Did he say that he had counted?

ERDEMOVIC: Yes.

HARMON: Now let me ask you, Mr Erdemovic, what was the attitude of the bus drivers who drove the victims to Pilicza Farm?

ERDEMOVIC: They were horrified. I think those men did not know that they were being driven to the execution ground. They probably thought they were being led for exchange and that is what this man that I talked to, the one between 50 and 60 actually told me that it had been promised them. However Brano Goykovic entered the bus and gave an automatic rifle, a Kalashnikov, and ordered each driver to kill at least one of those Muslims so that they could not testify.

HARMON: Can you estimate, Mr Erdemovic, how many civilians were killed by your unit on the 16th of July?

ERDEMOVIC: 16th. Somewhere about 1,000, 1,200. I don't know. I estimated the number according to the arrivals of the buses.

HARMON: Are you able to estimate how many people you killed?

ERDEMOVIC: (*Long intake of breath.*) I don't know exactly. I can't estimate. But to be quite frank I'd rather not know how many people I killed.

HARMON: Now you mentioned, Mr Erdemovic, that the Lieutenant Colonel who you had seen earlier that morning returned to the farm after or during the course of the executions. Is that correct?

ERDEMOVIC: Yes. Yes. He came at the end.

HARMON: In your opinion was it…did he see the dead bodies that were covering the field?

ERDEMOVIC: Of course. Yes. He saw them.

HARMON: Did he make any comments about seeing those bodies?

ERDEMOVIC: No. He made no comments. But he said in the place of Pilicza there were another 500 of those Muslims of Srebrenica, and that we had to go to finish off that work. I said aloud that I would not. That I didn't wish to kill anyone. That I was no robot for the extermination of people. Then I was supported by some individuals from the unit so we didn't go, but the group from Bratunac went.

HARMON: Mr Erdemovic, why did you refuse to follow that additional order?

ERDEMOVIC: Because I just couldn't take it anymore.

HARMON: Mr Erdemovic, shortly after the killings of Pilicza Farm, and after you had returned home, were you shot by a member of the 10th Sabotage Unit who had participated in the massacres at Pilicza Farm?

ERDEMOVIC: Yes.

HARMON: Did you suffer extremely serious injuries as a result of that shooting?

ERDEMOVIC: Yes. Yes.

HARMON: Which of the members of the 10th Sabotage Unit shot you?

ERDEMOVIC: The man who bragged that he had killed most Muslims, Savanovic Stanko.

HARMON: All right Your Honour, I have concluded my examination of Mr Erdemovic. Thank you, Mr Erdemovic.

JORDA: Mr Erdemovic, the Prosecutors would like to pose questions. Would you rather that we have a recess before we address those questions?

ERDEMOVIC: No. I would rather go on, your Honours, to get this over with as soon as possible because I am finding it very hard.

JORDA: That's what I thought. Judge Riad, do you have any questions?

RIAD: I am sorry to go back to the executions. Were you, did you make sure, your troop, make sure that everybody was executed before you left?

ERDEMOVIC: I personally did not. And I don't think that most of those men would check because this was really something awful. I don't know. We didn't check.

RIAD: You said that, this is my last question, you said that at after you left Pilicza Farm, you were shot at by this man called Stanko. Why did he shoot at you?

ERDEMOVIC: Well, my assumption is that someone, one of those men, and I think it was Brano Goykovic had conveyed to the commander of my unit my behaviour at the farm. And that probably they had reached the conclusion that I just couldn't stand it, and that perhaps, I don't know, that I might do what I am doing today, that is testifying against it.

RIAD: You mentioned that, sorry to add this question, you mentioned that in April 1994 you joined the army of Bosnian-Serbs. You being a Croat, what pushed you to join this army?

ERDEMOVIC: Your Honour, the war in Bosnia-Herzegovina was quite awful. Firstly I was in the army of the Bosnian Muslims, then of the Bosnian-Croats and, at the end, of the Bosnian-Serbs. I didn't want to join the army but I had no other choice. I had to join the army to have somewhere to stay because I had my wife with me who was pregnant. And that was the only motive I didn't have anywhere to go to join the army.

RIAD: Thank you.

JORDA: Mr Erdemovic – Why did you want to testify? What feelings underline that, and what do you feel now that you're before the International Criminal Tribunal?

ERDEMOVIC: I wanted to testify because of my conscience. Because of all that happened. Because I did not want that. I was simply compelled to, forced to, and I could choose between my life and the life of those people, and if I had lost my life there that would not have changed the fate of those people. The fate of those people was decided by somebody holding a much higher position than I did. And, as I have said already, that really got me, and it's completely destroyed my life and that is why I testified.

Appendix: From the evidence of Witness A

This edited extract, from evidence given by an anonymous witness (Witness A) to the United Nations War Crimes Tribunal in The Hague on Thursday 4 and Friday 5 July 1996, was not included in the play as performed for reasons of space.

WITNESS A gave evidence from behind a screen, and was under the protection of the court. From his own account he was an elderly Bosnian farmer who fled from the Bosnian Serb Army invasion of Srebrenica on 11 July and was deported from Potocari by Bosnian Serb Troops under Ratko Mladic's command on 12 July. The part of his evidence which follows describes the 36 hours after his capture.

WITNESS A: Ratko Mladic appeared at the door and all of us cried out: 'What are you doing with us here? Why are you killing us? Why don't you take us away? What are you doing?' He replied, 'Exchanges aren't easy to arrange. If the exchange had been easier to arrange we would already have done it. But when the exchange is done you will go to Kalesia. We only need to count you to find out how many you are so that I can arrange the transport for each one of you.' There was one amongst us who got up to count us and he said, 'All together here there are 296 of us', and he replied, 'All right I will arrange transport for all of you'; and then he left. Then later on we heard the noise of the arrival of a vehicle. At that moment there was someone who said, once again, 'Come on, buses have arrived, leave one by one.' So, we got up and went out of the hangar. At nightfall the buses started up going in the direction of the River Drina and Serbia. We arrived at the bridge over the Drina. We didn't cross it, we continued along the left bank of the Drina which is Bosnian territory. We arrived at a school. There the buses stopped and there once again there were fifteen Serbian soldiers who were waiting for us and gave us the order to get out. We got out and went into a room, the gymnasium of the school.

We sat down, and a little while later one could hear a car again, and again a group of younger men came in. They were brought into the hall. Maybe there were 50 or more of them. And they kept bringing in people until noon, and the hall became packed full. Then we cried out for water. There were people fainting. About midday Ratko Mladic appeared at the door, then we all as one cried out, 'Why are you choking us in here? Why are you keeping us here? Why don't you take us somewhere?' And he said, 'What am I to do with you when your government doesn't want you, and I have to take care of you? I will move a group of you to Kladusa and another group to Bijeljina.' 'And why don't you give us water?' He said, 'You will get water on the way out of the hall.' And then he went away. And so we sat there and they told us that we would be going out of the longer end, one by one. The vehicles had come, and then those nearest the door got up, and started walking out and so they went on. And then we heard from our people that they were blindfolding people. And we said, 'Did you ask them why?' and they said because you would be passing through Serb territory, so as not to see their military equipment.

And so we were filing out, people were filing out, about 7.30 in the evening. It was my turn to leave. When I actually got to the door you couldn't see outside because there is a wall. Then you pass the table, you have a drink of water, then they blindfold you from behind. And then you turn right behind the table, and then you notice a small lorry of two tons carrying capacity. Then you have to climb up and sit down. I was the one but last, because it was already full. There was a cover on the lorry, but it was folded. When I entered the lorry two soldiers closed it, and the lorry took off. There was a red car escorting the truck. Next to the driver was a man in uniform with an automatic rifle. He opened the door a little, and he threatened that he would kill us if we talked. I don't know exactly for how long the trip took, but it wasn't long. When we got to a field we saw to the left a lot of dead people. Then we realised where we were going. We passed those corpses, and the truck went on, across some pasture land, and when it turned we saw to the right the same number of dead. The truck stopped, the small car went back. Two Serb soldiers opened the back. They told us to come down quickly, not to look, just come out. And so we came out, we were lined up. As soon as the small lorry went off, they started firing at us from behind. There were some people standing behind me, and they fell on top of me, so I fell on my stomach, and they fell on top of me. Then the firing stopped, and then they started shooting individually. If anybody gave any signs of life, he would be killed. I kept quiet. They moved away, and again they would refill their automatic rifles. They were firing from automatic rifles. And then another small tan truck came near me, and when the third came the red car didn't go back, but out of the car the man who was sitting next to the driver came and Ratko Mladic came out. Ratko Mladic watched as people were being forced out of the truck and lined up. The lorry moved away. Mladic stood until all of them had been killed and had fallen. Then Mladic returned to the small red car, sat next to the driver and they went back from where they had come towards the hall.

There were two trucks, one truck was going in one direction, and the other in another, and there was one red car escorting both these trucks. As the truck arrived to the spot the car would return to accompany the second truck, and then again it would return, load and come back with a load full of the next truck. And this went on until the evening hours. I crawled out from under the dead, and I went to the pile of bodies where there was some small shrubs, and then I hid behind the shrubs. I don't know what time it was during the night when a small truck came again and somebody from the truck said, 'There are no more people in the hall, it's all over.' Then someone else asked, 'Are we going to stand on duty here during the night?' He said, 'If another truck comes then there will be no need for any night duty.' They stood around smoking. A little later another truck came. It reached them, they talked a while. The moon came up, it was a moonlit night. They climbed onto the truck. They all climbed on. I counted them just to see that no-one was left behind, and the truck went. I got up thinking to myself maybe there are some other survivors, so I shouted, 'Is anyone living? If you are get up so we can get away.' One man cropped up from among the dead and said, 'I am alive.' I said, 'Are you wounded?' 'No.' And I said, 'Come here.' He did, he got up, and so the two of us set off towards Kalesia.

THE REACTIONS TO SREBRENICA

A 'Parish-pump holocaust'

YUGOSLAVIA REPRESENTS, in Vulliamy's words, merely a 'parish-pump holocaust' occurring in the maelstrom of civil war, while what assaulted the Jews is to this day unprecedented: a vast death machine, bureaucratised and industrialised, that controlled most of a continent, especially the pacified areas.

Yet, in qualitative terms, there are similarities. As Vulliamy gruesomely documents, the daily life of people in the Serb-run concentration camps was not dissimilar to life in some Nazi-run camps. The manner in which women and children, whole villages even, were set upon, tortured, and practically incinerated by wild animals in uniforms bearing automatic rifles can indeed be compared to the experience of villagers in Eastern Europe in previous wars. So too can Europe's tepid response to the whole affair. And that is the ultimate comparison – the Nazi Holocaust and the slaughter in Bosnia will, for future historians, serve as bookends for the story of Cold War Europe.

From 'The Meaning of History' by Robert D Kaplan
(introduction to Seasons in Hell: Understanding Bosnia's War *by Ed Vulliamy (1994))*

Two eye-witness accounts of mass graves in Brcko, Bosnia

THE ELECTRICIAN

ANOTHER WITNESS to mass burial at the site was a Croat electrician who was forced to work by the Serbs.

His team laboured under armed escort, and one day in June was on the edge of the farm to fix damaged electrical cables strung along a series of pylons.

Walking beneath the cables at mid-morning, the team came to the crest of a hill and saw the mass grave 50 yards away. The bodies sprawled in the mud wore colourful clothing.

'We couldn't count them – we left immediately,' he said. He is now a refugee who escaped to a Croat pocket of Bosnia.

'It is difficult to estimate whether there were 10 or 15. We didn't speak about it, even among ourselves, because we were so afraid.

'But it's a fact that they were burying people there. If only half the people are killed who are said to be killed, then there are several mass graves,' he said.

THE DRIVER

ONE MUSLIM truck driver, who later escaped Serb areas, travelled the road to the farm regularly in May and June 1992. 'We knew immediately what the bulldozer was doing, digging a hole and burying bodies,' he said.

'I just had a quick look – they [Serbs] were unloading them and throwing them down. I saw four or five bodies just 15 yards off the road leading to the farm.

'We saw the trucks coming there all the time. They were big pits. I'm sure that there were two or three graves because it was changing all the time. One would be filled and then they would do another one.'

The driver had worked for the Bimeks company for 25 years and recognised the two-ton refrigerated Bimeks truck that was used during the killing to transport bodies to the farm. It had a distinctive yellow cab, and he remembers that its licence plate number was BR51915.

Long-time friends of his who drove other trucks told him that they had moved much of the rubble from Brcko's three blasted mosques to the farm. He remembers seeing the distinctive red bricks from one mosque at the grave.

The Bosnian Serbs have refused to co-operate with the Tribunal, though most of the mass grave sites alleged to exist by the UN are the work of Serbs and still in Serb-held territory... Local Serb denials that massacres took place are in stark contrast to a series of UN, Pentagon and State Department reports that allege there are at least 13 mass graves containing more than 500 bodies.

Daily Telegraph, *22 January 1996*
From an article by Scott Peterson

© *Telegraph Group Ltd 1996*

A Conflict of interest

On the first anniversary of the fall of Srebrenica Martin Bell launches a passionate attack on British policy in Bosnia that put national interest before principle.

I AM NOT a crusading or campaigning journalist, and indeed I tend to mistrust such journalists, on the grounds that they so often find what they are looking for and disregard the rest. But I do know what happens when politics and diplomacy fail. For I have been there.

I had not expected it – the first war and genocide in Europe, since the last war and genocide in Europe. I will concede that this war changed me. It has changed my way of doing things and seeing things, and my way of working. I was brought up in the old and honourable tradition of balanced, dispassionate, objective journalism. I would now call it bystander journalism. I would move from war zone to war zone without being greatly affected by any of them. And clearly I have been affected by the Bosnian war, enough passionately to wish to see an end to it. I am not sure about objectivity any more. What I believe in now is what I prefer to call the journalism of attachment; a journalism that cares as well as knows.

For all that we are accused in television, of distorting and exaggerating and wrenching out of context, in the Bosnian war we tended to understate and under-report and not show things quite as we found them. Sometimes courage failed. Certainly mine did. I believe we should show more than we do and take out less than we do on the grounds of taste. For war is a bad taste business. And in the real world people do not, as they do in television, expire gracefully out of sight.

Bosnia has shown that there is no middle course, no getting half in. And there is a strong case for staying out. No country willingly risks the lives of its young soldiers in a cause which is not their own and in a country of which they know little. But in Bosnia, for the first three years of war, we – not just the British, but many countries who could have helped but didn't – neither stayed out of it nor got into it effectively.

We came up with limited, symbolic measures, which may

have prolonged the conflict. One was using UN troops to escort aid to the victims of the war rather than to prevent the aggression. This was to pass food in through the window while the murderer stood at the door. Another was the plan for UN-designated safe areas without the troops and the mandate which would have made them safe.

War is diplomacy's failure. And the Bosnian war has left me with the conviction that a foreign policy based only on considerations of national interest, and not at all of principle, is not only immoral but inefficient. It cannot cope with the challenges of the new world disorder. What we do have is an interesting – and extremely British – discrepancy between what we do and what we say. What we do is to make a difference. The British people are a moral people with a profound sense of right and wrong. They hold coffee mornings and jumble sales to raise money for the victims of the Bosnian war. They take refugees into their homes. They drive convoys of aid into the war zones. Such people tend to be dismissed by my army friends as 'do-gooders from Bagshot'.

And the British, more than any other nation in Bosnia, have been doers of good. They included an Essex fireman who drove an old fire engine into Sarajevo across the airport, a free fire zone for the Serbs. It took five bullets but it got through. They included my friend Larry Hollingworth, the Father Christmas lookalike who ran the UN relief agency in Sarajevo and later in Central Bosnia, who stood up to the bandit-commanders at road blocks, and saved thousands of lives; Mark Cook, the former British army officer, who raised a million pounds to rebuild orphanages at Lipik in Croatia and Sarajevo; the ODA, the 'good works' department of the Foreign Office, under the leadership of Baroness Chalker. Now look at the pronouncements of officialdom, public and private, and you will find very different signals.

Malcolm Rifkind, in his first policy speech on becoming foreign secretary, quoted with approval Lord Palmerston's dictum that 'the furtherance of British interests ought to be the sole object of a British foreign secretary'. In which case we may perhaps wonder, whatever happened to British principles? Don't we have them anymore? And if we don't, what kind of people are we?

Let me make an example. The example is Srebrenica, the Muslim enclave of 50,000 people which fell to the Serbs a year ago. It was supposed to be a UN-protected safe area. As the Serbs overran it, some 2,000 Muslim men slipped out or fought their way out through Serb lines to Tuzla. The women and children were bussed out or trucked out or finally walked to safety, though some of them died on the way. But 3,000 to 5,000* men were separated from them and disappeared. We now know that most of these were killed by the Serbs in a series of cold-blooded, organised mass executions. It was the greatest war crime in Europe since 1945. In the words of the UN War Crimes Tribunal, 'these were scenes from hell, written on the darkest pages of human history'.

Now here's the point. On a strict calculation of national interest, Stebrenica was none of our business. It did not touch our security, our prosperity, or any of the usual political and electoral nerve-endings. It was not the business of any of the countries of the European Union except Holland, for there were 309 Dutch troops in the enclave at the time. And the national interest of the Dutch was to get them out as quickly as possible and at whatever cost, which is what they did. So Srebrenica was no one's business.

But put history into re-wind for a moment, track this argument back over 50 years, and you will see its destination with chilling clarity. Was Buchenwald none of our business? Was Belsen none of our business? Were Auschwitz and Birkenau none of our business? The case collapses under the weight of history, and of course its own invidiousness.

I come home from war zones and find that the great and good of journalism are much concerned about the position of Eurosceptics in the cabinet – and the great moral issue of the day, which is whether the winner of the National Lottery is entitled to anonymity. I ask myself: is this my country? Is it even my planet?

There is little discussion or none at all of whether there should be some consideration of principle in foreign policy. Of whether genocide matters to us even when our own security is not threatened. Of what risks and casualties we are willing to take in the cause of peace.

Not only are these issues not raised, they are actively avoided. It is not generally known that Britain's first contribution to UNPROFOR, when it was formed to keep the peace and police the ceasefire in Croatia, was delayed for two months so that it should not become an issue in the general election of April 1992.

What was this contribution? Was it armour, artillery, combat infantry? No, it was a field hospital which would save the lives and contribute to the safety of our UN troops. No-one was willing to stand up and make the case even for that. Of the quality and character of that decision, judge for yourselves.

The question that this raised for me, and which has been rattling around in my head ever since, is: what kind of people are we?

What we are, perhaps, is an unled people. Or a people who have had to find leadership within themselves, which no longer comes from the quarters it used to. This was the case with the British soldiers who served under a blue helmet in Bosnia, it was the case with the aid workers who served in Bosnia. It was even the case, sometimes, with members of that unfashionable underclass, the journalists, who served in Bosnia. What else were we to do? Pass by on the other side, wring our hands, and declare it was none of our business? It was all of our business. And it still is.

This is an edited version of a speech delivered on 11 July 1996 at Chichester Cathedral.

© *Martin Bell 1996*

Who cares as judgement falls on Serb hell camp?

Ed Vulliamy was among journalists who revealed the brutality of Omarska in 1992. At The Hague War Crimes Tribunal he wondered why there is so much apathy about one of the darkest chapters in European history.

A TRAIL OF BLOOD-CURDLING evidence laid before the international war crimes tribunal in The Hague last week has cut to some dark, bitter core – not only of Bosnia's war and the Omarska concentration camp but, it felt at times, of the human condition itself.

The testimony from survivors of the inferno of Omarska was wounded and forthright, especially when challenged as lies and fiction by the lawyers of Bosnian Serb defendant Dusko Tadic, charged with multiple war crimes.

'That's what you say,' they would retort to suggestions from Stephen Kay QC that they were fabricating their evidence. Or: 'I didn't see you in Omarska. I was there.'

'I have sworn that I would speak the truth,' retorted a man called Muharem Besic. 'I'm sorry that you are paid to do what you do.'

Whatever the final verdict on Tadic himself, the recollections of the Omarska survivors took us further into the nether depths than any other account of Bosnia's carnage to date. The savagery they describe wove a grotesque tapestry of what life in the camp was like – new dimensions of recreational and sexual sadism, and the macabre intimacy of that cruelty, inflicted by neighbour against neighbour, friend against friend.

At the centre of the evidence was an infamous scene described by an Omarska survivor, Halid Mujkanovic. It concerned a prisoner forced to perform fellatio on a fellow inmate, then ordered to bite off his testicles.

The victim was Fikret Harambasic, and the man forced to castrate him in order to save the lives of his room-mates (threatened with execution if there were no 'volunteers') is codenamed by the tribunal in The Hague as 'G'.

This is what Mujkanovic witnessed as he crouched behind a glass door and peeped through his hands. 'I saw someone held down by the arms... "G" had to bow down in his crotch and it was ordered that he must bite off his genitals. When I looked a second time, there was screaming. "G" got up, with his mouth full of I don't know what and covered with blood and oil.

'A little time passed. One of the soldiers brought the person [who had been castrated] a dove. He was lying on the concrete and he was given this dove or pigeon – it was still alive and it was given to this person to eat.'

Throughout, said Mujkanovic, the crowd of Serb guards who oversaw this barbarity 'looked as though they were attending a sports match, supporting a team'.

Although this incident was the pivot of the week's evidence, it was the setting that was most extraordinary, that the inner workings of the Omarska camp were being detailed in a courtroom.

For these men knew each other: the victims knew each other, and they knew some of their killers and torturers. Witness after witness comes through the courtroom to face the same opening questions. 'How well did you know Tadic?' The answers vary only slightly. 'I helped him work on building his café'; 'I have known him since he was a child'; and even: 'When I was a boy, he was my hero. I used to watch him do karate through the window of the gym.'

And they end up answering another: 'Do you see Tadic in court?', and they point.

These Muslims soon found themselves in a column, surrendering to the Serbs, Tadic allegedly cruising in a police car, helping soldiers from outside to sort out the women and children from the men.

Mehmed Alic, 73, whose rugged peasant manners seemed at odds with the formalities of the court, remembers it all well. On the road to Omarksa, soldiers questioned his daughter. 'She's a deaf mute. She said nothing and the soldier hit her with a rifle butt. I stepped in and said, "She can't hear or talk", and he said: "Shut up or else I'll hit you".' That was May 1992.

Alic had two sons: one, Ehkrem, was shot dead by the Serbs

on that road. He then found the other, Enver, in Omarska, to whom he broke the news of Ehkrem's death through a keyhole between cells. Within a month, Alic would – he told the court – see Tadic and others kick and beat Enver to death in camp Omarska.

Alic had been interned in 1943 and 1945, 'but this camp was unimaginable'. There were 'beatings on the way to and from the toilet every day'. The names of those selected for beatings were called out 'every night and every day'. This calling of names echoed out all the time. 'They would bring them back and throw them into the room, and there were people who never came back.'

These men would either return 'in blankets, barely alive', said another witness, Husein Hodzic, 'or else not at all'. Tadic is charged with the murder of Jasko Hrnic, who lived on a table. 'He was so beaten up, it was a more comfortable place for him,' said his friend Armin Kenjar. Another man, Emir Karabasic, with whom Hodzic shared floor space, lived in mortal fear of Tadic, because he had 'seen something I wasn't supposed to'. It was the first basic rule, that the more you knew the greater the chance you would be killed. Brother would counsel brother to say nothing.

Halid Mujkanovic had his name called out one night by a man called Baka. 'He said to lean over a table, and started whipping me with a cable. When I fell from the table, he told me I had 10 minutes to bring him 20 billion dinars. I asked around. We were all in the same situation and he beat me again. He said he was on tomorrow's shift and unless I had 20 billion he would kill me.'

Mujkanovic spent the night begging his comrades for his life. He managed to harvest a watch and a silver chain. 'I brought to him everything I had. He hit me a few times and told me to run. I left the room, but another soldier hit me with his rifle butt and started kicking me in my stomach, intestines, on my head. My colon was protruding and he had smashed my ear,'

As every witness says, Omarska's great hangar was like a battery farm for bloodied humans. Men on stairways, men in corridors, men living on top of lockers and tables for months on end. Explaining why it took a man called Jasko Hric so long to cross a room and reach his executioner waiting at the doorway, one witness said: 'You could not put your foot down without treading on someone's foot, hand or head.'

What emerged last week was among the most gruelling portraits of a concentration camp in Europe, which echoed themes of the Nazi Holocaust. As remarkable, therefore, was the absence of listeners from the wider world wanting to hear it. Omarska is, by any standards, a dark phenomenon, a terrible emblem of our times. And this Tribunal is nothing if not a historic attempt to confront its causes.

But who was there to listen? There were 13 people in the press area, and six in the public gallery on Wednesday when the evidence about the castration was heard.

Two of the 13 journalists were from the tribunal press office, and one each from Reuters, Associated Press and Agance France-Presse, all of which have given near-blanket coverage to the trial. One from *Corriere della Sera,* one from the *Guardian* and the rest were from Holland, where agencies, press and television are closely stitched into this nightmare unfolding in their civilised cities.

Le Monde has run page after page on the case. Two Swiss dailies – the *Nouveau Quotidien* and the *Journal de Genève* – have been especially attentive. The *Washington Post,* the *Guardian* and *The Times* have been regular visitors. The BBC World Service has been diligent, but no other branch. And – apart from a mêlée of 700 on the opening day and a wave of interest during the international arrest hearing on Radovan Karadzic and General Ratko Mladic – that's about it.

This is not for lack of effort on the tribunal's part. The chief prosecutor, Richard Goldstone, has spent so much time as its ambassador and advocate that staff have become surprised to see him in The Hague.

Information is organised by an office made up of a chief spokesman and four efficient press officers, including an international lawyer. It puts out a monthly bulletin on various cases, the budget and personalities involved. 'I understand no one can afford to cover every day of the trial,' concedes spokesman Christian Chartier, 'and I confess some of this is our fault. We are unable to tip off in advance, since we cannot give out any information that might identify a witness, who anyway has the right to withdraw until the last moment.

'But I have to say that the lack of interest baffles me. This thing is going much deeper than just the trial. I can't understand why there aren't philosophers here, or historians.'

What is happening at The Hague is part of the reckoning in the painful aftermath of Bosnia's carnage. Judge Gabrielle Macdonald asked one witness: 'Why...did this happen?'

For the wider world, the war and the diplomats' attempts at peace were the easy bit. But now the questions are being asked not by diplomats squealing their rhetoric but by the more concentrated minds of two attorneys from America, Michael Keegan and Alan Tieger, who happen to have called the survivors of Omarska into court.

In that court, their questions are simple: 'When you were sitting with your hands over your face, did you look up to see what was happening?' Outside court, these are the questions the world dare not answer about itself.

The Observer, *28 July 1996*

© *Guardian Newspapers Limited 1996*

'To bury my brothers' bones'
A REPORT BY AMNESTY INTERNATIONAL

MORE THAN 6,000 Bosnian Muslims were unaccounted for after Bosnian Serb forces captured the Srebrenica enclave in eastern Bosnia-Herzegovina in July 1995. In the year since then, very few of them have been found to be in detention or otherwise accounted for. Although relatives cling to the hopes and rumours that their family members are in detention or in hiding, there is little hard evidence to suggest that many of the 'missing' are alive. This report summarises the events surrounding the capture of the Srebrenica enclave, incorporating information released since September 1995, when Amnesty International published its report *The Missing of Srebrenica* (AI Index: EUR 63/22/95). Amnesty International delegates have conducted two missions to Bosnia-Herzegovina to talk to relatives of the 'missing', in July 1995 and April 1996. In the scores of interviews conducted with individuals approached randomly, the organization has never spoken to any Muslim displaced from Srebrenica in 1995 who did not personally know someone now among the 'missing', the vast majority being immediate relatives. The emphasis of the report is on the relatives of the 'missing' of Srebrenica, in particular the feelings and wishes of the relatives of the more than 6,000 people estimated still unaccounted for, on their need to find out the fate of their loved ones and on the obligations of the international community to help them achieve this goal and bring those responsible for grave abuses of human rights in Srebrenica and elsewhere in Bosnia-Herzegovina to justice.

As Bosnian Serb Army (BSA) forces took control of the Srebrenica enclave on 10 July 1995, approximately 15,000 Bosnian Muslims (primarily men who had served with the Bosnian Government Army), gathered on a hill outside Srebrenica. They departed on foot across the forested and mountainous terrain to try to reach Bosnian Government territory, approximately 50 kilometres to the north-west. Those who travelled through the forests were subject to ambushes by the BSA and many of those who were captured have never been seen since. The approximately 25,000 remaining civilians went to Potocari, an industrial town four kilometres north of Srebrenica where United Nations Protection Forces (UNPROFOR) had its main base in the enclave, to await evacuation to Bosnian Government territory. At Potocari, the BSA separated men from the women and took them to an unknown location.

An enormous number of the men separated from the civilians at Potocari or captured while fleeing to Bosnian Government-held territory were deliberately or arbitrarily killed by BSA forces. This is the inescapable conclusion of most observers, based on evidence including the testimony of those who claim to have survived the executions, witnesses' testimonies, a confession from a BSA soldier who claims to have participated in mass executions, on-the-spot investigations by journalists, preliminary exhumations, and photographic evidence from United States intelligence sources. The killings, in what appears to be an extensive BSA operation, took place either at the site of capture, while prisoners were temporarily detained in one of many improvised centres, or after they were transported to one of various sites used for mass executions.

While important for the prosecution of those responsible, the mere confirmation that mass executions took place is of little solace to the family members who want to know what happened to particular individuals: to be reunited if they are alive, and to have a place to mourn them if they are among the dead. Although some of the grave sites may have been irrevocably tampered with and a comprehensive picture may never be possible, until all detention centres have been reported and the mass graves are exhumed, it will be impossible to satisfy the wishes of the relatives to know what happened to the individuals who comprise the more than 6,000 unaccounted-for Srebrenicans. Finding out the truth about all the 'disappeared' and 'missing' is a crucial component of the future stability of the region, and for many of those relatives who have also been displaced by the conflict it is a precondition for returning to their homes. Halil Mehic, whose missing relatives include two brothers, told Amnesty International, 'I would want to go back [to Srebrenica] only if it were possible to find somewhere the bones of my brothers, to bury them. Otherwise I wouldn't. Otherwise I'd never go back.'

Srebrenica, because it was a UN-protected 'safe heaven' until July 1995, occupies a special place in the concern of the international community. The 'missing' of Srebrenica, however, comprise only a fraction of the more than 27,000 people estimated unaccounted-for following the conflicts in Bosnia-Herzegovina, and this paper also calls upon the international community to provide the necessary resources to resolve these cases. These endeavours must satisfy both the pressing and legitimate needs of the International Criminal Tribunal for Former Yugoslavia to gather admissible evidence and the deeply human desire of relatives to know the fates of their loved ones. The international community should, as a priority, provide the necessary staff, equipment and funding to carry out a program of action to resolve all cases within three years and to return bodies which can be identified to families or communities, in full co-operation with the UN expert on missing persons in the former Yugoslavia.

This report summarises a 26-page document (11,900 words): Bosnia-Herzegovina: *To bury my brothers' bones* (AI Index: BUR 63115196) issued by Amnesty International in July 1996. Anyone wishing further details or to take action on this issue should consult the full document.

International Secretariat, 1 Easton Street, London
WC1X 8DJ, United Kingdom

Bosnia war crimes judge condemns half-hearted West

[...] RICHARD GOLDSTONE (Chief Prosecutor of the International War Crimes Tribunal) expressed his 'tremendous frustration and unhappiness' at NATO's refusal to hunt down the Bosnian Serb leader and his military commander and bring them to justice, while he attacked the West's 'hands-off' approach as 'highly inappropriate, to put it mildly'.

Dr Karadzic and General Mladic face international arrest warrants for allegedly 'instigating, planning and ordering the genocide and the ethnic cleansing in Bosnia'.

So far, 74 arrest warrants have been issued for suspected Bosnian war criminals, but only eight are currently in custody, and the peacekeeping forces in Bosnia are under orders to arrest individuals only if they come across them in the course of their duties.

'They know where these people are, and according to our information the men on the ground are as frustrated as we are and would like to go out and get them,' the judge said.

The West's reluctance to apprehend the suspects is 'very much a political decision,' he added, noting that the US is particularly unwilling to risk possible bloodshed and domestic political criticism by attempting to round up the indicted Bosnian Serb leaders.

'Any decent, rational human being must recognise how inappropriate it is for the international community not to arrest these people when you look at the massive crimes they're charged with. Compare it to a national situation. It would be ridiculous to suggest that the police shouldn't go and arrest massive criminals like this because they might get injured,' Mr Justice Goldstone said. He noted that his successor as chief prosecutor, Judge Louise Arbour, of Canada, faces a daunting job when she takes over on October 1.

The court at The Hague 'is effectively being prevented from doing the job it was set up to do, and if this continues too long, it's going to destroy the credibility of the tribunal', he said. [...]

An intense man, whose passionate belief in the Tribunal's

moral role contrasts with a clipped, often legalistic turn of phrase, Mr Justice Goldstone believes that the importance of the court is primarily symbolic, but he also emphasised that the proceedings provide a unique opportunity to build an international legal code to deal with war crimes, and perhaps render them less likely in the future.

'The central function and purpose of the Tribunal is to establish individual as opposed to collective guilt. That was the importance of Nuremberg. It enabled the German people to come to grips with their own terrible inheritance from the Third Reich,' Mr Justice Goldstone said.

But whereas the war crimes trials then were staged by the victors and involved the conviction of key criminals on the basis of voluminous evidence, the Tribunal at The Hague is hampered by lack of funds and international co-operation. 'We decided our strategy must be to go for the leaders because of the small number we could put on trial...but without the big fish, the symbolic power is dissipated,' the judge noted bitterly.

The judge, who will be returning to South Africa next month to take his seat at the constitutional court, said he felt 'substantial satisfaction' that the machinery for prosecuting Bosnia's war criminals had been put in place, but 'unhappy and frustrated that so few arrests have been made, notwithstanding the issuing of arrest warrants' [...]

From an interview with Ben Macintyre in The Times, *21 September 1996.*

© *The Times/NI Syndication*

The sentencing of Drazen Erdemovic

A BOSNIAN CROAT was jailed for ten years yesterday for taking part in mass executions after the fall of the Muslim enclave of Srebrenica in July last year.

But in handing down its first sentence, the International War Crimes Tribunal in The Hague highlighted the fact that, while some of the most junior participants in Bosnia's atrocities had been caught and were being tried, their commanders were still at large. Of the 74 people indicted by the tribunal since its inception three years ago, only seven are in its custody. No attempt has been made to arrest the two men believed to be most directly responsible for war crimes: Radovan Karadzic, the former president of the Bosnian Serbs, and Ratko Mladic, his former military commander.

'There should be no slackening in the effort to bring to justice those who carry the greatest responsibility,' said Menzies Campbell, the Liberal Democrats foreign affairs spokesman, last night. The Foreign Office called on the parties to the Dayton peace accords to comply with their obligations under international law and to arrest all those indicted.

The man sentenced yesterday, Drazen Erdemovic, 25, had pleaded guilty to being part of an eight-man execution squad that gunned down up to 1,200 unarmed civilians north of Srebrenica. He was jailed without parole by a three-judge panel which rejected his plea that he had carried out the orders to shoot only because he feared for his life if he did not.

'Your honour, I had to do this,' Erdemovic said at his original hearing. 'If I had refused I would have been killed together with the victims. They told me, "If you're sorry for them, line up with them and we will kill you too".'

Erdemovic fought with the Serbs in the notorious 10th Sabotage Detachment. He said the victims of the massacres after the fall of Srebrenica were ferried the 40 miles to the killing site in buses. His attorney, Jovan Babic, said Erdemovic would appeal against the sentence, which was the maximum sought by the prosecution, although the harshest sentence available to the Tribunal's judges is life imprisonment.

The presiding judge, Claude Jorda of France, said the court had taken into account Erdemovic's remorse and his co-operation with the tribunal, but nonetheless it had to impose a stiff sentence in line with 'the extremely serious nature of the crimes.' The judges considered neither his age – he was 23 at the time – nor his subordinate role as mitigating circumstances in sentencing Erdemovic.

The judgement said the defence had failed to prove the 'extreme necessity' of obeying orders. Erdemovic is expected to serve his jail term in Italy, Norway or Finland. All three have volunteered cells for war criminals convicted by the Tribunal.

Christian Chartier, a spokesman for the Tribunal, said: 'We distance ourselves from the small fry and big fish argument. Think about it: this man admits he killed between 10 and 100 people. In Britain or France he would be the criminal of the century.'

Mr Chartier also repeated the call for all those indicted to be handed over. 'If this does not happen, the consequences might be worse than if the Tribunal had never been set up. It would undermine the authority of international institutions,' he said.

Report by Christopher Lockwood, Diplomatic Editor,
Daily Telegraph, *30 November 1996*

© *Telegraph Group Ltd 1996*

The Srebrenica question

ONCE IT WAS the bombing of Guernica, captured in all its barbarism and terror in Picasso's painting, that epitomised a crime against humanity. This has been superseded by the fall of Srebrenica, in July 1995, when 7,000 Muslim men and boys were executed by General Mladic's Bosnian Serb army and 23,000 elderly men, women and children were transported. This particular exercise in 'ethnic cleansing' needs no artist for its *frisson*: that is provided by the astonishing fact that this rankest of crimes was committed under the noses of the UN's 'Blue Helmets', and in some respects with their complicity. NATO commanders deliberately decided not to save this 'safe haven' by deploying aerial bombardment, although Security Council Resolution 819 charged them with taking 'the necessary measures, including the use of force' to protect it from attack. The fall of Srebrenica exemplifies the dangers of a fashionable human rights policy when it is decreed by states unwilling to lose a single life in its enforcement. The men of Srebrenica were caught in a human rights death trap, sacrificed to the good intentions of cowardly countries.

To state this does not detract from the prime responsibility of the Bosnian Serb commanders, who planned the massacre down to the last truck needed to transport the men – civilians and soldiers – to their mass graves. Their attack on the town was in aggressive defiance of international law. By executing prisoners-of-war, they committed a war crime in breach of the Geneva Convention. By executing civilians, the crime was against humanity as well as the Geneva Convention. As the siege intensified, General Mladic was pictured on the hill overlooking Srebrenica. He turned to his tame Serb TV crews, and emoted: 'Remember that tomorrow is the anniversary of our uprising against the Turks. The time has now come to take revenge on the Muslims.' His deliberate destruction of a community on ethnic and religious grounds counted palpably as genocide. It matters not how Srebrenica is characterised, because it was the worst war crime committed in Europe since the fall of Hitler – and it was committed several years *after* the United Nations had established the Hague Tribunal as a means of deterring exactly such offences.

Did Srebrenica, then, signal the futility of expecting the prospect of punishment to deter those hellbent on committing crimes against humanity?

This is an important question, but it must be remembered that by the time of the massacre – July 1995 – the Hague Tribunal was still very much a paper tiger. The intercept evidence which proves that the idea actually frightened the Bosnian Serb leaders when the Tribunal was first mooted in August 1992 (and this fear seems to have contributed to a lull in the fighting) shows that insouciance quickly returned to their headquarters as the Tribunal stumbled and delayed and failed to get itself off the ground. By July 1995, it had only one prisoner, a footsoldier named Dusko Tadic, whom it had yet to put on trial. Its very impotence may have convinced Mladic that he could breach international criminal law so blatantly and barbarically, and avoid punishment.

In the racially jumbled geography of Bosnia, Srebrenica was a Muslim city surrounded by predominantly Serbian countryside. It might have made sense to surrender it to Serbia with guarantees (that was the Vance–Owen plan) or even – since guarantees were often dishonoured – to transport its entire population to safety, but by 1993 this would have been an unconscionable reward to the Serbs for their brutality. Instead, at the suggestion of the Red Cross, the city was one of those declared a 'safe area' by Security Council Resolution 819, passed in April 1993 – a promise to its people that international law and, 'if necessary', international forces would protect them. To fulfil this promise, the UN correctly assessed the need for 34,000 soldiers on the ground, but none of its members stepped forward to offer troops. Eventually, some 7,406 were mustered for six enclaves (sarcastically referred to as 'safe areas lite'). Srebrenica was vouchsafed a Dutch battalion, the Netherlands being one of the few countries idealistic enough to send troops to patrol the safe areas, and naïve enough not to recognize the absurdity of sending a 'peacekeeping' force to a place where there was no peace to keep.

The Dutch troops' task was doomed from the start, but it is instructive to ask why simple defeat was allowed to become a disgrace. The insufficiency of numbers, of course, meant that they simply cowered when the Serb attack came, and watched apologetically during the subsequent preparations for 'ethnic cleansing' by evacuation and massacre. But their very presence prevented the UN from taking the one action which would have saved the town and honoured the promise of Resolution 819: ordering NATO air strikes to halt the Serb advance. The fear that Dutch soldiers would become hostages and that the battalion might suffer casualties caused the Dutch government (and the UN representative on the ground) to veto the essential air strikes. Unhindered, Mladic's army took the town and put into operation a carefully planned exercise in which males of arms-bearing age were separated from their families and, within sight of the Dutch 'peacekeepers', taken away ostensibly to be 'screened' for complicity in war crimes but in fact to be carted off to fields where they were killed, then buried in mass graves which have now yielded corpses with hands tied behind backs, shot from behind. The scenario is common in ethnic war: what made this massacre so horrific is that the international community stood back and allowed it to happen, as the price for protecting the peacekeepers who were there protecting the victims. The Dutch troops received heroes' welcomes on their return to the Netherlands a week after the massacre, a celebration of the fact that they were 'safe' which appeared grotesque precisely because those to whom they had promised safety had been left behind, in mass graves. The politicians who had sent these soldiers and the generals who had commanded them imposed a rule of silence which served to cover up not only their acquiescence in the genocide, but (for some months) the fact of the genocide itself. As one history of this appalling incident concluded, 'in hindsight, the Dutch failure to speak out after they left the enclave was worse than their conduct during the Serb offensive'.

Srebrenica was allowed to happen because of the Mogadishu factor: states intervening from humanitarian motives refused to risk the lives of their own soldiers to make that intervention effective. The case can be put more bluntly: The Dutch government preferred to dishonour promises and to allow Muslims to die in their thousands rather than to suffer one more Dutch casualty. This was the conclusion of the Netherlands

Institute of War Documentation, whose seven-year investigation published in April 2002 caused the Government to resign in shame (although only one month before its term of office was due to end). It had sought prestige by sending poorly prepared troops on an ill-defined mission, then panicked and ordered them to hand the Muslims under their protection over to the merciless Mladic. The same national funk took hold in Belgium the previous year, when its army was 'peacekeeping' in Rwanda: it failed to take action which might have prevented massacre (eg by closing down the radio stations which were inciting the Hutus to genocidal attacks on the Tutsi and by sending tanks against the killers on the streets). This would have been to 'take sides', stepping down from the fence on which UN peacekeeping missions can get impaled. Like the Dutch battalion in Srebrenica, the Belgians watched the massacre, and then withdrew as soon as they began to suffer casualties.

Both the Dutch and the Belgians were morally guilty for making a fashionable gesture of sending soldiers under the impossible condition that they should not be required to fight. But the problem was more fundamental: it stemmed from the diplomatic mindset that assumed peace could be secured without justice. If the UN is to protect a city or a people, it must have a clear idea of who it is protecting them from, and treat these aggressors as the enemy. Soldiers must be sent to fight, and politicians at home must be prepared for soldiers to die, in the cause of protecting the innocent (or at least the people promised protection) from attack. There is little doubt that General Mladic, a cunning calculator of odds, would have retreated under aerial bombardment and would not (at least for long) have provoked the international community by holding Blue Helmets hostage. But he knew his enemy's weaknesses: a Dutch public desperately opposed to sacrifice and a United Nations which wanted and needed him to talk about peace. The UN diplomat responsible, along with the Dutch defence minister, for vetoing air strikes was UN Special Representative for Bosnia, Yasushi Akashi: he defended his conduct on the grounds that 'the man you bomb today is the same man whose co-operation you may require tomorrow for the passage of a humanitarian convoy'. This is a very good reason for leaving humanitarian assistance to the Red Cross while the UN decides which men are in the wrong and have to be bombed. The writer Michael Ignatieff confronted the UN Secretary General as Srebrenica was falling: 'Why,' he asked, 'insist on being neutral in the face of a clear aggressor and a clear victim, when that neutrality daily undermines the UN's moral credit?' Boutros Boutros-Ghali could only reply: 'We are not able to intervene on one side. The mandate does not allow it.' Until mandates to keep the peace are interpreted by the UN as mandates to fight aggressor factions, if this is the only way the peace can be kept and genocide prevented, there will be many more Srebrenicas, and (much worse) more Rwandas. Or else there will be more unilateral humanitarian enforcement action, such as NATO's intervention in Serbia over Kosovo.

Five years on, the cries from the mass graves still being excavated around Srebrenica are more haunting than ever, as war crimes prosecutors gather further evidence to incriminate the Serb commanders and to shame the Dutch army and the UN. The most moving scenes were recorded on private camcorders, the grainy images of Muslim men and boys huddled in fields, surrounded by soldiers who wait impatiently to shoot them come nightfall. The most incriminating footage comes from Serbian television: it shows Mladic toying with the lives of his terrified hostages, and blowing lies and cigarette smoke into the face of the pathetic Dutch commander, Colonel Karremans. This soldier is seen disgracing his country and his calling by accepting drink and gifts from Mladic – a reward for following Dutch government orders and handing over thousands of Muslims who had sought refuge in their UN compound. This was the moral nadir reached by UN peacekeeping, rivalling the behaviour of the Belgian and Ghanaian 'peacekeepers' in Rwanda who handed over the Tutsis they were meant to be guarding to Interhamwe hit squads. It was this complicity in the slaughter which provoked a bleak joke about UN peacekeeping: 'If the UN had been around in 1939, we would all be speaking German.'

As the first half-century of the Universal Declaration drew to a close, the failure to make its provisions stick in most countries of the world seemed both abject and irremediable. Talk of a 'new world order' after the Cold War, the Gulf War and the Vienna Conference was just talk, by voices shrill if challenging universality or tremulous if contemplating another Mogadishu. The diplomats had drafted all the treaties necessary to define human rights, and the politicians had signed them because they would have no practical or legal effect, since violators would not be called to account other than through a polite and powerless UN committee system. What they overlooked was the gathering strength of the human rights movement and its NGO networks, galvanised by interrelated victories in the struggle for global justice at the century's close: Pinochet and Lockerbie and the ICC Treaty, Kosovo and East Timor and the work of the Hague Tribunal.

> *Geoffrey Robertson, 'The Srebrenica Question', from* Crimes against Humanity *(2nd edition, Penguin, 2002)*
>
> © *Geoffrey Robertson 2002: reprinted with permission of Penguin Books Ltd*

Bosnian Serb panel links 17,000 to roles in Srebrenica massacre

A BOSNIAN SERB COMMISSION said Tuesday that it had identified more than 17,000 people who had taken part directly and indirectly in the Srebrenica massacre in 1995, the worst slaughter of civilians in Europe since World War II.

The commission, which has been compiling the report since 2003, said the names would not be released publicly. Instead, they will be turned over to the state prosecutor's office for review and possible charges.

The panel said it had submitted the report to the office of the top international official in Bosnia, Paddy Ashdown, who requested it as part of efforts to bring to justice those responsible for the massacre of up to 8,000 Muslim men and boys toward the end of Bosnia's civil war.

The panel said 19,473 members of various Bosnian Serb armed forces and civilians had taken part in the massacre, and of those, 17,074 had been identified by name. About 24,000 Bosnian Serb troops converged on Srebrenica, a United Nations-designated haven for Bosnian Muslims seeking refuge from the Serbs.

The commission did not establish which participants were directly involved in the killing because its mandate 'was not to establish the level of responsibility in the killings,' said Smail Cekic, a panel member.

The state prosecutor's office said authorities would treat as a 'special priority' anyone on the list who holds public office or works in law enforcement or the judiciary.

The bloodshed began on 11 July 1995, when Serbian forces stormed past the eastern enclave's hopelessly outnumbered and outgunned Dutch peacekeepers and rounded up its inhabitants. At a car battery factory on the edge of town, men and boys were separated from women and girls and then were hauled away, forced to strip, and shot one by one.

A United Nations war crimes tribunal judge described the killing as 'scenes from hell written on the darkest pages of human history'.

Mr Ashdown's office issued a statement on Tuesday acknowledging that the Bosnian Serb government had finally 'taken its obligations seriously' in providing details about the massacre.

About 260,000 people were killed and 1.8 million driven from their homes during the 1992–5 civil war, which pitted Bosnia's Muslims, Catholic Croats and Orthodox Serbs against one another.

MORE SREBRENICA REMAINS FOUND IN TUZLA

Forensic experts have recovered the remains of 213 more victims of the Srebrenica massacre in 1995, an investigator said Tuesday.

The mass grave in the northeastern Bosnia village of Liplje has so far been found to contain '212 incomplete and one complete body', said Murat Hurtic, the head of the forensic team.

The bodies found Tuesday were originally buried elsewhere but later dug up by bulldozer and moved to Liplje to cover up the massacre, Mr Hurtic said. About 1,000 victims were found in four other mass graves previously discovered in Liplje, he said.

After the remains are found, DNA is extracted from the bones of victims and matched with DNA from living relatives. Thousands of victims from the 1992–5 Bosnian war have been identified this way, Hurtic said.

United Nations and local forensics experts in Bosnia have exhumed 16,500 bodies from more than 300 mass graves. Thousands of people remain missing and are presumed dead.

Associated Press report
Published in the New York Times, *5 October 2005*

© *Associated Press 2005*

THE COLOUR OF JUSTICE

BASED ON THE TRANSCRIPTS OF
THE STEPHEN LAWRENCE INQUIRY

Editor's Note

THE LAWRENCE INQUIRY consisted of 69 days of public hearings. The evidence is still sinking in and continues to be debated in police circles, among lawyers, in Britain's black community, and elsewhere. Sir William Macpherson and his inquiry team published their final report in February 1999, nearly six years after Stephen Lawrence's death. Its conclusions will provoke further controversy. It may be years before its full impact can be appreciated.

The transcripts of the inquiry amount to more than eleven thousand pages, which I have distilled into about a hundred – less than one per cent. Inevitably I have had to make brutal choices about which witnesses and which exchanges to include. It has not been easy. I have not included the evidence of Detective Superintendent Ian Crampton who was in charge of the case for the first few days and took the vital decision to delay arresting five suspects. 'One of the things I have to say with hindsight,' he told the inquiry, 'is that knowing what I now know I would have arrested earlier.' He later conceded that the police had 'reasonable grounds' to arrest two days after Stephen's murder.

I have not included the evidence of Detective Superintendent Brian Weeden, who took over from Crampton. He, too, failed to arrest, suggesting at one point that he did not have the authority. Michael Mansfield QC, the Lawrence family's counsel, asked Weeden, 'Do you not find it rather disturbing that it has taken all this time for you to recognise a basic tenet of criminal law?', to which Weeden replied, 'I think it is regrettable.'

I have not included the evidence of Sir Paul Condon, the Metropolitan Police Commissioner, who apologised to Doreen and Neville Lawrence but denied that racism played a role in the investigation into Stephen's murder. He urged the inquiry not to label his force as 'institutionally racist'.

Also not included is the evidence of Imran Khan, the Lawrence family's solicitor, who did so much to bring Stephen's murder, and the police handling of the case, to public attention. Also this play does not cover the inquiry's later evidence heard outside London.

I set out to include the most telling exchanges for a theatre audience, many of whom did not hit the headlines at the time but which reflect the interlocking threads which ran throughout the inquiry – police incompetence, conscious or unconscious racism and stereotyping, and the hint of corruption in the background. And I have included exchanges which reflect the personal tensions between the police and the Lawrence family – for example, Doreen's anger when she saw Detective Chief Superintendent William Ilsley, who supervised the investigation, 'fold up' as he put it, 'screw up' as she said, a piece of paper she handed him containing the names of suspects.

Above all, I wanted to select evidence of the inquiry which presented as fair, balanced and rounded a picture as possible. It was not an easy task. But if it contributes to a greater understanding of all the issues involved, it was, I hope, worthwhile and valuable.

The Colour of Justice is the fourth of what have come to be known as The Tribunal Plays performed at the Tricycle Theatre in London. The first, in 1994, was *Half the Picture*, a dramatisation of the Scott 'arms to Iraq' inquiry, which was followed by *Nuremberg* and *Srebrenica*.

Richard Norton-Taylor
London 1999

Chronology

1993

Thursday 22 April 10:30pm
Stephen Lawrence stabbed to death.

Friday 23 April
A letter giving names of the suspects left in a phone box. Statements made to the police by various people about the attacks. 'Grant', a young man who had previously provided information, goes to the police station and accuses the Acourts of the murder.

Sunday 25 April
Neville and Doreen Lawrence approach Imran Khan to act as their solicitor.

Monday 26 April
Police surveillance of the suspects' homes begins.

Tuesday 27 April
Detective Sergeant Davidson informed that an eyewitness, 'K', had been on a bus which passed the site of the murder.

Friday 30 April
More evidence obtained that the Acourts had been near the site of the murder on the evening of 22 April.

Tuesday 4 May
Press conference held. Neville Lawrence states, 'Nothing has been done. There have been no arrests and the police won't tell us what is happening.'

Thursday 6 May
The Lawrences meet Nelson Mandela.

Friday 7 May
The Acourts and Dobson arrested and made to appear in an identity parade.

Saturday 8 May
An anti-racist march held in protest at the British National Party (BNP) bookshop in Welling.

Monday 10 May
Luke Knight arrested.

Thursday 13 May
Duwayne Brooks identifies Neil Acourt in an identity parade.

Wednesday 19 May
Interview of alleged eyewitness, 'K'.

Thursday 3 June
Duwayne Brooks identifies Luke Knight in a further identity parade.

June
After the date for the criminal proceedings is set, Stephen Lawrence's body is released and buried in Jamaica.

July
The Crown Prosecution Service (CPS) drops the prosecution. The identification evidence from Duwayne Brooks is not considered good enough to secure the conviction of Neil Acourt and Luke Knight: 'After careful consideration of the available evidence in this case, we have decided there is insufficient evidence to provide a realistic conviction.' The five suspects are discharged.

October
Duwayne arrested and charged with criminal damage and violent disorder during the protest rally at Welling held on 15 May. Detective Chief Superintendent Barker brought in to review the police investigation. The Barker Report finds that the investigation had progressed satisfactorily and that all lines of inquiry had been correctly pursued. Later, in the inquiry, he admits that he intentionally covered up any criticism of Detective Superintendent Weeden, the Senior Investigating Officer. Later in the year the inquest opens, with Michael Mansfield QC appearing for the family. Mansfield asks for an indefinite adjournment.

1994
The renewed police investigation gives evidence to the CPS.

April
The CPS refuses to prosecute. 'Despite the police's painstaking and thorough investigation, we concluded that on the basis of

the information available there is insufficient evidence to take action against any individual.'

May
Detective Superintendent Weeden, who was in charge of the investigation, meets the Lawrences for the first time. At this time the family starts to consider taking out a private prosecution, an action which is exceptionally rare. After meeting Sir Paul Condon, the Commissioner of the Metropolitan Police, and informing him that they would be pursuing the private prosecution, a second police investigation is set up, led by Detective Superintendent Mellish.

December
Duwayne appears in court charged with criminal damage and violent disorder, arising from his participation in the Welling march. According to Duwayne Brooks' lawyer's final submission to the inquiry, 'The trial judge made it clear that, because of Duwayne Brooks' trauma, any conviction would result in an absolute discharge. He invited the CPS to offer no evidence. The CPS, exceptionally, declined and persisted with the prosecution. The judge stayed the prosecution as an abuse of the process of court.'

1995
April
The private prosecution starts. Neil Acourt, Luke Knight and David Norris are arrested. Jamie Acourt is already in custody.

August
First stage of the prosecution heard at Belmarsh magistrates' court in Woolwich.

September
Neil Acourt and Luke Knight sent for trial at the Old Bailey. Doreen Lawrence makes a statement outside the court: 'No family should ever have to experience the last two years of our lives. This is the worst kind of fame. We have been brought into the public spotlight, not because of our acts but by the failure of others who were under a public duty to act. The decision of the court today stands as the first clear indictment of that failure.'

1996
April

The private prosecution heard in the the Hight Court against three of the accused. Cases against Jamie Acourt and David Norris already dropped at the committal proceedings, on the basis of poor identification evidence. The case against the other three fails when the judge rules that Duwayne Brooks' identification evidence cannot be put to the jury, because the statement from Detective Sergeant Crowley calls it into question. Crowley had accompanied Duwayne to one of the identity parades.

1997
February

The inquest is resumed, during which the five suspects refuse to answer any questions. The evidence from the police confirms the view of the Lawrences that the investigation into Stephen's murder was seriously flawed. The jury return the verdict of an unlawlful killing 'in an unprovoked racist attach by five white youths'. The Lawrences lodge a formal complaint about the behaviour of the officers on the night of the murder and subsequently, Herman Ouseley, the chair of the Commission for Racial Equality, supported by 19 Labour MPs, calls for a public inquiry.

14 February 1997, *Guardian*

A coroner's jury went beyond the bounds of their instructions to issue an extraordinary condemnation of the killers of Stephen Lawrence, the teenage victim of a racist murder. After just 30 minutes of deliberation, the jury returned a verdict of unlawful killing 'in a completely unprovoked racist attack by five white youths'.

The condemnatory words exemplified the strength of feeling the case has provoked during the Lawrence family's four-year campaign for justice. Juries are required only to return a verdict as to whether a death was unlawful, accidental or 'open'.

Doreen Lawrence, in a statement read by her sister, condemned the police handling of the initial investigation. 'The wall of silence was not only in the surrounding area where my son was killed but with police officers investigating the crime,' she said.

Mrs Lawrence described parts of the inquest as a 'circus' after watching five white youths – Neil and Jamie Acourt, David Norris, Gary Dobson and Luke Knight – all refuse to answer questions, claiming a common-law right of privelege against self-incrimination. Earlier, clearly angry and close to tears, she told the reopened inquest at Southwark coroner's court that the justice system was racist.

The family's lawyer, Imran Khan, said that the inquest confirmed to the family for the first time that there were a number of lost opportunities on the night that Stephen died as far as the police were concerned. 'The coroner has indicated that had those lost opportunities been taken up by the police there might have been a difference in what has happened over the last four years. There might have been a prosecution by the CPS.'

He said that a formal complaint would be lodged with the Police Complaints Authority against officers who were in charge of the investigations. The Metropolitan Police yesterday pledged their willingness to follow up further lines of inquiry.

...The chairman of the Commission for Racial Equality, Herman Ouseley, said important questions remained unanswered after the inquest verdict. He called for an independent inquiry to investigate 'what went wrong in the investigation of this case'.

(*Extracts written by Duncan Campbell and Alison Daniels.*)

February
Immediately after the inquest verdict, the Lawrences meet with Jack Straw, the shadow Home Secretary.

July
Now Home Secretary, Jack Straw announces the calling of a judicial public inquiry to be chaired by Sir William Macpherson. It is scheduled to start after a Police Complaints Authority report, undertaken by the Kent Constabulary, is completed.

December
The Kent Report, as it has become known, goes to the Home Secretary. It supports the Lawrence family's claim that the police investigation was flawed, stating that there were 'significant weaknesses, omissions, and lost opportunities in the conduct of the case'.

Jane Shallice, London 1999

Where Stephen Lawrence was killed

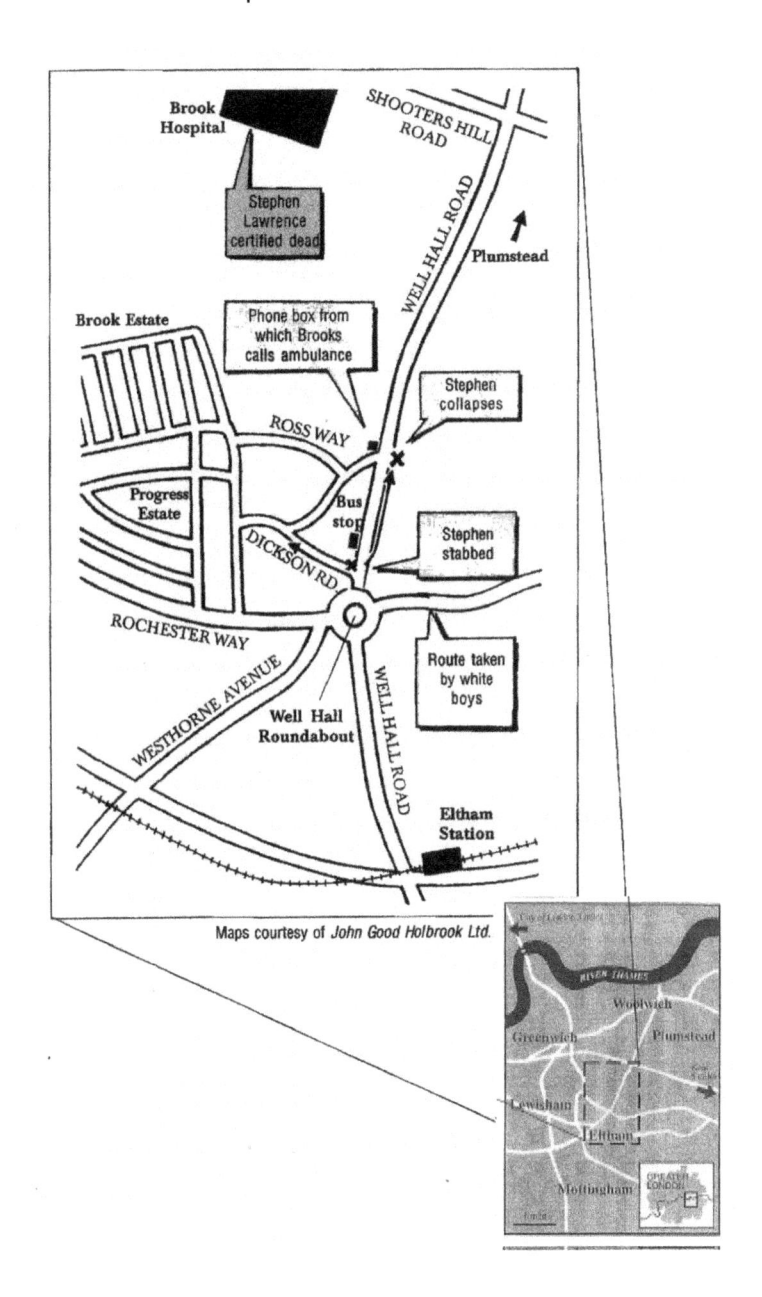

The Colour of Justice was first performed at the Tricycle Theatre, London, on 6 January 1999, with the following cast:

SIR WILLIAM MACPHERSON OF CLUNY *Chairman to the inquiry*, Michael Culver

The Lawyers

EDMUND LAWSON QC *Counsel to the inquiry*, James Woolley

ANESTA WEEKES *led by Mr Lawson*, Jenny Jules

MICHAEL MANSFIELD QC *Counsel for the Lawrence family*, Jeremy Clyde

STEPHEN KAMLISH *led by Mr Mansfield*, Joseph Alessi

MARTIN SOORJOO *led by Mr Mansfield*, Ravi Aujla

MARGO BOYE-ANAWOMA *led by Mr Mansfield*, Jenny Jules

IAN MACDONALD QC *Counsel for Duwayne Brooks*, Hugh Simon

RAJIV MENON *led by Mr Macdonald*, Alex Caan

JEREMY GOMPERTZ QC *Counsel for the Commissioner of the Metropolitan Police*, Michael Stroud

SONIA WOODLEY QC *Counsel for three Superintendents*, Deborah Wilding

MICHAEL EGAN *Counsel for officers of federated rank*, Roderic Culver

The Witnesses

POLICE CONSTABLE BETHEL, Hilary Maclean

CONOR TAAFFE, Tim Woodward

POLICE CONSTABLE GLEASON, Roderic Culver

POLICE SERGEANT CLEMENT, Ken Drury

HELEN ELIZABETH AVERY, Michelle Morris

INSPECTOR GROVES, Thomas Wheatley

MR JOHN DAVIDSON *formerly Detective Sergeant*, William Hoyland

DETECTIVE CONSTABLE HOLDEN, Jan Chappell

DETECTIVE INSPECTOR BULLOCK, Ken Drury

Mr William Ilsley *formerly Detective Chief Superintendent*, Mark Penfold

William James Mellish *formerly Detective Superintendent*, Michael Attwell

Ian Johnston *Assistant Commissioner Metropolitan Police*, Tim Woodward

Jamie Acourt, Christopher Fox

Howard Youngerwood *Crown Prosecutioner*, Thomas Wheatley

Mr Neville Lawrence, Tyrone De Rizzio

Mrs Doreen Lawrence, Yvonne Pascal

Duwayne Brooks, Leon Stewart

Grace Vaughan *Computer operator*, Nalina Tobierre

Stephen Wells *Secretary to the inquiry*, Martin Newcombe

Court stenographer and others played by the company.

Director, Nicolas Kent, with Susan Fletcher-Jones

Designer, Bunny Christie

Costumes, Heather Leat

Lighting, Chris Davey

Production Manager, Shaz McGhee

The play transferred to the Victoria Palace in the West End on 3 March 1999, and for that production the part of Howard Youngerwood was deleted, and Stephen Kamlish was played by Paul Mari, Conor Taaffe by Michael Cochrane and Ian Johnston by Thomas Wheatley.

OPENING STATEMENTS BY MACPHERSON OF CLUNY, EDMUND LAWSON QC, MICHAEL MANSFIELD QC AND JEREMY GOMPERTZ QC

MACPHERSON: The procedure of the hearings will be reasonably informal: nobody need stand to ask questions unless they wish to do so. And of course people may come and go exactly as they please.

Inevitably this room looks rather like a court, but the stricter rules of procedure and evidence do not apply to us in our search for the truth.

Our hope is that, at the end of the day, we will establish what happened and what may have gone wrong over these last years in connection with the investigation and management of this case.

To Mr and Mrs Lawrence, these years must have been dreadful. We hope sincerely that while nothing can alleviate the pain and loss which they have suffered, they may accept that all of us have done our best to establish what was done so that the future may not see repetition of any errors which may be uncovered during our hearings.

We will now turn to Mr Edmund Lawson, Queen's Counsel.

LAWSON: Stephen Lawrence was brutally murdered. The attack upon him was obviously cowardly, was unprovoked and was demonstrably racist. He was attacked in the street. He was black. His attackers were white.

No-one has been convicted for his murder. It might be appropriate just to remind the Inquiry and to inform those who listen of this description of him by someone who knew him at the Cambridge Harriers Athletic Club of which he was an active and successful member. Quite coincidently the someone was a policeman who knew him at the club because his son was involved. "During the period I knew Stephen," he said, "I never saw him display any form of aggression and would describe his temperament as the same as his father – quiet and unassuming, exemplary character." He was a young man who had never come into contact with, or the notice of, the police.

It appears that in a number of very material respects the police conduct of the investigation went badly wrong, not least in the decision to delay arrests of the principle suspects who were identified from various sources immediately after the murder. We will be inviting you to consider, and producing evidence to assist you to answer the question: were any of the errors due to simple, or perhaps more accurately, gross incompetence, or were they as some vociferously asserted – and as police officers have vigorously denied – attributable to or contributed to directly or indirectly by racism?

Nobody, police or civilian, has any proper basis for declining to assist this inquiry in its quest for the truth and that includes those who I will be referring to as the five suspects: Neil and Jamie Acourt, Norris, Dobson and Knight.

Neither Stephen Lawrence nor Duwayne Brooks did anything to provoke an argument, let alone a fight. They moved away a little from the bus stop looking to see if there was a bus coming when a group of some five or six white youths approached them. Duwayne Brooks recounted that he heard at least one of them make a reference to "nigger". He shouted to his friend to run, but Stephen could not because he was surrounded by thugs, attacked by one or more of them and knocked to the ground.

The first issue to be considered relates to first aid. It appears from the evidence that no police officer sought to administer first aid.

It seems, as a matter of tragic fact, that Stephen's injuries were so severe that first aid would not, in any event, have helped him. But questions do arise – whether first aid was denied by the police because "they did not want to dirty their hands with a black man's blood", as Mrs Lawrence asked after the inquest into her son's death. A witness on the night told her that Jamie and Neil Acourt were walking around the corner. Apparently one of the Acourt brothers carries a machete down his right hand trouser leg.

That information came to the police on the 24th of April. Apparently no action was taken until a week later.

On the 13th of May, Mr Brooks did identify Neil Acourt. On the 3rd of June, he identified Knight on another parade. The identifications led to each of those two men being charged with the murder of Stephen Lawrence. Unfortunately, a Sergeant Crowley asserts that at the time of the parade when Knight was identified, Mr Brooks made some comments to him suggesting that he had received information before the parade which may have enabled him to make the identification or prompted him as to who to identify.

Mr Brooks disputed Crowley's account. The importance of it is obvious. Mr Brooks' identification of those suspects was vital. The private prosecution that followed much later was forced, in effect, to be abandoned once Mr Brooks' evidence was excluded by the judge.

On the evening of the 23rd of April, there first came on the scene a man who has been given the name "Grant".

He accused the Acourts and Norris of Stephen Lawrence's murder.

The message stated: "The Acourt brothers call themselves the Krays. In fact, you can only join the gang if you stab someone."

Some of the suspects were under surveillance from the 26th of April. What was the object of this surveillance operation? There was a particularly crass failure. A photographer was put in place to keep surveillance on the Acourts. Before he got his camera set up, he saw somebody leaving their house with what appeared to be clothing in a bin bag, get into a car and clear off. He made no report at the time of either of these events.

This was a racist murder, there is no doubt about that. It was recognised as such by the police. I am bound to say that it is repellant that anybody who commits a murder should get away with it and anyone who does so and murders for racist motives and should escape is doubly repellant.

MANSFIELD: The magnitude of the failure in this case, we say, cannot be explained by mere incompetence or a lack of direction by senior officers or a lack of execution and application by junior officers, nor by woeful under-resourcing. So much was missed by so many that deeper causes and forces must be considered.

We suggest these forces relate to two main propositions. The first is that the victim was black and racism, both conscious and unconscious, permeated the investigation. Secondly, the fact that the perpetrators were white and were expecting some form of protection.

The fact that the same teenagers are equally capable of killing or maiming anyone in their way does not preclude them from being racist; racists rarely concentrate their venom on the black population or the Jewish population or whoever happens to be the ethnic group which they regard as barely worth living. When Doreen Lawrence first left home after this appalling crime, merely to go shopping locally, in a car park she was confronted by a woman who indicated that her son would not have been killed if he had not been there.

It went on, this racist force. Their tyres have been slashed, their home has been watched by white youths and barely two weeks ago, the memorial plaque was desecrated, painted, daubed, and smashed with a hammer. These are activities that the Jewish population are only too familiar with. It was on the spot where Stephen died.

GOMPERTZ: Sir, it is a matter of the greatest regret to the Commissioner and to the Metropolitan Police Service that no one has been successfully prosecuted for the callous murder of Stephen Lawrence.

With hindsight, the Metropolitan Police Service acknowledges that it should have done better. The Metropolitan Police are determined to learn every possible lesson from any constructive criticism which emerges from this inquiry.

Although it is right and proper that their actions and attitudes should be closely scrutinised, the broad allegations of racism are unfair to all of those officers to whom many people owe a great debt of gratitude. Stephen's murder was a callous, evil, act committed by callous, evil, people. It is they and they alone who should bear the guilt for ending such a promising and optimistic young life.

FROM THE EVIDENCE OF POLICE CONSTABLE BETHEL, 25 MARCH 1998

LAWSON: I propose to call the first witnesses who attended the scene. The first two on-duty officers were Mr Gleason and Miss Bethel. I am going to call Bethel first because she has a pressing engagement.

MACPHERSON: Yes.

LAWSON: Can I ask her to come in, come to the witness box and perhaps be sworn.

BETHEL: I do solemnly, sincerely and truly declare and affirm that the evidence I shall give shall be the truth, the whole truth and nothing but the truth.

MACPHERSON: Do be seated please. I do not think there is any need for any witness to talk, so to speak, at the microphone. They are very sensitive.

LAWSON: Your name, I think, is Linda Jane Bethel, is it not?

BETHEL: That's correct, sir.

LAWSON: Is it Miss or Mrs?

BETHEL: Mrs.

LAWSON: The first of the identified issues, which is principally concerned with the first aid given or not given at the scene. By way of background, it might, I think, be helpful if I were to just briefly divert to the chronology. You do not have this in front of you – Mrs Bethel just bear with me if you will – but, as we can see, this refers to some events that occurred during the evening of Thursday, the 22nd of April 1993 when Stephen Lawrence and Duwayne Brooks were out together. It deals at the bottom of the second page in very brief terms with the incident and the attack upon Stephen Lawrence is timed at around 10.40. A 999 call; you can see the timing of it: 22.44 on that evening. The location is given, the number of the phone box that was used.

And the message is: "Assaulted with an iron bar" and the name of Mr Brooks is given.

That night, Thursday, the 22nd of April, you were on duty with Constable Gleason, is that right?

BETHEL: That's correct.

LAWSON: When you got the call, the information you were given – there had been a suspected use of an iron bar, is that right?

BETHEL: That's correct.

LAWSON: There were no difficulties as far as you were concerned in seeing the blood coming from his body?

BETHEL: No, not at all.

LAWSON: When you saw the large amount of blood, you immediately called your control room asking them to hurry up the ambulance?

BETHEL: Yes, that's correct.

LAWSON: Did you have a first-aid kit in your police car?

BETHEL: To the best of my knowledge, yes.

LAWSON: Was it ever taken out of the car that night?

BETHEL: No.

LAWSON: Do you know the reason for that?

BETHEL: It wasn't deemed that we could actually use the first aid kit to any great benefit.

LAWSON: What would your training indicate to you should be done if you came across somebody who has apparently suffered a wound from which he is losing a lot of blood?

BETHEL: We were told that Stephen had a head wound. He was in the recovery position when we arrived. There was no obvious wound to see where the blood was coming from. We believed an ambulance would be there within minutes.

LAWSON: You have indicated that your attention was drawn to Duwayne Brooks, as you now know him to be?

BETHEL: Yes, that is correct.

LAWSON: You said he was walking around the scene very distressed?

BETHEL: Yes.

LAWSON: You asked what happened, who had done this? And he said: "A group of six white men."

BETHEL: Yes.

LAWSON: Then afterwards saying: "Where is the fucking ambulance? I didn't call the police"?

BETHEL: That's right.

LAWSON: You told him the ambulance was coming. You said you tried to get him to explain what happened but he was very excitable and upset and all he could tell you was that he had told his friend Stephen to run with him away from the youths.

BETHEL: That's correct.

LAWSON: You sent other officers who arrived off to search for the suspects; is that correct?

BETHEL: Yes, that's correct.

LAWSON: You did say: "I did try to find a pulse." How did you seek to check his pulse?

BETHEL: I believe I would have put my fingers to his neck.

LAWSON: Can you explain why you say, "I believe"?

BETHEL: The main reason being I think having dealt with Duwayne for quite a while beforehand it was obviously quite a hyped-up situation and in retrospect it is quite likely I felt my own pulse.

LAWSON: Mr Taaffe says: "At no point when I was at the scene do I recall anybody establishing that Stephen's injuries were stab wounds." You would not disagree with that?

BETHEL: No, no.

LAWSON: Still you didn't know it was stabbing?

BETHEL: No.

LAWSON: The suggestion that has been made publicly is that perhaps an explanation for the lack of first-aid attention was "police officers not wishing to dirty their hands with a black man's blood". Tell us your feelings about that.

BETHEL: I don't see myself as a racist. I don't think I act in a racist manner. I don't believe I am racist.

LAWSON: That is all I want to ask you. Thank you very much.

KAMLISH: I am going to deal with this witness. Can I do it sitting down? I am Stephen Kamlish. I am acting for the Lawrence family. Can I ask you about your first aid training? You do accept, do you not, that one of the most important matters for a person with a first-aid qualification attending a bleeding person is to try and staunch the blood?

BETHEL: If we hadn't been told it was a head injury, then perhaps I would have started searching through his clothing. It was dark.
I believed the best thing to do for Stephen was to leave him where he was.

KAMLISH: Why is the fact that it was dark relevant?

BETHEL: Because I couldn't see where any blood was coming from; it wasn't obvious.

KAMLISH: You had a torch in your car?

BETHEL: Yes.

KAMLISH: That was parked a few feet away?

BETHEL: Yes.

KAMLISH: Did you go and get the torch?

BETHEL: No.

KAMLISH: Did you ask somebody else to get the torch?

BETHEL: No.

KAMLISH: Why not?

BETHEL: I don't know.

KAMLISH: Nobody mentioned the word "stabbing" at the scene?

BETHEL: No.

KAMLISH: Were you concerned that you had not in fact looked for the injury?

BETHEL: Obviously, because of the amount of upset it has caused and the amount of attention there has been on it, yes. I do now regret that I didn't look at the injury.

KAMLISH: It is fair to say, is it not, that no one while you were there tried to identify the wound?

BETHEL: Not that I saw.

KAMLISH: No police officer?

BETHEL: Not that I saw, no.

KAMLISH: Is it fair to say that once you saw the fact that Stephen's chest was drenched in blood, coupled with his unconsciousness and the fact you believed he had a head injury, you must have by then felt that his injury was life-threatening?

BETHEL: I appreciated it was much more serious than I anticipated. I hadn't assumed it was life threatening. I hadn't assumed he was going to die.

KAMLISH: You went back to the hospital the next day to speak to the sister who cared for him?

BETHEL: It was because we were upset and we wanted to talk about it with somebody who obviously knew exactly what had happened.

KAMLISH: One of the reasons you went back was wondering whether you could have done more?

BETHEL: Mmm.

KAMLISH: Yes?

BETHEL: Yes. And she said no.

KAMLISH: In view of the questions I have asked you and the answers you have given about your failure to touch Stephen, can I just ask you some questions on another connected topic. Do you have any experience of equal opportunities or race-awareness training?

BETHEL: I believe we had training at Hendon.

KAMLISH: What ways do you consider in this country racism manifests itself?

BETHEL: Obviously in all sorts of ways…

MACPHERSON: I do not think that as broad a question as that is probably appropriate, Mr Kamlish.

KAMLISH: Perhaps these questions will relate to other officers. Perhaps I will ask a more focused question, dealing with your personal experience. Have you ever been present when someone has suffered racism in whatever form?

BETHEL: No.

KAMLISH: Never?

BETHEL: No.

KAMLISH: Never heard a racist comment in the Metropolitan Police by any police officer?

BETHEL: I'm aware that comments are made and, yes, they are heard, but I can't specifically recall any. I am not saying it doesn't exist.

KAMLISH: Thank you.

GOMPERTZ: Would you have behaved in exactly the same way if the victim had been white?

BETHEL: Yes.

GOMPERTZ: Can I ask you, please, to look at your interview? Perhaps it can be put on the screen. I hope we will find it at PCA (Police Complaints Authority) 48, pages 239 and 240. Can you look, please, at the next page, because you are asked there, just towards the bottom of the part that is on the screen now: "What is your stance on racism?" You answer: "It is despicable. There is absolutely no need for it whatsoever. I don't understand why it exists and why people have a problem with other people." Does that accurately summarise your feeling about racism?

BETHEL: Yes.

GOMPERTZ: Thank you very much.

MACDONALD: Mrs Bethel, can I say that I represent Duwayne Brooks. When you arrived, there is absolutely no dispute about this, it must have been quite clear to you that Duwayne Brooks was clearly very distressed?

BETHEL: Oh yes.

MACDONALD: Duwayne Brooks told you that the incident had started off when one of the white boys had said words to the effect: "What, what, nigger?"

BETHEL: I don't doubt he said that. I can't remember. I'm sure he did.

MACDONALD: Do you remember him saying something like this: "I fucking told you where they went. Are you deaf? Why don't you go and look for them?"

BETHEL: I certainly don't remember it, but there were an awful lot of aggressive swearing comments made. He could well have said that.

MACDONALD: Or something like it. It was in that context, I suggest, that he asked you if you could not take his friend in the police car to the hospital?

BETHEL: Again, I don't remember that being asked. It might well have been, I don't know.

MACDONALD: Is it within your police experience that you stopped someone like Duwayne in the street, or driving a car, or whatever it is, and when you stop them they get mad at you, they swear at you, they call you names and maybe end up assaulting you?

BETHEL: It is my experience with some people that you can end up getting that reaction.

MACDONALD: Is that something from your police experience that you would find when you are dealing with young black men?

BETHEL: No, I am saying generally.

MACDONALD: It is not something, is it, you are likely to experience with little old ladies?

BETHEL: No, but generally speaking it can happen. I mean, I have had a little old lady try and bite me.

MACDONALD: Your reaction to seeing Duwayne in the state that you have described is that you understand now that he was traumatised by the event that had taken place?

BETHEL: At the time I was a police officer there with him and he was, you know… He hated my guts.

FROM THE EVIDENCE OF CONOR ANDREW TAAFFE, 26 MARCH 1998

MACPHERSON: Thank you very much for coming. Mr Taaffe, you have been involved in giving evidence so much that I understand that your personal life has been disrupted.

LAWSON: Your name is Conor Andrew Taafe, is it not?

TAAFFE: That's right, yes.

LAWSON: You and your wife had gone to a prayer meeting at the local Catholic church?

TAAFFE: Correct.

LAWSON: You left about 10.35 and started to walk down towards the Well Hall roundabout. Is that right?

TAAFFE: That's correct, yes. Mmm.

LAWSON: Then there came to your notice a couple of young black boys who were jogging along?

TAAFFE: Yes.

LAWSON: As you thought at first, jogging?

TAAFFE: Yes, yes.

LAWSON: Of course, you know now they were not jogging, or simply jogging. Now you appreciate that one of them, the one in front, was Duwayne Brooks?

TAAFFE: Yes.

LAWSON: And the one behind was Stephen Lawrence?

TAAFFE: Mmm. When I say jogging, I didn't so much mean that I thought they were out jogging for exercise, just to sort of describe the pace. They seemed to be running. I did sense immediately something wrong, something dangerous, something suspicious straight away. It just – you just knew, you know.

LAWSON: You saw Stephen, to use your words, "crash onto the pavement", is that right?

TAAFFE: Mmm.

LAWSON: In your statement, you describe noticing at first Duwayne Brooks who was standing in the middle of the road?

TAAFFE: Yes.

LAWSON: And he appeared to be trying to flag down passing cars?

TAAFFE: He was, yes.

LAWSON: Once you had appreciated, and very quickly you did, as your wife had said, that this was something serious, you went straight over towards where Stephen had fallen, did you not?

TAAFFE: Yes, yes.

LAWSON: You went and bent down by Stephen; is that right?

TAAFFE: That's right, yes. He was definitely still alive at that stage.

LAWSON: You carried on holding Stephen's head with your hand on his back?

TAAFFE: Mmm.

LAWSON: And I think you were praying over him?

TAAFFE: Yes.

LAWSON: Then the first police car arrived?

TAAFFE: Mmm, yeah.

LAWSON: That as we know had a woman and a male police officer?

TAAFFE: Yes, yes.

LAWSON: Did the woman police officer pay any attention to Stephen as opposed to asking you what happened?

TAAFFE: She immediately came to his head.

LAWSON: She put a finger to the front of his mouth?

TAAFFE: Yes.

LAWSON: She said she thought there was some breathing?

TAAFFE: Yes, that's right.

LAWSON: You tried and felt nothing?

TAAFFE: Yes.

LAWSON: Did you see her take or feel for a pulse?

TAAFFE: I don't think so. I don't think so.

LAWSON: At the scene at that time did you have any inkling he was suffering from stab wounds? Did anyone say anything about that?

TAAFFE: I don't recall anyone mentioning stab wounds.

LAWSON: I am grateful to you. Would you wait there please.

KAMLISH: Mr Taaffe, when you first saw Stephen and Duwayne you saw Stephen holding his upper chest?

TAAFFE: Yes.

KAMLISH: The blood you saw was clearly coming from the upper body?

TAAFFE: Yes.

KAMLISH: There could not have been any doubt in the WPC's mind, could there, that this was extremely serious; that this was either life-threatening or his life was extinct?

TAAFFE: I think she was aware this was a very serious situation and that, therefore, her response to it was to get things happening: get an ambulance, find out what had happened. Do you know what I mean? I suppose she is a police officer, not a first aider, doctor, surgeon, paramedic.

KAMLISH: She is in fact first-aid trained.

TAAFFE: Oh, right. Oh, right.

KAMLISH: Your wife cradled Stephen's head at some point?

TAAFFE: Yes, yes, and she spoke in his ear. I thought it was such a lovely thing for her to say because Louise and I both knew that hearing is one of the last things to go, and so, while he was there, she said: "You are loved. You are loved." I had some blood on my hands. When I went home – this isn't material, but I will say it anyway – I went home and washed the blood off my hands with some water in a container, and there is a rose bush in our back garden, a very, very old, huge rose bush – rose tree is I suppose more appropriate – and I poured the water with his blood in it into the bottom of that rose tree. So in a way I suppose he is kind of living on a bit.

MACPHERSON: From the moment he fell into the position you have described, Stephen was not moved by anyone at all?

TAAFFE: No, no.

MACPHERSON: Yes, Mr Gompertz.

GOMPERTZ: You have said that when the WPC arrived, she crouched down?

TAAFFE: Yes, yes.

GOMPERTZ: So whether she did the right thing or the wrong thing, she was certainly being attentive to Stephen?

TAAFFE: Absolutely, yes. I wasn't aware that the WPC was a first aider. But having said that I wonder what difference it would have made. I mean, if someone stabs you and punctures an artery close to your heart even if a surgeon had been on the scene, he wouldn't have had the equipment. What could you do?

MACDONALD: Mr Taafe, I think we all appreciate that you did a wonderful thing that night. I just wanted to ask about the moment before you crossed the road, you had some fears about what was happening? You sensed danger.

TAAFFE: Yes, yes. I sensed that something was amiss, something suspicious, something dangerous. Perhaps they were running away from somewhere, perhaps they had been involved in a violent fight, you know.

MACDONALD: You have two young black men running along the road?

TAAFFE: Yes.

MACDONALD: You thought they might be about to commit a mugging or something like that?

TAAFFE: The thought flashed through my mind, being wary of the situation, that perhaps it was a ploy. One would fall down and you would think: "Oh my God, there's something wrong." You would go over and the other might get you. That did pass through my mind.

MACDONALD: Was that because it was two young black men running along the other side of the road?

TAAFFE: I would say that that was part of my assessment, yes.

FROM THE EVIDENCE OF POLICE CONSTABLE GLEASON, 26 MARCH 1998

MACPHERSON: Mr Gleason, will you sit to give your evidence and Mr Lawson, counsel to the inquiry, will start.

LAWSON: Thank you, sir. For everybody's information, the primary sources of evidence for this witness, is his temporary statement, PCA 38, and extensive interviews with the Kent Constabulary.

Constable Gleason, we are told you have had first-aid training?

GLEASON: Yes, sir.

LAWSON: You went to the hospital, yes, escorting the ambulance?

GLEASON: That's correct sir, yes.

LAWSON: Do you have any training, Mr Gleason, as to how you should deal with bereaved relatives?

GLEASON: No specific training, no, sir.

LAWSON: You will appreciate, of course, the trauma, the distress such people would feel?

GLEASON: Yes.

LAWSON: And the need for information?

GLEASON: Yes.

LAWSON: What did you do about that to comfort them or to give them information at the hospital?

GLEASON: As far as I recall I can remember speaking to Mr Lawrence outside the resuscitation room. What the context of that conversation was,
I am afraid I just cannot remember.

LAWSON: So you had some conversation with him?

GLEASON: Yes, I did.

LAWSON: Did you have any sort of conversation with Mrs Lawrence?

GLEASON: No, I didn't.

LAWSON: At no stage?

GLEASON: At no stage, no.

LAWSON: With hindsight, PC Gleason, do you not think you should have made an effort?

GLEASON: I believe I did make an effort on the night, sir.

LAWSON: Make an effort to speak with Mrs Lawrence, speak with the family?

GLEASON: I can remember Mrs Lawrence was very, very, upset. Understandably so. I spoke to Mr Lawrence and I can also remember speaking to other members of the family as they left the hospital later in the morning.

LAWSON: You also spoke to Duwayne Brooks, did you not?

GLEASON: I did speak to Duwayne Brooks, yes.

LAWSON: You described his excitable state at the scene. What was his state at the hospital?

GLEASON: At first he was still excitable until I actually managed to calm him down and take the necessary information that is in my pocket book.

LAWSON: You better tell us about the information you got from him. For these purposes can we have on the screen PCA 45 at page 72. This is your handwriting, is it not?

GLEASON: Yes.

MACPHERSON: Do you want the witness to read it?

LAWSON: It would be quicker.

GLEASON: (*Reads.*) "We got on a 286 bus at Eltham bus station. We got off at Well Hall roundabout. We waited until 10.40 pm and we walked slowly down to the roundabout and I saw about six white boys coming up Well Hall Road on the other side of the road.

"I said to Steve that there was a bus coming. Steve was about ten yards from me. I saw the youths cross the road towards Stephen. I said to Stephen: 'See the bus.' One of the youths who had blue jeans, his hair was bushy, light brown and stuck out, he was about nineteen or twenty, he said: 'What, what, nigger?' I knew they were coming for us and I shouted: 'Steve, run.' I ran but I then turned back to see if Stephen was running. I saw the same youth who was in front of Stephen strike down with one of his arms on Stephen's head, I think.

"Stephen fell to the floor and I ran back towards him. The youths ran off and Stephen got up and ran across the road. I was telling him to run. He said: "Look at me, what is wrong?' I could see blood trickling down his chest. He then just fell. Before striking Stephen I saw the youth pull something from his jacket. It could have been a wood or metal bar."

LAWSON: Thank you. Then the next note, you say: "I was present when Mr Neville Lawrence identified the body of his son at the Brook hospital in the resuscitation room one."

GLEASON: Yes.

LAWSON: You appreciated the seriousness of the stab wounds only really at the hospital. Is that right?

GLEASON: That is when I realised he had been stabbed, yes.

LAWSON: Did you understand, as some others did, that he had been hit on the head with an iron bar?

GLEASON: That was the information that first came out: "Hit over the head with an iron bar."

LAWSON: Which, if your evidence of your examination is true, you quickly realised was wrong information?

GLEASON: I could not see any wound to the head.

LAWSON: Thank you.

MACPHERSON: Yes, Mr Kamlish.

KAMLISH: You did not find anything on the head. You saw the blood coming from elsewhere. That is right, is it not?

GLEASON: I didn't know where the blood was coming from.

KAMLISH: It is the most obvious thing at the time, is it not, that he might have been stabbed?

GLEASON: Well, it wasn't obvious to me, no, sir.

KAMLISH: Why did you not move him slightly to see if there was a wound, such as a chest wound, which you could staunch the flow of blood from?

GLEASON: Because I didn't want to move him.

KAMLISH: Why?

GLEASON: Because an ambulance was on its way and I felt that he was best left in the position he was in.

KAMLISH: What, to bleed to death, as we now know happened?

GLEASON: I didn't know he was going to bleed to death.

KAMLISH: He was unconscious, was he not?

GLEASON: Yes, he was.

KAMLISH: You say you checked his pulse?

GLEASON: Yes, sir.

KAMLISH: Where did you check it?

GLEASON: On the wrist.

KAMLISH: Which wrist?

GLEASON: I cannot remember, sir.

KAMLISH: You really cannot remember all of this?

GLEASON: No, sir, it is a long time ago.

KAMLISH: It is a long time ago, but it is probably one of the most significant events in your life, is it not?

GLEASON: Yes, sir.

KAMLISH: You went to the hospital. Why did you decide that Mr Lawrence was the person you should take to the identification?

GLEASON: He appeared to be very calm.

KAMLISH: Very calm?

GLEASON: Yes.

KAMLISH: I see. Did you ask him whether he would mind doing it?

GLEASON: I honestly do not remember.

KAMLISH: What was said about the identification; do you remember any of the words at all?

GLEASON: I am afraid I cannot say what the words were.

KAMLISH: You see, Mr Gleason, the family had been in to identify Stephen about half an hour before. So if you are telling the truth, this would be a completely unnecessary event?

GLEASON: I am not aware of that.

KAMLISH: You are aware, are you not, that not a single member of the hospital staff recalls this event, your going in with Mr Lawrence to identify the body. You know that?

GLEASON: No, I don't, but it is noted in my pocket book that this has happened.

KAMLISH: Did you ask him to sign your pocket book to confirm that he had made the identification?

GLEASON: No, I didn't.

KAMLISH: Why not?

GLEASON: I felt it was traumatic enough to see his son there. There was no way I was going to thrust a pocket book on to him and say, please sign here for this identification.

KAMLISH: Do you know why, in the light of what you just said, the family were taken formally to identify their son on Saturday at the mortuary?

GLEASON: No, I don't, sir.

KAMLISH: Just describe what happened when you got into the resus room, please?

GLEASON: Mr Lawrence identified his son.

KAMLISH: Who went where and who did what?

GLEASON: I don't remember where we stood.

KAMLISH: Come on, Mr Gleason, what was Mr Lawrence's reaction?

GLEASON: Distressed, shocked.

KAMLISH: Did he cry?

GLEASON: I honestly cannot remember.

KAMLISH: Did he touch his son's body?

GLEASON: I don't know. I cannot remember.

KAMLISH: This did not happen, did it?

GLEASON: Well, it did happen because it is noted in my pocket book.

KAMLISH: With Stephen still there?

GLEASON: Yes.

KAMLISH: So you wrote your witness statement in the resuscitation room with no-one else in there except Stephen's lifeless body?

GLEASON: I believe WPC Bethel came up at some point but it was just myself and Stephen.

KAMLISH: You say that you radioed Duwayne Brooks' account?

GLEASON: It was radioed out what he said, yes, whether they recorded it, I don't know.

KAMLISH: They would have to receive it, would they not?

GLEASON: Everyone would receive it in that area.

KAMLISH: Exactly. It is probably the most crucial information that the Metropolitan Police Service would have received that night at that early stage, a description of the suspects?

GLEASON: Yes.

KAMLISH: There is no recording of this radio message, you know that, do you not?

GLEASON: No, I don't.

KAMLISH: May I ask you briefly about your experience of racism? Have you experienced racism in the police force?

GLEASON: I have probably been present when comments have been made.

KAMLISH: By other police officers?

GLEASON: By other people in general. I can't recollect…

KAMLISH: Other police officers?

GLEASON: I'm sorry, I cannot remember any specific racist remarks being made by police officers.

KAMLISH: How long have you been a police officer, I am sorry?

GLEASON: Fourteen years.

KAMLISH: And you have never heard a police officer make a racist remark?

GLEASON: I cannot remember a police officer making a racist remark. I am not denying that may ever happen.

MACPHERSON: Mr Gleason, you were actually the only police officer who was at the hospital more or less throughout, were you not, from the time that Stephen was taken there until you left at four o'clock in the morning?

GLEASON: That's correct, sir, yes.

MACPHERSON: I think I have to say this, that it looks to me very much as if the liaison with the family was hopeless because they feel very much that no attention was paid to them at all. You understand what I mean, do you not? You may have done your best in what you say you did, but who would have been responsible for sending somebody to do that job specifically? Who was your boss, so to speak?

GLEASON: Who was actually overall in command of the incident I don't know.

FROM THE EVIDENCE OF SERGEANT CLEMENT, 27 MARCH 1998

LAWSON: On that particular night, the night we are looking at, you with other officers were on board what I think are called a group carrier?

CLEMENT: Yes, that's correct.

LAWSON: Roughly how many of you would there be and of what rank?

CLEMENT: Possibly an inspector, sergeant and six PCs on each vehicle and the inspector... (*Inaudible.*) ...all three vehicles.

LAWSON: You let your voice drop occasionally. Was the inspector with you that night?

CLEMENT: Yes.

LAWSON: Is that Inspector Groves?

CLEMENT: Inspector Groves, yes.

LAWSON: You were called to the scene of what we know now to be Stephen Lawrence's murder?

CLEMENT: We responded to a call, to an emergency call there and chose to accept the call and went there.

LAWSON: Do you have any notes, Sergeant Clement, of the incident?

CLEMENT: I do not.

LAWSON: I wonder if we could look, please, at the screen, PCA 38 page 228. This is a printed, or typed, version of your witness statement made on the 1st of May 1993. Do you see that?

CLEMENT: I can see the statement. I can't see the date. I have got the date now, yes.

LAWSON: These computer print things are not easy to read sometimes. I am going to ask you to have a look at this. You described there responding to a call that related to an assault with an iron bar?

CLEMENT: Yes.

LAWSON: You then say: "We began to search the vicinity for a group of six males concerned"?

CLEMENT: That's correct.

LAWSON: On your arrival, you searched the vicinity. Where did you search, can you remember, on your first search?

CLEMENT: The first search we did, that was in our carrier – a mobile search – would have been the streets along Downman Road, Phineas Pett Road, the general side streets around there and back to the roundabout, from what I can recall, and past where Stephen was laying up to the Welcome Inn.

LAWSON: You then said in your statement: "You gave directions for a sweeping search"?

CLEMENT: Yes.

LAWSON: It does not seem at the time you made this statement that Dickson Road meant anything in particular to you. Is that a fair comment?

CLEMENT: Yeah, we knew of Dickson Road because we searched that Dickson Road, because the suspects had made off down Dickson Road.

LAWSON: You moved down Dickson Road searching for any kind of weapon?

CLEMENT: Anything really. Evidence, maybe a jacket discarded, anything.

LAWSON: Is this your entire team, so to speak?

CLEMENT: Yes, probably half a dozen to a dozen officers.

LAWSON: What were their instructions?

CLEMENT: We searched the gardens…

LAWSON: Forgive me, what were they being told to look for?

CLEMENT: The original call was of a male being attacked by an iron bar.

LAWSON: Anyone told you different before you went off on your search?

CLEMENT: I can't remember.

LAWSON: Did you have any artificial lighting, torches or anything of that sort with you?

CLEMENT: We had a rechargeable torch about that size.

LAWSON: Just one torch?

CLEMENT: As far as I remember, one. We had a supply of slightly smaller plastic ones which take the big Eveready battery. They were very unreliable. Often the bulbs wouldn't work or the batteries were flat.

LAWSON: And then you sent them out doing house-to-house enquiries?

CLEMENT: On certain houses. I didn't say, "Knock on every single door." Some houses had their lights on.

LAWSON: Would this be a rather cursory house-to-house enquiry?

CLEMENT: It would have been.

LAWSON: Just explain to me and some of us here as a layman: why was the house-to-house one put after the cursory search of the road? Surely, some might think it would be more important to find out if anybody had said: "Yes, they went that way."

CLEMENT: I don't know why.

LAWSON: Was that a sensible question or suggestion?

CLEMENT: It is a sensible question, yes.

LAWSON: In the weekend immediately following the murder, you remember the apparent thoroughness of the briefings you received?

CLEMENT: Yes.

LAWSON: You said: "I was aware that there were some suspects being mentioned as possibly being involved, but I couldn't remember the names." As you know, sergeant, there has been for some years a great deal of publicity in relation to certain names in this case, so I need not…

CLEMENT: I can't remember what names were mentioned.

LAWSON: Do you recall whether you were told that the Acourts were suspected?

CLEMENT: I can't remember, no.

LAWSON: Have you ever heard of them before?

CLEMENT: I hadn't, no.

LAWSON: Have you heard of the name Norris before, I venture to suggest?

CLEMENT: Yes, yes.

LAWSON: It is somewhat infamous, some might say?

CLEMENT: Yes.

LAWSON: Were you actually told names before you did your house-to-house briefing?

CLEMENT: No.

LAWSON: Would it not have been a good idea if you were going around getting information from people in the neighbourhood if you had known who the supposed suspects were?

CLEMENT: Yes.

LAWSON: But nobody told you that?

CLEMENT: I didn't know the names.

MACPHERSON: So if you had walked into a house and found several Acourts in it, it would not have meant anything to you at all?

CLEMENT: Probably not.

MACPHERSON: It strikes me that in that case your visit to the houses was totally useless?

CLEMENT: The reason – I see what you're saying. I was never aware of the names of the suspects at that early stage of that enquiry.

LAWSON: May we please have back on the screen, still on the house-to-house inquiries, PCA 37, page two, please.

We see, there is in this chronology, the first reference to any of the suspects. At 1.50 pm there is the anonymous male telephoning with information about Neil Acourt and David Norris, do you see that?

CLEMENT: Yes.

LAWSON: During the course of the weekend, as we can see, if more information came in making similar allegations against similar people, as we understand it, none of that was passed to you or those under you carrying out the house-to-house inquiries.

CLEMENT: As far as I can remember, yes, that is the case.

LAWSON: Can we just look back, please, at PCA 37, page two. On Friday the 23rd of April, at 7.45 pm, there is a record of "an anonymous male" – in fact we know him as Grant – "visiting the police station" and alleging specifically, I should say, "that the two Acourt brothers of 102 Bournbrook Road, together with others, were responsible for the murder".

CLEMENT: Yes, I can see that, yes.

LAWSON: That is information that as far as you know was never passed to you?

CLEMENT: Not that I can remember at this time, no.

LAWSON: That is just the sort of information that presumably you would say from your experience that you would want to ensure very promptly got passed to the investigating officer...

CLEMENT: Absolutely, yes.

LAWSON: ...for urgent action?

CLEMENT: Yes.

LAWSON: Thank you.

KAMLISH: So that the officer understands:

It is not accepted by the Lawrence family that this officer got to the scene when he claims he did;

> It is not accepted he carried out the early searches in the way he claims he did or at all;
>
> It is not accepted that he made the thorough enquiries he claims at the scene;
>
> It is not accepted that he went to the Welcome Inn;
>
> And other parts of his evidence are not accepted from the scene.
>
> Can I first of all ask you about records. Now, you have no records whatsoever compiled by you from the night of the 22nd/23rd of April, do you?
>
> Exit LAWSON.

CLEMENT: That's correct, yes.

KAMLISH: Not a single note?

CLEMENT: Not a single note.

KAMLISH: One record that might assist the inquiry as to whether you are telling the truth about what you did that night and what your vehicles did, would be the so-called tag sheets from the carrier. Yes?

CLEMENT: Yes, I see what you are saying. A tag sheet is just a sheet of paper. There is hundreds of them in a tray so they wouldn't tend to prove anything, really.

KAMLISH: No, but it is a log of what the carrier is doing on a particular occasion?

CLEMENT: Yes, that's right.

KAMLISH: It would record who is on it?

CLEMENT: That's correct, yes.

KAMLISH: You know, do you not, that all the tag sheets for this night for your vehicles have all gone missing?

CLEMENT: I have been informed of this, yes.

KAMLISH: Have you been involved in trying to search for them?

CLEMENT: No.

KAMLISH: When you arrived on the night, who exactly was there?

CLEMENT: I don't know the officers.

KAMLISH: What about a young man in a hysterical state running up and down, shouting, screaming, perhaps arguing a bit in a state of, I suppose, extreme hysteria, standing around and moving around where Stephen was lying?

CLEMENT: No, I never saw him.

KAMLISH: You were not there, were you, at this time?

CLEMENT: Oh yes, I was there.

KAMLISH: I suggest it was impossible to have missed Duwayne Brooks in the state that he has been described if you had been there at the time he was there?

CLEMENT: I was there.

GOMPERTZ: If my learned friend is moving to another topic – I did not want to have to interrupt, and I see that Mr Lawson is not in the chamber at the moment – we are becoming increasingly concerned, sir, about what is happening. This witness was asked to come here without the service of any form of Salmon letter* upon him. All kinds of allegations have been put to him of which he has had no notice whatsoever.

MACPHERSON: If this is going to happen again, I must have notice of it, because fairness works both ways, and if officers are going to be asked questions in the way they are being asked they must be given notice that that is going to happen. Because they may need representation.

What is said now is that officers not only told lies but they have actually invented their presence at the scene.

MANSFIELD: Well, sir, we obviously have all been discussing outside the concerns that we have. I accept in fairness there should be some notice.

MACPHERSON: I am grateful to you.

KAMLISH: You went to Phineas Pett Road, that was one of the roads that was searched?

CLEMENT: Yes, I see that road, yes.

KAMLISH: Can we have Law nine, page 537 up, please. Law 00090537.

Gary Dobson's alibi notice: "Gary Dobson lived with his parents at number 13 Phineas Pett Road." You have no record of having gone to the door of that house nor has anybody else?

CLEMENT: I certainly have no record, no.

KAMLISH: I am just giving this as an example of how your earlier visits to houses could blow somebody's alibi out of the water.

CLEMENT: I agree, of course, yes.

KAMLISH: Your failure to record who you spoke to and the houses you went to would have lost the prosecution the advantage forever, would it not?

CLEMENT: You use the word "failure". I do not think we failed in anything we did on that evening. We were very professional and expedient in our enquiries on that evening.

MACPHERSON: The point is that you did not go to any houses beyond Dickson Road.

KAMLISH: Thank you very much, no further questions.

MACDONALD: One of the things is when a group of attackers disappear off up a side street, they may have a car parked up there which they get into?

CLEMENT: Yes, there is always that possibility, yes.

MACDONALD: So, no doubt, you were on the look-out for cars that might contain youths of that general description?

CLEMENT: Yes.

MACDONALD: You in fact saw such a car, did you not?

CLEMENT: We saw a vehicle, yes. A red vehicle, yes. Drive along Well Hall Road on two occasions on that night.

MACDONALD: A red Vauxhall Astra?

CLEMENT: Yes, that is the case, yes.

MACDONALD: How many people did that vehicle contain?

CLEMENT: From memory, I said it was full of white youths, I believe.

MACDONALD: You would not have logged that car unless there was something suspicious about it, would you?

CLEMENT: That is right, yes.

MACDONALD: You were told the occupants were laughing as they looked on?

CLEMENT: Yes.

MACDONALD: Was that what was suspicious or that they fitted the general description that originally came from Duwayne Brooks of five or six white youths, male?

CLEMENT: That would obviously make you consider this vehicle may have had something to do with it, why they would be laughing?

MACDONALD: A week later you see the same car, do you not?

CLEMENT: Yes.

MACDONALD: And stop it?

CLEMENT: Yes.

MACDONALD: You spoke to the driver and took details, did you not?

CLEMENT: That is the case, yes.

MACDONALD: That was Daniel Copley?

CLEMENT: Yes, aged eighteen.

MACDONALD: Were you aware that Daniel Copley had been convicted in connection with an attack on Nathan and Rolan Adams; he was part of the attacking group which led to the murder of Rolan Adams a little bit earlier?

CLEMENT: What you are telling me now is the first indication of that that I am aware of.

MACDONALD: Ciaran Highland, no one told you that he was a leading light in NTO, the Nazi Turnout, a racist organisation that operates in the Eltham area?

CLEMENT: I was never informed of that either.

MACDONALD: Did anyone tell you from subsequent enquiries that those two who were in the car when you stopped it were in fact in the car on the night in question going past the scene?

CLEMENT: No, I did not speak to anyone about those connections.

MACDONALD: No. You can see the obvious significance of it now, can you not?

CLEMENT: Yes.

MACDONALD: You were never told that those people you had seen, had noted and eventually stopped, were involved in the Rolan Adams inquiry?

CLEMENT: I was never aware of that, no.

MACDONALD: Thank you.

MACPHERSON: Thank you very much.

FROM THE EVIDENCE OF HELEN AVERY, 27 MARCH 1998

LAWSON: Your name is Helen Elizabeth Avery?

AVERY: That's right.

LAWSON: You had been out for the evening with your mother and your stepfather, had you not?

AVERY: That's right.

LAWSON: And got back to find, amongst other things, a police car with a flashing light outside your home. When you went to go towards your house, you became aware of Stephen Lawrence, who was lying on the pavement. Correct?

AVERY: Yes.

LAWSON: You knew a bit about first-aid, did you?

AVERY: Yes. I've been a first aider since I was about eleven.

LAWSON: Do you belong to any organisation?

AVERY: Yes. St John's Ambulance.

LAWSON: You actually belong to St John's Ambulance?

AVERY: That's right.

LAWSON: At this stage you were what – what were you, about fifteen?

AVERY: I was just coming up to fourteen.

LAWSON: Fourteen. Anyway, you went inside, yes?

AVERY: Yes.

LAWSON: No doubt obviously you kept an eye on what was going on through the window?

AVERY: That's right, yeah.

LAWSON: Thank you very much.

KAMLISH: I think you actually held a first-aid certificate since you were eleven?

AVERY: That's right, yeah.

KAMLISH: So you get the same training as older people in that first-aid training course?

AVERY: Yes.

KAMLISH: When you have a first-aid training course, stemming the flow of blood is one of the most important features you are taught?

AVERY: Yes.

KAMLISH: Because it can save somebody's life?

AVERY: Yes.

KAMLISH: You never saw anybody either looking for where the blood was coming from or trying to stop the flow?

AVERY: That's right.

KAMLISH: When you first arrived back from where you had been, you actually spoke to a police officer, did you not?

AVERY: That's right.

KAMLISH: Or your stepfather did?

AVERY: Yes, my stepfather did.

KAMLISH: He actually asked one of the officers who was there, was there by Stephen: "Can we be of any assistance?"

AVERY: That's right, he did.

KAMLISH: What did the police officer say?

AVERY: They declined any assistance. They told us that he had been attacked and that the ambulance was on its way.

KAMLISH: But the officers you were talking to were not either then or shortly before or after attending to Stephen himself?

AVERY: No, I didn't see anybody attending to Stephen.

KAMLISH: It is also right, is it not, that you have never been asked to make a statement by the Metropolitan Police?

AVERY: That's right.

KAMLISH: Nor have you ever had a knock on the door and been asked for an account of that night?

AVERY: That's right.

KAMLISH: Nor have you had a message left for you by the police to get in touch with them to tell them what had gone on that night?

AVERY: That's right.

KAMLISH: Thank you very much.

GOMPERTZ: Miss Avery, you went upstairs to join your sister, I think?

AVERY: That's right.

GOMPERTZ: Because she has described a rather different picture to that which you give us – that there was a lady police officer who was either knelt by or crouched over Stephen by the pavement. Do you think that could be right?

AVERY: I could be mistaken, but I don't remember anyone attending to the body. I don't really remember anybody crouching down, but I mean it was a very hectic night. There were a lot of emotions going around.

FROM THE STATEMENT OF NEVILLE LAWRENCE, 27 MARCH 1998

MACPHERSON: Mr Mansfield, Mr Lawrence is happy that his statement should be read this morning. Does that suit everybody?

MANSFIELD: Yes.

SOORJOO: (*Statement of Neville Lawrence.*) "I was born on the 13th of March 1942 in Kingston, Jamaica. I came to England in 1960 at the age of eighteen. When I first came here I lived in Kentish Town which at the time was notorious for teddy boys and things like that. I was available to work as an upholsterer because I had done my apprenticeship and was therefore qualified. Unfortunately, I was not able to get a job. I believe this was because of racism. The racism that we experienced then was not as bad as that we now experience. In those days it was mostly verbal, not physical. The violence is much worse nowadays.

"I experienced racism when I first arrived here but I did not recognise it as such at the time. People used to make jokes about us in a way that you did not realise it was actually being racist. They used to call us 'coons' and the like but then you thought it was like a nickname.

"Stephen was born on September 13th 1974 at Greenwich District Hospital. Stephen was very talented at school. His favourite subject was art. One of the things we discovered was that he wanted to be an architect; he was very good at drawing.

"Stephen has never been in trouble. We brought our children up to respect the law. As far as I know, Stephen had never even spoken to a policeman. The children attended Trinity church in Woolwich from an early age. Stephen was christened there.

"In the early 1990s, there were several murders of black people in our area. I had not thought that racism was so bad in the area.

"On the morning of April 22nd 1993 Stephen came into our bedroom overlooking the road and said 'seeya later'. He asked me if I was okay and I said yes. He went down and returned upstairs and said: 'Are you sure you are all right, Dad?' I said, 'yes'. Because I was not working I was not feeling all that good about myself. I watched Stephen go down the road with his rucksack over his back. That is the last time I saw him alive.

"Ten-thirty pm there was a ring at the doorbell. I thought it was Stephen. It was Joey Shepherd. Joey told me that Stephen had been attacked down the road at a bus stop by the Welcome Inn Pub by about six white youths. Doreen called the police who told her that they knew nothing about the incident. We drove to the Brook hospital which was a few minutes away.

"I was just praying that he was not dead. We just sat there. All sorts of things were going through my mind. They came in the door. I do not remember the exact words they used, but I do remember they said that Stephen was dead, we could phone our relatives or something like that. It still did not hit me. When they said Stephen was dead, Duwayne went wild. I just sat there. I was numb.

"Nobody actually told us what happened to Stephen. Nobody. None of the policemen at the hospital spoke to us. I am sure I would have remembered if they did.

"The next day is very cloudy. We still did not know how Stephen had been killed. We were introduced to the two liaison officers, DS Bevan and DC Holden. Holden made a remark about woollen gloves and a hat being found. It was clear she was implying that Stephen was a cat burglar.

"There were incidents where our car tyres were slashed. It made us feel even more threatened.

"We had fears about burying Stephen here because of the situation surrounding his death. In June 1993, we flew out to Jamaica with the body. He is lying beside his grandmother in Clarendon in Jamaica."

FROM THE EVIDENCE OF INSPECTOR GROVES, 1 AND 2 APRIL 1998

LAWSON: You're an inspector serving in the Metropolitan Police?

GROVES: Yes, that's right.

LAWSON: Currently serving where?

GROVES: Westminster.

LAWSON: Mr Groves, already on the screen is a copy of the statement made by you in May 1993. The matters you were being asked particularly to address, page 24 of volume 50, it is right there: questions of consideration being given to neglect of duty in respect of failure to ensure a record was kept at the scene and a failure in respect of first-aid treatment?

GROVES: That's right, sir.

LAWSON: Moving back to PCA 38, page 303, may I ask you this – this is obviously dealing with the events of the evening of the 22nd of April 1993 – I understand, is this correct, that you have no surviving notes?

GROVES: No, sir, I have not.

LAWSON: There was reference to you having a clipboard at the scene?

GROVES: I still have the clipboard. I don't have any notes.

LAWSON: What happened to them, do you know?

GROVES: The notes I made that night were fairly comprehensive. They were taken by me at their request to Shooter's Hill Police Station a little while later.

LAWSON: Are you able to give an indication of what time you got to the scene?

GROVES: No, not really, I would think about 10.45.

LAWSON: Would you regard yourself as having been in charge of the scene?

GROVES: Yes.

LAWSON: Had you been given an inkling as to what had happened to Stephen Lawrence, apart from the fact that you had been told he had been assaulted with an iron bar and had serious head injuries?

GROVES: No sir.

LAWSON: Had you asked anybody at the scene if they could assist with what had happened?

GROVES: Yes.

LAWSON: What were you told?

GROVES: I did not have any information.

LAWSON: The very distraught young man who was there was Duwayne Brooks – WPC Bethel managed to calm him down sufficiently to get some account from him about what happened, but that was never passed to you?

GROVES: No, sir, I don't think so. I carried on walking to the pub.

LAWSON: You learned nothing from that?

GROVES: No, nothing at all.

LAWSON: Your account is that a variety of streets in the neighbourhood were directed by you to be searched by police, some with dogs, is that right?

GROVES: The one that happened at midnight, the main search, the very, very, thorough search.

LAWSON: Nothing, in fact, was found, was it?

GROVES: I have a feeling that the only thing one of them found was – I do not think it was anything to do with this. I think it was a salt pot.

LAWSON: Was a report made to you that night about the red Astra. Does that mean anything to you?

GROVES: No, sir. I don't think so. I don't recall.

LAWSON: Thank you.

MANSFIELD: So everybody knows exactly what it is that is being suggested on behalf of Mr and Mrs Lawrence in relation to you, I just want to pick out some of those.

First of all, it is suggested that you failed to take proper control of the scene upon arrival as the first senior officer.

Secondly, you failed to discover relevant information in order to exercise proper control.

Thirdly, that you failed to order and monitor an effective and immediate search for offenders by means of mobile, house-to-house and witness search.

Fourthly, the failure of one to three arose because of your assumptions about the nature of the offence and the victim – race.

The first question I want to ask you, officer, is looking back on it all now, is there anything you think first of all that went wrong as the senior officer between 11 and 1.30 in the morning with the investigation under you?

GROVES: No, sir, I don't think so.

MANSFIELD: Nothing?

GROVES: With the investigation, no.

MANSFIELD: Right. I am going to suggest to you that there was a great deal more that you could have done which might have resulted in something, it might not, do you follow?

GROVES: Yes, sir, certainly.

MANSFIELD: To use your own words to the Kent investigation: "Unless you search an area thoroughly and quickly, then you are losing evidence all of the time"?

GROVES: That's right, sir.

MANSFIELD: And I suggest to you that you were losing evidence every minute that went by that night, were you not?

GROVES: I would absolutely agree with you.

MANSFIELD: Right. So where did it go wrong, officer?

GROVES: Where did what go wrong?

MANSFIELD: Let us start with a fairly basic matter. Which carrier were you on when you went to the scene?

GROVES: I am not sure. The carrier that had Clement on it, 325 I believe.

MANSFIELD: Clement was in charge of 325, was he?

GROVES: Yes.

MANSFIELD: Clement was in charge of 326.

GROVES: Was he?

MANSFIELD: Was he? Well, do not ask me. I am asking you. Before we get going on this, Mr Groves, I am going to suggest this inquiry cannot rely on a single word you are saying. Do you think you are totally unreliable?

GROVES: No, sir.

MANSFIELD: I want to ask you very carefully about those notes. When did you last see them?

GROVES: In 1993.

MANSFIELD: What did you do with them?

GROVES: I took them to Shooters Hill.

MANSFIELD: When?

GROVES: A little while later.

MANSFIELD: When? The same day? The next day? Within a week?

GROVES: I am not sure.

MANSFIELD: I would like you to think.

GROVES: Well, I have thought about it for five years.

MANSFIELD: I am sure you have.

GROVES: You will get the same answer: I am not sure.

MANSFIELD: I suggest there is a very strong possibility that there were never any notes. Do you follow, Mr Groves?

GROVES: Yes, I do.

MANSFIELD: How many sheets were involved, roughly speaking?

GROVES: I don't know, sir. I could not answer that.

MANSFIELD: And the notes have never come to light, have they?

GROVES: No, they haven't.

MANSFIELD: No one has seen these notes with diagrams, dustbins and all the rest of it, no one but you?

GROVES: It would certainly make both our lives very much easier had I got my notes.

MANSFIELD: You talk about photocopying. Now what happened to the photocopies?

GROVES: I keep copies of most documents I think I might need. I certainly think I would have kept copies of this.

MANSFIELD: So where are they?

GROVES: This is five years ago. I have not got my copies any more. I have not got them. It would help not only me but it would help the inquiry if I could find the copies. I have not got them. I cannot say more than that. I have not got them.

MANSFIELD: Have you destroyed them?

GROVES: Very probably, yes.

MANSFIELD: Well, did you, and if so when, and why did you not tell Kent: "I destroyed them"?

GROVES: I cannot recall destroying them.

MANSFIELD: Why would you destroy them?

GROVES: I had no reason to keep them past three years.

MANSFIELD: This case you knew was trundling on in one way or another? You knew that from the publicity?

GROVES: Yes, of course.

MANSFIELD: Is there any possibility, officer, that you just never took any notes that night because you were not that bothered about this incident? Is that a possibility?

GROVES: No. When somebody dies it is something that I remember for the rest of my life. I don't just – whether they are black or white is irrelevant, if that is what you are getting at.

MANSFIELD: When you went to the scene, Mr Groves, you did not treat this as a murder enquiry, did you?

GROVES: I think I certainly did…

MANSFIELD: I want you to think very carefully. The question is, when you first went to the scene, you did not treat this as a murder enquiry, did you?

GROVES: Well, not when Stephen was alive.

MANSFIELD: He was dead, I suggest, when you got there?

GROVES: I don't think he was. When I knew Stephen had died this was something very, very different. It was now a murder inquiry.

MANSFIELD: Let us get utterly clear what you thought about this when you first got to the scene. What did you think about it?

GROVES: I thought that what we were dealing with here was possibly a fight.

MANSFIELD: A fight?

GROVES: Sir, if you keep interrupting me, I shall just slow down. It is important that I am allowed to give my answers here and it is not easy with you interrupting. When I arrived at the scene, I saw an unconscious person and my concern was who had done that to that person and I had to think about what I was going to do about finding the person or persons responsible.

MANSFIELD: I am waiting because I did not…

GROVES: I have finished. Please…

MANSFIELD: Now, may I use these words, which I suggest are your words. When you first got to the scene, it was just an assault and that is all.

GROVES: It was a serious assault. We had to act on the information that we had.

MANSFIELD: I am going to put to you, Mr Groves, that I suggest to you very clearly this is one of your assumptions because it is a black victim, was it not?

GROVES: No, sir. You are accusing me of being a racist now and that is not true. I would like it noted that I do not think that is fair either. You have no evidence that I am racist.

MANSFIELD: If I ask you if you are a racist what will you say?

GROVES: Of course I am not. I could not do my job if I was racist, it would not be possible, it is not compatible.

MANSFIELD: You agree you describe the assault as a fight and you say that was based on information?

GROVES: I think what I said was that is what I thought I was dealing with, an assault, a fight. That is right.

MANSFIELD: I am going to ask you carefully. I am going to suggest this is where the approach or attitude of mind to race is important. You did say before that was the message, that it was a fight. Is that right that you had information or was that an assumption by you?

GROVES: I have now said that five times. I have said five times that the information that I had was this was a fight. Do you want me to say it six times for you, would that make it clearer for you? I am not going to elaborate on this.

MANSFIELD: I suggest to you, Mr Groves, I am going to interrupt, there was no information being fed to the police that this man suffered an injury as the result of a fight?

GROVES: In that case you are wrong.

MANSFIELD: Where did you say it came from?

GROVES: I think the call we got, the original call was possibly from the information room.

MANSFIELD: You see, the information that the inquiry has been told was effectively, an assault with an iron bar, quite different to a fight. In other words, somebody being attacked. That was your information, Mr Groves?

GROVES: Sir, of course, I would agree with you.

MANSFIELD: You translated, I suggest to you, the information of an assault into: black man on pavement involved in fight. Is that a possibility?

GROVES: Of course that is a possibility, absolutely. Absolutely.

MANSFIELD: Yes.

GROVES: It is not an assumption, it is a possibility.

MANSFIELD: If you saw a police officer on the ground with injuries and you had been told about an assault with an iron bar, would you assume a fight?

GROVES: I would have to consider it, of course.

MANSFIELD: Moving forward, you were asked specifically questions about the race issue, were you not, by Kent?

GROVES: Yes.

MANSFIELD: What is the word that you use most regularly to describe non-white people?

GROVES: Black people.

MANSFIELD: Do you?

GROVES: Coloured people.

MANSFIELD: Coloured people is the word you most commonly use, is it not?

GROVES: Okay. I am in a sort of quandary here. He is a white man, that is a coloured woman. (*Indicating.*) What else can I say. I have to make some description. I do not think that is being racist. He is a white man, he is a white man, that is a coloured man. (*Indicating.*)

MANSFIELD: I am going to bring it back to the scene, as it were. Did the thought that night, since you kept your options open, ever come across your mind this was a racist attack?

GROVES: Not initially, no.

MANSFIELD: No.

GROVES: Not until I had enough information to make, using your word, an "assumption".

MANSFIELD: Yes, thank you.

MACDONALD: Were you aware that Duwayne Brooks had told WPC Bethel that as they were coming across the road to attack, they had shouted some racist abuse?

GROVES: No, sir, I was not aware of that.

MACDONALD: "What, what nigger."

GROVES: No, sir.

MACDONALD: You told us that you understood that the injuries that Stephen Lawrence had came from a fight?

GROVES: No, that was the information we had.

MACDONALD: Can I ask you this: is that why you went to the pub?

GROVES: A pub is an absolute mine of information. You can learn more from pubs from people who have had a drink than knocking on doors at 11 o'clock.

MACPHERSON: Thank you very much, Mr Groves.

FROM THE EVIDENCE OF JOHN DAVIDSON, FORMERLY DETECTIVE SERGEANT, 24 AND 27 APRIL 1998

LAWSON: Your name is John Davidson, is it not?

DAVIDSON: It is, sir.

LAWSON: On the Friday, 23rd April as you can see, there had been various bits of information being received referring in particular to the Acourts. Yes?

DAVIDSON: Yes sir.

LAWSON: One perhaps slightly inaccurately referred to as "an anonymous male" visiting the police station. That is the man who became known as James Grant?

DAVIDSON: I believe so, sir.

LAWSON: The message accuses the Acourts and David Norris of the murder. And you saw Grant on other occasions which appear to be unrecorded?

DAVIDSON: They were recorded. The record of them appears to have gone missing, sir.

LAWSON: As an experienced detective officer, you recognised that there was certainly by the weekend, if not before, more than enough information to justify arrest?

DAVIDSON: I recognised there was more than enough information to arrest them, yes sir, but I wasn't aware that, in fact, there were surveillance units and such set up on the houses. I could only imagine that there were other reasons.

LAWSON: For deferring arrest?

DAVIDSON: For deferring arrest.

LAWSON: Were you involved in the investigation after 1993?

DAVIDSON: I was called back in, as I was in the Regional Crime Squad, and I assisted Mr Mellish in observation and eventual arrest of Norris' father – in order to take him away from the scene and perhaps get witnesses to come forward because there was a big fear in the estate of the Norris name. This man was a very dangerous and frightening individual, sir.

LAWSON: There was a series of photographs showing Dobson and Norris together at a car immediately outside the Acourts' house?

DAVIDSON: I have only been made aware of that within the past three weeks.

LAWSON: Does it not strike you as being absolutely extraordinary, if that is not an inadequate adjective, if the sole purpose of the surveillance operation was to gather evidence of association, no one bothered to tell you about the fact they had evidence of association?

DAVIDSON: I am very surprised. I am shocked that I never was shown the photograph and I don't know the reason why.

LAWSON: Thank you.

MANSFIELD: Did anything strike you about the assault, about the witness statements from people who had been at the scene?

DAVIDSON: In what way, sir?

MANSFIELD: No, no, no, this is my question; did anything strike you stand out, when you read those statements?

DAVIDSON: A boy was murdered, a young lad was murdered by four or five other young lads outside a bus stop, what would strike me about that, sir?

MANSFIELD: I just wondered if it occurred to you that it was a race attack?

DAVIDSON: I do not think in my own mind this was a racist attack. I believe this was thugs attacking anyone, as they had done on previous occasions with other white lads.

MANSFIELD: During the Dobson interview you made it clear that you personally did not think this was a race attack, did you not?

DAVIDSON: By that time I didn't, no sir.

MANSFIELD: That is your view today, is it not?

DAVIDSON: It is, sir.

MANSFIELD: Do you know the Association of Chief Police Officers' definition of a racial incident?

DAVIDSON: No, sir.

MANSFIELD: Has anyone ever told you what it is?

DAVIDSON: I would imagine, from my memory and my experience in a job, a racial incident is one which is caused by or through racism. It can be anything from a shout, to an out-and-out racist attack, but because these lads had attacked whites before, I believed they were thugs. They were described as Krays. They were thugs who were out to kill, not particularly a black person, but anybody, and I believe that to this day that that was thugs – not racism, just pure bloody-minded thuggery.

MANSFIELD: I do not want to debate with you about the nature of racism, but do you recognise that thugs who may kill white people for a variety of reasons, but who kill blacks because they are blacks are committing a racial crime?

DAVIDSON: Yes, sir, I recognise that if they were killed because they were black, that is racist.

MANSFIELD: That is exactly what this case was about but you refused to recognise it, did you not?

DAVIDSON: I still refuse to recognise it, sir. I am very surprised that anybody knows it is about that because it has never been cleared up anyway, sir.

MANSFIELD: I want you to think again about when it was that you were deputed to speak to a particular individual which we all know as James Grant. During the late afternoon or early evening of Friday the 23rd of April this person walked into the front office of Eltham police station. Would you just listen to this sentence: 'DC Budgen interviewed this man initially and later the same day with DS Davidson.' That is Friday the 23rd. Is that possible?

DAVIDSON: No, sir. You have the duty sheets here. You will see that I wasn't on the inquiry until 12 o'clock on Saturday.

EGAN: My learned friend can find them on 00320096 and 00320097.

MACPHERSON: It does bear out in fact what Sergeant Davidson says, does it not?

MANSFIELD: His duty sheet does.

DAVIDSON: I am not going to do something and not put it on the duty sheet. I got paid a lot of money at the time by the police.

MANSFIELD: Please be careful, Mr Davidson.

DAVIDSON: I am very careful, sir. I am not going to do something on a Friday for the police and not show it on the duty sheet on a day I am off playing golf.

MANSFIELD: Really?

DAVIDSON: I would never, ever, go and do something for the police when I was playing golf elsewhere. Good God, what are you suggesting, sir? Are you suggesting that I would falsely say I was somewhere when I was somewhere else?

MACPHERSON: Mr Davidson.

DAVIDSON: I am not here for this, sir. I am not here for this at all.

MACPHERSON: You must calm down because Mr Mansfield is entitled to ask the questions.

DAVIDSON: He is not entitled to suggest I would do that, sir.

MACPHERSON: Take a pause. You have dealt with that point, Mr Mansfield.

MANSFIELD: You do recognise that this person – Grant – is, in fact, providing what has been described as crucial information, is he not?

DAVIDSON: Yes, sir.

MANSFIELD: There is in fact absolutely no record, is there, in relation to any of the meetings – and there are quite a number of them – that you had with this man?

DAVIDSON: That's correct, sir.

MANSFIELD: Why not?

DAVIDSON: The docket went missing, sir.

MANSFIELD: To put it bluntly, you really did not want this informant's material to be effectively followed up. Do you follow the point?

DAVIDSON: I can see what you are suggesting, sir, and I would always give my all in every murder. I don't like your suggestion, sir. I would give everything in every murder to solve it and I don't like the fact you are inferring I would do anything different in this. I am sorry, I don't want to sit and take this, sir. Do I have to sit here? He is accusing me of trying to stop this murder by racism. I have been in loads of incidents…

MACPHERSON: Just stop for the moment.

DAVIDSON: I won't have that, sir, he is accusing me of racism in a public inquiry.

MACPHERSON: Mr Davidson, you must take a pause, if you will. You must know what the suggestion that is made in this case is.

DAVIDSON: I have never been accused directly of racism, sir, and I don't accept it.

Slight pause.

MANSFIELD: Grant then went on to say that he may have found a witness, right?

DAVIDSON: (*Pause.*) Yes, sir.

MANSFIELD: This is somebody who is on a bus, there is a description of the stabbing, where on the body, and who did what?

DAVIDSON: Yes, sir.

MANSFIELD: It names, effectively, Neil Acourt and David Norris stabbing him, does it not?

DAVIDSON: Yes, it names Neil and David, yes sir.

MANSFIELD: So this person, Grant, appears to have found somebody who actually saw the stabbing or part of it?

DAVIDSON: Yes sir.

MANSFIELD: This is extremely important, is it not?

DAVIDSON: Yes sir.

MANSFIELD: Having got some information about somebody on the 27th of April, the person on the bus was not seen until the 19th of May. What is the delay for tracking down and seeing this person?

DAVIDSON: I can't properly tell you, sir. Eventually, his mother, when I saw him, suggested that the lad was open to suggestion. At the end of it, I put him down as undoubtedly a Walter Mitty.

MANSFIELD: Do you have a record of the conversation and meetings with this man?

DAVIDSON: I have nothing, sir.

FROM THE EVIDENCE OF DETECTIVE CONSTABLE LINDA HOLDEN, 5 MAY 1998

MACPHERSON: Thank you for coming. I am sorry you have been kept waiting. Miss Weekes will ask you questions on behalf of the inquiry.

HOLDEN: Detective Constable Linda Holden.

MACPHERSON: Thank you. You do not need actually to lean forward over the microphone but bring the microphone close to you and then everybody will hear what you say. But speak up so the stenographer can hear you across the room.

WEEKES: You were one of those officers that received the notice that pointed out: "in your dealings as family liaison officer to Mr and Mrs Lawrence, you failed to provide them with adequate support and information concerning the murder of their son, Stephen on the 22nd of April 1993 and the subsequent police investigation"?

HOLDEN: That's correct.

WEEKES: Did you receive at the time any special training for family liaison?

HOLDEN: No specific training as such but in the manuals there are actually sections of different roles as police officers and there is actually a section for family liaison which tells officers what they would do or what they would expect.

WEEKES: You had not been appointed as family liaison before on any other murder?

HOLDEN: Yes, I had.

WEEKES: Oh?

HOLDEN: In 1991 I was the family liaison officer for a black family whose baby had been thrown into the Thames and a few months later I was the family liaison with an Asian family whose fifteen-year-old had been shot in the head.

WEEKES: So you had some experience with a black family and an Asian family at least two years prior to Stephen Lawrence?

HOLDEN: Yes.

WEEKES: Can I go to the Lawrence family. The relationship with Mr and Mrs Lawrence became very difficult?

HOLDEN: Unfortunately yes, it was very, very difficult, yes. There was so many outside agencies from different sorts of parties. I couldn't – I couldn't really get a close relationship with the family because there seemed to be a lot of barriers put up.

WEEKES: Outside agencies; who were they as far as you knew?

HOLDEN: Well, there was some people from the Anti-Racial Alliance.

WEEKES: Yes.

HOLDEN: There was obviously a solicitor.

WEEKES: Is that Mr Khan?

HOLDEN: That is Mr Khan, yes.

WEEKES: Did Mr Khan put any barriers to your communication with Mr and Mrs Lawrence?

HOLDEN: Yes, he did at times, yes.

WEEKES: Perhaps you will help us. What barriers?

HOLDEN: There were things we needed to know about Stephen's background to try and find out whether he had any enemies, whether he had anyone who did not like him, about his friends, certainly about the girlfriend, and just general different things that could have helped the inquiry.

WEEKES: It is quite important, are you saying that Mr Khan stopped the family giving that information?

HOLDEN: No, not at all.

WEEKES: How was it that it did not get to you because of Mr Khan?

HOLDEN: I felt that sometimes we always had to sort of go through Mr Khan. He would sort of say: "Well, if you speak to me and then I will go back to them," and sometimes you would be waiting for his reply.

WEEKES: But you would get the answer?

HOLDEN: Eventually, we would get the answer, yes.

WEEKES: So the problem was going through Mr Khan?

HOLDEN: Yes.

WEEKES: Not that you were stopped from getting information?

HOLDEN: That's right.

WEEKES: Did you think of speaking direct to Mr Khan or getting the Senior Investigating Officer to have a meeting with yourself and Mr Khan as it was you that appeared to have been having a difficulty with the family liaison. Was that done?

HOLDEN: I don't believe it was, no.

WEEKES: No. Any reason why it was not done?

HOLDEN: I really can't answer that.

WEEKES: Did you provide them with information about the inquiry? For example, when the suspects, five suspects, were to be arrested was it yourself that told the Lawrences before or after the arrest?

HOLDEN: I told them the night before that there was going to be arrests made the following day.

WEEKES: I want to ask you about the use of your mobile phone late at night. One of those occasions was, in fact, by Mr Khan?

HOLDEN: That's correct.

WEEKES: He rang you?

HOLDEN: Yes.

WEEKES: To give you information?

HOLDEN: Yes.

WEEKES: About some suspects?

HOLDEN: Yes.

WEEKES: Did that upset you, irritate you in any way?

HOLDEN: When he phoned I think it was about 12.15 at night. He gave me two names of two suspects. He said to me they were tooled up. By this I took it that he meant they were armed and he said they were going to do a burglary. With that I thought he meant straight away, like that particular night. So I said: "Well, do you mean, now?" He said: "No, that was on the night of the murder." This was now a week later. So I must admit I did say to him, I would put it into the system. There wasn't anything I could do at that time of night.

WEEKES: Did you mind him having your mobile number?

HOLDEN: I didn't actually give him my mobile number.

WEEKES: Did you mind him having your mobile number?

HOLDEN: No.

WEEKES: You expressed a view to the Police Complaints Authority that you did not think there was any need for him to have it. Why did you say that?

HOLDEN: I didn't think there was any need for him to have it but if he had said to me: "May I have your mobile number?", then he could have had it.

WEEKES: It would have been natural, as the solicitor representing the family, that he would have got hold of your mobile?

HOLDEN: Probably if he had asked me but he must have obviously got it from the family which is...

WEEKES: Did you tell him you thought there was no need for him to have it?

HOLDEN: No, I didn't, never.

WEEKES: Alright. If you would wait there.

KAMLISH: You say that you informed the family the night before the arrests that there were going to be arrests the following morning by telephone?

HOLDEN: Yes, I did, yes.

KAMLISH: Where is the truth here? Did you tell them the night before or did you not tell them until the following day after the arrests?

HOLDEN: Sorry, you are right. I didn't tell them about the arrests the night before obviously for operational reasons but I did tell them as soon as we made the arrests the next day. So that is absolutely correct, yes.

KAMLISH: You actually gave your mobile number to Mr Khan on the only occasion you met him at the Lawrence's household on the Sunday, did you not, even though you said in evidence a few moments ago that you did not?

HOLDEN: I know I gave two telephone numbers to the family, but I can't recall giving my mobile number to Mr Khan.

KAMLISH: Can you look at this note, please. It is one of Mr Khan's account slips. Is this your handwriting?

HOLDEN: I can't see it from there. (*Handed.*) That is my handwriting, but that is not my mobile telephone number.

KAMLISH: What you did was on the Sunday you gave him those numbers and you must have written down the wrong number, initially. It is your handwriting?

HOLDEN: That is definitely not my mobile telephone.

KAMLISH: You wrote it?

HOLDEN: That's right, but that it is not my number.

KAMLISH: It is the wrong number?

HOLDEN: That's right.

KAMLISH: You remember there came a time when you were made fully aware of the fact that the Lawrences were dissatisfied with the paucity of information coming from you to them and they became upset about this, did they not?

HOLDEN: That's correct, yes, they did.

KAMLISH: And the plan was to invite them to the incident room?

HOLDEN: That's correct.

KAMLISH: They were told specifically, were they not, that Mr Khan could not come?

HOLDEN: That did not come from me. The decision had been made by the senior officers and it was not for me to go and say to them: "Why are you doing that?"

KAMLISH: It was your job to do precisely that?

HOLDEN: No, it wasn't.

KAMLISH: Perhaps that is a convenient moment.

MACPHERSON: Yes. We will break off now for twenty minutes until 11.25. Do not, of course, talk about the evidence. Thank you very much.

Interval.

HOLDEN: Sir, can I clarify one point about my mobile phone.

KAMLISH: You are going to tell us it was your old number, are you not?

HOLDEN: I am, yes. I had time to reflect that I have actually changed my mobile phone number so that is the correct number.

KAMLISH: That can be the only answer, can it not?

HOLDEN: That's correct, sir.

KAMLISH: What was your view as to the motive for Stephen being killed at the time you were acting as family liaison officer?

HOLDEN: I was obviously aware that it was a racist murder, but what the motive was I couldn't say.

KAMLISH: Is not racism a motive? A motive is racism?

HOLDEN: Yes, that's right.

KAMLISH: Stephen was killed by a bunch of sadistic racists. Do you not accept that?

HOLDEN: I do, but I can't say what was in their minds at the time.

KAMLISH: Do you accept he was killed because he was black?

HOLDEN: I really can't answer that.

KAMLISH: You must have been aware of what the eyewitnesses were saying. Yes?

HOLDEN: Yes, I was but…

KAMLISH: I am sorry for interrupting you, but let me summarise. There were three white people at the bus stop near where Stephen fell, one of whom was a teenager, Jospeh Shepherd?

HOLDEN: Yes.

KAMLISH: Plus Mr Westbrook. And a young French woman?

HOLDEN: I think she was on top of the bus.

KAMLISH: She got on to the bus. According to Mr Westbrook, there were other white people. Do you remember him saying that?

HOLDEN: Yes, yes.

KAMLISH: This group of five or six white youths came straight up to Stephen Lawrence and Duwayne Brooks? Do you remember that evidence?

HOLDEN: Yes I do.

KAMLISH: Then they immediately surrounded them and knifed Stephen, and Duwayne got away. Yes?

HOLDEN: I believe that's correct, yes.

KAMLISH: And in the course of the attack or just before the attack, the words: "What, what nigger" were heard?

HOLDEN: That's correct, yes.

KAMLISH: Yes. So two young black men targeted for no apparent reason but racist language spoken, both of whom were strangers to the five or six white men, were they not? That was clear after a while?

HOLDEN: I believe so, yes.

KAMLISH: Can I ask you again to tell us what you think the motive was for this killing?

HOLDEN: I accept all the circumstances surrounding it and I know what you are saying but I can't say what was in the minds of those thugs that killed him. I don't know what their motive was. I can't answer that.

KAMLISH: Did you treat this as a motiveless killing when you were dealing with the Lawrences? You must have done.

HOLDEN: I think what I believed it to be was a tragic murder of a young man who had everything to live for, whether he was black, white, whatever. That's how I saw it.

KAMLISH: Shortly after the murder there was a press release by the Metropolitan Police Service in which this killing was described as a racist murder?

HOLDEN: Yes.

KAMLISH: You can understand, or can you, the way in which this family would have felt about that. You understand there is more…

HOLDEN: Yes, I do, yes.

KAMLISH: …there is more suffering, more fear, yes? A community not wanting to express their emotions to white people within days of their son being killed by white people in a racist killing. You can understand all of that, can you?

HOLDEN: Yes, perhaps I can, but I didn't look at the family like that. All I saw them as was a family who had lost their son.

KAMLISH: You do not understand how a black family might feel when their son has been killed in a racist attack then?

HOLDEN: I do. From the age of fifteen months old to the age of seventeen, I was actually brought up in Africa, so I do know and understand black people.

KAMLISH: Does that make you understand white racists in a white, suburban neighbourhood?

HOLDEN: I can't answer what those people were doing on that night. I can't answer that.

KAMLISH: You do not have the point, do you?

HOLDEN: I have got the point, but I can't say what was in their minds.

KAMLISH: Moving to questions that you were asking the Lawrences about Stephen himself. This also caused a problem and was handled extremely insensitively by you, was it not?

HOLDEN: No, it wasn't. We were trying to, the same way we would ask any family, what type of – I mean, I knew the type of person that he was and the type of young lad that he was from what I had heard, but in any enquiry we try to establish what the person is like, whether they have got enemies. It is just basically to get information about him.

KAMLISH: Do you not understand how they would have viewed those sort of questions when the police were accepting from the first day that he was killed in either a motiveless or a racist – or both – attack by people he did not know?

HOLDEN: I'm sure the family would have been very, very upset, but unfortunately with the type of enquiry that we were conducting it was necessary to try and establish any type of information we could find out.

KAMLISH: Why?

HOLDEN: To find out who could have been responsible for his murder, whether there was anyone else that might be involved.

KAMLISH: It went on, did it not? Enquiries and results about Stephen went on. You can see, can you knot how it might hurt the Lawrences that you are asking, not only his school headmaster, but his college principal what sort of person he was, whether he had any enemies? You can understand that, can you not?

HOLDEN: Yes, I can, yes.

FROM THE STATEMENT OF DUWAYNE BROOKS, 1 MAY 1998

MACPHERSON: Mr Menon, Mr Duwayne Brooks sits beside you?

MENON: On my left, sir.

MACPHERSON: We are very glad that he has come and we are grateful for his assistance. Thank you very much, Mr Brooks. Mr Menon, I understand, will read the statements of Mr Brooks. Thank you very much.

MENON: (*Reads.*) "Stephen Lawrence was one of my best friends. We met on our first day of secondary school – the Blackheath Bluecoats Church of England School. Both Stephen and I were eighteen when Steve was murdered. We saw each other regularly…"

MACPHERSON: I am so sorry to interrupt. Can you go a little slower because it has to be taken down.

MENON: "In the evening we were hurrying to get home as soon as possible. We were just looking for a bus on Well Hall Road. We were attacked by a group of white boys, one of whom shouted 'What, what nigger?' I can't bear to go into the details…

"As were we running from the attack, Steve fell to the floor. I stopped on the pavement. I went back and I bent down and looked at him. He was lying by a tree. He was still breathing. He could not speak. I saw his blood running away.

"I ran across to the phone box and dialled 999. I asked for an ambulance. I left the phone hanging to run round the corner to see if the boys were coming back up the road.

"I saw a white couple. I have since been told they are called Taaffe. They just ignored me. They looked at me and sort of shimmied away. I see he thought we might be going to rob them. A car stopped by Steve. I now know the driver was an off-duty policeman, Mr Geddis, who was with his wife.

"I was pacing up and down, up and down. I was desperate for the ambulance. It was taking too long. I was frightened by the amount of blood Steve was losing. I saw his life fading away. I didn't know what to do to help him. I was frightened I would do something wrong.

"WPC Bethel said, 'How did it start? Did they chase you for nothing?' I said one of them shouted, 'What, what nigger?'

"She asked me if I had any weapons on me. She was treating me like she was suspicious of me, not like she wanted to help. If she had asked me of more details of the boys' descriptions or what they were wearing I would have told her. Those would have been sensible questions.

"None of the uniformed officers were doing anything for Steve. They should have known what to do. They should have done something for Steve. They just stood there doing nothing.

"The ambulance arrived. They carried Steve to the ambulance on a stretcher. His unopened ginger beer can fell from him on to the floor. I picked it up. I took it home and kept it in my room, until one day it exploded. I am told I called the police 'pigs' and used the word 'c…t'. I did not. I don't use those words.

"I was driven to Plumstead Police Station. I now know that in their statements the police said I broke a window in the front office. I didn't. I wasn't even in the front office. It just shows they were treating me like a criminal and not like a victim. They kept saying, 'Are you sure they said, "What, what nigger?"' I said, 'I am telling the truth.' A senior officer said, 'You mean you have done nothing wrong to provoke them in any way?' I said, 'No, we were just waiting for a bus.'

"On the 8th of May, I went to a large anti-racist demonstration outside the British National Party headquarters in Welling. I went to protest against Steve's murder and the way the police were handling it. In October 1993, I was arrested and charged with offences arising out of the demonstration. They waited until the Crown Prosecution Service had decided to drop the prosecution against the killers. It was devastating. It felt like the police and prosecutors decided to get at me to ruin my reputation – and the chance of any future prosecution for the murders. But the judge at Croydon Crown Court wasn't having any of it. In December 1994, he stopped the prosecution saying it was an abuse of the process of the court.

"I think of Steve every day. I'm sad, confused and pissed about this system where racists attack and go free but innocent victims like Steve and I are treated as criminals and at the outset ignored me when I pointed out where the killers had run and refused to believe me that it was a racist attack.

"I never knew Steve to fight no-one. Steve wasn't used to the outside world. He wasn't street-aware of the dangers of being in a racist area at night-time. I shouted to run. He had ample time to run as the boys were on the other side of the road. Steve didn't understand that the group of white boys was dangerous.

"I was taken to the identification parade. I saw a skinhead there, Stacey Benefield. He said the boys who stabbed him were known to stab people and not to get done for it. He said they knew people in the police. I now know that the person I picked out was Neil Acourt.

"On the third identification parade, I now know I identified Luke Knight. Sergeant Crowley said something to the effect that I was guessing. I got angry. I recognised the attackers from the attack and not from any outside information. Nobody described the Acourt brothers to me. I did not know how important Sergeant Crowley's lies were until I heard it on the news that the two men who had been arrested had been released and it was to do with my evidence not being good enough.

"I never told the officer that friends told me descriptions of the people to identify before any parade. If the officer has said I could not identify Stephen's attackers by their faces, he has misunderstood what I said. During the course of general conversation, I said to the officer that I was anti-police and that I wanted to seek revenge for Stephen's death myself and also that I had only called for an ambulance on the night of the murder and not the police.

"I wanted to put down that Sergeant Crowley was a liar, but the officer would not write that down. I recognised the attackers from the attack, not from any outside information."

FROM THE EVIDENCE OF DETECTIVE INSPECTOR BULLOCK, 18 AND 19 MAY 1998

LAWSON: Benjamin Bullock, I believe you still hold the rank of detective inspector, do you not, in the Metropolitan Police Force?

BULLOCK: Yes, sir.

LAWSON: You were appointed the Deputy Senior Investigation Officer fairly early on the 23rd of April 1993?

BULLOCK: That's correct.

MENON: Mr Bullock, you do appreciate that a large number of what were material decisions in this case do not appear to have been recorded in the policy file?

BULLOCK: That is correct, sir.

LAWSON: As the weekend wore on, there became certain named prime suspects, did there not?

BULLOCK: Yes, sir.

LAWSON: The Acourt brothers, Dobson and Norris, in particular?

BULLOCK: Yes, sir.

LAWSON: During the course of Saturday the 24th of April the investigating team received sufficient information to justify making arrests, had you not?

BULLOCK: We had sufficient information to give reasonable ground, yes sir.

LAWSON: You could have arrested, made some arrests on the Saturday?

BULLOCK: Yes, sir.

LAWSON: The decision was not to arrest. Why was that?

BULLOCK: We had no evidence up to then.

LAWSON: But you could, in your opinion, lawfully have arrested, is that right?

BULLOCK: Yes sir.

LAWSON: You had information on the night of Friday the 23rd that the Acourt brothers did live at 102 Bournbrook Road. Mr Bullock, the justification you gave for not affecting arrests, that you had insufficient knowledge of the Acourts' address, do you think on reflection that really holds water?

BULLOCK: No, we had information of their address, but we couldn't verify that by other means.

LAWSON: Over these first few days what inquiry did you make about the Acourts, Norris, Dobson, racist attacks in the area. You were receiving information from a variety of sources?

BULLOCK: Yes, sir.

LAWSON: Saying they were a violent, nasty bunch?

BULLOCK: Yes.

LAWSON: Did you see whether there was any similar information available from police officers?

BULLOCK: Yes, I am sure we did, sir.

LAWSON: Then information was received which contains at least a positive prospect of an eyewitness being found. There still seems to be an unreasonable delay in doing anything about it, yes?

BULLOCK: Yes, sir.

LAWSON: Why is that?

BULLOCK: I have no answer for that.

LAWSON: No answer?

BULLOCK: No answer.

LAWSON: It does seem a chapter of disasters?

BULLOCK: That's correct.

LAWSON: Let us go to Friday the 30th, to PCA00320009, please.

There is a note suggesting that one of the sources had actually seen Norris and the Acourts in the vicinity on the night of the murder? Again important information?

BULLOCK: Yes sir.

LAWSON: Again requiring action?

BULLOCK: Yes sir. Unfortunately none of these people put this in writing after a number of attempts.

LAWSON: The 6th of May, this is the eve of the arrests, is it not?

BULLOCK: Yes, sir.

LAWSON: What prompted the decision to arrest on the 7th?

BULLOCK: A knife being found, and also a witness who comes out with a remark of "J" or "Jamie".

LAWSON: The arrests took place in the form of dawn raids?

BULLOCK: That's correct.

LAWSON: I want to ask you about knives, please. The Acourts and/or Norris, yes, were fascinated by knives and usually hide them under the floorboards?

BULLOCK: Yes, sir.

LAWSON: What instructions were given for looking under floorboards?

BULLOCK: I don't think there were instructions given to look under the floorboards but the team that was at that address did pull away carpet to look if floorboards were loose, etcetera, but I don't think people went in and just jimmied up floorboards.

LAWSON: You allocated your most experienced sergeant, Davidson, to Dobson, did you not? Did you brief him about the surveillance operation that had been carried out?

BULLOCK: I am not certain if he knew who was involved in the pictures from the surveillance.

LAWSON: He has told us that no one told him anything about them?

BULLOCK: I didn't know Norris was in the photograph.

LAWSON: Do you not think you could or should have found out who Norris was by the time he was arrested and being interviewed?

BULLOCK: I obviously would have liked to, sir. That is why we carried on observations at 102.

LAWSON: Let me ask you, please, about the Grant information coming in. You showed little or no interest in this information when it was being reported to the police station on the Friday night?

BULLOCK: There was interest in the message but at the time I was up to my eyeballs in other things.

LAWSON: But the information he was giving was potentially of great significance, was it not?

BULLOCK: Yes sir.

LAWSON: Not only identifying or purporting to identify the Acourts as being responsible for the murder of Stephen Lawrence, but implicating them in other violent assaults.

BULLOCK: Yes sir.

LAWSON: And it merited your immediate attention, did it not, as the Senior Investigating Officer on duty?

BULLOCK: If I have one regret it is that I didn't see Grant.

LAWSON: Mr Bullock, the arrests on the 7th of May, were there extraneous considerations, that is not connected to the evidence or information, pressures from outside, that contributed?

BULLOCK: No, sir.

LAWSON: You were presumably aware of Mr Mandela's much publicised visit on the 6th?

BULLOCK: Yes sir.

LAWSON: And you were aware of the threatened demonstrations which took place on the 8th of May?

BULLOCK: I believe I was, yes.

LAWSON: And you were obviously aware that there had been well-publicised criticism of the police, including complaints from the family, for inactivity?

BULLOCK: Yes, sir.

LAWSON: Did any of those factors have any bearing at all on the decision that was made?

BULLOCK: No, not at all.

LAWSON: With hindsight, is it the case, do you think, that the arrest should have been made more promptly?

BULLOCK: If I had to do it again sir, then yes, I would agree they should have been made more promptly.

LAWSON: You are speaking very quietly. Can the witness be heard by everyone? It was a racist attack?

BULLOCK: Yes, yes, without a doubt.

LAWSON: Let me ask you this: you referred to the victims of the assault, Stephen Lawrence and Duwayne Brooks, as the two young coloured lads?

BULLOCK: Yes.

LAWSON: Do you understand now that using the expression "coloured" is regarded as offensive?

BULLOCK: I didn't know that before, sir.

MANSFIELD: Officer, as you are aware, I represent Mr and Mrs Lawrence. Looking back over the first weekend and throughout the two vital weeks thereafter and for a longer period, what things do you think you would change?

BULLOCK: I would say an earlier arrest, I would have deployed somebody with that surveillance team, I would have tried to meet the family, obviously tried to contain the media a bit more.

MANSFIELD: The media?

BULLOCK: Try and use Mr Mandela in a positive way with the police. He could perhaps have appealed for witnesses, I don't know.

MANSFIELD: I want to turn to surveillance. The whole operation starting on the Monday really was a complete waste of time, money and resources and, effectively helped to delay arrest. Do you follow, that is the suggestion?

BULLOCK: I did say to you, sir, one of my regrets is that I did not put an officer with the surveillance team.

MANSFIELD: The whole operation would not have been improved by one officer being added to it. I am going to suggest root and branch, the whole operation was a nonsense start to finish, the way you did it.

BULLOCK: It wasn't, sir.

MANSFIELD: There is no tasking document from you that still exists?

BULLOCK: As you say, it doesn't exist, sir.

MANSFIELD: You see, Mr Davidson and others have said, effectively, if only they had known about photographs in the interview with Dobson, they would have used them. Do you follow? Can you explain how Mr Davidson was completely in the dark?

BULLOCK: I can't, no.

MANSFIELD: Unless, of course, the surveillance was really a sham, was it? Was it a sham? Did you really not want to use it?

BULLOCK: That's not true.

MANSFIELD: Where is the record of evaluation by you, namely, this shows Neil Acourt doing so and so. This shows a bin bag leaving the premises. Any record of that?

BULLOCK: I don't think so.

MANSFIELD: Why not?

BULLOCK: I don't think I made a record.

MANSFIELD: Why not, officer?

BULLOCK: I have no answer for that, sir.

MANSFIELD: You knew the name Norris was a criminal name but it has not rung any bells that this man could in any way be related to the famous or notorious, rather, name. That is your position?

BULLOCK: Yes.

MANSFIELD: You did not have an idea of what Norris looked like before he was arrested?

BULLOCK: That's correct.

MANSFIELD: Photographs, bin bags, removing clothing – by the Monday morning, the 26th, you had plenty of material to affect an arrest, did you not?

BULLOCK: Yes.

GOMPERTZ: Mr Bullock, on behalf of the Commissioner, if I may. What is being suggested in this inquiry is that there was a corrupt conspiracy between officers charged with the investigation of the murder of Stephen Lawrence to pursue that inquiry as their duty required they should, to drag their feet, putting it at its lowest, and to try and ensure that David Norris at least, and perhaps other defendants, escaped prosecution. Do you understand that?

BULLOCK: That is totally wrong, sir, totally wrong and offensive.

FROM THE EVIDENCE OF MR ILSLEY, FORMERLY DETECTIVE CHIEF CUPERINTENDENT, 2–4 JUNE 1998

LAWSON: Mr Ilsley, you remained Detective Chief Superintendent in charge of the on-going Stephen Lawrence investigation?

ILSLEY: That is correct, sir, yes.

LAWSON: Mr Ilsley, you in fact have expressed yourself to be angered and outraged by allegations made, that the investigation was affected by racism and/or collusion with a known criminal?

ILSLEY: That's correct, yes.

LAWSON: Do you acknowledge that there were serious deficiencies in the first murder investigation?

ILSLEY: I acknowledge there were deficiencies in the first murder investigation, yes, sir.

LAWSON: And serious or significant deficiencies?

ILSLEY: Significant I think is the right word.

LAWSON: You were aware, indeed you were part of the Barker review?

ILSLEY: Yes, sir.

LAWSON: You remember, presumably, his reporting that the investigation, the first investigation, had been progressed satisfactorily and all lines of enquiry correctly pursued?

ILSLEY: Yes, sir.

LAWSON: That is not tenable, is it?

ILSLEY: That's correct, sir.

LAWSON: You met with the Lawrences on the 6th of May, did you not?

ILSLEY: Yes, I did sir, yes.

LAWSON: There was handed to you this note which contained a list of suspects, is that right?

ILSLEY: That's correct, sir, yes.

LAWSON: And you know that Mrs Lawrence, in particular, was distressed because you appeared, in effect, to scrumple it up as if you were going to throw it away?

ILSLEY: That's correct, sir, yes.

LAWSON: She said, having handed the note to you, she saw you fold the paper up so small she found shocking. In fact, the original note is available. Can you take it please. (*Handed.*) It does bear the signs of having been folded and folded and folded again into a tiny piece of paper?

ILSLEY: Yes, sir, it does.

LAWSON: Do you think you must have done that, in fact?

ILSLEY: I certainly did, sir, yes.

LAWSON: Was that just you being blunt, tactlessness?

ILSLEY: Not tactlessness, no, sir.

LAWSON: It appeared you were not treating it seriously from what she could see?

ILSLEY: No, I dispute this. I think Mrs Lawrence has said that I screwed it up. I didn't screw it up. I folded it. Why I folded it like that, I don't know, but it went straight into the system.

LAWSON: What Mrs Lawrence said is: "He rolled the piece of paper up in a ball in his hand. I was shocked by what I saw."

ILSLEY: I didn't do that, sir.

LAWSON: But you did fold it up?

ILSLEY: I did fold it, absolutely, sir.

LAWSON: Could you pass it to the chairman, please. (*Handed.*) Is what you are telling us that you were not intending to be dismissive of this information?

ILSLEY: Certainly not, sir, no. How could I be dismissive?

LAWSON: The point, Mr Ilsley, is that you gave the appearance of at least of not treating it seriously?

ILSLEY: Why? By folding it up like that, sir?

LAWSON: Yes.

ILSLEY: I am sorry if I did, but it wasn't intentional in any way whatsoever. What can you say? How you fold something up is how you fold it up. According to Mrs Lawrence, I screwed it up into a ball, which I didn't do.

LAWSON: In due course, on the 6th of May, a decision was made to arrest?

ILSLEY: Yes.

LAWSON: And the basis for that decision was recorded.

Can we look, please, at PCA00450205: "One. All are known associates"?

ILSLEY: Yes

LAWSON: "Two. Artist's impression, similar to Acourts"?

ILSLEY: Yes.

LAWSON: "Three. Information from numerous sources", yes?

ILSLEY: That's correct, sir, yes.

LAWSON: "Four. Norris and possibly others thought to possess a knife". "Five. Strong possibility they were in the area around the time of the murder"?

ILSLEY: Yes, sir.

LAWSON: In terms of information that had been available most, if not all, of those grounds existed the previous two weeks, did they not?

ILSLEY: Yes, sir.

LAWSON: That is all I wish to ask this witness. Just before Mr Mansfield, if you will forgive me, one of your advisors has helpfully suggested it might be sensible *vis-à-vis* the note if I just ask Mr Ilsley to refold it in apparently the way in which it was folded up. (*Short pause.*) Hold it up so everyone can see it. Thank you very much.

MACPHERSON: I have a bit of useless information for you, that you cannot do it more than 8 times, however large the sheet of paper.

MANSFIELD: If there had not been first a complaint by Mr and Mrs Lawrence, you would still be saying there was nothing wrong with the first investigation, would you not?

ILSLEY: I would, sir, yes.

MANSFIELD: That is, to say the least of it, a very unhappy and unsatisfactory situation?

ILSLEY: It is, sir, yes.

MANSFIELD: You agree with all of that?

ILSLEY: I do, sir, yes.

MANSFIELD: I think you agree that reveals a shocking state of affairs, does it not?

ILSLEY: Yes, sir.

MANSFIELD: In the Metropolitan Police?

ILSLEY: At that particular time, sir, yes.

MANSFIELD: It was perfectly proper and obvious that you could have arrested the first weekend?

ILSLEY: Absolutely.

MANSFIELD: You had the legal powers to do it?

ILSLEY: Yes, sir.

MANSFIELD: Nobody would be criticising you for an arrest even if you did not have all the evidence, would they?

ILSLEY: No, sir.

MANSFIELD: The real day you could have gone in, it does not require hindsight, was Monday the 26th?

ILSLEY: I accept that, sir.

MANSFIELD: That happens to be the day on which the first plastic bag disappears before the cameraman is able to set up his camera?

ILSLEY: Yes, sir.

MANSFIELD: That was the day, had you gone in, you would have been in a much stronger position to recover the clothing which might contain fibres – every chance of gathering the smallest amount of evidence has to be taken, does it not?

ILSLEY: I accept what you are saying, yes, sir.

MANSFIELD: I want to deal with Mr Grant, the man we know as Grant. Grant provided the first information to police as to who was responsible for the murder of Stephen Lawrence.

ILSLEY: Yes, sir.

MANSFIELD: Do you know what Grant is saying happened with the Met? He is complaining that from the beginning he told the Met, your officers, who the source was for the information and the identity of somebody who was a witness. Did you know that?

ILSLEY: No, sir.

MANSFIELD: "Hasn't given us anything, won't pay him £50, uncooperative." That was your view of Grant?

ILSLEY: That was my view at that particular time.

MANSFIELD: Your view is that you did not want Grant at the forefront of this investigation because he was too hot to handle?

ILSLEY: What does that mean, sir?

MANSFIELD: He knew too much and you did not want to arrest at the first weekend, so Grant had to be kept out?

ILSLEY: How ludicrous. That is absolutely disgusting that you say something like that, sir.

MANSFIELD: I am going to suggest to you there is only one inference, because of your lack of action and information, do you follow, Mr Ilsley?

ILSLEY: What are you saying, sir? Are you saying that I am corrupt?

MANSFIELD: I am suggesting very clearly that you did not in fact use the very person who was prepared to give you precise information. The very thing you claimed you put off the arrests for was neglected and kept out of the way essentially?

ILSLEY: Because I am corrupt, that is what you are saying.

MANSFIELD: Do you think you are corrupt; is that what you are saying?

ILSLEY: That is what you are saying, sir.

MANSFIELD: You see, Mr Davidson – you are perhaps not aware of this – agrees that a name was given by Grant and an address.

ILSLEY: Well, I didn't know that, sir.

MANSFIELD: That message is a description of a stabbing whereby Norris commits a stab wound and so does Neil Acourt. Do you follow?

ILSLEY: Okay sir, I accept that.

MANSFIELD: It is important. It is somebody claiming to have seen two assailants attack Stephen Lawrence?

ILSLEY: Yes.

MANSFIELD: You are saying, are you, that you never knew that Grant had actually provided you with the name of an eyewitness?

ILSLEY: No, sir, only afterwards did I know, but not during the investigation, no.

MANSFIELD: You never knew it came from Grant?

ILSLEY: I didn't, sir, no.

MANSFIELD: Until now, today?

ILSLEY: Until today, yes.

MANSFIELD: Were you aware a Metropolitan Police Officer was consorting with Clifford Norris?

ILSLEY: No, sir.

MANSFIELD: Are you sure?

ILSLEY: Positive. I can't remember that. I might have known at any time. I can't remember it now.

MANSFIELD: We are calling "XX". It would be completely out of order for that officer to have meetings with Clifford Norris on the pretext of nurturing him as an informant; that would be completely out of order?

ILSLEY: It would, sir. Totally. Especially as a professional criminal, yes.

MANSFIELD: You became aware that David Norris was the son of Clifford Norris?

ILSLEY: Yes.

MANSFIELD: Did you then decide: "Well, one of the things we better do perhaps in this case since Clifford Norris is wanted, is to make sure we arrest him and get him off the scene." Did that occur to you?

ILSLEY: No sir.

MANSFIELD: Why not?

ILSLEY: Well, he is a wanted man.

MANSFIELD: Yes, why not get him arrested fast?

ILSLEY: If he could have been arrested he would have been arrested fast. I assume once someone is wanted, they are wanted.

MANSFIELD: You see, perhaps you cannot answer the question of how it is that he stays at large and then when a senior officer takes over from you, Mr Mellish, decides that the time has come to remove the Norris threat, he is then arrested. Can you help us as to how it is that Clifford Norris stays at large?

ILSLEY: I can't, sir. We were under tremendous pressure as far as resources were concerned.

MANSFIELD: You had a wonderful opportunity to get David Norris off the streets, did you not, in this case?

ILSLEY: Yes.

MANSFIELD: You knew by the Monday that Clifford Norris was related?

ILSLEY: I probably did, yes.

MANSFIELD: We go to the 6th of May, a final decision about an arrest. Was it being done in a rush for a particular reason, Mr Ilsley?

ILSLEY: Not as far as I know sir, no.

MANSFIELD: I would like you to think carefully. The 6th was a particularly important day, was it not?

ILSLEY: The Nelson Mandela...

MANSFIELD: That is right. It had a massive effect – your words – on the publicity in relation to this case?

ILSLEY: It did sir, yes.

MANSFIELD: It was not a good effect from your point of you, was it?

ILSLEY: You are probably right, sir, yes. We had not arrested anyone, that's right.

MANSFIELD: It is not good news to have perhaps one of the world's foremost statesman in London and picking up the fact that a squad under your command have not managed to pick somebody up. That is not good news from a public relations point of view, is it?

ILSLEY: I can see what your saying, yes, sir.

MANSFIELD: In relation to race. In this case, if anybody in your squad were to say that it wasn't racially motivated, that would beggar belief, would it not?

ILSLEY: As far as I was concerned it was a racially motivated crime and it was obvious from day one. As far as the other people are concerned, they have got to answer for themselves.

MANSFIELD: There was a great attempt by Davidson, Holden and others in this inquiry to try and make a distinction between a racist murder and racially motivated murders and so on, do you follow?

ILSLEY: I do sir.

MANSFIELD: Do you find that reprehensible?

ILSLEY: I find it incredible, yes.

MANSFIELD: You find it incredible. Thank you.

MENON: Mr Ilsley, I ask questions on behalf of Duwayne Brooks.

ILSLEY: Yes, sir.

MENON: When XX was interviewed he said the various meetings with Clifford Norris in public houses was by pure chance and that, although unauthorised by any senior officer, he was meeting Mr Norris for the purpose of cultivating him as an informant. That is what he told the internal inquiry. That inquiry concluded that there was more to the relationship between XX and Clifford Norris than XX was prepared to admit?

ILSLEY: Yes, sir.

MENON: Yet for reasons best known to that internal inquiry, they chose not to discipline him, but simply give "words of advice"?

ILSLEY: Yes.

MENON: Bringing it back closer to home, XX, we have discovered recently, guarded Duwayne Brooks on at least one night during the period of the private prosecution. Can you think of any less appropriate officer in the Metropolitan Police to have been chosen to protect Duwayne Brooks whilst he is giving evidence at the Old Bailey as part of the private prosecution?

ILSLEY: If the facts are what you say and I accept they are true, yes, I do, sir, I find it incredible.

FROM THE STATEMENT OF DOREEN LAWRENCE, 11 JUNE 1998

LAWSON: Sir, the proposal now is to invite the completion of the reading of Mrs Lawrence's statement, and then for the questioning of Mrs Lawrence.

MACPHERSON: Mrs Lawrence, thank you very much for being here. There is a glass of water there should you wish it. If you want to pause at any time let me know, will you not? Do not hesitate to tell me.

BOYE-ANAWOMA: I am going to carry on reading Mrs Lawrence's statement.

(*Reads.*) "The police were not interested in keeping us informed about the investigation. We were simply regarded as irritants.

"It was also claimed that the police found dealing with our solicitor a hindrance. Basically, we were seen as gullible simpletons. This is best shown by Ilsley's comment that I had obviously been primed to ask questions. Presumably, there is no possibility of me being an intelligent, black woman with thoughts of her own who is able to ask questions for herself. We were patronised and we were fobbed off. As the meetings went on, I got more and more angry. I thought that the purpose of the meetings was to give us progress reports, but what actually happened was that they would effectively say: stop questioning us. We are doing everything. That simply was not true, and it led me to believe then and now that they were protecting the suspects.

" In September 1993 we hoped to get some feedback from the Barker review. We met with him too. He said that he couldn't give us a copy of the report, but he promised that we would meet again so that he could tell us what he had found out. That was the first and last time we ever saw him. The second investigation started with meeting Commissioner Condon in April 1994. We discussed the Barker review, and that was the first time we met Ian Johnston. We were still kept in the dark about some things in the second investigation. We weren't told exactly what was happening, but we heard rumours that things had gone wrong with the first investigation, and I think there was some cover-up about what was going on. It was then decided that the Crown Prosecution Service wouldn't take matters further. I felt we had no choice but to take a private prosecution, and I don't believe they would have been acquitted if we could have presented everything to the jury. On the first day at the Old Bailey I was extremely optimistic, but from the minute the judge opened his mouth, my hopes were dashed. It was clear from the outset he had come with the intention of not letting the matter proceed further. The judge instructed them to return a verdict of not guilty. When he told them that there was no alternative they actually went outside to consider it and then came back in. They didn't want to do it.

"I believe that the Kent Police Complaints Authority Report has not got to the bottom of what went on, it scratched the surface. At the beginning the Kent Police Complaints Authority Report was saying that the police officers were not racist in their attitude. If it wasn't racism what was it? Incompetence? Corruption? That only goes some way to explain. We are told these officers have years of experience investigating murders. What went wrong? Something did. Their attitude tells me that it was racism.

"It has been suggested that we were telephoned on the morning of the 7th of May 1993 to be told of imminent arrests. We had a meeting with Ilsley on the evening of the 6th of May and nothing was told to us or mentioned either. We complained then to senior officers that we had not been notified of an arrest in advance and, on the second arrest date, we were telephoned. We assumed first. Half an hour later we saw it on the television.

"I would like Stephen to be remembered as a young man who had a future. He was well loved and had he been given the chance to survive maybe he would have been the one to bridge the gap between black and white; he just saw people as people."

MACPHERSON: Mrs Lawrence, there is just one matter I would like you to clarify. There has been a lot of debate over the incident with the information you gave to Mr Ilsley in note form and what exactly happened. I wonder if you could just decide for everybody what happened to that piece of paper?

MRS LAWRENCE: On the evening when we went to the police station, as I walked in, at the time I didn't know his name, I handed the piece of paper with the names on to this officer. He took the paper from me, he folded it in small pieces in his hand, and then he had it in his hands like this, crunched up in his hand like a ball, and he held it like that, and as I was walking out through the door, I said to him: "You are going to put that in the bin now, aren't you?" And he was shocked because he didn't realise I was watching him, and he quickly said: "No, we treat all information that comes to the police."

GOMPERTZ: Mrs Lawrence, I want to ask you some questions on behalf of the Commissioner. In doing so can I make it absolutely clear that my purpose is not to criticise you and your husband. Secondly can I make it clear that I am mindful of the Chairman's ruling that was made a long time ago that counsel who wish to ask you and your husband questions should confine themselves to matters of fact and not opinion.

Can I ask you please to look at your note. Those are the names, are they not, that you wrote on the piece of paper and took with you when you went to see Mr Ilsley?

MRS LAWRENCE: Yes.

GOMPERTZ: You see, the reason I ask you is that if all the names were written on this piece of paper, they did not include the names Norris or Knight, did they?

MRS LAWRENCE: No, people were confused about the names when they came to us.

GOMPERTZ: Can I ask you about something quite different now: your journey home from the hospital on the night in question. You went, did you not, to the Welcome Inn?

MRS LAWRENCE: No.

GOMPERTZ: Where did you go then?

MRS LAWRENCE: Can I ask a question here? Am I on trial here or something here? I mean, from the time of my son's murder I have been treated not as a victim. Now I can only tell you or put into my statements what I know of went on that night. And for me to be questioned in this way, I do not appreciate it.

MACPHERSON: Mr Gompertz, I think your discretion should be exercised in favour of not asking further questions.

GOMPERTZ: Sir I will, of course, accept your guidance.

MACPHERSON: Thank you.

EGAN: Can I just ask one matter of Mrs Lawrence, please. Do you remember you had a conversation with Holden, one of the police officers tasked with family liaison and, as a result, she delivered a birthday card to your daughter who was on an outward bound course. Do you remember that?

MRS LAWRENCE: Yes.

EGAN: Why do you think she did that?

MRS LAWRENCE: She wanted to be helpful.

MR MCDONALD: We have no questions.

MACPHERSON: Thank you very much, Mrs Lawrence.

FROM THE EVIDENCE OF WILLIAM MELLISH, FORMERLY DETECTIVE SUPERINTENDENT, 11, 15 AND 16 JUNE 1998

LAWSON: We are now leaving what might be called the first investigation and going into the second, which was conducted by Mr Mellish.

MACPHERSON: Mr Lawson, on behalf of the inquiry, will question you first.

MELLISH: Yes, sir.

LAWSON: Mr Mellish, we are grateful to you for volunteering your assistance to the inquiry. It is right, is it not, to say you were not involved in the investigation that was carried out by the Kent police.

MELLISH: That is correct.

LAWSON: No complaint or allegation having been made against you or relating to the second investigation?

MELLISH: No, sir.

LAWSON: Mr Mellish, it was in the middle of 1994, was it not, that you assumed the mantle of Senior Investigating Officer?

MELLISH: Yes, sir.

LAWSON: Can I ask you in the most general terms, your own experience of racism within the Metropolitan Police Force?

MELLISH: I would say there is some racism in some officers, in a minority of officers.

LAWSON: Over your last ten years, did it get better, get worse, or stay much the same, would you say?

MELLISH: I would say much the same.

LAWSON: Your investigation – you decided to take an entirely fresh approach? No one had been prosecuted to conviction.

MELLISH: Yes.

LAWSON: You were aware this was racially motivated?

MELLISH: Yes, sir.

LAWSON: By virtue of Duwayne Brooks' evidence of the shout of, "What, what nigger", before the gang attacked?

MELLISH: Yes, sir.

LAWSON: Your belief that this was a racially motivated murder was hardened up as a result of the use of intrusive surveillance methods?

MELLISH: Yes sir.

LAWSON: You knew that David Norris' father was Clifford Norris, wanted for a large-scale drug importation and that his presence in South-East London could have a significant intimidatory effect, both on witnesses and sources of information, including any supergrass, and that it would be profitable to bring about his arrest?

MELLISH: Yes, sir.

LAWSON: You seemed to arrest him quite quickly.

MELLISH: There was a point where David's birthday was coming up and we hoped that old man Norris would come and visit the boy. We searched the dustbin of David Norris and his mother received a birthday card from the husband which was our first indication that he was in the country and was in communication.

We did surveillance on mum and the boy and we were very lucky. She went down into the country and visited some oast house cottages near Battle, Sussex. We carried on observations and Norris went for a drink. My sergeant got in the pub and gave me a positive ID: it was Norris. I sought permission for an armed operation. The next morning Norris stopped for breakfast at the local café and was arrested.

LAWSON: Thank you. That came about thanks to a combination of surveillance operation, looking in a dustbin and a bit of luck?

MELLISH: Yes, sir.

LAWSON: Your report refers to loaded firearms, handguns, a sawn-off shotgun, and another weapon, an Uzi?

MELLISH: An Uzi machine gun.

LAWSON: And a large amount of ammunition?

MELLISH: Yes, sir.

LAWSON: I will move on, if I may. Intrusive surveillance – that included inserting the video-audio probe into the flat occupied by Dobson? The probe was inserted, in effect making a film?

MELLISH: Yes, sir.

LAWSON: Of what Dobson and his mates, including some of the other suspects, including some Acourts, were saying amongst themselves and doing in the flat?

MELLISH: Yes.

LAWSON: You have described an edited product of that probe revealing amongst that group of young men "a propensity for violence and the carriage of knives and raving bigotry"?

MELLISH: Yes sir.

MANSFIELD: Can I go to MET00510149, it is also PCA00450286. There it is.

The first thing that we see is that, despite Dobson's denials in interviews, he plainly is associating with the very people, one of whom he denied knowing, namely David Norris?

MELLISH: Yes, sir.

MANSFIELD: The purpose of the exercise was to produce evidence against the suspects of motive?

MELLISH: Yes, sir.

MANSFIELD: And that it did in abundance, did it not?

MELLISH: On racism, yes sir.

MANSFIELD: Can I extend it. It is beyond racism. It is racism conjoined with an obsession to extreme violence?

MELLISH: I would agree with that. I think I would add to that, "with knives".

MANSFIELD: There are vast tracks when often Neil Acourt is toying with knives of the very kind that it is thought by the pathologist inflicted the injuries on Stephen?

MELLISH: That is correct, sir.

MANSFIELD: There is another feature – the toying with knives. We can see before they leave through a door in the rear, they will go to the window sill, pick up the knife and they will put it in the inside of their trousers so it cannot be seen whilst they are walking along?

MELLISH: Yes.

MANSFIELD: In addition to all of that, Neil Acourt can be seen on more than one occasion actually demonstrating what I am going to call the modus operandi of this particular stabbing in the Lawrence case.

There are some racially obscene comments throughout the whole of this recording but perhaps the high water mark is when Neil Acourt is heard to say words to the effect: "I reckon that every nigger should be chopped up, mate, and they should be left with nothing but fucking stumps."

Then later David Norris indicates he would like to "go down Catford and places like that with two sub-machine guns and I am telling you, I'd take one of them, skin the black cunt alive, torture him, set him alight." In relation to comments like that by all of the four suspects, is it right to say consideration was given to prosecuting these men for incitement to racial hatred?

MELLISH: Yes, sir.

MANSFIELD: It is the Public Order Act 1986, section 18 (2). May I just read it so that it is clear to the public why no action has been taken. "An offence under this section may be committed in a public or a private place, except that no offence is committed where the words… are used…by a person inside a dwelling and are not heard or seen except by other persons in that or another dwelling."

That was seen to be providing a real practical problem in bringing a prosecution based on this recording?

MELLISH: That is true, sir.

MANSFIELD: Can I just ask, the officer we are calling XX. This is becoming like a Pinter play with surreal references. There is an officer named there in relation to Clifford Norris.

MELLISH: I am pretty sure he was on the Flying Squad at Tower Bridge with me when I was in charge. I was aware that XX had met a criminal in bad circumstances and was disciplined.

MANSFIELD: Neil Acourt was extremely conscious of the fact that something had happened in his room. There is a lot of concentrated interest on the plug and socket and that they are being recorded in the socket. Somebody has tipped them off?

MELLISH: I don't think so. The people at my end were people of utter integrity. There is another possibility which has always been my thoughts on the subject of how and why they suspected from the very first day, if I may give it to you.

MANSFIELD: Yes?

MELLISH: A day or so after the murder, David Norris is involved in it and gets hold of his father. The father sits the boys down wherever, somewhere in London, somewhere out of London, and gives them a very firm lesson in why they must keep their mouths shut, which they have done ever since.

Gives them a very firm lesson in methods of interception.

MANSFIELD: Right?

MELLISH: On technical and telephone. These eighteen-year-old spotty thugs were using the telephone box in the public street and not their own telephone. They had to be briefed by somebody, that is my point.

MANSFIELD: In relation to the Old Bailey trial, the private prosecution, had you known that XX had, in fact, been consorting with the father of one of the suspects – that is Clifford Norris – presumably you would have thought it quite improper, unwise, undesirable, whatever term you may use for him, that that is XX, to have anything to do with protecting, helping, or guarding the main eye witness, victim, Duwayne Brooks, in this case?

MELLISH: What you say is correct.

FROM THE EVIDENCE OF IAN JOHNSTON, ASSISTANT COMMISSIONER OF THE METROPOLITAN POLICE, 17 JUNE 1998

JOHNSTON: Ian Johnston, Assistant Commissioner, Metropolitan Police, sir.

LAWSON: Mr Gompertz informs me that you wish, on behalf of the Metropolitan Police, to make a statement.

JOHNSTON: Mr Lawrence, I wanted to say to you that I am truly sorry that we have let you down. It has been a tragedy for you, you have lost a son, and not seen his killers brought to justice. It has been a tragedy for the Metropolitan Police, who have lost the confidence of a significant section of the community for the way we have handled the case.

I can understand and explain some of what went wrong. I cannot and do not seek to justify it. We are determined to learn lessons from this. A great deal has changed and yet will change. We have tried over the last four years since the first investigation to show imagination and determination to prosecute Stephen's killers.

I am very, very sorry and very, very sad that we have let you down. Looking back now, I can see clearly that we could have and we should have done better. I deeply regret that we have not put his killers away. On behalf of myself, the Commissioner – who specifically asked me to associate himself with these words – and the whole of the Metropolitan Police, I offer my sincere and deep apologies to you. I do hope that one day you will be able to forgive us.

Finally, I would like to add my own personal apologies for supporting the earlier investigation in ways in which it has now been shown that I was wrong. I hope the reasons for my support will be understood, and I hope that, eventually, you will forgive me for that as well, Mr Lawrence.

LAWSON: You know it has long been suggested by the Lawrence family and by others that the investigation was tainted by racism? What, if any, views do you wish to express about that?

JOHNSTON: It is my firm view that is not the case.

LAWSON: Mr Johnston, soon after you became involved, in the spring of 1994, as far as you were aware, the Barker report was a competent report?

JOHNSTON: I certainly believed it to be so at the time. I accept that it has been totally discredited.

LAWSON: Thank you.

MANSFIELD: May I begin by making it very clear on behalf of Mr and Mrs Lawrence that your initial statement today apologising for what has happened is both welcomed and appreciated.

JOHNSTON: The apologies were heartfelt, sir.

MANSFIELD: Can I go back to some other stages. The Barker review. I want to come to a particular document, MET00890004. This is one of the first meetings you had with the family.

JOHNSTON: In fact, how it happened was, I sat down, I had Mr and Mrs Lawrence on either aside and I read through to them the details, it is the opening page, which in essence gave the investigation, quite wrongly, a clean bill of health.

MANSFIELD: The unexpurgated version had not been written down, namely there were observed criticisms, errors, omissions, and shortcomings which had not been written down.

JOHNSTON: I am absolutely appalled by that. It really is totally, utterly unacceptable.

MANSFIELD: When one turns to the aspect of corruption. Corruption may take many forms. It may not necessarily just be the obvious form of money changing hands but collusion in a wider sense, namely, there is an understanding occurring between organised crime and some people who investigate organised crime. You appreciate the risk?

JOHNSTON: There are subtleties around corruption as there are around racism.

MANSFIELD: There is an officer, who we have been calling XX. Do you know who I mean?

JOHNSTON: I think I know who you are talking about.

MANSFIELD: There was a much closer relationship between Clifford Norris and the officer than he was prepared to admit to. Do you follow?

JOHNSTON: Yes.

MANSFIELD: The first tribunal came to the conclusion that he should be dismissed before he appealed, and he was reduced to the rank of Detective Constable. The question really is this. It really is, would you agree, astonishing that he should be an operational police officer in the detective branch dealing with crime in the very area where the Norris family are thought to have an influence. Would you agree with that?

JOHNSTON: On the fact as put to me, I am appalled that this particular individual is still working for the Metropolitan Police.

KAMLISH: Mr Johnston, I am going to ask questions on the issue of race. You are aware of a recent Met report which shows that black people were four times more likely to be stopped and searched in a street as white people?

JOHNSTON: If we look at the people who are likely to be out on the streets, youngsters who are truanting and excluded from schools, who are over-represented in the statistics, it is young black children. If you look at who else is out on the streets, it is the unemployed. If you look at the differential rates of unemployment, black people, for a range of reasons, some of which are understandable, some of which are abhorrent, are unemployed.

If you look at police where police do their stop and search, it is in high crime areas. High crime areas tend to be areas of social deprivation. Who lives in areas of social deprivation? For a range of reasons, coloured people.

FROM THE EVIDENCE OF JAMIE ACOURT, 29 JUNE 1998

J. ACOURT: I do solemnly, sincerely and truly declare and affirm that the evidence I shall give shall be the truth, the whole truth and nothing but the truth.

MACPHERSON: Mr Acourt, would you be seated?

LAWSON: Your name is Jamie Acourt, is it not?

J. ACOURT: That's right.

LAWSON: You understand, do you, Mr Acourt, that in common with all other witnesses giving evidence to this inquiry, you enjoy immunity in the sense that you cannot be prosecuted for anything that you admit to or say today?

J. ACOURT: Yes.

LAWSON: You understand, do you, that you cannot, by direction of the High Court, be asked any questions about whether you did or did not participate in Stephen Lawrence's murder?

J. ACOURT: Yes.

LAWSON: You appreciate that you are required to tell the truth?

J. ACOURT: Yep.

LAWSON: Are you willing to assist the inquiry?

J. ACOURT: Yes.

LAWSON: Let me ask you about knives, first of all. When you were arrested by police on the 7th of May 1993 at your home, as you know, a number of weapons were found, were they not?

J. ACOURT: Yes.

LAWSON: They included a tiger lock-knife and a Gurkha-type knife that were found in an upstairs bedroom. You are aware of that?

J. ACOURT: Yes.

LAWSON: Whose were they?

J. ACOURT: It wasn't my bedroom. I'm not sure.

LAWSON: Whose was the sword and scabbard found under the cushions on the sofa downstairs?

J. ACOURT: Those was ornaments, those was in the house.

LAWSON: Ornaments?

J. ACOURT: Yes.

LAWSON: Why under the cushions on the sofa?

J. ACOURT: I have no idea

LAWSON: Any particular reason, or is that where they are usually kept?

J. ACOURT: I have no idea.

LAWSON: Suggestions that you as a group commonly carried knives are completely untrue, are they?

J. ACOURT: Yes.

LAWSON: Can you proffer any suggestion as to why those suggestions might have been made?

J. ACOURT: No idea.

LAWSON: So the allegation of your being knife-carriers is wholly untrue, you tell us?

J. ACOURT: Yes.

LAWSON: What about the allegations of racism, are they wholly untrue?

J. ACOURT: Yes.

LAWSON: What about your brother, Neil, is it true of him?

J. ACOURT: No.

LAWSON: Your friend, Norris?

J. ACOURT: No.

LAWSON: Dobson?

J. ACOURT: No.

LAWSON: Knight?

J. ACOURT: No.

LAWSON: You attended a committal hearing when you were charged with Stephen Lawrence's murder. Did you see a surveillance video made by the police?

J. ACOURT: Yes.

LAWSON: That was peppered with references to racial comments?

J. ACOURT: I can't remember.

LAWSON: Did you remember all the references to niggers, Pakis?

J. ACOURT: No.

LAWSON: Have you ever come across racists?

J. ACOURT: No.

LAWSON: Is that the truth?

J. ACOURT: Yep. Not what I know of.

LAWSON: You know, do you not, that on the 20th of April you were photographed coming out of 102 Bournbrook Road* with a black bin liner containing something?

J. ACOURT: Yes.

LAWSON: What were you taking in the bin liner?

J. ACOURT: Dirty washing.

MACPHERSON: I asked you originally if you were willing to assist the inquiry and you said yes?

J. ACOURT: Yes.

LAWSON: Do you mean that?

J. ACOURT: Yes.

MACPHERSON: Before anyone else asks you questions I want to ask you one or two: you said you were willing to help insofar as you can by speaking the truth.

J. ACOURT: Yes.

MACPHERSON: As to the racism attitudes of yourself and particularly your brother and the others, having seen the surveillance video, you must know that they showed the most terrible racism. Do you not know that?

J. ACOURT: I can't speak on behalf of other people.

MACPHERSON: No. You have seen the film?

J. ACOURT: I have seen it once and it was a long time ago.

MACPHERSON: The only warning that I will therefore give you is this: you have immunity in connection with the matters which have been investigated in the past but if you commit perjury you may be prosecuted, do you realise that?

J. ACOURT: I understand that, I understand that.

MANSFIELD: It's the 3rd of December 1994, you're in custody. You're not there, it's 11.30 at night. I am going to ask you about a specific passage, near the beginning of the transcript. By strange, ironic coincidence, football is the topic of the day. Luke Knight complaining about the commentators wanting the Cameroons, "fucking niggers," to win. Your brother says: "Makes you sick, doesn't it?"

Neil Acourt says, whilst picking up a knife from a window ledge in the room and sticking it into the arms of a chair says: "You rubber lipped cunt. I reckon that every nigger should be chopped up, mate, and they should be left with nothing but fucking stumps." Now, Jamie, have you forgotten that?

J. ACOURT: Yes, I have, yeah.

MANSFIELD: Right. Shocked are you? An honest reply, please.

J. ACOURT: I ain't shocked. It is nothing to do with me. I ain't shocked.

MANSFIELD: David Norris is saying: "I'd go down Catford and places like that, I am telling you now, with two sub machine-guns and, I am telling you, I'd take one of them, skin the black cunt alive, torture him, set him alight."

Then a little further down: "I would blow their two legs and arms off and say, and say, 'Go on, you can swim home now'," and he laughs. Neil Acourt, your brother, says: "Just let them squirm like a tit in a barrel." Do you find all this shocking?

J. ACOURT: I have no comment on it.

MANSFIELD: You indicated that you did know Clifford Norris.

J. ACOURT: I met him when he was younger.

MANSFIELD: After your arrest on the 7th of May did you meet him at all?

J. ACOURT: Not what I can remember, no.

MANSFIELD: Well you know David Norris?

J. ACOURT: Yes.

MANSFIELD: Did he say his father was wanted for major crime?

J. ACOURT: No.

MANSFIELD: Mr Norris never tipped you off about what police might do to listen to you, to watch you?

J. ACOURT: No.

MANSFIELD: You do carry knives in public, do you not?

J. ACOURT: No.

MANSFIELD: In January '93 the police stopped you, you were found in public with a folding lock-knife, were you not?

J. ACOURT: I can't remember all the details.

MANSFIELD: Had you forgotten that you possessed a weapon in public?

J. ACOURT: Until you mentioned it, then I remembered.

MANSFIELD: At 102 – that is the address you were at at that time – quite a large number of weapons were found, were they not?

J. ACOURT: They weren't a large number of weapons, no.

MANSFIELD: Were you present when your room was searched?

J. ACOURT: Yeah.

MANSFIELD: It is clear two just ordinary kitchen knives were found in your bedroom? Did you do cooking in your bedroom?

J. ACOURT: Where was they found in the bedroom?

MANSFIELD: One was found behind a television.

J. ACOURT: No, that weren't in my bedroom.

MANSFIELD: It says: "Downstairs bedroom, Jamie Acourt, two knives."

J. ACOURT: Okay.

MANSFIELD: The revolver. That is a very life-like heavy revolver. What ammunition did you use?

J. ACOURT: It was broken, but it had a pump. I've never used it.

MANSFIELD: In an upstairs bedroom, there was a white jacket which had on it what appeared to be blood staining the right sleeve. Do you know anything about the white jacket?

J. ACOURT: No.

MANSFIELD: In the living room, found between the cushions on the settee, was a sword in a scabbard – this sort of length. What was it doing down the cushions of the sofa?

J. ACOURT: I don't know.

MANSFIELD: I would like you to look at this please. (*Green shirt handed to Acourt.*) This was found on a chair in your bedroom. Is that your shirt?

J. ACOURT: I suppose so.

MANSFIELD: I am going to suggest to you that you carried knives quite regularly and in the spring of 1993 this shirt demonstrates how you carried them. This shirt, do you see, has six cuts in it?

J. ACOURT: Yes, I can see that.

MANSFIELD: Just kindly tell us how those cuts got there?

J. ACOURT: I couldn't tell you; I wouldn't know.

MACPHERSON: You may leave the witness box.

FROM THE EVIDENCE OF HOWARD YOUNGERWOOD, CROWN PROSECUTOR, 1 JULY 1998

WEEKES: Mr Youngerwood, your full name is Howard Youngerwood.

YOUNGERWOOD: Howard Alexander Youngerwood.

WEEKES: In 1990 you became a Crown Prosecutor. I want to flag up, if I may, the code for Crown Prosecutors. Two very important paragraphs.

YOUNGERWOOD: These were the core of the code.

WEEKES: "If the case does not pass the evidential test, it must not go ahead, no matter how important or serious it may be.

"If the case does pass the evidential test, the Crown Prosecutors must decide whether a prosecution is needed in the public interest."

YOUNGERWOOD: A code is no better than its contents. However desirable, however much people might want to prosecute, if on your assessment and in all conscience and under analysis there is insufficient evidence that you simply stop there, whatever private thoughts you might have and however much you want to proceed.

WEEKES: Speak a bit slower?

YOUNGERWOOD: I am sorry.

WEEKES: Can I move on to the Stephen Lawrence inquiry itself. You undoubtedly had the assistance of other Crown Prosecutors who worked on this case.

YOUNGERWOOD: Yes.

WEEKES: We know that the discontinuance notice was dated the 29th of July 1993?

YOUNGERWOOD: Yes.

WEEKES: I would like to know how it came about, the actual notice itself.

YOUNGERWOOD: I became aware roughly at the end of June 1993 that Mr Grant Whyte and Mr Medwynter, between them, were acutely concerned about the state of the evidence.

These were difficult, chaotic days. I sensed that there was perhaps an understandable fear to take a decision they thought was inevitable and they wanted me, quite properly, to take that decision. A fear because of the understandable public concern and apprehended backlash which was entirely understandable.

WEEKES: Right. What happened?

YOUNGERWOOD: My first contemporaneous note made very unhappy reading. Unhappy in both a professional and human being sense. The evidence in my view was even worse than I had been led to believe.

The issue was simply this: the issue was not, was this a racial murder? Anyone who deludes themselves that it was not is not living in this land. But the legal issue basically is the difficult one of identification of a wicked racial murder.

The only identifying witness at that stage was Mr Duwayne Brooks.

The point was that Duwayne Brooks was not identifying the stabber. He had no reason to witness anything that the suspects had done, except they were in a group. Of course he had seen a group. He had described them as young, white men in jeans, but when I was looking at the vital question of identification, the important thing, especially when you compare it with what the other witnesses are saying, is did Mr Brooks see anything of relevance? When you take Mr Brooks' evidence *in toto*, apart from seeing a group converging on Stephen, he had not seen – I do not blame him for this – he had not seen any other battery, physical assault.

WEEKES: Right, we move on to the second point, which is corroboration. What did you understand that to be?

YOUNGERWOOD: There were one or two other witnesses who could have given valuable evidence about a group attack, but on the key difficult issue of identification, we had only one witness, Mr Brooks.

WEEKES: Thank you, Mr Youngerwood.

WOODLEY: I ask questions on behalf of the Senior Investigating Officers in the first investigation. What was your attitude when you heard that the Lawrence family solicitors were planning to launch a private prosecution?

YOUNGERWOOD: I was very, very worried. The evidence was, and I know it causes problems, the evidence was, I can't repeat it enough, sadly, hopeless at that stage.

I was telling Mr Khan I was not behaving like a faceless, boring official.

I was trying to speak to him as a human being who had suffered from racism. It scars my personality. When Mr Khan announced they were going ahead with a private prosecution, I was so desperate, I collapsed in the street. I was ill at home. I had to be physically helped into the office by my wife.

I conveyed increasingly desperately my views, to try and stop this prosecution going ahead, not for improper motives but because I feared what would happen, that we would never get justice.

Blackout.

CLOSING STATEMENT BY MACPHERSON OF CLUNY

MACPHERSON: Thank you very much. Ladies and Gentlemen, that concludes the evidence which will be heard by this public inquiry in connection with the matters arising from the death of Stephen Lawrence. I should indicate, however, that the future holds much activity and much work still to be done.

Finally, it seems to me right that we should end as we started with a minute of silence to remember Stephen Lawrence and to couple with that our congratulations, if that is the right word, on the courage of his parents.

Would you stand with me for a minute's silence.

A minute's silence.

Thank you very much for your attendance today.

The End.

JUSTIFYING WAR

SCENES FROM THE HUTTON INQUIRY

Characters

THE RIGHT HONOURABLE LORD HUTTON

THE LAWYERS

JAMES DINGEMANS QC

PETER KNOX

THE WITNESSES

PATRICK LAMB

ANDREW GILLIGAN

SUSAN WATTS

MARTIN HOWARD

ALASTAIR CAMPBELL

JAMES BLITZ

ANDREW MACKINLAY MP

GEOFF HOON MP

WING COMMANDER JOHN CLARK

GAVYN DAVIES

DR BRIAN JONES

MRS JANICE KELLY

Justifying War was first performed at The Tricycle Theatre, London on 30 October 2003, with the following cast:

THE RIGHT HONOURABLE
LORD HUTTON, James Woolley

The lawyers

JAMES DINGEMANS QC, Mark Penfold

PETER KNOX, Adam Barker

The Witnesses

PATRICK LAMB, Thomas Wheatley

ANDREW GILLIGAN, William Chubb

SUSAN WATTS, Sally Giles

MARTIN HOWARD, David Beames

ALASTAIR CAMPBELL, David Michaels

JAMES BLITZ, Thomas Wheatley

ANDREW MACKINLAY MP, Roland Oliver

GEOFF HOON MP, Kenneth Bryans

WING COMMANDER JOHN CLARK, David Beames

GAVYN DAVIES, David Fleeshman

DR BRIAN JONES, William Hoyland

MRS JANICE KELLY, Sally Giles

Director, Nicolas Kent with Charlotte Westenra

Designer, Claire Spooner

Lighting, Johanna Town

Sound, Shaz McGee & Mike Thacker

Producer's Note

Lord Hutton's Inquiry into the circumstances surrounding the death of Dr David Kelly sat for 25 days and heard from 75 witnesses. These edited transcripts are taken from the evidence of 12 witnesses in the first part of the Inquiry.

The evidence is presented chronologically, with the exception of that of Dr Jones. He gave his evidence two days after Mrs Kelly. It is presented here before her evidence. Of the witnesses we have chosen, all but five (Watts, Blitz, Mackinlay, Mrs Kelly and Dr Jones) were recalled for crossexamination in part 2 of the Inquiry.

The main purpose of the second part was to allow the earlier evidence to be tested in cross-examination by opposing counsel representing the Government – both ministers and officials – Dr Kelly's family, and the BBC and to be questioned further by counsel for the Inquiry itself.

Lord Hutton is expected to present his report to the Government in the New Year.

The text in square brackets indicates an addition [made for clarification purposes] to the original hearing script.

The following text was correct at the time of going to press.

USHER: Ladies and gentleman, could you please switch off your mobile phones.

Silence. All rise.

Opening Statement by Lord Hutton, 1st August 2003

HUTTON: This Inquiry relates to a very tragic death. Therefore, ladies and gentlemen, I think it would be fitting if we stood for a minute's silence in memory of Dr Kelly. My terms of reference are these: 'Urgently to conduct an investigation into the circumstances surrounding the death of Dr Kelly.' First of all, my primary task is to investigate the circumstances surrounding the death and that will involve a detailed and careful examination of the relevant facts. Secondly, my terms of reference require me to conduct the investigation urgently, and that means I must proceed with expedition. Thirdly, I must ensure that the procedures at the Inquiry are fair to those who give evidence. It is also important that I should emphasise that this is an Inquiry to be conducted by me – it is not a trial conducted between interested parties who have conflicting cases to advance. I do not sit to decide between conflicting cases – I sit to investigate the circumstances surrounding Dr Kelly's death.

Patrick Lamb, 11th August 2003

DINGEMANS: While we are waiting we might as well get have DOS 1/55. Mr Lamb, could you tell his Lordship your full name?

LAMB: My full name is Patrick Lamb.

DINGEMANS: And what is your current occupation?

LAMB: I am presently the deputy head of the Counter Proliferation Department in the Foreign and

Commonwealth Office. I worked very closely with David Kelly.

DINGEMANS: Can I deal with the dossier. Now I think you have disclosed that Dr Kelly was involved in April 2002 in the first draft.

LAMB: Correct.

DINGEMANS: Was he involved in the May additions?

LAMB: Yes, he was. At all times we would show the text to David and we would very much rely on his expertise and knowledge, as the source and person who could verify the accuracy of what we were producing.

DINGEMANS: That was because of his involvement in the UNSCOM inspections?

LAMB: Very much so. He obviously had direct involvement. Often, I can recall, if I had to make a choice between a textual choice and Dr Kelly, I would often back Dr Kelly ahead of the textual source

DINGEMANS: But it appears that David Kelly had further involvement, is that right?

LAMB: He had further involvement through me, which is that after the decision by the Prime Minister on 3rd September that there would be a public dossier there was obviously a revision of the constituent parts. Our relationship with Dr Kelly was a very easy one, a very relaxed one; and when he came into the department we would, as a matter of course show him drafts if drafts were available and we would discuss them with him. This was, as I say, on an informal basis.

DINGEMANS: Looking at the contents page [of the dossier], those bits of the chapter that you, in the Foreign and Commonwealth Office, would have discussed, if I can use that term, I hope fairly, with Dr Kelly would be part 2, History of UN Weapons Inspection and chapter 3, The Current Position; is that right?

LAMB: That would be correct. I would add, however, there is also part 3, Iraq Under Saddam Hussein, which became known, informally at least, to those of us involved in the Cabinet Office meetings, as the human rights element of the dossier. There we would have discussed that also with Dr Kelly.

HUTTON: Can I just ask you Mr Lamb on part 2 of the September dossier Dr Kelly would have commented on that, he did not actually write it, he commented on it, but he actually wrote, did he, the first draft of the box on page 38?

LAMB: He would have written what eventually became the first draft in the box on page 38. He also contributed in particular on pages 11 and 12 that relate to the chemical weapons and biological weapons agents developed by Iraq, their lethality and so on; and obviously he acted as technical adviser in that respect.

HUTTON: Yes; but when you say 'contributed', do you mean that he made comments on a draft that you or someone else had written or that he wrote it himself?

LAMB: With respect to Iraq's biological weapons programme, he wrote that himself.

HUTTON: I see, yes. Thank you very much.

DINGEMANS: Is that all that you can help with on the drafting of the dossier, from your point of view?

LAMB: I believe that it is, sir, yes. We worked extremely well in a very happy manner in many respects. It was not a labour of love, it was something we thought was extremely important, continue to believe to be extremely important. I am only very saddened that that happy atmosphere has the shadow of Dr Kelly's death hanging over it.

Andrew Gilligan, 12th August 2003

DINGEMANS: Can you tell his Lordship your full name?

GILLIGAN: Yes, it is Andrew Paul Gilligan. I am the defence and diplomatic correspondent of the Today Programme on Radio 4.

DINGEMANS: Can you tell us when you first met Dr Kelly?

GILLIGAN: Yes, it was in the early months of 2001. I cannot tell you exactly when because I have lost my appointments diary for that year but it was probably in January or February. I was going to Iraq and I wanted to speak to him to discuss, you know, Iraqi related issues with him.

DINGEMANS: How had you come on his name?

GILLIGAN: He had been initially recommended to me by a colleague at the BBC, and I had then found his details in fact in our central contacts database. There is a sort of potted biography of him and it starts by saying: 'If David Kelly were a tax inspector he would recoup Britain's entire national debt.'

DINGEMANS: Did he describe his role in the dossier?

GILLIGAN: He did in outline terms. I said something like: what was your involvement? He said it was to advise on all claims relating to his expertise in the dossier.

DINGEMANS: And what did you understand his expertise to be?

GILLIGAN: Chemical and biological weapons. He had spent a great deal of time in Iraq. He was pretty close to the subject.

DINGEMANS: What view did he convey to you of the Iraqi regime?

GILLIGAN: He was extremely suspicious of them; and I mean he had been involved in many confrontations with them when he was an UNSCOM inspector.

DINGEMANS: Who was responsible for the meeting on 22nd May? Did you contact him or did he contact you?

GILLIGAN: No, I contacted him.

DINGEMANS: Can I take you to diary entry BBC/7/55? You have written 4 o'clock. Did you actually meet at 4 o'clock or could it have been afterwards?

GILLIGAN: I was slightly, you know, maybe 10 or 15 minutes late. He was waiting when I got there.

DINGEMANS: I think you have seen his evidence where he said the meeting was at 5. Does that accord with your recollection?

GILLIGAN: No, I think it was at 4. It was certainly fixed for 4 and then I went on to something else; and I am pretty sure, you know, it would not have started later than about 4.10 or 4.15. I have a drinks receipt, I bought drinks for us.

DINGEMANS: We will come to that. Can we turn to BBC/7/56. You did not have something to eat [at] this time?

GILLIGAN: I do not think so. We might have had some sandwiches or more drinks but that is the only thing I can find.

DINGEMANS: That shows a bottle of Coke and a bottle of Appletize. Can you help me with the time on that?

GILLIGAN: That says 4.15, 16.15. That is the time I went to the bar to buy the drinks.

DINGEMANS: You still have this receipt because I imagine you put this through the BBC accounts, do you?

GILLIGAN: Yes, I need to claim it back for expenses.

DINGEMANS: The notes you made on 22nd May 2003, were those made with a pen and pencil or with some other means?

GILLIGAN: They were made on my personal organiser.

DINGEMANS: Can we turn to BBC/7/57? This is the printout from your personal organiser?

GILLIGAN: Yes.

DINGEMANS: Yes, just reading the note through, if that is alright.

GILLIGAN: 'Transformed week before publication to make it sexier. The classic was the 45 minutes. Most things in dossier were double source but that was single source. Most people in intelligence weren't happy with it because it didn't reflect the considered view they were putting forward. 'Campbell: real information but unreliable, included against our wishes. Not in original draft – dull, he asked if anything else could go in. 'It was small…', this is the programme, I think. 'It was small because you could not conceal a large programme.' I cannot read it, the type is a bit faint.

HUTTON: It looks like 'thin'. Is it 'I think'?

GILLIGAN: 'I think it is 30 per cent likely that Iraq had an active chemical warfare programme?

HUTTON: Is it 'chemical warfare' or 'chemical weapons'?

GILLIGAN: Either really. We started by talking about other things and then we got on to the dossier; and I said: What happened to it? When we last met you were saying it was not very exciting. He said: 'It was transformed in the week before publication'. I said: To make it sexier? And he said: Yes, to make it sexier. Then I said: What do you mean? Can you give me some examples? And he said the classic – he did not use the word example, he said the classic was the 45 minutes, the statement that WMD could be ready in 45 minutes.

DINGEMANS: Then there is the entry which is just a single word, 'Campbell'. Was there any question that gave rise to that entry?

GILLIGAN: Yes, it was something like: how did this transformation happen?

DINGEMANS: Right.

GILLIGAN: And then the answer was that, one word.

DINGEMANS: He said just 'Campbell'?

GILLIGAN: Yes.

DINGEMANS: And what question led to the next entry?

GILLIGAN: Well I was surprised and I said: What, you know, Campbell made it up? They made it up? And he said: No, it was real information but it was unreliable and it was in the dossier against our wishes.

HUTTON: May I just ask you, Mr Gilligan, looking at the first paragraph, you put the question: Was it to make it sexier? And Dr Kelly replied: Yes, to make it sexier?

GILLIGAN: Yes, to make it sexier, yes, so he adopted my words.

HUTTON: Now are you clear in your recollection that you asked how was it transformed, and that the name Campbell was first spoken by Dr Kelly?

GILLIGAN: Yes, absolutely.

HUTTON: It was not a question by you: was Campbell involved in this?

GILLIGAN: No, it was him. He raised the subject of the 45 minutes and he raised the subject of Campbell.

HUTTON: Yes

DINGEMANS: Was there anything else that you did to confirm or deny the story?

GILLIGAN: Well, I went to look at the dossier itself, and to sort of do a sort of textual analysis of the dossier itself.

DINGEMANS: Is there any passages you would like to refer us to?

GILLIGAN: There is a passage on page 18.

DINGEMANS: Page 18 of the dossier, DOS/1/73.

GILLIGAN: This is the right page. It starts off by saying: 'In mid-2001 the Joint Intelligence Committee assessed that Iraq retained some chemical warfare agents from before the Gulf War. These stocks would enable Iraq to produce significant quantities of mustard gas within weeks and of nerve agent within months.' 'Would enable Iraq to produce'. Then you go down to paragraph 8, this is on the next page, on page 19.

DINGEMANS: DOS/1/74.

GILLIGAN: Then you see standing almost on its own a very bald statement: Intelligence 'shows… Iraq has continued to produce chemical agent.' That is not what the earlier bit says. It says it could produce it within weeks. This says it has continued to produce it. There is a paragraph about 'Recent Intelligence' somewhere.

DINGEMANS: The paragraph headed 'Recent Intelligence' is paragraph 5 on DOS/1/73.

GILLIGAN: If you look at what they say the recent intelligence consists of, there is no recent intelligence about production capabilities. So there are inconsistencies in this document; and in all cases it was the harder – the firmer statement, that they actually had weapons rather than just the ability to produce weapons. Those are the statements that make it into the executive summary, into the Prime Minister's foreword.

DINGEMANS: Was there anything else you did?

GILLIGAN: I knew already that the Government had embellished another dossier. They published a dossier in

February 2003 on Iraq's infrastructure of concealment, deception and intimidation. The Prime Minister described it as further intelligence. A good part of it anyway was copied off the Internet. It was copied almost word for word, including the spelling mistakes actually in some cases, but one of the figures was embellished, and a couple of the claims, some of the language was embellished. In the student's original PhD thesis, the wording –

DINGEMANS: What student are you referring to?

GILLIGAN: This is Ibrahim al Marishi. He wrote the thesis which was then copied without acknowledgment. Marishi wrote the Iraqi Mukhabarat had a role in aiding opposition groups in hostile regimes, and that was changed in the February dossier to supporting terrorist organisations in hostile regimes, which is quite a substantial change.

DINGEMANS: Can we then turn to the broadcast itself on the [29th May]? Do you have the second broadcast? Can we look at BBC/1/5? Slightly less dramatically, could you be Andrew Gilligan at the bottom and I will be Mr Humphreys. If we pick it up halfway down the page: '[John] Humphreys: 28 minutes to 8. Tony Blair had quite a job persuading the country and indeed his own MPs to support the invasion of Iraq; his main argument was that Saddam had weapons of mass destruction that threatened us all. None of those weapons has been found. Now our defence correspondent, Andrew Gilligan, has found evidence that the government's dossier on Iraq that was produced last September was cobbled together at the last minute with some unconfirmed material that had not been approved by the Security Services. Are you suggesting, let's be very clear about this, that it was not the work of the intelligence agencies?'

GILLIGAN: No, the information which I'm told was dubious did come from the agencies, but they were unhappy about it, because they didn't think it should have been in there. They thought it was – it was not corroborated sufficiently, and they actually thought it was wrong.

DINGEMANS: At the top of page 6 you continue.

GILLIGAN: I mean let's go through this. This is the dossier that was published in September last year, probably the most substantial statement of the government's case against Iraq. The first thing you see is a preface written by Tony Blair. Tony Blair's words were voiced up by somebody on the production team. Those words were: 'Saddam's military planning allows for some weapons of mass destruction to be ready within forty five minutes of an order to deploy them.' Then it is back to me again: 'Now that claim has come back to haunt Mr Blair because if the weapons had been that readily to hand, they probably would have been found by now. But you know, it could have been an honest mistake, but what I have been told is that the Government knew that claim was questionable even before they wrote it in their dossier. 'I have spoken to a British official who was involved in the preparation of the dossier, and he told me that until the week before it was published, the draft dossier produced by the Intelligence Services, added little to what was already publicly known. He said…' Again, this is a voice up. 'It was transformed in the week before it was published, to make it sexier.'

DINGEMANS: Can we go back to BBC/1/4, which is the transcript for your first broadcast which I think took place shortly after 6 in the morning [of the same day] is that right?

GILLIGAN: Yes, this was at 6.07.

DINGEMANS: Was this contribution to the programme scripted?

GILLIGAN: No, it was not.

DINGEMANS: So this was you speaking from the studio or from home?

GILLIGAN: From home. This is me speaking live and unscripted.

DINGEMANS: Can I take you to this: [You say] '…and what we've been told by one of the senior officials in charge of drawing up that dossier was that actually the Government probably, erm, knew that that forty-five minute figure was wrong, even before it decided to put it in.' Now, we have all been through the note you say you made of Dr Kelly's meeting; this does not appear to be in that note.

GILLIGAN: No. This is not intended to be a direct quote from David Kelly. We were trying to convey the essence of what the source had said.

DINGEMANS: So it was not a direct quotation from the source and you did not portray it as a direct quotation. Was it supported by what Dr Kelly had told you?

GILLIGAN: I believe so.

DINGEMANS: If it was not entirely supported by what Dr Kelly had said, why did you not go back and check it with him?

GILLIGAN: As I say, what this was was a product of a live broadcast. It was, I do believe, a fair conclusion to draw from what he said to me. But I think, on reflection, I did not use exactly the right language. It was not wrong, but it was not perfect either.

DINGEMANS: Was this allegation ever withdrawn at any time before Dr Kelly died?

GILLIGAN: Well, I never returned to the form of words I used in the 6.07 broadcast. Subsequent broadcasts were scripted. The word I used in the 7.32 broadcast, the scripted one, was 'questionable', which I was happier with.

DINGEMANS: Can I then turn to [the Foreign Affairs Committee] FAC/1/94? Can I take you to the final passage, Mr Hamilton['s question]: 'Did you say anything which Mr Gilligan might reasonably have interpreted as identifying Mr Alastair Campbell as wanting to change the dossier or 'sex it up' in any way or make undue reference to the 45 minute claim?' Dr Kelly [says]: 'I cannot recall that. I find it very difficult to think back to a conversation I had six weeks ago. I cannot recall but that does not mean to say, of course, that such a statement was not made but I really cannot recall it. It does not sound like the sort of thing I would say.'

GILLIGAN: I noted that that was not a denial in some respects. I mean, you know 'I cannot recall but that does not mean to say, of course, that such a statement was not made'.

DINGEMANS: Can I take you on to your publication in *The Mail on Sunday* which was BBC/1/27? Why did you name Alastair Campbell in The *Mail on Sunday* piece when you had not on the BBC piece?

GILLIGAN: I had had a difficult relationship with Mr Campbell during the Iraq war. He complained about my coverage several times; and I thought he had a particular issue about some of my reporting. I did not want to be the first to name him in this context. But some of that press follow up did name Mr Campbell in this context, so I thought: well, I am not the first.

DINGEMANS: Can I take you to another complaint that Mr Campbell had made about your reporting in the war. BBC/4/146. This is a letter of 1st April 2003 that Mr Campbell writes to [the BBC Director of News, Richard] Sambrook: Dear Richard, Andrew Gilligan claimed on Radio Five that 'people here are saying the Republican Guard hasn't really been damaged at all and they could be right. Who told him the Republican Guard hasn't been damaged – the Iraqi Ministry of Information? Was this report monitored? Does Mr Gilligan have a minder? Then there are a couple more. Can I take you to the reply at 148? Sorry, at 148 there is another letter from Mr Kaufman making a similar complaint effectively.

GILLIGAN: It is, in fact, identical language, the words are identical.

DINGEMANS: Yes. Then page 149: 'Dear Richard, On Radio 4 this morning, Andrew Gilligan said: 'I'm not quite sure where these intelligence assessments come from. It might just be more rubbish from Central Command.' Do you believe that final sentence was justified? That, as I understand it, was a reference to American central command, is that right?

GILLIGAN: Yes.

DINGEMANS: Then page 150, the response by Mr Sambrook of 2nd April: 'Dear Alastair, Thank you for your letter. Gerald Kaufman has written in strikingly similar terms.'

DINGEMANS: The only purpose of taking you to that correspondence is to show you what I think you have already disclosed, that even if it was not a personal relationship with Alastair Campbell as a professional relationship it was pretty frosty?

GILLIGAN: These are good examples of the kind of relationship that Alastair Campbell has; and it is a good example of the reason why I was reluctant to be the first to name him in the context of transforming the dossier.

DINGEMANS: Can I take you to CAB/1/352. This is the letter dated 26th June 2003 from Alastair Campbell to Mr Sambrook. Can I take you to page 353, where he asked this question : 'Does the BBC still stand by the allegation it made on 29th May that Number Ten added in the 45-minute claim to the dossier? Yes or no? Does it still stand by the allegation made on that day that both we and the intelligence agencies knew the 45 minute claim to be wrong and inserted it despite knowing that? Yes or no?' I think you accepted that your appearance at 6.07 was unscripted, that the language was, I am afraid I do not have the transcript in front of me but not exact?

GILLIGAN: Was not perfect, I think I said.

HUTTON: But you had made the allegation, it was you who had said this on the programme.

GILLIGAN: As I said, the wording in that first two-way was not a fair reflection of how the whole story was covered either by me or by the BBC; and I had repeatedly said, in subsequent broadcasts, that nobody was accusing Downing Street of lying, nobody was accusing Downing Street of making the intelligence – of making the 45 minutes claim up. We made it clear on repeated occasions that it was real intelligence. So if a misleading impression was given and it was given unintentionally, it already had been corrected.

DINGEMANS: You are an experienced reporter - did you think that Dr Kelly would have had the faintest idea what he was letting himself in for?

GILLIGAN: I mean, I think he was pretty experienced at dealing with journalists; I cannot speculate on what Dr Kelly may have felt but he was experienced with journalists.

Susan Watts, 12th and 13th August 2003

WATTS: My full name is Susan Janet Watts and I am a BBC reporter.

HUTTON: Yes. Thank you.

DINGEMANS: What programme do you work with?

WATTS: I work with BBC Newsnight. I am the science editor.

DINGEMANS: Biological and chemical warfare was something you covered?

WATTS: Yes.

DINGEMANS: And in the course of that, on a professional basis, did you come across Dr David Kelly?

WATTS: Yes, I did.

DINGEMANS: How had you got into contact with him?

WATTS: I was given his name by a Foreign Office official.

HUTTON: The Foreign Office gave you Dr Kelly's telephone number.

WATTS: Yes.

DINGEMANS: Your conversations with him, were they all on the same basis, attributable or non-attributable?

WATTS: They were all non-attributable – the information was to be used but not identified as having come from him.

DINGEMANS: Did you have a conversation in April 2003?

WATTS: Yes, we did. We had quite a long telephone conversation. During that conversation he mentioned having had lunch with Geoff Hoon, the Defence Secretary.

DINGEMANS: Did he say what he had talked about at lunch?

WATTS: Well, yes. He talked about – he and I were talking about the process of the search for WMD and Whitehall's attitude to the fact that nothing of significance had been found by then; and Dr Kelly said that Mr Hoon had said to him, rather cryptically Dr Kelly implied, and I quote – Geoff Hoon said to Dr Kelly, 'One sees the mosaic of evidence being built up'.

DINGEMANS: What did you understand Dr Kelly to understand by that rather cryptic comment?

WATTS: Very little in fact. He chuckled about the fact that it was fairly meaningless.

DINGEMANS: What else did Dr Kelly say on that occasion?

WATTS: He expressed a firm wish to return to Iraq and some frustration at not having been asked to go back yet. He talked about the fact that he felt perhaps the security – there was not sufficient security for him to return. During the same conversation we discussed the uranium Niger intelligence issue and my shorthand notes show that he said, and I am quoting, 'That obviously was an improper analysis'.

DINGEMANS: Did you form any view about his access to Government information?

WATTS: Well, from the variety and breadth of it, I formed the view very definitely he had extraordinary access to Government information across the board.

DINGEMANS: Did he tell you in terms what access he had?

WATTS: Not specifically, no. Again, I would say that he was passing information to me that was not sensitive in any way, not operational information.

DINGEMANS: It was not anything that was going to compromise anyone's safety?

WATTS: No, and not whistle-blowing in any sense.

DINGEMANS: Do you have any notes of any other contacts to him?

WATTS: 7th, 12th and 30th of May.

DINGEMANS: Can we go back to the 7th May?

WATTS: Hmm, hmm.

DINGEMANS: Can you, first of all, tell us who initiated the contact?

WATTS: I did I rang him at home, I think, and probably from my home.

DINGEMANS: Did you discuss anything in particular, any development in Iraq?

WATTS: Well, we talked about the most recent developments; and Dr Kelly's view that the process of looking for weapons of mass destruction would likely be a lengthy one unless the teams were to 'strike it lucky'.

DINGEMANS: What was your understanding of Dr Kelly's views about the prospects of finding weapons of mass destruction.

WATTS: My impression is that he very definitely thought that there were weapons programmes. It might well be a lengthy search to find that evidence and it would be a process of pulling together many, many bits of information and that that process is really only beginning.

DINGEMANS: Did you discuss the 45 minutes claim in the Government dossier?

WATTS: Towards the end of the conversation we did, yes.

DINGEMANS: And what did he say about that?

WATTS: Dr Kelly said to me that it was, and I quote: 'A mistake to put in Alastair Campbell seeing something in there, single source but not corroborated, sounded good.'

DINGEMANS: Right. And what was the nature of the way in which he imparted this information? Was it as if this was a revelation or this was a chatty aside?

WATTS: Certainly not a revelation at all, I would characterise as a gossipy aside comment.

DINGEMANS: When Dr Kelly discussed with you the 45 minutes claim, did he discuss any weapons that might have been used to launch chemical and biological weapons?

WATTS: Yes. We talked a bit about why such a precise timing might be used, 45 minutes rather than 43 or 40. He said that he was – he made clear that he, in his word, was guessing; but he said that in 1991 the Iraqis were, and I quote, 'playing around with multibarrel launches and that these take 45 minutes to fill'. So that was his best guess, if you like, as to where that figure had come from.

DINGEMANS: Was he then suggesting that the 45 minutes claim was false?

WATTS: He was not suggesting it was necessarily false. But I think he was suggesting to me it might not necessarily only have one interpretation.

DINGEMANS: So that supported your view that he was a man with extraordinary access?

WATTS: Absolutely.

DINGEMANS: Did you make notes of the conversation on the 30th of May?

WATTS: I started to make notes in the same way as I usually would i.e. the shorthand aide memoire which I would note to myself the key parts and come back if I felt I wanted to. Because I was taping that conversation, I stopped after a few moments because I felt I could rely on the tape.

DINGEMANS: With what type of machine were you taping the conversation?

WATTS: This was a hand-held dictaphone, quite an old hand-held dictaphone.

DINGEMANS: Were you holding it to the receiver or did you have him on speakerphone?

WATTS: No, I had, again, quite an antiquated set-up, I suppose. It was one of these stick-on microphones attached to the receiver. Again, it was an aide-memoire to a private conversation for me to – an equivalent of notes.

DINGEMANS: And did you tell Dr Kelly that you were taping the conversation?

WATTS: No, I did not tell him.

DINGEMANS: You say: 'Okay, um, while I'm sure since you've been in New York I don't know whether you've been following the kind of rumpus that's erupted over here ... What prompted me to ring you, was the quotes yesterday on the Today Programme about the 45 minutes... 'Mr Kelly [said]: It was a statement that was made and it just got out of all proportion. They were desperate for information...that was one that popped up and it was seized on. [You say] 'Okay, just back up momentarily on the 45 minute issue. Would it be accurate then as you did in that earlier conversation to say that it was Alastair Campbell himself who...? And Dr Kelly says 'No, I can't. All I can say is the No 10 press office. I've never met Alastair Campbell so I can't. You interrupt. 'They seized on that?' Who were you referring to when you said 'they seized on that'?

WATTS: The No. 10 press office.

DINGEMANS: And [Dr Kelly] replied: 'But I think Alastair Campbell is synonymous with that press office because he's responsible for it'.

WATTS: Hmm, hmm.

DINGEMANS: Can we turn to SJW/1/53? And this is a summary of what you are going to say to the camera and indeed did say? It's really on page 54 if we can go to that, that we get any report of your conversation with Dr Kelly. It's about half way down. You introduce your anonymous source, making it clear that you cannot name him. 'Our source said...' Perhaps you can read that out?

WATTS: Yes. The direct quote from Dr Kelly is: 'That was the real concern – not so much what they had now, but what they would have in the future. But that unfortunately was not expressed strongly in the dossier, because that takes away the case for war – to a certain extent.'

DINGEMANS: Then I think at the top of page 55 [on] Newsnight, on 2nd June. Can you read those?

WATTS: 'It was a statement that was made and it just got out of all proportion. They were desperate for information, they were pushing hard for information which could be released. That was one that popped up and it was seized on, and it's unfortunate that it was. That's why there is the argument between the Intelligence Services and No. 10 – because they picked up on it and once they've picked up on it you can't pull it back from them.'

DINGEMANS: Any other comments from him?

WATTS: 'It was an interesting week before the dossier was put out because there were so many people saying, 'Well, I'm not so sure about that', or in fact that they were happy with it being in, but not expressed the way that it was – because the word-smithing is actually quite important. The intelligence community are a pretty cautious lot on the whole – but once you get people presenting it for public consumption then of course they use different words.'

DINGEMANS: And that was the material that you had obtained from your telephone conversation with Dr Kelly.

WATTS: Yes.

DINGEMANS: There came a time when the BBC paid for you to take independent legal advice through a firm of solicitors; is that right?

WATTS: I should just clarify I think why that happened.

DINGEMANS: Right.

WATTS: And it was for two reason, two important reasons. Firstly, that I felt under some considerable pressure to reveal the identity of my source.

DINGEMANS: Pressure from?

WATTS: The BBC

DINGEMANS: Yes.

WATTS: And I also felt that the purpose of that was to help corroborate the Andrew Gilligan allegations and not for any proper news purpose.

DINGEMANS: Did you consider that they corroborated Andrew Gilligan's story?

WATTS: No, I did not.

DINGEMANS: Why not?

WATTS: Because there were very significant differences between his report and my report namely, that I did not include the name of Alastair Campbell. And I did not refer to my source as being a member of the Intelligence Services and that the claim was not inserted by either Alastair Campbell himself or any member of the Government. It was for those two reasons, the pressure to identify my source and what I felt to be a misguided strategy in the use of those Newsnight reports, on which I sought independent legal advice.

DINGEMANS: Is there anything else that you would like to say to his Lordship?

WATTS: Only one thing, which is that during the process in the news suite on the Friday

DINGEMANS: The day on which Dr Kelly's body has been found?

WATTS: Everybody was very upset. There were many different concerns being juggled, sensitivities to the family, the needs of straightforward objective news reporting by the BBC. But I was concerned that it not be apparent that it was Dr Kelly's death that had prompted me to feel able to reveal his identity. It was not his death. For me when he gave evidence to the Foreign Affairs Committee, I formed a view on listening to that evidence that if I had been called to the Committee which was a possibility, I would have felt that he had relieved me of my obligation of confidence to him and I would then have felt able to reveal him as the source of my stories. And the reason for that is because under questioning he was given some – loosely quoted – the quotes from him in my reports. I saw the transcript the following day, he appears to deny that those are his quotes. I felt that together with his having acknowledged having spoken to me, although I think he was less than frank in describing the full nature of our relationship and conversations, that those factors together relieved me of my obligation to protect his identity as a confidentiality source.

Martin Howard, 14th August 2003

DINGEMANS: Mr Howard, we had a dossier on 20th June 2002. Do you recollect that?

HOWARD: Yes, I do.

DINGEMANS: We had a dossier of 5th September 2002, we had a [published] dossier on the 19th September 2002.

HOWARD: That is right, yes.

DINGEMANS: 5th September, no 45 minutes claim.

HOWARD: Hmm, hmm.

DINGEMANS: 19th September, 45 minutes.

HOWARD: Hmm, hmm.

DINGEMANS: Can I take you to DOS/2/7 [draft 10/11 September] 'Envisages the use of WMD in its current military planning, and could deploy such weapons within 45 minutes of the order being given…' Can we now look at the dossier that comes in on the 16th September? That is DOS 2/58. 'The Iraqi military may be able to deploy chemical or biological weapons within 45 minutes of an order to do so.' It seems to have got a little bit weaker; is that fair?

HOWARD: Well I was not involved in this process, it's very fine shading.

DINGEMANS: And then go to the dossier as it turned out, DOS/1/59, that his military planning allows for some of the WMD to be ready within 45 minutes of an order to use them.' This is noticeably harder, is that fair?

HOWARD: I think that is fair, yes.

DINGEMANS: These changes, which may be considered significant by intelligence personnel, you understood to be causing some of the concerns?

HOWARD: I think their concerns were about how it had been presented in the Prime Minister's foreword and in the executive summary.

DINGEMANS: Which is where, I suppose, the No.10 element became the strongest, because that was in the foreword.

HOWARD: I think that is probably true to say.

DINGEMANS: Can I then turn to other matters that I think you are going to help us with? Did you have any involvement in the broadcasts that had been made by Andrew Gilligan?

HOWARD: His broadcast on 29th May?

DINGEMANS: Yes. Did anyone contact you and ask you to undertake any investigations?

HOWARD: Yes, on 4th June the permanent secretary Kevin Tebbit wrote to the chief of defence intelligence, to identify more closely who might have been involved in passing this information to Mr Gilligan.

DINGEMANS: Did you have any other conversations at about this time?

HOWARD: Yes, it was a reception at the Security Service headquarters at Thames House, and in a conversation that I had with Mr Lamb and others it emerged that Dr Kelly had told Mr Lamb that he had spoken to Mr Gilligan –

DINGEMANS: So what did you do in response to that?

HOWARD: Well, I thought about it overnight and I decided to report this to Sir Kevin Tebbit,

DINGEMANS: You had seen Dr Kelly's letter, is that right, dated 30th June?

HOWARD: That is right.

DINGEMANS: Did you then become involved with [his] interview on 7th July?

HOWARD: Sir Kevin Tebbit was proposing to write to [the Prime Minister's security coordinator] Sir David Omand

DINGEMANS: Why had it gone up a level, as it were?

HOWARD: I think this was a judgment made by Sir Kevin Tebbit, that we had a letter which, you know, clearly showed that there had been a meeting between Dr Kelly and Andrew Gilligan, that it was clearly unauthorised, that it had certainly touched upon matters which were the subject of Andrew Gilligan's report. It was, you know, potentially quite a serious issue; Sir David recorded the Prime Minister's views that before we decided on what are the next steps that should be taken, it would be sensible to try to go into the differences between what Dr Kelly had said and what Andrew Gilligan had claimed.

DINGEMANS: Your broad understanding lower down, although not that lower down the chain, sorry, was that people at a higher level had become involved and there was then going to be a second interview?

HOWARD: Yes.

DINGEMANS: After the second interview were you convinced by what Dr Kelly had said?

HOWARD: I had no reason to doubt what Dr Kelly said. I still felt it most likely that he was the source that Andrew Gilligan had referred to.

DINGEMANS: Did you write to anyone about Dr Kelly's views as expressed in the interview?

HOWARD: I wrote to Sir John Scarlett, who is chairman of the JIC. Sir John Scarlett – not Sir John Scarlett yet. John Scarlett had asked me if I could provide a short summary of what I understood Dr Kelly's views to be on Iraqi WMD.

DINGEMANS: Right, we have got to the 8th July. You know, do you not, that the MoD issued a press statement –

HOWARD: Yes.

DINGEMANS: – saying that an undisclosed official has come forward? Do you know why it was proposed to issue a press notice?

HOWARD: I think the feeling was that this was a matter of, you know, very considerable public interest, that the Foreign Affairs Committee had themselves recommended that the Government should investigate links with Andrew Gilligan; and there was a very great concern that this would come out by other means.

HUTTON: In the report I think the F[oreign] A[ffairs] C[ommittee] said that Mr Gilligan's sources should be investigated. That would seem to suggest that the Ministry of Defence themselves would investigate that, but it does not necessarily mean, does it, that if the source was found that he would be asked to go to be a witness before the FAC?

HOWARD: No, it does not mean that automatically, my Lord, I agree. But it was part of a number of reasons, which included the fact that this was an issue or had been an issue of great public interest.

HUTTON: Yes.

HOWARD: That we had very unusually an individual who had written and said he had spoken to a journalist in this area in an unauthorised way. And the overall judgment reached, I think at all levels, from Ministers downwards, was that really it would be necessary to make the fact that this had happened public.

HUTTON: Can you just elaborate a little on that?

HOWARD: The accusation had been made that the Government had exaggerated the dossier.

HUTTON: Quite, yes. Then was the thinking that if Dr Kelly's name was made public and Dr Kelly came forward and said that he had not made the comments which Mr Gilligan had reported, that would show that Mr Gilligan's account was incorrect? Was that, in essence, the thinking?

HOWARD: It was more that this was information that was germane to an issue which had been of great public concern and great public debate.

HUTTON: But if the civil servant was not going to be named and if he was not going to give his account of what he said to Mr Gilligan, how would it advance the public knowledge to say that an unnamed civil servant had come forward?

HOWARD: Well, first of all, the fact that it had happened at all was very unusual; and there was a concern that if it came out from other sources that we might well be criticised for not having made this public. We might have been criticised for covering up for a whistle blower.

DINGEMANS: On that point. I mean, if the concern was to ensure that the public knew as much as possible, then the F[oreign] A[ffairs] C[ommittee] had actually asked for the drafts of the dossier, had they not?

HOWARD: I believe they had, yes.

DINGEMANS: Had they been given them?

HOWARD: Not to my knowledge. That is a matter for the Foreign Office to answer.

DINGEMANS: As far as the defensive Q and A material was concerned –

HOWARD: Hmm, hmm.

DINGEMANS: – this was material prepared by the Ministry of Defence to be given to their press personnel –

HOWARD: That is right.

DINGEMANS: – to brief the media with on the 8th/9th July?

HOWARD: Hmm, hmm.

DINGEMANS: Were you involved in the preparation of that at all?

HOWARD: Yes. It was discussed at the rather lengthy meeting which took place on 8th July.

DINGEMANS: What was the reasoning behind this defensive Q and A material?

HOWARD: Defensive Q and A material overall was to provide material that the press office could draw upon if they were asked questions by the media in the aftermath of the public statement.

DINGEMANS: Can I take you to MoD/1/63, which is part way through this defensive Q and A material? It says this, 'It is unprecedented for a Government Department to make a statement of this sort. Why have you done it?'

HOWARD: It was actually quite an unusual situation that we found ourselves in. So I think that really is reflected there.

DINGEMANS: Part of the reason appears to be that 'the official involved volunteered the information to us.' That is hardly likely to encourage others to do that, is it?

HOWARD: Well, I could not argue with that.

DINGEMANS: Now, on Monday 14th July we know that you took part in a briefing of Dr Kelly?

HOWARD: That is right. Sir Kevin Tebbit asked me if I would see Dr Kelly, to explain to Dr Kelly, as we would before any witnesses going before Select Committees, how Select Committees worked

DINGEMANS: Can I take you to a document which is CAB/1/106? 'DCDI' That is you, is it not?

HOWARD: That is me.

DINGEMANS: '…is to brief David Kelly this afternoon for his appearances tomorrow before the FAC and ISC, and will strongly recommend that Kelly is not drawn on his assessment of the dossier and stick to what he told Gilligan. Kelly is apparently feeling the pressure, and does not appear to be handling it well.'

HOWARD: I do not recall saying that.

DINGEMANS: Was the effect of this interview that Dr Kelly was being given a certain steer as to how his evidence should go?

HOWARD: No, certainly not.

Alastair Campbell, 19th August 2003

DINGEMANS: What is your occupation?

CAMPBELL: I am the Prime Minister's Director of Communications and Strategy.

DINGEMANS: Throughout the course of your evidence I am going to be referring to some documents that you very kindly supplied to us. You have also supplied to us copies or redacted copies of your diaries. Can you just, first of all, explain how you keep your diaries?

CAMPBELL: I write a diary not every day but several times a week. It is not intended for publication. It is a series of observations about what I do and what I witness.

DINGEMANS: When were you first aware that a dossier was being written or produced?

CAMPBELL: I had been aware for some months of a different dossier on the general issue of WMD. On the specific Iraq dossier, I became aware of that during – the intention of doing one during August, when the Prime Minister and I were both on holiday and we were discussing the way that the Iraq situation was developing.

DINGEMANS: Can you help us: what was identified as the toughest question?

CAMPBELL: Sorry: what new evidence was there? The Prime Minister said the debate had got ahead of us so we were going to do the dossier earlier, in the next few weeks. The debate, particularly in the United States, had really moved on to a different level. And what he was saying there was that any case that we make for why Saddam Hussein's regime is a serious and credible threat has to be based on evidence, and he wanted to share as much of that evidence as possible with the public.

DINGEMANS: And what did you record at the time that you needed to show in relation to the dossier?

CAMPBELL: That it had to be revelatory; we needed to show it was new and informative and part of a bigger case. I emphasised that the credibility of this document depended fundamentally upon it being the work of the Joint Intelligence Committee.

DINGEMANS: Can I then take you to a document dated 5th September? That is CAB/11/17, which was an email from Jonathan Powell to you. We start at the bottom of the page, simply working our way up in chronological sequence. You can see, 1.50, what did you decide on dossiers? And there is a first comment that has been redacted. Up the page you say: 'Regarding the dossier, substantial rewrite with JS...' Who is that?

CAMPBELL: John Scarlett [chairman of the Joint Intelligence Committee.]

DINGEMANS: John Scarlett will take to the US next Friday, and be in shape Monday thereafter. Structure as per TB's discussion.' I imagine that is the Prime Minister?

CAMPBELL: Yes.

DINGEMANS: 'Agreement that there has to be real intelligence material in their presentation as such.'

CAMPBELL: Hmm.

HUTTON: Did you receive any indication that there might have been unhappiness in the lower ranks of the intelligence agencies about the writing of the dossier, about what would be in it?

CAMPBELL: Not at that stage.

HUTTON: Yes.

DINGEMANS: If we go to DOS/2/7: 'Envisages the use of weapons of mass destruction in its current military planning, and could deploy such weapons within 45 minutes of the order being given for their use.'

CAMPBELL: Hmm, hmm.

HUTTON: You did not know where the entry of 45 minutes had come from in the sense you did not know what it was based on?

CAMPBELL: I knew it had come from the JIC but I was not aware either of the raw intelligence on which it was based or of the sourcing. What is more, I did not make any effort to find out.

HUTTON: No.

DINGEMANS: Can I just then, at the moment, come to the issue about dissatisfaction of members of the intelligence staff about some of the comments being made –

CAMPBELL: Hmm, hmm.

DINGEMANS: – and take you to an email at CAB/3/21 specific about Dr Kelly. This is 10th September [at] 11.41.

CAMPBELL: Hmm, hmm.

DINGEMANS: You can see the subject is 'Dossier – Iraq'. The person who sends it says this: 'I have just spoken to Dr David Kelly... about the growth media which Iraq claimed it used in BW work. But Iraq has not revealed its production documents therefore this amount is unaccounted for. The existing wording is not wrong – but it has a lot of spin on it'.

CAMPBELL: Hmm, hmm.

DINGEMANS: Were you aware of comments of this nature being made at the time amongst Defence Intelligence personnel?

CAMPBELL: No.

DINGEMANS: And the only other document, can I take you to MoD/4/9, which was a document which is dated in July 2003, and it is for a briefing, but this relates to concerns that were expressed contemporaneously. You can see that concerns were expressed into three main groups: recent production of [CBW] agent; the 45 minute claim; and Saddam and the importance of CBW.

CAMPBELL: Hmm, hmm.

DINGEMANS: One can see in relation to the 45 minutes claim, if I can just deal with that –

CAMPBELL: Yes.

DINGEMANS: – that concerns had apparently related to the level of certainty expressed in the foreword and executive summary.

CAMPBELL: Hmm, hmm.

DINGEMANS: That, at the least, indicates there were some people who were unhappy with some of the wording that was going on; you were not aware of that?

CAMPBELL: I was not aware of that.

DINGEMANS: Can I take you to some emails making the rounds on September 11? CAB/11/23 There is Daniel Pruce's email, it is to you and copied to others. It is subject: 'Draft Dossier (J Scarlett version of 10th September).' Daniel Pruce is?

CAMPBELL: He is a Foreign Office press officer based in Downing Street.

DINGEMANS: He said: 'The foreword is good but whose voice is it? Do we need a Minister to sign it off?' That is what starts the process running, I suppose, until the Prime Minister –

CAMPBELL: It is not actually. Danny Pruce is a very, very good press officer, but this is him making contributions effectively above his pay grade. The foreword process was already under discussion between myself, the Prime Minister, and John Scarlett.

DINGEMANS: And who had, in fact, drafted that?

CAMPBELL: I prepared a draft based upon a discussion with the Prime Minister, and with others, about what should go into that draft.

DINGEMANS: CAB/11/53. This is Jonathan Powell's email to you. I imagine his comments were comments that you took seriously, is that right?

CAMPBELL: I had certainly read them.

DINGEMANS: And he says –

CAMPBELL: Sorry, that was no offence intended there.

DINGEMANS: 'I think it is worth explicitly stating what TB keeps saying, this is the advice to him from the JIC?' He goes on to deal with this: 'We need to do more to back up the assertions.' He suggests some wording. And: 'In the penultimate paragraph you need to make it clear Saddam could not attack us at the moment. The thesis is he would be a threat to the UK in the future if we do not check him.' At page 69.

CAMPBELL: Of the dossier?

DINGEMANS: Sorry CAB/11/69. On the same day, but later on, he appears to have made some comments to John Scarlett, but he has copied you into those. Here the tone of his email seems to be slightly different to the effect that the document does nothing to demonstrate a threat. I am third line down: 'Let alone an imminent threat from Saddam in other words it shows he has the means but it does not demonstrate he has the motive to attack his neighbours let alone the west.'

CAMPBELL: Hmm, hmm.

DINGEMANS: Do you know, from any discussions you had with John Scarlett, whether those were taken up with – whether he accepted any of those, et cetera?

CAMPBELL: I think what Jonathan is doing there is making an observation which is actually consistent with what John Scarlett had been doing. I mean, this dossier is sometimes described as the Prime Minister 'making the case for war'. What it was actually doing was setting out in as factual a way as possible the reason why the Government was concerned about Saddam's WMD programmes.

DINGEMANS: Can I then take you to a document, CAB/11/70 which is a memorandum, if we go to page 71 at the bottom, you can see is from John Scarlett. Effectively the gist of what he appears to be doing is taking on some comments about strengthening the language on current concerns and plans, is that right?

CAMPBELL: I think it showed he took on some of my comments and none of the Prime Minister's on the structure. The structure stayed the same and some of the detailed points he took.

DINGEMANS: Can I turn back to CAB/11/69, with Mr Powell's comments. What he says is: 'We will need to make it clear in launching the document that we do not claim that we have evidence that he is an imminent threat.' Is there any part of the dossier that actually makes that explicitly clear?

CAMPBELL: I know that what we always said was: a serious and credible threat to the region and therefore the stability of the world.

DINGEMANS: CAB/11/103 Jonathan Powell's email at the top, the third line down says: 'Alastair, what will be the headline in the Standard on the day of publication?'

CAMPBELL: Search me.

DINGEMANS: If we look at BBC/4/90, this is what the headline was '45 Minutes From Attack'. Did you have any hand in the headline?

CAMPBELL: I did not. I do not write headlines for the Evening Standard.

DINGEMANS: Now, so you can deal with some of the points that have been suggested, did you have any influence on the inclusion of the 45 minute claim in the dossier?

CAMPBELL: None whatever. The words that you read out earlier were the words that were in the draft of the dossier that I saw on the evening of September 10th; and I had no input, output, influence upon them, whatsoever at any stage in the process.

DINGEMANS: I am proposing to move on to complaints about BBC reporting. Can I then take you to the coverage of the war in Iraq by the BBC and take you to a document at BBC/4/131. Can you tell us what this is?

CAMPBELL: (*Pause.*) This is a letter from myself to Mr Sambrook, BBC Director of News, making a number of complaints about BBC coverage during the Iraq...

DINGEMANS: 2nd April, BBC/4/149, you say: 'On Radio 4 this morning, Andrew Gilligan said ...[his] final comment, was: 'I'm not quite sure where these intelligence assessments come from it might just be more rubbish from Central Command.'

CAMPBELL: Yes.

DINGEMANS: And we get the response to that at 158. Mr Sambrook had agreed that his final phrase was unacceptable and made some points about that. It does seem, looking through the file, that there were a considerable number of complaints that were being made at this time. Is that fair or unfair?

CAMPBELL: Unfair, because there was a considerable amount of coverage that was giving us cause for concern.

DINGEMANS: That is because your perception was, there was unfair or inaccurate coverage?

CAMPBELL: Yes, our perception was that BBC viewers and listeners were at times being given a sense of moral equivalence between the democratically elected governments that were involved on one side and the Iraqi regime on the other.

DINGEMANS: Can I then turn to the broadcast on 29th May? First of all, where were you on 29th May?

CAMPBELL: I was in Kuwait.

DINGEMANS: What was your reaction to those reports?

CAMPBELL: I was torn really, because, on the one hand, I did not imagine anyone would have taken them terribly seriously, because it is such an extraordinary thing to say, that the Prime Minister and the Government would do that. Given my close involvement in the production of the dossier, I knew the allegations to be false. The reason why I then got more concerned as the day wore on was because shortly after the Prime Minister spoke to

British troops when we were in Basra it was clear to me that the travelling press party were frankly more interested in this BBC story than they were in what the Prime Minister had been saying to the troops and his visit to Iraq.

DINGEMANS: On 1st June, looking at your diary, what was your reaction to all this press coverage?

CAMPBELL: I said it was grim. It was grim for me and it was grim for TB and there is this huge stuff about trust?

DINGEMANS: And did you speak to John Scarlett at all?

CAMPBELL: I did.

DINGEMANS: And what was the gist of that conversation?

CAMPBELL: The gist of that conversation was that John expressing his absolute support. Could I just add to that? I have just seen what he went on to say. He said: 'You are the brutal political hatchet man and I am the dry intelligence officer and we've been made to [ac]cord to our stereotypes'.

DINGEMANS: Mr Campbell, if you look on your screen you will see the reference is CAB/1/244. You can see there the letter you wrote to Mr Sambrook. Can you just tell us how you concluded the letter?

CAMPBELL: I predicted that he would seek to defend the story because, in my experience, Mr Sambrook generally does. I then concluded by saying that: 'On the word of a single, uncorroborated source, you have allowed one reporter to drive the BBC's coverage. We are left wondering why you have guidelines at all, given that they are so persistently breached without any comeback whatsoever.'

DINGEMANS: That seems a reasonably strong letter. Does that give proper vent to your feelings at the time?

CAMPBELL: It does.

DINGEMANS: Did you also speak with the Prime Minister about the dispute with the BBC?

CAMPBELL: Yes. Yes, I did.

DINGEMANS: And what was the gist of that discussion?

CAMPBELL: At that stage, the Prime Minister was saying to me: look, this is clearly quite an intense row that is going on. It is fine, keep going, but then we have to just after a day or two just leave this to the [Foreign Affairs] committee. During that discussion the Prime Minister was saying to me: how on earth are we going to get back on to a domestic political agenda? I said that until we could somehow change this dynamic that was currently prevalent in the media, it was going to be very difficult.

DINGEMANS: We then come on to the 8th July. The Prime Minister is prepared, in the morning, for the Commons Liaison Committee. Then at 11.30 am he returns and there is a discussion about whether or not Dr Kelly's name should be made public. Were you party to that discussion?

CAMPBELL: I was party to parts of that discussion.

HUTTON: Mr Campbell, I would just like to ask you a general question: suppose at this discussion on 8th July someone had said: let us just hold on for a minute, this is a civil servant who has given very distinguished service to his country, he has admittedly been indiscreet in speaking to a journalist as he has, but if we release his name we are going to subject him to very considerable strain. Is it right that we should do this?

CAMPBELL: I think you could have done that, but I think it would still have ended with all the media pressure because I think it would have come out, because these things do.

HUTTON: References have been made to the concern that if his name was not given to the [Foreign Affairs

Committee] and/or the [Intelligence and Security Committee] and if it leaked out, that the Government would be accused of a cover-up?

CAMPBELL: Part of the discussion that I recall involving the Prime Minister and others was about what Dr Kelly might actually say if he was called before a select committee. The Prime Minister did have some concerns about the Government's position.

HUTTON: So the concern was that if his name was not given by the Government but it was later revealed, it might transpire that Dr Kelly had views which were quite or strongly critical of the Government?

CAMPBELL: That is right.

DINGEMANS: Can I ask you on 9th July, two aspects of your diary in that respect. What was, as you perceived it, the biggest thing needed at this stage?

CAMPBELL: I felt that at that time, if we were going to bottom out this story and have it established beyond doubt that the allegations were false, then I felt that Dr Kelly appearing before a [parliamentary] Committee probably was the only way that was going to happen.

DINGEMANS: So you were keen by 9th July that Dr Kelly's name should be out?

CAMPBELL: I felt – we all felt that was going to happen, and I thought that that was the only way this was going to be resolved. But I did not do anything to bring that about because I was under strict instructions not to.

DINGEMANS: At CAB/1/93 can I take you to an email that is sent to you. You have Tom Kelly here, the Prime Minister's Official Spokesman, writing an email saying: 'This is now a game of chicken with the Beeb – the only way they will shift is [if] they see the screw tightening.' Was this the mindset that was dominating No. 10 at this stage?

CAMPBELL: I do not think it does reflect the mindset really. I think I know what Tom is saying there. I think emails that are sent between colleagues who are very close and work together very closely can look very different when you are staring at them in a screen in a courtroom.

DINGEMANS: We hear, on 17th July, that Dr Kelly goes out and his body is found the next day. Is there anything you wanted to say in relation to that

CAMPBELL: (*Pause.*) I just wanted to say that I think, like everybody, I have found it very distressing that Dr Kelly who, was clearly somebody of distinction, had died in this was and obviously I have, like everybody I am sure has thought very, very deeply about the background to all this. So I think all I would say is that I just find it very, very sad.

DINGEMANS: Is there anything further about the circumstances surrounding Dr Kelly's death that you can assist his Lordship with?

CAMPBELL: I do not think so.

HUTTON: Thank you very much Mr. Campbell. Thank you. We will sit again tomorrow morning at 10: 30.

USHER: All rise.

Houselights up to full.

James Blitz, 21st August 2003

BLITZ: My full name is James Simon Blitz.

DINGEMANS: What is your occupation?

BLITZ: The political editor of the *Financial Times* newspaper.

DINGEMANS: On 10th July you wrote an article in the *Financial Times* which named Dr Kelly as the individual who had come forward to the Ministry of Defence? Can you tell us the circumstances which led to you obtaining the name?

BLITZ: On the afternoon of Tuesday 8th July the MoD press release was published which suggested that an individual had come forward.

DINGEMANS: So what did you do when you got that press release?

BLITZ: I wrote a story for the 9th July edition of the FT.

DINGEMANS: Did that relate to Dr Kelly or not?

BLITZ: The name of Dr Kelly was not in the story that appeared on the 9th July.

DINGEMANS: Did you then carry on trying to find out who this anonymous person was?

BLITZ: I was not actively pursuing for the purposes of that article in the morning the question of who the individual was who had come forward in the MoD press release.

DINGEMANS: Did you change your attitude during the course of Wednesday 9th July?

BLITZ: Yes, I did.

DINGEMANS: Why was that?

BLITZ: Because I attended the Lobby briefing at 3.45 for Lobby journalists.

DINGEMANS: And we have an extract from that. It is at FIN/1/46. I am very sorry, it is not going to come on the screen. Can I read a short extract: 'Asked if the person who had come forward was a man, the [PM's Official Spokesman] said that journalists had a 50 per cent chance of being right. Asked whether he had been suspended from his job, he declined to get into personnel matters. Put to him that the person did not work for the MoD, the PMOS said the person was a technical expert who had worked for a variety of Government departments including the MoD with whom he was currently working, salary paid by another department.' Then some further questions. Was that the matter which had triggered your further interest?

BLITZ: That is precisely the matter that triggered my further interest and in the course of the Lobby briefing I asked a question specifically as to whether the name of the individual would in any way be publicised at some stage.

DINGEMANS: What was the answer you got?

BLITZ: The answer which was recorded in the official transcript put up on the Downing Street website was that the Prime Minister's official spokesman did not know of any plan to publicise that name.

DINGEMANS: What struck you about that briefing?

BLITZ: There were two aspects of the briefing that struck me, namely that details about this individual were coming forward; the fact that he worked for the MoD but was paid for by another department; the fact that he was a technical expert in the area of chemical and biological weapons. I took the view that there could be very few people who could fit such a description and that it would be possible to relatively quickly come to that person's name.

DINGEMANS: How did you go about trying to find the actual identity?

BLITZ: I went back to my office which is in the Parliamentary press gallery and I began to make inquiries.

DINGEMANS: What inquiries did you make?

BLITZ: Would you like me to go through this in detail at this point?

DINGEMANS: Yes, you tell me.

BLITZ: My first reaction was to open the Civil Service Handbook which lists the names of most key civil servants. The thought on my mind was that since the individual was paid for by another Government department he might be listed under such a department. I called my colleague, the FT security correspondent, in the paper's main office. I told him that I was determined to try and get the name of the individual and asked him if he would help. I called a Whitehall official and asked whether the individual worked in the DTI.

DINGEMANS: Were you given any information?

BLITZ: The only thing I wish to say about this conversation, because it was an off the record conversation, is that at the end of it I came to the conclusion that the individual was paid for by the Foreign and Commonwealth Office. I gained no other information whatsoever from that conversation.

DINGEMANS: What do you do to continue?

BLITZ: At this stage my colleague, on of the four members of the team which I lead at Westminster, came into the room.

DINGEMANS: You tell him what is going on. How does he help you?

BLITZ: Mr Adams, like myself, does not specialise in defence or intelligence work, so with very little information with which to establish the identity of the individual, he chose to conduct a search on the Internet.

DINGEMANS: Right, and he put some key words in.

BLITZ: 'Ministry', 'defence' 'consultant', 'chemical' and 'weapons'.

DINGEMANS: And who popped up on the search?

BLITZ: The first search produced a list of references where the key words appeared. Mr Adams reviewed the results of that search and told me of one individual. I looked at the name of the individual and I took the view that this was not somebody who matched the description that has been given out at the 3.45 briefing.

DINGEMANS: Right.

BLITZ: He continued his research and selected from the list the reference to www.Sussex.ac.uk which produced a document.

DINGEMANS: Was Dr Kelly's name on that document?

BLITZ: It was on that document, yes.

DINGEMANS: Had you ever heard of Dr Kelly before that?

BLITZ: No, I had not.

DINGEMANS: So what did you do to take the matter further forward?

BLITZ: Mr Adams and I concentrated our attention on that name. We proceeded to have a series of conversations with Whitehall official at the start of which we put the name of Dr David Kelly as the possible individual.

DINGEMANS: Right, and what was the first response Mr Adams got?

BLITZ: One moment please.

DINGEMANS: 44.

BLITZ: Yes I wish to be very faithful to the witness statement I have given you if I may.

DINGEMANS: Right I hope this is based on your recollection.

BLITZ: This is based on a very firm recollection and Mr Adams' recollection of what happened this afternoon. Mr Adams spoke with the first Whitehall official that he contacted. He understood the conversation to be off the record. The official declined to comment when Mr Adams put Dr David Kelly's name to that person.

DINGEMANS: Does he speak to anyone else?

BLITZ: He spoke to a second Whitehall official on the same off the record basis. The official did not confirm Dr David Kelly as the individual and referred Mr Adams to the MoD press office. Mr Adams then pursued his inquiries around the name of Dr David Kelly. Asked about Dr David Kelly's job and background, this official replied that he was seconded to the MoD from the Porton Down defence establishment and that his salary was paid by the FCO [Foreign Office].

DINGEMANS: What did Mr Adams do after that?

BLITZ: Mr Adams then tried to speak to [Miss] Pam Teare, the head of the MoD press office, on the telephone but she was engaged on another telephone call.

DINGEMANS: Following that lack of success?

BLITZ: Mr Adams spoke to a third Whitehall official on an off the record basis and pressed that person with Dr David Kelly's name. At the end of this conversation Mr Adams believed that Dr David Kelly was the individual mentioned in the MoD press statement the night before.

DINGEMANS: How was the individual actually identified?

BLITZ: It was only a few moment later that Mr Adams again called Miss Teare. He put the name of Dr David Kelly to her and she immediately confirmed he was the individual in the MoD statement.

DINGEMANS: Having confirmed the name, he obviously told you, did he?

BLITZ: That is correct.

DINGEMANS: And what did you do then?

BLITZ: I then proceeded to speak to other – to continue with inquiries. Although I had confirmation of this, you must understand this was a most unusual situation. I telephone another Whitehall official and spoke to that official on an off-the-record basis. I indicated to that person I had good grounds for believing that Dr David Kelly was the individual mentioned in the MoD statement. This official did not expressly confirm my belief, but the language used left me in no doubt that Dr David Kelly was indeed the person in question.

DINGEMANS: Did you then start to produce any article on the basis of this information?

BLITZ: I did not, at that point, do that. Before writing the article I telephone Ms Teare myself. Ms Teare told me the MoD had a policy to confirm the name to any journalist who offered it.

DINGEMANS: And then did you become aware, later on, that other journalists had identified –

BLITZ: Dr David Kelly?

DINGEMANS: Yes.

BLITZ: Around one hour after I filed the story, I was informed by a journalist on another newspaper that the *Times* and *The Guardian* had also discovered the name of the individual in the MoD press statement. This was the first moment at which I was aware of this fact.

Andrew Mackinlay MP, 26th August 2003

DINGEMANS: Could you tell his Lordship your full name.

MACKINLAY: Yes, my Lord. I am Andrew Mackinlay. I am the member of Parliament for Thurrock. I was elected in 1992 so I am in my third term.

DINGEMANS: You were party to the Foreign Affairs Committee's [decision] to investigate the decision to go to war in Iraq?

MACKINLAY: Correct an enthusiastic advocate, some were not. The reason why I was enthusiastic we should investigate this matter of the Government's justification for going to war was against a backdrop of many people, many very good people who either were opposed to war initially or then had doubts afterwards. There was currency in the press and in the political world that the Government had exaggerated the case; and it seemed to me that Parliament had a duty to look, albeit retrospectively, as to whether or not the Government had exaggerated that case. Also it is against a backdrop that for the first time in our history Parliament actually voted an affirmative resolution to commit our armed forces to a conflict situation – is has never happened before, and all 650 of us had to wrestle with our consciences. The historic duty of Parliament is one of scrutiny. It seemed to me no greater duty than to scrutinise this issue. The very final point I make on this is in a way after all the Prime Minister [has] offered no other inquiry in the open on this.

DINGEMANS: There was a meeting when it was decided to call back Dr Kelly. Did you support the idea that Dr Kelly should be called to give evidence?

MACKINLAY: I did.

DINGEMANS: Mr Hoon says [In a letter to the FAC]: 'I am prepared to agree to this on the clear understanding that Dr Kelly will be questioned only on those matters which are directly relevant to the evidence that you were given by Andrew Gilligan and not on the wider issue of Iraqi WMD and the preparation of the dossier'. Were you aware of those proposed restrictions on Dr Kelly's evidence?

MACKINLAY: Yes I was. I did not agree with them. I consider it a monumental cheek of the Secretary of State to try and tell us what we should and could inquire into.

DINGEMANS: We know that Mr Gilligan had sent some emails to members of the Committee. At BBC/13/17 we can see an email dated 30th June. This is obviously before the inquiry has completed its report.

MACKINLAY: Hmm.

DINGEMANS: 'John, as promised here is my analysis of the Campbell evidence. I've added some further notes at the bottom. Andrew.' He talks about the dodgy dossier, various questions that have been asked, et cetera. Were you aware of these communications?

MACKINLAY: No, I was not until it had come out in this Inquiry some few days ago in relation to David Chidgey MP.

DINGEMANS: What is your attitude to persons who themselves appeared before the Committee making suggestions to members of the Committee?

MACKINLAY: I think this highly inappropriate.

DINGEMANS: Can I turn to 15th July? What do you recall of Dr Kelly's appearance at the beginning of the session?

MACKINLAY: Apart from the question he was softly spoken, I thought very controlled, except for – I mention this in my witness statement – two people who accompanied him and sat immediately behind him. To me that was quite significant.

DINGEMANS: FAC/4/15 question 105, which is towards the bottom of the page. You are asking him about the journalists.

MACKINLAY: Yes.

DINGEMANS: Dr Kelly: 'I have met very few journalists'. 'Andrew Mackinlay: I heard 'few', but who are the ones in your mind's eye at this moment? What are their names? Dr Kelly: That will be provided to you by the Ministry of Defence.' This continues over the page: 'Andrew Mackinlay: No, I am asking you now. This is the high court of Parliament and I want you to tell the Committee who you met.' I think you wanted to say something in relation to that?

MACKINLAY: Yes. My Lord, if I may.

HUTTON: By all means. Do you want to look at your witness statement?

MACKINLAY: Yes. Thank you very much. It is against a backdrop – that question is against the earlier questions when I had said: Can you tell me the journalist? He said: 'see the Ministry of Defence'. I asked him again. See the Ministry of Defence. I asked him again. So I say: could you let us – by Thursday, by Thursday. He again said: the Ministry of Defence. I thought this a prevarication, unnecessary, inappropriate. It was a challenge to the whole business of Parliamentary scrutiny. You see, my Lord, just supposing in a moment, my Lord, you were to ask me a question and I said: see the chairman of my constituency party. Probably because you are a disciplined man not a muscle in your face would move. Then you asked me again and I said the same thing, my Lord, and again. Then you try and help –

HUTTON: You thought Dr Kelly should answer because he was before a Committee of Parliament?

MACKINLAY: Absolutely. Absolutely. I then went on in my witness statement: 'The power of the House to punish for contempt is well-established and its origin is probably to be found in the medieval concept of the English Parliament as a primary court of justice.'

DINGEMANS: Can I ask you some questions about your other questioning towards the end of the session? FAC/4/[25]: Perhaps you can read out your question? Number 167.

MACKINLAY: 'I reckon you are chaff; you have been thrown up to divert our probing. Have you ever felt like a fall guy? You have been set up, have you not?'

DINGEMANS: Did you consider that to be a fair question?

MACKINLAY: Yes, I do think it is; and because it is against a backdrop of where the Government had indicated they think that Dr Kelly is the sole source. He then comes along to us. He has convinced me that he is not the source – the Gilligan source, very impressively, very impressively indeed. I mean, I have had lots of hating emails and letter since. A lot of people do not understand the word 'chaff'.

DINGEMANS: What did you understand?

MACKINLAY: Well, chaff to a weapons expert is what is thrown out by our destroyers and from our fighter aircraft to deflect incoming –

DINGEMANS: Exocet missiles?

MACKINLAY: Absolutely. No offence was meant. Our Committee – the paradox, the irony was that my Committee did suffer from chaff because we were successively diverted.

HUTTON: Mr Mackinlay, may I ask you, coming back to your thought that Dr Kelly had been set up.

MACKINLAY: I do not buy this business of him coming forward voluntarily. I think by this time the heat was on.

DINGEMANS: After the hearing you pursued some Parliamentary questions, at TVP/2/15.

MACKINLAY: Yes.

DINGEMANS: We see your question: 'To ask the Secretary of State for Defence which journalists Dr Kelly has met over the past two years, for what purpose and when the meeting took place.' What was your purpose in pursuing those questions?

MACKINLAY: Because Dr Kelly, if you remember, said: ask the Ministry of Defence. That is precisely what I did do. I am tenacious, I will not be thrown off on a thing like this.

HUTTON: Yes. Thank you very much indeed.

MACKINLAY: Is that all?

DINGEMANS: Is there anything else you want to say?

MACKINLAY: There is, my Lord. I deeply regret the death of Dr Kelly. If there is any way that my questions contributed to his distress or stress, I deeply regret that, and I expressed my condolences to his wife and family. After that my Lord, I have not had dealings with any journalists. Just to complete the picture, my local newspaper had daubed on its walls, 'Kelly's blood on Mackinlay's hands'. I have shown the utmost restraint and I want to continue to do so. It is difficult. Even yesterday afternoon the Today Programme phoned up my house wanting me to go on this morning, presumably to save you the trouble of listening to me because you would have heard it on your way in my Lord. My whole basis as an MP is based upon reputation and I have not been able to hit back or to respond. But you see I am like a sprung coil this morning, my Lord. I am very, very angry because I think not only Mackinlay is at stake but the future of Parliament because, my Lord, this could go either way. Your report could either very welcomely open up a whole new vista of openness in Government or it could be used as the Hutton rules whereby it buttresses all this sort of thing in the future. I think we are at a crossroads as regard Parliament. I am desperately anxious that nobody has spoken up for Parliament. The final thing, sir –

HUTTON: I think Mr Mackinlay I should just say, as I am sure you appreciate, the Bill of Rights itself provides that the affairs of Parliament should not be commented on other than in Parliament. Therefore you will appreciate it will not be appropriate for me to express views on the affairs of Parliament. That is a matter for Parliament itself.

MACKINLAY: In a way that makes it more difficult for me to be restrained, but I will continue to be restrained. Lord Hutton, there is one final point you might want to consider. The Government refused us access to documents and to people who we all now see. The irony is that all these people and documents are given to you and I am very much pleased you have them but you also can put them on a website. If it was so critical that they should not be out in the public domain. They will not let Parliament have them; now the balloon has gone up, they are available.

Geoff Hoon MP, 27th August 2003

DINGEMANS: You are Secretary of State for Defence?

HOON: Yes, I am.

DINGEMANS: Did you have any involvement in the drafting of the dossier that was published by the Government on 24th September 2002?

HOON: I saw two drafts relatively late, and I did not offer any comments or suggest any changes to it.

DINGEMANS: Were you aware of the Defence Intelligence Staff involvement with the drafting of the dossier?

HOON: I was not aware of what specific contribution they had made.

DINGEMANS: Were you aware of any unhappiness expressed by members of the D[efence] I[intelligence] S[taff] with the dossier, either before or after publication?

HOON: Not at the time.

DINGEMANS: Can I then turn to a lunch that we have heard from Ms Watts that Dr Kelly reported having with you in about April time. Did you, in fact, have lunch with Dr Kelly at any time?

HOON: No, I did not. It is my practice from time to time to eat in the Old War Office Building canteen. On this particular occasion at the end of lunch we were approached by an official, I did not know who it was. We talked about Iraq. We discussed the Government policy, which the official said he strongly supported; and it was not a formal occasion in any sense at all. I did not know that it was Dr Kelly at the time.

DINGEMANS: We have been told about investigations that were carried out after the broadcast on 29th May. Were you aware of any of these investigations?

HOON: No, I was not.

DINGEMANS: Were you told anything about a letter that the official had written?

HOON: I was told that he had set out, in some detail, that he had had this meeting with Andrew Gilligan. The significant thing was that although he had recognised some of the things that Andrew Gilligan subsequently broadcast as being attributable to him and to his conversation, he did not believe that he was Andrew

Gilligan's single source because there were other things in the broadcast that he did not recognise.

DINGEMANS: Did you have any initial reaction to this information?

HOON: I think my first – my very first reaction was that this was something that could well lead to disciplinary proceedings. Immediately, perhaps almost at the same time, I was also concerned at the Foreign Affairs Committee hearings because any disciplinary process will take some considerable time to complete.

DINGEMANS: Did you decide, when you were talking to [your Permanent Secretary] Sir Kevin Tebbit, what to do in relation to Dr Kelly, about interviews or anything else?

HOON: Well, I did not decide because it has always been my practice, in the Ministry of Defence, to ensure that appropriate responsibilities are dealt with by appropriate people. Therefore, as far as any personnel issues were concerned, the responsibility was clearly that of the Permanent Secretary.

HUTTON: Was correcting the public record a personnel matter?

HOON: It was important to the Ministry of Defence and indeed to the Government as a whole that the public record should be corrected.

DINGEMANS: Did you speak to Mr Campbell about your initial reactions on hearing the news of Dr Kelly coming forward?

HOON: Yes, I did. I emphasised to him my concern about any suggestion that the Government should be covering up [to the Foreign Affairs Committee] the fact of a potential witness coming forward.

DINGEMANS: We know that there was a draft press statement, prepared by the Ministry of Defence, and draft

Q and A material, also prepared. Were you any part of this Q and A material and were you consulted about it?

HOON: No, I was not.

HUTTON: Before we proceed, may I just ask, Secretary of State: with regard to the BBC, suppose you had given in confidence to the BBC Dr Kelly's name and that the BBC had then confirmed that: yes, he was Mr Gilligan's source. What was your thinking after that? What did you think might happen or that you might bring about?

HOON: He could indicate what he had and had not said to Andrew Gilligan, so the public, Parliament, we would all have been in a position to know whether Andrew Gilligan had or had not exaggerated the material that he had been provided with by Dr Kelly.

HUTTON: Yes. But that would have involved Dr Kelly coming forward into the public domain and stating what he had said and what he had not said to Mr Gilligan?

HOON: I was not aware that Dr Kelly necessarily had any concerns about his identity remaining secret.

DINGEMANS: Were you aware of any doubts being expressed about whether Dr Kelly had told the whole story, at this stage?

HOON: I was not aware doubts were being expressed.

DINGEMANS: Right. We can see that the Ministry of Defence are preparing some press statements. But these are now being at least altered or improved by Downing Street. Were you aware that Downing Street was involved in helping the Ministry of Defence with their press statements?

HOON: I was not directly aware of that, but it would not be a particular surprise given the involvement of Downing Street in these events.

DINGEMANS: At this stage, did you understand whether or not Dr Kelly was happy for his name to be given to any newspaper or press statement?

HOON: That, at that stage, obviously had not been discussed with Dr Kelly.

DINGEMANS: We have seen the defensive Q and A material that was actually deployed. Can I take you to some draft Q and A material which we have received, CAB/21/5 – If you can look down to the fifth question: 'Is it X (i.e. the correct name)? 'If the correct name is put to us we will need to tell the individual we are going to confirm his name before doing so? The actual Q and A material put out later has a rather different look to it. If you look at MoD/1/62, you can see: 'If the correct name is given, we can confirm it...' That is a reasonably substantial change. One is saying: we need to go back to the individual and tell him first. Do you know whether or not Dr Kelly was told about the draft Q and A material and the Q and A material as deployed?

HOON: I do not, no. But can I make clear that I did not see either of these documents.

DINGEMANS: We have heard about some meetings that took place in Downing Street on 8th July, when it is decided that Dr Kelly's name ought to be supplied to the Intelligence and Security Committee, copied to the FAC, and because it is going to be copied to the FAC, it is going to be made public. Were you being told at all what was being decided at the meeting in Downing Street?

HOON: I was certainly told that there was a proposal to contact the I[ntelligence] S[ecurity] C[ommittee] and to use the ISC as a means of perhaps persuading the BBC to reveal privately their source.

HUTTON: May I ask you, Secretary of State, did you understand that there was any thought that the ISC would go rather beyond that and would examine Dr Kelly for the purpose of coming to the conclusion that Mr Gilligan's main criticism was incorrect?

HOON: I was not present at that meeting, but what I understood to be the case was that by giving the name of Dr Kelly to the ISC on our side might encourage the BBC to reveal their source on their side. The fall back was for me to write to the BBC and to publicise the fact that an official had come forward.

DINGEMANS: Whose plan or strategy was it, as far as you understood?

HOON: I was given a message to the effect that it was now appropriate for me to write to the Chairman of the governors.

DINGEMANS: The fall back plan is coming to you from No. 10?

HOON: Yes.

HUTTON: Is it your evidence, Secretary of State, that this MoD statement was issued solely for the purpose of trying to persuade the BBC to reveal its source or was there another reason behind it?

HOON: That was certainly part of it, but throughout I had been concerned that we were in possession of significant information about a potential witness relevant to Parliamentary proceedings, relevant to the public debate.

DINGEMANS: Effectively there are a number of pieces of information which are going to assist any journalist to identify Dr Kelly. Is that a fair analysis of this defensive Q and A material?

HOON: I did not see this Q and A and played no part in its preparation.

DINGEMANS: Going to your correspondence with [chairman of the BBC governors] Mr Davies. You give the name, in confidence, to Mr Davies of Dr Kelly. What is the purpose behind this correspondence?

HOON: By then I had accepted that the BBC were not going to volunteer the name of their source. I thought it might assist them in assessing the reliability of what Andrew Gilligan might have said to them to indicate privately to Gavyn Davies the name of the official who had come forward.

DINGEMANS: Did you get any assistance from anyone else about [the] decision to put Dr Kelly before both the ISC and the FAC? Were you aware of anyone else's views?

HOON: I was certainly aware that the Prime Minister took the view that it would be extraordinarily difficult to explain to Parliament and to the Foreign Affairs Committee why we were refusing permission for an official who clearly had something relevant to say about their previous deliberations, why we would refuse permission for him to appear before that select committee.

DINGEMANS: How had you been aware of the Prime Minister's views in relation to that?

HOON: I had not spoken to him directly. I think that came in a view from Jonathan Powell.

DINGEMANS: Were you aware that Dr Kelly had some views that might be considered uncomfortable on the dossier and Iraqi weapons of mass destruction?

HOON: This was just one official who had particular views. But his views were not characteristic of the policy that the Government had developed or established.

DINGEMANS: We know that Dr Kelly's body was found on 18th July. Can I take you to TVP/3/238, which is an interview with Peter Sissons. Mr Sissons says this: 'This is a very great personal tragedy. He killed himself after your department, indeed you personally outed him as the probable mole.' You say this: 'We followed very carefully established MoD procedures, and at all stages, certainly as far as I personally was concerned, we protected his anonymity.' We have heard that in fact the department confirmed his name to journalists. We have heard from you that the department issued a press statement to the effect that a man had come forward, all at a time when no-one knew for sure that he was the single source. Do you still hold by your answer that the Ministry of Defence followed established procedures and protected his anonymity?

HOON: Yes, I do.

Wing Commander John Clark, 27th August 2003

KNOX: Could you tell the Inquiry your full name and your occupation?

CLARK: My name is Wing Commander John Clark. I am a Wing Commander in the Royal Air Force. My current job title is CPAC, CONAC 1.

KNOX: CPAC, am a right in thinking, stands for Counter Proliferation Arms Control?

CLARK: Correct, and the CONAC stands for Conventional Arms Control.

KNOX: I want to ask you one or two questions about your contact with Dr Kelly.

CLARK: Yes. We worked quite closely because he really was the fount of all knowledge in respect of Iraq.

KNOX: Can I ask you about Dr Kelly's press contacts. Were you aware he had a number of press contacts?

CLARK: Yes. In fact he made no secret of that fact. He was quite proud that he had many press contacts, from diverse backgrounds.

KNOX: Did you at any point before the hearing in front of the FAC discuss the forthcoming appearance with him?

CLARK: I felt it would be inappropriate to ask him the obvious questions that clearly the hearings were there to ask him. I asked him how he felt. He was tired. He was clearly not looking forward to the hearings.

KNOX: What was the atmosphere, as far as you could tell, at the Foreign Affairs Committee hearing?

CLARK: It was uncomfortable to – certainly from where I was sat it was extremely warm. The fans or the air conditioning had to be switched off because the Committee could not hear David – Dr Kelly, and they were continually asking could he speak up, speak up. He was quite a softly spoken individual, and he was obviously having difficulty being heard.

KNOX: Did Dr Kelly comment on any of the questions that he had been asked?

CLARK: Yes. He was totally thrown by the question or the quotation that was given to him from Susan Watts. He spoke about that when he came back to the office. He did say that threw him. He had not expected or anticipated that that would have come to the fore at that forum.

KNOX: Can you be a bit more precise about what that question was?

CLARK: A member of the Committee read out a very long quotation from Susan Watts which apparently David or Dr Kelly had said. Now, in response to that Dr Kelly said it was not his quote.

KNOX: So after the hearing he says to you: that really threw me?

CLARK: Yes he did.

KNOX: There has been some speculation that perhaps Mr Mackinlay was a bit brusque with him. Did he mention anything about that?

CLARK: No, I think Dr Kelly accepted he was doing his job.

KNOX: And Thursday 17th July, did Dr Kelly come into work?

CLARK: No, he did not. We had two Parliamentary Questions that had to be responded to that had been tabled by Andrew Mackinlay.

KNOX: These were the two Parliamentary Questions that you or Dr Kelly were trying to answer on the 17th?

CLARK: Yes they are.

KNOX: Did you play any part in assisting Dr Kelly to answer these Parliamentary Questions?

CLARK: Yes, I played the role of facilitator. What had been agreed on the previous day, the 16th, was Dr Kelly would provide the detail that was required by about 10 o'clock the next morning.

KNOX: Could you go to MoD/20/12? This appears to be an email from Dr Kelly to you sent at 9.22.

CLARK: Correct.

KNOX: You will see it says: John: 'I have compiled the information as best I can. The list of journalists is the most difficult because some may date before 2002 and some may have nothing to do with Iraq whatsoever.' Could you go to MoD/20/12? This appears to be an email from Dr Kelly to you sent at 9.22.

CLARK: Correct.

KNOX: You will see it says: 'John: I have compiled the information as best I can. The list of journalists is the most difficult because some may date before 2002 and some may have nothing to do with Iraq whatsoever.' Over the page he lists the journalists he has contact with.

CLARK: Yes. So I added the detail in accordance with Dr Kelly's email.

KNOX: There is another set of emails at MoD/20/22. You see here another email which you are sending at 13.59. You are now sending it to Parliamentary Questions. Who is that?

CLARK: That is the organisation we send completed Parliamentary Questions to.

KNOX: We know there appears to be another draft which you can see at MoD/20/27. There is a reference to 'journalists whose business cards Dr Kelly has in his possession.' Did you talk to Mr Kelly about this at all?

CLARK: Yes. It was decided that the reference to the business cards would remain.

KNOX: Can you recall what conversations you had with Dr Kelly in the course of the 17th July, apart from the emails?

CLARK: We had a number of calls. The first one was about 10 o'clock in the morning to say the information required is on the Internet machine. We also had a general discussion of developments, how he was feeling. He was feeling still tired but in good spirits, although at that stage – and David Kelly was a very private man and very rarely mentioned his family – he had come in later on the 16th [July] because of a personal problem at home. That was because he had obviously come back from Cornwall and his wife had been left in Cornwall and he some way had to work out how to get his wife, who has arthritis, back from Cornwall. That is why he had been making arrangements on the 16th and that is why he was somewhat later in. On the 17th, when I asked him how he was going, he basically said he was holding up all right but it had all come to a head and his wife had taken it really very badly. Whether that was in association with the additional pressure of having to get back the day before under her own steam, I do not know, but he did say that his wife had been very upset on the morning of the 17th.

KNOX: In the course of these conversations were you told by anyone that any further contacts with journalists had to be checked with Dr Kelly?

CLARK: Yes, I was contacted by the Secretary of State's office and he brought up the subject of the article that had been published on 13th July, written by Nick Rufford [of the *Sunday Times*]. Now, Dr Kelly had made no reference to that meeting in his one-to-one meetings, and I was asked to check with Dr Kelly if that meeting had taken place and, if it had, then really it ought to be included in the response.

KNOX: At what time did you attempt to ring Dr Kelly?

CLARK: It was – I have since been told by the police – I thought it was close to 3 o'clock but it was about 3.20, and I was told by his wife who answered the telephone that Dr Kelly had gone for a walk at 3 o'clock.

KNOX: Can you recall what the last telephone conversation you actually had with Dr Kelly was before that attempt to get hold of him?

CLARK: Yes, I had a call with him which was just before 3 o'clock. That was the one where we discussed the business cards.

KNOX: And after you had not been able to get hold of Dr Kelly, what did you do?

CLARK: I was surprised that I could not get two-way with him because he was always very proud of his ability to be contacted. He took his mobile phone everywhere.

KNOX: Did you try again?

CLARK: I rang his wife because clearly I needed to get the staff work taken forward and I needed to speak to Dr Kelly. I spoke to her and said I had not been able to contact Dr Kelly on his mobile and I thought she might say something but she was quite matter of fact and said, you know – did not really record the fact. I then said: could you ask Dr Kelly when he returns, could he give me a ring. That is how the message was left with his wife.

Gavyn Davies, 28th August 2003

DAVIES: My name is Gavyn Davies, I am the Chairman of the BBC.

DINGEMANS: Did you hear the broadcast by Mr Gilligan on 29th May?

DAVIES: I did. I heard the whole of the Today Programme.

DINGEMANS: Do you listen to it every morning then?

DAVIES: I do, I am afraid, yes. Not always from 6 o'clock, but –

DINGEMANS: At the time, as a member of the listening public but perhaps paying more attention than others might, what was your understanding of the original thrust of the story?

DAVIES: Well, my understanding of the thrust of the story was that Mr Gilligan was saying that he had a source who he believed to be a senior and reliable and credible source, who believed that the September 2002 dossier on intelligence had been sexed up by No. 10. There was no mention of Alastair Campbell, I seem to remember. And that some of the information in the dossier was not fully approved by the Intelligence Services.

DINGEMANS: We have heard from the Prime Minister about the denials that were issued and his hope that the story would go away with those denials.

DAVIES: Yes.

DINGEMANS: Were you aware of those denials being reported, et cetera?

DAVIES: Yes. I was aware that the Prime Minister and others, I think Alastair Campbell too, had that week said things to the effect that the programme – that the report was rubbish.

DINGEMANS: Right. But as a Chairman of Governors, are you involved at that stage?

DAVIES: No, I mean essentially I have to say that at that stage I thought that the Gilligan reports were just another of those episodes which Today tends to trip over occasionally.

HUTTON: What do you mean Mr Davies by appear to trip over?

DAVIES: What I mean is the programme – it is probably Britain's leading forum for political debate. It is a programme which attracts enormous attention; and from time to time it becomes the centre of that debate. That is really all I meant.

HUTTON: It is just the words 'trip over', if you could just explain what you mean by trip over?

DAVIES: I think I meant encountered, my Lord.

DINGEMANS: Then Mr Gilligan, continuing with the chronology if I may, giving evidence to the Foreign Affairs Committee on 19th June. Mr Campbell gives evidence on 25th June. What was your view about Mr Campbell's evidence on the debate between the Government and the BBC?

DAVIES: I mean, I felt this was an extraordinary moment. I felt it was an almost unprecedented attack on the BBC to be mounted by the head of communications at 10 Downing Street. Mr Campbell accused the BBC of lying directly. He alleged that the BBC had accused the Prime Minister of lying, something which I never believed the BBC had done. And he accused the BBC of having followed an anti-war agenda before, during and after the Iraqi conflict.

DINGEMANS: We know that Mr Campbell wrote Mr Sambrook a letter of 26th June. He asked for a response to some specific questions, I will go straight to the response which was on the 27th of June, CAB/1/355. Were you a party to this letter of response?

DAVIES: No I was not a party to that, I was aware Richard Sambrook showed me the letter from Alastair Campbell. He also showed me a draft of the reply he was going to send.

DINGEMANS: Can I take you to page 7 of the letter. And [one of] the questions that Mr Campbell had asked: 'Does the BBC still stand by the allegation it made on 29th May that No. 10 added in the 45 minute claim to the dossier?' [Answer] : 'The allegation was not made by the BBC but by our source – a senior official involved in the compilation of the dossier – and the BBC stands by the reporting of it.' There is a distinction between the BBC and the source. Was that how you saw it at the time?

DAVIES: I read this letter, Mr Dingemans, I did not write it. I believe that what this letter was doing was giving, on behalf of BBC management, our best and most truthful explanation to Mr Campbell of what we had reported.

DINGEMANS: This is when you have also decided to call a Governors' meeting. Did it become apparent that the matter was not going to go away?

DAVIES: Well, I was hoping it might go away, but in this period the Government continued in its press briefings daily, at No. 10, to bring the matter up with a fairly high degree of volume.

HUTTON: Did the Governors know that the first part of Mr Gilligan's report on 29th May was unscripted?

DAVIES: I believe they did, my Lord, yes.

HUTTON: Does that make any difference to the question of editorial control?

DAVIES: Well, I think it raises an issue. It does raise an issue, in my mind, about whether reports of this nature should be unscripted.

HUTTON: Yes.

DINGEMANS: Then you put on record [in a press release] that the BBC had not accused the Prime Minister of lying.

DAVIES: Yes. Here is a very, very strong statement and extremely unusual statement for the Board of Governors to make.

HUTTON: If you were satisfied that the Prime Minister was not lying, might it not have called for perhaps even a qualified withdrawal of the first part of the report?

DAVIES: Well, my Lord, I did not think that the BBC had any evidence to suggest that the source would have wished to withdraw his views. Now, sometimes in life you get the same event being watched by two different people with two different interpretations of the same event.

HUTTON: Quite. Yes.

DINGEMANS: You get a letter on 8th July. Can I take you to MoD/1/66 from Mr Hoon. 'Dear Gavyn, 'I am writing to draw your attention to an MoD statement which we shall be issuing later today... 'You will see that we have not named the official... We would, however, be prepared to disclose his name to you in confidence... in the interests of resolving what has become a management problem for both our organisations.' What was your reaction to that?

DAVIES: At the time I was puzzled by what he meant by management problem. I did not really know what the tactics or strategy lying behind the letter was. In any event, I could not have disclosed the name myself because I did not know the name.

DINGEMANS: Was there any correspondence after that?

DAVIES: Yes. First of all, on this one, Mr Dingemans, my suspicions that something was up were raised when I found out that the letter from Mr Hoon to myself had been released to the press, and that made me more suspicious about that, maybe something was going on that I had not fathomed.

DINGEMANS: Was there any reason that you felt that the source should not be confirmed?

DAVIES: Well, at this particular stage he had not named the source to me. He did that the following day

DINGEMANS: Can I take you to his letter of the following day? MoD/1/71.

DAVIES: Yes.

DINGEMANS: He now gives you the name Dr Kelly. So what is wrong, now, with saying: yes, it is Dr Kelly?

DAVIES: Well, I think what was wrong was first of all I did not, of course, know yet whether Dr Kelly was the source. So I was unable to confirm or deny it. What occurred to me here was: look, I do not know whether Dr Kelly is actually Mr Gilligan's source, but if he is he has probably said some very different things to Mr

Gilligan to what he has said to his employer; and my feeling was that if we had come forward and said: yes actually that is the source, we would have been betraying the confidence, number 1, because the source had never suggested that we should divulge his name, and number 2 we would have effectively been telling his employer that he had told Mr Gilligan more than he was now owning up to [to] his employer.

DINGEMANS: So what steps did you take to deal with the letter?

DAVIES: What I did was I was the only person that saw the name 'David Kelly'. I Tipexed that out and I showed the redacted letter to the Director General; and I think within a very short time we heard that the name of David Kelly was circulating among journalists and, you know, I did not know how that had happened.

DINGEMANS: Dr Kelly comes to give evidence to the Foreign Affairs Committee on 15th July. We have heard about that. We have also seen, now, an email that Mr Gilligan has sent that is FAC/6/62 and he was suggesting some questions for Dr Kelly. If you go down to the bottom of the page you can see: 'He told my colleague Susan Watts, science editor of Newsnight…' If you read that as a lay person you might think that he is suggesting that Dr Kelly was Susan Watts' source. Did you know of this email?

DAVIES: I had absolutely no idea whatsoever, no.

DINGEMANS: And what is your view on journalists sending this type of email to members of the Foreign Affairs Committee?

DAVIES: I think this is something the Director General may wish to look at.

DINGEMANS: Is there anything else that you know of the circumstances surrounding Dr Kelly's death that you can assist his Lordship with?

DAVIES: I think on behalf of the whole BBC I would like to put on record that we enormously regret the death of Dr Kelly. The BBC has the deepest sympathy for Dr Kelly's family; and all of us in the BBC are profoundly sorry about the tragic events of the last two months and we will do our utmost to learn important lessons for the future.

HUTTON: Thank you very much indeed, Mr Davies.

Dr Brian Jones, 3rd September 2003

HUTTON: Sit down please.

DINGEMANS: Can you tell his Lordship your full name.

JONES: It is Brian Francis Gill Jones.

DINGEMANS: What is your occupation?

JONES: I am a retired civil servant.

DINGEMANS: Before you retired?

JONES: I was a branch head in the Scientific and Technical Directorate of the Defence Intelligence Analysis Staff.

DINGEMANS: What is your personal opinion about weapons of mass destruction?

JONES: My personal opinion is that almost all – almost all – nuclear weapons truly fit this concept of being a weapon of mass destruction, that some biological weapons are perhaps reasonably described in that way because they could be used to produce very large numbers of casualties on the same sort of scale perhaps even as nuclear weapons, but there are many biological weapons that struggle to fit into that. Some are incapacitants for example rather than lethal.

DINGEMANS: Those are biological weapons you think do not fit into that character. What about the chemical weapons?

JONES: I think chemical weapons almost struggle to fit into that category. There are certain agents and certain scenarios where I would think that chemical weapons truly are describable as weapons of mass destruction. Sorry, could I take a sip of water?

DINGEMANS: Yes of course.

HUTTON: Do I gather, Dr Jones, that there is perhaps some debate in intelligence circles then about the precise meaning of 'weapons of mass destruction'? You are expressing your own view. Do I take it that there are others that might take a different view?

JONES: There may be. I mean, I think 'weapons of mass destruction' has become a convenient catch-all which, in my opinion, can at times confuse discussion of the subject.

HUTTON: Yes I see. Thank you, yes.

DINGEMANS: Mr Scarlett, I think, told us that Dr Kelly may have been confused about the difference between missile delivery of chemical weapons and artillery delivery. Do you think there is a difference between the two.

JONES: In terms of weapons of mass destruction? I think I would struggle to describe either as a true weapon of mass destruction.

DINGEMANS: Do you know whether Dr Kelly had seen the earlier drafts of the dossier?

JONES: I discovered on 18th September, when I met him then, that he was actually looking at the latest draft at that time.

DINGEMANS: Did you discuss with Dr Kelly his view of the dossier as so far drafted?

JONES: At that point, I did. He said he thought it was good.

DINGEMANS: And were there others in your group who had differing views?

JONES: Some of my staff had said that they were unhappy with all the detail that was in the dossier. My expert analyst on C[hemical] W[arfare] expressed particular concern. I had, I think, at the time I spoke to David, begun to look at his problems, to look at the bits of the dossier that he had problems with.

DINGEMANS: And what was your CW expert's particular concern?

JONES: Well, at its simplest he was concerned that some of the statements that were in the dossier did not accurately represent his assessment of the intelligence available to him.

HUTTON: May I just pursue: changes had been suggested. Is it your understanding they were passed on to the assessment staff but they were not adopted?

JONES: That is correct.

DINGEMANS: And those concerns had not been accepted?

JONES: Some had, but there were significant ones that had not been accepted.

DINGEMANS: And how did your CW expert feel about that?

JONES: He was very concerned.

HUTTON: Could you just elaborate a little on his concern?

JONES: My Lord, they were about language but language is the means by which we communicate an assessment, so they were also about the assessment, yes.

HUTTON: Quite. Yes.

JONES: I mean, if I can just refer to a note I have here…they were really about a tendency in certain areas, from his point of view, to shall we say over-egg certain assessments in relation particularly to the production of CW agents and weapons since 1998. And he was concerned that he could not point to any solid evidence of such production.

DINGEMANS: Did any of the personnel who were working under you know that people within the communications side of No. 10 had been making suggestions on the dossier?

JONES: I think there was an impression that they were involved in some way.

DINGEMANS: The 45 minutes is the next area. Were you aware of any concerns about the 45 minutes?

JONES: Yes, I had some concerns about the 45 minute point myself; yes. My concerns were that Iraq's chemical weapons and biological weapons capabilities were not being accurately represented. In particular, I had seen – on the advice of my staff, I was told that there was no evidence that significant production had taken place either of chemical warfare agent or chemical weapons. We had problems about the source. Our concern was that what we were hearing was second-hand information. And the information did not differentiate between whether these were chemical weapons or whether they were biological weapons; and that is an important matter. There was a lack of detail on whether the agents, the weapons, what scenarios were being discussed. It was a fairly nebulous general statement that concerned us.

DINGEMANS: Can I take you to one final reference, CAB/29/15? This was Mr A's email. Just at the bottom Mr A makes the comment: 'Another example supporting our view that you and I should have been more involved in this than the spin merchants of this administration.' Was there a perception, right or wrong, amongst D[efence] I[ntelligence] S[ervice] personnel that spin merchants were involved with the dossier?

JONES: Well, 'spin merchants' is rather emotive. I think there was an impression that there was an influence from outside the intelligence community.

DINGEMANS: And were people in the intelligence community happy with that?

JONES: No.

Janice Kelly, 1st September 2003

HUTTON: Good morning Mrs Kelly. As I think you know, Mr Dingemans will take you through your evidence and if at any time you would like a break, please just say so.

KELLY: Thank you, my Lord.

DINGEMANS: Mrs Kelly, I hope you can see me. We can see a still picture of you. Can you hear me clearly?

KELLY: I can see you and hear you.

DINGEMANS: You married Dr Kelly in 1967?

KELLY: That is correct.

DINGEMANS: Where had you met?

KELLY: We had met when he was at Leeds University. I was studying at Birmingham Training College at the time before I moved on to Birmingham University.

DINGEMANS: Mrs Kelly, you will need to keep your voice up a wee bit, if that is all right.

KELLY: That is fine.

DINGEMANS: After university, what had he gone on to do?

KELLY: He went on to do a Doctorate at Oxford University.

DINGEMANS: Do you know what that was in?

KELLY: Not entirely. It was something to do with viruses and insect viruses.

DINGEMANS: Dr Kelly was asked to get involved in the UNSCOM, United Nations Special Commission on Iraq. And we have heard that in 1988 the UNSCOM inspectors were removed from Iraq.

KELLY: That is right.

DINGEMANS: And what was his view on that?

KELLY: Yes, he felt that his job there was not finished, that Iraq did indeed have plenty of weapons to discuss and to reveal. It was quite a frustrating time I think when they were effectively thrown out of Iraq.

DINGEMANS: And it seems at about that time that he had started working more directly for the Ministry of Defence. Were you aware of that?

KELLY: It was always a bit unclear as to who he was working for. Sometimes he would be paid for some things by the Foreign and Commonwealth Office and sometimes by the United Nations.

DINGEMANS: We have heard at some time Dr Kelly became a member of the Baha'i faith. Do you know anything about that?

KELLY: Only a little. He kept it very privately to himself. It was a few years ago, perhaps five or six years ago, when I realised he was reading the Koran and he was becoming perhaps gentler in his ways, in some ways. It really was a spiritual revelation for him.

DINGEMANS: How was his mood in January time?

KELLY: In January time he was a little more tired than he had been. It was fine. He had some trepidation though about the war coming up. He believed in it but was obviously sad that we seemed to be moving towards that position.

DINGEMANS: And had he talked about his retirement, at that stage?

KELLY: Yes, but only in general terms. He was a little bit worried about his pension requirements there and we still had a mortgage to pay on the house, so he was going to leave it as late as he could.

DINGEMANS: And do you know what he was doing work-wise then?

KELLY: He was working at the United Nations.

DINGEMANS: And did he take any other holiday time, so far as you are aware?

KELLY: No, he was not good at holidays. He was always on call. He always had his mobile phone on and he took a minimum amount of time. He would try to slot in his gardening duties, mowing the lawns and so on between work, either in the evening or very occasionally he would take a day in lieu.

DINGEMANS: Did he have a weekend earlier on this year?

KELLY: Yes, he did. Our field and the lawns had got very, very long and he seemed to be driven. He really had to spend a long time doing that and he was extremely tired afterwards. We have a very old, battered ride-on mower and that was a seven hour job, and he made himself stick at it all day with just breaks for water and food. He was extremely tired. This was fitted in tightly between two visits.

DINGEMANS: In May we have heard that he met Mr Gilligan, on 22nd May. Were you aware of that meeting?

KELLY: Yes.

DINGEMANS: He did not tell you the nature of the meeting?

KELLY: No, he would never tell me the nature of his meetings.

DINGEMANS: On 30th June we know that Dr Kelly wrote a letter to his line manager. Were you aware of that at the time?

KELLY: Not at the time, no. The only thing I was aware of was that he became very much more taciturn. He became withdrawn and we as a family expressed this worry to each other, we each noticed it.

DINGEMANS: When can you date that from, if you can?

KELLY: The last week of June, I would think. We were worried about him before then. He was tired and looking his age. He seemed to have aged quite a bit.

DINGEMANS: We also know between 5th and 11th June he went out to Baghdad.

KELLY: That is right. He was really glad to be going. He was slightly nervous of what he might find there. He knew it was an occupied country. So a little bit of trepidation.

DINGEMANS: Had he enjoyed his trip?

KELLY: Yes and no. He came back with mixed feelings. So much had changed, he was quite sad for the Iraqis.

DINGEMANS: Was there anything that you noticed at the end of June, any long walks or anything?

KELLY: Yes, yes. He worried me somewhat one evening, by suddenly getting up from his chair, having been quite withdrawn and worried I think. He said he was going to walk to the Hind's Head at the other end of the village and off he went, seeming very preoccupied. That again would have been just before that letter was sent. About half an hour later he came back and I said: 'You have been quick' and he replied: 'I went for a walk instead to think something through.' He said it slowly. I immediately thought perhaps he was worrying about me or something. So he said: 'No, no, it is not you, it is a professional thing' I said: 'Do you want to talk about it?' He said no.

DINGEMANS: That brings us, I think, to 4th July. We know from documents we have seen that Dr Kelly was interviewed on 4th July about the letter he had written on 30th June.

KELLY: Right.

DINGEMANS: Did you know about that at the time?

KELLY: No, I was totally unaware of anything other than the feeling that he was not enjoying his work so much, that he was more withdrawn.

DINGEMANS: He was travelling back home on the Tuesday 8th July. How did he seem then?

KELLY: Quiet. I was busy. I was busy interviewing some people for my local History Society. So I did not actually talk to him for long at that immediate point on his return. It was a little bit later we spoke.

DINGEMANS: What was said?

KELLY: Well, we had a meal. He seemed a little bit reluctant to come and watch the news. The main story was a source had identified itself. Immediately David said to me 'it's me'.

DINGEMANS: The story, we have seen a press statement that was put out by the Ministry of Defence on 8th July, was that the story that was on the television?

KELLY: That is right. My reaction was total dismay. My heart sank. I was terribly worried because the fact that he had said that to me, I knew then he was aware his name would be in the public domain quite soon.

DINGEMANS: How did he seem to you?

KELLY: Desperately unhappy about it, really really unhappy about it. Totally dismayed. He mentioned he had had a reprimand at that stage from the MoD but they had not been unsupportive, were his words. I deliberately at that point said: would it mean a pension problem, would it mean you having to leave your job? He said it could be if it got worse, yes.

DINGEMANS: And what was his reaction to the fact that he thought his name was going to become public?

KELLY: Total dismay.

HUTTON: Did he say, Mrs Kelly, why he thought his name might or would become public?

KELLY: Yes. Because the MoD had revealed that a source had made itself known, he, in his own mind, said that he knew from that point that the press would soon put two and two together.

DINGEMANS: On the 9th July, do you know where he was?

KELLY: Yes. He was supposed to be going to London so I was quite surprised when he said he was going to work in the garden all day.

DINGEMANS: Did you have any visitors that day?

KELLY: Yes, we did in the evening. It turned out to be Nick Rufford [of the *Sunday Times*]. No journalist just turned up before this, so I was extremely alarmed by this.

DINGEMANS: And did you speak with Dr Kelly after the conversation?

KELLY: Yes, I did. He came over to me and said that Nick had said that Murdoch had offered hotel accommodation for both of us away from the media spotlight in return for an article by David. He, David, was to be named that night and that the press were on their way in droves.

DINGEMANS: And did you get the impression that he was happy or unhappy that this press statement had been made?

KELLY: Well, he did not know about it until after it had happened. So he was – I think initially he had been led to believe that it would not go into the public domain. He had received assurances and that is why he was so very upset about it.

DINGEMANS: Having heard that the press were on their way in droves, what did you do?

KELLY: We hovered a bit. I said I knew a house that was available to us if we needed it in the south west of England. The phone rang and he went in to answer it, came out, and he said: I think we will be needing that house after all. The MoD press office have just rung to say we ought to leave the house and quickly so that we would not be followed by the press. We immediately went into the house and packed and within about 10 minutes we had left the house.

DINGEMANS: You set off down to Cornwall I think? Which town did you drive to?

KELLY: Weston-Super-Mare. We had a rather sleepless night but we stayed overnight there en route to Cornwall.

DINGEMANS: You were staying in a hotel?

KELLY: We were. We had asked for *The Times* to be delivered. We just read it as we finished our breakfast. We just read a couple of articles that were about David.

DINGEMANS: What were the articles about David saying?

KELLY: There was a run down of his career given I presume by an MoD source naming him as a middle-ranking official.

DINGEMANS: How did Dr Kelly seem about that?

KELLY: Well, there was several references to his lowly status. I do not know whether it was more my reaction or his but he was rather knocked back by that. I was trying to say to him how nice Cornwall was. I was trying to make conversation to relax him and try and turn this in some way into a holiday. On the Friday we decided to go to the Lost Gardens of Heligan. We spent a long morning there during which he had taken a call from several people from MoD explaining about the Foreign Affairs Committee on the Tuesday. One was from Bryan Wells. Who told him it would be televised.

DINGEMANS: How did Dr Kelly take that news?

KELLY: He was ballistic. He just did not like that idea at all. He felt it – he did not say this in so many words but he felt it would be a kind of continuation of a kind of reprimand into the public domain.

DINGEMANS: How was he after receiving this news?

KELLY: He was really upset. He did not see the gardens at all. He was in a world of his own. He was really quite stressed, very strained, and conversation was extremely difficult.

DINGEMANS: Coming on to Saturday, are you still down in Cornwall?

KELLY: We are indeed. We set off to the Eden Project. It is a huge quarry which has some biospheres in it with tropical and warm temperate plantings within.

DINGEMANS: Did he enjoy seeing it?

KELLY: No. Although it was a lovely World Heritage site, he seemed very grim, very unhappy, extremely tense, but accepting the process he was going through. It was a very grim time for both of us. I have never known him to be as unhappy as he was then.

DINGEMANS: His unhappiness you could feel?

KELLY: It was tangible. Absolutely, palpable.

DINGEMANS: Right. 13th July is a Sunday?

KELLY: That is right. I stayed in Cornwall. David wanted to set off early.

DINGEMANS: Did he go by train or by car?

KELLY: No, he drove by car. I was worried about this. I asked him to drive extremely carefully and to take his time. He was extremely tense. The MoD had offered, by now, to put him up at a hotel in Horse Guards but we all thought especially our daughter Rachel, he would be more comfortable with her. So he set off about 11.30.

DINGEMANS: Did he read anything in the papers that day?

KELLY: Yes, and it did not help. There were other comments about his junior status, about – it was just a total belittling in some ways.

DINGEMANS: What did he think of the belittling of his status as you put it?

KELLY: He was in dismay. I think it was on this day that he said that somebody had told him over the phone while we were down in Cornwall that Jack Straw, who he had supported a few weeks earlier at the Foreign Affairs Committee –

DINGEMANS: I think that was some time in September 2002.

KELLY: Jack Straw had said he was upset at the technical support at that Committee meeting, he had been accompanied by somebody so junior.

DINGEMANS: How had Dr Kelly taken that?

KELLY: He laughed. It was kind of a hysterical laugh in a way. He was deeply, deeply hurt.

DINGEMANS: 15th July we know he goes off to the Foreign Affairs Committee. Did you speak to him at all that day?

KELLY: Later on. This was our 36th wedding anniversary so I was constantly thinking of him all day. He rang that evening and said it had been a total nightmare. Certainly from the television pictures I saw later he really did look very stressed, I could see that.

DINGEMANS: And where does he spend the night on 15th July?

KELLY: At my daughter Rachel's.

DINGEMANS: 16th July we know he goes off to the [Intelligence and Security Committee]. Do you speak to him at all on that day?

KELLY: I spend the day returning from Cornwall by train. I met up with him at Rachel's house.

DINGEMANS: How was he then?

KELLY: He was able to converse a little, but it was very, very strained. He was sort of used up. We made our way home. He did not speak at all during that journey. He was very tense and very, very tired.

DINGEMANS: 17th July is a Thursday. How did he seem?

KELLY: I have no idea. He had never seemed depressed in all of this, but he was very tired and very subdued.

DINGEMANS: Did he have any work to do that day?

KELLY: He said he had a report to write for the MoD. This is the one that somebody on the Foreign Affairs Committee referred to as his 'homework' I think.

DINGEMANS: Some Parliamentary Questions that were tabled?

KELLY: That is right.

DINGEMANS: Do you know whether he made any telephone calls that day?

KELLY: Yes, he was certainly on the phone quite a bit I think. I left the house for a few minutes to meet somebody and pick up some photographs. I came back, went into his study to try and lighten the atmosphere a bit by showing him some photographs and some other data I had got for the History Society. He smiled, stood up and then said he had not quite finished. But a few minutes later he went to sit in the sitting room all by himself without saying anything, which was quite unusual for him, but he went and sat in the sitting room.

DINGEMANS: When was he sitting in the sitting room?

KELLY: From about 12.30 I would think.

DINGEMANS: Did he say anything?

KELLY: No, he just sat and he looked really very tired. By this time I had started with a huge headache and begun to feel sick. In fact I was physically sick several times at this stage because he looked so desperate.

DINGEMANS: Did he have any lunch?

KELLY: He didn't want any lunch he did have some lunch. I made some sandwiches and he had a glass of water. We sat together at the table opposite each other. I tried to make conversation. I was feeling pretty wretched, so was he. He looked distracted and dejected.

DINGEMANS: How would you describe him at this time?

KELLY: Oh, I just thought he had a broken heart. He looked as though he had shrunk, but I had no idea at that stage of what he might do later, absolutely no idea at all. He could not put two sentences together. He could not talk at all. I went to go and have a lie down after lunch, which is something I quite often did just to cope with my arthritis. I said to him, 'What are you going to do?' He said, 'I will probably go for my walk'.

DINGEMANS: What time do you think you went upstairs, so far as you can remember?

KELLY: It would be about half past 1, quarter to 2 perhaps. He went into his study. Then shortly after I had laid down he came to ask me if I was okay. I said: yes, I will be fine. And then he went to change into his jeans and put on his shoes. Then I assumed he had left the house.

DINGEMANS: And did he, in fact, go straight off for his walk?

KELLY: Well, the phone rang a little bit later on and I assumed he had left so I went downstairs to find the telephone in the dining room. By this time the ringing had stopped and I was aware of David talking quietly on a phone. I said something like: I thought you had gone out for a walk. He did not respond of course because he was talking on the phone.

DINGEMANS: Do you know what time this was?

KELLY: Not exactly, no. Getting on for 3, I would think.

DINGEMANS: Do you know who the caller was?

KELLY: I assumed it was the MoD, I am not sure.

DINGEMANS: And did Dr Kelly go out for his walk?

KELLY: He had gone by 3.20.

DINGEMANS: What time did you start to become concerned?

KELLY: Probably late afternoon. Rachel rang, my daughter rang to say: do not worry, he has probably gone out to have a good think. She made a decision to come over. She said: I will go and walk up and meet Dad. She walked up one of the normal footpaths he would have taken. She came back about half an hour or so later.

DINGEMANS: What time was this?

KELLY: This must have been about 6.30 perhaps by now. I am not sure of the times. I was in a terrible state myself by this time trying not to think awful things and trying to take each moment as it came.

DINGEMANS: What was decided to be done?

KELLY: Well, we had delayed calling the police because we thought we might make matters worse if David had returned when we started to search. I felt he was already in a difficult enough situation. So we put off calling the police until about 20 to 12 at night.

DINGEMANS: The police are called. Do they turn up?

KELLY: They turn up. And the search begins.

DINGEMANS: Did you hear any other news?

KELLY: Not initially, no. It was during the morning of the Friday, I think, the 18th by now, that the police came to inform us of David's death.

DINGEMANS: We have heard about the circumstances of Dr Kelly's death and the fact that a knife was used. Were you shown the knife at all?

KELLY: We were not shown the knife. We were shown a photocopy of I presume the knife which we recognised as a knife he had had for many years and kept in his drawer.

DINGEMANS: We have also heard that some co-proxamol was used.

KELLY: Indeed.

DINGEMANS: Do you take any medicine?

KELLY: I do. I take co-proxamol for my arthritis. I keep a small store in a kitchen drawer and the rest in my bedside table.

DINGEMANS: Finally, after Dr Kelly's death there were some reports in the press about him being a Walter Mitty character. What was your reaction to that?

KELLY: I was devastated. That was totally the opposite. He was a very modest, shy, retiring guy. He did not boast at all and he was very factual and that is what he felt his job was. That is what he tried always to be, to be factual.

DINGEMANS: Is there anything else you would like to say?

KELLY: Yes. Lord Hutton, on behalf of my family I would like to thank you and your counsel for the dignified way in which you are carrying out this Inquiry into my husband's death. We would also like to acknowledge the support our family have received from so many people all over the country and elsewhere and, finally, may I take this opportunity to ask the media to continue to respect my family's privacy. We are a very private family. Thank you.

HUTTON: Mrs Kelly, thank you very much indeed.

KELLY: Thank you, my Lord.

HUTTON: I think this will be an appropriate time to adjourn.

USHER: All rise.

For Further Reading

The transcripts of the evidence to the Hutton inquiry and the documents provided to it by Government departments are on the inquiry website:
www.the-hutton-inquiry.org.uk

The Commons Foreign Affairs Committee report on the Decision to go to War in Iraq was published in July 2003, reference number HC 813-1, ISBN 0 21501162 7 available from TSO, The Stationery Office email:
book.orders@tso.co.uk

The Parliamentary Intelligence and Security Committee report on Iraqi Weapons of Mass Destruction – Intelligence and Assessments, was published in September 2003. Reference number: Cm 5972, ISBN 0 10 159722 3 available from TSO (as above).

GUANTANAMO

'HONOR BOUND TO DEFEND FREEDOM'
TAKEN FROM SPOKEN EVIDENCE

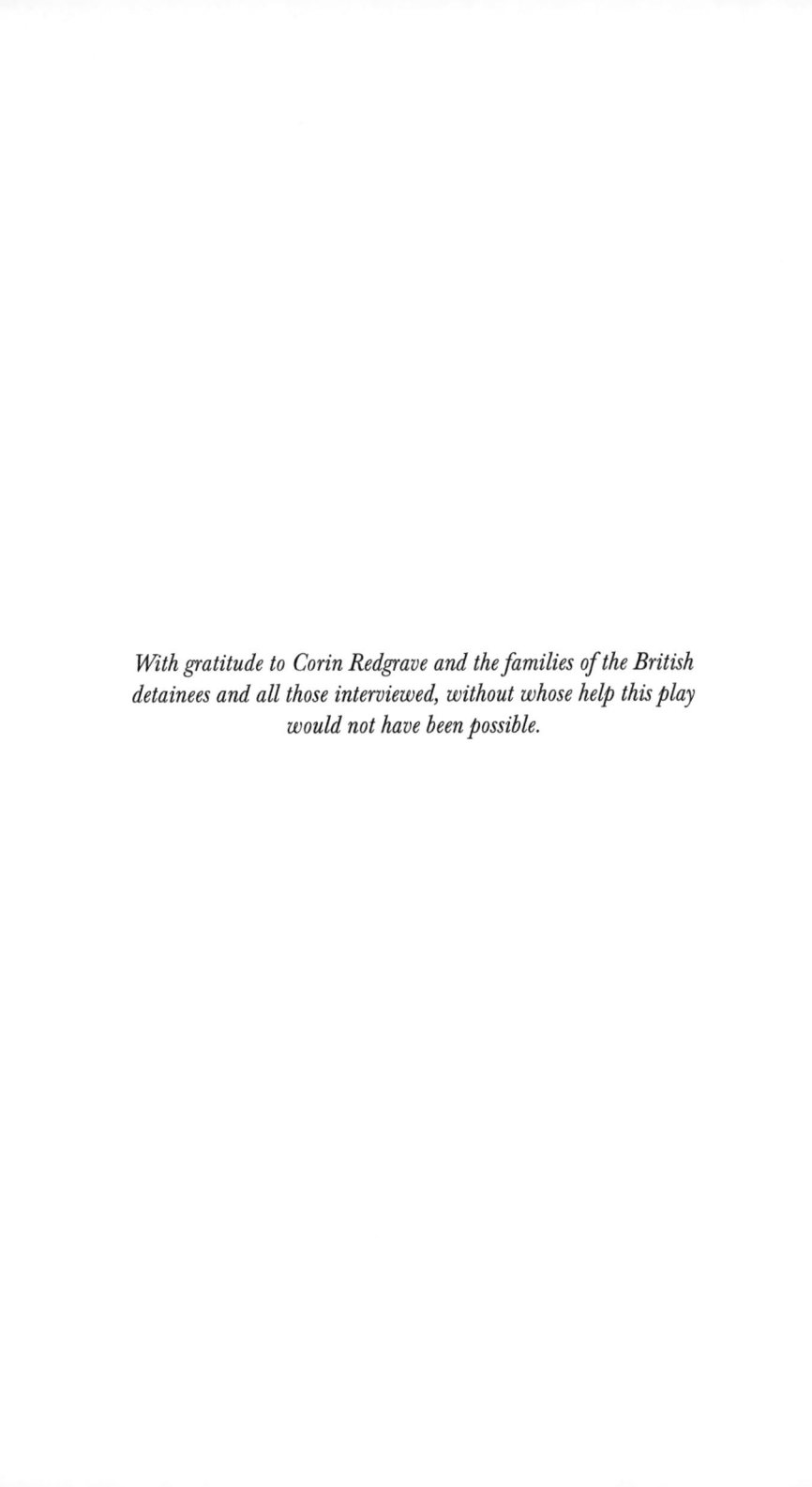

With gratitude to Corin Redgrave and the families of the British detainees and all those interviewed, without whose help this play would not have been possible.

Characters

LORD JUSTICE STEYN

MR BEGG

WAHAB AL-RAWI

JAMAL AL-HARITH

GARETH PEIRCE

MARK JENNINGS

BISHER AL-RAWI

MOAZZAM BEGG

DONALD RUMSFELD

TOM CLARK

CLIVE STAFFORD SMITH

RUHEL AHMED

JACK STRAW

GREG POWELL

MR AHMED

MAJOR DAN MORI

Guantanamo was commissioned, from an idea by Nicolas Kent, by the Tricycle Theatre in January 2004. The five British detainees were released in late February. The interviews for the play were conducted at the end of March and beginning of April 2004. Numerous attempts were made to get the viewpoint of members of the government (both in the Lords and the Commons) for this play, but no one was prepared to be interviewed.

The first performance of *Guantanamo: 'Honor Bound to Defend Freedom'* took place at the Tricycle Theatre, London, on 20 May 2004, with the following cast:

LORD JUSTICE STEYN, William Hoyland

MR BEGG, Badi Uzzaman

WAHAB AL-RAWI, Aaron Neil

JAMAL AL-HARITH, Patrick Robinson

GARETH PEIRCE, Jan Chappell

MARK JENNINGS, Alan Parnaby

BISHER AL-RAWI, Daniel Cerqueira

MOAZZAM BEGG, Paul Bhattacharjee

DONALD RUMSFELD, William Hoyland

TOM CLARK, Theo Fraser Steele

CLIVE STAFFORD SMITH, David Annen

RUHEL AHMED, Tariq Jordan

JACK STRAW, David Annen

GREG POWELL, Alan Parnaby

MR AHMED, Paul Bhattacharjee

MAJOR DAN MORI, Daniel Cerqueira

Directed by Nicolas Kent and Sacha Wares
Designed by Miriam Buether
Lighting by Johanna Town
Sound by John Leonard

Act One

House lights on. From the auditorium comes Lord Justice Johan Steyn, up on stage to a podium.

Written on the dot matrix: '27th F A Mann Lecture, given by Lord Justice Johan Steyn on 23 November 2003.'

LORD JUSTICE STEYN: The most powerful democracy is detaining hundreds of suspected foot soldiers of the Taliban in a legal black hole at the United States naval base at Guantanamo Bay, where they await trial on capital charges by military tribunals. This episode must be put in context. Democracies must defend themselves. Democracies are entitled to try officers and soldiers of enemy forces for war crimes. But it is a recurring theme in history that in times of war, armed conflict, or perceived national danger, even liberal democracies adopt measures infringing human rights in ways that are wholly disproportionate to the crisis. Ill-conceived, rushed legislation is passed granting excessive powers to executive governments which compromise the rights and liberties of individuals beyond the exigencies of the situation. Often the loss of liberty is permanent...

The purpose of holding the prisoners at Guantanamo Bay was and is to put them beyond the rule of law, beyond the protection of any courts, and at the mercy of the victors... At present we are not meant to know what is happening [there][1]. But history will not be neutered. What takes place today in the name of the United States will assuredly, in due course, be judged at the bar of informed international opinion.

The regime applicable at Guantanamo Bay was created by a succession of presidential orders. It can be summarised quite briefly. The prisoners at Guantanamo Bay, as matters

---
[1] [ ] are used throughout to indicate words added to the transcripts for clarification, or to signify a cut.

stand at present, will be tried by military tribunals. The prisoners have no access to the writ of habeas corpus to determine whether their detention is even arguably justified. The military will act as interrogators, prosecutors, defence counsel, judges, and when death sentences are imposed, as executioners. It is, however, in all respects subject to decisions of the President as Commander-in-Chief even in respect of guilt and innocence in individual cases as well as appropriate sentences. It is an awesome responsibility. The President has made public in advance his personal view of the prisoners as a group: he has described them all as 'killers…'

As STEYN leaves house light dim.

The pre-dawn call to prayer: sung from the stage.

VOICES: Alaahu Akbar
Bishmillaahi-r-Rahmaani-r-Raheem
Al-hamdu Lillaahi Rabbi-i-aalameen (*Etc.*)

MR BEGG: I will start with his childhood so you have the full picture of [Moazzam].

He was born in

MR BEGG hesitates for a fraction of a second.

… '67 on 5th June and he was very well looked after by his mother and by me. When he was a little bit grown up he went to a Jewish junior school. His reports were quite good. His teachers, especially the Headmaster Mr Levy, I don't know whether he's alive or not but he was very, very good. He saw that there is good potential in my sons, so he took them after certain questions and examination. He was quite happy with Moazzam.

WAHAB AL-RAWI: (*He is smoking.*) I came into the UK in '83. [My brother Bisher], came one year later.

In the early 80's, my father was arrested – the Iraq secret service went to his office and arrested him and they took him and he disappeared for eight months. And when we found out where he was, then he was moved from one secret service to another, and he disappeared again. Eventually we found him and we used some influence at that time to just get him to go to trial. Of course he was tortured and he was abused. A year and a half he spent with the Iraqi secret service which is one of the worst in the world. Finally he went to trial. The judge found him innocent and he was released, but by then the Government has confiscated a lot of his properties and so we decided to leave Iraq for the UK.

None of us ever asked for asylum. We were very well off at the time.

MR BEGG: Moazzam did his initial schooling there and one day he said: 'Dad I want to make a society' and I smiled [because he was too young to talk about society] and said: 'what kind of society are you going to make son?' He said: 'A society to help older people, feeble people, and people with disabilities and all that.' So, I said: 'This is a very good thing, it's a noble thing. I'll not stop you doing that.' I don't know how far he went...

WAHAB AL-RAWI: I was studying GCSEs at a school in Cambridge and [Bisher] came to do the same thing. We were teenagers living on our own in one house. It's the first time we've ever gone anywhere, so it was a mess. Every day there was a fight. We'd make peace and then we'd go back and break the peace. So the next year, my mother split us apart. I went to study my A-levels in Shrewsbury and he went to Millfield College to finish his GCSEs and then do his A-levels.

[Bisher] finished A-levels, went to University. He was very physical, he was very active – this is why he loved it in Millfield – he did all the sports, wrestling, archery, climbing. Even he was a parachutist. He had 63 jumps. He had PPL – private pilot's licence. He studied on helicopters as well. Deep sea diving – he's got all the equipment for deep sea diving. He was a biker. Every sport you can imagine. If he's interested in something, then he takes it on completely. He absorbs it in his blood and veins. It's a profession. Then he leaves it and goes on to another thing.

WAITER: There's no smoking in this area.

WAHAB AL-RAWI: Oh. Okay. No problem. I'll put it out. (*Putting out his cigarette.*) I don't like to break the law.

MR BEGG: [Moazzam] was about seven [then]. Seven I think, yes he was, because it was one year before his mother died. So, he was doing this sort of thing and after one year I married again. Moazzam [was my] second born. First born had a bit of a tussle with my [new] wife (*Laughter.*) but Moazzam never had that. He was quite alright with her and he in fact supported me that we had to have somebody in the house. So, Moazzam was very co-operative. He was very, very polite, very nice, very intelligent because any question I asked he replied with proper intelligence at the age and I was surprised sometimes that he had that sort of intelligence.

After finishing the school [he] went for Law.

WAHAB AL-RAWI: [Gambia] was my idea. My idea was I build a mobile oil processing plant and because of…obviously because of the title…because you're mobile you need to go to where the peanuts are.

MR BEGG: I'm a banker by profession [but] I opened another business [an Estate Agent] and [with] Moazzam ran [it] four or five years. Without [Moazzam] I would have not done [it]. [He] was attending the College as well at that time – going to the University part time. Then, when I finished from that business and everything he said: 'Dad, I want to get settled now. I want to get married.' I said: 'Son, I wanted you to finish these studies', as every father would think, 'and after that, you may do whatever you feel like.' He said: 'No it's all too tiring now, I can't do any more.' I said: 'Alright, take a break and next year you do what you will want to do' and he said: 'Yes, I'll do it later on.' But… er…he got married and settled down and he opened a shop, an Islamic bookshop and an Islamic clothing shop. So, that was unusual and he was running it very nicely, I think he was making a reasonable profit.

WAHAB AL-RAWI: And we decided for the experimental stages to go to a small country like Gambia and then there would be a stage two. We decided to go to Gambia because we knew somebody there. I met the first secretary for the Ministry of Agriculture and he encouraged me – I met a lot of people who encouraged me in the UK as well. I met the Gambian High Commissioner. He encouraged me – everybody encouraged me. And I thought what better to do? You go to Africa where there's poverty, you produce labour, you give these people wealth and at the same time you help yourself.

MR BEGG: [Moazzam] always used to pray in the midday because we pray, well, when I say we pray – practising Muslims I should say – pray five times a day. One early in the morning before the rise of sun, and then midday, and then we pray in the afternoon at about four or five o'clock. After that, at the time of sunset and then before going to bed. So, this five times prayer is supposed to be done by practising Muslims. I never did it (*laughter*) unfortunately. Apart from that we have got to keep fast – one month fast. So this is all good things. I don't have any objection to it, leaving that fundamentalism aside. It is not only the prayer, it is the physical exercise you do, mental exercise you do, concentration you [get].

WAHAB AL-RAWI: [My idea was] we buy the peanuts from the farmers. We process it. We produce cooking oil, which we sell back to the farmer and the by-product is animal feed which you can use to raise chicken or beef or whatever. So, everything is produced on the ground and everything is sold on the ground. And it is very, very profitable.

And my brother's position was that he was going to come over with us for a couple of weeks to help us just set the factory, build the factory – and then he'd come back. His ticket was for one month. When I asked him what he was going to do with the extra two weeks, he said, well, I'm going to go for a walkabout, see Africa.

MR BEGG: [Moazzam prayed] at least three or four times a day [and] in midday he used to put the shutter down of the shop. Not just him, there were two or three persons more used to come to the prayers. So, Moazzam prays here, in this house; in his house; in his shop; whenever he had time for prayers.

He used to call me: 'Come on down dad, this is the time of our prayer'. I'd say: 'I'm coming in a minute, I want to take a shower' (*laughter*) because you can't pray until you are absolutely clean – top to bottom and you wash your hands, you wash your mouth, you wash your face and then you wash your feet – each time – and then it's time for prayers. So, Moazzam was used to remaining very clean all the time otherwise he can't do the prayers.

[But] when he was putting the shutter down and putting the light little, people got suspicious. What this man is doing? Why the half shutter and so forth – what is he doing? So, somebody, possibly of different faith took it that something funny was going on, and informed and the shop was raided.

WAHAB AL-RAWI: I went in advance of the party to reconnaissance, to set up the company, to lease the warehouse, to lease the house for us to stay in the city, to do the banking, to get the equipment out of the port.

When I left London at the airport I was called into a room with two British officers and they interrogated me for about twenty-five minutes. They asked me: why was I going to Gambia? What did I have business in Gambia? Did I know these people – they named a few people –Abu Qatada. Did I know any Algerians? Which mosque did I frequent? All of these questions and then they were satisfied and they let me go.

MR BEGG: [The police] said that [Moazzam] must be having some connections with Taliban or somebody. He said: 'I don't, I don't know what you are talking about'. They raided his house. They couldn't get anything, nothing at all, but they were after his computer. They said there must be something in the computer, a code in computer and you have got to tell the code. [Moazzam] said: 'There is no code in computer – whatever is there is there and you can check it. You are [the] experts have it checked.' He was very unhappy. He said: ' What for are they accusing me? I know what the law is, I work according to the law, I haven't done anything wrong at all.'

[So] they took him to the court, I mean to the police station, questioned him and immediately released, and afterwards they apologised. They said we are sorry that we bothered you but we were informed or misinformed or whatever. I don't know what reason was that, but he came out very clear and there was nothing wrong and he was running his business as usual.

JAMAL AL-HARITH: I went to Pakistan on tableeg. That's sort of like when you want to find out about the religion like but you also visit villages and all that. But I didn't actually get there. It was October 2001 and I was told by the money changers, they said obviously that Americans and British wouldn't be welcome there because they were the ones who were going to be attacking, they said. Like it's 60% Pashtoun in Pakistan so they are like the people of Afghanistan. This is what I was told.

MR BEGG: I told you in the beginning [Moazzam] was very much interested to help people all the time. He somehow, had it in his mind that the Afghan people are the people in the world who are most deprived. He talked to me about it. He said: 'I want to go and start some educational institutions there'. I said: 'Who's going to back you? Do you know how the money is going to come? Is it a big project?' He said: 'No, I'll work with a small project. My wife, because they don't like mixing of woman with man or girls mixing with boys, so I'll take my wife and my wife will be teaching the girls' side of the school and I'll be teaching the boys' side.' I said: 'Well, it's a good idea if you can do that.' Then suddenly I received a letter – I was suffering from angina – I received a letter from the hospital that we have made arrangements for you to go to hospital.

JAMAL AL-HARITH: I decided to [travel] to Turkey, through Iran to Turkey. [A guy got a truck full of people] and the truck went off and then in the journey it was stopped. I was in Pakistan and then they stole the truck and I was just handed over. Gun-toting Afghanis. They didn't steal the truck to get me, they stole the truck because they wanted the truck themselves.

When the truck was being pulled over, you don't really think anything. You think, oh, they're just going to look in the truck or it's some road toll you know. That was what was crossing my mind, they were just going to check the truck or whatever. But then they just ordered everyone out, and then you know me and the driver's mate were put in their jeep or whatever to take away. Then I start to think, oh well, things aren't, you know, going as I planned – there's something wrong here, something's wrong. And obviously you're scared, your stomach's turning over and you just…

MR BEGG: Moazzam he was preparing himself to go to Afghanistan [but when] he heard that his father was going to have an operation, he came to me and he said: 'I'll drop the idea of going to Afghanistan until you are well'. I say 'No, you go. I'm in safe hands and you cannot do much here so you'd better go. I'll be alright, don't worry.' But he said 'No, this is a bad time, I need to be with you, I'll not go.'

He is a good son. He is the best son of mine. I told him 'You are wasting your time here, you are wasting your money here. They are not going to wait for you, you had better go and start the job and you can come later on, come and see me.' After about a week of intensive conversations, he somehow agreed. But he had small children. I said 'I don't particularly like that area because Afghan people are very different people as compared to us or to English people. We are more like English person: how can you live with Afghans?' He said, 'No I won't live with them, I'm teaching them but as far as living is concerned I'll be confined to my wife and children and that's it.'

He was very upset when he was going and his wife was upset too and she was crying badly that she is going. I said 'Why are you crying, what you are worried about, I'm not going to die, don't worry, I'll be alright.'

JAMAL AL-HARITH: [I was handed over to the Taliban.]

WAHAB AL-RAWI: My brother, [and my partners tried to join me in Gambia but] at Gatwick they were taken. They were held for, I think four days altogether. Our homes were searched and the whole case went in front of a judge and the judge found there was absolutely nothing, I mean he asked the secret service why did you arrest these guys and they showed him a piece of equipment, electrical equipment and our solicitor, Gareth Peirce, she said…

GARETH PEIRCE: [One of Mr Al-Rawhi's partners Mr Al Banna had] a visit from special branch two days before he was leaving saying we know you are going. And he said do you have a problem with that? And they said no. Two days later they get to Gatwick and they're all taken off, away from embarking on the plane, their luggage searched, held on a completely false pretext for two or three days, said that there was a suspect item in the their luggage, which turned out to be a battery charger. So that we were able to go down the road from Paddington Green Police Station to Argos and get a catalogue saying here's the battery charger, while they were busy saying they were flying a forensic expert from Bali to inspect this thing.

WAHAB AL-RAWI: The judge dismissed the case.

GARETH PEIRCE: However, they then go to Gambia and are immediately arrested.

WAHAB AL-RAWI: ...all of us, my brother, my two partners, myself, my driver, my contact in Gambia, we were all arrested by the Gambian secret service.

MR BEGG: [After Moazzam] went [to Afghanistan] he was ringing me up all the time from there, telling me: 'I have submitted the application to Taliban government. I'm in everything and I'm going and coming every day and there is little movement.' He felt that they are not very keen to have English or Maths or education in the country and he started getting a bit disappointed.

JAMAL AL-HARITH: [They took me to Afghanistan and] I was put in some building for three days and questioned, well not really questioned really – the main questioning was in another place. And then that's when I, you know, the kicking and all that. And then they took me out to the main prison, a political prison that they have. And then I was in isolation for two weeks but in that two weeks was when I was questioned. They asked me...where do I study, surprisingly, and all this stuff. What education have I got. Then they said I'm part of some unique special forces from England obviously, some British special forces military group that was trying to enter Afghanistan and that, er, where are the rest of the other guys, you know? And what rank do I hold in the British army? Oh and, what mosque did I go back home? Would you believe it, what mosque do I pray at back home? (*laughs*) Even the Americans asked me that.

WAHAB AL-RAWI: They took us to the secret service HQ in Banjul and they started interrogating us, it's a routine investigation. They asked us about the business. What we were coming to Gambia to do, who did we know in the Gambia? All of the stuff that were routine to the Gambians. At the end of all this two Americans came in. [They] introduced themselves as Mr Lee, and the other guy I can't remember what. Mr Lee said, I'm with the American Embassy, we're here working with the Gambians, can I ask a few questions? I said, you can't ask me anything, you have no authority over me. I want to see a solicitor. I want to see my High Commissioner. [Mr Lee] turned to the other guy and said, this guy's going to be trouble and he left the room.

JAMAL AL-HARITH: The Americans had started bombing while I was in there, and after two or three weeks I'm not sure, they released me out into the normal population, the prison population that is.

WAHAB AL-RAWI: We were separated and put in different rooms in the Gambian HQ. I was in the conference room with a mat on the floor. They told me to relax and take it easy. I was very very upset. I was shouting and screaming and being abusive. I knew that I hadn't done anything and I didn't know who had, I mean I suspected that the British authorities had ordered the arrest, but I didn't know why.

MR BEGG: One day Moazzam, he said that I have got another idea in my mind, to put in hand pumps for people living far, far away from the water source. I think that in a week's time the water was there. He called me and said 'People are very, very happy – they are dancing, they're kissing my hands, and I'm very happy'. I said 'Son, I'm happy too, that you have done that very gentle work, very high class work [but] what happened to your applications?" He said 'Well, it hasn't... I haven't got any answer to it but I'll keep on going until I haven't got funds – would you like to join me?' I said, 'When I'm well I'll come.'

WAHAB AL-RAWI: We were all moved into a house in the suburbs of Banjul. There were three or four Gambians, but I wouldn't say guarding. Don't forget this was Ramadan in Africa, so it was hot and people were fasting. It was low security. I was preparing breakfast on most occasions because the food they were bringing wasn't so tempting, so actually once I went out of the house and did some shopping on my own. Well, the guy was with me, supposedly.

[After two days] we were taken back to the Gambian secret service headquarters. [In the interrogation room] was the two Americans in front of me, and the two Gambians beside me. They went over the whole thing again and again. About the business; about who I knew. And then after they had finished about the business, they go onto fanatical questions.

About what did I think of Mr, what is his name, not the Taliban, the Qaeda guy, what's his name…em… – Bin Laden. I said, I don't know Mr Bin Laden, you probably know him more than I do, you trained him. They said, do you know any terrorists? I said, of course I don't know any terrorists. They say that we think you have come here to do so, so and so. And I say, well this is stupid because there is no basis for that.

One idea was that [we] were in the Gambia to build a training camp. The division of labour as follows: I was the cover, going to run the business. [One of my partners] was to keep an eye on me just in case I did something wrong, so he was to be my policeman, and my brother, because of his skills, is supposed to be the trainer of the camp.

I said have you found any training equipment or military stuff? They said no. I said: my brother is supposed to be training these people but he only has a visa for one month. How can he set up a camp and train people in one month?

At the next meeting they brought another theory. We were supposed to come to the Gambia to blow up something. So I told him OK, name two targets in the Gambia that are worth blowing up and he could only name one –

the American Embassy. There aren't any targets in the Gambia. Point one. Point two is: if I was coming over to blow up something, why would I come through the airport, you have two hundred miles of porous borders – no police, no nothing – I could have easily slipped through these borders. Third, where is the equipment that I was supposed to use to blow up anything? Have you found a bullet or a gun or explosives? No.

MR BEGG: Moazzam did about four water pumps in different villages, in a province called Herad. He was [putting in] the fifth one [when] the [American] bombardment started. He rushed to his house in Kabul, took his wife and children, crossed the border and came to Pakistan and during that time as there was no telephone call from him so I was very much worried – what is happening? – but he reached there and he telephoned me that we are all safe, children are all safe.

JAMAL AL-HARITH: When the Taliban, the government, fell and the new Afghan government came in to power, we were told we could leave and they were offering us money to travel to Pakistan with some guards…and I said, well, it's quicker for me to go to Kabul, thinking it would be quicker to go to Kabul because I heard the British had an embassy there. So they got hold of the Red Cross [and the Red Cross] said, okay then you stay here and we'll be in touch with the British in Kabul and then you can, you know, make arrangements to travel.

WAHAB AL-RAWI: They told us they were going to move us to a better place, I understood later they were actually using my tools and my equipment and my timber to build a jail. You heard they were boarding the windows and blocking the doors. The funny thing is they were using the food we had brought with us to feed us as well. We were hooded and handcuffed, and we were moved at two o'clock in the morning to this house one at a time. We didn't see each other.

At every single interview and every single occasion, whenever the subject comes along, I would ask to see the High Commissioner. Every single time they said the High Commissioner doesn't want to see you, sometimes they tell me, who do you think ordered your arrest? The British already knew you were in this situation.

MARK JENNINGS: I was working three days a week doing case work for Ed Davey, the local MP, and Ed happened to say to me [he had a case that] turned up to one of [his] surgeries: an Iraqi guy nabbed in the Gambia. I met the family and I got to know them as friends and it struck me that no way are they fanatical about anything. [What I learned about] Bisher was that, yes, he was reasonably devout but he's the sort of guy that can sleep for England – he used to sleep through morning prayers.

WAHAB AL-RAWI: [The Americans] had files on us. They were asking me about Abu Qatada and what Abu Qatada said about us.

MARK JENNINGS: [The connection to Bisher] is suspicious immediately because first of all, yes he's a Muslim, [and] there's Abu Qatada; also in 1998 he did a pilot's licence to fly small light helicopters, little two / four seater things, it's hardly 737s if you want to get into that, and he's a bit of a speed freak, he's got a collection of seven motorbikes, well we think there's seven – they're all in different stages of disassembly in the garage and in various places and he likes parachute jumping, he likes the adrenaline thrill. But then on the other hand he's a young man with probably slightly more money than sense so I think the only connection to any Al-Qaeda is Abu Qatada and I mean we've held Abu Qatada in Belmarsh prison for getting on for eighteen months, if not longer. We haven't been able to charge him with anything.

[With] Bisher [and Abu Qatada] certainly I think it was a friendly relationship. Bisher strikes me, from what I've heard, as being very popular with his neighbours, Muslim and non-Muslim. He's the sort of guy that's helpful. As far as I know he and Wahab, Bisher's elder brother, used to take Abu Qatada's kids swimming. I think Abu Qatada's got quite a few kids. I think the other thing they used to do was take Abu Qatada's wife to the hospital, which again is hardly the stuff of terrorism.

WAHAB AL-RAWI: One day they came into my room. Mr Lee, he came into my room and he asked me if I worked for the British secret service. I said, well I really can't answer this question, you will have to go to them and ask them politely. What kind of a question is that, I mean? So I thought about it, and I thought they must have asked him to release me.

If I tell you exactly what happened, you would never be able to come up with an answer to this problem. It's very very stupid. It's dumbfounding.

JAMAL AL-HARITH: [The Red Cross took my details] and so on, so on... Then the games began. They were in contact with the British Embassy. They said oh you know the British will be sorting something out for you. I was using the journalists' phones, they had satellite phones, so I was phoning the British Embassy all the time to speak to the guy, said yeah, yeah, we're sorting it out, you know, we're going to get either someone down, or we are going to fly you up.

[We were] constantly in touch for about over a month [then] the Special Forces came – the American Special Forces – and they questioned us to give our stories and then the Red Cross came like the day after and said like 'Oh you're going back now' said 'you're going to fly out in a plane from the American base to Kabul' and the British obviously will meet [you] there. This was arranged by them they said.

Two days before I was booked to fly out then the Americans come in and go, you know, 'You're not going anywhere. We're taking you to Kandahar' to their base.

They took me to their base obviously but put me in jail or in a concentration camp and they questioned us. Even though MI5 were there at the time in Kandahar questioning other British people that were there, they refused to see me for some reason, I have no idea what for. I spoke to some SAS guy. And then I spoke to American Intelligence – American military.

[They asked] mainly my details in England, where I lived, what jobs I had. Didn't really seem interested in anything else. Mainly just where did I work in England? At what time? My education and so on, so on. Where did I go? Where did I pray? They just seemed more interested in getting all that out than why I was here, it seemed. And the SAS guy said – he interviewed me about twice, at night, cold – he said 'I can't release you'. He didn't actually say 'You are going to be sent to Cuba', but, 'the decision is going to be with the Americans whether you get let out or not'.

WAHAB AL-RAWI: After two weeks of interrogation and threats and all of that stuff, he comes into my room, Mr Lee that is, he says, there's your passport and your ticket, you're going home, this is not a joke, we're not playing with you, you're really going home. And then he starts to relax and starts, you know, acting normally instead of the formal way.

He told me that [he had freed my one partner the day before and now, he said,] we're getting rid of you, [so] I can concentrate more on your brother.

It doesn't make sense. I'm friends with Abu Qatada, why was I let go? The whole thing doesn't make sense. If it is because we know Abu Qatada, ok, I know Abu Qatada, why release me – do you see what I mean? – and take my brother. It doesn't make sense.

MARK JENNINGS: The only difference between [the two brothers] is that Wahab al-Rawi has British citizenship and Bisher doesn't. When [they came here from Iraq] they left behind quite a large nice house plus some other assets, and they thought, well, Bisher is the youngest member of the family, if he keeps Iraqi citizenship, if there's ever a change in the regime – and I hasten to add they were very anti the war – if there was ever a beneficial change in the regime in the future, there's no problem for him as an Iraqi citizen for him to go back and say, we want our house back, thanks very much.

WAHAB AL-RAWI: Mr Lee asked me if he could keep my Iraqi passport – I had an expired Iraqi passport – and he said he wanted to keep it as a souvenir and I said no, you can't keep it as a souvenir. He said, can we give this to the guards – we had some brake pads and some expensive equipment, he said, can we give that to the guards? And I said, no you can't give that to the guards. You can give this to the guards – and we were trying to negotiate what I can keep and what I can't. And then again I was hooded, I was taken to the airport, I was taken into a lounge on my own with the Americans. We sat down talking normally and the Gambian security guard came in at that point and asked them about my property. He denied ever knowing anything about it. He said what property? I said my factory, my lorries, my equipment, my cars, my generators. He said, no we don't know anything about it, so I understood it was all gone… Altogether about a quarter of a million dollars.

[My one partner] and myself [had been held for] 27 days.

My brother and [my other partner Mr Al Banna] have been in prison ever since.

MR BEGG: [Moazzam] [and his] three children and his wife moved to Islamabad – capital of Pakistan – and they rented a flat or a house, something like that. So, he rang me up from there. I said: 'Why don't you come back now, enough is enough.' He said 'No, I've just started and I'm quite happy with it and this thing will stop in a week's time and I will go again and do that whatever I was doing and eventually I will do the school as well', but, it never happened.

Long pause.

One night two Pakistanis…two American soldiers, assisted by two Pakistani officers, burst into his house, took him as prisoner, threw him to the floor, bundled him up and put him into the boot of their car – in front of other neighbours and the little child, who is about seven now, seven or eight now, she saw that and – they took him away. I received a telephone. It was between twelve and one at night. I received a telephone call…it was whispering…I think he had his mobile with him or what …he said – just like that

MR BEGG drops his voice and whispers.

'Dad',

Raising his voice to normal.

I said: 'Who is that?' He said:

Dropping to a whisper again.

'Moazzam'.

Normal voice.

I said: 'Why you are talking like that?' 'I have been arrested.' I said: 'By whom?' He said: 'two Pakistanis… two American soldiers and two Pakistani soldiers.'
I said: 'Where are you?' He said: 'I'm in the car and they are taking me away, I don't know where. My wife and children are in Pakistan, please take care of them and don't worry,' and then either somebody saw him talking or something.

Well, I was so shocked for ten minutes I was just looking as if something had happened to my mind – it didn't work at all. I didn't know why? How? I couldn't make out anything. I couldn't make out anything.

My wife got up as well and she said 'Well, you calm down, nothing will happen'. I said 'In that [area] people kidnap people for the sake of money and they kill them and throw their bodies and take the money and so – that area is very dangerous…'

WAHAB AL-RAWI: The law in Gambia is that you can't hold somebody for more than 40 days or something like that. So, we moved immediately to get the solicitors to work on his behalf, but just before the expiry of that deadline, [Bisher] was moved with [my other partner Mr Al Banna] to Bagram airbase [Afghanistan].

MR BEGG: Moazzam said that two Americans assisted by two Pakistanis [had taken him], but who knows whether they were Americans or Pakistanis but it comes to my mind that they could be Afghans, dressed up as Americans or something. How could I think that? – that Americans will catch my son, he's from England. I couldn't think of anything like that.

WAHAB AL-RAWI: It's worse than kidnapping. It's like, if you take it from the American standpoint, we want to make sure that our people in America think that these people are terrorists. So they came not from Gambia, they came from Bagram airbase, from Afghanistan, so they must be terrorists.

We don't know exactly [how long they were held in Bagram] Because Bagram everybody knows is a no-go zone for anybody – there's no human rights, nothing.

MR BEGG: I used my resources, whatever we have in Pakistan in army – because we come from army you see. For generations we have been with British army so we do not know any civil life except recently.

Some [of my relations] are quite high ranking officers. I rang them up – I never talk to them, never took any help off anybody in my life [but] when [the Foreign Office] didn't give me any answer, proper answer, I rang up one of my cousins who is Brigadier General there. I asked his help and he straight away said: 'very sorry about it, I'll do whatever I can.' Then I rang up General Begg who was Chief of the Army Staff some time ago, and then I got in touch with several officers, the high ranking officers to search and find out if Moazzam is dead – but nobody could find that Moazzam is dead. They said that Moazzam is not here; he must be either as you say kidnapped by local Patans or [he] is with Americans.

WAHAB AL-RAWI: [We got one letter from Afghanistan.]

BISHER: Dear Mother, I'm writing this letter from the lovely mountains of Afghanistan at a US prison camp. I am very well. The conditions are excellent and everyone is very very nice. I hope that you, my brother, my sister and all the family are well. Give my salaam to everyone and I hope we meet soon. p.s. Tell

BISHER mouths a few names (to indicate censored words).

that the food is very good and I can pray as much as I want. Your loving son, Bisher.

MR BEGG: I was like a madman for one month because [Moazzam] was very precious to me. After one month I receive a telephone call from Red Cross. A gentleman called Simon rang me from a province called Kandahar. Kandahar is next to Pakistan province – and he said 'I am speaking from Red Cross. This is about your son. He is in the custody of Americans and he sends you regards' – that's all. I said: 'Tell me please more', he said: 'I'm not allowed, nor I know. I can't tell you anything more.'

On one hand I was happy that [Moazzam] was alive and on the other hand I was shocked that he was in custody and I thought that possibly he is there for a week or two and then he would be released. Now, Red Cross people, Birmingham Red Cross people came down and [they] had a letter from Moazzam. We all got very excited to read the letter.

MOAZZAM: In the Name of Allah

To dad, As Salamu alaikum

I am writing this letter after around 4 wks, I am in good health and ok. I don't know what is going to happen with me, but I believe everything will eventually be ok. Please contact my wife and ask her to go back to the UK and stay with her mother. I am sorry to put you all through this, but I didn't want any of this to happen.

MR BEGG: [The letter was] from Kandahar. We wrote a reply back and gave it to the lady so that she took it away. Later on we came to know, after about two or three weeks, that he was transferred to – from Kandahar to – there's another American base which is known as Bagram, it is near Kabul. So, he was transferred there, so we think, alright, shortly they are going to sort it out or something and in the meantime we went to the Foreign Office and they say 'Well, unfortunately we don't have any access to American military bases, they won't allow anybody, so, go to the Red Cross', and that's it.

JAMAL AL-HARITH: I actually thought I was going to be released, because they said before we left [Kandahar], they said 'you have to complete the process'. The guy he said 'the process is that you are going to be [in Cuba] for one or two months and then you'll be sent home, but anyone who comes to our prison in Kandahar [has] to go to Cuba', he said. So I said 'OK then', well I didn't say 'OK', but 'if I have to go, then I have to go' and then they sent me.

End of Act One.

Act Two

TOM CLARK: [My sister] was very independent, capable, flexible – an enormously liberal-minded person who... she was a very...you can't talk about someone's life without saying something insipid... I don't know charming, attractive, sensible, intelligent person, enjoying her life in New York. We live[d] together for a while, for a couple of years, in New York actually, because I was studying there and my sister had a successful job and she offered to support me in my time of need. So I lived with her...first it was a kind of convenience thing and we hadn't really spent any time together since we were kids, but it worked out really really well. It was interesting, we never used to fight or argue, until we got home of course, you know what siblings are like when you put them in a domestic environment, things just go tits up. But you know it was wonderful. It was the happiest couple of years of my life, and in a way, you know I look back and know that I was very lucky to have had that – it would have been a much greater shame if I hadn't had the chance to spend so much time with her.

I don't call it 9/11, I've got an issue with that. It's not what I said before, so why should I say it now. I've always had this thing with American dates.

She's someone who worked in Public Relations, I mean it wasn't anything to do with her life, she was always politically minded, she studied Politics at college and that's what she was always going to be interested in. She got into Public Relations through working for the European Commission, I think that's how she got into it. But...it was, I don't know, I remember thinking that [injustice in the Middle East] was something we spent so much time thinking about and [she] actually genuinely cared about. And that was one of the great...the things that made me the most sad. I mean obviously her loss was the most sad thing, but all of the things peripheral to it, of all the injustices and wrongs, the fact that she actually did care about the things that led some people to think that was a smart thing to do some sort of clever stunt…that really upset me.

Call to prayer – 2nd. Noon: over loudspeaker.

MOAZZAM: [Bagram airbase]
In the Name of Allah
Dear Dad, Mum, Twins and Motard,
As-Salamu alaikum
I was very happy to receive your letter today, and I hope that you are all fine and well. Thank you for staying in touch with Sally and the children. Two letters have arrived from her and they should allow me to read them today or tomorrow. I have been extremely worried about them, and don't know even if they were left with any money. Please, help them in whatever way you can and I will repay you as soon as I can. Don't let my children want for anything due to any financial problems. I am doing well here and treatment has been good. Food, water, clothes and Quran are all provided. I am now about to complete my 7th reading of the Quran, and have memorised many chapters, praise be to Allah. The days go by slowly, but my ability to speak English has been a tremendous help. I cannot tell you much about what is going to happen, but I remain patiently hopeful and pray that soon I will see you all again. This is the hardest test I have had to face in my life and I hope I have not caused you too much distress, but I will pass this test by the will of Allah and your prayers. I love and miss you all very much. I thank you for all that I never did thank you for (both you and mum).
Your loving son, Moazzam.

DONALD RUMSFELD in press conference.

NEWSPAPERMAN 1: Mr Secretary…

NEWSPAPER MAN 2: Mr Secretary…

RUMSFELD: We were able to capture and detain a large number of people who had been through training camps and had learned a whole host of skills as to how they could kill innocent people – not how they could kill other soldiers. We've got a good slug of those folks off the street where they can't kill more people.

BISHER AL-RAWI is putting on the orange boiler suit of Guantanamo marking his transition from Bagram to Guantanamo.

BISHER: Dear Mother,

I'm writing to you from the seaside resort of Guantanamo Bay in Cuba. After winning first prize in the competition, I was whisked to this nice resort with all expenses paid. I did not have to spend a penny. I and Jamil [Al Banna] are in very good health. Everybody is very nice. The neighbours are very well behaved. The food is first class, plenty of sun and pebbles, no sand I'm afraid. Give my salaam to everybody and my special salaam to Wahab. I wish him the very best with his life, religion and business. I hope to see you soon if you want. Your son, Bisher.

p.s. Please renew my motorbike insurance policy.

RUHEL AHMED is wearing the boiler suit.

RUHEL: Assalamwa-alakum

Hi, how are you all. I'm fine and well. I recieve your letters and photos. Well about my eyes u can send me contact lenses. Get them from Sandwell hospital [Eye Clinic] and solution for Boots. Its call [Boston advance care]...and I need protein tablets to clean them... [Total Care tablets for hard contact lenses]. Both solution and tablets for hard contact lenses. Its going to cost total of £30.00. I need 2 packets of tablets and 1 packet of solution. You don't need to worrie about me. They army cool with me and everyone. Well what can I say to u all. The solders call me by the name of Tiger and Slimshady for some reason. Im know very well. All the army know me as U know everyone me back home as I used to be centre attration where ever I went. ...Hope to see you very soon inshallah, assalemalaykum, love Ruhel Ahmed.

RUMSFELD points at one of the newspaper men.

NEWSPAPERMAN 1: But have you determined [the detainees'] status individually, on an individual?

RUMSFELD: Yes, indeed, individually.

NEWSPAPERMAN 1: So you know which are al Qaeda and which are Taliban?

RUMSFELD: 'Determined' is a tough word. We have determined as much as one can determine when you're dealing with people who may or may not tell the truth.

NEWSPAPERMAN 1: Right.

RUMSFELD: So yes, we've done the best we can. They are not POWs, they will not be determined to be POWs. Don't forget we're treating these people as if the Geneva Convention applied.

GARETH PEIRCE: There are a number of concepts which are deliberately confused by the American administration. It seized people for purposes that are clearly the obtaining of information and having seized those people, it transferred them to a place which it believed would be beyond the reach of courts in America. It claimed that it had seized people on the battlefield, there were frequent references to capture on the battlefield, and then, having presented it to the world in this way, found itself stuck with the immediate response, well if these are prisoners of war, they are entitled to give name, rank and number and no more, and they deserve to be treated as the Geneva Convention dictates and not to be made the subject of interrogation. So having at first flush grabbed the nearest label, finding that it meant that there were international treaty obligations to provide prisoners of war with rights, the regime very quickly had to redefine what it had, and therefore it said these were unlawful combatants who were not wearing uniform and were not conforming to the norms of warfare.

RUMSFELD: We said from the beginning that these are unlawful combatants, and we're detaining them. We call them detainees, not prisoners of war. We call them detainees. We have said that, you know, being the kind of a country we are, it's our intention to recognise that there are certain standards that are generally appropriate for treating people who were – are prisoners of war, which these people are not, and – in our view – but there – and you know to the extent that it's reasonable, we will end up using roughly that standard. And that that's what we're doing. I don't – I wouldn't want to say that I know in any instance where we would deviate from that or where we might exceed it.

MOAZZAM: [Bagram airbase] [To Sally Begg]

In the Name of Allah, Most Compassionate Most Merciful
Dearest Zaynab, As-Salamu alaikum

I am writing this message late at night, which is usually when I cannot sleep, because of thinking and worrying all the time, the heat and bright lights. I have written several messages to you and it appears that you have not received any except the first one! Please let me know exactly what messages you got (the date I wrote on the message) and I will see what has happened. These past few weeks have been more depressing than usual especially since the birth of our son, May Allah bless and protect him and all my family. Time is dragging on so slowly and things don't change here at all, if they do it is very slowly. I still don't know what will happen with me, where I will go and when, even after all this time! There is nothing here to do to occupy time, except read the Quran which I have finished so many times. There are many rules here which does not make this wait any easier. The food has been the same for 5 ½ months, 3 times a day, first meal in the morning and last in the late afternoon, and most of the time I am hungry. I miss your cooking so much.

MOAZZAM mouths words (censored words).

The most difficult thing is my wife being away from you and the kids, and being patient.

MOAZZAM mouths words.

I miss you and love you as much. Moazzam

CLIVE STAFFORD SMITH: I run a [legal] charity called Justice in Exile in the US, which is devoted to representing the people in Guantanamo Bay. Guantanamo Bay is a massive diversion. It's got nothing to do with the real issues – none of [the people that they think are] the real bad dudes are in Guantanamo Bay, because the American Government would never put them there while there is a possibility that we'll get jurisdiction to litigate to get them out of there. So all of them are in Bagram air force base and places like that.

GARETH PEIRCE: [There are] 700 in Guantanamo, [there are] however many thousands around the world, distributed in places where Guantanamo would probably look quite humane. And there is a process of shipping people for instance to Egypt, where you know they'll be tortured. [You] torture something out of them, then get them back to Guantanamo. [It's] a grotesque international redistribution. And what are you getting out of it? Well maybe that's where the weapons of mass destruction came from. Certainly the product you'll get is bound to be complete nonsense, bound to be, once it's ricocheted off 700 people, any cocktail of invention will have happened.

RUMSFELD: Anybody who has looked at the training manuals for the al Qaeda and what those people were trained to do, and how they were trained to kill civilians – and anybody who saw what happened to the Afghani soldiers who were guarding the al Qaeda in Pakistan when a number were killed by al Qaeda using their bare hands – has to recognise that these are among the most dangerous, best trained vicious killers on the face of the earth.

NEWSPAPERMAN 3: Mr Secretary, there was a debate…

RUMSFELD: And that means that the people taking care of the detainees and managing their transfer have to be just exceedingly careful for two reasons. One, for their own protection, but also so these people don't get loose back out on the street and kill more people.

RUMSFELD points at NEWSPAPERMAN 3.

NEWSPAPERMAN 3: Mr Secretary, there was a debate yesterday in the British Parliament. I happened to notice.

RUMSFELD: Oh I read some of that. Just amazing.

NEWSPAPERMAN 3: And it – well it was interesting. And one of the comments made was that [the] handling of John Walker, a United States citizen, has been different from the handling of the others, and that this demonstrated that the United States would not treat one of its own people the way that it has treated these others. And I would ask your reaction to that?

RUMSFELD: Well, it's amazing the insight that parliamentarians can gain from 5,000 miles away. I don't notice that he was handled any differently or has been in the past or is now.

NEWSPAPERMAN 3: Well, will he be put in an eight by eight cell that has no walls but only a roof?

RUMSFELD: The…just for the sake of the listening world, Guantanamo Bay's climate is different than Afghanistan. To be in an eight-by-eight cell in beautiful sunny Guantanamo Bay, Cuba is not a – inhumane treatment. And it has a roof. They have all the things that I've described. And how each person is handled depends on where they go. And Mr Walker has been turned over to the Department of Justice. He will go where they want him. He will not go to Guantanamo Bay, Cuba.

Points to NEWSPAPERMAN 4.

NEWSPAPERMAN 4: On a related question, there are British citizens at Guantanamo Bay.

RUMSFELD: Yeah.

NEWSPAPERMAN 4: Can you clarify – did the United States tell the British government about moving these detainees from Afghanistan to Guantanamo Bay? That we were taking this step?

RUMSFELD: I don't know, my – the United Kingdom is working very closely with us. They have liaison in Tampa, Florida. They are part of the coalition. They're leading the international security assistance force. People talk at multiple levels with the UK every day of the week, every day of the – just continuously. And do I know whether someone called them up on the phone and said: Gee we're thinking of doing this, that, or the other thing? I just don't know the answer to that. You could ask them.

NEWSPAPERMAN 4: Well their claim is that they weren't told, and they seem pretty upset about it. And I'm just wondering…

RUMSFELD: 'They' – who's 'they'?

NEWSPAPERMAN 5: Several members of the British parliament are claiming that the British…

RUMSFELD: They are not the government. The 'they' is the UK government, and if I'm not mistaken, I read that Prime Minister Blair and the other representatives of the government said things quite the contrary to what you're saying.

RUMSFELD points at Newspaperman.

Yes.

NEWSPAPERMAN 5: Mr Secretary, you've said that you reserve the right to hold the detainees until the end of the war. You've also said that there won't be a signing ceremony on the Missouri in this war.

RUMSFELD: Right.

NEWSPAPERMAN 5: So when exactly is the end of the war? And are we talking about the war on terrorism or the conflict in Afghanistan?

RUMSFELD: Well, at the moment, we all know the conflict in Afghanistan is going on, so we're not past our deadline or our due date. I don't know how to describe it, and I suppose that will be something that the president would make a judgement on, as to when it was over.

MOAZZAM: [Bagram airbase]

...When I wrote about all those insects etc – that was in the Summer; now it's well into Winter. The camel spider is the only 10 legged spider in the world, and, I believe, is not an arachnid: (technically not a spider). But it grows to bigger than the human hand-size, moves like a race car and has a bite that causes flesh to decay – if untreated. In the Summer there were plenty here, running into the cells and climbing over people; one person was bitten and had to be treated. Apart from that, there is the usual melee of scorpions, beetles, mice and other creepy-crawlies. Thank God it's Winter! I have done a lot of reading in the past few months (45 books or so); just having read about the US Wars of Independence and Civil War.

MR BEGG: I received a telephone call from the Foreign Office...and the person in charge of the case she told me that [Moazzam] has been transferred to Guantanamo Bay from Bagram air base... It was a surprise yes. I was not expecting him to go there. I was expecting that he was going to be released. He's an innocent person and he didn't do anything wrong as far as we know, and so I thought that possibly he's going to be shortly released. And then I received a message that he was going to Guantanamo Bay, that he'd been transferred to Guantanamo Bay.

[Moazzam's] oldest daughter here, she understands. She understands that her father has been taken away by

Americans and they…she gets at times nightmares. She says at times, 'my father is being beaten up, his head is bleeding'.

JAMAL AL-HARITH: When I first arrived [in Cuba], they put me in a block where there was some English people there from Birmingham, the guys from Birmingham or one from London, or two from London. I was only there for an hour, because when I came in, obviously the plane journey with a mask, and everything, and goggles, I nearly fell out there unconscious from the plane. [Then they] moved me to the hospital. The guy took blood pressure and x-ray and then he just gave some tablets. Didn't say anything apart from 'How do you feel now?', I said 'OK', 'No, how do you feel?' and I said 'like my muscles are just relaxed'. He had given me a muscle relaxant. And he said 'Oh your blood pressure was one of the highest I've seen here'. But the reason why was cos the chains on my foot.

You had four or five different types of chains. It depended on how your interrogation was going to go. If they came with chains that made you sort of hunch up and have to walk like that then you knew they were going to be hard on you when you get to the interrogation. Or if the chains were where you can actually stand up, easier and walk, then they want something from you, so there're going to be nice, and they might offer you tea or something like that, or a drink of water.

The Americans would change their interrogators every three month, so you had new interrogators coming in. The British, some of the guys would come back again, but mainly you'd get someone different each time with the ambassador he would come. Round about six or seven times, I was interviewed by them. But the British, they didn't come just for us. Cos they were like given free rein in the Camp. Anyone like who had took a transit in England and spent like an hour on a plane, stopped in England for an hour, were questioned by the British.

GARETH PEIRCE: I think slowly the world has become aware that Guantanamo Bay is a convenience, it's a resource pool for American intelligence, and even more disturbingly perhaps, the intelligence services of the rest of the world, who are deemed to be allies, or even those who are perhaps not deemed to be allies. There is a huge range of nationalities captured there.

JAMAL AL-HARITH: I found a lot of the guards were stupid. Just young coming in like they were in training, and I would say to them, especially when they said 'Oh, we've put your name and your picture through like Interpol, all the Intelligence Agencies of the world or whatever, First World countries, and nothing came back on you, you haven't even got a parking ticket. I said 'That's because I haven't done anything'. And I said 'You know I'll walk out from here when I leave, free, because I haven't done anything at all, but your problem is that you've got me here and you can't release me without having something on me.'

They have these names they use. In [Delta] it was 'reservation'. 'You're going for reservation.' It means interrogation, but they didn't like to use the word 'interrogation'. 'You're not really being interrogated, we're investigators.' They use all these words. In Delta it was – no sorry in X-Ray it was 'exhibition'. 'You're going for exhibition' this meant interrogation.

They use words but there's evil behind it man. There's malice.

Pause.

I got put in isolation for [the first time], because I refused to wear my wrist band. I said 'In concentration camps they were given tattoos, and now they've given us these, it's just the same really. I said 'As a matter of principle', I'd keep saying 'As a matter of principle' – I'd keep saying it, and that would easily get me into trouble. So as a matter of principle every time they gave me a wrist band, I'd rip it off. The cages [had] little bits sticking out, I'd just put the band on it until its cut then I'd rip it off and [then] I used to throw it out. And this went on for a couple of weeks, and after a certain time they just said 'We've had enough, mate', so they put me in isolation for four days.

They took me in chains out down to isolation. There was nothing in the isolation cell except bare metal – just like a freezer blowing cold air for 24 hours, so it turns it into a freezer box, a fridge. I had to go under the metal sheet because the cold air was blowing in. I tried to go to sleep but you can't because you're just shaking too much. I said, oh I can't do this to myself. I said I can't do this.

Some people admitted to stuff in Kandahar, because of the beatings and they used electricity on some of the people there as well, but in Cuba they changed their minds, they said 'Oh no, what we said wasn't right. It isn't true'. I know some people signed papers, but I don't know what they signed. I know under pressure that people have admitted to stuff, but I said 'No way, am I doing that'. I mean without being arrogant, but internally I am mentally stronger than a lot of people.

CLIVE STAFFORD SMITH: We have learnt shocking things. For example in the first few months at Guantanamo they had 32 suicide attempts and then suddenly the suicide attempts [seemed to stop]. There was effort on behalf of the powers that be down there to act as if, ah, everyone's calmed down now, they're taking their Prozac, there's no problem. But then we discover that far from suicide efforts stopping, they'd just been re-classified by the military into Manipulative Self-Injurious Behaviour. There were more than 40 of those in a six month period, since the re-classification of suicide attempts.

MR BEGG: It's very personal but I'll tell you [this]. I talk to [my son]. Because I love him. When you are in deep love with somebody you tend to talk to him – in your dreams, in your life, when you are alone.

At times I see that he is sitting here and I'm shouting, and he puts his head down, and quietly listening to him. He's a grown up man, he's a married man, he's got children, he's a responsible person and I was shouting at him – telling him off – [and he just sits there].

WAHAB AL-RAWI: The times that are awkward are when you're on your own at night, when I don't sleep, and then you start to say what can I do, is there anything I can do, and you end up on a nightmare, and I keep getting these stupid nightmares. Just ugly ones – I'm walking in a tunnel, and I turn to my left and just near the staircase my brother is there and he's getting beaten up by four guys, and he just turns to me, and he doesn't say anything, he just turns to me and gives me this look, as if 'why aren't you doing anything about it?' and I wake up sweating and angry and I just want to punch something. You tell me what can I do about it?

JAMAL AL-HARITH: I used to sometimes think 'Gosh, I'm from Manchester, what am I doing here?' I'd look at the cage, and think 'Is Beadle going to come round or something.'

I had a dream a year in that I was going to stay there for two years. And that's one of the big things in there – dreams. People had dreams and they would tell it to everyone, and raise everyone's spirits. So dreams was a big thing, and you had interpreters of dreams as well there.

In Kandahar, I [dreamed] myself back home, watching the news, with some guys about Cuba. So I said 'That's the sign for me that I'm going back home'. And I would take it as a sign that's my personal sign to me that I'm going back home. But some people would say 'No, you can't take it, it's just a dream' and I'd say 'No, no'. You have to hang on to something, because that was my hope. I freely admit that when I did see that dream, I said to myself 'I know I'm going back home'. And I just had to keep on believing. No-one swayed me on that.

GUANTANAMO: ACT TWO

JAMAL AL-HARITH: I did more worship [in Guantanamo] because you're in that situation, you just do, you don't have a choice but to have patience, because you can't do anything. But I did do a lot more worship – at night praying and so on. I think if I didn't then I would have been mentally more affected. It was a release for me. It was something to hang on to.

Call to prayer – 3rd. 4pm: over loudspeaker.

RUHEL AHMED: ...the US army has made a new prison. We got tranfered here on 27/04/2002 and its better in some ways. We have a toilet and a bed. We hardly see the sun or moon anymore cause we are in side buildings in the old prison it used to be open air u could see different animal and stuff like that.

All of u pray all time not for me, for urselfs cause on day of judgement u all have to answer for ur own actions and deed. No one will want to know anyone on that day. Are you excesizing Shian, Junel and Juber. Keeping healthy if not start, stay in shape. Me myself excercis all day long about 4 hours a day. Got a nice pack of six pack now & looking good as always. Mom and Dad How are U. I hope u all forgive for the pain I brought too u both in these last few years. I know I haven't been a good son. Hope u can forgive me. Luv u all and miss u. inhsallah. See U soon. Assalamwaalaykum. Luv Ruhel.

CLIVE STAFFORD SMITH: [I've done death penalty work] for the last 20 years. It's all about hatred. About how you get a huge group of people to hate a small group of people and in that way you get them to quit blaming their problems on the Government. You hate black people because that avoids you blaming the Government for your own problems, and [you] hate people on death row and blame them all for the problems in the world.

[But] OK, [so] we hate people on death row. If they hate us back, it doesn't have any impact, because they have no power. Yet when we translate this onto [Guantanamo, and] the international stage, and we hate Muslims, and let's be honest that's what's going on here, despite the pathetic attempts to pretend that's not true. There are one billion Muslims around the world, and when we [hate them] we create a world which is a very very dangerous and unpleasant place. Translated onto the international scene, it's terrifying.

WAHAB AL-RAWI: I am angered by my Government and I don't see what difference is between Saddam Hussein and Bush and Blair. Saddam Hussein did exactly the same thing to my country and that is why we came there and we came here and we end up with the same misery – ten times over – because this is supposed to be a land of freedom and laws.

I even thought about putting [on] a suicide belt, but that doesn't help [Bisher]. But that doesn't help him. That doesn't help anybody.

TOM CLARK: I remember thinking more about the Guantanamo Bay thing – when you mentioned you were doing this, I sort of thought, well, what do I think, what is my attitude because it changes and it swings over time. But, you know, [my sister] would have been incensed.

…But then, she, you know, was incinerated publicly, live on television, for an hour and forty minutes…

Let's say for the sake of argument that among those detained at Guantanamo Bay are some of the people who led to her death – who murdered her essentially – that's a little difficult for me to, you know, it's difficult for me to say it was a bad thing that they were there.

Suicide bombing is a completely bizarre thing. It is…if there was such a thing as evil, I've lost the belief that there is…but if there was, that would be the most evil thing. So yeh, lock 'em up, throw away the key.

JAMAL AL-HARITH: [I stopped talking to the guards], because I couldn't justify myself laughing and joking with them, [after] they're beating upon this guy, I turned away from them. I wouldn't communicate with them. Sometimes I wouldn't even ask for salt. And the guys through the holes in the cells, used to pass me salt and so on, because they knew that I had a principle that I was not going to back down on.

[There's one detainee] an Arab. They hate him, the guards, the Americans, hate him. Because he organised. If someone was in trouble, say not giving medicine to someone, cos if you were ill they wouldn't give you medicine until you drop out or there's blood, because then it's not counted as serious. So if you're in pain, it doesn't matter, be in pain. He would, if it was in his block, say: 'Right, no-one's taking food', or: 'We're not going off to showers, no-one's going to go in interrogation', and everyone would just stand firm and say 'We're not going until this guy gets seen to by a doctor', and we had to do that quite a few times as well.

That same guy [who] organised people said like every block's got to have an Emir that people if people have a question you ask. And then if something happens everyone gets together, because only when you get together can you stay strong and sane. So they try to implement it but anyone who was elected Emir would get put in isolation. So they were trying, and then the thing is [that guy], he read the Geneva Convention in Arabic, and it said that you are allowed to do this, I think it was Red Cross someone said you are allowed a leader. But the Americans said 'There's no law here, it does not apply'. So when we tried to organise Emirs, they kept putting them [in isolation] so people were afraid to become Emir now. So [we] tried to use codes, and one of the codes was like 'Have you got a cook in your block?' Yeah, Yeah'. 'No, we haven't got a cook', 'Well you need to get one.'

RUHEL AHMED: ...It's getting hot again here as summer is around the corner. Bros getting married which I cant belive and Im stuck in Fucking Cuba mind my French couse it bad… Everytime I write a letter I can't think what to write. Suppose don't do anything here except the same thing day in day out. I myself don't know how long its going to be until come home but Inshallah soon.

TOM CLARK: [So] Part of me is like, yeh, throw away the key, let 'em rot. Who gives a shit really?

Part of me wants to say it's completely fine. [But] another part of me [wants to understand why] have they been detained for so long. I mean what the hell have they been doing up there? The American Government put a ridiculous amount of resources into this, they've got so much money to spend on the war against terror surely, they could have them processed quicker? Surely, they could figure out which ones? At least if they decided they needed detaining in some way, to do it in the eyes of, either their own people or an international court or something, at least to illustrate what they're doing to these people, why they're detaining them longer because, although their initial reaction I think I'm comfortable with, given the extremes, I can't understand why detain them for longer.

If I had to sum up, it would be: I'm furious at the length of detention of these people, furious because those who are innocent have lost three years of their life, much as I lost, as I've been living in a sort of private hell since my sister was murdered, and although at least I've been able to recover and get over it and deal with, and still sort of have my life, they've had theirs taken away. And that's …and they'll never get it back and I'd buy them a drink if I met them, you know, if in truth they had done nothing wrong, I can't imagine a worse thing for any person, they deserve all of our sympathies and all of our efforts to sort of make sure they do actually get the justice that they deserve.

End of Act Two.

Act Three

Call to prayer (sunset – the prayer itself, or first two stanzas, out loud: last one silent): over loudspeaker (or from stage).

On dot matrix: 'The Minister of State for Foreign Affairs, the Right Honourable: Jack Straw. MP. February 2004.'

JACK STRAW: Good afternoon. I am going to make a statement concerning the nine British citizens detained at Guantanamo Bay.

In July 2003, two of the British detainees were designated by the United States authorities as eligible to stand trial by the United States Military Commissions.

The British Government has made it clear that it had some concerns about the Military Commission process. Consequently, the Prime Minister asked the British Attorney-General to discuss with the United States authorities how the detainees, if prosecuted, could be assured of fair trials which met international standards. Our discussions are continuing.

In the meantime, we have agreed with the United States authorities that five of the British detainees will return to the United Kingdom They are:

Ruhel Ahmed
Tarek Dergoul
Jamal Al Harith
Asif Iqbal
Shafiq Rasul

GREG POWELL: So finally Jack Straw tells us that my client Ruhel Ahmed is going to be released, but there is no date given. So what you have is journalists ringing me up saying it's going to be whenever. Tuesday and it's going to be at Northolt Airport, and they should arrive at 8 o'clock on a plane. Well it's news to me you know, because no-one tells the lawyers. It's all been leaked out to [the] Press, who then ring the lawyers and tell you, and then you ring the family and tell them, then you ring the Liaison Police Officer and tell him and he says 'Well, I don't know about that', then he has to then ring somebody else and find out about it. At the airport the backpacker Jamal, who has been jailed by the Taliban and then handed over to the Americans, is released.

JAMAL AL-HARITH: If I am the worst of the worst, and obviously the scum of the earth, and people should fear me, of course, why then have they been released? After two years in there, I mean they still didn't give me a reason for being in there.

GREG POWELL: The other four, which include the Tipton three, are taken off to Paddington Green to be interviewed by the anti-terrorist squad. When we arrive at the freezing cold Paddington Green Police Station foyer, [there are] thousands of policemen outside, and they've got Press and they've got barriers up, and created a one-way system round the police station, high security and all that.

It was maybe half ten by the time we had finished the booking in procedure. And all the Police are going to do, they tell us, is take fingerprints and DNA and that's going to be it for the night. [But first] we have this farce over fingerprinting. We go into a little fingerprint room [with] quite a large officer, who is fat and a bit tired, and obviously hasn't taken fingerprints for a long, long time. There is no live-scan computers: they are going to do it on a Victorian ink block. So he gets out the ink block and inks it all up, but the block doesn't quite fit on the little spindle. It's not quite stable and it rocks. And he's got lots of bits of paper, and he's going to put fingerprints on them. He is putting the right hand ones on [when he sees] he's [using] the left hand piece of paper. He start(s) again with the left hand piece of paper and he [sees] that he has done the right hand.

The [trick is to] take the finger and roll it in a certain way,

GREG POWELL now using his index finger to demonstrate.

make a certain movement with it, [but] because he had not done it for a long time, he's not very good. He [can't get] clear images. So he gets another officer to help, then [one more] officer turns up to help him [with] a Finger Print Case [and a] different roller. [And all] this takes over two hours to do. The officer is getting hot, he's beginning to sweat and knowing he's having to do it again, and he feels really uncomfortable because it is all humiliation for him: there's this high-tech, top of the tree, top class, anti-terrorist squad officer taking over two hours to fingerprint somebody. Not to mention the bits of paper, you can't imagine how many bits of paper there are in this room at this point. [My client] is trying his best to help. At one point [they decide] that the thing is too low and they put it up on another piece of board, and [my client] is twisting his fingers, and doing his stuff, and the officer is getting ink on his shirt, and I say to them at one point: 'I'm sure I've seen something like this on Blue Peter'.

It was the biggest farce really, at the end of it, can you imagine, two and a half years in Guantanamo Bay, you arrive back in the country, you go to Paddington Green High Security Police Station and you end up you know at 1a.m. with this pile of fingerprint paper and this officer up to his knees in Victorian ink. The next day all four which include my client Ruhel are released, so the three boys from Tipton can finally go home.

GARETH PEIRCE: One of them, the tallest of them, has problems with his joints, real problems, because the space in which they had to exercise. And one of the young men had problems with his eyes, a particular dislocation of his eyes, which require contact lenses, they require them to stop something horrible happen[ing] to the eyes, he hasn't had them for two years. Ultimately the eye breaks if it isn't held in.

MR AHMED: [When I first go to meet my son, Ruhel after he came back from Guantanamo I thinking of him like] a small boy. [Before he went he had], no hair, no beard. Now he have very long beard up to there…

Gestures down almost to his waist.

I'd like to cry but I can't cry. I do not cry. He look like people who walk around the streets. I don't cry.

My heart filling, I see my boy like it was two years, I want to hold him, I want to cry myself, but I can't do it. [When somebody] hitting you, you can cry, somebody beating you, you cry – but without reason you can't cry, but when I see him in this condition I'm surprised…
I did. I did want to see him. But how I'm supposed to think when he look like this?

[I] want to cry but I don't know how. He said to me: now give me telephone. I say to him, I give you mobile and he [press the numbers like this].

MR AHMED holds up a make-believe mobile to show how his son held his face really close to the phone – illustrating how bad RUHEL's eyes are.

and then my cry comes out. [And] I don't want it coming out… This make me so upset because he is my son, he is a young boy and I am old man… [and] …he could not see anything. So I am crying myself. And he said don't cry, this time is gone.

MR AHMED drops his voice.

Don't cry, it will be alright.

On the next night…we go with his mother – we were crying everybody… He say, don't worry Daddy I'm OK, don't cry… He's got less feeling, less feeling than before. He always talk. He always talk.

Two nights he stay here. The whole night he walks. He walk himself…around the house…from there. To there.

Gesturing.

I left him here.

Pats the sofa.

If he's coming home, I have no room, over two years now we are all set up so I have no room for him. So I said to him, you go to my bed. I said: Me and my wife sit down here and you go of my bed. He say; 'no, mine's too [big]. I need small room. Small places, I don't sleep all night.' He say: 'I'll close my eyes and sit down, I'll be OK.' He could not sleep apparently. So, he walk round all night... I've been to bed, come back five o'clock... He walk round here.

Indicating how RUHEL walked.

Walk round here...I say: 'what you doing?'... So I said go on, go to my bed, so he go to bed. Nine o'clock he come back...

GARETH PEIRCE: The [boys] are three young British lads who are like all our children – they're people who are very familiar, very easy to feel immediately comfortable with. And yet the story they tell is one of terrible stark medieval horror. It's like going back in time to something unimaginable from beginning to end of what they say, of being bodies in a container suffocating to death, waking up to find everyone around you dead, to being tortured in a prison in Afghanistan, being interrogated with a gun to your head, being transported like animals to a country you don't know where you are, and being treated like animals from start to finish for two years.

I think perhaps we're very calloused. We read, we watch, we hear about atrocities – we know what man's inhumanity to man consists of, we know all that, but we don't sufficiently register it. We don't have the capacity to take it in and react in the way we should as human beings. But when you have [in front of you] men you're getting to know and they're talking about it, not because you're interrogating them, but it's tumbling out and they're reminding each other, they're telling things that they haven't told anyone. Maybe it's the testimony of every survivor from a concentration camp or a massacre or a… How do you tell it? How do ordinary words tell it? But yet they do, if you are realising the people who are telling it to you are the people who've survived it, and there isn't any… I'm sorry, I'm not able to convey this to you well…

It is happening to our children, in that sense, yes, it's happening to our children and, perhaps, the disguising feature of it is the absolute lack of any artifice, or pretence, or contrivance, so that the words come tumbling out [from] young men who were busy at the same time looking at their new mobile phone, and seeing…trying to work out how it works. It's a complete ordinariness of where they are now, suddenly, from something so extraordinary. It's as if they've come from another planet.

Pause.

[There's] two contradictions. [There's] Guantanamo where there is continuous interrogation for the purposes of making people talk. [And there's] the converse here under internment [in Belmarsh] where 16 foreign nationals have been certificated by the Home Secretary since December 2001 as requiring to be detained indefinitely without trial [and] none of the[se] people have been asked a single question, they're simply locked up.

CLIVE STAFFORD SMITH: Belmarsh undercuts our ability to be patronising to the Americans when we're doing the same thing. It's shocking, the [idea] that somehow because you're a foreigner you are more dangerous than a British person. Let's assume we buy into the whole process that [they have done something wrong]: then you try them for it. If they didn't, then you don't. The concept that we can just detain people is just like *Minority Report*, I mean [it's as if] we're going to predict that these people are going to be violent in the future.

GARETH PEIRCE: What Blunkett wants for everybody accused of terrorism, he wants to abolish jury trials, have judge only, half of it in secret. He's on the way, yes. I think that Guantanamo is an experiment in how you obtain information from people and it's an experiment in whether anyone is going to protest about that.

JAMAL AL-HARITH: It made me stronger. Made me stronger but it opened my eyes, sometimes I do think it's a war on Muslims, a war on Islam. That came to mind when I was over there.

MR BEGG: If my son has done anything wrong he should be brought back to this country. Let him see his wife, his children and us. Let him be normal. If he is [medically and physically] alright take him to court, and let the court decide whether he is guilty or not. If he is guilty he should be punished. If he is not guilty he shouldn't be there for a second.

GREG POWELL: [There are] many features inside the criminal justice system which allows government to exercise very powerful social control from different areas of criminal law. Take football hooligans – football hooliganism established the right to take away your passport, the right to make you report to the Police Station on certain days, and the right to ban you from travelling abroad and attending some certain social functions; Anti-Social Behaviour Orders aimed at children on estates establish a whole series of things; Anti-Social Behaviour [Orders] can be for life, it can be that you are not allowed to speak to a named list of people or associate with them, you are not allowed to meet in public with more than two or three people at a time, and you must stay out of a quarantined area, a geographical area. Releasing prisoners on licence introduces home detention curfews and tagging, so you must stay at a certain place between certain hours. And finally [there's] prisoners staying in Guantanamo Bay and Belmarsh without trial.

It does not take a genius to add these together [and] you slightly reinvent the world. It means that if you fall under suspicion, you can be subject to a special tribunal, you can be, not necessarily, incarcerated for a long period of time, but you can be made subject to special measures if you like, and you could be electronically tagged, you could be denied access to certain people, you could be put in a certain geographical area, you could be limited where you go. All those features that I just described can be made applicable to you, so effectively you have this fantastic level of social control by some individuals inside the community. And having done it to terrorists…you can just extend it to the whole population of people who upset you because they commit crimes. So you can enter a whole new era of social control.

You can't start to think like this unless something like Guantanamo exists. In a way is an experiment but it leads you on into a much more controlling social control criminal justice system.

MR BEGG: I have quite a lot of letters [from Moazzam]. A lot have been lost. In the beginning I didn't bother about them because I think well he's coming out in a month or two or three or maybe four – so I didn't keep track. But I've got ten or eleven letters.
[In his letters] he didn't mention anything about er his life there, he talked his normal. [Then] one day I wrote [to him. I wrote, my heart is better now] I am absolutely alright, I go to the park, I walk, I do so many things which I could [not] do before and…er there is nothing wrong with me.

After this we received a letter that [is always] on my mind. Because he wrote in reply to my letter, Dad I'm pleased to know that you're well…and you can do so many things, but my situation is different. I've been treated like an animal. Most of the time I'm in chains and they throw me into cells or what do you call it…

MR BEGG, choking back tears.

I'm thinking something that is cell but is not cell –[yes, not cells,] cages –

As he tries to bite back his tears the caged MOAZZAM reads this letter.

MOAZZAM: Dear Dad,

As Salaam Aleikum

I received your message and am glad to hear all is well with you and the family. It is nearing a complete year since I have been in custody and I believe…that there has been a gross violation of my human rights, particularly to that right of freedom and innocence until proven guilty. After all this time I still don't know what crime I am supposed to have committed for which not only I, but my wife and children should continually suffer for as a result. I am in a state of desperation and am beginning to lose the fight against depression and hopelessness. Whilst I do not at all complain about my personal treatments, conditions are such that I have not seen the sun, sky, moon etc for nearly a year!

MOAZZAM mouthing (censored words).

since it is the same three times a day, everyday – for all the time that I've been here! My situation here is unique in so many ways – for 'good' and 'bad' but mostly bad. I believe it is wrong for me to be kept like this and I have more than served enough time for whatever has been perceived about me, yet I still see no end in sight.

MOAZZAM mouthing (censored words)

and passed to

MOAZZAM mouthing (censored words).

I hate so much to place this burden upon you, and do as a last resort to alleviate this injustice. Please remember me in your prayers. Your son, Moazzam.

MR BEGG: (*Wiping tears away.*) [I have another letter.]

MOAZZAM: As-salaama 'alaykum.

MR BEGG: ...that means, 'Peace be upon you'.

MOAZZAM: I 'eid...wa barakaat Ramadan.

MR BEGG: ...that means congratulations for the festival... and Ramadan blessings.

MOAZZAM: Dear dad, I hope and pray all is well with you and the family. I am in receipt of your ICRC messages and I'm glad to hear that all is sound. I have written countless ICRC messages and letters by US mail to you (list of inaudible names). I expect that after this 'bombardment'...

MR BEGG: Letters he means...

MOAZZAM: Bombardment of news, I have 'inflicted' upon the authorities here, that some may found their way to you. My experience thus far however, has left me to believe that much of my mail to and from home has been deliberately constrained.

Including even, pictures of the family. I have yet to receive them father. I have not received any communication that was brought over by the visiting British delegation despite the fact that they informed me that they were hand over

MOAZZAM mouthing (censored words).

to all the family, Moazzam

please forward my greetings to T and others.

MR BEGG: This is the last letter I received.
He wrote it in 2003.
I received this one about two weeks [ago] I think.
[in March 2004]
Sometimes [the Foreign Office] tell us on telephone that [Moazzam's] alright, he sends you regards and all that but I don't know whether his hands are working, or his eyes are working or his brain is working because today I hear that they were giving injections to detainees.

[The Red Cross] say that the Censor Board is not letting us have the letters.

GARETH PEIRCE: We know that Moazzam Begg is in solitary confinement, we know he's been in solitary confinement since he was designated as an enemy combatant last summer. We have very good reason to think he's been driven into mental illness from oblique and unattributable comments that have been made to us – not by our Government, not by the American Government, but we believe that he is in a very bad way now and that's what this letter is saying. We believe he's in a very bad way.

CLIVE STAFFORD SMITH: He has confessed, apparently, Moazzam Begg, to being an Al-Qaeda agent who was going to take part in a plot to send an unmanned drone aircraft from somewhere in Suffolk to drop anthrax on the House of Commons. That's the confession right. Now what do you think? You as the jury. Do you feel that that's a credible allegation?

[I say] if you believe that, you believe in the tooth fairy… Number one, the only people who have drone aircraft in the world are the Americans, they cost $50 million each, they don't ever hit the target anyway and if you want to drop anthrax on someone, you just stick it in the damn air-conditioning system, and the whole thing is ludicrous… Now you think about what happened to the Tipton lads and you see the incredible good fortune that they had, because they confessed to being at the Al-Farouq training camp – every single person I've come across so far has confessed to being in the Al-Farouq training camp, they must have had millions of people in it at one point – and they confessed to being there in 2000. And the Americans got very excited when they confessed to that, they put them in a solitary cell and were getting all fixed to prosecute them for being vicious Al-Qaeda terrorists. Well fortunately, and purely by good fortune, MI5 checked the story for the US. [And they] proved that they really weren't in the Al-Farouq training camp, they were working in Currys in Birmingham at the time. So the reason those kids didn't get charged with that and they got let out of the whole solitary confinement, was that purely by fortune an alibi was proven.

MAJOR MORI: [I am a Defence Counsel at the Military Commissions. My client, an Australian, who will be one of the first of four cases against Guantanamo detainees for violating the law of war.] I was working as a Head Prosecutor for the Marines [when I got this job]. It was half a challenge, half just wanting to find out if it really was going to be like they were planning.

The US Court Martial system is an efficient and fair criminal justice system [that has] jurisdiction to try Law of War violations and its rules and procedures specifically gear to battlefield type cases. [But] all of a sudden you see this step back to before the Geneva Convention has come into play. [These Guantanamo military commissions are] doing away with all the safe guards and checks and balances in the justice system that are there to ensure that innocent people aren't convicted. I don't understand it. It seems very contrary to fundamental fairnesses. In my introduction to the Military, and through my legal training, these are very basic protections that are needed in the justice system. You need to have an independent judge, you need an independent review process. The system can't be controlled by people with a vested interest only in convictions.

One of my fears is that they're not going to bring someone just to testify against my client, they are going to bring some document written by some investigator of what Mr Smith told him, and they are going to use this document, and I'm never going to have the opportunity to cross [examine] Mr Smith, all the fundamental protections of a fair trial have been removed.

The problem with this system [is] it's not a justice system, it's a political system.

MR BEGG: [This] is a human rights issue. I'm not asking mercy from anybody. I am asking justice.

MAJOR MORI: I worry about [not being able to do my duty to my client properly]. There is no independent judge in this process, and our criminal justice system both in the Military and the Civilian in America has recognised that you need an independent judge to serve certain functions to ensure that there's a fair system, that both sides get an equal shot at putting on their case, and equal access to evidence, that there is an independent person not part of the prosecution to rule on motions.

MR BEGG: Justice in process. Justice. Human rights justice.

GARETH PEIRCE: I would like to be wrong, but with the people we represent [in Belmarsh] we don't want to mislead them. [They] want to know, can I win my appeal? [They] want to know, is there any point me participating in the process? They want to know, our case is going to the House of Lords, is there any hope? Will I see my wife and children again in the foreseeable future, or is this it? And one has to be truthful at the same time as wanting to give hope, it isn't right to give false hope, and it's that growing feeling, knowledge, not just feeling, knowledge that you're not meant to get out of this and that you might be there forever and the feeling that if you were not a good Muslim who found the concept of killing yourself abhorrent, that you might be going on the view that your wife and children, for instance, might be better off without you...

MAJOR MORI: When they let the [five] Britons go home, and the Foreign Secretary, Mr Straw said that the remaining four should either receive a trial under international legal standards, or should be returned home. That was a very strong stand... Well, I'm telling you I really think it's up to Britain. It's up to Britain if they're going to tolerate this sub-standard form of justice for people...

LORD JUSTICE STEYN: At Guantanamo Bay arrangements for the trials are proceeding with great efficiency. A court room with an execution chamber nearby has apparently been constructed. But the British prisoners will not be liable to be executed. The Attorney-General has negotiated a separate agreement with the Pentagon on the treatment of British prisoners. He has apparently received a promise that the British prisoners of war will not face the death penalty. This gives a new dimension to the concept of 'most favoured nation' treatment in international law. How could it be morally defensible to discriminate in this way between individual prisoners? It lifts the curtain a little on the arbitrariness of what is happening at Guantanamo Bay, and in the corridors of power on both sides of the Atlantic [...]

The question is whether the quality of justice envisaged for the prisoners at Guantanamo Bay complies with minimum international standards for the conduct of fair trials. The answer can be given quite shortly: It is a resounding No [...]

Trials of the type contemplated by the United States government would be a stain on United States justice. The only thing that could be worse is simply to leave the prisoners in their black hole indefinitely [...]

The type of justice meted out at Guantanamo Bay is likely to make martyrs of the prisoners in the moderate Muslim world with whom the West must work to ensure world peace and stability [...]

It may be appropriate to pose a question: ought our government to make plain publicly and unambiguously our condemnation of the utter lawlessness at Guantanamo Bay?

John Donne, who preached in the Chapel of Lincoln's Inn, gave the context of the question more than four centuries ago:

> 'No man is an Island, entire of it self; every man is a piece of the Continent, a part of the main;...any man's death diminishes me, because I am involved in

Mankind; And therefore never send to know for whom the bell tolls; it tolls for thee.'

Call to prayer: Isha: sung from the stage.

Text on dot matrix – or a voice-over:

VOICE: UK citizens Feroz Abassi, Moazzam Begg, Richard Belmar and Martin Mubanga, and UK residents Bisher al-Rawi and Jamil Al-Banna are among more than 650 prisoners held in Guantanamo. Most are from countries with even less power than Britain to influence events. They are being held indefinitely.

End.

BLOODY SUNDAY
SCENES FROM THE SAVILLE INQUIRY

Characters

THE RT HON LORD SAVILLE

Lawyers

CHRISTOPHER CLARKE QC,
Counsel to the Inquiry

MICHAEL MANSFIELD QC,
Representing some of the Families

EDWIN GLASGOW QC,
Representing some of the Soldiers

CATHRYN McGAHEY,
Assistant to C Clarke QC

ALAN ROXBURGH,
Assistant to C Clarke QC

PETER CLARKE,
Representing some of the Soldiers

EILIS McDERMOTT QC,
Representing some of the Families

BARRY MacDONALD,
Representing some of the Families

Witnesses

BISHOP EDWARD DALY
MICHAEL BRIDGE
BERNADETTE McALISKEY
WILLIAM PATRICK McDONAGH
ALICE DOHERTY
GERALDINE McBRIDE
GENERAL SIR ROBERT FORD
MAJOR GENERAL ANDREW MacLELLAN
COLONEL DEREK WILFORD
SOLDIER S
SOLDIER F
REG TESTER

Bloody Sunday was commissioned by the Tricycle Theatre and was first performed at the Tricycle Theatre on 7 April 2005 with the following cast:

SAVILLE, Alan Parnaby
C. CLARKE, Nick Sampson
MANSFIELD, Jeremy Clyde
GLASGOW, Thomas Wheatley
McGAHEY, Hilary Maclean
ROXBURGH, Theo Fraser Steele
P. CLARKE, William Hoyland
McDERMOTT, Rita Hamill
MacDONALD, Gerard O'Hare
DALY, Michael O'Hagan
BRIDGE, Charles Lawson
McALISKEY, Sorcha Cusack
McDONAGH, David Beames
DOHERTY, Carole Nimmons
McBRIDE, Julia Dearden
FORD, Michael Cochrane
MacLELLAN, John Castle
WILFORD, William Hoyland
SOLDIER S, David Beames
SOLDIER F, Charles Lawson
TESTER, Michael Cochrane

Director: Nicolas Kent with Charlotte Westenra
Designer: Claire Spooner
Lighting: Jon Driscoll
Sound: Michael Thacker
Production Manager: Shaz McGee
Casting: Suzanne Crowley and Gilly Poole

The Inquiry opened on 27 March 2000. The hearings were held in the Guildhall in Londonderry up until the soldiers' evidence which was heard in the Central Hall, Westminster. The Inquiry returned to Londonderry at the end of 2003 for its closing stages. The Inquiry's final hearings were in November 2004. The Inquiry's report is due to be published late in 2005 or some time in 2006. The Inquiry took 2500 witness statements and heard oral evidence from 921 witnesses.

INQUIRY INTO THE EVENTS ON 30 JANUARY 1972 WHICH LED TO LOSS OF LIFE IN CONNECTION WITH THE PROCESSION IN LONDONDERRY ON THAT DAY

SUMMARY OF LORD WIDGERY'S CONCLUSIONS
Conclusions 11 and 12

11. None of the deceased or wounded is proved to have been shot whilst handling a firearm or bomb. Some are wholly acquitted of complicity in such action; but there is a strong suspicion that some others had been firing weapons or handling bombs in the course of the afternoon and that yet others had been closely supporting them.

12. There was no general breakdown in discipline. For the most part the soldiers acted as they did because they thought their orders required it. No order and no training can ensure that a soldier will always act wisely, as well as bravely and with initiative. The individual soldier ought not to have to bear the burden of deciding whether to open fire in confusion such as prevailed on 30 January. In the conditions prevailing in Northern Ireland, however, this is often inescapable.

Widgery, 10 April 1972

27 MARCH 2000

C CLARKE: On Sunday, 30th January 1972, thirteen identified people are known to have died and a similar number to have been wounded, probably in the course of no more than thirty minutes on the streets of this city not far from where I now stand. Several of them were teenagers.

Serious, then, as were the immediate effects of the shootings, what happened on 30th January 1972 has affected the lives of many more people than those who were directly involved.

That those events should be fully understood and the facts publicly established is, therefore, not only a matter of acute, albeit private, interest to those most immediately affected, but also a subject with a wider public importance.

Whatever happened, whatever the truth of the matter, was a tragedy, the pain of which many have endured down the passage of years. The tribunal's task is to discover as far as humanly possible in the circumstances, the truth. It is the truth as people see it. Not the truth as people would like it to be, but the truth, pure and simple, painful or unacceptable to whoever that truth may be. The truth has a light of its own. Although it may be the first casualty of hostility, it has formidable powers of recovery, even after a long interval.

BISHOP EDWARD DALY
6 FEBRUARY 2001

Clapping in the gallery.

SAVILLE: Bishop Daly, if you look to your right you will see who is talking to you. I am the chairman of the Tribunal. The questions will come from counsel who are sitting in front of me. All I would ask you to do at this stage is to try and remember to keep your face fairly close to the microphone, more or less where it is now, so that everybody can hear what you have to say.

C CLARKE: Do you have with you, Bishop, your statement made to this Tribunal?

DALY: I have.

C CLARKE: You describe how you celebrated noon Mass at the cathedral and what you did between then and going down towards Rossville Street and William Street. Can you help us on this: had the church in Derry taken, as it were, any particular line about the march?

DALY: No, there was no line certainly amongst the priests in the cathedral that I was aware of, or city-wide that I was aware of.

C CLARKE: Was any announcement made about the march at the Mass?

DALY: Yes, towards the end of the Mass, the administrator in the cathedral, Father O'Neill, came to the altar and he said to me: 'There is a lot of activity going on outside. There are paratroopers there and just ask the people to be calm and to go home and to not, not to get into any confrontation with them.'

C CLARKE: If we come to paragraph 5 of your statement, you describe how you came to go towards the Rossville Street area.

DALY: Yes, I moved on down past Rossville Street and went down. I stopped in the doorway of Porter's [radio] shop and observed what was happening there. At the beginning there was shouting and cat-calling and then gradually it deteriorated into missiles being thrown and a response by the Army.

C CLARKE: You describe scenes we have seen on the television film: water cannon, CS gas and a 'moment of panic', I think you put it –

DALY: Yes, I remember – I have a clear recollection of the crowd racing to get away and another crowd rushing down to get a better view.

C CLARKE: You describe in paragraph 10 of your statement hearing two or three shots ring out which sounded much sharper and louder than the normal report of a gas grenade or a rubber bullet being fired, and them moving close to the wall at the end of Kells Walk to take cover.

Could you tell me in which direction the shots had been fired?

DALY: Well, it appeared they came from the west of William Street. The reaction of the people who were in Rossville Street was, they all looked in that direction and most people moved to take cover from gunfire coming from that direction.

C CLARKE: You describe speaking to a number of residents in Kells Walk who were concerned about the shooting, and seeing a number of stragglers at the end of the march and a number of young people still throwing stones sporadically at the Army.

DALY: Yes, I think down in William Street which would have been within my hearing. Rioting is a rather noisy business.

C CLARKE: Then you describe how your attention was drawn to the revving up of the engines of the Saracens and you saw them coming down Rossville Street followed by soldiers on foot and you, together with everybody else, ran in the opposite direction towards Free Derry Corner?

DALY: Yes, that moment, the revving up the engines is something I remember very, very clearly because it alarmed me and um, it alarmed most of the people there. They were revved up quite loud and then they started moving in our direction and –

C CLARKE: Had you – I did not want to interrupt, sorry.

DALY: They started moving in our direction and most people started just moving away slowly at first, but then they gathered speed, they came across to William Street and we expected them, I think most of the people expected them, to stop at the junction, I think, of Eden Place which would normally – there was almost a kind of choreography that everyone observed, and I think what caused the panic that day at the beginning was that the choreography was not followed and once the Saracens came past Eden Place, everyone there sensed that this was different than what had happened before. I think at that stage panic set in, people started running in all directions, including myself.

C CLARKE: You then ran with the crowd. Can you tell us where you were in the crowd, were you at the front, the middle, or the back?

DALY: I think I was towards the rear of the crowd, um people came from all directions, running and my memory is that I was towards the rear of the crowd.

C CLARKE: You describe running into the courtyard of the Rossville Street flats, looking back to see if the armoured cars and the soldiers were still coming. You describe a young boy running beside you.

DALY: I became conscious of him because he was smiling or laughing. That was the reason he caught my attention. I think it was – I have wondered since – but I think all of us were kind of excited, exhilarated, and frightened and scared, so I think the laughter is more of that than of humour.

C CLARKE: I think in your evidence to Lord Widgery you said that 'he appeared to be smiling at the sight of the priest running so fast'?

DALY: I thought that at the time, but I have thought a lot about that; this is one of the events in my life I have thought an awful lot about over the years, and I think possibly all of us were frightened and scared. I think that possibly the reason he was laughing, it was nervous laughter more than anything else. We are just speculating but I know, I am quite clear in my mind, how I noticed him was the fact that he was laughing.

C CLARKE: Did you overtake him as you ran?

DALY: He was running and I was running. I know when he was struck he was just behind me.

C CLARKE: You describe when you reached the courtyard, you heard a shot?

DALY: Yes.

C CLARKE: You looked around and the young boy fell on his face.

DALY: I was running, I was looking back to see where the soldiers were coming or where the Saracens were moving to and, um, at one point the shot rang out.

It was a very clear – over the general noise the shot was quite distinctive, quite clear. With that he gasped and he fell on his face just behind me, just a few feet from me.

C CLARKE: Were you conscious, in addition to that shot, of rubber bullets being fired anywhere at this stage?

DALY: No, I do not think so. I think there was not any reports either of rubber bullets or anything else at that particular time.

C CLARKE: Had you noticed at this stage, by which I mean up to the time when you saw Jack Duddy fall, any form of hostile action against the Army, from stone throwing to firing guns?

DALY: Not at that time. People, at that time, were interested in getting clear. Most people were just trying to get out of the way as quickly as they could.

C CLARKE: You describe a mass of panic-stricken and frightened people, a woman screaming and yells and screams of fear, is that right?

DALY: Yes. There was, there was first of all a single shot. There was a single shot. Jack Duddy fell. I moved on seeking to get out of the area, and then there was a burst of gunfire and that really caused terror and panic, and that was the time the air was filled with yells and screams of fear. I think the priority changed from getting away from it to getting cover.

C CLARKE: The burst of gunfire, where did it appear to be coming from?

DALY: It came from the area of the waste ground.

C CLARKE: In the end, you got to the low wall or close to it?

DALY: Yeah.

C CLARKE: You saw the young boy now lying on his back with his head towards you. You made your way out to him?

DALY: Yeah.

C CLARKE: And Charles Gray, the Knight of Malta, appeared at your side?

DALY: Yes.

C CLARKE: We know that, at some stage, Liam Bradley was with you by Jack Duddy's body?

DALY: Yes.

C CLARKE: Can we have a look at EP26.12, the one of the very well-known photographs of this scene? There is you on the left?

DALY: Liam Bradley is in the centre and Charles Glenn, who is the first aid man, yes.

C CLARKE: You describe in your statement how you felt that you should administer the last rites to Jack Duddy and did so, and how the gunfire started again at around this time. Was that from the same direction as before?

DALY: My recollection, my clear recollection is that the gunfire all came from the direction in which the soldiers were.

C CLARKE: Can I ask you something about that. One of the major questions for this Tribunal to decide is whether the Army opened up with live bullets for no understandable reason, or whether, on the other hand, they were faced with fire from a number of different sources.

DALY: Uh-huh.

C CLARKE: Is it possible that in the noise and confusion and fright, you simply did not notice any firing at the Army that was going on?

DALY: Well, I can only speak about the square of Rossville Flats and I certainly was not conscious of any gunfire directed towards the Army. Certainly there was no threat posed to the Army at the time they opened fire, none, and I do not think there was any justification for it.

C CLARKE: You then describe how a young man with long, fair hair dashed past you. I think we can now be pretty certain that that man was Michael Bridge.

DALY: I distinctly remember those arms in the air waving around. He became – I suppose we were all very distressed and shocked by what had happened. I think he became quite hysterical and angry, I suppose with some justification.

C CLARKE: You say: 'I saw a soldier stepping out from the gable end of block 1, going down to one knee, taking aim and firing at him and the young man staggered, and then he started running crazily around for a few moments'? You have a recollection of that, do you?

DALY: Absolute clear recollection of that. It is one of the, um, things I remember from that day particularly, yeah.

I remember the soldier stepping out from the end of the – the Eden Place end of the Rossville Flats – of that block, coming out and firing, and Michael Bridge was dancing around or shouting at the soldiers. I remember him being shot, I remember his body after he was shot, and then he just staggered out of my sight line but I knew that he had been hit.

C CLARKE: May we have a look at paragraph 24 of your statement at H5.6. It is the portion of your statement in which you – paragraph 24 please – describe seeing a man move along the gable wall of the last house in Chamberlain Street and produce a small handgun from his pocket and fire two or three shots around the corner at the soldiers. Do you remember that?

DALY: Yes, I remember that, yes.

C CLARKE: Did you scream at him to stop?

DALY: Yes, we screamed at him to go away and, um, we were frightened that, that the soldiers might think the fire was coming from the group in which we were, and I think the words that we used 'for Christ's sake, get out, go away, clear off'.

C CLARKE: Did he fire any more shots?

DALY: He fired two or three shots.

C CLARKE: You say that you cannot recall the soldiers reacting or firing in his direction, is that right?

DALY: Yes. Actually I have thought about this over the years. I do not think the soldiers were aware of his presence. I think had they been aware of his presence, I think they would have riddled him. I do not know the range of guns, but I do not think that a handgun would have the range even to reach the soldiers, with body armour and flak jackets and so forth.

C CLARKE: There was gunfire coming in again. That caused you to change direction?

DALY: We discussed a long time what we would do. I was not sure whether Jack Duddy was dead or not and we had an idea first of all to try and get out. We decided it was imperative to get him to the hospital as soon as possible but, um, I do not know at what stage Jack Duddy died.

C CLARKE: Eventually, after [carrying his body to the ambulance] you went down to the Rossville Flats?

DALY: Yes.

C CLARKE: You describe seeing several dead bodies and others who appeared to be very seriously wounded, and administering the last rites to many of them, though you do not know how many?

DALY: I just do not know. I think I administered the last rites to Bernard McGuigan, and, I think, to one or two others, I'm not sure. But a lot of priests, a lot of us administered last rites.

I remember I was just aghast at what I saw there. There were a lot of people lying around injured as well as dead and a lot of other people, very, very distressed.

C CLARKE: If you can think back to the position before the day: had you expected anything serious to happen on the march?

DALY: No, absolutely not.

C CLARKE: Had you thought there might be some rioting and stone throwing?

DALY: Yes, but rioting and stone throwing were every day occurrences, unfortunately, at that time and, um, no, there was no premonition of anything sinister or anything out of the ordinary. My plans for that evening were to rehearse a play that I was producing and to meet the cast at half seven. I did not anticipate that I would be late.

C CLARKE: These are all the questions I have to ask but there may be others.

SAVILLE: There will be some more questions, Bishop Daly. Would you like to take a five minute break at this stage?

DALY: No, I am fine, sir, thank you.

MANSFIELD: Bishop, I represent the family of William Nash and the family of Barney McGuigan. May I also extend, at the beginning, their gratitude to you for your care, courage, and commitment, on that day.

Just a few questions. Was there any occasion on which a civil rights march was used as a cover by paramilitaries, obviously meaning the IRA in this case, for gunmen to shoot at the Army or the police?

DALY: Never.

MANSFIELD: At the point in time on 30th January 1972 when the Saracens, Pigs, or armoured personnel vehicles entered Rossville Street there was in your view no threat posed to the Army?

DALY: No.

MANSFIELD: I want to ask you this, specifically, at any time that day did you see or hear fizzing nail bombs, petrol bombs, or acid bombs?

DALY: No.

MANSFIELD: Thank you.

GLASGOW: My name is Edwin Glasgow and I represent a very large number of soldiers. I think it is right to say that in your long and distinguished vocation you have been an outspoken opponent of violence in all its forms.

Bishop, it was a matter of concern to you, indeed on Bloody Sunday, that a peaceful march had, to some extent, been taken advantage of by rioters?

DALY: Yes, but I think that was a, was a hazard that you had. I mean, do you cease to protest at all? Internment, I considered, and many people in Derry considered, was a grave injustice and, um, people wanted to express their feelings about it in a public manner. Um, do you, do you cancel all marches because there might be a fringe group that would cause a row. I am sure you have riots at London at marches and Derry is no exception. But I do not think – I think the right to protest about something that is perceived as a great injustice is a very important right in a democracy, and I think that the risk that there is a risk, one has to live with.

GLASGOW: One of the reasons why I thought it right to emphasise your own not only abhorrence, but outspoken objection to violence, is that there were men of violence in this city?

DALY: Yes.

GLASGOW: And they would not, by definition, be likely ever to have taken you into their confidence of all people?

DALY: No, but I would point out to you that the men of violence were not just civilians.

GLASGOW: No?

DALY: And men of violence on that particular day certainly were those in uniform.

SAVILLE: Bishop Daly, thank you very much indeed for coming here to assist this Inquiry.

DALY: Thank you, sir.

Clapping from the public gallery.

MICHAEL BRIDGE
15 MARCH 2001

SAVILLE: Mr Bridge, I am the chairman of the Tribunal. As you have probably heard from previous witnesses, the questions will come from the barristers sitting in front of me.

C CLARKE: Do you have with you your statement to this Tribunal which we have beginning at AB84.2?

BRIDGE: Yes.

C CLARKE: If we could come to the first page. You describe in paragraph 8 and 9 how you were approached by an English girl who you think had something to do with the organisers and asked, together with others, to be stewards and given a white armband; is that right?

BRIDGE: That is correct.

C CLARKE: Who did you understand were the organisers?

BRIDGE: Oh, it would have been NICRA [The Northern Ireland Civil Rights Association].

C CLARKE: You are a little far away from the microphone. Do you think you can come a little closer or move the microphone a little closer.

May we go over the page and take paragraphs 12 to 14, if we may. You describe there being ahead of the platform lorry?

BRIDGE: Yes.

C CLARKE: As it turned right into Rossville Street and you say in paragraph 13: '...the bulk of the marchers followed the platform lorry as it turned...but a number of young lads proceeded down William Street towards the Army barrier', and you and seven or eight other stewards went down William Street to get in front of them. What were you aiming to do?

BRIDGE: To direct them over, to direct them over to Free Derry Corner and follow the lorry. The lorry was going to Free Derry Corner, to direct them behind the lorry, keep the march intact the way it was.

C CLARKE: Paragraphs 14 to 17? You describe there recollecting that, at least in the early stages, you were successful in persuading some of the marchers to go to Free Derry Corner, but after a time stones were thrown and it turned more serious after the Army responded with gas and rubber bullets. And you say: 'Suddenly, there were shouts by people in the crowd that the Saracens were coming in.'

BRIDGE: Yes.

C CLARKE: Then you and most others believed that if you were on William Street you would be arrested and so you ran down Chamberlain Street, is that right?

BRIDGE: Yes.

C CLARKE: Paragraphs 22 to 24. Your memory is that the Saracen was not moving when you first saw it, is that right?

BRIDGE: That is right, yes.

C CLARKE: But two, or possibly three, soldiers you saw climbing out of the back. You describe them as definitely firing their rifles as they did so, are you sure about that?

BRIDGE: That is correct.

C CLARKE: As they came out, where were they firing towards?

BRIDGE: Well, my impression was that they were firing towards William Street down towards where I was, at the mouth of Eden Place.

C CLARKE: Firing towards William Street?

BRIDGE: Yes.

C CLARKE: Could you see what they were firing at?

BRIDGE: I seen them, I seen them firing. What they were firing at is, effectively I cannot tell you, but in a situation like that, you would assume that they were firing at you, that would be the impression.

C CLARKE: It was at that stage that one of those who were coming up the street shouted out that a boy had been shot up there, meaning somewhere in the car park?

BRIDGE: Yes.

C CLARKE: You went down [on] Chamberlain Street and came out at the bottom of the street, can we now go to paragraph [28]? You describe there how you saw Jack Duddy lying on the ground and went up to him.

When you saw him, do you recall whether he was face up or face down?

BRIDGE: Yeah, he was face up.

C CLARKE: You were able to see that there was blood over his face. Your recollection is of only two or three people, one of them Father Daly, presumably, and the other the first aid man, is that right?

BRIDGE: Yes, that has always been my – it is, yes.

C CLARKE: You describe in paragraph [31] how, when you had got to within a couple of yards of Jack Duddy, you turned and saw a soldier standing with his rifle in an aiming position at his shoulder, pointing in your direction, a couple of feet off the corner of the backyard wall of the first house in Chamberlain Street, is that right?

BRIDGE: Yes.

C CLARKE: You describe having a vague recollection that there was another soldier somewhere behind him, is that right?

BRIDGE: Yes.

C CLARKE: You also recall there being a soldier in a kneeling position at the north-east of block 1. You walked three or four paces towards the soldier [in your position C], who you believed was responsible for shooting Jack Duddy?

BRIDGE: Yes.

C CLARKE: You describe giving the soldier a mouthful of abuse because you were annoyed and upset by the sight you had seen of Jack Duddy's body, is that right?

BRIDGE: Yeah, probably putting it mildly.

C CLARKE: You recall saying, 'Shoot me, shoot me'?

BRIDGE: I am told I shouted, 'Shoot me' or something like that, but I really cannot remember anything. In fact I get scared to think of what I did.

C CLARKE: As you walked towards the soldier were you conscious of bullets flying as you did so?

BRIDGE: One bullet hit me, but I have the sense of other bullets flying round me.

C CLARKE: You did not actually see, or have you no recollection of seeing the soldier who shot you?

BRIDGE: No.

C CLARKE: The last matter I have to put to you is this: it is right, is it not, that in 1965 you were convicted at Leeds Assizes on a charge of unlawful wounding. Is that right?

BRIDGE: It is quite correct, but could you, please, explain to me what it has to do with 1972?

C CLARKE: Let me just finish what I am asking at the moment – and you were sentenced to three years imprisonment?

BRIDGE: That is right, yeah.

C CLARKE: And that involved, I think, a stabbing of a civilian in Bradford. Is that right?

BRIDGE: That is quite right.

C CLARKE: Those are my questions.

BRIDGE: Sorry, Mr Clarke, could you tell me what that has to do with Bloody Sunday?

C CLARKE: Yes, I can. The Tribunal, in considering the evidence of all witnesses, whether they be civilians or soldiers, needs to know whether or not they are persons who have significant convictions because that may bear on their credibility, or may, if the conviction is one of violence, give some indication of the character of the person with whom they are dealing, that is the relevance.

BRIDGE: So what you are saying is, it is effectively – it is not addressing the actions on Bloody Sunday, it is addressing the credibility of people, of actions other than Bloody Sunday would have which, in your opinion, would effectively discredit their evidence.

C CLARKE: It is nothing to do with my opinion. It is the Tribunal's. It is the credibility and character of witnesses.

BRIDGE: Would the same – would I be given the same facility from the soldiers that is going to appear here.

C CLARKE: If there are convictions of like nature in relation to the identity of the soldier, the answer is yes.

BRIDGE: Excuse me, sir, in a clear and precise way, in relation to the soldier.

C CLARKE: I am sorry, I do not understand what you are saying.

SAVILLE: I think Mr Bridge is asking you some question about the identity of the soldiers. That really is a rather different topic, Mr Bridge. I expect your counsel will be able to explain the position to you.

BRIDGE: Sir, yeah, yeah, the answer is, yeah.

C CLARKE: If it helps, we are attempting to discover the identity of the soldier who shot you. We have not so far done so because no soldier has accepted that he did or given evidence that somebody whom he knew did either.

SAVILLE: Thank you, Mr Bridge. As we said at the outset, as we have continued to say throughout, it is our intention to conduct as open an Inquiry as it is possible for us to do.

BRIDGE: Thank you, sir.

BERNADETTE MCALISKEY
15 MAY 2001

C CLARKE: Mrs McAliskey, can we recall the position in 1972: you were then, if I am right, the member of the Westminster Parliament for Mid Ulster?

MCALISKEY: I was, yes.

C CLARKE: And indeed had been, I think, elected in April 1969 at a by-election?

MCALISKEY: Yes.

C CLARKE: As we know from your statement, you went on the march. I wonder if we could have on the screen a photograph which appears at P334A. This is a photograph that was taken on the day. It has been suggested that the person at whom I am pointing an arrow on the screen is you. Do you know whether that is you? It is sometimes difficult to recognise oneself.

MCALISKEY: I would have to say in all honesty I have no reason to believe that it is not me. I looked like almost every other young long-haired person of my age and I have probably been on hundreds, if not thousands, of demonstrations of that nature. I could not actually say, but I have no reason to believe to the contrary that this is not a photograph of the day in question, and there is a very good likelihood that that young person is me.

C CLARKE: Were you concerned in any way in the organisation of the march?

MCALISKEY: No.

C CLARKE: Could we have on the screen KD4.30? This is a document we have obtained from people who were making a documentary on the 25th anniversary of Bloody Sunday for Channel 4. This particular note under the heading of your name says:

'There was an understanding between the Provos and the civil rights people that there would be no guns in the city that day – not just no guns on the march.'

Do you remember being interviewed for a Channel 4 documentary?

MCALISKEY: I would have no clear memory.

C CLARKE: You will appreciate that the reason I am asking you is that it looks pretty likely that we will be told that these notes were taken by people who noted down what the subject of the note said?

MCALISKEY: Which given the standard of journalism in this country may not necessarily bear any resemblance to what was said.

C CLARKE: Can we then concentrate on your own words. If we look at KD4.20, paragraph 29, what you say in that paragraph, about six lines down, 'Paragraph 4 of the note refers to (I will insert the letter X) who, the note says, negotiated a "no arms" agreement with the Provos. I would have no knowledge of that. I believe that (X) was politically active with the Officials and was not involved with the Provos.' Is that a fair statement of your present recollection?

MCALISKEY: Yes, a fair statement of my own recollection.

C CLARKE: You describe your belief that the person in question was politically active with the Officials and not involved with the Provos. Were you aware one way or another whether he was a member of the Official IRA?

MCALISKEY: Again in my statement – before the split in the Republican movement, nobody was called an Official and nobody was called a Provo. After the split, Officials referred to all those Republicans who were not Provos. It was a broad terminology, and therefore the person whom I spoke of has clearly recalled being politically active with the Officials as opposed to being connected with the Provos. It does not infer that he was a member of any armed organisation, and the broad base of people, including on occasion people like myself would have been designated because of our political opinions as belonging to something or another.

C CLARKE: I quite follow the statement that somebody was politically active with the Officials does not entitle one to infer that he was a member of an armed organisation, but my question to you was whether you knew whether he was or not?

MCALISKEY: No, I did not.

C CLARKE: Forgive me for chopping around. I am trying to keep in some form of logical and approximately chronological sequence. Could we have a look at KD4.16, paragraph 23? You are dealing with the position of Police Superintendent Lagan. You say this: 'I have also been asked whether Superintendent Lagan was told that there would be no IRA guns in the Bogside that afternoon. I do not know. All of the avenues of knowledge were open to him and in my view it was inconceivable that he did not know.' Did you mean anything by that other than that being a local man and a member of the Catholic community he would be in a position to know what was happening on the street, as it were, or did you mean something else by that?

MCALISKEY: No. It would have been a very simple reference to the country was riddled with informers, probably in 1972 as well as now and therefore the police were probably perfectly well informed of what we ate for our breakfasts in the morning.

C CLARKE: Could we then go to your statement at KD4.7. You describe in the second line reaching the point where the march could either turn right across Rossville Flats towards Free Derry Corner or proceed further to the barricade preventing access to the town:

'It was unclear to me which way the procession was actually going. There appeared to be a log jam of people in both directions, some confusion and the usual barricade aggro.'

Can you help me on this? When the march began and as you went along with it, where did you think it was going to end up?

MCALISKEY: In hindsight there was no doubt in my mind that it was going to end up at Free Derry Corner.

C CLARKE: May we then come over the page and could we have highlighted the first three paragraphs.

We have got, in this part of your description, to you being on the platform constituted by the coal lorry at Free Derry Corner, and you describe being handed the microphone when [Lord] Fenner Brockway was either getting on or getting off the platform as you began to speak. Is that right?

MCALISKEY: Yes.

C CLARKE: You describe the crowd widening and filling out towards the front and almost as soon as you spoke hearing several shots in your right ear coming directly from your right?

MCALISKEY: I know that almost as soon as I started, I heard the shots. I turned in the direction of them. People in front of me are concerned. They think that some somebody has fired at me. I have not actually said anything other than probably the standard 'people of Derry' or whatever it was I used to say and I hear the shots.

I say to the people something to the effect that they would not dare shoot us, something to the effect of 'stand your ground'. There are more shots. The shots come in three different waves, shots there, shots here, then shots there. At that point everybody –

C CLARKE: Everybody runs away?

MCALISKEY: Yeah – they do not run away. They do not run away.

C CLARKE: What does everybody do?

MCALISKEY: Everybody almost moves like a body. There is nowhere to run with thirty thousand people. This was not a scattering match in the street, this was thirty thousand people like one wave. One minute I was looking at faces looking up at me, the next minute I was looking at the crowns of people's heads. It was like a wave, they were moving that way and I was telling them to stay down, I was telling them to get off the streets, but they were still at that point moving as a body forward and there was not an opportunity to actually run until the streets were nearly clear.

There are more shots and therefore more panic. In that space of time I am no longer standing on this coal lorry telling people anything, I am under it. I am either under the vehicle beside the wheel, or I am behind it beside the wheel. My view has now dramatically altered. I remember saying 'do not run' because I felt if people ran they would be shot because it was now clear to me that the Army were shooting the people of the streets, thirty thousand people were being fired on. The only clear memory I have, which I have as I speak of it, is terror. That is all I remember, sheer terror. I remember my mouth was dry. I think I could taste the coal dust, that may have been what it was. There was a pain in the bottom of my back, my stomach was like lead and yet I could not feel anything at all. I was looking at something and yet it was happening in front of my eyes in slow motion. That is all I remember reliably about that.

C CLARKE: Could we go to KD4.4? This is part of the *Sunday Times* archive in 1972. What is recorded there, rightly or wrongly is this:

'Essentially the NICRA have become a shell. The politics of Derry had dissolved. The situation was now one of violence and by calling out the people NICRA unleashed forces which it must have known it could not control.' Is that a sentiment that you would have expressed?

MCALISKEY: No, it is a very simplistic summary. NICRA was an organisation, it was only one of several organisations involved within the broad civil rights movement. I was an active part of the broad civil rights movement. There were more intricate politics going on in this city than anywhere else in Northern Ireland.

C CLARKE: Let us look at the next paragraph. 'BD [you] says it was inconceivable that the Provos would have started anything with thirty thousand people around, that is just not their style. Much less certain of the Officials and indeed was very worried that they might be more ruthless than the Provos.'

Were you apprehensive that the Officials might use violence on this occasion?

MCALISKEY: No, that whole paragraph is nonsense. I challenge the whole rationale behind that because there is an implication behind it that somebody was attempting to persuade armed organisations not to do things on the day when the reality is that there is no history from '68 on, there is no history, or from '72 after, there is no history of either or any Republican armed grouping organising armed activity in, out, through, during, or in conjunction with, the marches.

C CLARKE: The statement that appears to be attributed to you, that you knew the Provos in Derry very well?

MCALISKEY: I do not think that is even attributed to me and I come to the point again, where I do not see the point of me spending an afternoon going through a statement that I do not even think is attributable to me.

SAVILLE: Ms McAliskey, they were words which, apparently, were written down round about 1972 shortly after Bloody Sunday and in order for us at the end of the day to gauge whether we can believe what these people wrote down, we must ask you some details about them. Having the advantage of you here this afternoon will give us an aid in trying to discover where the truth lies; that is why we are doing it.

MCALISKEY: I appreciate that – I do not believe that this is the way to do this. I do most deeply believe that the Government of the day conspired, or organised, or authorised, in violation of its governmental duties, the killing of the citizens. I believe that people who believe that, should bring charges against that Government through the proper procedure in the International Court of Justice at the Hague.

SAVILLE: I would ask you, if you would, to bear with us. We are doing the best we can.

MCALISKEY: So am I, and I would prefer – well, I would really prefer not to be here, and every time I keep feeling that I am being drawn further and further into matters of no consequence that I believe at the end of the day will become part of a great big cloud that will confuse the final issue: that the Government of the day ordered the Army to shoot the citizens, and that to me is all that matters. I actually do not care, and I do not think that it matters if the entire Brigade of the Provisional IRA, aided and abetted by the Official IRA and anybody else that they could gather up for the occasion were conspiring to take on the British Army on that day, even if that – which I do not believe – even if any of it and all of it were true, it did not justify the Army opening fire on the civilian population on that demonstration. This should be somewhere, this should be somewhere else where the accused is not running the party.

Clapping in the public gallery.

That is not against the Inquiry, you are doing your best and so am I and when I get out of here today, I will not be back. And all the High Court writs in Christendom will not be getting me back after this day.

SAVILLE: Ms McAliskey, you have expressed your views about this Inquiry, but it still remains for me to thank you very much for coming to assist us and I hope you will accept our assurance we shall do our best.

MCALISKEY: I have not wanted to come here. I have done so out of respect for the relatives.

What is very easy to forget about Bloody Sunday is the actual enormity of what it was. Before that day, although people were being shot, I did not have a belief that death was an integral part of the equation of seeking justice in this country. After Bloody Sunday, I believed that it was.

I never for thirty years raised my voice against the arming and taking of the war to the British Government. For thirty years, as a consequence of Bloody Sunday, my policy was death is part of this equation. The British Army declared war on the people seeking justice in this country on that day. Three thousand and more coffins followed and years of imprisonment and torture and pain. It is highly arguable that without Bloody Sunday where we are today we would have been in 1972 and I cannot forgive the British Government for that.

WILLIAM PATRICK MCDONAGH
24 MAY 2001

MCGAHEY: Mr McDonagh, do you have with you, please, a copy of the statement that you made to this Inquiry?

MCDONAGH: I have.

MCGAHEY: You tell us on the first page that you went on the march, went up as far as William Street and, having seen a few lads throwing stones at the soldiers, decided to go back to see your girlfriend who lived in block 1 of the Rossville Flats, is that right?

MCDONAGH: Yes.

MCGAHEY: If we go over the page, please, if we could highlight paragraphs 8 and 9, you tell us that the flat was on the first and second storeys of block 1?

MCDONAGH: Yes.

MCGAHEY: If I show you a photograph, I wonder if you can place the flat for us on the map. If we could have P301. This photograph was taken after the day, but it shows block 1 of the flats?

MCDONAGH: Yes.

MCGAHEY: Looking at that photograph now, can you tell us where your girlfriend's flat was?

MCDONAGH: Yes.

MCGAHEY: If Mr McDonagh could be given control, could you mark the screen. If you touch it with your finger, it should make a mark for you.

MCDONAGH: Up here (*Indicating.*) on up. That is the door, number 4.

MCGAHEY: That is the door. Is that the lower floor?

MCDONAGH: Yes. They are actually second and third storeys, because they are like maisonettes; there is an upstairs and downstairs.

MCGAHEY: So the window we see immediately above the arrow would be the upper floor of the flat?

MCDONAGH: Yes.

MCGAHEY: Could we save that image, please, as AM192.9?

You say that you looked in the courtyard and saw a man who you thought at the time to be quite elderly, being seized by two or three soldiers who were standing behind a Saracen?

MCDONAGH: Yes.

MCGAHEY: You recall there were a couple of boys in the courtyard who tried to get to the old man but you do not believe that they reached him?

MCDONAGH: No.

MCGAHEY: On to paragraph 11:

'At the same time that the man was being held by the soldiers, more soldiers got out of the Saracen. One of the soldiers took up a position to the west of the Saracen and aimed his rifle towards the gap between blocks 1 and 2 [of the Rossville Flats].'

MCDONAGH: I know that in this statement which is twenty-seven years later, I have said 'he took position and aimed a rifle'. He was not aiming.

MCGAHEY: He was not aiming?

MCDONAGH: No.

MCGAHEY: What do you recall him doing?

MCDONAGH: He was firing indiscriminately from, roughly, I would say, midriff – waist or midriff.

MCGAHEY: Could you actually see him firing?

MCDONAGH: Well, at the time I heard a crack of at least two shots, and I am sure it was him. But it was pandemonium in that square. People were running.

MCGAHEY: You say the next thing you recall is seeing a boy fall. It happened at the same time you saw the soldier take aim and fire?

MCDONAGH: Not take aim.

MCGAHEY: Same time?

MCDONAGH: Same time as he fired.

MCGAHEY: Did you believe he had been shot by the soldier who you saw fire?

MCDONAGH: It was my impression that that is what happened. But in saying that, as soon as the live rounds were fired, I was back in the flat. I did not hang around that balcony. It happened so quickly, so I am not one hundred per cent sure.

MCGAHEY: You say that as you heard the shots you saw a boy clutch his leg and fall down. He was two feet away from the west side of block 1?

MCDONAGH: Yes.

MCGAHEY: You say that after a lull in the shooting you looked out and saw two men lying at the rubble barricade, the first lying to the south, and you could see only his torso and his legs?

MCDONAGH: Yes.

MCGAHEY: And the second person appears roughly to be on top of the rubble barricade?

MCDONAGH: He could have been on top of it, but he was at the barricade.

MCGAHEY: You noticed a third man waving a handkerchief?

MCDONAGH: Yes.

MCGAHEY: Was he near to either of the bodies that you had seen on the barricade?

MCDONAGH: Yes.

MCGAHEY: To which one?

MCDONAGH: The middle one.

MCGAHEY: Going on to paragraph 24, you saw a Saracen come down Rossville Street –

MCDONAGH: Yes.

MCGAHEY: – towards Free Derry Corner, and it stopped ten to fifteen feet north of the rubble barricade. You saw two soldiers carrying a body?

MCDONAGH: Yes.

MCGAHEY: Did you know where that body had come from?

MCDONAGH: I am nearly sure they took it from the barricade.

MCGAHEY: Did you see that?

MCDONAGH: No. I only seen them putting it into the back of the Saracen; not putting it in, actually throwing it in.

MCGAHEY: In 1972, when you made your statement, what you said then was: 'I saw two of the soldiers laughing at the bodies at the barricade. These soldiers had no respect for the dead. One of them grabbed one of the bodies by the collar and the other by the belt.' Do you remember that happening?

MCDONAGH: I remember the soldiers having the body. One had him by the collar and the other had him by the belt.

MCGAHEY: That was one body?

MCDONAGH: It was the one body I seen, yeah. I am not standing staring out all the time at this because I am afraid they are going to fire up at the flats.

MCGAHEY: As far as you could see, did the person who was being carried appear to be dead or alive?

MCDONAGH: I could not say for definite. I know that when the body was thrown into the back of the Saracen, when there was a lull in the shooting and it seemed like time stopped, you would have heard a pin drop then. I know I heard groans from the back of that Saracen.

Witness upset.

MCGAHEY: Sir, I wonder whether Mr McDonagh would like a break.

SAVILLE: Yes, I think that might be a good idea. Mr McDonagh, would you like a break or a minute or two?

MCDONAGH: I will be okay.

GLASGOW: Mr McDonagh, my name is Glasgow. I represent many of the soldiers. When you looked out into the courtyard, did it occur to you that the incident that was going on might be an arrest operation of any kind?

MCDONAGH: It looked to me like it was an arrest operation.

GLASGOW: You had, of course, seen – I do not suggest you participated in it – a riot at barrier 14 in William Street?

MCDONAGH: Yes.

GLASGOW: And following that riot, it did not surprise you that, whatever may have happened, soldiers tried to make arrests following that riot? That did not surprise you?

MCDONAGH: It did not surprise me, but when those soldiers came in, when the paratroopers came in, there was no rioting. There was a lull in the rioting. Everybody had drifted away.

GLASGOW: Whether or not they got all the right people it looked as if the soldiers might have been chasing people who had been rioting?

MCDONAGH: It might have looked that way, but we all know the right way of it.

GLASGOW: Sorry, I missed the last bit.

MCDONAGH: I say it might have looked that way in people's eyes, but we know the right way of it.

GLASGOW: Yes, yes, I follow. I am sure we all –

MCDONAGH: I am sure there was a game plan in the town that day.

GLASGOW: I am now coming to the incident of the bodies you saw at the barricade. You believe that a Saracen drove down Rossville Street towards the barricade?

MCDONAGH: Yes, when there was a lull. I cannot remember how far now away from it, but stopped at the barricade.

GLASGOW: And the soldiers went to the barricade, collected one body?

MCDONAGH: No, I did not see them lift [it] from the barricade. I just seen the body, when I went back to the window, getting put into the Saracen.

GLASGOW: And you formed the impression at that time that that body that you saw being carried was dead?

MCDONAGH: Yes.

GLASGOW: That is the only one you saw carried, and it is only because you heard a noise afterwards that you believed it was possible that somebody else in the Saracen was not dead; is that what it amounts to?

MCDONAGH: Yes, I heard moans coming from the back of that Saracen, cries.

GLASGOW: It is that –

MCDONAGH: As I said – excuse me, if I can finish. As I said, they were not cries of panic or – they were cries of people that were hurt. And there is nothing put in my mind. There was people in that Saracen that were not dead.

GLASGOW: That was an impression that you had?

MCDONAGH: It was not an impression, I heard the cries coming from it, and the moans. I know I heard crying coming from the back of that Saracen, and moans.

GLASGOW: It may not come as any comfort to you that the Tribunal has the medical evidence concerning the three bodies that were placed in the back of that Saracen to the effect that their death would have been extremely rapid, and I do suggest to you – because they were examined by a first class medical orderly just a very short time after you would have seen them – that they were all dead. Can you comment further on that?

MCDONAGH: I cannot, I cannot.

GLASGOW: Thank you very much, Mr McDonagh.

SAVILLE: Do you have any further questions?

MCGAHEY: No thank you, sir.

SAVILLE: Mr McDonagh, thank you very much indeed for coming here to assist this Inquiry. Thank you.

ALICE DOHERTY
4 SEPTEMBER 2001

ROXBURGH: May we have on the screen, please, AD60.36? Mrs Doherty, do you have with you a copy of the statement that you made to this Inquiry, of which we have the first page on the screen now?

DOHERTY: I should have.

ROXBURGH: Please take your time, if you would like to have the paper copy. Otherwise we can also look at it on the screen.

DOHERTY: Aye, on the screen.

ROXBURGH: You tell us in the statement that in 1972 you were a superintendent in the Knights of Malta and you attended the march in that capacity, is that right?

DOHERTY: Yes.

ROXBURGH: I wonder if we could have a look at AD50.28, please. This is the first page of your statement that you made at the time. You will see that it says: 'On Sunday 30th January, being a superintendent in the Knights of Malta Ambulance Corps I took part in the march as a first aid worker. When the march stopped in William Street, I was opposite the former site of Richards shirt factory.'

DOHERTY: Yes.

ROXBURGH: Would this be right, Mrs Doherty, that you started off that day intending to operate as a pair with Angela Coyle, but that you quickly became separated?

DOHERTY: Yes, we did, yes.

ROXBURGH: A general question, Mrs Doherty: you have described in your statement to this Inquiry and in the statements you made at the time a large number of different incidents involving various people who were dead or injured?

DOHERTY: Yes.

ROXBURGH: How clear are you now in your own mind as to the order in which the various events happened?

DOHERTY: Well, I can only go by what my statement has said because, like you are talking thirty years ago and things do change, your memory just does not stand up. I came here to tell the truth for the families, and I may make mistakes, but I hope they will forgive me for them.

ROXBURGH: Of course, but do you think it possible that in some respects your recollection may have become –

DOHERTY: Blurred, yes, I will accept that.

ROXBURGH: Can we come to the incident involving the armoured personnel carrier on Rossville Street?

DOHERTY: Yes.

ROXBURGH: Can we look at paragraph 10 of your statement, please, which is on the screen at the moment? You say in that paragraph that a male bystander told you that there were three people dead or injured inside one of the Saracen personnel carriers parked in Rossville Street?

DOHERTY: Yes.

ROXBURGH: Going on to the next page, paragraph 11, you say: 'At this point I became aware of high-pitched shots being fired, coming in blasts'?

DOHERTY: Yes.

ROXBURGH: Did you locate the source of those shots?

DOHERTY: No, no, because everything was so quick, everything was going on in a panicky sort of way and I just did not pay no attention to what direction the shots was coming from.

ROXBURGH: Can we go back to AD50.39, paragraph 17. You say that you heard a moaning sound from inside the Saracen?

DOHERTY: Yes.

ROXBURGH: And you reached forward and grabbed the door but the soldier kicked it shut?

DOHERTY: Yes.

ROXBURGH: And then you say that you immediately opened the door again?

DOHERTY: Yes.

ROXBURGH: And you saw one of the feet of the boy at the bottom give a slight twitch?

DOHERTY: Yes, that is correct.

ROXBURGH: Apart from that twitch and the moaning sound that you heard –

DOHERTY: Yes.

ROXBURGH: Did you at any stage either see anything or hear anything that enabled you to tell whether these boys were dead or alive?

DOHERTY: Well, when we heard the fizzle or the moaning that went on inside the Saracen, we immediately tried to grab the door again. My only interest was trying to get in and see if there was any possibility of saving a life.

ROXBURGH: Can we go back to AD50.39, please, paragraph 20? You say that you noticed two bullet cases on the ground near the Saracen?

DOHERTY: Yes, that is correct.

ROXBURGH: You picked them up?

DOHERTY: Yes.

ROXBURGH: And they were split wide open like flowers?

DOHERTY: Yes, that is correct.

ROXBURGH: Can we be clear you are talking about spent cartridge cases, not actual bullets?

DOHERTY: Spent, yes.

ROXBURGH: You say you thought they were dum-dum bullets?

DOHERTY: Yes, because of the way they were opened, they were almost like daffodils.

P CLARKE: Mrs Doherty, my name is [Peter] Clarke, and I represent a number of the soldiers.

[A] soldier has to have fired these shots before they had got into the Saracen, does he not?

DOHERTY: But them bodies was already, them bodies was already shot and them – [a] small soldier, he fired while I was there, he definitely did.

P CLARKE: Three shots?

DOHERTY: Three shots?

P CLARKE: And cartridge cases that opened like daffodils?

DOHERTY: Yes.

P CLARKE: And you came to the conclusion that they were dum-dum bullets?

DOHERTY: Yes.

P CLARKE: Why?

DOHERTY: Because everyone was saying that day that if they spread like daffodils, they were supposed to be dumb – I know nothing about guns or rifles –

P CLARKE: Or dum-dum bullets?

DOHERTY: I know nothing about anything like that.

P CLARKE: You will appreciate, Mrs Doherty, that as a Knight of Malta, you are a person who is regarded as neutral as possible?

DOHERTY: Yes, that is correct.

P CLARKE: At least in theory you would tend to a wounded soldier as much as a wounded civilian?

DOHERTY: Yes, I have letters from a couple of different British regiments thanking me for my work.

P CLARKE: Why are you accusing people of using dum-dum bullets when you have not the faintest idea of what they are?

DOHERTY: I am only going on what I was told.

P CLARKE: Do you not think that is quite irresponsible?

DOHERTY: Well, I suppose so.

P CLARKE: I am not disputing, madam, that you saw a number of unfortunate people on the ground, but is there not the possibility that you have added to your memory unconsciously some images you have seen?

DOHERTY: No.

P CLARKE: Absolutely sure in your own mind?

DOHERTY: No, positive.

P CLARKE: Thank you.

ROXBURGH: Sir, I have no further questions of this witness.

SAVILLE: Mrs Doherty, the chairman again, if you look to your right. That is the end of your evidence, thank you very much indeed for coming here to help the Inquiry.

GERALDINE MCBRIDE
20 – 24 SEPTEMBER 2001

C CLARKE: Do have in front of you your statement to this Tribunal which you signed on 28th January 1999?

MCBRIDE: Yes, I do.

C CLARKE: Could we have on the screen AM45.2, paragraphs 6 to 8? In this part of your statement you describe how there came a time when you and [Hugo] your now husband stopped at William Street between Rossville

Street and Chamberlain Street and as you stopped a water cannon was directed at the crowd from the barricade and there was a massive scramble and you lost Hugo in the crowd and got separated from him outside Porter's television and radio shop.

Did you ever meet up with him again on the day?

MCBRIDE: No.

C CLARKE: You describe how as the crowd surged back from the barrier you went back towards Rossville Street, made your way to a spot on the wasteground at the corner of William Street and Rossville Street and decided to wait there for Hugo.

At this stage, when you go to the position where you waited for him, what had happened to the main body of the march?

MCBRIDE: They were still down in William Street, the main body was still down there. There was some scattered people around the open area, but it was quiet, there was not too many people about.

C CLARKE: When you mean the 'open area'. Do you mean the wasteground around Rossville Street?

MCBRIDE: Yes.

C CLARKE: You describe in paragraph 8 how you were not expecting anything to happen and did not feel apprehensive. You thought that the crowd were rioting in William Street and the Army would react in the usual way, but you did not think they would enter the Bogside. How far did you think they might come?

MCBRIDE: Well, I thought they would a went round by William Street and sort of cordoned off and get snatch squads. I did not feel that they would come into the Bogside.

C CLARKE: You describe how as you were standing waiting you met up with the young man you later found out was Hugh Gilmore and there was some friendly banter between you.

All of a sudden the barrier at Little James Street opened and the Army vehicles came in as a result which you ran, with Hugh Gilmore and the young man he was with, as fast as you could down Rossville Street towards Free Derry Corner, running towards the rubble barricade. Were there others who were doing the same at this stage?

MCBRIDE: Yes, there was, there was a lot more people about at this stage.

C CLARKE: When you were at about halfway down Rossville Street you stopped, the three of you stopped. Hugh Gilmore and the other boy picked up stones and each of them threw a single stone towards the direction of the Army vehicles which had now stopped, is that right?

MCBRIDE: That is right.

C CLARKE: Was anybody else throwing stones at that stage?

MCBRIDE: Yes, there was.

C CLARKE: Could we have please, back on the screen, AM45.35? You describe how, as you looked up Rossville Street, you recall seeing three Army vehicles bunched together. Soldiers got out of the back of them and you remember three soldiers who got out of the middle vehicle, two of whom went to the Chamberlain Street side and a third came round the Kells Walk side of the vehicle to the front, bent down on his knee and started shooting and you realised that he was firing live bullets.

You realised that it was not a snatch squad because the soldiers were not carrying shields and were firing real bullets and you could see people running.

MCBRIDE: Yes.

C CLARKE: You then describe how when the kneeling soldier started to shoot, Hugh and the other man and you ran towards the rubble barricade and there was more shooting from the north which was sporadic, but the same sound as that which had appeared from the gun of the kneeling soldier. Did you at this stage hear the firing of rubber bullets as well?

MCBRIDE: No.

C CLARKE: You describe how you ran past block 1 and Hugh was running close to the wall saying, 'The bastards are killing us', and as you reached the rubble barricade you noticed that there were people on it throwing stones. You describe how Hugh Gilmore and you stumbled over the rubble barricade, continuing running towards the Free Derry Corner, is that right?

MCBRIDE: Yes.

C CLARKE: You heard two shots which came from your right, felt the bullets rush past in front of you and heard Hugh gasp and say that he had been hit, is that right?

MCBRIDE: That is right.

C CLARKE: When you say you felt that, do you mean that you heard the sound or felt a sort of whoosh or what, exactly?

MCBRIDE: Felt a sort of whoosh.

C CLARKE: And then Hugh gasped and said that he had been hit?

MCBRIDE: Yes.

C CLARKE: May we come, please, to paragraphs 19 and 20 on AM45.4? You describe how Hugh only managed to stumble a few paces after he had been hit and he stumbled forward and his legs went from under him and a young fellow and you grabbed him, pulling him backwards and helped him round the corner of the southern end of block 1 [of the Rossville flats].

When you got round the corner, you laid him down and a Knight of Malta came to assist.

MCBRIDE: That is right.

C CLARKE: Can you remember how many people you saw lying behind the barricade?

MCBRIDE: Well, there was people lying down, you know, because of the shooting and squealing and roaring, people were lying down, people were running and people were trying to get to safety.

C CLARKE: After Hugh died, you could hear the Army vehicles much closer and heard a crash at the rubble barricade and [you] knew they had come through it and a couple of men pulled you to the telephone booth at the southern end of block 1, one of whom was Mr McGuigan.

MCBRIDE: Yes.

C CLARKE: Could we then go back to paragraphs 24 to 26. You describe the circumstances in which Barney McGuigan came to be shot. You describe how he walked away from the group at the gable end [of block 1] and you say that all the time that he was walking you could see the left-hand side of his face and you were calling to him all the time to come back and he kept 'looking back towards us'. You say that you could see bullets going past you and Mr McGuigan from all directions. Did those bullets land anywhere before Mr McGuigan was hit or were you just conscious of them going past you?

MCBRIDE: I was just conscious of them going past.

C CLARKE: You describe hearing two distinct shots, after the first of which Mr McGuigan turned back towards you. You think he turned his whole body and the second shot hit him and blew his head up. You are quite sure, are you, that it was the second and not the first shot?

MCBRIDE: It was the second shot.

C CLARKE: Those are my questions.

MANSFIELD: Mrs McBride, I represent the family of Barney McGuigan. When Barney McGuigan walked out, away from the wall, do you mean he was literally walking – I am going to demonstrate to you, as if he was walking like this. How was he walking?

MCBRIDE: He was half down, shaking, putting his hand out in front of him, you know. Not fully up, you know, crouching down. That is the way he walked.

MANSFIELD: Hand out, with a handkerchief in it?

MCBRIDE: Yes.

MANSFIELD: And I am sorry to ask you, it is important, as he is walking out, he is walking out with his back towards the gable end of the wall where you were?

MCBRIDE: Yes.

MANSFIELD: But holding out the handkerchief in front of him?

MCBRIDE: Yes.

MANSFIELD: Is that the position?

MCBRIDE: (*Witness nodding.*)

MANSFIELD: As he walked out from the wall. This is as he gets shot, I need to know – if you can remember, please stop me if you cannot. As he is walking out, is his back to block 1 where you are standing?

MCBRIDE: I could demonstrate, you know.

MANSFIELD: Please do, that is acceptable. Do stand up, if it is not too much trouble.

MCBRIDE: He went out like that there. (*Indicating.*)

MANSFIELD: He is walking out with his left arm out with the back of his right shoulder towards where you are?

MCBRIDE: Yes. When he was walking out, he was looking at us.

MANSFIELD: So he is turning towards where you are?

MCBRIDE: Yes.

MANSFIELD: Holding his left arm out with a handkerchief in it?

MCBRIDE: Aye.

MANSFIELD: You indicated it was the second shot that hit him and it was after the first shot he turned back towards you. The first shot misses, but the second shot hits him. In what position is he when the second shot hits him, is he looking directly at you at the wall, or is he turned away, can you remember?

MCBRIDE: (*Pause.*) He was looking over at us like that – (*Indicating.*) You know, he was looking at us.

MANSFIELD: He was looking at you with his body front on to you or just his head?

MCBRIDE: He jumped, you know, he looked and then he was shot, you know and then…

MANSFIELD: Is it right to say, because you were so upset by what you had seen, and affected, that really you do not have much of a memory of what happened thereafter?

MCBRIDE: No. I went hysterical after Mr McGuigan got shot.

MANSFIELD: That is perfectly understandable.

GENERAL SIR ROBERT FORD
29 OCTOBER – 12 NOVEMBER 2002

SAVILLE: General Ford, if you look to your left you can see who is talking to you. I am the chairman of the Tribunal. The questions in the main will come from the barristers, the people in front of me.

C CLARKE: Can we have on the screen B1,208.019. General, that is the first page of your statement to this Tribunal which you signed on 23rd March 2000. Are the contents of that statement true to the best of your knowledge and belief?

FORD: They are.

C CLARKE: You describe how you were told in April 1971 that you were to become Commander of Land Forces in Northern Ireland. You describe the arrest operation on internment. You describe how, because the arrest operation was directed at every large Catholic area, it threw up enormous hatred against the Army, and particularly in Londonderry.

The Army, or at any rate Lord Carver and General Tuzo, did not believe internment was necessary in August 1971, in military terms although it was a course favoured by Brian Faulkner, the prime minister.

Could we have a look, please, at 1,208.003.001. This is an interview with you. You record the taking of the interment decision by Faulkner, Maudling, and Carrington. You are recorded as saying: 'This was a major decision and in my opinion the totally wrong one. I backed it at the time because I thought it was the right way. Now I know I was dead wrong. But I had only been there a few hours.' He is accurately recording your opinion?

FORD: I think he – I think he is.

C CLARKE: May we come, please, to B1,208.2[3]. Internment was implemented on 9th August. You describe on 19th August how 8 Brigade mounted an operation to remove the Bogside and Creggan barricades. You say: 'It was a failure and there was major Catholic reaction.'

FORD: I cannot really remember anything about this operation, excepting that it was a failure in that all the barricades went up again.

C CLARKE: You record that, thereafter, to avoid provocation, no routine military patrolling was carried out in the Bogside and Creggan. Am I right in thinking that that was in fact an approach that you disagreed with?

FORD: It was a unilateral decision by General Tuzo and he told me later that it was not just the strong views of the middle class Catholics who appealed to him to give them a chance to stop the rioting in the city, but that also he was particularly and especially persuaded by Chief Superintendent Lagan.

C CLARKE: In paragraph 3.1[5] of your statement, you then record that at [a] meeting on 6th October [1971] Sir Edward Heath, the prime minister, said that the first priority was the defeat of the gunmen using military means and the inevitable political consequences must be accepted.

On 26th October, you issued your directive for future internal security operations and the mission given to 8 Brigade was to progressively impose the rule of law on the Creggan and Bogside.

Would it be fair to say this represented a deliberate change of gear?

FORD: It was a change of gear, and in relation to the new instructions which had come down from above.

C CLARKE: Could we have on the screen G41.263, please. This is your appreciation of the situation of December 1971. 'Adopt a much more offensive attitude than in previous months.' Did you know that your recommendation had been approved by the Secretary of State?

FORD: Yes.

C CLARKE: Could we have on the screen G48.299, which is the report you made to the GOC [General Officer Commanding]. You say this: 'The weapons at our disposal, CS gas and baton rounds, are ineffective. I am coming to the conclusion that the minimum force necessary to achieve a restoration of law and order is to shoot selected ringleaders among the DYH [Derry Young Hooligans] after clear warnings have been issued.

'I believe we would be justified in using 7.62 millimetre bullets but in view of the devastating effects of this weapon and the danger of rounds killing more than the person aimed at, I believe we must consider issuing rifles adapted to fire high velocity .22 ammunition.'

The conclusion you were coming towards was that, after warning, selected ringleaders of the DYH should be shot, is that right?

FORD: I was suggesting – I have no recollection of this at all, of course – I was suggesting that this weapon which had apparently been developed by the Ministry of Defence in the UK for possible use in Northern Ireland. Of course, eventually, it would have to go to the Government who, no doubt, would seek legal advice.

C CLARKE: You say that .22 ammunition has been described somewhere in the Ministry of Defence as 'marginally lethal at two hundred yards'. What does 'marginally lethal' mean?

FORD: That is very interesting. I do not think any officer would really know. I saw this weapon being used to incapacitate and cause less casualties. The chance of killing anyone was much reduced once you introduced it.

C CLARKE: You were proposing that ringleaders should be shot after warning. It is right, is it not, that soldiers are taught to 'shoot to kill'?

FORD: Yes, with a 7.62.

C CLARKE: If they are taught to 'shoot to kill' by firing at a position on the body where the bullet is likely to kill them, the same is highly likely to arise even if they use a .22 bullet?

FORD: It is likely to arise, but less likely. There again, this was purely a first thought which needed detailed examination.

C CLARKE: I appreciate that, but I want to understand the nature of the proposal. It is that ringleaders should be shot by soldiers who are trained to 'shoot to kill' in circumstances where it is likely that people shot at will be killed. That is what it amounts to.

FORD: That is true, but less likely, much less, with a .22.

C CLARKE: If you fire a .22 at somebody, at fifty yards range, if you are attempting to kill him and are a well-trained soldier, you are likely to do so, are you not?

FORD: It depends on the accuracy of the weapon, and I know nothing about that.

C CLARKE: Did you appreciate that it was probably unlawful.

FORD: I do not think an idea is unlawful.

C CLARKE: Were you aware that in general soldiers are subject to the law as much as anybody else?

FORD: I was, yes.

C CLARKE: And are entitled to use such force as is reasonable in all the circumstances to protect either themselves or others whom it is their duty to protect?

FORD: But this might well become the only way they could carry out their duty.

C CLARKE: But this proposal was not limited to protecting soldiers or those whom it was their duty to protect. It was a proposal to give warnings that, unless they dispersed or something of the kind, ringleaders amongst the hooligans would be shot?

FORD: Yes.

C CLARKE: You then deal with the march. You say: 'It is the opinion of the senior commanders in Londonderry that, if the march takes place, however good the intentions of the NICRA may be, the Derry Young Hooligans, backed up by the gunmen, will undoubtedly take over control at an early stage.'

Were you aware of a civil rights march ever having been taken over by gunmen before?

FORD: Well, there had not been one in Londonderry.

C CLARKE: Did it ever occur to anybody that if the IRA or any other offshoot were to use the march as cover by sniping at the Army, they would be shooting themselves in the foot because it would emasculate the effect of a peaceful civil rights march, quite apart from endangering the lives of people who might be sympathetic towards them?

FORD: I am sure it did.

C CLARKE: Thank you, those are my questions.

MCDERMOTT: General Ford, I represent the family of the late Patrick Doherty. Might I ask you a little about your memory. You have absolutely no independent memory of the events of this day and you are relying entirely on the documents that have been provided?

FORD: That is correct.

MCDERMOTT: Mrs Doherty is present here, and of course this is the first opportunity that she has had of being in the same room as the Commander of Land Forces at the time. Can you give her any explanation as to what happened to her husband?

FORD: I am extremely sad that it happened, but sadly I can give no explanation as I did not see anything of that event.

MCDERMOTT: Did you foresee that thirteen citizens would be shot dead on the streets of their own city?

FORD: No, never.

MCDERMOTT: When you were writing out your own account of the events of that day, if B1126 could be put up for a moment, please, you say: 'At about 16.10 barrier 14 was lifted…it was about this stage that I heard shots fired from the direction of the Rossville Flats.'

At the bottom of the page: 'I spoke to CO 1 Para who confirmed my view that his troops had been fired upon and had returned fire.' I suggest to you that you could not possibly have had a proper view that the troops had been fired on first?

FORD: I had no view, but I meant my mental view. My mental view was that 1 Para would have been fired on first before they opened fire, because that is the normal way in which they would operate. I knew that the soldiers do not open fire without good reason. I therefore assumed the shooting had come from the other side, shall we say.

MCDERMOTT: That was an assumption on your part?

FORD: Yes.

SAVILLE: It would be the case, would it not, General Ford, from these diary entries as a whole, that you would not know who had fired first? Is that not right?

FORD: That is true, sir.

SAVILLE: I am a bit puzzled by this part of the diary: 'I spoke to CO 1 Para who confirmed my view…' because you did not know whether the troops had been fired on, or whether they had fired?

FORD: That is true, sir. I do not know why I wrote it that way. I had only a mental view. I saw nothing.

SAVILLE: It could be suggested, could it not, that you wrote that, General Ford, because it would assist the Army's case?

FORD: I hope I did not, sir, and I do not believe I did.

MCDERMOTT: Might X2.256.6 be put up on the screen, please. This is a transcript, General Ford, of a conversation between two Army officers.

Male Voice The whole thing's in chaos…obviously, I think it has gone badly wrong in the Rossville…the doctor's just been up the hospital and they are pulling stiffs out there as fast as they can get them out.

Male Voice There is nothing wrong with that.

Male Voice Well, there is because they are the wrong people…there is about fifteen killed by the Parachute Regiment in the Rossville area, they are all women, children, fuck knows what, and they are still going up there…I mean their Pigs are just full of bodies…

Male Voice The padre is a bit upset. He is going off to see the commander about all the ill-treatment.

Male Voice General Ford.

Male Voice He was lapping it up.

Male Voice Who was?

Male Voice Ford.

Male Voice Was he?

Male Voice Yeah…he said it was the best thing he had seen for a long time.

Were you lapping it up?

FORD: I was not.

MCDERMOTT: Do you have any comment to make about anything else that appears in that?

FORD: We do not know who they are and they are talking – well, quite honestly there is no truth in what they said at all. It is highly emotional and exaggerated.

MCDERMOTT: Thank you, those are my questions.

MANSFIELD: General Ford, I think I am the last one to ask you questions on behalf of families. I want to put two propositions to you. First, that what you had in mind for the operation on 30th January 1972 necessarily entailed a serious risk that far more unarmed civilians than gunmen would be killed. The corollary to that, it is proposition number two, it is astonishing throughout the time then and the thirty years since that you never managed to discover how such highly trained, disciplined, and focused troops managed to hit so many targets that were unarmed. Do I make the position clear?

FORD: You have made the position clear, yes.

MANSFIELD: You recall that you met, on a street corner, Colonel Wilford for the first time and he told you at that stage that the only rounds that had been fired by the Army were three. That was your recollection of what he told you, was it not?

FORD: Apparently, yes.

MANSFIELD: Then you, at some stage, are back at the observation post, there comes a time, having spoken to the TV reporters, you try to track down the commander of 8 Brigade, do you not?

FORD: I do.

MANSFIELD: And you do track him down?

FORD: Yes.

MANSFIELD: According to your third draft statement, you spend about an hour with him discussing matters?

FORD: That is true, yes.

MANSFIELD: Did you keep any notes?

FORD: No notes at all.

MANSFIELD: Why not?

FORD: I may have kept notes, but they have been destroyed.

SAVILLE: Was it your practice to keep notes?

FORD: I normally kept notes of all important conversations, yes sir.

SAVILLE: This would be an important conversation, would it not?

FORD: Yes, it would be, sir.

MANSFIELD: I suggest from this very early stage, you were not interested in the truth, which is why you did not keep a note?

FORD: That is untrue.

MANSFIELD: I want to move forward to 1998. The position was this: the Prime Minister said that those who died should be regarded as innocent of any allegation that they were shot while handling firearms or explosives. That was echoed in rather stronger terms by Mr Hague: 'I believe it was right for my right honourable friend, the member for Huntingdon, Mr Major when he was prime minister, to say that those who died on Bloody Sunday were innocent victims of the troubles, and the prime minister has today reaffirmed the statement of my right honourable friend.' Therefore three leading politicians were saying in 1998 that the victims were in fact not gunmen, nailbombers, petrol bombers, do you follow?

FORD: I do follow.

MANSFIELD: That must have concerned you in 1998?

FORD: Actually, it did concern me, if I remember correctly, because it seemed to me that they were jumping the gun, as it were, before the work of this Tribunal.

MANSFIELD: Why were the thirteen shot at by paratroopers?

FORD: I do not know. That is what this Inquiry is presumably going to find out?

MANSFIELD: This Inquiry has one duty, I suggest you have another: it has always been your duty as Commander of Land Forces, to be able to come here where there are relatives, and in Derry where they are sitting now watching the screens, so that you finally would be in a position to explain why thirteen unarmed civilians were shot [dead] by paratroopers?

FORD: I am not in a position to explain why thirteen apparently unarmed people were shot by the paratroopers. It is obviously a long and complex problem.

MANSFIELD: I suggest to you there is no complexity and I will make it clear why. In the case of Mr McGuigan, he was a man in his early forties, he had six children, he was standing in the street sheltering by a telephone kiosk, he was not in a firefight. He held up a white handkerchief in order to go the rescue of someone else and was shot through the back of the head.

Did you know of any of that?

FORD: I did not know, no. I am very saddened to hear of that, of course I am.

MANSFIELD: And it has nothing to do with a firefight, do you appreciate –

FORD: I do not agree. I do not agree.

MANSFIELD: If you do not agree, General Ford, how is it that you know something the rest of us do not?

FORD: All the evidence I have seen indicates there was a firefight, for instance –

MANSFIELD: Around a telephone box at the end of the Rossville Flats?

FORD: I do not know where the firefight took place.

MANSFIELD: If you do not know where the firefight took place, why do you disagree with what I have just put to you?

FORD: I am talking about the position in general.

MANSFIELD: You know nothing about the position in general, do you?

FORD: Yes.

MANSFIELD: Mr Nash, Alex Nash, fifty-two at the time, a family man, also shot but not dead, going to the rescue of his son with his arm in the air, requesting the shooting to stop. Did you know that?

FORD: I am greatly saddened by what you have just told me.

MANSFIELD: General Ford, what I put simply is: you have never taken the slightest interest in the victims, have you?

FORD: Of course I have.

MAJOR GENERAL ANDREW MACLELLAN
19 – 25 NOVEMBER 2002

C CLARKE: If we look at your statement, you describe how you took over command of 8th Infantry Brigade on 27th October 1971. I presume that you became aware on takeover, that initially, after internment was introduced in August 1971, General Tuzo had tried a softer approach in Londonderry?

MACLELLAN: I was aware.

C CLARKE: Do you recollect expressing generally a gloomy view of things?

MACLELLAN: I recollect describing the situation as I saw it, but I personally regarded it as unacceptable that we should have a no-go area in a third of a city in the UK, a third of a city the size of Winchester if you like, and it was simply impossible to do anything about it.

C CLARKE: G48.299, paragraph 6. General Ford expresses to General Tuzo this proposition: 'I am coming to the conclusion that the minimum force necessary to achieve a restoration of law and order is to shoot selected ringleaders amongst the DYH [Derry Young Hooligans], after clear warnings have been issued.'

Did General Ford discuss with you or did you otherwise become aware that he was coming to [this] conclusion?

MACLELLAN: No.

C CLARKE: You say in your statement to this Tribunal, that had you been asked about the proposal to adapt 7.62 weapons to fire high velocity .22 ammunition, you would have advised strongly against its adoption?

MACLELLAN: Yes.

C CLARKE: Why is that?

MACLELLAN: I believe I was disturbed by the fact that to shoot perhaps a fifteen-year-old boy throwing stones would not have a helpful effect in our ultimate political or military aim of trying to encourage the moderates to alienate the extremists.

C CLARKE: I think it follows you never authorised their use?

MACLELLAN: I don't think they ever were used.

C CLARKE: You met with [chief superintendent] Lagan and his deputy [to debate] how best to deal with the march. Following the meeting, you sent a signal to [General Ford]. G70A.411.02. It records that [Lagan] believes that massive confrontation with the security forces would: 'shatter such peace as is left in the city, create intense violence and remove last vestiges of moderate goodwill. He urges identification and photographs followed by usual court proceedings rather than direct confrontation.' What was your view?

MACLELLAN: It was pie in the sky, because if you brought someone to court you would have to have witnesses, you would have to get them out of the Bogside and Creggan, which would have been a major operation and I just thought it was an impractical suggestion.

C CLARKE: You decribe how you were given a direct order by General Ford to launch an arrest operation if the soldiers were attacked by the hooligans and he specifially allotted 1 Para for the task. Was there any discussion about the allocation of 1 Para for the task?

MACLELLAN: This was not a sort of debating association. It was what the Army would call an orders group, he would say: 'This is what you are going to do – boom, boom, boom.'

C CLARKE: Do you remember whether there was any discussion about how the arrest operation was to be affected.

MACLELLAN: Do you mean the moment the operation was launched?

C CLARKE: Yes, the mechanics.

MACLELLAN: Can I try and explain that when you, in military terms, if you issue an operation order, that is really to get everybody to the start line, to the off. But as I think von Clausewitz said, no plan survives first contact.

C CLARKE: If we look at B1279.034, you record this: 'The General's plan was 1 Para should go round behind the rioters, to stop them running away, to arrest those who were causing trouble at the barriers.' 1 Para would have to get behind the rioters if they were going to have any chance of arresting them in any sufficient numbers, is that right?

MACLELLAN: He referred to a scoop-up, which implies a sort of pincer movement behind, as you are implying.

SAVILLE: What appears to be puzzling is how are you going to get round behind the hooligans in order to arrest them, the corollary of that being, on the face of it, there does not seem to have been much to stop the hooligans simply running south into the Bogside and escaping in the manner which one might have expected.

MACLELLAN: Yes. (*Pause.*)

SAVILLE: You see –

MACLELLAN: I see what you are getting at, sir, yes. What I do not see is the correct reply, at the moment. I think all I can say is that one can merely give a concept and then the man on the ground has to do as best he can.

C CLARKE: One of the matters the Tribunal may have to address is whether this was a plan that was incapable of successful conclusion because, if you thought about it, the notion that you could actually get behind the rioters by going from the places where the troops were, was impossible, or very difficult at any rate. What had been contemplated originally, was it not, was that the arrest operation would be conducted on foot?

MACLELLAN: It was conducted on foot.

C CLARKE: Only in the sense that you cannot actually arrest somebody when you are in a Pig?

MACLELLAN: They did not, they got out.

C CLARKE: The operational order would have been sent to the Ministry of Defence in London, is that right?

MACLELLAN: I assumed it would have gone back.

C CLARKE: If we look at B1232, in this draft of a statement for the purpose of Lord Widgery's Inquiry, you expressed yourself as follows:

'I was prepared to allow the maximum possible separation of the hooligans from the main body of the NICRA marchers, even if this meant a reduction in the number of arrests.' Is that an accurate depiction of your views?

MACLELLAN: Yes, I can explain it further if you wish.

C CLARKE: Add any qualification or observation you would like.

MACLELLAN: One thing about the march was that it was highly likely to contain members of the families or relations of the extremists, and it seemed to me they would be, so to speak, shooting themselves in the foot if they used the march as cover and had their own casualties.

C CLARKE: I want to come, if I may, to the events of the day. You have said for this exercise ever to take place at all that there should be a wide separation between the arrest force and innocent civilians; that is right, is it not?

MACLELLAN: That is right, yes.

C CLARKE: And the position, I have to suggest to you, is that on the information that was available to you [at HQ] when you gave the order that you gave, you had no means of telling whether there was a wide separation or not?

MACLELLAN: I, rightly or wrongly, was under the impression that adequate separation had been achieved.

C CLARKE: May we come to the actual orders themselves. Could we have on the screen W47? This is the 8 Brigade log which records: 'Orders given to 1 Para at 1607 hours for one unit of 1 Para to do scoop-up through barrier 14. Not to conduct running battle down Rossville Street.'

The log appears to indicate that the order you gave was for one unit of 1 Para to do a scoop operation through barrier 14, and that was it?

MACLELLAN: My recollection is that I authorised the arrest operation to start, and that the plan for how it was conducted was that of CO 1 Para.

SAVILLE: Does that last answer mean, General MacLellan, you did not know what the plan was?

MACLELLAN: I did not know the detailed plan, sir, no.

SAVILLE: As I understand it your evidence is that your recollection is that you simply, in effect, said to 1 Para: carry out your plan, is that right?

MACLELLAN: That is in effect –

SAVILLE: Without knowing what the plan was?

MACLELLAN: Yes, sir.

SAVILLE: The evidence you have given us is that, at five to four when you get the request, you were not satisfied that separation had taken place. At about ten minutes past four, according to the Brigade log, an order is given which is in almost precisely the same terms as the request. If you were so keen, as you say you were on separation, you could not have simply given an order to 1 Para to carry out whatever arrest operation they had in mind unless you knew what it was? Do you see what I am getting at?

MACLELLAN: I think I do, sir, yes.

C CLARKE: If the order was simply in general terms, any number of companies could go almost anywhere?

MACLELLAN: As regards going 'almost anywhere', they were instructed not to get sucked in. But if the circumstances altered – I mean, if firing started and so on, then the whole situation changed.

C CLARKE: The aim of the operation was to arrest as many hooligans as possible. The operation was only to be launched, in whole or in part, on your orders?

MACLELLAN: Correct.

C CLARKE: So there were limits on what Colonel Wilford could do. They were that C Company was to go through William Street and pick up rioters and arrest them. That is something quite different from driving through [the] barrier down into Rossville Street and the wasteground to the side of it?

MACLELLAN: Yes.

C CLARKE: I think this is right, is it not, that when you gave the order you had no idea, in fact, that ten vehicles would go through [another] barrier, is that right?

MACLELLAN: That is right.

C CLARKE: You did not know that one of the vehicles would go as far as the car park of the Rossville Flats?

MACLELLAN: That is right.

C CLARKE: One of the things you were concerned about was the importance of legality in the making of arrests, do you remember that?

MACLELLAN: Yes, I remember the –

C CLARKE: That means, does it not, that soldiers should only arrest those who they could see, or who they had seen, were guilty of riotous behaviour or the like?

MACLELLAN: Yes.

C CLARKE: One effect of them arresting people in the car park of the Rossville Flats is that they would have no chance of determining he – or possibly she – had been rioting, would they?

MACLELLAN: I have not read the accounts or the evidence given by soldiers, so I do not know what they all say.

C CLARKE: If what you see is somebody running away, that does not actually tell you they are part of a rioting crowd, does it?

MACLELLAN: No, it does not, but it implies they might have been, would it not? Why would they have been running away otherwise?

C CLARKE: Because ten rather fast-moving vehicles were driving down a principal street.

MACLELLAN: Yes, I see what you are getting at, yes. Yes, I accept your point.

C CLARKE: You have made it plain that you were anxious for there to be a wide separation between marchers and rioters. The effect of driving down Little James Street is that you overtake people, and you have the effect of destroying at a stroke the separation which was the precondition of the operation taking place in the first place, do you not?

MACLELLAN: I think the short answer is: 'Yes'.

C CLARKE: It looks as if from start to finish of whatever happened, Brigade [HQ] did not have any information as to what was going on?

MACLELLAN: I think that is true.

C CLARKE: If the Paras had not been used on this occasion, do you think that the outcome would have been different?

MACLELLAN: If there had been no arrest operation I assume that we would have contained the march, which would have gone off peacefully. I mean, that is hindsight.

C CLARKE: Could we have a look at B1279.003.014, this is part of [the journalist] Hamill's notes. He records you as saying:

'Where it all went wrong was at the arrest operation. It was carried out by 1 Para. These were General Ford's favourite "shock troops" and he stood there and urged them to "go and get them". The Paras cry anyway was "go, go"…'

MACLELLAN: Well, I think each battalion has a character of its own.

SAVILLE: Before we leave this page, look at the last sentence on that page, General MacLellan.

'My orders were specifically not to allow troops to get sucked into the Bogside.'

One reading of that would be that you accepted that troops had, to use your own words, 'got sucked into the Bogside', contrary to your orders. Would that be a misunderstanding of what you were saying?

MACLELLAN: I am really, I think now looking back at this carefully, was putting in other words the final order, that they were not to conduct a running battle or to get sucked in and –

SAVILLE: Not to conduct a running battle down Rossville Street but what, on one view at least, would seem to be the case, is that they did almost precisely the opposite, and did conduct a running battle down Rossville Street by going through a different barrier and straight down Rossville Street in vehicles. Is that view quite misconceived?

MACLELLAN: I think that – sorry, sir. I think, as you say, that they went further than I had expected.

SAVILLE: It is a bit more than that. Not further than you expected, it is they did something which, on the face of it, was contrary to your order?

MACLELLAN: Why I have been hedging my answers to an extent on this is that once a tactical battle had started, if they had been shot at, for example, then they had to react in accordance with the circumstances.

SAVILLE: I follow that, but the reason why they had to react was because they disobeyed your orders and went deep into the Bogside. They were not going deep into the Bogside because they were being shot at.

MACLELLAN: No, I accept that.

SAVILLE: They went in trucks deep into the Bogside and on one view at least, there started a running battle precisely contrary to your instructions.

MACLELLAN: That is correct. I mean, I am agreeing with your proposition.

SAVILLE: Ms McDermott?

MCDERMOTT: I represent the family of the late Patrick Doherty. I want to refer you to one sentence in the Hamill interview. You say: 'Maybe my policy was considered too soft. Whitelaw got it in the neck constantly.'

MACLELLAN: I cannot remember now what the background to that remark was.

SAVILLE: I think Ms McDermott's question to you is that the new CLF [Commander of Land Forces] General Ford, when he arrived, was of the view that the softer approach was one that he was not going to adopt?

MACLELLAN: I think that is true, sir, yes. I mean my war was with people who tried to shoot the soldiers and to blow up the premises, not with people who may have thoroughly disapproved of the Stormont Government and the Army and the rest of it, but they were non-violent people. I was, so to speak, a policeman dealing with the law breakers, not with people's political views.

MCDERMOTT: I will move on and ask you about your order not to conduct a running battle down Rossville Street. Did you make any inquiries as to why your order was disobeyed?

MACLELLAN: No.

MCDERMOTT: Why not?

MACLELLAN: I was not aware at the time that it had been disobeyed. I mean, the Inquiry was done by Lord Widgery, if you recall, and that was who was going to inquire into these matters.

MCDERMOTT: After Lord Widgery's Inquiry was over, you were obviously aware by then, if not before, that your order had been disobeyed. Did you make inquiries at that stage?

MACLELLAN: I accepted Lord Widgery's findings.

COLONEL DEREK WILFORD
25 MARCH – 10 APRIL 2003

C CLARKE: Colonel Wilford, on 21st July 1971, you became the commanding officer of the 1st Battalion of the Parachute Regiment, then on a two-year tour based at Belfast. Would it be fair to say that the 1st Battalion of the Parachute Regiment would go in fast, and in strength, and hard when a local battalion needed reinforcement?

WILFORD: When we were directed to do so, yes.

C CLARKE: At this stage, you had never been to Londonderry, that is right?

WILFORD: No, I had not.

C CLARKE: Could we have a look, please, at B1110.125. This is part of the order that deals with the task of 1 Para, 'to conduct a scoop-up operation of as many hooligans and rioters as possible'.

When you received this order, did anybody discuss with you how you might successfully arrest as many hooligans and rioters as possible?

WILFORD: No. Whatever happened it would require a pincer movement if I was going to make arrests.

C CLARKE: Can you help me on this? How in practice did you think you could get behind the rioters. They would seem to have means of escape down Rossville Street to the wasteground. So that as soon as they could see you coming, they could run away, without a great deal of difficulty.

WILFORD: Nothing is perfect in this world of riots; all sorts of things can happen. And to have a fixed plan, of course, would be pointless. You have to be absolutely flexible.

C CLARKE: Did you realise that if [the Para's] Support Company were to drive down Rossville Street the likely effect would be that the arresting soldiers, far from being separated from peaceful marchers would become embroiled with them?

WILFORD: No, I did not see that as a possibility.

C CLARKE: Why not?

WILFORD: Because I recognised that in fact, once we went through the barriers after the people, at the rioters, this situation would not prevail. There might have been some hangers-on; people, if you like gawping. There are always gawpers, I am afraid, on the edge of a riot.

C CLARKE: If what you do is to take [the Para's] Support Company in vehicles down there, the likely result of that, is it not, is that soldiers coming out of those Pigs are going to find themselves among people who may have absolutely nothing to do with rioting at barrier 12 or 14?

WILFORD: You have to remember that my deployment[s] were dependent on the brigade commander's say-so.

SAVILLE: Your evidence is that you were going to use troops through both barriers?

WILFORD: Well, sir, I have to say that when people are rioting, there is a kind of mesmeric effect with rioters and they take courage from each other and at that time, of course, they are absolutely at their most dangerous, so in order to destroy that danger one has to go in very, very hard and very, very fast and break up that cohesion.

C CLARKE: Are you aware of the evidence Brigadier MacLellan has given to this Tribunal?

WILFORD: No, I am not, I am not clear, I do not know.

C CLARKE: I think I ought to tell you what it is. He was unaware of the motorised operation going through barrier 12 and regarded going down to the Rossville Flats as a breach of that order because it involved getting sucked in and mixing up with peaceful marchers. You were aware of that evidence?

WILFORD: No, I was not.

C CLARKE: Could we look, please, at B1110.016. This is a transcript of a radio interview which took place shortly after Bloody Sunday on the *World at One*. In the course of it you are recorded as saying this: 'We got sniper fire. Certainly, I personally saw a man with an M1 carbine on the balcony of a flat. It was also highly inaccurate and indiscriminate firing from the other side.'

You were questioned about this in your evidence to Lord Widgery. Do have any recollection of this now?

WILFORD: (*Witness shaking head.*) No, no. I mean, I recollect what I said because I have looked at the Widgery thing again, but that is all. I do recall hearing M1 carbine shots passing over my head, or close to me, and that is it, that is all I recall.

C CLARKE: Do you recollect in which block of flats was the balcony in which you thought you saw a man with an M1 carbine?

WILFORD: No, I do not, and I think in fact I got muddled up over that.

C CLARKE: That looks rather as if you had not seen the man?

WILFORD: Seen the man himself, yes, yes it does.

C CLARKE: You had not seen the circumstances in which any of the thirteen were killed or the fourteen injured on Bloody Sunday?

WILFORD: No.

C CLARKE: But your position is this, is it not: you cannot believe that any of your soldiers were guilty of misconduct or worse?

WILFORD: That is so.

C CLARKE: And it is on that basis, belief but not knowledge, that you have loyally said that your soldiers behaved admirably?

WILFORD: Yes.

C CLARKE: I want to come, if I may, to certain statements of yours in the immediate aftermath of 30th January. Could we have a look, please, at B1107. It is a transcript of what was broadcast by ITN.

Question But what exactly was seen by you or your company commander before your men opened up?

Answer A man with a Thompson sub-machine gun was seen from the area of the Rossville Flats. He came round the corner and fired in indiscriminate bursts of fifteen to twenty-five rounds which hit the ground in front of the company commander. They then dived for cover – for cover, and returned fire.

That is not something that you had witnessed yourself, is it?

WILFORD: No, it is not.

C CLARKE: Those are my questions.

SAVILLE: Mr Mansfield.

MANSFIELD: (*To WILFORD.*) You are prone, Colonel Wilford, do you agree, from time to time, to make false assertions, are you not?

WILFORD: I do not think that is fair.

MANSFIELD: Do you not?

WILFORD: No.

MANSFIELD: Your evidence to Widgery, and since, is that you ran out of the observation point and you are at the junction, Aggro Corner, and it has only taken you two or three minutes to get there?

WILFORD: Yes. If I said it at the time, yes, that is okay.

MANSFIELD: Which means that you must have been in the Rossville area in a position to see the majority of the gun battle which takes place, from seventeen minutes past four, you must have been there?

WILFORD: Well, I did not see it.

MANSFIELD: Does it come to this; that you cannot explain why you did not see effectively ninety-nine per cent of what is described in this gun battle?

WILFORD: I think there is one explanation, and it is simply this: that being a soldier on – in this sort of situation, there is a lot of noise, there was a lot of shooting, there were a lot of bangs, there was a lot of shouting, there was a lot of screaming. The answer is: I did not see ninety per cent, I think you said –

MANSFIELD: Ninety-nine per cent?

WILFORD: Ninety-nine per cent – no, please, I did not see ninety-nine per cent of this action.

MANSFIELD: On the log – and there is no dispute about this – there are over one hundred rounds fired in Rossville Street, in the Rossville Street area, by your troops. Yet your statement and your evidence since has been that you only saw one soldier firing?

WILFORD: Yes.

MANSFIELD: And effectively you did not hear, other than that one, any SLR firing.

WILFORD: Not that I recall.

MANSFIELD: You managed to tell the radio at the time that you had actually seen a man with a carbine on a balcony of Rossville Flats, did you not?

WILFORD: Yes, I did.

MANSFIELD: That was not true, was it?

WILFORD: Well, apparently not, no.

MANSFIELD: I want to ask you now, because this may be one of the last opportunities you have: do you now accept that those who were killed – and I represent two of the ones who were killed and two who were injured – were innocent, do you accept that now?

WILFORD: I cannot accept anything, because I do not have the evidence.

MANSFIELD: You are obviously not aware that what has been conceded on your behalf is that the identified civilians who were killed were not armed terrorists, did you know that?

WILFORD: No I did not know that.

GLASGOW: Could I deal with the matter that my learned friend Mr Mansfield put to you about the concession that had been made on your behalf. You should know that the document included the statement, I [will] just read it to you:

'That those of our clients [soldiers] who fired live rounds aimed and shot at, and only at, those whom they believed to be gunmen or nail bombers threatening lethal violence to them or others. However, it does not follow that those who have been identified as having been killed or wounded on 30th January 1972 were themselves gunmen or nail bombers.'

Witness nodding.

'What none of our clients [the soldiers] did was to conceive or to carry out any plan to provoke violence or to take advantage of the violence which we will say they undoubtedly encountered, and none of them did anything which he believed was other than fully and lawfully justified by that violence.'

We shall see whether or not it is fair or proper to express that conclusion at this stage, that there were no gunmen or a bomber on that day. Accordingly, we are not instructed to contend that those individuals who have been identified were armed with lethal weapons.

Do you have any problem with that?

WILFORD: No, I do not.

SOLDIER S
14 – 15 MAY 2003

SAVILLE: Soldier S, as we have to call you, if you look across to your left, you can see who is talking to you. I am the chairman. The questions in the main will come from the barristers, they are the people in front of me.

C CLARKE: May we go to B724.003, you describe in paragraph 18 how you were engaged in exchanges with a gunman or gunmen and that your only recollection is that the exchange was over quickly. Do you have any recollection now of what it was that caused you to fire?

SOLDIER S: Do I have a recollection now?

C CLARKE: Yes, that is my question.

SOLDIER S: No.

C CLARKE: Let us look at your contemporaneous statements, by which I mean the statements made in 1972.

SOLDIER S: Excuse me, sir, can I just stop you there?

C CLARKE: Yes?

SOLDIER S: I want to make a little bit of a statement myself about those statements, if I may.

C CLARKE: Say anything you want.

SOLDIER S: Well those statements were made when I was an eighteen-year-old soldier on the day of Bloody Sunday. They were sort of – there are definite inaccuracies in those statements and I am not proud of that fact and I am conceding to the fact that those statements are inaccurate. Making a statement to the RMP [Royal Military Police] can be quite a frightening affair.

C CLARKE: Thank you for that. In the light of that I think we will have to go through the statements quite carefully so that you can tell us what is inaccurate and what is not. If you look at B692. The sentence reads as follows: 'nail bombs and acid bombs were thrown from the top of flats on the men from my unit who were making arrests'.

SOLDIER S: Yes, I think maybe that is, that is something that is an inaccuracy and I would apologise for that.

C CLARKE: Can we just – did you want –

SOLDIER S: I was just going to say I am just saying that that is an inaccuracy that has got in there from maybe an RMP maybe sort of trying to collate some evidence of several soldiers together.

C CLARKE: Your evidence was of hearing gunfire before you engaged with the gunman between block 1 and block 2?

SOLDIER S: Yes.

C CLARKE: It is correct, that you have now no actual recollection of firing twelve shots, four bursts of three at thirty second intervals, injuring one man twice or two men once?

SOLDIER S: No, I have no recollection of it now, no.

C CLARKE: Could we then go to B703 which is your second statement to the RMP. There you said this: 'I saw a gunman open fire from a ground floor window from the south-east corner of block 1 of the flats. He fired about six shots directed at members of the company who were deployed around one of our APCs.' Is that a truthful account or not?

SOLDIER S: Well, first of all, I think that part of that is something that the RMPs maybe – obviously not deliberately, but there is an inaccuracy there so far as the direction and the distance anyway. There are a lot of inaccuracies in that statement.

C CLARKE: What I would like to know is whether that was your true recollection at the time or whether you are saying something that was put into your mouth?

SOLDIER S: Well, I am, I am not saying that it was put into my mouth, but I am saying that things may have been altered to, to suit things at the time – the RMPs, I mean, I think you have to understand that when you are an eighteen-year-old soldier at the time and the RMP come along and they tell you: this is what, you know, actually happened to you or – but if I wanted to make some sort of supplementary statement, you know, they would more or less tell you to shut up and be quiet.

C CLARKE: Can the Tribunal treat as reliable the basic fact of your having seen a gunman open fire with about six shots from a ground floor window in the south-east corner of the flats?

SOLDIER S: (*Pause.*) No.

C CLARKE: Could we have P627. Here is one of the photographs of the scene which in fact shows Father Daly, as he then was, with two others by the body of a boy named Jack Duddy. Do you have any recollection of seeing something like that?

SOLDIER S: It is a dreadful scene. I am sorry, but I do not have any recollection of it, dreadful as it is.

C CLARKE: There is a large body of evidence that Jack Duddy was shot as he was running with other people towards the exits from the flats. Is it possible that you shot towards a crowd of people –

SOLDIER S: No.

C CLARKE: – and caught him?

SOLDIER S: No.

C CLARKE: Very shortly after this photograph was taken, Michael Bridge fell, shot in the leg. We know that he was shot in the leg, he has given evidence to this Inquiry. Did you witness somebody being shot in the car park?

SOLDIER S: I do not believe so, no. No, I cannot say that I – to be honest, I do not know what I said in my Widgery evidence on that, but I do not recall it sir, I am sorry.

C CLARKE: Those are my questions.

MACDONALD: Soldier S, my name is MacDonald and I represent some of the families of those who were killed or wounded on Bloody Sunday. Among those that I represent are the family of Jack Duddy who was seventeen on Bloody Sunday and was shot dead in the courtyard of Rossville Flats. His sister, Kay, and his brother, Gerry, are here today.

SOLDIER S: Yes, sir.

MACDONALD: Can I ask you whether you regret anything that you personally did on Bloody Sunday?

SOLDIER S: I regret the whole incident, yes. Can I just – will you bear with me a moment, please, sir, even the man that I identified as a gunman, even if I did hit him and kill him, it is still a tragedy to his family, is it not, it is still – somebody grieved him? This is a tragedy, a tragedy for everybody. I realise that and I am sorry that innocent people got killed.

MACDONALD: In your statement at B724.012, the very bottom of the page, you talk about nail bombs and acid bombs being thrown from the top of the flats. That was false, was it not. You did not see any nail bombs or acid bombs being thrown?

SOLDIER S: I would not say it was false. It is inaccurate.

MACDONALD: It is inaccurate because it did not happen, did it?

SOLDIER S: Things were being thrown from the top of the flats.

MACDONALD: You did not see any nail bombs or acid bombs being thrown, did you?

SOLDIER S: I saw objects being thrown.

MACDONALD: Did you see any nail bombs or acid bombs?

SOLDIER S: No, I did not.

MACDONALD: Why did you suggest these things?

SOLDIER S: Because of the nature of the way the things were done at the time.

MACDONALD: They said: Look, Soldier S, you saw nail bombs and acid bombs, did you not, just put it in your statement. Is that what happened?

SOLDIER S: Probably.

MACDONALD: Yes, and because you were eighteen at the time you allowed yourself to sign this statement when you knew you had not actually seen nail bombs or acid bombs?

SOLDIER S: I would say that is a fair assumption.

MACDONALD: You left the Parachute Regiment shortly after Bloody Sunday?

SOLDIER S: Yes.

MACDONALD: Why was that?

SOLDIER S: I left to join another unit.

MACDONALD: You have said you were injured in a firefight in the Middle East. I am not going to probe this in such a way as to require you to expose details of special forces, but can we take it you were not involved in a separatist war as a mercenary?

SOLDIER S: Yes, you may – yes.

MACDONALD: But as a member of the British Army?

SOLDIER S: That is correct.

MACDONALD: And you were involved in firing thousands of rounds in total?

SOLDIER S: Yes.

MACDONALD: Do you know how many people you killed?

SOLDIER S: (*Pause.*)

SAVILLE: We have to be a bit careful.

MACDONALD: Have you in fact killed lots of people?

SOLDIER S: (*Pause.*)

MACDONALD: Have you?

SOLDIER S: Yes.

MACDONALD: On 30th January 1972 you had no compunction about shooting and killing civilians.

SOLDIER S: That is not true.

MACDONALD: And I suggest that you fired twelve shots at least on this day in circumstances which are so indefensible that you had to invent a ridiculous story about how you discharged your twelve rounds?

SOLDIER S: No.

SOLDIER F
1 – 2 OCTOBER 2003

Sworn.

(SAVILLE: Will people sit down. If people want to have a conversation, will they please go outside at once.)

C CLARKE: [Soldier F], according to your evidence to Lord Widgery, you fired thirteen rounds on Bloody Sunday. Had you fired as many as those before in an operation?

SOLDIER F: No.

C CLARKE: This must, therefore, must it not, have been a pretty dramatic day?

SOLDIER F: It was, yes.

C CLARKE: And are you being truthful when you say that you remember practically nothing whatever about it?

SOLDIER F: That is correct.

C CLARKE: Were you not told that there was going to be a big civil rights march and that rioting might take place and that 1 Para were to be used as an arrest force if it did?

SOLDIER F: I cannot remember.

C CLARKE: You cannot remember even that?

SOLDIER F: No.

C CLARKE: Do you remember receiving any orders from anybody before you started moving down Rossville Street?

SOLDIER F: No.

C CLARKE: This is the first statement that you made to the Royal Military Police [in 1972]: 'We advanced about thirty yards and came under sniper fire. These shots came from the direction of Rossville Flats.'

> Pausing there, the account which you gave to the military police was of coming under sniper fire from the direction of the flats as you advanced and coming under further fire from the flats as you took up a position. Do you have any recollection at all of that now?

SOLDIER F: I know obviously that this is what I saw at the time and the statement I made, but I cannot recall that now at all.

C CLARKE: You refer to a wall at a building known as Kells Walk. Do you have any recollection of firing and killing someone from that wall?

SOLDIER F: No, I do not.

C CLARKE: Do you have any recollection of receiving, when you were at Kells Walk, any orders from anybody to fire?

SOLDIER F: No.

C CLARKE: Do have any recollection now of approximately how many times you fired your weapon?

SOLDIER F: No, I do not.

C CLARKE: We know that in this area at least seven people were killed or wounded?

SOLDIER F: Yes.

C CLARKE: That is something that you must have seen happening, must you not?

SOLDIER F: I do not remember.

C CLARKE: May we have on the screen, photograph P728. The man who was shot at the base of block 1 of the Rossville Flats is the man in the foreground of the photograph, Bernard McGuigan. Do you recognise that scene?

SOLDIER F: No.

C CLARKE: Did you shoot that man?

SOLDIER F: I said in my statement, I did, but I do not remember it.

C CLARKE: You did not say in your statement that you shot Bernard McGuigan, you said that you shot a man with a pistol at the far end of the Rossville Flats.

SOLDIER F: Yes.

C CLARKE: Are you saying you shot this man?

SOLDIER F: I am not sure.

C CLARKE: Could we have B1565.047 please. This is [Soldier] 027's statement where he is dealing with events in the back of the Pig. What he says to the Tribunal is this: 'The mood in the back of the Pig was not so much euphoria as a release of tension. There was almost a silence and a sort of a feeling of "bloody hell what happened there". If you think there has been a transgression you hang together and look for way of protecting yourself. There was already a recognition that there was a problem that had to be explained away.'

Was that the atmosphere and the feeling amongst the platoon at the end of the day?

SOLDIER F: No, I do not remember.

C CLARKE: You do not remember?

SOLDIER F: No.

C CLARKE: Are you saying that may well have been the position?

SOLDIER F: No. But, um, I do not think that would have happened, but I cannot remember that instance anyway.

C CLARKE: Thank you, those are my questions.

MANSFIELD: I represent the family of Bernard McGuigan shot dead at the end of block 1 of the Rossville Flats. You were the only soldier, as far as you were aware firing towards the south of the Rossville Flats?

SOLDIER F: Yes.

MANSFIELD: I would like clarification from you now: you did shoot Barney McGuigan, did you not?

SOLDIER F: The person I shot was the man with the pistol.

MANSFIELD: Why did you presume he was the man with the pistol? Or is that the way you operated on the day?

SOLDIER F: I did not operate on the day any way. I was under the impression that photograph I was shown was the person who had the pistol, that was the impression I was under.

MANSFIELD: All right, I will ask it one more time only: from where did you get that impression?

SOLDIER F: That is what the impression I got, what I had formed in my mind, that the person who I had shot with the pistol.

MANSFIELD: Could we have on the screen, please, [P] 818. I suggest you can see there in the faces of these unarmed civilians the terror being inflicted, I suggest, by you. You can you see it, can you not?

SOLDIER F: I see the picture, yes.

MANSFIELD: Come on, I am only asking for a very obvious comment. Fear, terror, upset, anguish; it is all there, is it not?

SOLDIER F: Yes.

MANSFIELD: There are several who have given evidence. One of them, her name is Geraldine McBride, provided a statement to the Inquiry of what she saw because she knew Barney McGuigan. Could we have AM45.5, please. I am going to read it with you. Paragraph 25: 'Barney McGuigan, one of the men huddled at the wall with me was a community man and was generally looked up to. After a short time, Mr McGuigan said that he could not stand the sound of the [wounded] man calling any longer and that if he went out waving a white hanky, they would not shoot at him. We tried to dissuade him from going out. We told him they would shoot him. However, he was brave and he stepped away from us holding the white hanky in his hand. He kept looking back towards us. I could see bullets going past us and Mr McGuigan from all directions.'

I do not wish to read the next paragraph out in public, it is there for you to see. Would you read that to yourself, please?

Pause.

SOLDIER F: Yes.

MANSFIELD: You will accept, I think, that the injury suffered by this man who had no more than a handkerchief in his hand, was truly horrific; was it not?

SOLDIER F: Yes.

MANSFIELD: That is the result of what you did. I am going to ask you because, as you fully recognise and have been informed many times, it is virtually the last occasion this family can expect from you, at least a recognition of what you have done; are you prepared to make that recognition?

SOLDIER F: As I have said in my previous statements, the person I shot from that corner had a pistol in his hand; that was it.

MANSFIELD: If you have noticed, I have not relied on a memory that does not exist; you do not have a memory, do you, do you?

SOLDIER F: If you say so, yes.

MANSFIELD: No, you have said so.

SOLDIER F: At that particular time I have no recollection of it, that is correct.

MANSFIELD: If you have no recollection, there is no way that you can stand here today and suggest you did not shoot this man, Mr McGuigan, is there?

SOLDIER F: No.

MANSFIELD: Would you, for the benefit of his wife, who is here and his six children, finally accept and recognise that is what you did, are you happy to, or are you prepared to, at least accept that?

SOLDIER F: Yes.

MANSFIELD: When you came to make your first statement you did not mention this at all. You left it out, I suggest, not because you had forgotten, but because you recognised that what you had done in killing the man with no pistol, but only a handkerchief really could not be justified, that is why it was left out, was it not?

SOLDIER F: Not in my opinion, no.

MANSFIELD: Not in your opinion.

People crying, leaving gallery.

SAVILLE: Just wait one moment, Mr Mansfield.

MANSFIELD: You were not prepared to face them, but you are today?

SOLDIER F: Yes.

MANSFIELD: I say on behalf of the family they are grateful that you have done that, but you do recognise that if you shot an unarmed man in the back, that is murder, is it not?

SOLDIER F: As far as I was concerned, as I say in my statement, the man had a pistol.

MANSFIELD: But not this man, you see, no-one suggested this man had a pistol. If you shot a man who is unarmed only with a handkerchief in the back of the head, it is murder, is it not?

SOLDIER F: I said I fired on a person who had a pistol.

C CLARKE: Just a few matters. The allegations are that you killed up to four people, possibly even more. Firstly, Michael Kelly and we know that you killed him because of the forensic evidence that a bullet from your gun was found in his body?

SOLDIER F: That is correct.

C CLARKE: Do you accept that you shot Patrick Doherty?

SOLDIER F: Yes.

C CLARKE: There is evidence that might lead to the conclusion that you shot William McKinney, do you follow?

SOLDIER F: Yes.

C CLARKE: What is alleged in relation to four people is that you shot them without justification, that is to say, that you murdered them, do you follow?

SOLDIER F: I follow, it is not correct, but I follow, yes.

C CLARKE: And you say it is not correct because?

SOLDIER F: Because, as I refer to my statements, the people I shot were either petrol bombers or a person who had a weapon.

C CLARKE: I am sure you understand; in case you do not, I wish to make it plain that the suggestion is that the evidence you have given to the Royal Military Police, to Lord Widgery, and to this Tribunal is false, both as to what you have said and to what you have not revealed, do you follow?

SOLDIER F: Yes.

C CLARKE: And that is evidence which constitutes perjury, do you follow?

SOLDIER F: I do.

C CLARKE: The suggestion is that the reason why that evidence is false is because you have needed to conceal unlawful activities on your part and the part of your colleagues, do you follow?

SOLDIER F: I do.

C CLARKE: Is there anything more that you would wish the Tribunal to take into account or to hear from you in relation to those matters?

SOLDIER F: No, I have nothing to add.

SAVILLE: Thank you, Soldier F.

REG TESTER
22 JANUARY 2004

C CLARKE: May we, please, have on the screen AT6.1, para 1. You record there that at the time of Bloody Sunday you were a command staff quartermaster to the Official Irish Republican Army and you describe how there were around thirty or forty members at the time. I will come back to that in a moment. You say that you were third-in-command of the local brigade.

Is it right that there would have been a large number of people in Derry who knew who their members were and what their rank was?

TESTER: There would have been quite a good number.

C CLARKE: Can you remember how many the command staff was in all?

TESTER: Probably about five or six.

C CLARKE: May we come, please, to paragraph 25. You say in your statement, as indeed have others, that there were less weapons than there were members and you list in this paragraph what you can remember of the weaponry that you had.

Some well-used Lee Enfield .303s, some .22s, some shotguns, a .306 rifle, a Sterling sub-machine-gun and an old antique Sten gun. Then you say: 'Initially we had a couple of Thompson machine guns and a selection of pistols and revolvers' and a new M1 carbine that you had just got. What is the force of the word 'initially', what does that signify?

TESTER: One, I believe, became – I think it died of natural causes. It just got wore out. I mean, they were very old weapons, propbably dating back to before the second world war.

C CLARKE: Do you remember where the new M1 carbine came from?

TESTER: I think it came up from Dublin, actually.

C CLARKE: And there was only one was there?

TESTER: We only had one, yes

C CLARKE: What I am about to ask may be a Donald Rumsfeld unknown unknown, but is it reasonable to suppose that some members of the Official IRA may have had weapons that were not under your control?

TESTER: I very much doubt it.

C CLARKE: Why?

TESTER: Because I kept me hands on the lot.

C CLARKE: The Tribunal has received conflicting evidence about the respective styles, if that is the right word, of the Provisionals and the Officials. Could we have H1.7. What is about to appear is the statement to this Tribunal of Father Bradley: 'The Official IRA were mainly disliked in the city. It was an old Catholic thing. They were seen as Marxist left-wing. They were considered to be "gangsterish". The

Provisionals were much more careful about who was allowed in and were more disciplined.'

Were there some very irresponsible people in the Officials at the time?

TESTER: No, there were not.

C CLARKE: Could we have on the screen S34. This is the *Sunday Times* note of a conversation with what they say is you: 'There were to be no weapons in the Bogside except those kept in safe dumps. All other Official weapons were to be kept in two cars which would be on hand in the [neighbouring] Creggan. Nobody was to initiate firing on the Army.'

Is that what happened in the period leading up to Bloody Sunday, so far as orders were concerned?

TESTER: Yes.

C CLARKE: If that is so, would that mean that although the Officials were not to initiate firing on the Army, they could return fire or retaliate if the Army fired?

TESTER: It would have depended on how many people were around. I mean, if the Army opened fire and somebody fell in the middle of a crowd, you would hardly open up and risk even more being shot?

C CLARKE: Once any form of fire had been opened up by the Army, could a volunteer think that in those circumstances, provided he thought it was safe to do so, it was open to him to fire at the Army?

TESTER: I would say so.

C CLARKE: Could we have on the screen AT6.7, paragraph 12. You say there: 'On Bloody Sunday, I knew there were three weapons out.' As I understand it, the three weapons are the rifle that was used to fire across William Street, the pistol that was used by Father Daly's gunman, and the weapon issued to a volunteer. That is right, is it not, Mr Tester?

TESTER: That is correct.

C CLARKE: Could we come, then, to the events of the day. In paragraph 10 you describe how both cars stayed at the centre of the Creggan that day: 'We drove around a bit and then stopped and parked for a while and then drove around a bit again.' You did not hear any shooting at all?

TESTER: No, I mean, while we were driving around we would not have heard it because of the noise of the engine. We stopped at the top of New Road.

C CLARKE: It is at this stage you heard something had happened.

TESTER: Yes.

C CLARKE: Paragraph 12, please. You describe how you took the new M1 carbine out from the car and tried to fire it. But the gun jammed and you were unable to unjam it. Did you succeed in firing any shot at all?

TESTER: No, I did not.

C CLARKE: What were you trying to fire at?

TESTER: Military personnel who were down by the Rossville Flats.

C CLARKE: Were you aiming at an individual soldier?

TESTER: Yes, only he moved, apart from everything else.

C CLARKE: Were there any ambulances around at that stage?

TESTER: No.

C CLARKE: Or civilians?

TESTER: Well, that is what I realised, after I had failed to get a shot off. I could see them moving around and it suddenly dawned on me, bearing in mind that I was extremely angry and upset, like anybody else in my position, I wanted to strike back, but I realised after a minute that, thank God, that my rifle had jammed, because I could not see the soldier really clearly enough and there was still civilians wandering around.

C CLARKE: And when you learnt that some volunteer had fired, was the command staff not concerned to find out exactly what happened after so cataclysmic an event as Bloody Sunday?

TESTER: Well, I think as far as as the command staff were concerned, and probably everybody else in the entire area, a massacre had been inflicted upon the civilian population, quite coldly and quite deliberately. What reason? Well you can make up your own mind on that, whether it was just to try and put the fear of God into the local population, make the IRA back off, I do not know.

C CLARKE: One view that the Tribunal might be invited to take is that the Official IRA could not have realistically have maintained a fiction that no shots were fired.

TESTER: For us to have, um, at those early stages, admitted quite openly that we had fired, whether it was one shot, two shots, or three shots even, would have simply been to give the authorities all the scope they needed to excuse what they did. Therefore, certainly for a long time, the fact we had actually fired shots – and bear in mind that not everybody knew that those shots had been fired by any of their colleagues – um, was simply played down.

C CLARKE: Mr Tester, I quite follow what you say; that to accept in 1972 that the Official IRA had fired at all was thought to distract attention from what is said really to have happened, that the soldiers had killed and wounded a number of civilians without justification, but you would I am sure, accept that in fact it is quite undeniable but that a number of shots were fired on the day by members of the IRA?

TESTER: Well, you cannot deny it, no.

SAVILLE: Mr Tester, it is the chairman again. Thank you very much for coming here to give evidence to us. Thank you.

End.

CALLED TO ACCOUNT

THE INDICTMENT OF ANTHONY CHARLES LYNTON BLAIR
FOR THE CRIME OF AGGRESSION AGAINST IRAQ –
A HEARING

All the interviews (except two) for this play took place in offices in London between 5 January and 15 February 2007. Scott Ritter's evidence was taken on two separate occasions on a conference call to the United States, and Juan Gabriel Valdes' evidence on a conference call to Santiago, Chile.

Altogether about 28 hours of evidence was taken from 14 witnesses – a further eight witnesses were approached but declined to take part.

The Tricycle Theatre is enormously indebted to all the witnesses who volunteered to commit to this process and answered questions rigorously; and to the dedicated legal team of Philippe Sands QC, Julian Knowles, Alison Macdonald and Blinne Ní Ghrálaigh who worked tirelessly and pro-bono on this project from November 2006 to March 2007.

Nicolas Kent and Richard Norton-Taylor
April 2007

Characters

THE LAWYERS

Philippe Sands QC, Prosecution

Alison Macdonald, Prosecution

Julian Knowles, Defence

Blinne Ní Ghrálaigh, Defence

THE WITNESSES

Dr Shirwan Al-Mufti

Scott Ritter

Michael Smith

Sir Murray Stuart Smith

Clare Short, MP

Michael Mates, MP

Edward Mortimer

Juan Gabriel Valdes

Bob Marshall Andrews QC, MP

Richard Perle

Sir Michael Quinlan

Called to Account was first performed at the Tricycle Theatre, London on 19 April 2007, with the following cast:

PHILIPPE SANDS QC, Thomas Wheatley
ALISON MACDONALD, Morven Macbeth
JULIAN KNOWLES, David Michaels
BLINNE NÍ GHRÁLAIGH, Charlotte Lucas
DR SHIRWAN AL-MUFTI, Raad Rawi
SCOTT RITTER, David Beames
MICHAEL SMITH, Ken Drury
SIR MURRAY STUART SMITH, William Hoyland
CLARE SHORT, MP, Diane Fletcher
MICHAEL MATES, MP, Roland Oliver
EDWARD MORTIMER, Jeremy Clyde
JUAN GABRIEL VALDES, James Woolley
BOB MARSHALL ANDREWS QC, MP, Terrence Hardiman
RICHARD PERLE, Shane Rimmer
SIR MICHAEL QUINLAN, William Hoyland

Director, Nicolas Kent
Designer, Polly Sullivan
Lighting Designer, James Farncombe
Assistant Director, Phil Honour
Sound, Paul Kizintas

The Prosecution's Opening Statement

SANDS: In accordance with Article 15 of the [International Criminal Court] statute, the prosecutor seeks the authorisation of the Court to investigate the facts, to ascertain whether they provide a basis for indicting Anthony Charles Lynton Blair for the crime of aggression. As the Court assesses the evidence, we invite you to focus on four facts: One, what was Mr Blair's true purpose in using force against Iraq: was it Regime change or the elimination of WMD? Two, when did Mr Blair commit himself to use force: was it in March 2003, or was it earlier, in March 2002? Three, did Mr Blair manipulate the presentation of the evidence on WMD, and did he willfully disregard evidence and advice that would have been unhelpful to his case, including the legal case? Four, what was Mr Blair's true state of knowledge as to the legality of the use of force?

The prosecutor recognises that the crime of aggression is the most serious of crimes. This application is not made lightly. We invite the Court to consider the evidence.

The Defence's Opening Statement

KNOWLES:

1. This case is not about politics. It is about law. There could not be a more serious allegation than that made by the prosecution in this case. But legal condemnation should not result from political opposition.

2. And you should certainly demand the most cogent evidence before deciding the prosecution's case is made.

3. In defending this case we do not rely alone on the Security Council's failure to declare the Iraq war to be unlawful, even though that is a powerful factor, if not a complete defence, to the charge. Nor do we rely on the refusal of many of the prosecution witnesses to accuse others in the Government of a crime, even though, if the prosecution's charge were well-founded, they should be here too. We say the prosecution's evidence lacks cogency and comes from peripheral figures who cannot speak with authority about relevant matters. Heart-felt opinions are no substitute for hard evidence.

4. The prosecution ask you to consider a number of issues. Some of these have already been examined in other inquires. As you will hear, those involved in those inquiries found no evidence to suggest that the Prime Minister manipulated intelligence or disregarded advice. None of the opinions offered by the prosecution's witnesses, however passionate, can displace that stark conclusion.

5. Finally, we would remind you that the crime of aggression requires proof that the Prime Minister intended to act in breach of international law. When you have heard the evidence you will be certain that what the Prime Minister did, he did with the legal authority of the Government's legal adviser, whose good faith the prosecution and its witnesses accept.

Act One

SCENE 1: DR SHIRWAN AL-MUFTI

KNOWLES: Could you give us your name and your occupation please.

MUFTI: My name is Shirwan Al-Mufti. I am a Senior Research Fellow at Cardiff Centre for Astrobiology. I am an astronomer by profession.

KNOWLES: And where were you born, and where did you grow up?

MUFTI: I [was] born in Sulaymaniyah in 1947. I grew up in Baghdad until 1979. So 1979 I came to the UK.

KNOWLES: And what were the circumstances in which you came to the UK?

MUFTI: I came to continue my study. Really the first time I came in 1973, I did an MSc in Reading University, and then I went back to the University of Sulaymaniyah and in 1979 I came to continue my PhD.

KNOWLES: On your ethnic background, you are a Kurd?

MUFTI: I am a Kurd, yes.

KNOWLES: How does the [Iraq] population break down in terms of Kurds, Shi'as, Sunnis – what are the approximate proportions?

MUFTI: We always go back to the 1957 census. The breakdown, they normally take it as 20 per cent Kurd and 80 per cent they said Arab, but now they are talking 60 per cent Shi'a Arabs, 13 per cent Arab Sunnis.

KNOWLES: Just for focusing obviously in particular on the Kurdish community of which you are member, what was life like for the Kurds under Saddam?

MUFTI: The first two years, after the breakdown between Kurds and Ba'ath party, '74 until '76/'77 it was very bad.

KNOWLES: It was bad in what way?

MUFTI: They had the right to do whatever they liked. I mean if they suspect anybody. In one circumstances, which I was witness for, because at the time I had one of my relatives ill, so I took him to the emergency hospital, and suddenly one of these pick-up cars belonging to the general security arrived with three bodies in it. They say 'these are the guerrillas', and apparently they were three secondary school students, they were studying early in the morning, because of the heat, near the cemetery, so at that time, a group of the security men were there, and they just killed them in cold blood.

KNOWLES: That sort of incident – just random executions?

MUFTI: Just random executions.

KNOWLES: If I said the word 'Halabja' to you. What would that mean?

MUFTI: Halabja when it happened back in 1988, I was in Cardiff anyway, but Halabja is this place when chemical weapons being used by the admission of the Iraqi government themselves, so there were about 5,500 victims of Halabja.

KNOWLES: Just explain to us how Halabja happened and what happened?

MUFTI: Halabja, the geography of it is, it is attached to Iranian border. And apparently the Patriotic Union of Kurdistan, which was one of the big parties against the government at the time, took control of Halabja and apparently they had some kind of relation with the Iranian forces, and because Iraq was at war with Iran, so they wanted to make Halabja as an example. So that they authorised the chemical attack, the only people killed were women and children.

CALLED TO ACCOUNT: ACT ONE

KNOWLES: Saddam, as we know, was a Sunni, how were the Shi'a majority generally treated?

MUFTI: After the start Iran/Iraq War, the way he was thinking that the Shi'a, [w]as a fifth column, and that was the problem. Because Saddam Hussein, he ran the government as a dictator, he was controlling everything, and in the South the Shiite clerics, all the Ayatollahs they have a very big power among the population, so that's why he tried to get rid of these big Shiite families for that reason. Like the Al-Sadr.

KNOWLES: What did he do?

MUFTI: Really, he dealt very harshly with them. He used the army and his secret service to shoot at whoever demonstrated. And after, in 1991, he killed roughly, they took about 300,000 people in the South after the Kuwait War.

KNOWLES: I want to come to the use of torture. Was the use of torture by Saddam's regime widespread?

MUFTI: Very much so.

> It is not only against the Kurds. I mean... If I give an example, which I know. In 1973 [his Chief of Security] was against the Iraqi Communist Party a lot. So they captured, I think, one person was responsible for the Baghdad area, so he said nobody touch this person, no torture, nothing like that. They kept him in solitary confinement for one week, and then in the afternoon he called this chap to his office, and he opened bottles of beer and he asked him to drink beer. And this chap he couldn't believe it, that's a Communist. I'll drink it. I think he has about five bottles of beer. After that he asks these people, excuse the language, so they tie his penis to stop him from going to the toilet and eye witnesses were saying that they were hearing this chap shouting all night until he died.

KNOWLES: The situation obviously in Iraq at the moment is violent and difficult and dangerous. When that ends and

Iraq has a democratic government, in your view will it be a good thing or bad thing that Saddam is no longer in power?

MUFTI: The majority of the Iraqi people they were happy with the removal of Saddam Hussein's regime. But the mishandling of the situation by, especially the Americans prolongs this thing. Especially after [11th] September 2001, you try to control or get rid of any, what you called it, militant Islamic things, and when you are against Iran for a very long time, which is all Shi'a society and suddenly you come and you support the Shi'a society [in Iraq], all the Islamic society in Iraq that really puzzles me, I can't understand it.

KNOWLES: Yes, thank you. That's all I ask.

SANDS: Dr Al-Mufti, I am appearing on behalf of the prosecutor in this case. Can I ask what your view is on the rule of law?

MUFTI: Really I, as I explain now, I came from a society which nobody gave a damn about the rule of law.

SANDS: So the Iraq, that you were born into and lived in as a young man and then left, was a country that had no respect for the rule of law.

MUFTI: I can say, yes, especially after '68.

SANDS: I think we can all agree in this room that the record shows that Mr Saddam Hussein was not a good person who respected human rights?

MUFTI: Yes.

SANDS: Mr Hussein is not on trial in this case. The question is whether an indictment should be issued against Mr Blair for not having complied with the rule of law. This is what the Attorney General says in July 2002: 'the desire for regime change was not a legal base for military action. There were three possible legal bases:

self defence, humanitarian intervention or UN Security Council Authorisation. The first and second could not be the base in this case.' End the quotation there. The facts in Iraq in the summer of 2002 do not justify humanitarian intervention. Does that come as a surprise to you?

MUFTI: Really 2002 humanitarian, if you compare it with after Kuwait's war, the humanitarian side of it wasn't as grave as it was then.

SANDS: It would have been more justified in 1991 or 1988?

MUFTI: Yes.

SANDS: Can I now take you to a document that you do have. It's the famous legal advice of the Attorney General. It's at Tab 3. I wonder if you could read out paragraph 4.

MUFTI: 'The use of force to avert overwhelming humanitarian catastrophe has been emerging as a further, and exceptional, basis for the use of force. It was relied on by the UK in the Kosovo crisis and is the underlying justification for the no-fly zones. The doctrine remains controversial, however. I know of no reason why it would be an appropriate basis for action in present circumstances.'

SANDS: Do you have any reaction to that argument by the Attorney General?

Long pause.

MUFTI: His advice is against it, against using force, isn't it?

SANDS: Against force on humanitarian intervention grounds. What's your reaction to his legal advice? I appreciate you are not a lawyer...

MUFTI interupts.

MUFTI: I am not a lawyer really, I mean. 'Overwhelming humanitarian catastrophe', what it is? Is it like what happened in '91 when people were in the mountains dying from cold, or running from Saddam's forces, 3,000/4,000 people killed in one week while the regime is doing his dirty business [Saddam] will kill 3,000 in one month. That's the problem. So I don't know, what he mean by 'humanitarian'.

SANDS: I think what he's expressing is concern that if countries start using human rights arguments to use force, then the door is opened to any country saying we don't like what someone else is doing to their people, we are going to use force. The Government has been told by legal advisors, by the Attorney General, that you can't use human rights arguments to invade Iraq. What you have to say is that Iraq is violating its obligations on weapons of mass destruction. So what I put to you is that the human rights situation, was not the argument made by the British Government to justify the use of force in March 2003.

MUFTI: But there is a strong link between the British Government, or the policy of British Government and the United States. The American was going for the regime change while all the advice from the British Foreign Office that they were against the regime change. But I didn't see any policy evolve after that. So whatever happened after that, I think it was just going in tandem with the United States, because they made their mind.

SANDS: Well the prosecutor says that Mr Blair also made his mind, very early, to go with the United States irrespective or whether or not there was a legal justification.

MUFTI: They started on a wrong thing when they just kept talking about the weapons of mass destruction. In my opinion, or the majority of the Iraqi people, the regime of Saddam Hussein, it was our weapon of mass destruction itself. And there was no way, I know as I am an Iraqi and probably I know a bit of the country, there wasn't a way you can change that regime without an external power.

SANDS: But is it your view then, the argument on weapons of mass destruction was really an artificial argument?

MUFTI: Really in my opinion, if I was an advisor to the British Government, I wouldn't let them to put that argument in the first place. If it was for me.

SANDS: Why?

MUFTI: Because that argument probably it's good for public opinion in the West, because when you talk about weapons of massive destruction, atomic weapons, nuclear weapons, the public opinion always has something against it, so it will go with it. It's like…frightened of it.

SANDS: So might it be fair to say that in a way that this was a slightly dishonest argument?

MUFTI: (*Chuckles.*) We are coming to the legality of it.

SANDS: I don't mean dishonest in the legal sense.

MUFTI: The legality of it as far as I understand for a layman like myself. When you read any Security Council Resolution it is so elastic, you can interpret it the way you like it.

SANDS: The question was, 'was this really about weapons of mass destruction?'.

MUFTI: I answered you. If you asked me personally my gut feeling. No.

SANDS: Dr Al-Mufti, thank you very much indeed.

KNOWLES: I just have one question in. Do you think a time will come when Iraq will be a peaceful, stable democracy?

MUFTI: Yes, I think if the intervention from the neighbouring countries will stop. I remember very well before, when the invasion started, President Bush was saying that we make Iraq a democratic country and it will be an example for the region. Okay if you look at the countries surrounding Iraq, you have Iran which is not a democratic country, you have Syria which is again a part of the Ba'ath Party. Now if you want to make an example for a very progressive, democratic entity in the middle of these countries, it means if I am the King of Saudi Arabia, the first thing I think of [is] 'Okay I am next', if I am [President] Assad of Syria I think 'I am next, America is going to topple me as well'. So what is the obvious thing to do? – prevent this experience from succeeding. It is as simple as that.

SCENE 2: SCOTT RITTER

RITTER: My name is William Scott Ritter Jr.

SANDS: And what is your professional background and training?

RITTER: I was a Commissioned Officer with the United States Marine Corps, and since 1987 I have been serving in an intelligence role in the armed control and disarmament aspects of US Government Policy. From 1991 to 1998, I served in a similar capacity with the United Nations Special Commission on Iraq.

SANDS: At that time in 1998, what was your view as to the situation concerning Iraq's possession and capability of chemical, biological and nuclear weaponry?

RITTER: I was tasked with preparing a document that set out in speculative fashion what the Iraqis might be capable of having hidden from the inspectors. We could account for around 95–98 per cent. We were concerned about the unaccounted-for material.

SANDS: Can I ask, what was the position of Tony Blair's Government in 1998 on the issue?

RITTER: In 1998, the Special Commission sent a high level delegation, including myself, to London where we met with people from the Foreign Office, from the Ministry of Defence, and at that time the British Government cautioned the Special Commission from pursuing a line of investigation that lacked substantive, factually based information. Meaning that they could not support confrontational inspections with the Iraqis unless we had hard data. The British Government was not able to provide the Special Commission with hard intelligence data.

SANDS: Would you then infer from that, that the position of the British Government, and presumably of the Prime Minister was that, in 1998, there was insufficient evidence to justify that type of aggressive inspection?

RITTER: Yes, I wouldn't infer. We were told this by the British Government in no uncertain terms.

SANDS: Do you have any reason for believing that that decision had come right from the top of Government?

RITTER: We were never told right out that this is the position of the Prime Minister, we were told this is the position of the British Government.

SANDS: Are you saying in 1998 the British Government was taking the position that there was no hard evidence that Saddam's Government was continuing to produce biological and chemical weapons?

RITTER: Correct, there was nothing but circumstantial evidence.

SANDS: In the bundle, can you turn to Tab 6. That is the dossier produced by British Government, its assessment of Iraq's weapons of mass destruction. We're now in September 2002, and you've just been extremely clear, if I may say, on the situation in 1998. Have you got page three in front of you?

RITTER: Correct.

SANDS: Foreword by the Prime Minister, the Right Honourable Tony Blair MP. About two thirds of the way down is a sentence that begins 'What I believe…' Could you read that out for the Court, that paragraph?

RITTER: Okay. 'What I believe the assessed intelligence has established beyond doubt is that Saddam has continued to produce chemical and biological weapons, that he continues in his efforts to develop nuclear weapons, and that he has been able to extend the range of his ballistic missile programme. I also believe that, as stated in the document, Saddam will now do his utmost to try and conceal his weapons from the UN Inspectors.'

SANDS: Can I ask your view on the accuracy of that statement in September 2002?

RITTER: Well, I think I'm on record as saying that when somebody uses the term 'has established beyond doubt' that that leads one to believe that there is irrefutable fact to back up this statement, there was always doubt, especially when it came to the charges that Saddam Hussein's Government had either retained, or had reconstituted weapons of mass destruction capability. But this is an absurd statement because in 1998, the International community had the freshest information derived from the inspection process. What transpired between '98 and 2002 that would change the Prime Minister's mind, I don't know.

SANDS: Would you say that it's seriously misleading?

RITTER: I will preface this by saying that I'm not privy to the data that was shared with the Prime Minister, but based upon my understanding of the intelligence data as of 1998 and a further understanding that no new substantive intelligence information was gathered by the British Government from 1998 to 2002, that this was a deliberately misleading statement.

SANDS: How would you summarise the conclusions respectively of UNMOVIC and the IAEA [on the eve of war in] March 2003?

RITTER: The ground truth that the inspectors were finding was of an Iraq that had been fundamentally disarmed. They weren't in a position to make a final conclusion. They still believed that work needed to be done. When they went before the Security Council El Baradei was much more conclusive when he talked about the Iraqi nuclear programme, saying there was no programme.

SANDS: I think, Mr Ritter, that covers all the questions I wanted to raise.

KNOWLES: Mr Ritter, would you agree that you do have some strong views?

RITTER: Let's say that I have well informed views, which carry some strength.

KNOWLES: Well let's look at that. Have you said on occasions that the United States is at war with Iran?

RITTER: I have said that the United States has engaged in acts that can be classified as warlike in nature with Iran, yes.

KNOWLES: I am looking at a report that you wrote in 2005, where you are quoted as saying: 'The reality is that the US war with Iran has already begun.' Have you been quoted correctly there?

RITTER: Correct.

KNOWLES: Is that a view that is widely shared?

RITTER: I think it is increasingly shared today as people become more and more cognisant. I believe that at the time I made that statement, no, it was not a widely held view.

KNOWLES: We are talking June 2005, so we are talking a little over 18 months ago. You say it is increasingly the view that is shared, what is your evidence for that?

RITTER: I would guide you to the newspapers and news articles that appeared in the last few weeks and indeed many American politicians are very concerned about confrontation between the United States and Iran.

KNOWLES: You are aware that two Inquiries in the UK specifically set up to look at aspects of use of intelligence on Iraq both concluded that there was no deliberate distortion by the UK Government's intelligence. The Butler Report concluded: 'Before the War the Iraqi regime had the strategic intention of resuming the pursuit of prohibited weapons programmes including, if possible, its nuclear weapons programme.'

RITTER: I disagree and I think that the facts that have emerged post 2003 back up the basis of my disagreement, namely the audio and video tapes that have been captured by coalition forces of internal meetings held by Saddam Hussein in his inner circle where it is quite clear that the Iraqi Government had given up weapons of mass destruction.

SCENE 3: MICHAEL SMITH

SANDS: Mr Smith, I'd like to ask a few questions about a number of documents that have come into your possession. I wonder if you could begin by explaining about your professional background and the manner of which you came by this material.

SMITH: I am a newspaper journalist. I developed a number of sources within Whitehall, who were, both on the defence and the intelligence side. The source was someone who came up with this completely out of the blue, asked me if we could meet up for a drink, presented me the first six documents, said was I interested in these? And obviously I was, when I read them, I thought, they were extraordinary documents and then obviously I am pushing for anything more I can get, and eventually some more came, two more came and they included what is now known as the 'Downing Street Memo'.

SANDS: You have in this period written for two reputable newspapers, you will have taken steps to ascertain the authenticity of this material.

SMITH: Indeed, we took extraordinary steps on the *Telegraph* I have to say and I really don't want to go too much into that. Obviously, when you get something like this, you have to approach the authorities and ask them what they think of it. But equally you have the problem that they might send in the police, particularly Special Branch and get a court to block your use of documents which they see to be theirs. I photocopied those photocopies, sent them back to the person who owned them or who handed them to me because their basis was the paper probably belonged to the Government and the Government could come along and say that's our paper.

SANDS: What might have motivated the source?

SMITH: I think, there was considerable anger within Whitehall that the Prime Minister had completely ignored all the advice. Not just on whether it was legal to go to war, although that figured, but whether it was sensible to go to war.

SANDS: Let's start with the text of the [Options] document that was prepared by Foreign Office lawyers in March 2002. Paragraph 31. I quote, 'as the ceasefire was proclaimed by the [Security] Council, it is for the Council to assess whether any such breach of these obligations has occurred. The US have a rather different view, they maintain that the assessment of breach is for individual member States, we are not aware of any other State which supports this view.' I've got this at Tab 21.

SMITH: Well, it's extremely significant. In March 8th 2002, the Foreign Office legal advice is that there isn't any way of this being legal at the moment unless the UN says it is legal.

SANDS: And they go on to say, do they not, that the only other justifications in law, the use of force as self defence and use of force by reason of humanitarian intervention are not available.

SMITH: Yeah, they can't really escape there.

SANDS: (*Interrupts.*) Turn to the letter of 14th March 2002.

SMITH: From David Manning to Blair.

SANDS: Who is Mr Manning?

SMITH: At the time he was Mr Blair's foreign policy advisor.

SANDS: And he described in this letter, a lunch he has had or a dinner he has had with Condoleezza Rice, who at the time who was not Secretary of State but was…

SMITH: National Security Advisor.

SANDS: I want to take you to the second paragraph: 'We spent a long time at dinner on Iraq. It is clear that Bush is grateful for your support and has registered that you are getting flak. I said that you would not budge in your support for regime change. But you have to manage a press, a parliament and a public opinion, which is very different from anything in the States.' Now, can I ask you what you understand of those words, 'you would not budge in your support for regime change'?

SMITH: On the 14th March 2002 David Manning is talking of going to war, he is talking about regime change. Nevertheless, regime change is not justified legally.

SANDS: Can one read into that, recognition by Mr Manning, that the personal consequences for the Prime Minister might be very serious?

SMITH: I don't read it as saying that I have to say, that there might be special consequences for Mr Blair on his own. I mean, I think it is part of this continued view within the Foreign Office that this was a very, very risky and dangerous business and you had to get it right.

SANDS: If now we go to the next letter, four days later, this is from the [British Ambassador] to the US, Christopher Meyer to David Manning at Number 10 Downing Street.

And this concerns a conversation with Mr Wolfowitz, who was the deputy to Mr Rumsfeld. And he has come to lunch on the 17th March. Paragraph 2. 'On Iraq, I opened by sticking very closely to the script that you used with Condi Rice last week. We backed regime change. But the plan had to be clever and failure was not an option. It will be a tough sell for us domestically, probably tougher elsewhere in Europe. The US could go it alone if it wanted to but if it wanted to act with partners, there had to be a strategy for building support for military action against Saddam. I then went through the need to wrongfoot Saddam on the inspectors and the UN Security Council resolutions.' I ask you, what's most striking to you about this paragraph?

SMITH: There are two phrases in there, 'the plan had to be clever' and 'the need to somehow wrongfoot the inspectors' that jumped out to me as a journalist. Further to that this is not a plan the US has drawn up, this is a plan coming from 10 Downing Street.

SANDS: So the plan on your view was premised on a refusal by Saddam to allow in the inspectors?

SMITH: Yeah.

SANDS: That of course didn't happen.

SMITH: No.

SANDS: Let me take you now to a document, briefing the British War Cabinet, on the 23rd July 2002. Paragraph 2: 'When the British Prime Minister discussed Iraq with President Bush at Crawford in April, he said the UK would support military action to bring about regime change provided that certain conditions were met. Efforts had been made to construct a coalition, shape public opinion, the Israel and Palestine crisis was quiescent. The options for action to eliminate Iraq's WMD through UN weapons inspectors had been exhausted.' End of quote. Could you explain to us what this paragraph is saying?

SMITH: It is saying that Mr Blair has told President Bush that he is going to back military action to achieve regime change. He's going to back an invasion of Iraq. It can't be read any other way.

SANDS: Are you saying Mr Smith that when the Prime Minister subsequently told the British Parliament and the British public that no decision had been taken, and he maintained that position right up until the 18th March 2003, is it your view that he misled Parliament and the public?

SMITH: Yes.

SANDS: Can we now, go to the final document. It is dated July 2002. [The Downing Street memo, 9 months before the war.] Now, that note is from a junior Downing Street official to David Manning and there is a number of people, to whom it is sent, who are quite striking really. It is sent to the Defence Secretary, the Foreign Secretary and the Attorney General, it is sent to John Scarlett. What was, is John Scarlett's position at that time?

SMITH: He was Chairman of the Joint Intelligence Committee.

SANDS: And it is sent to C. What's C?

SMITH: C stands for chief. It is the official title of the head of MI6.

SANDS: Moving back to the note of the meeting. Starting from the third paragraph: 'C reported on his recent talks in Washington. There was a perceptible shift in attitude. Military action now seen as inevitable, Bush wanted to remove Saddam through military action justified by the conjunction of terrorism and WMD, but the intelligence and facts were being fixed around the policy.' Can I ask for your comment on that paragraph?

SMITH: The meaning is very clear and that is confirmation basically I think, that most people sort of realised that the intelligence was being fixed to match up to the policy.

SANDS: Can we go on in the same note to the words of the Foreign Secretary, Mr Straw, and I quote, 'It seemed clear that Bush had made up his mind to take military action even if the timing was not yet decided. But the case was thin.' In July 2002, we have got the Prime Minister being told at this meeting that the case is thin.

SMITH: That is a remarkable statement but that is not a change of position because Mr Straw was telling Mr Blair that, before Mr Blair went to Crawford.

SANDS: Is it your view then that on the basis of this material that Mr Blair had taken an early decision to remove Saddam Hussein from office?

SMITH: I think, it is my opinion that Mr Blair recognised that there was a powerful clique in the administration which was dominant, and which was determined to do something about Iraq. I personally believe Mr Blair genuinely thought he could somehow control this if he was on board, therefore at Crawford, he decided to say, 'Okay we'll do it', despite the advice of all his key policy advisors. 'Okay we'll do it, yes with conditions.' But conditions actually weren't met.

SANDS: That is not what he told the British public though is it?

SMITH: No, course it's not and they continued to tell the British public that nothing was going to happen. Then they started preparing for war. There is evidence from inquests that throughout December the British Army, all the chiefs, all the military planners were told to go off, take two weeks for Christmas as usual, so that it didn't look like something was happening.

SANDS: Would it be fair to summarise this material as establishing that by July 2002, a decision had been taken, there was no intelligence evidence available to suggest that Saddam was a real WMD threat and there was no legal argument.

SMITH: Certainly by July, I would say, much of that by then.

SANDS: Thanks very much, Mr Smith.

KNOWLES: Mr Smith, your evidence is not, that you think that the Prime Minister acted in bad faith? Have I understood you correctly?

SMITH: No, I don't think that initially he acted in bad faith, but once he was on board this whole business, he was stuck in a position where he had to act on a number of occasions in bad faith.

KNOWLES: You said a moment or two ago that you felt by April 2002, it was put to you July, but you said April, that an unequivocal decision had been taken to go to war come what may.

SMITH: Yes.

KNOWLES: That's your evidence is it?

SMITH: That's my belief yes.

KNOWLES: That's your interpretation of the documents.

SMITH: Yes.

KNOWLES: So we won't see in any of these documents any caveats, any conditions, any reservations, anything of that nature.

SMITH: There are plenty caveats and plenty of reservations, most of them, in fact all of them, made by Government officials who were all along, very, very concerned about it and at any event six of these documents precede the [April 2002] Crawford summit, when Mr Blair agreed to go to war.

KNOWLES: Let's just look at the July 2002 [Downing Street memorandum], because you said even by this stage the decision has been taken. First conclusion: a) we should work on the assumption that the UK will take part in any military action but we needed a fuller picture of US planning before we could take any firm decisions. How is that consistent with what you've said, that by April a firm decision had been taken when here it's saying that we needed a fuller picture before taking firm decisions?

SMITH: Because we are talking about here firm decisions about how much support we would give the action, precisely what support, what military support it would be. We are also taking about a situation where we know already that British territories in Cyprus and Diego Garcia would be used by the Americans.

KNOWLES: With very great respect that is a complete misreading of the…what that conclusion says, it says we should work on the assumption that the UK will take part in any military action but we need a fuller picture etc before we can take any firm decisions. Let's just follow this through. If the Government and the Prime Minister, who heads the Government, take a decision that is in the UK's national interests, to conduct a military campaign, in and of itself there's nothing wrong with that.

SMITH: No, no, of course not.

KNOWLES: I mean subject to lots of conditions.

SMITH: Yeah.

SCENE 4: SIR MURRAY STUART SMITH

SANDS: Sir Murray, I wonder if you could give us a little bit of information about the circumstances in which you have come to, erm, face issues of the use of intelligence in decision-making.

MURRAY: Well, I was a Queen's Bench Judge and in 1989 I was appointed Commissioner for the Security Service and five years later I was Commissioner for the Intelligence Services. My actual function, I suppose, would be best described as a one-man judicial review of the Secretary of State's power to issue warrants to bug people, but in doing that I saw a good deal of the raw intelligence.

SANDS: Would you say you can express a view on what to call good intelligence, as opposed to intelligence that might be not so good?

MURRAY: Well, I think that um, if you take the three sources of intelligence. First of all human intelligence, which has been a source of secret intelligence for centuries. That can vary enormously um, in reliability. Reading the Butler Report, there are obviously great difficulties in relation to Iraq, it's a very difficult target. It's very dangerous for human spies to operate. I imagine it was very difficult for case officers to contact informants. One of the problems about human intelligence, erm human agents is how close they are to the source of information. Whether they are gaining first hand evidence or whether it's sub-source, from a sub-sub-source. So far as signals intelligence is concerned, the chief source of that is of course is GCHQ, supplemented by bugging, eavesdropping operations and or telephone taps. Now, so far as Iraq was concerned, I don't get the impression that there was any signals intelligence or not much at any rate. The other form of intelligence is…is photographic imagery. Um, I think that did play some part in, in this because there are some photographs in the Dossier, um and although the camera doesn't lie it's is not always easy to interpret actually what…what you're seeing.

SANDS: Is there any other body, apart from the J[oint] I[ntelligence] C[ommittee] that the Government and Prime Minister could have turned to, to obtain confirmation of its views on the intelligence in the best of your knowledge?

MURRAY: No, not to my knowledge. I, I don't think so. I think it all goes through the JIC.

SANDS: I'd like to take you now to Tab 3 of your bundle. You'll find two documents authored by the Attorney General. The first is his full advice on the 7th March 2003, and the second is his statement in the House of Lords on the 17th March 2003. At this point, I'm just concerned with the first document, in particular paragraph 29.

MURRAY: I need a marker pen.

SANDS: This goes to the argument that the authorisation to use force in resolution 678 has revived. The Attorney says, and I quote: '[The argument] will only be sustainable if there are strong factual grounds for concluding that Iraq has failed to take the final opportunity. In other words we would need to be able to demonstrate hard evidence of non-compliance and non-co-operation.' Is that substantially the same standard that was being put by the Cabinet Office a year earlier in March 2002?

MURRAY: Well, I would say so yes.

SANDS: Can I then take you three pages on, to the Attorney's statement in the House of Lords, ten days later on the 17th March 2003. The Attorney returns to the question of compliance and I quote: 'It is plain that Iraq has failed so to comply and therefore Iraq was at the time of Resolution 1441 and continues to be materially in breach.' End of quote. Now can I just ask you, between March 7th and 17th the passage of just ten days, what would be your expectation as to the evidence on intelligence to justify that rather clear conclusion by the Attorney?

MURRAY: Well, hard evidence I suppose, I mean. It would need to be very clear. What is…what is curious, is that where the Attorney General on the 7th of March is saying that's what we need, he seems to be satisfied on the 17th of March that that is what has been provided.

SANDS: Let me take you [to Tab 2] paragraph 383 of the Butler Report. The legal secretary to the Attorney writes to the private secretary of the Prime Minister on the 14th March 2003 seeking confirmation that it is 'unequivocally the Prime Minister's view that Iraq has committed further material breaches as specified in paragraph 4 of Resolution 1441'. And then paragraph 384: 'The Prime Minister's private secretary replied to the legal secretary on the 15th March saying that: 'it is indeed the Prime Minister's unequivocal view that Iraq is in further material breach of its obligations'. On what basis do you think the Prime Minister came to that unequivocal view?

MURRAY: Well, I don't know. He doesn't seem to have had any basis for that, but I don't know – your guess is as good as mine.

SANDS: If the Government takes the decision to go to war, would you expect the intelligence basis to be weak or to be strong?

MURRAY: Well, it's the gravest decision that any Government will ever take. Therefore I would have thought they would have a high degree of certainty.

SANDS: No further questions for the time being.

KNOWLES: Sir Murray, I have some questions on behalf of the Prime Minister. He stands accused of a crime of aggression, and the allegation means that he waged a war knowing that it was in breach of the UN charter.

MURRAY: Can I just come in here? I mean one of the problems is knowing that it was illegal, sometimes people believe what they want to believe and there is such a thing as being reckless. It is not for me to decide whether the Prime Minister was being –

KNOWLES: No, no absolutely –

MURRAY: Guilty of that?

KNOWLES: Is it also your understanding that the Attorney General while he is obviously a political appointee doesn't give political advice? Does not give legal advice that is politically expedient but gives legal advice in good faith?

MURRAY: Well he shouldn't do. He shouldn't give political advice, which is politically expedient he should give it in good faith. It's a difficult position he's in. But that is undoubtedly what should be the position.

KNOWLES: Here [in Tab 2 in the Butler Report] in paragraph 381, the Attorney General informed Lord Falconer and Baroness Morgan in a meeting of the 13th March of his view, that it was lawful under 1441 to use force without a further UN Security Council resolution. Do you have any comments on what's recorded there?

MURRAY: Well only that that doesn't seem to me what he's saying in his full written opinion. Certainly I've read this opinion several times now and I thought that his final view was on the whole that a second resolution was needed and that he couldn't advise the Prime Minister as he didn't have the second resolution, he would be safe from prosecution.

KNOWLES: We have first of all international law being very much on the agenda, would you agree? People are concerned to act within the law.

MURRAY: Well certainly, that's why they asked for the Attorney General's opinion.

KNOWLES: Quite so. They were concerned to act within the law. Thank you very much.

SANDS: You'll recall that in the Attorney General's minutes of the 7th March 2003, he directs the Prime Minister to take particular attention to the views of UNMOVIC. Its executive chairman was Dr Blix. You'll recall that in Resolution 1441, Mr Blix had the obligation to report back to the Security Council if he found Iraq to be in material breach. At Tab 17 you've got Dr Blix's report.

MURRAY: I've not seen it before.

SANDS: And nowhere in this document does Mr Blix say that Iraq is in material breach. He is a man of very careful words. Let me just take you to page [6]. The page number is in the right hand corner.

MURRAY: Yes.

SANDS: Mr Blix says in a wonderful Swedish way, 'It would not take years nor weeks but months, neither governments nor inspectors would want disarmament inspections to go on forever however it must be remembered that a sustained inspection and monitoring system is to remain in place to give confidence and to strike an alarm if signs were seen of the revival of any proscribed weapons programmes.' Now I put it to you Sir Murray this is not the conclusion of an executive chairman who has found Iraq to be in material breach.

MURRAY: Well it doesn't read like that.

SANDS: The minute of the 7th March was not the Attorney's final word?

MURRAY: No.

SANDS: The final word seems to have been the view he expressed on the 17th March. Now in that ten-day period what intervening events might have occurred to justify such a change?

MURRAY: Well, I mean there might have… I don't see what uh can have occurred to change the opinion of the law. The law was the same on the 7th March as it was on the 17th March. The problem is that it is differently expressed by the Attorney. I don't know why he changed his mind but he did change his mind.

SANDS: There are, there is an explanation Sir Murray.

MURRAY: Well obviously one explanation is that he was leant on to change his mind. But that's a serious thing to say.

SANDS: Thank you very much. I have no further questions.

KNOWLES: Under international tribunal rules I'm entitled to the last word. To a lay audience they may think the business of lawyering, the business of giving legal opinions is as straight-forward as looking up the answer in a book, and that everything is clear-cut. That is a naïve and simplistic view of the way the business of lawyering is done, wouldn't you agree?

MURRAY: Oh of course, I mean you've got to give weight to the conflicting argument but, um having listened to argument in court, having considered the papers and having considered the views of the experience of others, you come up with a judgement and having given that judgement you don't change it.

KNOWLES: The question is really this, changes of opinion do not necessarily betoken that there is bad faith in operation. It could just be the problem's difficult and that your mind has changed.

MURRAY: Well, um yes, I mean I would think you would need to have, um, to have been persuaded that you made a mistake. But what I don't think I would do, five or six days later say: 'Oh terribly sorry I've got that wrong, I've changed my mind.' I mean, it's a very odd thing to happen.

SCENE 5: CLARE SHORT

SANDS: Ms Short, you are a Member of Parliament are you not?

SHORT: I am, the Member of Parliament for Birmingham Ladywood, elected in 1983 as a Labour MP. And I, just a few months ago, resigned the Labour whip but I am still a member of the Labour Party.

SANDS: And you were in Cabinet as a Labour Minister for a certain period were you not?

SHORT: For six years, from 1997 till 2003, whenever it was, April I think.

SANDS: And what were your functions as Minister?

SHORT: I was Secretary of State for International Development.

SANDS: Was there any discussion of Iraq in Cabinet before July 2002?

SHORT: We had discussions from time to time. I brought it up a lot.

I can remember one, I think it must have been when we came back from the Summer recess, when Tony said, right, now we can have a discussion of Iraq, and people like Estelle Morris, erm, Alan Milburn, Patricia Hewitt were all speaking up, very sort of frankly and honestly and saying, what about the Palestinians? And what about the UN? And this was when people had been thinking freely and brought their thoughts to the table. But after that things were managed through the media and discussions were very much managed, but this is the style of the Cabinet by Tony Blair, Tony would intervene in a sort of chatty way, not anything like the constitutional image people have of a sort of serious discussion in the Cabinet with everyone giving a view and the Prime Minister summing up. They were little chats.

SANDS: You were not a member of the War Cabinet, so called.

SHORT: I was actually but the War Cabinet didn't exist till the war had started.

SANDS: Sorry, I am using the phrase War Cabinet inaccurately. I am talking about the inner grouping that met in July 2002.

SHORT: Ah yes. I don't think it would be accurate to call it a War Cabinet as it was predominantly officials. And this is how Tony runs everything…

SANDS: But…

SHORT: And the whole of the Iraq war…

SANDS: But…

SHORT: Was run…

SANDS: But...

SHORT: By little informal groups of sort of, his personal appointees and people close to him. That is the way Britain is governed.

SANDS: So...so you were excluded shall we say, from those select deliberations?

SHORT: Well I think that's correct in that my department had necessarily a role in any preparations for afterwards in relating to various UN bodies. Erm, I saw all the intelligence that was circulated in Whitehall. I was expressing doubts about the whole enterprise. The department had a legitimate role and couldn't be completely left out.

SANDS: Well, let's look at your book that we will use as a lengthy witness statement. And at page 141, you noted in your diary, and I quote: 'TB just keeps saying nothing decided.' End of quote, and this refers to September 2002. Were you surprised when after the war press reports started emerging [that] certainly by April 2002, the Prime Minister had expressed his commitment to President Bush that he was fully in support of regime change?

SHORT: Yes. The Downing Street Memo and so on. When that became available, it became obvious that Tony Blair had given his word absolutely firmly to President Bush at a time when he was telling his Cabinet, Parliament and country and me individually, that nothing had been decided. And there is no doubt –
it was just straightforward deceit and the documents prove it.

SANDS: Deceit or dishonesty?

SHORT: Both. Lies, half truths, deceit, hints, I actually think Tony, he doesn't sit down and say I'm going to tell a lie here, he's so much kind of – I can charm my way through this, I can, I can just sort of tell Clare this, or tell the

Cabinet that, and get through it and he thinks that's what politics is. He doesn't see it as lies, but I'm afraid it is lies.

SANDS: Can I take you to Tab 22? This refers to a memorandum which reflected a meeting on the 31st January 2003, several weeks before the war began and if I can just take you to the opening paragraphs. 'The starting date for the military campaign was now pencilled in for 10th March,' Mr Manning wrote, paraphrasing the President.

SHORT: Where are we sorry?

SANDS: (*Goes to her and shows her the document in bundle.*) This was when the bombing would begin.

SHORT: (*Reading.*) 'Our diplomatic strategy'…yes… (*Looking at SANDS.*) …yes.

SANDS: You were not aware that the President Bush and the Prime Minister had met on the 31st January 2003 and indeed agreed on a timetable for war?

SHORT: No but I was having meetings with the Head of SIS, as we call it, MI6, and it's funny I had always met with them over various crises in Africa or in Pakistan or wherever we were working, and then Blair tried to block my access to those people and, of course I was reading the intelligence that circulates in printed form through Whitehall, but I made a big fuss and he let me see them, and I can remember them saying, 15th February is the date. Which if you remember is the day of the big demonstration, it was also my birthday, I remember it really well, and they later said it slipped back to March.

SANDS: Did you form the view that they were under the impression that the Prime Minister had committed?

SHORT: Well they kept saying things like they were trying to help the Prime Minister, and there is a certain frisson and, you know, they are all going off to the White House, they sort of like all that, it's exciting, but when they're talking to me they're sort of worried too, and they are saying this is the US target date.

SANDS: [On] page 169, you describe in passing, the February 2003 Cabinet meeting and you mention that you stressed the need for UN authorisation of the war. When you raised the issue who is there to respond, to any concerns that you raised?

SHORT: Oh, the only person who ever responds on any of these questions is Tony Blair.

SANDS: And what response did he give you?

SHORT: He kept saying we will only proceed through the UN which is a crucial thing for people like me – most of the bulk of the Labour Party and so on. But he's a great one for a bit of wriggle room in the way he answers questions.

SANDS: But to cut to the chase, there was no one made available to you in Cabinet to address the legal concerns that you expressed in February. No advice or view from the law officers had been put to Cabinet. Is that correct?

SHORT: That is absolutely correct.

SANDS: So February 2003, you've had no word from the Attorney or the other law officer and nothing has been before Cabinet, then you describe in your book, you take the novel step, you say, of going off to consult with the Prime Minister's wife. What was that about?

SHORT: Because, well it was just, I'm getting more and more desperate about international law, and thinking, well Cherie is a human rights lawyer and you know, she and Tony have a very close relationship – why not give it a try? I know it's a very odd thing to do but I mean things were getting very extreme. Try anything.

SANDS: And what did that result in?

SHORT: I had a note that I had sent to Tony about international law, also the Geneva Convention, and the rules post-occupation and everything, erm, which I took a copy with me, she gave me a cup of tea, and was terribly nice, and was generally reassuring and said of course, Tony will always honour international law and gave me the very firm impression she was involved in detailing considerations of questions but sort of: 'Don't worry Clare, it will all be alright.'

SANDS: Let's then come to the Cabinet meeting on the 17th [March] which as you put it, the Attorney General is served up, he's served up along with a couple of sheets of paper. As you describe in the book and he takes the seat of Mr Cook who has now resigned from Cabinet.

SHORT: And didn't come to that meeting. I still think that's very odd, why didn't Robin come and argue, just resigned and went, it was kind of poignant, because the Attorney sat in his seat.

SANDS: What…what was on your desks?

SHORT: Well then they put these, I can't remember if it [was] two sheets or one sheet of A4 and it was just put round the table as we were coming in. There was a general fraught atmosphere and then in comes the Attorney General and he starts reading it out word for word. And we are all reading it, then we sort of say, it's alright we can read, and he sort of says, well that's it, and Tony says, Well that's it. Something like that: 'That's it, there's the legal advice.' And I say –

SANDS: Sorry can I just pause there, are you saying, the Prime Minister used those words, 'That's the legal advice'?

SHORT: I can't remember the exact words, but the whole thing was: here it is, that's the legal advice, okay, and they were trying to cut the meeting short.

SANDS: You were not aware of any other documents that the Attorney General might have authored.

SHORT: No, absolutely not.

CALLED TO ACCOUNT: ACT ONE

SANDS: This is the...

SHORT: I mean I was stunned by it, but I absolutely believed he had brought his legal advice to Cabinet and that's what it was.

SANDS: What surprised you about the document?

SHORT: Well, that it came so late and it was so firm. I started to say, well could you explain how it has taken you all this time, did you have any doubts, and they were all saying, Oh Clare be quiet. It was like everything is very fraught and they didn't want that discussion. I tried to get a discussion, I read it, I was astonished by it, and I have to say, I thought this is the Attorney General of Britain in his formal role as a law officer coming to the Cabinet on the brink of war. Stunning as it is, this was his legal opinion. I mean that's what it meant for the military, they were thinking of refusing the order but he produced this, which meant that they then didn't feel entitled to refuse the order.

SANDS: So he had his finger on the trigger?

SHORT: Absolutely. I've tried to make a complaint to the Bar Council since, when the full legal advice was out. They said he was acting, not as a barrister but as a Minister and, of course, the enforcement of the Ministerial code is dependent on the Prime Minister.

SANDS: And of course we know now that the Attorney had given a fuller advice.

SHORT: I just think it's completely dishonourable. He's unfit to be Attorney-General. We can't have a law officer that's meant to advise our Government system on the legality of war that's a crony, a personal appointee, who can be leant on in this sort of way and then distort the legal advice to give the Prime Minister what he wants, and this is, dishonours our whole system.

SANDS: What would have been the reaction, this is a matter of speculation obviously, amongst your colleagues in Cabinet if the full legal advice had been put before the Cabinet on the 17th March?

Pause.

SHORT: I don't know. But it would have been completely and absolutely different. It would have been a much longer meeting, much more complicated.

I think it would have been very much more difficult for Tony to get the yes.

SANDS: Thank you, I have no more questions.

KNOWLES: How many issues would you say you disagree with the present Government on?

SHORT: Well in any Government, any decent Minister will have little doubts and worries about all sorts of things that are going on. I mean that's the nature of...

KNOWLES: (*Interrupts.*) I mean central key themes.

SHORT: I thought broadly the first term was a pretty decent Labour government with lots of New Labour spin that got on people's nerves, but was fundamentally a decent Government. And then what went wrong was both Iraq and a whole series of other things, I think there was a change in the way in which the Prime Minister operated, from the second term on.

KNOWLES: And now of course you've resigned the whip and you sit as an independent Labour MP. The position has come when you are no longer even prepared to support the Government in Parliament.

SHORT: That's right.

KNOWLES: There was a time when you supported the Government on Iraq, and you in fact voted in favour of the war on the 18th March. Is that right?

SHORT: That's absolutely right, as everybody knows, I didn't believe it was the right thing, and I wasn't going to vote for it, but the Prime Minister entered into a negotiation with me, and er, promised well, one, if he could persuade me to stay he could probably persuade President Bush to come out to support the road map and we should have established a Palestinian State by the end of March 2005 – which he did, the President came out and said that. And secondly, he promised that the reconstruction would be led by the UN – internationalised. I knew by then we couldn't stop the war, so very painfully I voted for the war because the Prime Minister had made those promises.

KNOWLES: So you went into the... Was abstention not an option?

SHORT: No.

KNOWLES: Because you had to vote one way or the other...

SHORT: Actually my Permanent Secretary had negotiated and proposed that I would go to the UN and not be there for the vote. But then Gordon Brown came in and said that's impossible.

KNOWLES: So we then fast-forward two months or thereabouts, to May 12th which was the date of your resignation. What prompted the resignation so soon after the event?

SHORT: Well we'd...the whole question of the authority for the occupation, the powers of the occupying powers, what's the role of the UN? Tony was absolutely breaching the promise he had made to me on the UN lead.

KNOWLES: If we, if you and I read the Butler Report from the first page to the last we wouldn't find any suggestion in there that the Prime Minister lied or misled Parliament or misled the public.

SHORT: Well I think the Butler Report is a very good report, in a very British Mandarinese, understated kind of language.

KNOWLES: So the short answer?

SHORT: It wasn't taken as seriously as it should have been.

KNOWLES: The short answer, is no we wouldn't, we don't find any accusation against the Prime Minister of that nature.

SHORT: No I don't agree. I think the Butler Report makes very serious allegations. And I think Butler made the speech in the House of Lords that you might want to look at.

KNOWLES: No doubt, if there's anything there, Mr Sands will produce a book. My question for the third time of asking, is, and I suggest it is the case, that Lord Butler, having investigated the matter, made no conclusion about the Prime Minister's bad faith.

SHORT: What shocks me and I think should worry everyone is that this degree of deceit and manipulation of the legal advice that has been engaged in, no one has held the Prime Minister or our political system to account. People in Britain have lost faith in their political institutions partly because of all this.

KNOWLES: We know there were strenuous good faith efforts to get a second [UN] resolution?

SHORT: There were efforts but not good faith. They were in bad faith.

KNOWLES: You're saying there were efforts but the whole thing was a charade?

SHORT: I didn't want this. I really regret that the Government did this and so dishonoured itself and the Labour Party. But truth is profoundly important and I think it's the duty of all of us to try and stand up for truth about the serious questions and this is a monumentally serious thing for British history and British constitution and dreadfully sad thing for this Government and Tony Blair's historical record. But there it is.

End of Act One.

Act Two

SCENE 1: MICHAEL MATES

NÍ GHRÁLAIGH pours MICHAEL MATES a glass of water from a bottle on the table. As she pours:

MATES: I might need something stronger by the time I finish this. I should have brought Butler with me.

NÍ GHRÁLAIGH: (*Handing MATES a copy of the Butler Report.*) You can have that and give it back.

MATES: Here we go. (*Looking at KNOWLES.*)

KNOWLES: Shall I start then. Okay. You are Michael Mates.

MATES: Yes.

KNOWLES: And could you tell us a little bit about your career please?

MATES: I was an officer in the British army. I was elected to Parliament in 1974 – I have been there ever since. I was a Minister of State in John Major's Government. I then joined the Intelligence and Security Committee when it was formed thirteen years ago.

KNOWLES: Now you, um, were a member of Lord Butler's Committee that was appointed to look into intelligence matters after the war. I want to ask you a little bit about how the Committee carried out its work, you were working under constraints of time?

MATES: Yes, we were appointed as I recall in February and we were asked to report by the summer recess.

KNOWLES: This is February of 2004?

MATES: If you say so yes. Is there a list of all the people we saw? I'm not sure whether it's public. Who we went to.

SANDS: There is a list.

KNOWLES: Oh yes, it's page 161.

MATES: Oh, this is terrific.

Silence.

Yep, okay, it's on the record. Sorry, I thought I'd try – be a bit careful. We started off with a series of informal meetings, I think I can tell you one, I can break one confidence, when we saw Lord Hutton we had a pretty interesting chat with him about the various aspects of what he'd done and at the very end Robin Butler said: 'Well, thank you Lord Hutton very much, is there any final thing you'd like to say to us?' and he leaned back and put his fingers together and said in the very dour way that he had, 'Yes, don't report'. Which he said without a smile, I think he was heavily scarred by what had happened to him.

KNOWLES: Were you in particular looking at the issue of whether there had been deliberate misuse by the Government of intelligence?

MATES: Well the challenge was to decide whether that was accidental or deliberate. Conspiracy or cock-up? It is nearly always the latter in my experience.

KNOWLES: So if you had found that there had been deliberate and knowing distortion, misuse, overstatement of intelligence by the Government, the decision makers. Did that fall within the remit of the Committee?

MATES: Certainly, and we did report on some aspects, I think one of the phrases was 'more emphasis was put on this than the intelligence could bear' – isn't that a phrase that comes out of this somewhere? That may be wrong…but it's close.

KNOWLES: Did you meet with the Attorney General as part of your work?

MATES: We did, we took evidence from him.

KNOWLES: One of the allegations is that the legal advice that he gave to the House [of Lords] fitted the answer he knew he was expected to give in order to support the Government's case for war – that he gave dishonest legal advice is the suggestion.

MATES' mobile phone rings.

MATES: Sorry I should have switched that off. I will switch it off.

He switches it off.

Where were we?

KNOWLES: What is your comment on that suggestion? The Attorney General's section is 366 onwards.

MATES: 366?

KNOWLES: Yep.

MATES: Sorry, I must be very careful here.

Silence.

Now, the Attorney General was, and I think has never made any bones about it, in difficulty because his advice at some stage changed and that was really only over the United Nations resolutions. He was quite clear about why his advice changed, why he took one view initially and then took another.

KNOWLES: What did he say the reason was?

MATES: He said that things had moved on and that he had taken another look at the Second Resolution and I think it was difficult for him but he was, in the end, quite clear that yes his advice had changed and it had changed in good faith. He said he wasn't put under pressure. There was no evidence to the contrary.

KNOWLES: On the 17th March, the day of the House of Commons debate, the Attorney General submitted a shorter document of what his view of the legal position of the war was. It has been suggested that was produced for reasons of political expediency. Could you just tell us about that?

MATES: The fact that it was contrived, as a parliamentary answer is neither here nor there, that's just procedural. There was pressure, which actually was wrong, because people were saying the Chief of Defence staff refused to go to war without a certificate if you like.

KNOWLES: So the, just to be clear about it, the origin of the Parliamentary answer of the shorter statement, came from the soldiers, rather than the politicians?

MATES: No, no. My recollection is that there was enormous media pressure and political pressure, um to know what the legal advice was. At the same time, the Chief of Defence staff who was about to commit his troops said, 'Well I need my piece of paper please, telling me that this is legal.' And that would have happened in Kosovo, in Bosnia, you know, in all sorts of places.

KNOWLES: The allegation's been made that the Prime Minister knowingly lied to the House of Commons in the course of the debate on the war in order to procure a favourable vote. What is your reaction to that charge, based on the material that you have seen?

MATES: Had we thought that, it would have been very difficult, we'd probably have said so. We didn't think that. We did think that there was some extraordinary circumstances surrounding the facts, or alleged facts that the Prime Minister presented. I was going to come on to the 45 minute bit. It's in this report?

KNOWLES: Yes.

MATES: Can you point me to it? Sorry.

SANDS: It starts at 504.

MATES: Thank you, can I just take a look at that?

Silence.

Ah, you see, we did comment on it as well. We said it was unhelpful. Sorry, the Intelligence Committee said it was unhelpful, Butler agreed with that and took the firm view that the JIC should have included that judgement in its assessment and in the dossier. Nobody, except the experts, knew what it was referring to. And then you'll remember great maps appeared in the newspapers with rings around it, you know, that they could hit Cyprus within 45 minutes and all this and that.

KNOWLES: *Private Eye* said it could hit Neasden.

MATES: Yes, it was – Sorry what, was that?

KNOWLES: *Private Eye* said it could hit Neasden.

MATES: Ha, I missed that. And it was one of those things that there was fairly trenchant criticism about because it was a cock-up. We had no evidence that it was a conspiracy.

KNOWLES: The focus of this trial is on the Prime Minister's personal responsibility, rather than his broader collective responsibility, so on the charge of lying to Parliament you would acquit him?

MATES: Yes.

KNOWLES: Yes, thank you very much.

SANDS: [In Butler] you didn't express any view did you on the decision-making process on the political issues taken by the Prime Minister did you?

MATES: Yes we did, right at the end of the report we said that the 'style of Government –'

SANDS: Paragraph 611, I think.

MATES: '– may have had something to do with some of the errors that occurred.' I think that was it. Now that is a criticism, it's what we'd call in shorthand 'sofa-style' government. That a number of things didn't get minuted.

SANDS: Tab 12 [in the bundle], right at the end is the minute, 'Iraq, Prime Minister's meeting 23rd July [2002]'. Can I take you to the comment by the Foreign Secretary? 'It seemed clear that Bush had made up his mind to take military actions even if the timing was not yet decided, but the case was thin.' What we're hearing is a meeting of the most senior Cabinet Ministers, being told that the evidence is thin, and six weeks later the Prime Minister writes a foreword to a report saying there is no doubt as to what is going on. Does not that raise certain questions?

MATES: Well, he would probably with retrospect wish to have put the word 'reasonable' in.

SANDS: So it wasn't an accurate statement?

MATES: Well, I mean...

SANDS: Would you confirm that statement?

MATES: It's not my job to defend the Prime Minister.

SANDS: You're doing an excellent job at it, if I may say. But there's no hint in the Butler Report, is there, that senior Cabinet Ministers thought that the intelligence was thin? [One] of our witnesses, Sir Murray Stuart Smith whose reputation you will know, when asked which other body the Prime Minister could turn to for advice on intelligence, apart from the JIC, concluded that he knew of none.

MATES: Well, that's true.

SANDS: Is it then the case that the Prime Minister expressed his unequivocal view that Iraq was in further material breach i.e. after December 2002, without taking into account the views of the JIC? On what basis did he reach that view?

MATES: Well, I'm sure he reached it because he was in, at that stage, daily touch with the heads of the Intelligence

Service, particularly SIS. And this is, if you like a further reflection of the informality with which these things were done.

SANDS: Is it an appropriate way to take such a decision as grave as this with such informality?

MATES: I don't think it is, no.

SANDS: Well, let's go back then to the Attorney's advice. You voted for the war in March 2003.

MATES: I did.

SANDS: The resolution that was before the House referred to the opinion of the Attorney General and I think when you voted you had before you the one page document?

MATES: Yup.

SANDS: It's now entered into the public domain that there was a longer document. Were you surprised when that longer document appeared before you?

Silence.

MATES: Well.

Silence.

He says he set out his views of the legal position to the Cabinet by producing and speaking to the written answer.

SANDS: So were you surprised to discover that not only was there a one-page document but also a thirteen-page document, written just ten days earlier?

MATES: I would not have been surprised *per se*, provided that the one page was a faithful reproduction of the thirteen pages.

SANDS: You don't want to express a view do you as to the apparent lateness with which the Attorney's advice was provided to the Prime Minister?

MATES: Well, I don't know when it was provided.

SANDS: 7th March 2003, ten days before the war.

MATES: I think it is in the public domain, stop me if I'm wrong, but one of the things that the Prime Minister said was, 'I will ask for the Attorney's advice when I have come to a conclusion and I don't want it before.' Now is that public?

SANDS: It is public, it's in Robin Cook's book.

MATES: I think it's extraordinary that something like 23 Cabinet meetings between the summer I think and January when Iraq was on the agenda, the Attorney General was only present at one or two. I find that extraordinary, I'm speaking personally now, because Butler doesn't view this because that was none of our business.

SANDS: Because that was outside your terms of reference?

MATES: Because that was outside our terms of reference, yes. I think it is quite extraordinary in a system of Cabinet government when they are moving into territory as serious as this with legal consequences as profound as this, they don't have their legal advisor there. That was the Prime Minister's decision, I believe.

SANDS: And therefore, if that's the case, the decision for which he takes the responsibility.

MATES: Oh yes.

SCENE 2: EDWARD MORTIMER

SANDS: Mr Mortimer, could I begin by asking you about your professional background?

MORTIMER: Most of my life I've been a journalist but for the last eight and a half years I worked in the United Nations as Chief Speech Writer and latterly Director of Communications for the Secretary General, Kofi Annan.

SANDS: And were you, associated with the United Nations in the run up to the war in Iraq?

MORTIMER: Yes.

SANDS: At what point did you form the view that in the course of 2002 that war in Iraq was moving from the possible to something more likely?

MORTIMER: In the late summer probably. Gosh, it's hard to recall exactly the chronology of things but I think that probably from the time of the 'Axis of Evil' speech in January 2002 there was a quite widespread expectation that something like that would happen, and I, erm, seem to remember in August 2002 there were pronouncements by Vice President Cheney and others which rather reinforced that conviction.

SANDS: So we move to the autumn of 2002. Tell us a little bit about, what the atmosphere was like before Resolution 1441 was adopted?

MORTIMER: Well of course the key thing was, that started the ball rolling, so to speak, was Bush's speech to the General Assembly, which was sort of an ultimatum and the Secretary General was very concerned, if possible, to get Iraq to comply with that ultimatum, as he saw that as the only way of avoiding war. And he sort of gatecrashed a meeting of Arab Foreign Ministers, I think a couple of days after Bush's speech, and which included the Iraqi Foreign Minister and he basically said to them, look this is obviously very serious and you have got to comply with the Security Council resolutions, you have got to let the inspectors back in. And as a result of that a letter came from Baghdad but it was still a sort of if-ish but-ish kind of letter and there was a sort of sub-negotiation which actually went on, on the 38th floor where the Secretary General's office is. You might think that the Americans who had ostensibly been pushing for this would have been pleased that the Secretary General had made such efforts to get

Iraq to comply – in fact they were rather cross because they clearly expected and wanted the answer no.

SANDS: What was the British Government reaction to that set of events?

MORTIMER: Well I think they were more in sympathy with what the Secretary General was trying to do.

SANDS: They being?

MORTIMER: Well again I'm not privy to what the Prime Minister may have thought. If you'd asked me at that time I would probably have said I think the Brits would prefer not to have a war but they are very serious about disarming Iraq. Whereas the Americans want to disarm Iraq, but they want more than that.

SANDS: And that of course takes us straight on to Resolution 1441, and to justify the use of force. There must be some kind of further material breach.

MORTIMER: Well, as I interpret the Resolution, the Council were saying, we are giving Iraq one last chance and therefore if Iraq, now at the eleventh hour, complies with our requirements it will not be necessary to proceed to military action.

SANDS: The Secretary General had formed the view that it was only for the Security Council to decide and not the individual members?

MORTIMER: I believe that's right, yes.

SANDS: [He] had conversations with the British Foreign Secretary and the British Prime Minister –

MORTIMER: Yes.

SANDS: Is it possible that the Secretary General would have communicated to the Foreign Secretary or the Prime Minister that view?

MORTIMER: I think it's very likely.

SANDS: Can I take you then to the dates in early March, it must have been very frenetic days –

MORTIMER: Yes indeed.

SANDS: When the British put forward a possible resolution, can you describe what the atmosphere was like?

MORTIMER: Well the atmosphere was indeed very tense, as you say, I mean of course there had been these massive demonstrations around the world, there had been the famous article in the *New York Times* which said that the Third Superpower, or Second Superpower had been discovered which was world public opinion. There was an enormous pressure from both sides on the non-permanent members of the Security Council. And I think it became more and more apparent that there were, in those circumstances and at that time, not the votes.

SANDS: The description suggests to me that it was pretty clear, early on, on the 38th floor that a resolution was not likely to pass.

MORTIMER: Well I think it was fairly clear but I don't think it was certain because you know, the capacity of Great Powers to convince Small Powers to go along with what they want is very considerable. If you are a country like Mexico you don't go lightly against the wishes of the United States. But it did become gradually apparent that there was this countervailing force which I think, I've always thought was, ironically enough, a vindication of democracy, although many Americans took it the other way, I think actually it showed it's become more difficult to get governments to do something of which their people strongly disapprove.

SANDS: The pressures on the small countries must have been intense –

MORTIMER: (*Interrupts.*) Yes of course the French put pressure on African countries over which they have a lot of influence too. I don't want to make it out that it was a one-sided thing.

SANDS: What was your reaction later on when you learnt the news stories that some of the Security Council members may have been the subjects of bugging or eavesdropping?

MORTIMER: 'I was shocked', rather in the sense of Claude Rains in *Casablanca*.

SANDS: So, not unexpected. For the British public this might be a great revelation but for you on the 38th floor this was all part of Great Power Politics.

MORTIMER: I'm afraid that's the assumption we go on.

SANDS: And yet all of that under pressure didn't produce a second resolution. What was the British delegation's reaction?

MORTIMER: They were sort of dismayed – approaching to meltdown. It was actually sad and undignified when Greenstock and [the US Ambassador] Negroponte had to appear and say that they were withdrawing this. And I think among the British delegation there was some acrimony towards their American allies. They felt that Bush, paradoxically I think, they felt that Bush had not given as much support to this, not taken the negotiation of a possible new resolution as seriously as they would have liked.

SANDS: Would the office of the legal advisor at the United Nations have formed a view as to the legality of the war in Iraq without an explicit second resolution?

MORTIMER: I think that they would have thought that it was not legal, but I think that everybody in the Secretariat was aware that words carry an enormous political charge in these kinds of situations and the Secretary General at that time used the phrase 'not in conformity with the charter' and it was only a year and a half later and under pressure from [BBC reporter] Owen Bennett Jones that he conceded that that was effectively a paraphrase for the word 'illegal' from a UN point of view.

SANDS: Thank you very much. I have got no more questions for the time being.

NÍ GHRÁLAIGH: If we can just take a step back, the reason why we're here of course is to see if there is sufficient material in which to indict the Prime Minister for the crime of aggression and one of the reasons behind it, is that the second resolution didn't take place. Now based on your extensive knowledge of the UN, would it be fair to say that in all of the wars that have taken place since the creation of the UN in 1945, very few have been authorised by the Security Council?

MORTIMER: Yes. I mean the only ones directly authorised that I'm aware of were in Korea in 1950 and the first war against Iraq in 1990/1991.

NÍ GHRÁLAIGH: And that would include wars in which, or instances in which, the UK has been involved in, in the past?

MORTIMER: Well it would noticeably include the one in Kosovo in 1999 which many people in the UN thought was illegal, and indeed I think many thought that the legal justification was even thinner, in terms of the Security Council's resolutions, for that one.

NÍ GHRÁLAIGH: As you say the closest analogy is with and between the Iraq war and the Kosovo crisis.

MORTIMER: I didn't say that. I said this was an example.

NÍ GHRÁLAIGH: And with that as background, I'd like to return to what Kofi Annan's position was in relation to the military action in Kosovo. And for this I'd like to take you to a transcript of a conference that you gave in Washington last year, in October –

MORTIMER: You've certainly done your homework.

NÍ GHRÁLAIGH: That's also – these two pages. Can I take you to page 16? He goes to the General Assembly in September 1999 and says: 'Look the Security Council should take care, it shouldn't presume on its authority because if it is not able and willing to deal with a crisis like this, somebody is going to take the law into their own hands.'

MORTIMER: Yeah.

NÍ GHRÁLAIGH: So, two things stick out here really; the first is that you describe Kofi Annan's position here as being that it would be much more preferable that these things be decided by the Security Council, not that it's necessary. Kofi Annan didn't say that in 2000 –

MORTIMER: (*Interrupts.*) Here we're talking about what is now known as the 'responsibility to protect' populations from genocide, ethnic cleansing, war crimes, crimes against humanity. This was not the way that the issue about Iraq was presented to the United Nations in 2003. [The Secretary General] was very well aware of an acute tension between two principles, which to him were both very important. One was that sovereignty was not a licence to commit genocide or massacre or ethnic cleansing and the other was that if there was going to be military action that there should be some kind of international procedure for legitimising it.

NÍ GHRÁLAIGH: Nobody's tabled a resolution to state that the war in Iraq was illegal or a war of aggression or anything like that?

MORTIMER: That is true, not in the Security Council.

NÍ GHRÁLAIGH: By unanimous vote, the Security Council declared through 1441 that Saddam Hussein was in material breach. Saddam was to be given, as you yourself have described 'one last chance' to comply? What was to happen was that the Security Council was then to convene to consider the situation. The text doesn't stipulate that they have to discuss whether or not to take military action.

MORTIMER: Well, I'm sorry, I'm not a lawyer but I think it's a matter of common sense.

NÍ GHRÁLAIGH: You said that Britain was mainly interested in…in seeing previous resolutions enforced, that it wasn't in a rush to war in the same way that America was.

MORTIMER: That was my impression.

NÍ GHRÁLAIGH: And did that impression change?

MORTIMER: I was basically an observer, learning what was happening through the media like anybody else; but my impression was…the conclusion that one cannot avoid is that the British Prime Minister, if there was going to be a war, he wanted Britain to be in it.

SCENE 3: JUAN GABRIEL VALDES

SANDS: [Mr Valdes] I wonder if you could begin by giving us a bit about your personal background and your professional training?

VALDES: I am a diplomat, I was appointed after democracy came back to [Chile], as Ambassador to Spain, then I became Minister of Foreign Affairs [in Chile].

SANDS: Just to be clear on the timing, you were Foreign Minister during Pinochet's residence in London?

VALDES: That is correct.

SANDS: So you have a certain experience about proceedings of this kind?

VALDES: That is right. I became very much involved in the opposition against the dictatorship of General Pinochet.

SANDS: When did you move to the United Nations?

VALDES: In March 2000.

SANDS: What was your understanding as Ambassador to Chile of what [Resolution] 1441 set in motion?

VALDES: Our understanding was that even if it was a very serious situation, it did not imply a decision to attack Iraq.

SANDS: Were you familiar with Ambassador Greenstock's statement and the slightly different approach it had from that of ambassadors [from other countries]?

VALDES: Yes. I think so. I have the recollection of the French Ambassador telling me immediately after the vote that the Resolution was doomed with different interpretations.

SANDS: Ambassador [Mahbubani of Singapore], who was on the Security Council at the time, describes how Ambassador Greenstock told him after 1441 that it was clear a further Resolution would be needed. Do you have any recollection of that?

VALDES: To clarify your question, what you are saying is that Ambassador Greenstock said explicitly that a further…

SANDS: It was a private conversation?

VALDES: Yes but he implied that a second resolution would be needed?

SANDS: Yes.

VALDES: I not only have a recollection I believe that in my notes in discussions that came after that debate on the Resolution in my notes I have, Ambassador Greenstock saying exactly that.

SANDS: Did he ever say that to you?

VALDES: Yes, and not only that I believe that he said that publicly in one of the private meetings of the Security Council.

SANDS: You need to explain a little because people won't be clear what you mean by 'say something publicly in a private meeting'.

VALDES: Yes, you are right. Well as you know the Security Council has private sessions, public sessions. The private sessions are sessions in which Ambassadors examine the different issues that are in front of the Security Council...

SANDS: Of course...

VALDES: I have the clear impression that Ambassador Greenstock indicated that there was a need for a second resolution.

SANDS: Ambassador Greenstock has written a book. An extract did briefly appear on the website of publisher, Public Affairs, and that extract described the conflict as 'illegitimate'. I quote those words. Does that accord with your recollection of his view of the conflict?

VALDES: Well, that is difficult to say because I would say that Ambassador Greenstock was extremely receptive to our views as representatives of countries that would decide finally as the voters. In our case we don't have national intelligence on these issues. We [also] knew what [being a] developing country meant. We knew [that] to look for records everywhere was something not too reasonable. We knew that Intelligence Services were somewhat of a disaster because we had been the subject of intelligence reports ourselves and we knew how intelligence sources tended to distort and to have some empty sort of information...

SANDS: Let's turn to January 2003, what your impression was when you first took up your seat in relation to the reports by the inspectors of what did or did not exist in Iraq in terms of WMD?

VALDES: Okay, before addressing that, if you allow me one more word on what I was saying before. The fact that we didn't have intelligence didn't mean that we didn't have good common sense and that we tried to get information from where we thought it was better to seek it. I am referring to the Arab countries. We decided to have talks with every one of the members of the Arab group at the UN, who told us, in private, exactly what has happened historically in Iraq. It was not something very difficult to get that information, that if the war happens, Iran would take an enormous role, that the situation would be absolutely catastrophic, and that the turn of events would leave the USA and Great Britain to be involved in an atrocious political situation.

SANDS: The last session with the Inspectors was on 7th March 2003. Was it the view of the Council that Mr Blix and Mr El-Baradei had found Iraq to be in further material breach?

VALDES: Blix and El-Baradei consistently gave a negative response to the US or UK allegations.

SANDS: Did the reports of Mr Blix and El-Baradei constitute hard evidence of non-compliance and non-co-operation?

VALDES: Not at all. On the contrary.

SANDS: Did Ambassador Greenstock ever offer to make available to you, private briefings on British Intelligence?

VALDES: Yes, we were invited, both the Mexican Ambassadors and myself were invited at different times to the [British] mission to be presented [with intelligence reports] which, to say the least, we found not convincing.

SANDS: Were you given those presentations by two members of the British Intelligence Services, MI6?

VALDES: We supposed so.

SANDS: You said you didn't find it too convincing. Could you explain why not?

VALDES: Well our question was if Iraq is producing this amount of weapons, and these are the locations, why on earth don't you tell the Inspectors the same thing you are telling us.

SANDS: When you put these questions to the people you supposed were from MI6, did they give you the impression that they were convinced by their own intelligence?

VALDES: Frankly speaking I don't believe so.

SANDS: At what point did you become aware that your movements and your telephone conversations and other communications were being monitored and spied on by the British and the Americans?

VALDES: There was a moment which to me is clear. I invited our senior police in Chile to visit my mission and they gave me... After examining the mission, they told me that I had microphones in every place and in all the telephones.

SANDS: Do you believe the British Government behaved honourably and honestly on the issue of intelligence and related matters in the context of this series of issues in Iraq?

VALDES: I would say that I reserve my opinion or I prefer to wait on time and look at the records that I am sure will pop out some time.

SANDS: Thank you very much.

NÍ GHRÁLAIGH: I am going to ask you a number of questions on behalf of the defence, that is on behalf of the Prime Minister. The second [UN] resolution that was sought, by the British Government prior to the war. The position of the defence is this: 'I am sure a second resolution would of course have been politically preferable but it wasn't legally necessary that there is no crime committed because there was no secondary resolution.' So do you understand that is the view that we are putting forward?

VALDES: Yes, I understand that is your view.

NÍ GHRÁLAIGH: I was slightly taken aback earlier when you said that there was no evidence of non-compliance and non-co-operation.

VALDES: We believed that, these hurdles and what we called at the time 'breaches', have been proven in time to respond to the fact that Iraqis had no weapons of mass destruction and therefore their original declaration was not false. It is clear it was incomplete, it was clear that they didn't like to present that their scientists or their technicians, but at the end we found that the Iraqis were prepared to send their scientists to Cyprus, they were prepared to allow them to be interviewed even without minders, therefore the inspectors were surpassing all the hurdles that had been put in front of them. The question was, therefore, to decide, and this is a political decision, do we consider that any incomplete response or any hurdles put in front of the inspectors is sufficient to cancel inspections and to launch war? That was the problem.

NÍ GHRÁLAIGH: There is an accusation that the effort by the British Government to secure a second resolution were just a farce or a charade. But in fact they were very real weren't they?

VALDES: I fully agree with you on that.

NÍ GHRÁLAIGH: You have told us quite freely about conversations that you'd had with Mr Greenstock or your impressions of his views on whether or not a second resolution was needed, etc.

VALDES: Well yes, I believe that Ambassador Greenstock did his best to get the second resolution approved. It was no mystery to us that the political situation inside the UK was becoming extremely difficult for Prime Minister Blair.

NÍ GHRÁLAIGH: I wanted briefly to go through the statement that he did make just to touch on a few elements of it. He begins by stating that there is no shadow of a doubt that Iraq has defied the Security Council, and that is what is contained in operatives paragraph 1 of Resolution 1441. Then he goes on to say, 'there is no automaticity in this Resolution. If there is a further Iraqi breach of its disarmament obligations, the matter will return to the Council for discussion as required in operational paragraph 12. We will expect the Security Council to then meet its responsibilities'. So he uses the word 'discuss', doesn't he?

VALDES: Yes, that is right.

NÍ GHRÁLAIGH: So the UK's view as represented by Mr Greenstock was not that a second resolution would be necessary?

VALDES: I would be very surprised if that was true, because the United Kingdom made such an effort to persuade us to support a second.

NÍ GHRÁLAIGH: Politically necessary but not legally necessary. It was desirable but not legally necessary.

VALDES: We never heard [the argument] that it was not legally necessary, but politically necessary until the situation had finished and then the new opinion of the Attorney General was distributed among the members of the Council. Up to the end even when we were discussing the text that was circulated for a second resolution, there was no recognition by the UK or by the USA that, that Resolution meant war. War was never discussed at the Security Council.

NÍ GHRÁLAIGH: Thank you Ambassador, I have no further questions.

SANDS: Can I just come back to something you said right at the end, you said when the new opinion of the Attorney General made its way to the Security Council. What was the reaction of some of your colleagues when they saw this document?

VALDES: It was extremely ironical and well, it was an argument that had been…it was like a rabbit in the headlights.

SANDS: Were you aware subsequently that the Attorney General had given a different opinion just ten days earlier?

VALDES: I read it in the papers.

SANDS: Having now seen both opinions what is your…

VALDES: I fully agree with the first opinion, I have to say. I wholeheartedly believe that this was the opinion that Sir Jeremy defended during the debate in the Security Council.

SANDS: What is it about that first opinion that leads you to... what is in the first opinion...

VALDES: I am referring to the facts that the Attorney General that he believes that a second resolution is needed and that in case the second resolution would not be approved there could be consequences in terms of international law.

SANDS: Including the crime of aggression?

VALDES: That is what he says, yes.

SCENE 4: BOB MARSHALL ANDREWS QC, MP

ANDREWS: [Bob Marshall Andrews] a [Labour] Member of Parliament, for Medway, have been since 1997. I am a Silk, partly criminal, mainly criminal of late.

MACDONALD: I want to focus in particular on the vote in Parliament on the 18th March 2003. Firstly, I wonder if you could briefly explain what led you to vote against that motion.

ANDREWS: I didn't believe a word of it. I didn't believe any case had been made out on the main issue which was the weapons of mass destruction. I was not convinced, quite the reverse, I was not only not convinced, I believe that we were being deceived.

MACDONALD: And what was the basis for that view?

ANDREWS: I had read Blix. He had said in terms, 'I can find no WMD'. He said in the memorable phrase to the UN: 'I have just watched them destroy seventy out of ninety of their missiles. These are not matchsticks, these are lethal weapons.'

MACDONALD: I want to refer you to, I'm handed a copy by Mr Sands, the text of the Resolution that the Prime Minister put before the House of Commons on the 18th March 2003. 'This House recognises that Iraq's weapons of mass destruction and long range missiles and its continuing non-compliance with Security Council Resolutions pose a threat to International peace and security.' Did you feel that in this debate in Parliament and in his other public statements around that time, the Prime Minister knowing what you do now, honestly presented an accurate picture of the intelligence?

ANDREWS: No I don't. No, I don't. I think we were deliberately misled. It is absolutely clear that what was put forward as potential and possibilities was turned into certainties – irrevocable certainties and statements of opinion.

MACDONALD: Do you believe that those statements reflected the Prime Minister's honest opinions?

ANDREWS: I find this very difficult. We have all, in our professional life had clients who are not telling the truth but have managed to persuade themselves that they are. Query: Are they lying? It is a philosophical point. I simply do not know what the Prime Minister had persuaded himself to do, assuming he was not delusory. Yes we were deliberately misled. I believe he may well have misled himself as well.

MACDONALD: Moving slightly down the text of the Resolution – there. The Prime Minister asks the House of Commons to endorse the following proposition: 'That it notes the opinion of the Attorney General that Iraq having failed to comply, and Iraq being at the time of Resolution 1441 and continuing to be in material breach, the authority to use force under Resolution 678 has revived and so continues today.' Did you have a reaction at the time to that text?

ANDREWS: Yes, I did. It...

MACDONALD: What was your reaction?

ANDREWS: There was no way that the Attorney General himself could be under the opinion that Iraq was in material breach, because of course he is a lawyer, as we all are, he has to rely on somebody else's facts. [His] statements just had that bald assertion – 'Iraq is in material breach'. Now he must have got that from somewhere. It's a statement of fact, not a statement of law, and it seemed to me immediately that where he got that from must have been the Prime Minister. Now, of course, we know what happened, and with the benefit of that knowledge, this is probably one of the examples of Parliament being misled, and indeed the Cabinet being misled.

MACDONALD: Now at Tab 3 we have the Attorney General's opinion, the full opinion, when it was finally published. Did you consider that that opinion was consistent with the answer [in the House of Lords] that the Attorney General gave?

ANDREWS: It was completely inconsistent. Firstly is it fair to say the Attorney came to the conclusion that 678 was capable of being revived by 1441? It is not an opinion with which I would agree, but that is nothing to the matter, I mean, I can see that it is just possible to argue that – just possible, in which case of course you ought to tell your client it is just possible to argue this, not it is a certainty. What he is saying is you've got to understand that there might be actions brought against you which will be very difficult to defend.

MACDONALD: From your contact with other MPs at the time, was this statement by the Attorney General a material factor in their decision to vote?

ANDREWS: Yes. Yes, undoubtedly it was.

MACDONALD: Can I just look at the precise terms of the Attorney's conclusions. At paragraph 30 about half way down, he says: 'But a reasonable case does not mean that if the matter ever came before a Court I would be confident that the Court would agree with this view'. Now as a lawyer, can you explain how you read that – somewhat guarded use of language?

ANDREWS: He is saying it is arguable that there is a reasonable chance of success, but I can't guarantee it. That is a very long way away – I mean just as about as far away as it is possible to get in legal terms from the answer that came ten days later in the House of Lords. Something happened.

MACDONALD: Do you think that the advice, the full written advice that we have now seen could in good faith be summarised in the form that the Attorney General gave it to the House of Lords?

ANDREWS: No. No. Something happened between those two events, and I don't think that anybody can be in any doubt about that. And what happened came from the Prime Minister, the Prime Minister's Office. Something happened that we don't know about.

MACDONALD: As a lawyer, clearly the law did not change in that week, clearly the factual position in Iraq isn't likely to have changed in that week. Do you have any idea of what material change could have led the Attorney General to have changed his view?

ANDREWS: I have suspicions which are shared by a very large number of people – that is that it must have been the relationship between him and the Prime Minister. Whether he received from the Prime Minister assurance of fact which caused him legitimately to change his view is doubtful, because those factual assurances could not have been based on anything that we now know about. Therein lies the Attorney General's problem. But we don't know.

MACDONALD: I don't have any further questions for the moment. Thank you.

KNOWLES: You are not prepared to say that a dishonest legal opinion was provided by the Attorney General?

You accepted, I think, in answer to a question there was a tenable legal basis for going to war.

ANDREWS: Yes. It was tenable, I wouldn't agree with it. Just to follow it through. He got an unequivocal assurance. It is a matter of criticism, it seems to me, that he did not then, as any lawyer should or would have done, go back and say, 'What is the basis of this unequivocal factual position?'. I would have done. I have not the slightest doubt that you would have done, if a client on a serious matter – supposing we were going into Court, and your client said, 'I'm going to tell you there is unequivocal evidence', then all of us would say, 'What is it? You tell me.' Now let's assume that happened. If it did happen, then what he must have been told must have misled him.

KNOWLES: You are not prepared to say either, are you, that the Prime Minister knowingly told a lie to the House of Commons and knowingly took the country to war knowing that he had no legal basis to do so? You are not prepared to say…

ANDREWS: (*Interrupts.*) I think that when the Prime Minister said that things were 'unequivocal' in the House of Commons, he knew perfectly well that the intelligence would not sustain that and I think in those circumstances we were misled and it is impossible not to draw the conclusion that the misleading was deliberate.

KNOWLES: In any of the inquiries that there have been into the Iraq War and the surrounding issues, have you read anyone's opinion that the Prime Minister has lied?

ANDREWS: No, I haven't. None of them have said we believe that we were seriously misled by the Prime Minister. I tell you something, for either Butler or Hutton to have said that would have been the most extraordinary thing.

KNOWLES: The reason it would have been the extraordinary thing is, because it is an extraordinary thing for a Prime Minister to lie, isn't it?

ANDREWS: No, it was not their remit, and that has been one of our persistent complaints about these Inquiries, that the Government has repeatedly said there have been four Inquiries and we have been cleared throughout. It is rather like having a murder and saying that we have inquired very carefully into the surrounding circumstances, we've looked at the churchyard in which it took place. We've looked at the people who have assisted in the getaway, and we have looked at the Police Inquiry which followed it, as a matter of fact what we haven't looked at is the murder.

KNOWLES: Have you read anything in any of the reports that you have read which says that the Attorney General gave a dishonest legal opinion?

ANDREWS: No.

KNOWLES: Have you read anything that says the intelligence was deliberately distorted by the Government in order to support a decision to go to war?

ANDREWS: No.

KNOWLES: Thank you.

MACDONALD: We needn't turn it up, but are you aware of the terms of the resignation letter of [the deputy legal officer of the Foreign Office, Miss] Elizabeth Wilmshurst?

ANDREWS: Yes, I saw it at the time. I haven't read it since.

MACDONALD: I only want to refer you to two paragraphs. She says firstly, 'I regret that I cannot agree that it is lawful to use force against Iraq without a second Security Council Resolution.' 'I do not need to set out my reasoning, you are aware of it.' 'My views accord with the advice that has been given consistently in this Office before and after the adoption of Security Council Resolution 1441, and with what the Attorney General gave us to understand was his view prior to his letter of the 7th March. The view expressed in that letter has, of course, changed again as to what is now the official line.' Now Miss Wilmshurst's reference to her advice, in other words a second resolution is needed, being the consistent advice of the Foreign and Commonwealth Office throughout that period. What's your reaction to the terms of her letter?

ANDREWS: My reaction is that it needs careful investigation.

MACDONALD: I have no further questions.

SCENE 5: RICHARD PERLE

KNOWLES: Mr Perle. Could you describe your career for us in a word or two?

PERLE: Yes. I served in Ronald Reagan's Administration as Assistant Secretary of Defense. More recently I served as the Chairman of the Defense Policy Board, which is an advisory group to the Pentagon. I did that through the first two years of the first Bush term.

KNOWLES: President George W Bush comes to office in January 2001. Where would you say Iraq was on President Bush's agenda?

PERLE: It was under study. There was certainly no decision to change the policy toward Iraq – the policy inherited from the Clinton Administration. Because there is a lot of speculation that Bush had in mind something aggressive with respect to Iraq even before September 11. The fact is the Administration didn't – it changed on September 11.

KNOWLES: Just tell us what effect September 11th had on the thinking of the Administration.

PERLE: Well, I can tell you what I thought the [Administration] would think, that they had waited too long to deal with Osama Bin Laden, because by then we had had the Embassy bombings. We had seen Bin Laden in Afghanistan. We had seen the camps. We knew that they were embarked on a Jihad. We had also had the first World Trade Centre bombing in 1994, and it seemed to me a perfectly normal reaction for the President on September

11 to say, 'Why didn't we take action before now?'. The United States was the single largest source of economic assistance to the Taliban regime, which was harbouring Bin Laden. So I think there was a sense that the Administration would conclude that it could not again afford to ignore, or remain passive in the face of a visible threat.

KNOWLES: We come now to 2002 and the dust of 9/11 obviously has had time to settle. You by this stage are Chairman of the Defense Policy Group, is that right?

PERLE: Yes.

KNOWLES: And being in that position, is it right that you have access to classified material?

PERLE: Yes.

KNOWLES: Obviously I am not going to come close to that, but within what you are able to speak about, what was the state of intelligence knowledge about Saddam's weapons programmes in 2002, as you understood it to be?

PERLE: The intelligence community believed with great conviction that Saddam Hussein possessed weapons of mass destruction. His mission was to make sure that what they had hidden was not found.

KNOWLES: What was your view of the efficacy, thoroughness, and accuracy of the UN Weapons Inspectors?

PERLE: Well, I had real reservations about Blix. Among other things, Blix had been the Head of the [IAEA] during the period in which Iraq had a clandestine programme that astonished everybody when it was unearthed after the first Gulf War, and he missed it completely. I also had run into Blix and I knew him to be an ardent believer in the efficacy of arms control agreements and international arrangements. I found it hard to imagine an agreement with Saddam Hussein that one could count on. I think he found it less difficult to imagine that.

KNOWLES: So what you are saying is that he was of the view that one could reach [a] meaningful binding treaty or other international agreements with Saddam that would be efficacious...?

PERLE: (*Interrupts.*) Yes, I think he was ideologically committed. I always found it amusing that I and some of the others were referred to as 'ideologues' when it seemed to us that we were being deadly practical about the nature of Saddam's regime, and the real 'ideologues' were people who believed that international institutions could somehow overcome the characteristics of some of the regimes that make up part of what we call 'The International Community'. But there was more in evaluating Blix. He had a very small team and Iraq is a big country. It is the size of France. We are sitting in a room that is probably twelve by nine and a half feet. The amount of anthrax that could be stored in this room [is]...er...[is] probably equal to the whole inventory we believed Saddam [had]. The whole premise of the inspection seemed to me faulty. So you had to imagine that a grain of sand in the desert could be identified, and the inspectors could get there before the regime could move that grain of sand, and it seemed to me an impossible mission.

KNOWLES: What were the options for dealing with the Saddam Hussein problem? Sitting in the seat in which you sat at the time, the turn of the year 2002/2003, what was your own personal favourite option?

PERLE: I was in favour of establishing, asking the Iraqis to establish a Government in exile, and working with the Government in exile for the liberation of Iraq including by military means that would have meant a seamless transfer of authority from the moment Saddam fell.

KNOWLES: We see in various documents, regime change alone referred to – phrases like: 'The Administration is committed to regime change', or 'The Prime Minister says he will support regime change'. The phrase 'regime change' by itself is often read to mean invasion and overthrow of the type that happened, but in your view does it necessarily...

PERLE: (*Interrupts.*) No, indeed not, indeed not. The Iraq Liberation Act which passed in 1998, I think...

KNOWLES: The Clinton Act.

PERLE: ...called for regime change, and it certainly did not contemplate an invasion. Regime change under Franco of Spain did not mean invading Spain. Salazar's Portugal and Milosevic's Yugoslavia, the Orange Revolution – regime change by political means has an honourable tradition.

KNOWLES: I want now to ask you about legality and acting within the confines of international law. Is that something, which to your knowledge was of concern to the Administration?

PERLE: It always is. So the answer is yes. The interpretation of the laws are obviously open, it's never clear cut, particularly international laws. It's not statutory law.

KNOWLES: Tell us what your views are then and now?

PERLE: Well, I believe that the right to self-defence provided an adequate legal basis. A modern application of the right of self-defence, in my view, includes acting before one is struck, or the famous pre-emption.

KNOWLES: Thank you very much.

SANDS: You mentioned in the 1980s you were in the Reagan Administration. Now in the 1980s let's understand that the relationship between the United States and the Government of Saddam Hussein was rather different?

PERLE: Well during the Iran/Iraq War, it was the judgement of people who made these policies that we had an interest in Iran not winning that war, not quite the same as Iraq winning it.

SANDS: And famously there were photographs of people rather senior in the Reagan Administration visiting Iraq, visiting Baghdad and being seen in an embrace with Saddam Hussein.

PERLE: Was it an embrace? The Rumsfeld. I don't know which photographs you are referring to?

SANDS: It was certainly one in which there was physical contact. Whether it was a handshake or an embrace, it was not a relationship of antipathy, let's put it that way. Could you explain what it was that would have motivated that US Administration?

PERLE: I believe that it was simply a preference for the lesser evil.

SANDS: And the lesser evil, of course, at that time already possessed WMD, and very shortly after actually, very sadly, horrifically, used it.

PERLE: Yes, yes.

SANDS: And that didn't produce the type of reaction that came fifteen years later. Perhaps you could explain the political or other differences that led to…

PERLE: (*Interrupts.*) Yes, it was a shameful moral failure. We should have been down on them like a ton of bricks, and we didn't. We held a conference, the International Community, held a conference in Paris after the use of poison gas at Halabja, and they managed to spend three days in Paris without ever mentioning the word Iraq. Unbelievable.

SANDS: And of course Iraq's government used poisoned gas against the Iranians?

PERLE: Yes.

SANDS: And that didn't meet any objection, as far as I am aware, from the US Administration?

PERLE: If it did, I am unaware...

SANDS: So what changed over the fifteen years?

PERLE: Well, I think the end of the Cold War was part of it. We no longer regarded ourselves in a situation where we were so threatened we had to make various Faustian deals.

SANDS: You had strong views on the need to act in respect of a threat that you thought that was serious? And growing?

PERLE: Well, growing in the sense that the only thing that was preventing Saddam from a resurgence were the sanctions, and it was clear that the sanctions could only function for a limited period of time. The idea that we could, despite French objections, Russian objections, Chinese objections hold onto those sanctions forever – none of us believed that.

SANDS: And what about your relationships with the representatives of Her Majesty's Government in Washington at the time?

PERLE: Well, I have always regarded our two countries as the centre of the civilised democratic world.

SANDS: And you have a familiarity with British politics?

PERLE: I do.

SANDS: What do you think Tony Blair's role was in assisting President Bush to promote in 2002 his Iraq effort?

PERLE: The fact that we had allies, and not just Blair, made it far more legitimate than if we had acted alone. But if we had been forced to act entirely alone? I think that would have robbed the enterprise of some of its legitimacy.

SANDS: And would a lack of legitimacy have made the decision to go to war more difficult?

PERLE: I certainly did not use the word 'legitimate' to mean legal. Politically it's a lot more difficult if you have no allies.

SANDS: Are you aware that President Bush and Prime Minister Blair had a meeting in the White House on the 31st January 2003?

KNOWLES: Mr Perle has not seen the document and may want to, if you are going to ask him questions about it.

SANDS: There is a report of it, by Don Van Natta, in the *New York Times* which we've got at Tab 22 of the red folder. And about halfway down quoting from Mr Manning's memorandum, 'The start date for the military campaign was now penciled in 10th March. That was when the bombing would begin.' End of quote. It does seem that by January 2003 a decision had been taken.

PERLE: Well, it depends on what you mean by a decision. If you want to be in a position to use force, you have to assemble the elements of that force and to plan the use of that force, and that obviously has to be done before D-Day. Suppose Saddam had said, 'Alright, we'll give you records showing that we destroyed nerve agent and anthrax.' Would we have gone to war? I don't believe we would.

SANDS: What could Saddam Hussein have done as at 31st January 2003 that would have satisfied you and the President?

PERLE: Well he could have reported in detail about what had happened to the weapons of mass destruction. That would have been…show stuff.

SANDS: Assuming that was possible for him to do.

PERLE: Assuming that was possible for him to do, but the belief was that he was hiding the weapons, and that he had failed to provide the United Nations with the basis for validating his claims.

SANDS: But all of the beliefs that you've referred to, of course were shown to be wrong. He didn't have any WMD.

PERLE: That's right.

SANDS: So in those circumstances, what else could he have done?

PERLE: Well, presumably he could have told us what happened to those stockpiles, unless he just lost control of them. Can I quote Hans Blix? The quote sort of caught my fancy. He said, 'Nerve agent is not marmalade'. When you have it, you account for it, and if it is destroyed you have records of the destruction.

SANDS: And are you saying it doesn't matter at the end of the day whether or not anything was found? It was the right decision to use military force to remove him?

PERLE: Yes, yes. I don't think we did it very well after Saddam fell, but that's another matter.

SANDS: So the...

PERLE: (*Interrupts.*) I don't accept much of what has happened since Baghdad fell was inevitable. I believed we would turn things over to the Iraqis more or less immediately. I am not sure that the insurgency would have evolved out of that situation. I think we screwed it up.

SANDS: But if you knew then what you know now...

PERLE: If I knew then...

SANDS: Would you have unleashed military force?

PERLE: If I knew that we were going to send Jerry Bremer to Iraq with 8,000 Americans living in the Green Zone trying to design a new society for Iraq having sacked the military and the police force? I would have hesitated.

SANDS: So what were President Bush and Mr Blair doing between April 2002 when they talked for the first time, one to one, on regime change in Iraq and the period a year later? Surely they could have planned for all this?

PERLE: There was a lot of planning. Plans don't always go the way they are supposed to go, and there were endless documents prepared and you can't imagine the length of the list of catastrophes were thought about before they went in. Hindsight is perfect, now we can all see the mistakes that were made, but they did not have to be made.

SANDS: [At Tab 12 – the Downing Street memo] we can read what the Foreign Secretary [Jack Straw] had to say: 'It seemed clear that Bush had made up his mind to take military actions even if the timing was not yet decided, but the case was thin. Saddam was not threatening his neighbours and his WMD capability was less than that of Libya, North Korea or Iran.' Any reaction to that comment?

PERLE: I don't know what he based that on. Had Libya given up at that point? I think the key point here is that who you talk to makes a very large difference, and this Administration is unique in my experience in that the President is less in command of his Administration than any President I have ever observed. He's got a…he's had a method of operating in which he is the Chief Executive, and that he expects things to happen, and he doesn't superintend them very closely, and a significant number of the people who are nominally working for him don't agree with him, don't work very hard to implement his policies, and in some cases even work against him, and that was certainly true at the State Department. It was certainly true at the CIA.

SANDS: Is it your view that the intelligence that was held in late 2002 and early 2003 was an adequate base to justify the use of force?

PERLE: Well, are you asking me based on what we know now?

SANDS: Based on what was known then.

PERLE: Yes, it was adequate.

SANDS: In your view…

PERLE: It was wrong, but it was adequate.

SCENE 6: SIR MICHAEL QUINLAN

SANDS: If you could tell us your name and very briefly your professional background.

QUINLAN: My name is Michael Quinlan. I spent most of my main career in the Ministry of Defence. My final job there was as Permanent Under Secretary of State, retiring in 1992.

SANDS: Are you able to form a comparative view as to the circumstances in which Britain went to war in 2003 as compared for example, in 1991?

QUINLAN: It seemed to me that the case for going to war in 1991 was absolutely clear cut. What Saddam Hussein had done was intolerable by any possible standard of international acceptability. I took a markedly different view in 2003.

SANDS: Thank you.

KNOWLES: Is there anything wrong in principle if a government in the course of its decision-making decides that armed action by the forces of this country are in this country's interest providing that can be done legally?

QUINLAN: No. I am not a pacifist, and I do not think the country's tradition is pacifist. That said, I do believe there is a wider range of considerations besides just legality and national interest to be taken into account.

KNOWLES: What sort of considerations do you have in mind?

QUINLAN: I have in mind primarily the kinds of considerations that are enshrined in the 'just war' tradition. Is this the last resort? Is the damage which this war will do proportional to the ills it is reasonably expected to avoid?

KNOWLES: So what you have described to us is a balancing of matters of high principle, both high constitutional principle and high policy principle.

QUINLAN: That's right. I would add moral principle.

KNOWLES: It has often been said in opposition to the war: 'Why was Saddam Hussein singled out, there are plenty of other bad people that we can out go after?' Is that a view you subscribe to?

QUINLAN: Certainly he ranked very high among disagreeable rulers, but I took and take the view that in the current state of the international system, both legal and more broadly political, there isn't a right to remove such people by force. Perhaps there ought to be, but there isn't.

KNOWLES: Have you read in any of the voluminous materials which have been produced on the Iraq War – anything from any informed observer which has made a case backed by evidence that the Prime Minister was party to a knowing deceit in respect of the war?

QUINLAN: No, I have not. The only matter which caused me disquiet in that regard was the Prime Minister's public statement which I think was using words which were not, I think provided to him by the JIC or Mr Scarlett, that the evidence was 'extensive, detailed and authoritative'. And I couple that with Lord Butler in the House of Lords characterising exactly that same evidence later as 'very thin', and I do have some difficulty with the gulf between those two statements.

KNOWLES: But that does not necessarily follow that at the time the Prime Minister made that assessment that was not his genuine assessment.

QUINLAN: Oh no, I'm sure there was not cold-blooded, deliberate mendacity.

KNOWLES: Thank you.

The Prosecution's Closing Statement

You have now heard the evidence. Are there grounds for a full investigation as to Mr Blair's involvement in the crime of aggression? We say there are, and plainly so. The war in Iraq was undoubtedly illegal. It was an act of aggression under international law. The questions are: what were Mr Blair's intentions, what was his state of knowledge? The evidence shows that he committed himself to regime change as early as March 2002. He did so in the full knowledge that regime change was illegal under international law. He was so advised by the lawyers at the Foreign Office and by his Attorney General.

He constructed an alternative justification for war. Weapons of mass destruction. He argued that force had been authorised by the Security Council. The Security Council did not authorise force. Yet, Mr Blair took the decision that he alone could determine that Iraq was in material breach. To do all this he manipulated intelligence and turned a blind eye to the facts. And he manipulated the law. The UN lawyers advised that war would be illegal without a clear Security Council mandate. On 7th March 2003, his Attorney General gave him what was, to all intents and purposes, the same advice. Mr Blair withheld that advice from Cabinet. He misrepresented its contents to Parliament and to the British people.

He took his decision to go to war without the 'hard evidence' of Iraqi non-compliance and 'non-co-operation' that the Attorney General had secretly advised him was necessary to sustain any possible legal justification. He did not ask the Joint Intelligence Committee for hard evidence of non-compliance, because he knew he would get the wrong answer. He had no other authoritative basis to determine, as he did on 15th March 2003, that Iraq was in 'further material breach'. Whether the standard to be applied is knowledge that the war was illegal, or simple recklessness, the evidence clearly shows that there is a case for Mr Blair to answer.

The Defence's Closing Statement

KNOWLES: Ordinarily in a case like this a detailed closing speech would be necessary. But I'm only going to make a short speech. That is all that is needed, because the prosecution has so obviously failed even in the limited task it has set for itself. Sir Murray Stuart Smith said, 'hard evidence – it would need to be very clear'. But if you ignore the prosecution's rhetoric and instead concentrate on the evidence then you will be bound to conclude that they have not even come close to proving their case. Here are just a few reasons why I can say that to you with such confidence.

First, there cannot be a crime of aggression without an act of aggression. Where is the evidence for the prosecution's confident assertion that the war was illegal? Certainly the topic is hotly debated, but if you are going to indict a Prime Minister for a war crime then you might expect this rather important issue to be beyond debate. In fact, as Ed Mortimer told you, the UN Security Council, which has the power and the duty under the UN Charter to declare wars to be unlawful, has not done so in this case. So for that reason alone this prosecution should fail.

But let's grant the prosecution the indulgence of assuming the war was unlawful. That's only the start. In accordance with well established principles the prosecution must also prove that the Prime Minister intentionally took the country into an illegal war knowing that it was illegal. Here again the prosecution runs into trouble because all its assertions are contradicted by the evidence it chose to call. For example, the prosecutor asserts that the Prime Minister 'manipulated the intelligence'. The slight difficulty it faces is that its witnesses do not agree. For example, Robert Marshall Andrews agreed he'd read nothing to suggest intelligence was distorted. And Ambassador

Valdes declined the prosecutor's invitation to say that the Government had behaved dishonestly.

Also essential to the prosecution's case is its suggestion that a decision was taken to go to war in 2002. But this time it is the documents which contradict its case. The fabled Downing Street Memoranda show that at every stage the need to act within the law was axiomatic to the policies under consideration.

Also fatal is the fact that no witness – or at least none with any credibility – suggested that the Attorney General did anything other than act in good faith. On the evidence you've heard there is no doubt that the Prime Minister followed the proper advice of his Government's Senior Legal Adviser.

Self evidently, there is not the 'hard evidence' that is necessary.

At the close of his trial in 1953 Fidel Castro said 'Condemn me. It doesn't matter. History will absolve me.' At the close of this hearing I submit that you should find that Tony Blair does not need absolution. He has done nothing that justifies condemnation.

The End.

APPENDIX
Edited witness testimony not used in the staged play

PROFESSOR MAHBUBANI

SANDS: Should we refer to you as Ambassador Mahbubani?

MAHBUBANI: I used to be the Singapore Ambassador to the UN from '98 to 2004. Now my technical title is Professor Mahbubani.

SANDS: So you lived through the events concerning the run up to the decision to use force in Iraq?

MAHBUBANI: Yes.

SANDS: Were you personally involved in the discussions and deliberations during that period in the Security Council that related to Iraq?

MAHBUBANI: Well I think I attended probably every significant discussion there was on Iraq.

SANDS: And so would you say, therefore, that you have direct personal experience of the negotiation of Resolution 1441?

MAHBUBANI: Yes.

SANDS: Did the British Government in the summer of 2002... were they very actively involved on the issue of Iraq through their delegation in New York?

MAHBUBANI: Very much so. You see the British delegation traditionally played a very active role on most key issues in the UN Security Council. That was always the case.

SANDS: And the British delegation at the time was headed by Ambassador Greenstock, is that right?

MAHBUBANI: Yes.

SANDS: And how do you regard Ambassador Greenstock?

MAHBUBANI: He's a close personal friend and I have enormous respect for him.

SANDS: Can I then jump directly to Resolution 1441. In paragraph 4 the Council decides that false statements or omissions in the declaration submitted by Iraq shall constitute a further material breach of Iraq's obligations, and will be reported to the Council. What was the function of paragraph 4?

MAHBUBANI: Basically the thrust that the Resolution, essentially if you were to describe it in three words was to give Iraq one last chance.

SANDS: Can I be clear? When you say the purpose of the Resolution was to give Iraq one last chance, can it be said that the Resolution explicitly authorised the use of force against Iraq?

MAHBUBANI: No. In fact, that was what the debate was all about.

SANDS: So your interpretation was that this was the first of two steps?

MAHBUBANI: Yes. That was the general understanding, as far as I could tell in the Council.

SANDS: Was that the understanding of the British delegation?

MAHBUBANI: Yes.

SANDS: And then paragraph 12, which we say is the key, the Security Council decides to convene immediately upon receipt of a report in accordance with paragraphs four above in order to consider the situation. What was your understanding of what paragraph 12 was intended to achieve?

MAHBUBANI: I think the critical thing is that the Security Council should reconvene if there had been any further violation by Iraq of the Resolution. So, there should be no automaticity.

SANDS: And did paragraph 12 mean that it would be for the Security Council to reconvene and then decide whether or not force could be used?

MAHBUBANI: Yes, that was the understanding.

SANDS: Was that also the understanding of the British delegation?

MAHBUBANI: I would presume so. [In] the explanation of votes, it's very clear that that's what the British explanation of vote says.

SANDS: The British explanation of vote in the statement by Sir Jeremy Greenstock. Can you take us to which part of the explanation of vote...

MAHBUBANI: Yes, I think there's a sentence that says, 'If there is a further Iraqi breach...the matter will return to the Council for discussion as required in operational paragraph twelve.' Of course it goes on to add: 'We would expect the Security Council then to meet its responsibilities.'

SANDS: What did you understand that to mean though?

MAHBUBANI: It was the French and Russians who were very active on this. They said before the Council could take any further steps, before any negotiations on Iraq the Council had to reconvene again.

SANDS: Would it be for the Council to take a decision that Iraq was in material breach, or could an individual member state take the view that Iraq was in material breach?

MAHBUBANI: I don't think that anyone suggested that any country could do it on its own. But it's clear that the American interpretation of what it meant was different.

SANDS: As you know, Ambassador Greenstock has authored a book called *The Cost of War, Iraq, and the Paradox of Power*, which has unfortunately never been published due to the Foreign Office deciding in London that it didn't want it to be published. The only thing that appeared about that book at some stage on the website of the US publisher is an excerpt. In that excerpt Ambassador Greenstock is quoted as saying 'The conflict itself was politically illegitimate'. Do you have any recollection of conversations that you had with Ambassador Greenstock as to the need for a second resolution against the background of what appears to be his view that the conflict was politically illegitimate?

MAHBUBANI: I'm trying to see whether I'm being fair to him. I think he believes very strongly that any action should be taken with the existing authorisation of the UN Security Council. That's my sense of his view.

SANDS: The British and American governments of course ultimately justified the war on the basis of the revival theory, that the war had somehow been authorised by the Security Council in 1991. And their further argument was that the justification for the use of force could be revived by the decision of individual member states. Having regard to the discussion that took place on 1441, what's your reaction to that argument?

MAHBUBANI: I think if that was the case, the obvious question is why table a second resolution of the UN Security Council? I think the fact that the United States and UK tabled a second resolution seeking explicit authorisation for war against Iraq was a clear statement that a second resolution was needed. As you know they tabled the resolution and then withdrew it when they couldn't get enough support for it.

SANDS: Is it your position then that you did not understand Sir Jeremy to be implying unilateral use of force by the United Kingdom?

MAHBUBANI: Yes. I think it's…one of the few things…after five years one of the few things that stuck in my mind was a very categorical statement that there would be a second step before any action was taken in Iraq. And I was actually surprised by how strong this statement was.

SANDS: Was it the fact that it was so strong that it stuck in your mind?

MAHBUBANI: Well, I mean, to be candid with you, it was not necessary. To reassure the other side that, Hey this means that there's no automaticity, no hidden triggers…

SANDS: Professor Mahbubani, that's very helpful indeed. I have no more questions for the time being, and I hand you over to my colleague, Blinne Ní Ghrálaigh.

NÍ GHRÁLAIGH: Hello Professor Mahbubani, thank you for joining us. I'm going to ask some questions on behalf of the Defendant. I'll come first to the statement made by Ambassador Greenstock. When he talks about what the second step will be, he says that the matter will return to the Security Council for discussion. He doesn't state that it will return for a second Resolution, does he?

MAHBUBANI: No.

NÍ GHRÁLAIGH: And other countries made clear their view that a further decision of the Council would be required?

MAHBUBANI: Yes. They all had different levels of specificity on what the second step would be.

NÍ GHRÁLAIGH: But nevertheless that was the word that was agreed in operative paragraph 12. It wasn't that the Council was to reconvene to secure a further resolution. It was in order to consider the situation.

MAHBUBANI: Yes. If anything happened, if Iraq contravened any of the provisions of 1441, then the Security Council would reconvene immediately.

NÍ GHRÁLAIGH: Well, Professor Mahbubani, I would suggest that that is your interpretation and, as I have said, there are different interpretations. That isn't an interpretation that was shared by the Americans, and it wasn't one…

MAHBUBANI: You're right, the Americans had a different interpretation.

NÍ GHRÁLAIGH: In his explanatory statement to the public on the part that the British signed up to, he did not say there as a requirement for a second Resolution, he said there was a requirement for further discussion.

MAHBUBANI: Can I just tell you the message people heard?

NÍ GHRÁLAIGH: But you have already told me what the message people heard is, and I very much take that on board, and it's indeed a message that I know was heard by a lot of people. But there was also another message…

MAHBUBANI: I think to be fair, by the majority of the members of the Council.

NÍ GHRÁLAIGH: Well perhaps, but the explanatory…

MAHBUBANI: That was what the whole debate was about.

NÍ GHRÁLAIGH: Indeed, but Professor Mahbubani…

MAHBUBANI: All I'm saying is that such statements…you have to understand their meaning in the context in which they were expressed. And after spending months battling over these issues, in that context, to say they would come back to the Council, was a very strong and powerful statement.

NÍ GHRÁLAIGH: But in that context it was not stated that a second resolution was required. Is that correct?

MAHBUBANI: Yes, of course, you're right. It wasn't explicitly stated. All Security Council Resolutions are the result of a tremendous amount of political compromise, a lot of fudging and they're never, ever clearly explicit to the nth degree of what they really mean.

NÍ GHRÁLAIGH: Thank you and I think that we have finally got to the point that I was making, that the Security Council did not agree to a resolution that mandated the requirement for a second resolution, because the members of the Security Council would not have agreed on that.

MAHBUBANI: Yes.

NÍ GHRÁLAIGH: I have one last set of questions for you in relation to the crime of aggression, having regard of course to your experience within the UN. Article 39 of the UN Charter reads that the Security Council shall determine the existence of any threat to the breach of the peace or act of aggression. Are you familiar with that text?

MAHBUBANI: Yes. From memory, yes.

NÍ GHRÁLAIGH: And so under Article 39 the Security Council has competence to determine whether an act of aggression has been committed, is that right?

MAHBUBANI: Yes.

NÍ GHRÁLAIGH: And so in 1976 it made a finding that aggression had occurred, condemning South Africa for its aggression in Angola, for example, and again in 1979, it condemns Southern Rhodesia for its unprovoked acts of aggression against Zambia. So, the Security Council can and has pronounced acts that are deemed to be acts of aggression in the past, that's the first statement.

MAHBUBANI: Yes, when they reach agreement.

NÍ GHRÁLAIGH: But in the four years since the war in Iraq commenced the UN hasn't declared it to be an act nor a war of aggression?

MAHBUBANI: Factually that's correct, yes.

NÍ GHRÁLAIGH: The proper assumption must, therefore, be that the Security Council as a body does not regard it as an act of aggression. Is that not right?

MAHBUBANI: No. The silence of the Security Council can be interpreted in other ways. It can be interpreted either as, yes, they agree with what happened there, or it could be decided that there is no way they can get the Resolution passed. I'll give you another example. The Iraqi invasion of Iran, there's a general consensus that Iraq committed aggression against Iran. Did the Security Council say that aggression took place? No, it didn't. Did aggression take place? Yes.

NÍ GHRÁLAIGH: I have no further questions.

SANDS: Did Sir Jeremy Greenstock, or any other member of the British delegation say at any point at which you recollect that an individual member state is free to assess whether there's been a material breach?

MAHBUBANI: No, definitely not.

SANDS: And what would be the consequences for the international system of allowing any state to determine unilaterally that another state is in breach of Security Council obligations? What would be the consequences of that with the international system?

MAHBUBANI: I think it would be disastrous.

LORD LESTER

SANDS: Can I begin by inviting you to introduce yourself?

LESTER: I was born Anthony Lester and I am now Lord Lester of Herne Hill QC.

SANDS: Can I take you to Tab 20 in the folder, the big folder, the lever arch folder. Which is a copy of an extract from the Ministerial Code of Conduct, 2001 version?

LESTER: Yes.

SANDS: And the top paragraph is 22. I just wonder if you could read out paragraph 22?

LESTER: Yes: 'The law officers must be consulted in good time before the Government is committed to critical decisions involving legal considerations.' Certainly one would expect the advice to be formal, formally sought and given in sufficient time for the Prime Minister and the Cabinet to be able to make a decision one way or the other as to go to war.

SANDS: You've got at Tab 3 of the bundle the Attorney General's full legal advice of the 7th March and then a written answer to a parliamentary question, which expresses his view.

LESTER: Yes.

SANDS: Are you aware that, in relation to those two documents, only the later, the view was put before Cabinet on the 17th March 2002?

LESTER: Yes I believe that is true. In fact, it is worse than that because, I mean, I read the full opinion of the 7th March which is 13 pages long and very carefully reasoned and balanced and in my view correct. The précis that was provided to Parliament, ten days later, when the House of Lords debated the legality of invading Iraq, that précis did not give reasons, it gave conclusions and it didn't reflect the balanced view contained in the view ten days earlier. So that not only was the Cabinet given the full information, but when it came to the debate in Parliament, we were not given the opinion even though he sourced it. All we had was that summary of the conclusion which differed from what was in the opinion itself without any explanation as to the reasons for the differences.

SANDS: Did, just to be clear on this, are you saying that the legal opinion of the Attorney General and the statement to the House were different?

LESTER: Well they were different in the sense that the Attorney General's opinion was heavily qualified.

SANDS: Would it be absurd to say that the legal opinion of the Attorney General was different to his statement to the House?

LESTER: No, it was completely different.

SANDS: Can I read to you a statement made by the Prime Minister in the House of Commons on the 9th March 2005, that date is important because it predated the publication of the 7th March advice. So the members of the House were not aware of what was in the 7th March advice. This is what the Prime Minister said and I quote, 'If it is being said that the legal opinion of the Attorney General was different from the Attorney General's statement to the House that is patently absurd', end of quote. Can I ask you is that a misleading statement by the Prime Minister?

LESTER: Yes.

SANDS: Do you believe it to be a deliberately misleading statement?

LESTER: Erm.

SANDS: Take a moment to look at the statement. The question that I put to you was, assuming that the Prime Minister was familiar with the content of the 7th March advice, the full advice, was this statement deliberately misleading.

LESTER: Well, I mean, either he was forgetful and negligent and it was a kind of inadvertent error or it was deliberate and I have no idea which it was but I mean it's like the Hutton Inquiry, we don't have to establish bad faith in order to show that Parliament has been misled and I think Parliament was clearly misled.

SANDS: Let's go back to the advice and to the comparison of the advice and the view put in the statement to parliament. Over the ten-day period that passed between the dates of the two documents, were there any new facts of which you were aware that were material?

LESTER: There were no new facts that I was aware, I forget the chronology about the so-called 'dodgy dossier' and other security intelligence material and I don't know whether in that period, the Attorney General paid another visit to Washington DC because he refers to having heard the views of the US administration and, presumably on a previous occasion, I'm not aware of any further facts.

SANDS: Are you aware of any change in the law that took place between the 7th and the 17th March?

LESTER: No, no.

SANDS: There was no change of fact...

LESTER: Not that I'm aware of...

SANDS: As regards to the intelligence on Iraq's weapons of mass destruction or any of the material issues that could confirm the content of the advice.

LESTER: That is my understanding, yes.

SANDS: So what might have caused the Attorney General to move from his equivocal advice of the 7th March 2003 to the very unequivocal statement of the 17th March 2003?

LESTER: I don't know. All I know is that this was a clear breach of the Ministerial Code, which meant that the Cabinet were not properly informed when they took the key decision.

SANDS: But I want to come back to the differences between the shortcomings, the two documents are different, you've said that, there was no new material fact between the 7th and the 17th. There was no change of law between the 7th and the 17th, so I ask you again, what could have caused the Attorney General to change from an advice which essentially said a war would be illegal without a second resolution to a view that said it would be plainly legal. What caused that change?

LESTER: I can't think of any, anyone other than political pressure, which is one of the reasons, why I am so uneasy about having a politician who is the Attorney General.

SANDS: I have no more questions. To Mr Knowles.

KNOWLES: You have described the opinion as, I have noted the following adjectives, correct me if I have got any of them wrong, as balanced, objective, clear and scholarly.

LESTER: Yep.

KNOWLES: You're not saying are you, that in your view, that there is nothing legally wrong with the positive basis for war expressed in that opinion?

LESTER: He says there is an argument based on the negotiation history but he goes on to say it is a rather frail argument and he says, that the arguments of the US administration, which he rejects, he accepts on the basis of those arguments that a reasonable case could be made but what he then goes on to do, effectively is to say that's not good enough.

KNOWLES: That you need an evidential basis.

LESTER: You need a hard evidential basis and strong factual grounds.

KNOWLES: Turning to the Butler Report from [paragraph] 378 onwards, the history charted and then at paragraph 383 we have set out quotations reflecting what views the Prime Minister had reached.

LESTER: Yes.

KNOWLES: 'It is unequivocally the Prime Minister's view that Iraq has committed further material breaches specified in paragraph 4 of resolution 1441' and then we have a reply here on the 15th [of March 2003] in similar terms, 'It is indeed the Prime Minister's unequivocal view that Iraq is in further material breach' because, it quotes, of 'false statements' in the declaration submitted by Iraq. We have been told, and this is Lord Butler's committee quoting, we have been told that in coming to his view that Iraq was in further material breach, the Prime Minister took account of both the overall intelligence picture and information from a wide range of other sources, including especially UNMOVIC information. Well, what I suggest we see happening in the documents is we see the Prime Minister seeking to answer the question set for him by the Attorney General in the advice. Would you agree that is a reading of the sequence of events?

LESTER: Yes, I would agree. My difficulty goes back to something I said before about the evasiveness that the Government has shown previously about the first date on which legal advice was sought, and the reason I attach importance to that is, it finally emerged, that advice was first sought in about March 2002 shortly after the Prime Minister came back from meeting Mr Bush at his ranch and that made me wonder that from that moment the decision had been taken by both of them that, willy-nilly, Iraq would be invaded and it was then a question of looking for evidence and advice to support the invasion. That may seem a cynical view but it's a view I continue to hold. You are asking me to only look at the 10th March [2003] and the 17th March [2003] where I would look at the course of conduct from the previous March onwards and indeed what was exactly going on among all the players.

KNOWLES: I'll certainly take you to, we have something called the Downing Street Memorandum, which is dated July 2002, which you know?

LESTER: I remember that.

KNOWLES: And you remember the big controversy and one of the things that does in its very final paragraphs, and it is drawn up by Matthew Rycroft who is a Downing Street official and it says, we must not ignore the legal position, the Attorney

General must be consulted, and that is in July 2002. So we certainly know that at least by that date the Attorney General started to enter the picture even if he hadn't entered the opinion ahead of time. Just as to that, would you agree that is consistent with a Government seeking to operate within the law because that is why you go to the Attorney General to get legal advice?

LESTER: I think the fair way of putting it is a decision had been taken in principle to invade Iraq but because the chiefs of staff and no doubt members of the public could no doubt attach importance to the question of legality, it was important to obtain a legal opinion to justify the invasion and therefore from that summer, every effort was being made to ensure that appropriate legal advice would be given. It's not quite the same thing as you just said to me.

KNOWLES: But, you would agree, that if the Government had decided in the UK national interests, whatever political view one might hold, if the Government decides it's in the UK's national interest to fight a war or invade or whatever it might be, there is nothing in objectionable constitutional terms in and of itself in a Government making that determination.

LESTER: No.

KNOWLES: The objection, the objections that could be raised or the principle objection, which could be raised, is it may be unlawful.

LESTER: I suppose the question is whether the Government had prejudged the facts and in order to arrive at a result it wishes to arrive at and managed to use the facts to persuade the law officers to give advice in accordance with that prejudged view and that's what I think we are talking about here. Without going back over all the documents, it is pretty clear that from early the previous year both the President of the United States and the Prime Minister were contemplating invading Iraq. That's fair...and they needed a legal justification for doing so.

KNOWLES: But in a genuine legal justification for doing something that the Government exercising its governmental function wants to do, one can politically disagree with that but in constitutional terms and legal terms there is nothing wrong with that.

LESTER: Provided that the advice and the conclusion are correct in law.

KNOWLES: Well, in my initial questions you agreed with me this appears to be the Attorney General's genuinely held view.

LESTER: Yes, no, I agree with that, I'm accepting that, I'm not accusing the Attorney General of bad faith, I'm saying the question in the end is whether the answer was correct in international law because you can have an Attorney General who genuinely believes but gives bad advice for example and its bad advice leads to the fact you now have an unlawful invasion. You are not safe from the fact that the law officer gives bad advice. I'm not suggesting he did give bad advice, I think the advice itself is remarkably good advice.

KNOWLES: Just so you're aware, the Prime Minister stands charged with the crime of aggression and that he knowingly perpetrated an unlawful war. Not just took the country to a war that happened to be declared unlawful afterwards but doing so knowing that it was unlawful.

SANDS: No, no, that's –

KNOWLES: Well it is an issue between us, we will have to try and resolve it.

LESTER: I know the problem of defining aggression has eluded people for decades and has eluded people for that time...

DON VAN NATTA

SANDS: Mr Van Natta, my name is Philippe Sands, I appear on behalf of the Special Prosecutor in this case, and I'm just going to ask you a few questions in particular about an article that appeared in your name in the *New York Times* on the 27th March 2006. I wonder if I could begin just by asking you about your professional background?

VAN NATTA: I am an investigative reporter for the *New York Times*.

SANDS: If we just begin then, by reference to the materials you described in your article, you refer to a Memorandum dated 31st January 2003 that appears, according to your article, to have been written by David Manning.

VAN NATTA: That is right. It is a five page Memorandum written by David Manning, Mr Blair's Chief Foreign Policy advisor at the time.

SANDS: Turning to the Memorandum itself, could you tell us who is said to have attended the meeting, where it took place, and any other surrounding circumstances that might be relevant in your mind?

VAN NATTA: The meeting occurred in the White House, in the Oval Office. The meeting was attended by President Bush and Prime Minister Blair. Also attending the meeting was Condoleezza Rice, who was then the National Security Advisor. David Manning accompanied Mr Blair at the meeting, there were two other senior British officials attending the meeting, Jonathan Powell, who is Mr Blair's Chief of Staff, and Matthew Rycroft, who is a Foreign Policy Aide to Mr Blair.

SANDS: Now, can I just ask you by way of general introduction, what first struck you in terms of the information contained in that Memorandum?

VAN NATTA: I would have to say that the thing that struck me the most profoundly was the fact that this meeting occurred on January 31st 2003, at a time when both the United States and Britain were lobbying aggressively for a second United Nations Resolution condemning Iraq. And despite that public posture of both the United States and British Governments, the President and the Prime Minister basically had convened a War Council, and were discussing war as if it were inevitable, regardless of whether a Second Resolution was obtained or even if international arms inspectors continued to fail to find WMD, they were going to war. And there is a quote by Mr Manning that I feel in all of my years as a journalist, I've never seen a quote quite like it, and the quote is: 'Our diplomatic strategy had to be arranged around the military planning. The start date for the military campaign was now pencilled in for 10th March.'

SANDS: And of course it is the case, is it not, that the public statement to the President and the Prime Minister are that at that time, 31st January 2003, no decisions had been taken?

VAN NATTA: That's quite right.

SANDS: What you've just described to us is a paraphrasing by Mr Manning, apparently, of what President Bush had said. What, to the best of your recollection, is the British Prime Minister's reaction as set out in that Memorandum to what the President has said?

VAN NATTA: Well, my recollection is that the Prime Minister was there to try to persuade the President to go after this Second Resolution. In more than one place in the Memorandum Mr Blair is concerned that without a Second Resolution, things could get difficult, to say the least, for both the United States and Britain if the war were to go badly. In fact in one place he uses the phrase 'insurance policy' to describe the Second Resolution. But despite that motive that Mr Blair had at least in going into that meeting, when Mr Bush sort of pushes that motive aside and says well, even if we don't get a resolution, we are still going to go to war, Mr Blair acquiesces in that position and doesn't really take the fight, doesn't argue really too much, on that point.

SANDS: So your reading of the Memorandum is that the Prime Minister was committing the United Kingdom to support the United States in the bombing on the 10th March a few weeks later?

VAN NATTA: Yes, that's my reading of the Memorandum.

SANDS: Irrespective of the outcome of the Security Council discussions?

VAN NATTA: Yes. Yes, sir, that's my reading of the Memorandum.

SANDS: Can I take you to another aspect of the Memorandum that's referred to in your article? In my printout of it, it is on the second page, and it's under a heading entitled 'Discussing Provocation'.

VAN NATTA: Yes.

SANDS: And I'm just quoting now from your article: 'Without much elaboration the memo also says the President raised three possible ways of provoking a confrontation. Since they were first reported last month, neither the White House nor the British Government has discussed them', and I quote: 'The US was thinking of flying U2 reconnaissance aircraft with fighter cover over Iraq painted in UN colours, the memo says attributing the idea to Mr Bush. If Saddam fired on them he would be in breach.' That seems like a rather astonishing remark to attribute to the President of the United States. Are we sure it's accurate?

VAN NATTA: I am absolutely certain it is accurate.

SANDS: And what is your interpretation of that quotation, or comment attributed to the President in the context of the Memorandum and the general political background pertaining at the time?

VAN NATTA: Well, it certainly speaks for itself, but I think it's clear to any reasonable person reading the Memorandum that the President was prepared to take special steps to provoking Saddam Hussein if WMD was not found. And this was one of them.

SANDS: In short there was nothing, was there, that could happen after 31st January that could stop the US and Britain going to war. Would that have been your reading of the Memorandum?

VAN NATTA: That was the conclusion I drew from reading the Memorandum.

SANDS: Thank you very much. I have no more questions for the time being.

VAN NATTA: Thank you sir.

KNOWLES: Mr Van Natta, the Memorandum that you have seen does not purport to be, does it, a verbatim account of every word that was said by the two leaders, their advisors and others present in the meeting?

VAN NATTA: No, sir, it's not a transcript of the meeting, but it is a rather detailed recitation of the conversation that occurred at the meeting. There are some quotations included in the Memorandum, and often what Mr Manning does is he paraphrases the various participants.

KNOWLES: Does the Memorandum give any idea of how long the meeting lasted for?

VAN NATTA: Yes, it does. It was a two hour meeting.

KNOWLES: And how many pages does the Memorandum run to?

VAN NATTA: It's a five page Memorandum.

KNOWLES: So we have five pages compressing a two hour meeting?

VAN NATTA: Five pages compressing a two hour meeting; the five pages are single space, there's quite a bit of information on the five pages. But, yes, it's a two hour meeting compressed in five pages.

KNOWLES: But it's right, isn't it, that the Memorandum doesn't always clearly indicate the context in which things are said?

VAN NATTA: I don't know if I would say that. You really do get a feel, as you read the memo, that you're in the room with them, you have a fly on the wall aspect. And so although I would agree with you that the context is probably not always there, it's certainly there more often than not.

KNOWLES: Well, I put the suggestion to you and then you initially disagreed with me, and then you qualified that. But you do state, don't you, that some of the things, I think the President in particular said, the context is not clear from the Memorandum? I have in mind your paragraph talking about Mr Bush's plan to paint UN colours on planes in order to provoke Saddam to shoot them down.

VAN NATTA: Yes, on that particular issue, you're right, the context was not given. But, again, I think in the majority of the occasions where quotations are used, Mr Manning did his job well enough to give the context and make it clear what people are responding to when they say it, and you get the feel that you're eavesdropping on a conversation.

KNOWLES: Well the triggers for war, the painting planes in colours was suggested to you a few minutes ago by Mr Sands, and I think the context in which it was suggested to you here was a President behaving like a cowboy, willing to indulge in reckless things like dressing up planes in order to trigger war. But as I understand it, you're saying certainly as far as that is concerned, the context isn't clear and we shouldn't conclude that was the determined element of the plan?

VAN NATTA: The context of why that was suggested was not clear from the Memorandum, you're absolutely right about that.

KNOWLES: Thank you. Would you also agree that looking at a single document provides only a snapshot of the decision making process that both the US and the UK were going through during this period of late 2002, early 2003?

VAN NATTA: I would agree with that, but with this caveat. This two hour meeting came at such an important moment in the diplomatic run up to war, and it was so wide ranging in its subject matter that although it was just a snapshot it was a 20/20 snapshot, in my view, of the thinking of both the President and the Prime Minister at that time.

KNOWLES: So far as the President is concerned, is your evidence that this Memo that you've read shows the President absolutely desperate to go to war?

VAN NATTA: No, I don't know if I would say desperate. I think the word I would choose is that he was committed to going to war and was preparing for that eventuality, regardless of whether WMD was found, or whether the United States and Britain were able to obtain a Second UN Resolution.

KNOWLES: Some of the things the President said, some of them are open to interpretation, perhaps in differing ways. Would that be fair?

VAN NATTA: Oh I think that's fair any time the President speaks publicly. And I think the same could be said for the Prime Minister; any time a leader says something, what he or she says is open to interpretation.

KNOWLES: The suggestion has often been made in the United Kingdom that the efforts at the United Nations by the US and the UK to get a Second Resolution were not efforts made in good faith – in the sense that there was no genuine desire, effort or will put into the attempt to obtain a Second Resolution. Is that suggestion consistent or inconsistent with the Memorandum as you read it?

VAN NATTA: Well, the Prime Minister is quoted as saying that it is essential for both the United States and the United Kingdom to lobby for a Second UN Resolution against Iraq because, as he put it, it would serve as 'an insurance policy against the unexpected'. And he went on to say if anything went wrong with the military campaign, or if Saddam increased the stakes by burning the oil wells, 'killing children or fermenting internal divisions within Iraq, a Second Resolution would give us international cover, especially with the Arabs'.

KNOWLES: Certainly so far as the President is concerned, but here I'd like to draw a distinction between the two because obviously the criminal trial we're concerned with concerns the British Prime Minister. So what you're saying is certainly so far as he is concerned, the Memo, taken on its face, is consistent with good faith as being made by the UK to obtain a Second Resolution?

VAN NATTA: Well, again, you're asking me to make a judgment about what occurred after the meeting, and I don't feel comfortable doing that.

KNOWLES: So really to summarise, the situation is this. We have a Memo of a meeting between the two leaders about seven weeks or so before the war started in which the British Prime Minister is expressing concern to have a legal basis for the war that would be acceptable, yes?

VAN NATTA: It was a subject that was discussed between the President and the Prime Minister on more than one occasion. That's correct, sir.

KNOWLES: We have both leaders expressing the view that they would very much like a Second Resolution if possible?

VAN NATTA: Yes, they both do indicate that they would like to have a Second Resolution, absolutely.

KNOWLES: Yes, thank you very much.

SANDS: Mr Bush told Mr Blair that the bombing will begin on 10th March.

VAN NATTA: Yes, he said the start date for the military campaign was pencilled in, was the language for 10th March, and then there was another sentence saying this was when the bombing would begin. And that's Mr Manning paraphrasing the President's comment to Mr Blair and the other people present at the meeting.

SANDS: And in response to that, Mr Manning paraphrases Mr Blair as saying he was solidly with the President and ready to do whatever it took to disarm Saddam, did it not?

VAN NATTA: That's correct, it did say that.

SANDS: The words 'solidly with the President' don't admit of any ambiguity do they?

VAN NATTA: No, that is pretty clear. [And] I don't recall the Prime Minister ever saying that it was absolutely necessary for there to be a UN Resolution. Let me rephrase that. I don't recall the Prime Minister ever saying that he would not stand solidly with the President.

NADEEM KAZMI

NÍ GHRÁLAIGH: Could you please state your name and occupation?

KAZMI: I am Nadeem Kazmi, and am Director of International Development at the Al-Khoei Foundation, but I am not employed by them, I am a self-employed consultant in international development.

NÍ GHRÁLAIGH: And what is the Al-Khoei Foundation?

KAZMI: It is an international Shi'a Islamic charitable organisation that has general consultative status at the UN as an NGO. [It] is an educational research and welfare establishment based on the philanthropic teachings of Grand Ayatollah Khoei, who in the 1960s and '70s and part of the '80s, the supreme spiritual leader of the Shi'a Muslims of the world, so he was the predecessor to the current Grand Ayatollah Al-Sistani.

NÍ GHRÁLAIGH: What nationality are you?

KAZMI: British.

NÍ GHRÁLAIGH: And what is your ethnic origin?

KAZMI: Pakistani with a mixture of...well, let's keep it simple... Pakistani.

NÍ GHRÁLAIGH: And where did you grow up?

KAZMI: England. I was brought over here when I was three and a half months old.

NÍ GHRÁLAIGH: And did you ever live in Iraq?

KAZMI: No.

NÍ GHRÁLAIGH: I presume from your involvement with Al-Khoei, that you are yourself a Shi'a Muslim?

KAZMI: I grew up as a Shi'a Muslim. I am not particularly religious. I am not a practising anything.

NÍ GHRÁLAIGH: Can you explain to us whether you have any experience, or any knowledge of what Iraq was like under Saddam Hussein.

KAZMI: I don't have any direct experience in the sense that I never lived in Iraq, but I was one of the, I suppose, prominent non-Iraqis, who from the early '90s was involved in highlighting the plight of the Marsh Arabs of southern Iraq.

NÍ GHRÁLAIGH: If I could stop you there, could you explain that a bit more, please?

KAZMI: The Marsh Arabs?

NÍ GHRÁLAIGH: Yes.

KAZMI: The Marsh Arabs, they are the...one of the oldest surviving civilisations on earth. They go back more than five thousand years. They live on the water exclusively in the area of southern Iraq, and quite a unique civilisation that's been written about by the likes of Wilfred Thesinger and others. The name escapes me, but the author of *Tarka the Otter* also did a book called *Return to the Marshes* on that, but they were being wiped out systematically by Saddam Hussein for two reasons. One was Saddam, at the time, was claiming economical development and at the same time an engineer was discovered in the region, and he had on him some maps which spoke about the razing of villages and the total annihilation of the Marsh culture.

NÍ GHRÁLAIGH: When you say that they are being wiped out systematically – what do you mean?

KAZMI: Well, there is a policy of extermination which the Iraqi government at the time. Whole populations of villages were being forcibly removed, and the excuse that we had at the time from the Iraqi government was that it was because the marshes were also being used by people that were fighting the regime, were against the regime, and they were using the marshes as cover. So there were a number of excuses offered by the Iraqi government at the time as to why they were persecuting the Marsh Arabs, the majority of whom happened to be religiously Shi'ite as well.

NÍ GHRÁLAIGH: You spoke of whole villages being removed or moved. Could you explain a bit more exactly what the policy, from the evidence that you had...

KAZMI: (*Interrupts.*) Yes. Basically what it is. At the time Saddam Hussein was killing Marsh Arabs, but it was part of an overall policy of persecuting the Shi'as, and it was a systematic persecution, and this was perhaps more symbolic than other persecutions, because these were the indigenous people of Iraq – one of the oldest civilisations. He was trying to make a point. At the time, there were also economic development issues relating to Iraq wanting to develop, but not withstanding that, the Marsh Arabs were specifically targeted as an ethnic, I suppose, to some extent linguistic and also religious group to be completely annihilated.

NÍ GHRÁLAIGH: And how was this effected. Sorry for interrupting, but how was the policy of extermination effected? Are we talking people being shot, or…?

KAZMI: Sorry, yes I see. Yes, it was the burning of villages. Iraqi armed forces – armed brigades – physically going in and removing tribal elders, forcibly displacing them. Offering certain financial incentives for the leaderships to remove themselves from the region. Actual Iraqi Republican guard death squads going in and committing assassinations against Shi'as, because the system of…the cultural system within the Marsh Arabs, if you think the Arab culture is very cultural, if I can use that term in the sense that it has specific conditions that they are very loyal to, the Marsh Arabs even more so. There was also racist language used against the Marsh Arabs. They were termed 'monkey-faced people' and they were basically dehumanised. I personally saw the Marsh Arabs themselves, with the help of the Iranians, constructing shelter and housing and all that sort of thing. And that was in 1991, in May, about two to three months after the famous Shi'a uprising in April 1991.

NÍ GHRÁLAIGH: Again could you tell us how this persecution of the Shi'as manifested?

KAZMI: Yes. The looting of libraries, the burning of books, arrests and harassments of religious leaders, I don't think it was because Saddam was a Sunni, I think it was more because he just saw it as another enemy, because he was doing the same thing to the Kurds in the north, so it manifested itself – the persecution manifested itself in a number of ways, but it was obviously targeted at their religious identify.

NÍ GHRÁLAIGH: How long was the persecution of Shi'as ongoing?

KAZMI: Yes.

NÍ GHRÁLAIGH: Until when?

KAZMI: Until 2003, I think it was April 10th, when he was removed.

NÍ GHRÁLAIGH: We have heard allegations of torture by Saddam's regime. Do you have any evidence that that was taking place?

KAZMI: Again, the evidence that we have is from witnesses who spoke to us in the early 1990s. And I have accounts of individuals who were clearly suffering in front of me. One individual, for example, who had had his stomach bayoneted and was in Iran, and had walked to Iran literally holding on to his guts, because they were spilling out. But we do know that the refugees from Iraq that were continuing to come over to the United Kingdom and the US, even in 2000, 2001 were still telling the stories of torture and persecution. But the systematic nature of it, I feel may have been limited after a while, as part of the strategy. I still do not give Saddam's regime any credit for anything.

NÍ GHRÁLAIGH: I want to ask you one last area of questions as we are pressed for time, but that's about the invasion. How did you feel about the invasion?

KAZMI: I personally had questions about the invasion, and I'll tell you why. I will be very honest with you. Notwithstanding my experience and the work that I have done which has been a lot with Iraqi communities, and I am very well known within the community. Um, notwithstanding all that, I was uncomfortable with the invasion and I sort of almost...well let me put it this way. I thought that the removal of Saddam Hussein was really important, and I felt that it had to happen, and I will tell you why. Because in 1991 when I stood there on the Iran / Iraq border, and saw for myself the people flooding in, I was... I know that many of them were screaming for George Bush Senior to get rid of Saddam Hussein at that point, and I know throughout the 1990s there was an effort by many Iraqis in exile and inside Iraq as well, to want to get rid of, someone to get rid of Saddam Hussein. So, but the reasons that we were given as to why we went to war, well like anybody else, you know I don't entirely accept them, and I certainly don't accept the fact that we are now, we find ourselves in a quagmire of our own making where it's very difficult for the US to extricate itself, it's difficult for the UK – there was no real exit strategy, and I suppose I am one of those people who does on occasions talk to high officials, and you know, we have expressed this, I have expressed this personally that you know despite wanting the removal of Saddam Hussein, the way things have gone are not perhaps the way they should have gone.

NÍ GHRÁLAIGH: But that's with hindsight, but at the time?

KAZMI: At the time in 2003, I felt that it was important at some point – I had always felt that it was important to remove Saddam Hussein, and I had felt, I had always believed that the Iraqi people wanted the removal of Saddam Hussein, and as somebody who believes in democracy and wanted democracy for the whole of the Middle East – for Iraq – can never live under a theocracy or live under a dictatorship, it would be hypocritical of me to suggest to other people that it might be okay for them simply because they don't like a Westminster style democracy, or a US style democracy, but then again the other side of me says, you can't impose that sort of democracy, that style of democracy, you simply can't do it, but then on the other side without doubt my seventeen odd years with the Iraqi people has taught me that they definitely, the vast majority, even the ones who say they lived better under Saddam, the vast majority were screaming for the removal of Saddam Hussein.

MACDONALD: As you know we are prosecuting the defendant for the crime of aggression. And I think it is important to start by saying that the position of the prosecutor is not in anyway to condone the actions of Saddam Hussein, or to diminish in anyway the sufferings of the Iraqi people under his regime. We are looking specifically at whether the defendant should be found guilty.

KAZMI: Who is the defendant in this?

MACDONALD: Tony Blair.

KAZMI: Okay.

MACDONALD: And should be found guilty of the crime of aggression, which we define as knowingly waging an illegal war, and I want to start with one thing that you touched on earlier which was the ultimate justification when force was eventually used by the Government – what was the view of the arguments that were put forward in 2003 to support these reports?

KAZMI: You mean the chemical weapons issue? Weapons of mass destruction?

MACDONALD: Well, yes.

KAZMI: That's a really good question, and I will answer it honestly. I felt that Saddam had the capability to develop weapons of mass destruction. I think that there was some good intelligence to suggest that he had that capability, but I think that is a far cry from saying that he actually had weapons of mass destruction in his possession.

MACDONALD: Is it your view that humanitarian intervention was any part of the purpose?

KAZMI: I think it is always good to be wise after the event, and then to forget the passion and commitment that you had and why you had it at the time. But I know why I was passionately committed to the removal of Saddam Hussein – it was because I had spent so many years and so many hours of the day talking to people that had suffered, and looking their cases personally, and having to advise on specific issues – at various levels. At the level of the ordinary man, as well as at the level of government, so I felt that I had an insight. But I will be honest, I was not… I don't think there was that much of a humanitarian imperative contained within the reasons for going to war as perhaps they pretended, which is why you had a very confused PR from the Government at the time of the war. So you know, I am genuinely torn, because I still do believe it was important to remove Saddam Hussein,

MACDONALD: Kofi Annan in his much publicised BBC interview has described the war as illegal. Do you consider that the unilateral force by the US in Britain have a negative impact – respect for the rule of law internationally.

KAZMI: I think it has had…yes, I think rule of law is philosophically so important that…and it's a value, it almost this value that we have in terms of international relations and international law. And even now inside Iraq, the arguments rest on this idea of following the rule of law. For example, this whole proliferation of militias etc. Why should they disband when they feel that they're defending themselves against the Al Qaeda, or whatever, because we are not talking about disbanding the Al Qaeda, we're talking about ordinary militias. And of course the quick answer, the convenient answer is that if the Iraqis are really serious about governing themselves in a proper way, then they have to respect the rule of law, and the rule of law means – part of the rule of law means following those that govern over you – respecting those that govern over you; respecting the fact the use of force ought to be the domain of government, not the domain of militias. But in a way I find that contradictory from a country that has preparation of weapons you know in its own back yard, you only have to go to South Central Los Angeles, or…maybe I am wrong in demonising those particular areas, you know the United States, it's a bit fresh for the US to lecture other people, you know, on limiting weapons.

MACDONALD: Looking away from the Iraqi people themselves and looking at the International Community, can you see potential detrimental effects on the International Community as a whole if individual states act…

KAZMI: No, I am not trying to dodge your… What I am saying to you is that the – yes – on principle as a question of principle, yes that's not a good principle to have states going off and doing whatever they want. Unilaterally that is not good, but then again when was there ever consensus on anything in the International Community, and although I would like the United Nations to be respected and to have more power, but at the end of the day it is an organisation, it is not a country and it is not the police force of the world, and we are still living in this post-Westphalian conflict of States scenarios still exist.

MACDONALD: You mention the UN, and we know that in March 2003 the weapons inspectors had been in the country for a couple of months, and that they were asking for some more time to assess the situation. Do you feel that the UN was given every opportunity, or do you feel that the discussion was forestalled by the Coalition?

KAZMI: I think that the Coalition rushed. I do feel that the Coalition rushed. I'll give you that one. I do feel that the Coalition rushed into it. I feel that the UN should have been given more time. But having said that again the other side of the argument of course is that I for one had witnessed the Iraqi people for two decades screaming for the removal of Saddam Hussein, so for them that was not a rush. You know it came late, the Western World did not rush at all to their aid. In fact if anything they procrastinated and so that's I think what a lot of them will tell you. It depends on which side of the fence you stand. If you stand on the Western political analytical fence, then you can say that in terms of building consensus in the United Nations and what we consider to be the normal route of how this should have occurred, perhaps there was a little bit of impatience on the part of those that wanted to go to war. On the other side, there was nothing but procrastination, so again it is not black and white, it is not clear. It's a very, very complicated situation.

NÍ GHRÁLAIGH: Based on your experience of what was going on in Iraq during Saddam's regime, do you think that Tony Blair should be facing a criminal trial and a criminal conviction for a crime against peace for having removed Saddam Hussein and his dictatorship from power?

KAZMI: No. I don't believe he should be facing...

NÍ GHRÁLAIGH: And do you think that the majority of the Iraqi people – those people who you have described as 'screaming out for the removal of Saddam' – would they agree with you?

KAZMI: Yes. I think a lot of them, because they are living the reality of the chaos and the anarchy that is Iraq today, may perhaps say that things are not comfortable, but if they were honest with themselves, and they were to take themselves back to what it was actually like under Saddam Hussein, think they would agree that the removal of Saddam has to have been a good thing.

TACTICAL QUESTIONING

SCENES FROM THE
BAHA MOUSA INQUIRY

An Overview of the Baha Mousa Inquiry

Thousands of British soldiers took part in the US-invasion of Iraq, ill-prepared and badly-informed. Their commanders were under the illusion, based on poor intelligence, that the overwhelming majority of Iraqis would welcome them with open arms, that much of the Iraqi army would remain in place and help maintain law and order after Saddam Hussein was toppled. If there was going to be any problem at all it would be a humanitarian one with Iraqis desperate to escape the bombing.

Lack of preparation and inadequate training of British (and US) forces, so clearly exposed at the Chilcot inquiry, paved the way to a violent insurgency. A potentially welcoming and enthusiastic population became a deeply disappointed, disillusioned, and embittered one, that quickly came to see foreign troops as occupiers not liberators.

Gerard Elias, QC, Counsel to the Baha Mousa Inquiry put it this way: 'As well as increasing disorder, looting, and the activities of insurgent groups, soldiers were required to cope with very difficult environmental conditions. The temperature in Iraq in September regularly exceeds 50 degrees centigrade. Many soldiers suffered from heat exhaustion. In addition to the conventional military function of providing armed security, British forces found themselves in a civilian policing role and responsible for running much of the city's infrastructure. Soldiers were sometimes working very, very long hours, often with little respite'.

Colonel Jorge Mendonca, commander of 1 Battalion Queen's Lancashire Regiment (1QLR), who with six of his soldiers faced a court martial, told the Inquiry: 'I cannot begin to describe what it feels like to be in 58 degrees centigrade. When we turned up in Kuwait, I think it was 45 and I felt like I had walked into an oven'.

All this may help to explain, but not excuse, the abuse of Iraqi civilians. It became clear that British soldiers had little or no idea of the legal, let alone moral, boundaries of behaviour. The case of Baha Mousa and others in Iraq led General Dannatt, the former Head of the Army, to suggest that many members of the

Armed Forces lacked moral values when they joined up. 'I think you've got to look at the proportion of people who come into the Armed Forces from chaotic backgrounds', he said recently. Respect for others, he added, was 'almost the most important' of all the values soldiers were taught. Without it, he warned, 'that's when you're into bullying or abusing Iraqi citizens'.

Yet the soldiers' commanders and even the Ministry of Defence's own senior lawyers were uncertain and divided about the law. The chain of command appeared confused. They were unaware of the ban imposed by Prime Minister Edward Heath in 1972, following an official inquiry and ruling by the European Court of Human Rights, on what became known as the 'five techniques' – wall-standing, hooding, subjection to noise, deprivation of sleep, and deprivation of food and drink.

General Sir Michael Walker, Chief of the Defence staff at the time of Baha Mousa's death, said he didn't remember being aware of the Heath ruling and had 'no inkling' detainees were hooded for long periods.

Baha Mousa was a 26-year-old hotel receptionist, whose wife had recently died of cancer, aged 22. He was arrested, along with nine other Iraqis, at the Haitham Hotel in Basra on 14 September 2003 by soldiers from 1QLR. Rifles, bayonets and suspected bomb-making equipment were found at the scene. Many Iraqis traditionally had arms to defend themselves against criminals or tribal enemies. Many more did so in the chaotic aftermath of the US-led invasion. A month earlier, an officer serving with the QLR was blown up in a marked ambulance.

Mousa, the son of an Iraqi police colonel, was held at a temporary detention centre with the other civilians for 36 hours, more than 23 hours hooded. Two days after his arrest, on 15 September 2003, Mousa died. A post-mortem examination found he had suffered asphyxiation and at least 93 injuries to his body, including fractured ribs and a broken nose.

There is evidence that army officers and MoD officials wanted to cover up the circumstances of Mousa's death. Certainly they were in no hurry to have it investigated by the Military Police. Lord Goldsmith, Attorney General at the time, expressed his concern in a letter to Geoff Hoon in March 2005. 'I have been extremely concerned at the conduct of the investigations carried out in a number of the cases which have been referred to the Army Prosecuting Authority arising out of the Iraq conflict', he told Hoon. He added: 'I have become most concerned about the quality of investigation into the death of Baha Mousa and the assaults against others detained with him in an incident which occurred on 14/15 September 2003. The matter was not referred to the [prosecuting authority] until 23 June 2004'.

Martin Hemming, the MoD's chief legal adviser, admitted the MoD failed to seek the advice of Goldsmith, who held the view that British soldiers were bound by the European Human Rights Act in places such as detention centres, which they controlled. Colonel Nicholas Mercer, the army's chief legal adviser strongly opposed to hooding, walked out of a meeting with the Red Cross in Iraq because he was told by defence officials not to speak at it.

Major General Robin Brims, commander of all British forces in southern Iraq, issued an order banning hooding in April 2003, five months before Mousa's death. He admitted his order was distributed 'patchily'. Geoff Hoon, Defence Secretary at the time, said he was unaware of that.

Ministers, including Hoon and his Armed Forces Minister, Adam Ingram, appeared not to want to know what some British troops were up to in Iraq. Mendonca, who left the army in apparent disgust at the way he had been treated, told the Inquiry he was 'wholly unaware' of the state of his regiment's detention facility in Basra.

A six-month court martial – the most expensive in British history – ended in April 2007 with six soldiers of the QLR, now the Duke of Lancaster's Regiment, cleared of abusing civilian detainees and in Mendonca's case, negligence. A seventh soldier, 36-year-old Corporal Donald Payne, admitted inhumane treatment, was jailed for a year and dismissed from the army, becoming the UK's first convicted war criminal under the International Criminal Court Act. The judge presiding over the court martial accused QLR soldiers of erecting 'a wall of silence' around the case.

That was not the end of a matter which General Sir Mike Jackson described as 'a stain on the character of the British Army', and one that would remain until it had been solved. Lawyers for the Iraqis, notably Phil Shiner, applied to the High Court for a proper independent inquiry as required by the Human Rights Act in cases where agents of the state – in this case, British soldiers – were involved in abuses.

In March 2008, the Ministry of Defence admitted breaching the human rights of the detainees held in Basra. It agreed to pay £2.83m compensation to Baha Mousa's family and the nine surviving detainees held with him. The then Defence Secretary, Des Browne, admitted 'substantive breaches' of the European Convention on Human Rights which enshrines the right to life and prohibits torture. Browne said the court martial had highlighted important questions that needed to be answered. An Inquiry was important to 'reassure the public that we are leaving no stone unturned'. The Inquiry, under Sir William Gage, a recently retired appeal court judge, began in July 2009. He was expected to publish his findings this month, June 2011. The Inquiry revealed a litany of buck-passing, irresponsibility, ignorance, and incompetence. The MoD's defence was expressed by Bob Ainsworth, Browne's successor as Defence Secretary, when he said: 'Over 120,000 British troops have served in Iraq and the conduct of the vast majority has been of the highest order'. He added: 'Although there have been instances of misconduct, only a tiny number of individuals have been shown to have fallen short of our high standards'.

Richard Norton-Taylor

Tactical Questioning: Scenes from the Baha Mousa Inquiry edited by Richard Norton-Taylor was first performed on 2 June 2011 at The Tricycle Theatre, London.

Cast in order of appearance:
SIR WILLIAM GAGE (Chairman of the Inquiry), Alan Parnaby
GERARD ELIAS QC (Council to the Inquiry), Thomas Wheatley
DETAINEE 002, Lewis Alsamari
INTERPRETER, Rick Warden
AARON COOPER, Luke Harris
ADRIAN REDFEARN, Mark Stobbart
CRAIG RODGERS, Christopher Fox
DONALD PAYNE, Dean Ashton
MAJOR MICHAEL PEEBLES, Rick Warden
LIEUTENANT COLONEL NICHOLAS MERCER, David Michaels
THE RT. HON. ADAM INGRAM, Simon Rouse

Director, Nicolas Kent
Designer, Polly Sullivan
Lighting, Charlie Hayday
Sound & Audio Visual, Ed Borgnis
Assistant Director, Sophie Lifschutz
Production Manager, Shaz McGee
Company Manager, Lizzie Chapman
Deputy Stage Manager, Charlotte Padgham
Assistant Stage Manager, Chiara Canal
Casting Director, Marilyn Johnson
Set Construction, Russell Carr
Associate Producer, Zoe Ingenhaag

This play was commissioned with the support of The Joseph Rowntree Charitable Trust.

Any text in square brackets was inserted by the editor or company for clarity.

OPENING STATEMENT BY COUNSEL TO THE INQUIRY 13 JULY 2009

CHAIRMAN (SIR WILLIAM GAGE): Yes, Mr Elias.

ELIAS: Thank you sir. I appear as counsel to the Inquiry. The Inquiry is primarily concerned with the circumstances surrounding the death in September 2003 of Baha Mousa and the treatment of others detained with him in Basra, Iraq, by soldiers of the 1st Battalion The Queen's Lancashire Regiment. The death of any person in the custody of the state, other than by natural causes, is always a matter raising serious questions. Where the death has occurred in the custody of British forces serving abroad these matters are of clear and obvious public concern and importance which require an independent and thorough enquiry to ascertain where possible the truth of what occurred and, where appropriate, to attribute responsibility.

There is little doubt [the regiment] faced a very challenging operational environment in Iraq. As well as increasing disorder, looting, and the activities of insurgent groups, soldiers were required to cope with very difficult environmental conditions. The temperature in Iraq in September regularly exceeds 50 degrees centigrade. Many soldiers suffered from heat exhaustion. In addition to the conventional military function of providing armed security, British forces found themselves in a civilian policing role and responsible for running much of the city's infrastructure. Soldiers were sometimes working very, very long hours, often with little respite.

Early in the morning of Sunday 14 September, [1st Battalion, Queen's Lancashire Regiment] searched various hotels in Basra. 'Salerno' was the name given to that operation. The stated intention of Operation Salerno was to find 'former regime loyalists' and Iranian insurgents who were thought to be staying in hotels in Basra. Hotel Ibn Al Haitham was one of the hotels searched. Soldiers found a quantity of weapons, along with fake identity cards and other suspicious materials. Seven people, including Baha Mousa, were detained.

There can be little doubt but that the detainees, or some of them, were the victims of physical assaults. The detainees' evidence is that they were beaten more or less continually over the 48-hour period of their detention. The detainees say they were subjected to various other forms of physical and personal abuse. There is evidence that the detainees were made to endure disgusting conditions in the facility. Some soldiers say that the detainees had urinated and defecated in their own clothing and that they were effectively left in their own excrement. The detention facility was quite open. It had no doors and any soldier passing by would, it seems, be able to wander in. There was shouting, moaning and even screaming coming from the [facility] from time to time during the detention, according to some witnesses, and the Inquiry will hear scandalous accounts of an orchestrated 'choir' of victims' reactions.

Lastly and most importantly perhaps of the events that I outline now, there occurred the death of Baha Mousa in British custody. He died at around 10 o'clock in the evening, on Monday 15 September [2003]; that is to say approximately 36 hours after his arrival at [the detention facility]. A post-mortem was conducted six days later by a pathologist, Dr Ian Hill. Dr Hill found 93 separate injuries on Baha Mousa's body, including extensive bruising over his head, torso and limbs, a fractured nose and two fractured ribs. He concluded that the injuries were consistent with a systematic beating.

We now propose to play a short extract of video film. The video shows the early stages of the detention of these detainees during the daytime on the Sunday. It shows Corporal Payne using techniques of hooding and stress positions and noise. The voice that can be heard on the video is that of Corporal Payne. I would ask that that video be played at this stage.

[Video shown.]

TACTICAL QUESTIONING

Sir, I am moving to the approach of government, the Ministry of Defence and the army to so-called conditioning techniques from the time of internment in Northern Ireland in the early 1970s up to and including March 2003, which was, of course, the date of the invasion of Iraq. That was the decision of the Prime Minister, Edward Heath, given to the House of Commons on 2 March 1972. I am going to read [an] extract: 'The Government, having reviewed the whole matter with great care and with particular reference to any future operations, have decided that the five techniques will not be used in future as an aid to interrogation.' Nobody, so far as the Inquiry is concerned, appears to suggest that in the 30 succeeding years Parliament did authorise the use of these five techniques [wall-standing, hooding, subjection to noise, deprivation of sleep, and deprivation of food and drink] by the armed forces as an aid to interrogation. Yet, even if one considers only the video that we have just looked at, it may be thought to be entirely apparent that these detainees were being subjected to techniques which had been prohibited in 1972.

12 OCTOBER 2009

From the evidence of Witness Detainee 002 (D002 gave evidence in person on the 30th September 2009, but the hearing was discontinued when the witness broke down).

CHAIRMAN: Good morning, ladies and gentlemen. I am just going to say a word to Mr D002.
Good morning Mr D002. If you can hear me, I am going to explain – please sit down – that your voice I don't think can be heard in this room, but we shall be hearing the translation in this room. The next thing I want to explain to you – I would be grateful if you respond 'yes' – is that you understand that you are under oath. Translator, did he say 'yes'?

INTERPRETER: I couldn't hear him, sir.

CHAIRMAN: Mr D002, could you speak up please? The interpreters are having difficulty in hearing you.

D002: Yes.

CHAIRMAN: I think we all heard that. All right. You are still under oath.

ELIAS: Mr D002, I am going to ask you some questions now. Can you hear and see me?

D002: Yes

ELIAS: I want to ask you about your treatment when you were at that detention centre by putting to you a number of questions. First of all, when you were in the detention centre, was your head hooded with something?

D002: Yes, it was.

ELIAS: Through the period of your detention, were you hooded with one hood or ever more than one hood?

D002: Three hoods.

ELIAS: At what stage do you say the three hoods were put on, from the beginning or some later stage?

D002: At all stages.

ELIAS: After your arrival at the detention centre, how soon or how long after were the hoods put on your head?

D002: After about fifteen minutes.

ELIAS: Between that time [on] the Sunday when the hoods were put on your head and the Tuesday morning when you left the detention centre, were the hoods taken off your head for any reason that you can remember?

D002: Yes.

ELIAS: For what reason?

D002: When they brought us water and food.

ELIAS: Were you ever examined by a medic or doctor or a soldier who might have been a medic?

D002: No.

ELIAS: In that detention room, Mr D002, were you made – instructed – to try to hold any particular body position?

D002: Yes.

ELIAS: Can you describe that or demonstrate it so that we can see it on the screen?

D002: Many, many – I need to remember. Many positions, hands stretched forward like this *(Indicating.)* and also our legs bent while we were leaning on the wall.

ELIAS: I understand. Can you remember whether you were able to drink whenever you wanted to?

D002: But it was never enough. The water was never enough.

ELIAS: Over that period from the Sunday to the Tuesday, apart from the bags over your head and the positions that you were made to hold, can you tell us what was done to you?

D002: They hit me on the back and they hit me with metal they got off the pane of the window.

ELIAS: Apart from the metal from the window –

INTERPRETER: I'm sorry, there are lots of noises through my ear. I can't hear distinctly. Sorry about that.

CHAIRMAN: I am afraid that is coming through to all of us.

ELIAS: Mr D002, let me ask the question again. Are you able to hear me? Apart from the metal on your back, were you hit or struck with anything else?

D002: They hit me with a pipe.

ELIAS: Apart from the pipe, do you remember being hit or struck with anything else?

D002: The metal piece as well, in addition to punching and kicking.

ELIAS: I don't want you to guess, D002, but have you any idea, over the period of time that we are talking about, how many soldiers were involved in ill-treating or assaulting you?

D002: Many soldiers.

ELIAS: The blows that were struck to you, were they aimed at any particular part of your head or body?

D002: On the kidney area, on my chest as well.

ELIAS: Could you tell the chairman of the Inquiry, Mr D002, what was the effect on you of having these hoods on your head as you have described for hour after hour?

D002: They affected my breathing.

ELIAS: Do you mean you found it difficult to breathe?

D002: Yes.

ELIAS: You speak in your statement to the Inquiry – paragraph 53 – of there coming a time when you collapsed. Do you remember that?

D002: That's correct.

ELIAS: What caused you to collapse, do you know?

D002: The severity of the beating, I lost control of myself.

ELIAS: Can you remember what, if anything, happened to you when you collapsed?

D002: I remember when I fell, collapsed, a soldier came, and lifted me up while shouting at me in English and I don't know any English. Is this the justice? Is this the humanity? Where are the human rights?

ELIAS: So the –

D002: Britain is a great country. Where are the human rights? How come we have this treatment?

ELIAS: Mr D002 –

D002: How come? How? What a treatment? Why this treatment? You liberated us from Saddam Hussein and you did this to us. Why?

ELIAS: Mr D002 –

D002: Not only one soldier you can't single out, you know all the soldiers. Even those who treated us badly, you know them very well.

CHAIRMAN: Can we just pause a moment?

D002: Where is the justice? Where are the rights?

CHAIRMAN: I think we had better break off to find out whether he is able to continue.
We are going to break off, Mr D002.

AARON COOPER, 10 NOVEMBER 2009

CHAIRMAN: Good morning ladies and gentlemen, before we start our first witness, there is one thing I want to say about tomorrow. As I am sure nearly all of you know, or have remembered, tomorrow is Armistice Day. What I propose to do tomorrow is to take our ten-minute break between five to 11 and five past 11, so that during that time each person can observe Armistice Day in any way they chose. Thank you very much.

ELIAS: Thank you sir, then I call Aaron Paul Cooper, please.

CHAIRMAN: Please stand up, Mr Cooper. I am going to ask you if you want to take the oath. I think you want to affirm, is that right?

COOPER: Yes.

AARON PAUL ANTHONY COOPER (affirmed)

CHAIRMAN: If you would be kind enough to sit down.

COOPER: Thank you, Sir.

ELIAS: In the statement that you made to this Inquiry – paragraph 39, at the foot of the page you refer to your training and the 'classroom sessions' as you call them. You say this:

'The classroom sessions were all well and good, but I do not remember putting anything that we were taught in the classrooms into practice when I got to Iraq. We just followed instructions of our superiors. This is the way the army works. I trusted that what I was being told by my superiors was right, and the way things should be done.'

That is how you viewed it, is it?

COOPER: Yes.

ELIAS: I want to ask you a little, please, about Captain Dai Jones and his death. He was held in very high regard, was he?

COOPER: Yes, sir.

ELIAS: He died in August [2003], as we know. You describe his death in your statement as being a 'real standout event for everyone'.

COOPER: Yes.

ELIAS: What effect did his death have on the soldiers of 1QLR?

COOPER: We was quite upset, the fact we was going out there to do a job and trying to get Basra City back to some kind of normality after the war. We were – obviously – Dai Jones was attacked while in a marked ambulance. Obviously the lads was very angry, upset.

ELIAS: You say in your statement that [your multiple] became generally more aggressive.

COOPER: Yes.

ELIAS: 'In addition, after Captain Dai Jones' death our briefings with Lieutenant Rodgers were much more serious and "down to business".' True?

COOPER: True, yes.

ELIAS: 'We left the briefings feeling much more pumped up'.

COOPER: Yes Sir.

ELIAS: Can we move on, please, to Operation Salerno. You know what I'm talking about when I refer to that operation?

COOPER: Yes, I do, yes.

ELIAS: Did you ever hear any rumour, or anything said, that indicated these detainees had anything at all to do with the death of Captain Dai Jones?

COOPER: I do remember something being mentioned, I think by Lieutenant Rodgers.

ELIAS: What did he say? I don't mean the exact words; what was the gist of what he said?

COOPER: It was possible we were going to do some hotel – a hotel raid to find bomb making equipment and weapons, and there was a possibility that it could be in connection with the death of Captain Dai Jones.

ELIAS: Later that Sunday, did you go to the TDF?

COOPER: I did, yes.

ELIAS: About how many detainees did you see in that room at that time?

COOPER: 6 or 7.

ELIAS: In what condition were they? Were they standing; were they sitting; were they free to move about?

COOPER: No, they were in stress positions, hooded, plasticuffed.

ELIAS: What was the stress position they were in?

COOPER: Arms out in front of them, backs away from the wall.

ELIAS: And crouching, as it were?

COOPER: Some may have been crouching.

ELIAS: And what were conditions inside that room like when you went in?

COOPER: Not very good.

ELIAS: Why not?

COOPER: It's a small dark room. It didn't smell too pleasant.

ELIAS: What did it smell of?

COOPER: Excrement.

ELIAS: What was happening when you went into the room?

COOPER: The detainees were being shouted at to stay in the stress positions.

ELIAS: Who was shouting at the detainees?

COOPER: Other soldiers who were in the room.

ELIAS: Apart from shouting, were they doing anything?

COOPER: Yes.

ELIAS: What?

COOPER: Physically hitting the detainees.

ELIAS: Hitting detainees in what way?

COOPER: As you would normally hit in a fight.

ELIAS: Punches?

COOPER: Yes.

ELIAS: Punches with the fist?

COOPER: Yes.

ELIAS: And where were the blows being struck?

COOPER: Various parts of the body. Mainly the head, the abdomen region.

ELIAS: Can you tell us the names of any of the multiple who did throw a punch?

COOPER: Myself, Lieutenant Rodgers, Corporal Redfearn, Private Aspinall, Private Appleby, Private Allibone.

ELIAS: In that period of time, did you see Corporal Payne punching anyone?

COOPER: Yes, I did, yes.

ELIAS: So, would this be right, Mr Cooper – and don't just take it from me because I say it – when you went into that room, almost immediately what you saw was mayhem?

COOPER: Yes.

ELIAS: Soldiers having a go at detainees right left and centre?

COOPER: Yes.

ELIAS: Had you been prepared for that?

COOPER: No.

ELIAS: Why did you join in, as you say you did?

COOPER: Obviously – as I mentioned earlier, anger, frustration in regards to Captain Dai Jones. I just – I don't know, I just did what I felt inside.

ELIAS: So you went into the room, saw what you have told us you saw, joined in. How many detainees did you strike?

COOPER: I couldn't – I couldn't tell you.

ELIAS: Give us some idea?

COOPER: Three to five.

ELIAS: Three to five. What effect did your blows have on the detainees that you struck?

COOPER: I couldn't comment.

ELIAS: You have said that Lieutenant Rodgers was there striking a blow?

COOPER: Yes.

ELIAS: Is that right? Did you see that or is that something you were told?

COOPER: No I seen that myself.

ELIAS: Through that night, were there various visitors to the TDF?

COOPER: Yes, that's correct. There was various other soldiers from 1QLR and other regiments that did come into the TDF.

ELIAS: What was the purpose of the visits of those other soldiers, as far as you could see?

COOPER: Basically to do what had previously been done to the detainees in regards to throwing punches and mimicking them, and things like that.

ELIAS: Did you strike any blows after leaving the TDF on what I have called the first occasion?

COOPER: No, I didn't, no.

ELIAS: What caused you to change your conduct in that way?

COOPER: I felt quite guilty. I felt that the way that we had set upon them was out – you know, out of order, out of control.

ELIAS: So when did your conscience strike you?

COOPER: During that evening, after I had done what I had done.

ELIAS: So what was your feeling then?

COOPER: As I said, guilt. I mean, even if they did have a connection, the way that I had set upon them myself, and the others, you know, it – it was more animalistic than, you know, anyone else.

ELIAS: It was animalistic, and it wasn't justified on any basis, was it?

COOPER: No, not at all.

ELIAS: When did you first hear of the choir?

COOPER: On the Sunday evening. Basically Corporal Payne had got the detainees around him. He would poke them in the stomach for them to make a noise, and obviously because they all made different noises, they did it to each detainee once, and then went round them, and that's obviously where he got the choir from.

ELIAS: So that each detainee would make a different sound?

COOPER: Yes.

ELIAS: What was your reaction to the choir?

COOPER: At the time I found it quite humorous.

ELIAS: Did you laugh about it?

COOPER: At that moment I did.

ELIAS: Looking back on it, do you find it funny now?

COOPER: No.

ELIAS: Why not?

COOPER: Well, if I had been in their position, I'd be quite embarrassed.

ELIAS: Whilst you were at the TDF, were you aware of detainees being taken off for Tactical Questioning?

COOPER: I was aware of one being taken away.

ELIAS: How did you become aware of that?

COOPER: It was during my guard duty. The staff sergeant came in and took one of the detainees away.

ELIAS: What I want you to do, please, to assist the Inquiry, is to tell us what you remember about the incident that involved Baha Mousa.

COOPER: We more or less arrived [back] at the TDF, and we got off the vehicles. As we were stood outside I heard a scream – well not that scream, a cry for assistance. I entered the right-hand door.

ELIAS: When you went in, what happened? What did you see going on in that room?

COOPER: I seen Corporal Payne struggling with Baha Mousa. Baha Mousa wasn't wearing his hood; his plasticuffs were off. Obviously there was a struggle between the pair of them.

ELIAS: Just pause. In what position was Baha Mousa?

COOPER: Baha Mousa was stood up and Don Payne was to the rear of Baha Mousa trying to put his knee into the back of Baha Mousa's legs, to try and get him to the ground.

ELIAS: So Corporal Payne was behind. And what happened?

COOPER: Obviously I went to assist Corporal Payne in restraining Baha Mousa. We managed to get him to the floor. From that point, I'm not too sure if I found his arms or his legs, but I have held a piece of his body, you know, to stop him from moving about, because he was wriggling everywhere. Just to try to stop him from moving, to make it easier to get the plasticuffs back on to him.

ELIAS: And he went to the ground, did he?

COOPER: Yes.

ELIAS: To his knees, or further?

COOPER: I think it will have been further, all the way down to the floor.

ELIAS: Flat, facing downwards?

COOPER: Yes.

ELIAS: What happened then?

COOPER: As I have said, I assisted in trying to restrain him so Corporal Payne could get the plasticuffs on.

ELIAS: The plasticuffs are effectively put on then, on your account, are they, twice?

COOPER: Yes, that's correct.

ELIAS: The first time he breaks out of them, but they are reapplied? So what happened when Baha Mousa broke out of his plasticuffs for the second time?

COOPER: Obviously Corporal Payne was rather annoyed. I seen Corporal Payne stand up at that point. Corporal Payne has – in other words – give him a good kicking. Punches and kicks to his body.

ELIAS: Where on his body?

COOPER: Around the ribs. Rib area.

ELIAS: Did [Baha Mousa] try to get up?

COOPER: No, he didn't seem to be struggling as much.

ELIAS: And what happened to Baha Mousa?

COOPER: Obviously, with the strength of the kicks, Baha Mousa did bang his head against the wall.

ELIAS: So his head was banged against the wall, is that what you are saying?

COOPER: Yes.

ELIAS: By a kick?

COOPER: By a kick, and also previous – after that by Payne – Payne's hands as well. Corporal Payne also banged his head against the wall with his hands, by grabbing his head.

ELIAS: Again, so there is no ambiguity about it, do you mean that he was deliberately banging the head against the wall, or that was what happened as a result of his other actions?

COOPER: No, that's correct, [Payne] was doing it on purpose.

ELIAS: For how long did this attack by Corporal Payne go on?

COOPER: No more than 30 seconds.

ELIAS: What was it that brought it to an end?

COOPER: I think after Baha Mousa had stopped moving and stopped trying to protect himself, I think – I think – Payne just – to be honest Payne just stopped, and then obviously at that point there was no movement or sound from Baha Mousa.

ELIAS: So what happened when Corporal Payne stopped that?

COOPER: Obviously we was a little bit concerned, between – from myself really. I remember checking to see if there was a pulse. I couldn't feel a pulse.

ELIAS: What were you told by Corporal Payne?

COOPER: Payne basically said: '[He] banged his head against the wall, that's all'. You know, 'that's what happened, that's what we are going to say'.

ELIAS: In other words, you are saying he was putting you up to a story?

COOPER: That's correct.

ELIAS: It happened accidentally?

COOPER: That's correct.

ELIAS: Why did you go along with it?

COOPER: Obviously you are in the British Army, you all work as a team and try to stick as a team. [Then] there was a conversation between the [multiple] and Lieutenant Rodgers. He wanted to try and protect us and himself from anybody finding out about the treatment, the way that we treated them. So his suggestion was that all the blame be put on to Corporal Payne. That's the only reason I can think of for [why] things changed so dramatically. Mr Rodgers did not want anybody to find out the way that we had treated the detainees.

ADRIAN REDFEARN, 11 NOVEMBER 2009

ELIAS: You say in your statement to this Inquiry that you were put into stress positions during your own training exercises?

REDFEARN: Yes, I was.

ELIAS: Did you understand that stress positions could be used on civilians?

REDFEARN: No one had ever told me or shown me any part of any legislation or video where they were prohibited, sir.

ELIAS: What was the difference, as you understood it, Sergeant Redfearn, between the treatment of what I might call civilian detainees and prisoners of war?

REDFEARN: In my mind at the time, sir, the civilian detainees that we detained, they were prisoners of war. That was the way we had been taught.

ELIAS: From your perspective, as you understood the position, anyone who was detained, arrested, if you like, by soldiers, would be treated in exactly the same way whatever their status was?

REDFEARN: That's my opinion, sir, yes. I am not saying they would be placed in stress positions, what I'm saying is they should all be treated the same, sir.

ELIAS: Yes.

CHAIRMAN: Sergeant Redfearn, could you speak a little more slowly.

REDFEARN: I will, Sir.

CHAIRMAN: There is a good reason for that. What you are saying is being translated into Arabic and it is extremely difficult for those who are doing that work to keep up with you if you speak fast. It is a common fault that most people speak too fast, including myself very often. If you try, please, to slow down.

REDFEARN: I will do, Sir.

ELIAS: From your training or, indeed, from anywhere else, did you have as an individual soldier any guiding beacon, if you like, as to the way in which detainees should be treated?

REDFEARN: Yes, we had a video showed to us yearly but the video we were shown, sir, was well out of date. It was to do with basically fighting the Soviets and full-on war. It was nothing to do with fighting a building insurgency in Iraq.

ELIAS: When you arrived on that Monday morning, did you go into the [temporary detention facility] building?

REDFEARN: Yes, I did, sir, yes.

ELIAS: How many detainees were in that room?

REDFEARN: From what I can remember, either eight or nine, sir.

ELIAS: And what was their position and condition?

REDFEARN: They were sat down, cross-legged, basically in an U-shape against the wall, all hooded, all plasticuffed, and obviously –

CHAIRMAN: Please, not so fast.

REDFEARN: All plasticuffed and obviously in a lot worse condition than when they were taken away, sir.

ELIAS: Why obviously in a lot worse condition?

REDFEARN: Because when we arrested them, sir, they were still fully clothed, there were no marks on their bodies, there was no blood around the face. When we went in there, sir, it was a totally different scene.

ELIAS: What was it about their clothing?

REFEARN: Some of them were ripped. I think at least one of them was missing a top. But basically they were just in a lot – lot worse condition, sir.

ELIAS: Did you say something about blood?

REDFEARN: Yes, there was at least a couple of them had visible blood marks around the chin, around the neck, which I presumed had come from the nose or mouth, sir.

ELIAS: Were they hooded at this time?

REDFEARN: Yes, they was, sir.

ELIAS: And what condition physically did they seem to be in, apart from the marks?

REDFEARN: Worse for wear, sir, a lot worse for wear.

ELIAS: What did you think had happened to these detainees?

REDFEARN: That they had been assaulted, sir.

ELIAS: They had been beaten up?

REDFEARN: Yes, sir.

ELIAS: Did you say anything to Corporal Payne at this time?

REDFEARN: Not to Corporal Payne, sir, no.

ELIAS: Why not?

REDFEARN: Because I was intimidated and threatened by him, sir.

ELIAS: What, by merely the fact that he was who he was or as a result of something he did or said, or what?

REDFEARN: Merely by the fact that he was a bully, sir.

ELIAS: Did you take it up with anyone?

REDFEARN: Initially I sent for two medics, sir, that never returned.

ELIAS: Sent for two medics?

REDFEARN: Yes, sir.

ELIAS: No response?

REDFEARN: No response, sir.

ELIAS: The medics didn't come?

REDFEARN: Never came, sir.

ELIAS: Let's look at your statement to this Inquiry for a moment. BMI01805, paragraph 134. This is what you say:

'Conditions in the TDF were indescribable.' They were that horrific, were they?

REDFEARN: They were, sir.

ELIAS: 'When the detainees were originally arrested they were tidily dressed and not in any kind of distress. The next time I saw them in the TDF on Monday morning they all looked like they had been in a car crash.'

REDFEARN: Yes, sir.

ELIAS: It was as bad as that, was it?

REDFEARN: It was, sir.

ELIAS: 'The majority of their clothes were ripped and most if not all of them had had heavy bruising across their abdomens and upper arms.' True?

REDFEARN: Yes, sir.

ELIAS: You will go on in the next paragraph in the second line to say: 'Having seen what I had seen, I was "in bits".' What did that mean, Sergeant Redfearn?

REDFEARN: It meant I was upset, sir.

ELIAS: Did the detainees find it difficult, even on that Monday morning, to hold the stress position into which they were being put?

REDFEARN: They were obviously fatigued from being sat like that, sir, no sleep, and they were obviously distressed from the fact that they were hooded and they probably didn't know what was going to happen to them, sir.

ELIAS: Did they find it difficult to remain in the positions in which they were being held?

REDFEARN: Yes, sir.

ELIAS: What would happen if they did fall out of it?

REDFEARN: As soon as they started falling out when I was there, sir, I let them relax as best as I could.

ELIAS: What was Corporal Payne's attitude to allowing detainees to relax in this way?

REDFEARN: He went mad, sir.

ELIAS: In what way?

REDFEARN: He just went absolutely ballistic. I mean, I was not in there at the time, it was after I had been on [guard duty], but he came in and told other members basically that it was not to happen again, or basically what had been happening to the prisoners would happen to them, along them lines, sir.

ELIAS: I want to ask you, please, about Baha Mousa. You were aware of him being taken on a stretcher, were you?

REDFEARN: I was there, sir, yes. When I arrived and by this stage the events were already in full swing, sir.

ELIAS: I want you to tell us what you saw and heard, please.

REDFEARN: Yes, sir. As soon as I got out of the Saxon and I turned the engine off, I heard the screaming, sir, from the middle room. I believe Cooper [was] both shouting and screaming, obviously panicking. There had also been a bad power cut so there was no electricity, no lighting whatsoever, sir. As I entered the [facility], someone passed me a torch, ushered me towards the middle room and that's when I first started seeing the events, sir.

CHAIRMAN: Slowly, please.

ELIAS: Pause there. The shouting or the screaming that you heard was from soldiers, was it?

REDFEARN: Yes, sir. As well as detainees, sir.

ELIAS: You went in. You were handed the torch. You went to the middle room?

REDFEARN: Yes, sir.

ELIAS: What did you see when you got to the middle room?

REDFEARN: I saw Private Cooper and Corporal Payne struggling with a detainee towards the top left-hand side of the middle room, sir.

ELIAS: We know the detainee was Baha Mousa?

REDFEARN: Yes, sir.

ELIAS: In what position was he?

REDFEARN: He was laid flat on the floor. Obviously with Cooper and Corporal Payne on his back, sir.

ELIAS: What did the two soldiers, Cooper and Payne, appear to be doing?

REDFEARN: Panicking, shouting at each other, telling each other what to do. Cooper was saying stuff like, 'I am trying my best'.

ELIAS: What were they trying to do, apparently?

REDFEARN: Trying to get his plasticuffs back on, sir.

ELIAS: Was he hooded at this time?

REDFEARN: Yes, he was, sir.

ELIAS: And what happened?

REDFEARN: He was thrashing about on the floor. He was banging his head off the floor and the wall. I then left to the right-hand side –

CHAIRMAN: Do please take it a bit more slowly.

REDFEARN: I left to the right-hand side, sir, to see what was going on – as soon as there were two soldiers on top of him, sir, I thought that was under control. I then left to the next room to make sure that everything was under control in there, sir. When I re-entered, I saw Corporal Payne, Cooper stood back up –

ELIAS: Take it slowly, if you will.

REDFEARN: They were just stood up, sir, staring at him. I asked what was going on, but straightaway the hood was removed and straightaway you could see that there was something wrong with him, sir.

ELIAS: What told you there was something wrong?

REDFEARN: The fact that one minute he was thrashing about and then the next minute he was just silent, and just by looking at him, sir, I knew that he had stopped breathing.

ELIAS: So what happened?

REDFEARN: I shouted for [a soldier who gave] mouth-to-mouth, sir.

ELIAS: Did that produce any improvement?

REDFEARN: Not at all, sir, no, to be honest.

ELIAS: How long after Baha Mousa was taken away did you learn that he had died?

REDFEARN: Probably within 15 minutes, sir.

ELIAS: That was a great shock, was it, to you?

REDFEARN: It was – it wasn't a shock, sir, no, because the way things had been going it was only going to end one way, sir.

ELIAS: With somebody dying?

REDFEARN: Well, the way things were going, sir, yes.

ELIAS: If it was as bad as that, Sergeant Redfearn, didn't you feel impelled to tell somebody in higher authority that something needed to be done?

REDFEARN: As far as I was aware, sir, everybody in higher authority already knew what was going on, sir.

ELIAS: You had that, you say, from Mr Rodgers?

REDFEARN: And the fact that higher ranking officers had been in there and also the fact that the ops room was ten metres away from the TDF, sir.

ELIAS: You are telling the Chairman and this Inquiry that it became apparent to you that someone was likely to die to the extent that you were not shocked when it happened?

REDFEARN: No, I knew that there was going to be a serious incident, sir.

ELIAS: And yet you still didn't feel that you really had to shout it from the rooftops to somebody?

REDFEARN: There was no one in that camp, sir, as far as I was aware, that I could have told. Even the padre had been in there. If you can't turn to the padre, who can you turn to, sir?

LIEUTENANT CRAIG RODGERS, 11 NOVEMBER 2009

ELIAS: Please give the Inquiry your full name.

RODGERS: Craig Gerard Rodgers.

ELIAS: As far as you were aware, during the time that you were in Iraq, did your multiple do anything which was against the law of armed conflict or in the way of treating civilians in any way improperly?

RODGERS: At the time, I believed not.

ELIAS: Did you have any training before getting to Iraq in the handling of civilian detainees?

RODGERS: Not in the handling of civilians, no.

ELIAS: None at all.

RODGERS: No. The training that we had was based around war fighting, which is the rules that we were working off at the time.

ELIAS: So what was your understanding in relation to the use of hoods?

RODGERS: That any detainees that were believed to be former regime loyalists were to be hooded.

ELIAS: Sorry, why [was it] the former regime loyalists were to be hooded in this way?

RODGERS: We believed it was so they could not see where they were being taken.

ELIAS: So putting it in shorthand, it was a security issue, was it?

RODGERS: It was, yes.

ELIAS: I don't want you to speculate or to guess, Mr Rodgers, but taking the chain above you, do you know of officers above you who were aware of the use of hooding in the ways that you have described in Iraq in 2003?

RODGERS: It was a brigade policy, sir, so every officer in the brigade would have been aware. And I believe that it was also a British forces policy, not just brigade policy.

ELIAS: And what understanding did you have about the rights and wrongs of the use of stress positions?

RODGERS: At the time, sir, I believed it was in accordance with British forces policy. The same as hooding, it was a brigade policy.

ELIAS: When you say it was a brigade policy, was that something that you simply assumed?

RODGERS: It wouldn't have been an assumption, it would have been something I was specifically told. My job in Iraq was to follow orders and I didn't make assumptions, I followed orders that I was given.

ELIAS: And in the arrest and in the period that you were detaining, was there in your mind, Mr Rodgers, any – my words – guiding beacon as to how these individuals, former regime loyalists, if you like, should be treated?

RODGERS: Not that I am aware of.

ELIAS: For example, did you appreciate that you had a duty to treat them – indeed, I suggest all civilian detainees – humanely?

RODGERS: Absolutely, sir.

ELIAS: Where did you get that understanding from?

RODGERS: That's my own moral understanding.

ELIAS: Now, I want to ask you a little about the conditions under which you and the multiple were working in Iraq. You have said in your statement about the nature of the work that you were called upon to carry out. You have indicated that, I think, frequently you would be working 20 hours a day?

RODGERS: Yes, sir.

ELIAS: Did that apply to you or to the multiple, or to both?

RODGERS: I would suggest that applied to every single British soldier in Iraq at the time, sir.

ELIAS: The brief you were given by Corporal Payne with regard to the detainees, to the best of your recollection, what did he tell you?

RODGERS: I can't remember, sir.

ELIAS: Did you see the detainees at this time?

RODGERS: I think I saw them in the room, sir, yes.

ELIAS: Were they in stress positions?

RODGERS: I can't recall, sir.

ELIAS: Were they making any noise?

RODGERS: I can't recall, sir.

ELIAS: Did Corporal Payne show you any injury to any of the detainees at that stage?

RODGERS: He did, sir. He pointed out some bruising to one of the males.

ELIAS: Where was the bruising?

RODGERS: I think it was around his torso, sir.

ELIAS: Why was Corporal Payne pointing out bruising to you at this stage?

RODGERS: I believe it was to point out, sir, that they had been involved in fighting previously.

ELIAS: Why was that relevant to you?

RODGERS: I believe that we had not just wasted our time and arrested people who weren't at least involved in some kind of activity.

ELIAS: So Mr Payne was demonstrating to you that you had picked up men – or a man anyway – who appeared to have been involved in earlier fighting?

RODGERS: I believe so, sir, yes.

ELIAS: What were the conditions in the room itself at that time?

RODGERS: The room was hot, sir, and smelly.

ELIAS: What was the smell?

RODGERS: Just sweat and dirty bodies, sir.

ELIAS: You of course knew Corporal Payne?

RODGERS: I did, sir, yes.

ELIAS: Did he have any reputation?

RODGERS: He was a provost corporal, sir. All provost staff have a reputation as being tough and hard line.

ELIAS: Tough and hard line?

RODGERS: They enforce the policy of the regimental sergeant major for discipline.

ELIAS: So nothing unusual about that?

RODGERS: No, sir.

ELIAS: But – if you forgive me for putting it in shorthand – there was, for whatever reason, open season on these detainees and your [multiple] were permitted to have a pop at them?

RODGERS: No, not at all. Not at all.

ELIAS: You would not have tolerated that under any circumstances, would you?

RODGERS: I would not have tolerated that under any circumstances.

ELIAS: Did you at any time yourself use any violence on any detainee?

RODGERS: Never.

ELIAS: I now want to ask you about what you remember of the events at the time of the death of the detainee, Baha Mousa.
In your statement in October of 2003 you said that [Payne] said: 'There's a problem with one of the prisoners who stopped breathing and has had to go to the medic centre,' or words to that effect. Would that be correct?

RODGERS: If that's what I said, sir, then yes.

ELIAS: Was [Baha Mousa's death] a shock to you?

RODGERS: Yes, sir. It would be a shock to any reasonable human being but I was told by the commanding officer not to ask any questions as it would be a police matter.
Any death in custody – similar to the UK – would be a internal investigation matter and the internal investigation part of the military is the Royal Military Police. I was instructed by the commanding officer not to [ask any questions], and that's a direct order.

ELIAS: Is that the position to this day?

RODGERS: Absolutely, sir.

ELIAS: What did you know about your 'guys trying to fit up Don Payne'?

RODGERS: Nothing, sir. I was not aware of any plot to set up Corporal Payne.

ELIAS: You knew Captain Dai Jones, did you?

RODGERS: I did, sir.

ELIAS: Is it right his death was a very great shock to the whole of 1QLR?

RODGERS: It was a shock, sir, yes.

ELIAS: Did you ever hear any suggestion that the detainees who had been brought in, the Baha Mousa detainees as I call them, had anything to do with the death of Captain Dai Jones?

RODGERS: No, sir.

ELIAS: You certainly heard from one source, did you, at the time – from one source – that these might be people who had killed the RMP?

RODGERS: At that time, sir, I presume Major Peebles told me that on that evening.

CHAIRMAN: 25, you were, at the time. Is that right?

RODGERS: Yes, sir.

CHAIRMAN: What sort of relationship does a young officer have with fairly senior older NCOs?

RODGERS: It varies, sir. There is across the army a common thread that a lot of senior NCOs in particular – the ones that are longer in the tooth – believe that officers have no purpose in the army.

CHAIRMAN: The only other thing I want to ask you about is this: you have no doubt seen the injuries to the detainees, some of which are, to put it mildly, quite horrendous?

RODGERS: Yes, sir.

CHAIRMAN: A number of members of your [multiple] accept that they did punch detainees.

RODGERS: Yes, sir.

CHAIRMAN: You say, as I understand it, that you had no idea that this had happened.

RODGERS: No, sir.

CHAIRMAN: None at all?

RODGERS: None, Sir.

DONALD PAYNE, 16 NOVEMBER 2009

ELIAS: Mr Payne, it is right, isn't it, that you joined the army in 1988?

PAYNE: Yes.

ELIAS: You went straight into 1QLR?

PAYNE: Yes.

ELIAS: At about the turn of the century, 98/99, thereabouts, did you become a regimental policeman?

PAYNE: 1999, yes.

ELIAS: And did you remain on the provost staff until you were discharged from the army following your conviction at the court martial?

PAYNE: Yes.

ELIAS: I want then to begin with your training. At the moment I am dealing, please, with training that was not specifically for provost staff. Hooding: When did you first encounter hooding training in the army?

PAYNE: 1988.

ELIAS: What were you taught about it then?

PAYNE: Just to hood suspects who, you know, we caught, whether in Northern Ireland or in war.

ELIAS: You served in Northern Ireland?

PAYNE: Yes.

ELIAS: To your knowledge were suspects hooded after you joined the army in Northern Ireland?

PAYNE: If caught, yes.

ELIAS: Were you told what the purpose of hooding detainees was at that stage?

PAYNE: To disorientate them.

ELIAS: Did you receive any what I might call general training in how detainees, prisoners of war or detainees, were to be treated if captured?

PAYNE: We used to see a video once a year.

ELIAS: What, if anything, was the general message of that video as you remember it?

PAYNE: To treat them properly.

ELIAS: By 'properly', what do you mean?

PAYNE: Feed them, water them, make sure that they were safe.

ELIAS: Were you told that minimum force was to be the rule?

PAYNE: Yes.

ELIAS: Is there any doubt but that you would have known at the time of the events this Inquiry is concerned with that civilians must be treated humanely at all times?

PAYNE: Yes.

ELIAS: No doubt about that, is there?

PAYNE: No doubt.

ELIAS: Thank you. Was that something which you knew that the detainees in Iraq were entitled to?

PAYNE: No.

ELIAS: What did you believe that they were entitled to that differed from that care?

PAYNE: I don't understand your question.

ELIAS: Why did –

PAYNE: I didn't know any of this in Iraq. When we went to Iraq it was a new thing for everybody.

ELIAS: Yes. What I am asking you, Mr Payne, and I thought you were agreeing with me, was that as far as the detainees in Iraq were concerned you would have understood that they were entitled to be treated humanely, that is to say with respect, with fairness.

PAYNE: Yes.

ELIAS: Is that right?

PAYNE: Yes.

ELIAS: You would have appreciated that at the time, but I think you would agree now, would you, they plainly were not treated humanely, were they?

PAYNE: No, they weren't.

ELIAS: You refer in your statement to this Inquiry to training you were given in Catterick.

PAYNE: Yes.

ELIAS: Were there lectures, talks?

PAYNE: It was a 40-minute lecture.

ELIAS: Who gave it?

PAYNE: Two guys from the Intelligence Corps.

ELIAS: What was the content of the talk?

PAYNE: Basically it was on tactical questioning, to get them questioned as fast and as soon as we could.

ELIAS: What else were you taught?

PAYNE: Nothing.

ELIAS: If you look at where you refer to this training, you say it was a two-hour lecture given by the Intelligence Corps to senior NCOs. Your statement goes on: '... lack of sleep and to keep prisoners confused as much as we could.'

PAYNE: Yes.

ELIAS: Was anything said as to what the purpose of that was: Shock of capture, lack of sleep?

PAYNE: It was to aid the tactical questioner, or the interrogator.

ELIAS: Was anything at that lecture – and I don't want you to guess if you don't remember, Mr Payne – was anything at that lecture, that session, said about hooding or stress positions?

PAYNE: Not about stress positions, no.

ELIAS: Was anything said about hooding?

PAYNE: Yes.

ELIAS: What was that?

PAYNE: They were to be hooded.

ELIAS: Was anything said about the duration of hooding?

PAYNE: No.

ELIAS: Before you went out to Iraq, what was your position in relation to the use of stress positions on detainees? Was it appropriate or not?

PAYNE: We didn't know we'd be dealing with detainees, so I didn't have a position.

ELIAS: Where did responsibility lie for the detainees?

PAYNE: With Major Peebles, the overall –

ELIAS: Sorry? You are just dropping your voice a little.

PAYNE: The BGIRO [battlegroup internment review officer] was overall in charge.

ELIAS: Now, in relation to the manner in which detainees were to be treated and in accordance with what you say was the s.o.p. [standard operating procedure] can you help us, please, as to who was aware of that in the chain of command through you?

PAYNE: Everybody.

ELIAS: How did it go?

PAYNE: All the way up.

ELIAS: To whom?

PAYNE: The CO.

ELIAS: On Sunday – the day of their arrest and their being brought to the TDF – who was in charge?

PAYNE: Myself.

ELIAS: They arrive, they are met one by one, you say, by you. You search them. What happens to them when they are searched?

PAYNE: The plasticuffs are removed from the back and placed out in front.

ELIAS: What else?

PAYNE: Sandbags are reapplied.

ELIAS: Who applied the sandbags?

PAYNE: Me.

ELIAS: How many?

PAYNE: One.

ELIAS: We know that these detainees were detained until the Tuesday morning at some time when they were sent off to Umm Qasr.

PAYNE: Yes.

ELIAS: In that 48 hours or so, for what period of time did the hoods remain on these detainees?

PAYNE: 36 hours.

ELIAS: Until a particular event?

PAYNE: Yes.

ELIAS: What was that?

PAYNE: Death of Baha Mousa.

ELIAS: You have told us that you had them brought in one by one? Let's deal with the initial six. Was it apparent to you that some of these – and I hope I am not putting it too delicately – were older rather than younger?

PAYNE: Yes, they was old men, yes.

ELIAS: You put them into plasticuffs and hoods. Were they put immediately into stress positions?

PAYNE: Yes.

ELIAS: What was the stress position?

PAYNE: Back against the wall, knees bent.

ELIAS: Arms out in front of them?

PAYNE: Yes.

ELIAS: And they were expected to hold that position?

PAYNE: Yes.

ELIAS: Throughout the period that these detainees were in that detention centre – the 48 hours or so – who in authority to your knowledge – I don't want you to guess about it – knew of their presence there?

PAYNE: Everybody.

ELIAS: Meaning?

PAYNE: CO [Colonel Mendonca].

ELIAS: Mr Peebles?

PAYNE: Yes.

ELIAS: You say the CO. How did you know that he knew?

PAYNE: Because he would have to be informed.

ELIAS: Thank you. Over that period of time, emanating from the TDF would there have been shouting and screaming?

PAYNE: Yes.

ELIAS: Who would have been doing the shouting?

PAYNE: Myself, if I was there, and the guard.

ELIAS: Why would you have shouted?

PAYNE: To keep them awake.

ELIAS: Shouting of a kind that would have been heard – might have been heard – in, for example, the accommodation block opposite?

PAYNE: Yes.

ELIAS: Did your conduct in fact include kicking and punching –

PAYNE: Yes.

ELIAS: – routinely to detainees?

PAYNE: Yes.

ELIAS: And in relation to these detainees, the Baha Mousa detainees, why did you involve yourself in kicking and punching them?

PAYNE: No reason.

ELIAS: For no reason. I just want you to think about it. I am not suggesting it for one moment, but was it the case, for example, that you believed that they were involved in some previous killing?

PAYNE: Maybe, yes.

ELIAS: Was that something that had anything to do with your behaviour?

PAYNE: Yes. I think it was because we thought they had murdered the RMP[s].

ELIAS: Who is the 'we' in that sentence?

PAYNE: Everybody.

ELIAS: You go on in the statement to say this: 'Moreover at one time or another I saw all the members of the multiple emulate me.'

PAYNE: Yes.

ELIAS: Is that true?

PAYNE: Yes.

ELIAS: Why haven't you said that before?

PAYNE: Misguided loyalties.

ELIAS: You lied about almost everything, didn't you?

PAYNE: Yes.

ELIAS: We can go to innumerable other examples where you told the police investigating you had never assaulted any of them and you had never seen any such assaults, can't we?

PAYNE: Yes.

ELIAS: Your interview under caution on 9 March 2004. You were asked about the choir. You prodded detainees who made noises one after the other?

PAYNE: That was one of my checks when I came in to the detention –

ELIAS: To see if they were awake, you said?

PAYNE: Yes.

ELIAS: I am going to ask you, please, to look at a few photographs with me of some of the detainees, photographs taken a day or two after they left the TDF at Umm Qasr. Injury to the left flank, bruising. Do you know how those injuries were come by?

PAYNE: By being punched and kicked.

ELIAS: Should the Inquiry now understand that you will have kicked and punched each of these detainees?

PAYNE: Yes.

ELIAS: Forceful blows?

PAYNE: Yes.

ELIAS: Designed to hurt them?

PAYNE: Yes.

ELIAS: Injury to the nose of D003. Do you know how such injuries were occasioned?

PAYNE: No.

ELIAS: Were sandbags rubbed across their faces?

PAYNE: No, not by me.

ELIAS: Was there any eye gouging, moving of sandbags in that way?

PAYNE: No.

ELIAS: Grabbing around the face?

PAYNE: Yes.

ELIAS: You did that, did you?

PAYNE: Yes.

ELIAS: Grabbing around the face for what purpose?

PAYNE: To lift the head up.

ELIAS: In doing that, could you, if you like, have scuffed the bag across, for example, the nose of the detainee?

PAYNE: It could have happened, yes.

ELIAS: Why did you grab the head to lift up?

PAYNE: If the head had slumped.

ELIAS: If they were falling asleep or something?

PAYNE: Yes.

ELIAS: We see bruising and marking to the torso of D003's body. Would that have been kicking and punching too?

PAYNE: Yes.

ELIAS: When you saw others from the multiple kicking and punching, where were their kicks and punches directed?

PAYNE: Various parts.

ELIAS: Being?

PAYNE: Various parts.

ELIAS: What do you mean by 'various parts'?

PAYNE: Various parts of their body.

ELIAS: Yes, which parts?

PAYNE: Various parts.

ELIAS: Well, which parts?

PAYNE: I cannot be specific.

ELIAS: The feet?

PAYNE: Yes.

ELIAS: The knees?

PAYNE: Various parts.

ELIAS: The thighs?

PAYNE: Various parts.

ELIAS: The trunk?

PAYNE: Various parts.

ELIAS: The head? What, any? Any and all, is –

PAYNE: Yes.

ELIAS: – that what you are saying?

PAYNE: Yes.

ELIAS: Would you agree, Mr Payne, that it would seem to be apparent from photographs – forget any other evidence – that these detainees who suffered those injuries were not subjected to the odd kick or punch, were they?

PAYNE: Yes.

ELIAS: You would agree?

PAYNE: Yes.

ELIAS: You say, you told us, that you couldn't see, didn't see, any injury on any of them at any time up until and including the death of Baha Mousa, correct?

PAYNE: Yes.

ELIAS: What you said was – can I remind you: 'I could see the prisoners were being worn down, they were knackered through lack of sleep and having been in the stress positions for a long time.'

PAYNE: Yes.

ELIAS: That was very obvious to you, was it?

PAYNE: Yes.

ELIAS: And very obviously inhumane?

PAYNE: Yes.

ELIAS: Was that a matter that troubled you?

PAYNE: Yes.

ELIAS: Did you take it up with anybody?

PAYNE: Yes.

ELIAS: With whom?

PAYNE: The BGIRO.

ELIAS: Mr Peebles?

PAYNE: Yes.

ELIAS: At what stage did you take it up?

PAYNE: After the Tactical Questions had finished.

ELIAS: Tell us what transpired.

PAYNE: I was told [they were wanted] with the shock of capture still because they had intelligence to give.

ELIAS: So it was an explicit order, was it, to maintain the stress positions?

PAYNE: Yes.

ELIAS: And hooding?

PAYNE: Yes.

ELIAS: And you say that came from Major Peebles?

PAYNE: Yes.

ELIAS: From that time of assaulting the detainees on the Sunday evening through until the death of Baha Mousa, should the Inquiry understand – tell me this is wrong if it is – from your evidence that more or less whenever you went back to the TDF you would involve yourself in more violence of this kind?

PAYNE: Yes.

ELIAS: And you saw members of the multiple using violence?

PAYNE: Yes.

ELIAS: Punching and kicking?

PAYNE: Yes.

ELIAS: Would that be the guard on duty?

PAYNE: Yes.

ELIAS: When, if at all, were you first aware that Baha Mousa was, if you like, causing any problems?

PAYNE: Sunday teatime.

ELIAS: What were the problems?

PAYNE: He kept getting out of his plasticuffs and taking his hood off.

ELIAS: So was any decision come to as to how this problem was to be overcome or dealt with?

PAYNE: Yes, we was to place him in the middle room.

ELIAS: What were you told, if anything, to do with him in the middle room?

PAYNE: To plasticuff his thumbs together and his little fingers and place him laid down on the floor with his chin in his hands.

ELIAS: So on his stomach?

PAYNE: Yes.

ELIAS: And was he so plasticuffed, fingers and thumbs as well as wrists?

PAYNE: Yes.

ELIAS: Then placed on the floor?

PAYNE: Yes.

ELIAS: Did that solve the problem?

PAYNE: It seemed to, yes.

ELIAS: So now moving onto [the night one day later], the incident relating to his death.

PAYNE: Yes.

ELIAS: Well, then, please tell us what happened in this incident: where did you first encounter Baha Mousa?

PAYNE: Just inside the left-hand room.

ELIAS: So he was what, in the doorway, if you like, of the left-hand room, is that what you are saying, coming out of the small room?

PAYNE: Yes.

ELIAS: Hooded, plasticuffed?

PAYNE: No hood.

ELIAS: What was he doing?

PAYNE: Walking towards the door.

ELIAS: What did he do then?

PAYNE: He saw me. I screamed – well, shouted – that he was trying to escape. He then turned and I followed him, got him down to the floor in the middle room.

ELIAS: What happened there?

PAYNE: I placed my knee in the small of his knee at the back. Put my hand across his face, pulled him back, and knelt with my knee to push him forward. Got him to the ground. By this time Cooper came and helped me.

ELIAS: Had you been calling for help?

PAYNE: Yes.

ELIAS: Did you use any further force upon him other than that which you used to take him to the ground and hold his arms together?

PAYNE: Yes, I had my knee in his back.

ELIAS: Why did you have your knee in his back?

PAYNE: To control him.

ELIAS: In the thrashing about, do you say that any part of his body struck anything or anybody?

PAYNE: I heard his head, but I don't know whether it was the floor or the wall.

ELIAS: What did you hear his head?

PAYNE: I heard it whack.

ELIAS: What sort of a noise was it?

PAYNE: Like a whack.

ELIAS: Did that bang either to the wall or the floor stop the thrashing about?

PAYNE: Yes.

ELIAS: What happened after that?

PAYNE: I reapplied the plasticuffs. We sat him up. Cooper had checked for a pulse. He had a pulse, but I sent somebody to get the – a medic.

ELIAS: Mr Payne, It has been said that in the course of that incident you lost your temper and kicked out and punched out at Baha Mousa. Is that right?

PAYNE: No.

ELIAS: You didn't lose it and go into a sort of frenzy?

PAYNE: No.

ELIAS: When you realised that there was something wrong, did you stay with him or did you move away?

PAYNE: Moved away.

ELIAS: Why?

PAYNE: To let the doctor and the medic get there.

ELIAS: Subsequently, did you say anything to them about what had happened?

PAYNE: I was explaining it all to the adjutant. And I just kept saying, 'I can't believe he's dead. He only banged his head.'

ELIAS: 'He only banged his head'. Did you say anything to those members of the Rodgers multiple or, indeed, any other to the effect that it should be said that he only banged his head?

PAYNE: No.

ELIAS: In the sense of meaning 'we all know that worse than that happened, but that's the story we are going to tell'?

PAYNE: No, I never said that –

ELIAS: Nothing of that kind was said by you, was it?

PAYNE: No.

ELIAS: Can I then move on to just a couple of other aspects of the 48 hours that we have been talking about. Going back to your statement which you signed today, you referred to an incident involving Lieutenant Rodgers.

PAYNE: Yes.

ELIAS: Can you just tell us what happened, please?

PAYNE: It was early on the Monday morning. I came in to check on them to make sure that they got their breakfast, and the multiple was there, Mr Rodgers was in the middle room with the – the young lad. There was a open jerry can there in front of him.

ELIAS: Say again?

PAYNE: An open jerry can of petrol there in front of him.

ELIAS: In front of whom?

PAYNE: The young lad, so he could smell the fumes.

ELIAS: Was the young lad, as you call him, hooded at the time?

PAYNE: Yes, hooded.

ELIAS: What happened?

PAYNE: He poured water over him, took the jerry can of water away, removed the hood and then lit a match as if he was going to burn him.

ELIAS: So who poured water over him?

PAYNE: Rodgers.

ELIAS: Who lit the match?

PAYNE: Rodgers.

ELIAS: When you observed that, did you say anything to Rodgers or any other member of the multiple about it?

PAYNE: No.

ELIAS: Why not?

PAYNE: Because he's an officer.

ELIAS: So the match is lit. What happened then?

PAYNE: The young lad went hysterical.

ELIAS: How did it end?

PAYNE: I can't remember.

ELIAS: I will be corrected if I am wrong about it, I don't recall the young man suggesting that that happened to him. It did, did it?

PAYNE: Yes.

ELIAS: Not something that you are making up against Mr Rodgers or the Rodgers multiple?

PAYNE: No.

ELIAS: Did you ever have any conversation with the CO about what had happened –

PAYNE: Yes.

ELIAS: – to these detainees or to Baha Mousa?

PAYNE: Yes.

ELIAS: What did you tell him?

PAYNE: What had happened.

ELIAS: What you have told us?

PAYNE: Yes.

ELIAS: As to the struggle?

PAYNE: Yes.

ELIAS: What did he say to that?

PAYNE: He said, 'I hope it's right, because if it's not' – well, 'I hope it's right, because if it's not it's the end of my career and your career.'

ELIAS: What did you understand him to be saying by that?

PAYNE: That it was either me or him.

MICHAEL PEEBLES, 7 DECEMBER 2009

ELIAS: Sir, I call Michael Edwin Peebles, Major Peebles, please.

CHAIRMAN: Yes. If you would be kind enough to stand, as you are, Major, I will ask you to take the oath.
MICHAEL EDWIN PEEBLES (sworn)

CHAIRMAN: Please sit down, and if you would be kind enough to speak into the microphone, then hopefully we will all be able to hear you.

ELIAS: I want to ask you specifically about your BGIRO role.

PEEBLES: Yes, sir.

ELIAS: Had you ever heard of the role of BGIRO before you went to Iraq?

PEEBLES: No, I had not, sir.

ELIAS: When you were appointed to that role, what did you understand was that role and its responsibility?

PEEBLES: I understood it principally, sir, to be a quasi-judicial appointment in the sense that I had to come to a decision as to whether a detainee that had been brought in was to be released back into the population, handed over to the police force or sent down to the T.I.F. [Theatre Internment Facility at Umm Qasr] for further questioning and for prolonged custody.

ELIAS: So you took the internment decision?

PEEBLES: Yes, sir, I did.

ELIAS: Who had responsibility for detainees brought into BG main?

PEEBLES: In terms of looking after the detainees, the regimental police staff, were there to do that specific task.

ELIAS: Who had, ultimately, as you understood it, the responsibility for them?

PEEBLES: Overall? Overall, that would then go back to the commanding officer.

ELIAS: Yes.

PEEBLES: I had – there is no doubt I had a pivotal role over the co-ordination of dealing with the detainees, but in terms of the sole responsibility for the handling and welfare of detainees, I don't believe that came down to me, if that is the question.

ELIAS: Major Peebles, you are answering my question before I ask it, but let's deal with it since you have. You had a pivotal role in handling or dealing with the detainees? What was that pivotal role, please?

PEEBLES: That role in terms of – bringing in the evidence and coming to a decision as to what –

ELIAS: I am sorry to stop you, just so we make some progress. What was your role specifically in relation to what we might all understand as the handling of the detainees? If something was being done wrong, you would seek to correct it?

PEEBLES: Yes, I would.

ELIAS: Just dealing with the practicalities, if you like, of operating your role pre-Operation Salerno. You understand what I think, in this Inquiry, we have been calling the '14-hour rule', did you?

PEEBLES: Yes, I did.

ELIAS: What did that mean?

PEEBLES: That meant that we should try to get the detainees or internees down to the theatre internment facility [at Umm Qasr] within 14 hours.

ELIAS: Let me move on to Operation Salerno itself, then, please. You knew that prisoners had to be treated humanely –

PEEBLES: Yes, sir.

ELIAS: – and in accordance with the Geneva Conventions?

PEEBLES: Yes, sir.

ELIAS: You obviously knew that they had to be treated lawfully, that is to say for the purposes of this Inquiry anyway, not assaulted.

PEEBLES: Yes, sir.

ELIAS: You believed that conditioning was approved at brigade level, if not higher?

PEEBLES: Yes, I did.

ELIAS: And you saw yourself [as] having some general oversight where conditioning was being used to ensure that guards or provost staff were not going over the top?

PEEBLES: Yes, I think that's quite natural.

ELIAS: Did you visit the TDF when the Operation Salerno detainees were there on the Sunday, Monday and Tuesday?

PEEBLES: On the Sunday and Monday, yes sir.

ELIAS: Do you recall, over that period, how many visits you made to the TDF?

PEEBLES: I think it was approximately three to four on the Sunday and three on the Monday prior to the incident of the death.

ELIAS: Prior to the death of Baha Mousa?

PEEBLES: Yes.

ELIAS: So about seven visits?

PEEBLES: That would be approximately correct, sir, yes.

ELIAS: So that state of affairs, the conditioning, the hooding, the stress positions and so on, looking at matters now, Major Peebles, do you accept any responsibility for the detainees being subjected to conditioning over that period?

PEEBLES: I think it was part of the process and therefore I was involved in that process, but I don't accept full responsibility but –

ELIAS: But you accept some, do you?

PEEBLES: In part, yes. I was aware of the practice, yes, sir, and indeed I condoned it.

ELIAS: Did you go further than simply condoning it? Did you at any stage instruct that conditioning should be commenced?

PEEBLES: Yes, I did. I suggested it should start at about 16.30 hours [on the Sunday].

ELIAS: You ordered the guard to start conditioning?

PEEBLES: Yes.

ELIAS: When you gave that order, did you see whether they put it into operation?

PEEBLES: Yes, I am sure that they did. They were – I didn't hang around for that long but I saw them go in, shout at the detainees to get up and to get their hands up, i.e. to –

ELIAS: They were already hooded?

PEEBLES: Yes, sir.

ELIAS: Wasn't that part of the conditioning?

PEEBLES: Well, yes, it is, it is, but the hoods were – the hoods remained on for – the hoods remained on in that period because we felt that maybe they posed a potential threat and therefore the hooding was appropriate.

ELIAS: I think you say in your statement to this Inquiry that you became aware of the medical assessment having been carried out at 3 o'clock in the afternoon –

PEEBLES: Yes.

ELIAS: – by which time the detainees had been in army custody for six or seven hours or so.

PEEBLES: Yes, sir, they had.

ELIAS: Wasn't that something that concerned you?

PEEBLES: We had to wait for the tactical questioners [to arrive] and the questioning clearly wasn't going to happen for some time. We had a lot of information to sift through, a lot of documentation, et cetera. So I suppose there was – there could have been – there could have been an assumption on Corporal Payne's part – time for him to co-ordinate the medical visit. I wasn't sat there, honestly, just doing nothing and twiddling my thumbs, but –

ELIAS: Time for Corporal Payne to co-ordinate the medical visit? What was involved in this co-ordination?

PEEBLES: I presume he would go down to the regimental aid post and call for some medics to come and do the examination.

ELIAS: About 80 metres away?

PEEBLES: Yes, not far at all. It should have happened sooner, I plainly admit to you. I think it could have happened very quickly, but, for whatever reason, it appears that it didn't.

ELIAS: You know [Corporal Payne] told the Inquiry what he did?

PEEBLES: Yes, I am aware of that, sir, yes.

ELIAS: Routinely returning and gratuitously assaulting – unlawfully kicking and punching detainees. You never saw or heard anything of that kind?

PEEBLES: No, I didn't, sir. As I say, I hardly saw Corporal Payne over those two days, but obviously when a problem arose, he came and told me about it.

ELIAS: We are coming to the Baha Mousa incident in due course. So you have started the conditioning process, you say. You never called it off?

PEEBLES: No, not formally, no, sir.

ELIAS: Why, that Sunday afternoon, did you pass on the fact that you believed that these detainees might have something to do with the deaths of the three [Royal Military Police] men?

PEEBLES: Sir, I was either asked or I said in terms of passing on information to the guard that – I was either asked why these people were in custody, so I gave a brief explanation, or I just said it. It wasn't to – it was so that they were fully informed. I said, 'The reason we are questioning them is because we might believe that they would know something about the RMP incident'. I never said – well, you know, I never said that they were responsible because clearly, at that stage, we didn't know that.

ELIAS: Wasn't it highly irresponsible, to put it at its lowest, to spread the rumour that detainees being guarded by soldiers of 1QLR – wasn't it highly irresponsible to spread that possibility as a rumour?

PEEBLES: No, I thought it was appropriate that they know the people who we were dealing with, that they were a potential threat and –

ELIAS: Major Peebles, why did they need to know that?

PEEBLES: Sorry, sir?

ELIAS: Why did they have to know that these men might have something to do with the death of three RMPs?

PEEBLES: Well, sir, they may have been a potential threat. That's all. It's part of a briefing process, sir. You try to inform people.

ELIAS: Of course what you could have said to anybody who enquired is, 'Mind your own business'?

PEEBLES: Sir, they are responsible for dealing – for looking after detainees, and they have a right to know. If anybody escaped or tried to escape, et cetera, they should – you know, they should be aware of the type of people potentially they were dealing with. I didn't say to them – I certainly didn't say to them that they were responsible for. I did make it clear that we believe there might be an involvement.

ELIAS: It wasn't the case, was it, that by late on the Sunday evening, it was, for these detainees – if I'll be forgiven for [putting] it this way – open house on assaulting them because of that?

PEEBLES: With some of the evidence which has come out of here, I would agree that they found motive. It doesn't justify it though, sir, whatever you believe.

ELIAS: No. I suppose the question remains, doesn't it, Major Peebles why did you contribute in spreading that story?

PEEBLES: I did not want to spread a story, sir, and certainly, if I felt that it would result in such behaviour, I wouldn't have said anything.

ELIAS: What role did you play in the [Tactical Questioning]?

PEEBLES: I – there would be – I would take notes. I would – if there was guidance that needed providing, I would also look at whatever previous notes had been written, so I could feed questions into the tactical questioner if so required.

ELIAS: Do you recall one of those detainees being particularly young?

PEEBLES: I do, yes. D005.

ELIAS: Was he treated in any different way to the other detainees so far as tactical questioning is concerned?

PEEBLES: No, except for the way that he was placed outside, next to the generator, yes.

ELIAS: So D005 was placed next to the generator?

PEEBLES: Between questioning sessions, yes.

ELIAS: Who ordered that he be placed next to the generator between questioning sessions?

PEEBLES: I think it was the tactical questioner, but it wasn't – it was to place him somewhere where he could be put directly –

ELIAS: We will come to the reasons, Major Peebles, in a moment.

PEEBLES: But I was aware of that –

CHAIRMAN: Just listen to the question.

ELIAS: Did you give the order that D005 be put by the generator?

PEEBLES: I can't recall specifically giving an order of that nature.

ELIAS: Does that mean that it might have been you who did?

PEEBLES: It might well have been.

ELIAS: What was the purpose of putting D005 to the generator?

PEEBLES: The purpose of putting him there was that he was being fairly non-responsive to the first few questions that he was being asked.
It was more practical to send him just outside, which was close by where the generator was, then [he] could be brought back in within a few minutes for further questioning.

ELIAS: What, so this was merely an operation for convenience's sake, was it?

PEEBLES: Yes, yes.

ELIAS: Not, for example, to punish D005 because he wasn't being cooperative in answering questions?

PEEBLES: No.

ELIAS: No?

PEEBLES: I wouldn't say that it was punishment. The guy was already pretty scared. I saw him in interview. It was more a matter of practicality.

ELIAS: When he was placed by the generator, [was he] hooded?

PEEBLES: Yes, I believe he was.

ELIAS: Plasticuffed?

PEEBLES: Yes.

ELIAS: A guard with him?

PEEBLES: He either had a guard with him or there was a guard by the doorway. I don't know if there was a guard right next to him, actually.

ELIAS: The impression one gets, Major Peebles – correct me if I'm wrong – is that that was the plan with this detainee, that there would be a short session of questioning, he would be told to get out, taken out and brought back in. Was that the plan for him?

PEEBLES: Yes, I think it was – a sort of a naughty schoolboy routine, I think.

ELIAS: So when he was taken to the generator, you would now concede, would you, that it was part of what I might call 'unofficial conditioning' in his case?

PEEBLES: No, I would say it was a place to put him.

ELIAS: It was a punishment for him, wasn't it?

PEEBLES: It wasn't – the generator was not a punishment. The naughty boy syndrome is a way in which – what I am explaining is the way in which the tactical questioner acted with the individual involved, as a schoolmaster would at school.

ELIAS: And the generator was very hot?

PEEBLES: Sir, not for that reason, no.

ELIAS: But it was, wasn't it?

PEEBLES: The generator was hot, the conditions were hot and, as far as I'm aware, he wasn't placed right up against it.

ELIAS: The generator was noisy, wasn't it?

PEEBLES: It was noisy, yes.

ELIAS: These were not reasons that he was put there, were they?

PEEBLES: No, sir.

ELIAS: That is the truth, is it?

PEEBLES: That is the truth. It was convenient.

NICHOLAS JUSTIN MERCER

CHAIRMAN: Yes. Good morning, ladies and gentlemen. It may not have escaped the notice of the more alert of you that the Inquiry has not been able to get email in the last few days. I'm told that there's a problem in the Holborn area. BT are doing their best to resolve it. At the moment they have not resolved it and it's not certain when they will. However at around about lunchtime today, I hope that you will be notified of an alternative method of getting emails to the Inquiry through what I'm told is termed a 'solicitor's box' by another method. So I hope that will assist. As to when BT manage to get us back on our own email, I have no idea and I don't think, sadly they have.

ELIAS: Then I will call, if I may, Nicholas Justin Mercer, please. Colonel Mercer, please.

CHAIRMAN: Colonel, would you be kind enough to stand up, please, whilst I ask that you take the oath?

NICHOLAS JUSTIN MERCER (sworn)

ELIAS: Would you give the Inquiry your full name, please?

MERCER: Nicholas Justin Mercer.

ELIAS: Your current rank is lieutenant colonel.

MERCER: Correct.

ELIAS: I want to begin, please, by briefly asking you about your role in Iraq in 2003.

MERCER: Well, I was legal adviser for the 1st Armoured Division. I gave legal advice to the chain of command on all matters pertaining to military operations.

ELIAS: You have undertaken training in the law of armed conflict yourself, have you?

MERCER: Yes, I have.

ELIAS: That involved learning about the appropriate treatment of prisoners of war, amongst other things?

MERCER: Yes.

ELIAS: If there was a single message that emerged from that training in relation to the handling of prisoners of war, what was it?

MERCER: Well I use the phrase 'humanity and dignity'.

ELIAS: May I come, then, please, to training that you may have given in relation to Op Telic 1 [the overall operation in Iraq]. You say in the statement to this Inquiry – I don't think it need be put up, but it's your paragraph 17 – that all soldiers regardless of rank are supposed to receive annual training in the law of armed conflict.

MERCER: That's correct.

ELIAS: Paragraph 20 of your statement – you say this: '... given the training provided, I had no concerns about prisoner-handling prior to deployment as I believed it was well understood by all members of the division.'
By that the Inquiry should understand that you were saying you believed it was well understood that prisoners should be treated with humanity and dignity.

MERCER: Yes, I mean, this message is reiterated the whole time. The video that soldiers watch each year, which is a sort of old cold war relic or it was then, makes it absolutely clear: do not mistreat prisoners. This message is repeated and repeated and repeated.

ELIAS: At the time of your deployment to Iraq, what was your understanding about the rights and wrongs of the use of hoods on prisoners?

MERCER: I didn't even give it any thought because I just didn't envisage it. It hadn't happened [in the first Gulf War], so why would I have it in contemplation? It just didn't emerge – you know, it wasn't an issue.

ELIAS: So you were aware that hooding had been, can I put it this way in shorthand, ruled as being inhumane?

MERCER: Well, in contravention of the Convention on Human Rights, yes.

ELIAS: Thank you. Were you aware, prior to deployment to Iraq, that hooding was being used for any purpose?

MERCER: No, none whatsoever.

ELIAS: Would your view of the use of stress positions have been: 'They are off the menu entirely and not to be used under any circumstances'?

MERCER: Of course, both under Geneva and under the European Convention on Human Rights.

ELIAS: You say at paragraph 23: 'Although the UK maintained that it took its responsibilities under the Geneva Convention in relation to prisoners very seriously, this was not my experience. In my view, the issue of prisoners had very low priority and was treated more as an inconvenience than an obligation under international law.'

MERCER: Yes, I think that's correct.

ELIAS: If I may comment, that's quite a serious allegation to be making.

MERCER: It is. It's to do with resources. If you don't resource it properly, it is a low priority.

ELIAS: Could we have a look, please, at paragraph 21 of your second statement? We find that at BMI06901A paragraph 21. If we just go down three or four lines in the paragraph, you say this: 'However hooding was not banned by Permanent Joint Headquarters until after Baha Mousa's death and emails in May 2004 show that there was an information gap within the MoD about the practice of hooding.
Can we just look at the documents. MOD028354. A loose minute that's dated 25 November [1999]. 'Legal status of interrogation in situations other than general war.' 'The use of five interrogation techniques, i.e. keeping detainees' heads covered by a hood, continuous and monotonous noise, sleep deprivation, deprivation of food and water and making the detainees stand' essentially in stress positions ... 'amounted to inhuman and degrading treatment.'

Your reference to those documents in 1999 was a reference, was it, to the fact that there appears from that correspondence to be an indication that, for example, hooding was not to be employed?

MERCER: That's correct. It's clear that advice was sought in 1999 and the army made it very clear that these [five techniques] were prohibited. Then we bump into the issue again in 2003.
As soon as I saw hooding in the Joint Field Interrogation Team, I wrote immediately to the General [Officer Commanding] Robin Brims –

ELIAS: We are going to come to that.

MERCER: The point is, sir, that when I saw it for the first time, I put in an immediate complaint.

ELIAS: I want to ask you, please, about visits [in 2003] that you made to the [Joint Field Interrogation Team]. You kept a diary. Was that a diary intended for your own use, your own consumption, if you like, alone?

MERCER: Yes, my grandfather had kept one in 1939, so I rather wanted to repeat what he had done, so it was just personal.

CHAIRMAN: You have always kept a diary, have you?

MERCER: No, I've never kept a diary. I don't like them.

CHAIRMAN: Never.

MERCER: But I thought these were historic times.

CHAIRMAN: So this is a new departure for you?

MERCER: Yes.

ELIAS: What I really wanted to know, Colonel, was whether you were keeping a diary with a view to it being published to a wider audience.

MERCER: No, it was a private record and my wife very kindly typed it up at the end for me.

ELIAS: It was never intended to be anything more than that, was it?

MERCER: No. Quite frankly some of it is embarrassing.

ELIAS: When you say 'typed up' out of pure curiosity, does that mean that what we see as your diary in that rather neat writing is a font?

MERCER: It's a font, yes.

CHAIRMAN: I was for a moment lost with envy of anyone who is able to write as carefully as that, but …

ELIAS: If we look at your diary, please, can we look at 28 March [2003]. You refer to this, don't you, in the last half a dozen lines of this entry? 'I went by helicopter with General Brims to Umm Qasr to see the prisoner of war collation area.' Is that the occasion that you are now referring to?

MERCER: That would be correct, yes.

ELIAS: You say: '… a unique experience where I saw over 3,000 prisoners of war all in different compounds separated by large strands of barbed wire. Very few were in uniform, but all had been captured in various battles over the last seven days. Some looked terrified, others defiant.' Just before we go on, then, on that occasion who else apart from yourself and General Brims was present at the JFIT?

MERCER: We weren't going to see the [Joint Field Interrogation Team].

ELIAS: No.

MERCER: We were going to visit the Prisoner of War Camp.

ELIAS: I understand.

MERCER: The JFIT was situated at the entrance to the prisoner of war camp; in other words, as you walked into the camp, the JFIT was to your right and there was a guard on the gate. The General was met by a huge posse of people and I sort of tagged along at the back.

ELIAS: And what, if anything, did you see that caused you [to] have concern?

TACTICAL QUESTIONING

MERCER: Well, this was the first time that I'd seen what was going on [in the JFIT]. As I walked past, I saw two lines of prisoners, all kneeling in the sand, hands cuffed behind their backs, all with hoods on their heads.

ELIAS: All of them hooded. With what?

MERCER: Well, I saw sandbags on their heads and I'm pretty sure there were other bags as well...I mean, it's a bit like seeing a picture of Guantanamo Bay for the first time. It is quite a shock.

ELIAS: Would you describe the position in which the prisoners were being held – apart from the hoods on their heads – would you describe the positions as being stress positions?

MERCER: Yes, I mean I wrote – you have got my memo to General Brims.

ELIAS: We are going to come to that.

MERCER: If I just go back to the stress positions, the prisoners were cuffed behind their backs, up like this (indicates), so it looked extremely uncomfortable.

ELIAS: Did you speak to anyone as to what was going on?

MERCER: I did, I expressed my concern as to what was happening and my view that it was illegal.

ELIAS: So you sent this memo. Paragraph 6, please, where you say this: 'I visited the [JFIT] and witnessed a number of prisoners of war who were hooded and in various stress positions. I am informed that this is in accordance with British Army doctrine on tactical questioning.
'Whereas it may be in accordance with British Army doctrine (you went on to say), in my opinion, it violates international law. Prisoners of war must at all times be protected against acts of violence or intimidation and must have respect for their persons and their honour (you refer to Articles 13 and 14 of Geneva Convention III). I accept that tactical questioning may be permitted but this behaviour clearly violates the Convention.' If we look at paragraph 43 of your statement, please, where you say this:

> 'My complaint to General Brims ... (about hooding and stress positions) caused considerable disquiet.'
> How were you made aware of that?

MERCER: It was just obvious. It was not popular.

ELIAS: Say that again.

MERCER: It was just obvious. It was not very popular. I understand subsequently that the commandant of the prisoner of war camp had also seen it and raised his concerns and, of course, whilst I was being told I was wrong, at this point the Red Cross picked up on it and it was now – obviously once the Red Cross had got on it, it was a turbo-charged issue.

ELIAS: At those meetings where the ICRC [Red Cross] were raising concerns about hooding, was there any attempt to justify the use of hooding for any purpose by any of the British representatives?

MERCER: Yes.

ELIAS: What was your attitude to that when it was raised, that security was a reason for hooding?

MERCER: Well, I was – I didn't accept it for a minute. I thought there was no requirement at all and I thought it was not the way that hooding was actually being used when I'd seen it.

ELIAS: So it would be fair, would it, to say that you didn't believe that is why it was being used –

MERCER: I was hard over hooding. I just find the whole thing repulsive. In my view it amounts to violence and intimidation and it degrades the individual. So I don't like it at all under any circumstances.

ELIAS: And you made that clear at the meeting, did you?

MERCER: I was instructed not to speak at the meeting.

ELIAS: I want to ask you about that, of course. You were instructed not to speak about what?

MERCER: About anything.

ELIAS: And by whom were you so instructed?

MERCER: I think it's probably on the list of ciphers.

ELIAS: Did you walk out of any meeting at which the Red Cross were present?

MERCER: I did walk out at one point, yes.

ELIAS: Why did you walk out?

MERCER: Because I was very cross with some of the excuses that were being put forward, what I saw as excuses.

ELIAS: What, excuses for hooding?

MERCER: Yes.

ELIAS: Colonel Mercer, in the course of what I am going to categorise as general discussions about this issue of hooding and whether it was justified in any way, was the shock of capture referred to by anyone as any sort of justification to your recollection?

MERCER: I didn't understand it in the sense that you put a hood over someone's head – I mean, the shock is there because you have been captured.

ELIAS: I just want to ask you this about it: that was your assumption, was it, that the matter would go, as it were, all the way up to ministers?

MERCER: I am not sure how much I am allowed to say. But, yes, I think if the Red Cross is going to make an official complaint to a government, which is what it does, then there is no way that this thing would have stayed at the level of [senior military commanders on the ground]. It would have gone all the way up.

ELIAS: That's what you assumed would happen?

MERCER: I did, yes.

ELIAS: Moving on now to 20 May – [four months before Baha Mousa's death] you were advised by the [military police] that there had been a death in custody of someone held by a battlegroup and that that matter was being investigated.

MERCER: That's correct.

ELIAS: You were also led to believe that there may have been other deaths in British custody. Having been alerted to two deaths, what then did you do about it?

MERCER: Well, it wasn't just two deaths. There were a number of deaths – I thought the figure was higher.

ELIAS: Can I take you, please, to paragraph 99 of your statement, under the heading 'Conclusion', in which you say: 'There was a general indifference to prisoners which was reflected, initially, in the lack of manpower and resources provided.'
Again do you mean indifference brought about by a lack of resources or indifference demonstrated in other ways?

MERCER: I think by this stage this went wider. I think actually the lack of resources reflected a general lack of consideration for what was going to be a massive issue and indeed it was.

ELIAS: You reflect that, don't you, in paragraph 100, where you say: 'I am still amazed that we had to fight so hard for even basic Geneva Convention rights for prisoners.'

MERCER: That's correct.

ELIAS: You say: 'This indifference ... was exacerbated by the total strategic failure to plan for Occupation and the vacuum it created.'

MERCER: Yes.

ELIAS: Then this at paragraph 101: 'In my view, if the issue of prisoners had been properly resourced and we had been allowed to implement a proper reviewing and oversight mechanism then the tragedy which unfolded might never have happened.'

MERCER: Yes, I agree with that.

ELIAS: By the 'tragedy', are you referring to the particular matter that this Inquiry is investigating?

MERCER: Yes, I am here. I think if we had had a proper reviewing process in place, I think if we had had a judge in theatre, as we requested, with a detainee/internee management unit, if we had had an independent team for prisoners and I think if there wasn't this constant reluctance to accept high legal standards, then I think we could have avoided this tragedy.

ELIAS: You go on in the final two lines of your statement to say: 'Ultimately, however, given the vagaries of all warfare, in my view, it's also about proper education, training and the moral compass.'

MERCER: Yes.

ELIAS: Proper education, training and the moral compass for whom?

MERCER: This is the wider point. I mean, all staff officers deal with problems within a military operation, but let's face it whenever this is going on then every time a soldier abuses a prisoner, there is generally a junior NCO present who should know what to do, there is generally a senior NCO present who knows what to do. There is generally a Platoon Commander, there is generally a Company Commander overseeing that Unit. You cannot stop those sort of things simply by staff work. It is impossible. It pops up somewhere else. It's what happens on the ground and if soldiers are taught to intervene rather than turn a blind eye – and this is what I refer to as the moral compass.

ADAM INGRAM 2 JUNE 2010:
ADAM PATERSON INGRAM (affirmed)

CHAIRMAN: If I could ask you, please, to keep as close as you reasonably can – I think it is not all that comfortable – you have a fairly loud voice, if I may say so, so I am sure we will have no trouble in hearing you.

ELIAS: [In] June 2001, you were appointed Minister of State at the Ministry of Defence, responsible for the armed forces.

INGRAM: I was, yes.

ELIAS: And that was a post that you held, you tell us, until June 2007?

INGRAM: That's correct.

ELIAS: It follows that you were in that office in the spring of 2004, when abuse allegations, particularly relating to Iraq, surfaced in the media.

INGRAM: I was, yes. I was responsible across a range of issues. It was a very busy post.

ELIAS: Did you have any knowledge, at the time of planning for Iraq, as to whether it was or was not proper or appropriate for soldiers to hood or deprive of sight prisoners that they may take?

INGRAM: No, I wouldn't have any more than I would have had a close intimate knowledge of other operational requirements placed upon military personnel such as rules of engagement.

ELIAS: Are you telling the Inquiry, to the best of your recollection, that the issue of hooding was something that was never discussed with you prior to deployment to Iraq?

INGRAM: I would – that would be accurate, yes.

ELIAS: I am going to ask you this question or something like it perhaps a number of times. Let me ask you for the first time now: your position in taking on the responsibilities that you [had] as Minister of State, meant, of course, that you had responsibility for these areas, but you also had, didn't you, a duty, as it were, to be answerable to Parliament and through them to the public –

INGRAM: That is correct, yes.

ELIAS: So it might be said that you did need to know about certain matters where it was likely to be a matter that became public through the media or otherwise so that you could deal with it and answer questions, either [in] Parliament or outside Parliament, appropriately, fully and accurately.

INGRAM: Well, I would have been dependent upon the advice being forwarded to me through the Department and I would have to be dependent upon the quality of that advice as being accurate and honest.

ELIAS: It didn't occur to you that the armed forces would be acting in any way unlawfully.

INGRAM: Absolutely. I mean I would take the view that all military planning would have been done in full conformity with both domestic and international law. We would have expected all forces, to be sensitive to the needs of the local population: don't make enemies, make friends.

ELIAS: Does it mean that you would have regarded your involvement in these areas as only arising if and when something went wrong?

INGRAM: No, I think it would have been a case of mutual respect between ministers and those in the hot position in the front-line, and there had to be honesty at all levels in that.

ELIAS: You used the phrase 'honesty at all levels'. I just want to understand what you meant by that.

INGRAM: Well, it would be that. There would have to be people telling you – the phrase that would have been used would have been people telling you ground truth. There was no point trying to obscure or dissemble or to deny reality.

ELIAS: I think you will know that the Inquiry has been made aware that the ICRC [International Committee of the Red Cross] made a complaint or raised issues in relation to the handling of prisoners – hoods, being left out in the sun, the possibility at least of stress positions being used by our forces – in late March or thereabouts 2003. Did you know about that complaint at the time?

INGRAM: I have no recollection of being aware of it at the time.

ELIAS: You are likely to have a recollection, if indeed you were told, of ICRC [a Red Cross] complaint about hooding prisoners at a relatively early stage, are you not?

INGRAM: Well, I think my political antennae would have been alert enough in that sense to have been made aware that I was being told something that I should be aware of it, and if it was a request for action on my part, then I would have addressed that.

ELIAS: If we have a look, please, at MOD050331. You will be very familiar with these letters, Mr Ingram, where you are responding to an MP no doubt raising a matter on behalf of a constituent.

INGRAM: Yes, I am aware of that, yes.

ELIAS: This is May 2003. If we look at the last paragraph of this letter, going out in your name to Michael Foster MP, you say this at the third line: 'There were a small number of occasions at the start of the conflict where prisoners were hooded for short periods – this practice has now been stopped.' That's information that you would have accepted in a draft before you signed this letter, is it?

INGRAM: It wasn't just a case of being given a draft letter and signing it off. There would be a full explanation as to the content of that letter coming from those who had responsibility to properly report to me on this.

ELIAS: But the letter would also have been drafted for you, would it?

INGRAM: That's correct, yes.

ELIAS: If we read on in that last paragraph, please: 'But I would like to reassure your constituent that in all this we have worked very closely with the ICRC [Red Cross] who have expressed themselves content with the way we have treated prisoners and detainees throughout the conflict.' Had you known that the ICRC [Red Cross] had raised a complaint in March/April [2003], corroborated indeed by soldiers who have given evidence to this Inquiry, that prisoners were hooded, left out in the sun, [in] stress positions, could you have said that in this letter?

INGRAM: It would have depended upon the nature of what the originating complaint was. Of course, these letters were probably being generated by anti-war groups, by Amnesty International and by a range of other organisations.

ELIAS: Well, that's as may be, but it is the fact, isn't it, that if it is right that there was a complaint by ICRC [the Red Cross] and if it is right that prisoners were hooded, were left out in sun for hours, hooded, put in stress positions, it would not have been entirely accurate – forget the honesty bit – to say, 'The ICRC [Red Cross] have expressed themselves content with the way we have treated the prisoners and detainees throughout the conflict'. That simply would not have been accurate, would it?

INGRAM: I don't know whether it referred to the specific complaint that you have noted and whether that would have been brought to my attention, whether I would have had a knowledge of that. I need to see the background note. I would then need to judge why I would not have included that in the draft letter that had been presented to me.

ELIAS: Accepting the fact of a complaint, this letter, putting it neutrally, would not appear to have been telling accurately the ICRC [Red Cross] position and the British Government's position throughout the conflict, would it?

INGRAM: Well, I would need to see just what the ICRC [Red Cross] complaint was I have no recollection of being aware of it.

ELIAS: May I just ask this one last time and I shall then move on. The last two lines of the letter: 'The ICRC [Red Cross], who have expressed themselves content with the way we have treated prisoners and detainees throughout the conflict ...'
Would you have put your signature to that if you had known that, a month or so earlier, there had been a complaint made by the ICRC [Red Cross] which, in fact, complained that prisoners were hooded, left in the sun and possibly left in stress positions? Would you have put your signature to the letter as it is there drafted?

INGRAM: I would have probably tried to establish ground truth.
There was nothing to be gained from people telling something that wasn't true because the truth would always surface. So I don't think it was a denial of honesty. I think it was dealing with the ground truth at that point in time and correcting any feelings that may have arisen.

ELIAS: That doesn't quite address my question, Mr Ingram, which is really this: we know what you did write, we know what you signed because it is there in black and white.

Looking back even with hindsight, if you like, do you think now, given that you were going to be writing letters of that kind, it would have been better had you been told in March or April 2003 that the ICRC [Red Cross] have made a serious complaint about the way prisoners are being handled?

INGRAM: Without seeing the nature of what the ICRC [Red Cross] has said, I don't know whether it was serious or not.

ELIAS: Then I will move on. You tell us in your statement that you didn't see the Sky News footage, I think broadcast in April 2003, of Iraqi detainees hooded.

INGRAM: Yes. I do not recall seeing the footage. You know, I do not recall that, but it's – I may not have been in the country.

ELIAS: Again, if you had seen that, would it not have shocked you?

INGRAM: I think it would have done, yes.

ELIAS: If you had seen it, wouldn't it have been something that caused you to make some inquiry?

INGRAM: There's no evidence that I didn't make an inquiry.

ELIAS: If you didn't see it, which is your recollection, do you not find it astonishing that the fact that there was such footage was not brought to your attention, [as] the minister?

INGRAM: Well it may have been, but I don't recollect that being – I go back to my earlier comments. I was involved in that whole range of different issues.

ELIAS: Can I move on, then, please? Still looking at your state of knowledge, if you like, Baha Mousa's death, do you recall being told of his death?

INGRAM: I remember seeing – I have seen the briefing note that came up that referred to two incidents. One was his death; another one was the injury to a child.

ELIAS: You say in your statement to this Inquiry that when you heard of the death of Baha Mousa, as I understand it, you recall being shocked.

INGRAM: Yes, I do, yes.

ELIAS: What was it that shocked you, do you remember?

INGRAM: Well there were two elements to that. One was the injury to the child and the death of someone in detention. It is not something which should have happened.

ELIAS: Can we have a look at [what] would appear to be a briefing note to the Secretary of State, copied to you and your private secretary, MOD048699.

In paragraph 5, the detail that you were given in this document:
'Although the individual did not need to be forcibly restrained on arrest, advice from theatre suggests that he consistently struggled with his cuffs and hood during the day, repeatedly tried to escape and also allegedly lashed out at guards. At 18.40 Iraqi time the individual slipped his hood. Two members of the guard restrained him and replaced his hood. His pulse was also apparently checked at this time. Three minutes later the guard suspected that he might not be breathing.'

Pausing there, that, therefore, was telling you, wasn't it, that a detainee had been hooded perhaps within minutes of his collapsing and subsequently dying?

INGRAM: That's correct.

ELIAS: It goes on: 'The detainee was declared dead at 1905 hours.' Then you are given this additional information: 'At this point the individual had been in custody for a total of 36 hours. He had spent 23 hours and 40 minutes of this hooded, albeit not continually. We are continuing to investigate the circumstances surrounding the incident and will provide further information when we have it.'

If we look, please, at document MOD048704 dated 18 September, a similar updated briefing note; correct?

INGRAM: Yes.

ELIAS: You can see in the top right-hand corner a handwritten [note] says this, doesn't it? 'This could be very messy. 2 soldiers have been arrested. Minister (AF) ...' That would be you.

INGRAM: Yes, that's correct.

ELIAS: '... will deal as lead minister.'

INGRAM: Correct, yes.

ELIAS: Were you horrified to learn that prisoners were being kept hooded for 24 hours in 36?

INGRAM: Horrified? Strong word. It does say albeit not continually. I wouldn't have put a value judgement on it until I had established best information and ground truth on this.

ELIAS: When these matters were raised with you, did you stop then to think [to] yourself, 'Well, is this humane? Is it lawful? Is it a matter about which I need legal advice?'

INGRAM: I probably received that.

ELIAS: Was the fact that maybe there was something, as some witnesses had put it, thin about the written doctrine – inadequate about the written doctrine, if you like – was that fact or the fact that perhaps the training of forces in this area needed to be looked at, was that ever brought to your attention?

INGRAM: I have no recollection of that being brought to my attention. What I am saying is I have no recollection, but that's not to say that it wasn't brought to my attention.

ELIAS: I understand. What's the answer to my question?

INGRAM: They should have been.

ELIAS: Should it have been brought to your attention?

INGRAM: The answer to that is 'yes'.

ELIAS: Of course, you had responsibility not only for the Iraq conflict, but for the conduct of soldiers wherever they were deployed throughout the world, didn't you?

INGRAM: Correct.

ELIAS: Did you not consider, when these issues of hooding were being raised in this specific theatre, that what was needed was a clear direction, a clear legal view, if you like?

INGRAM: But there was a debate about the legal view and my recollection tells me that a similar discussion was taking place in relation to Afghanistan and the handling of detainees, insurgents or whatever else, and how we should deal with them, whether we should turn them over –

ELIAS: Wasn't this something that cried out for direction from the top?

INGRAM: There was no evidence that there was no direction from the top.

ELIAS: Did you give any on the use of hoods?

INGRAM: Did I give any on the – well, I don't have the paperwork to prove or disprove that that did or did not happen, but let me assure you that there was intensive discussion going on about the use of hoods and its appropriateness because there were differing legal approaches in all of this.

ELIAS: I don't misrepresent you, do I, if I say that your evidence is, then, that you have no recollection of taking any proactive step to ascertain a clear line for hooding to be cascaded down from the Ministry?

INGRAM: I don't accept that there was an omission on my part. I do not have the paperwork, I do not have the paper trail, to show whether it was proactive or not.

ELIAS: Now we have the extract from Hansard [MOD050379], what you actually said [on the 28th] June 2004; do you see? If we go into the right-hand column after the second half under 'Interrogation techniques', as a heading.

INGRAM: I have that, yes.

ELIAS: 'Mr McNamara: To ask the Secretary of State for Defence when he was first informed that UK forces in Iraq were practising the banned interrogation technique of hooding prisoners; if he will list the regiments in which the practice was identified; and on what date and on whose authority an order was issued to cease the practice.'

Your answer, [on the 28th] June 2004: 'We are not aware of any incidents in which United Kingdom interrogators are alleged to have used hooding as an interrogation technique.'

INGRAM: I see that yes.

ELIAS: We have also seen, haven't we, the briefing to the Secretary of State copied to you – which you would have read, you tell us – which said in terms that a prisoner had been hooded.

INGRAM: I would need to go back to see that. I need to see the precise term of that background note.

ELIAS: That might have affected the way that you answered the question, might it? Might it have affected the way that you answered the question?

INGRAM: It may have done or may not have done, but since it is something that has been brought to my attention, I think I would need to see precisely what was said in that background note.

ELIAS: Can we go back then, please? This is what you were being told in September 2003 MOD048704: 'In this instance the tactical questioning of the suspects was conducted by two Intelligence Corps Staff Sergeants, both fully trained in [tactical questioning]. It would appear that the hooding of the suspects took place on the advice of one of the staff sergeants.'
Do you need more?

INGRAM: No, I think – yes.

ELIAS: So if we go back to your answer [in The House of Commons], please – appreciating time has moved on – if you had had that in mind, Mr Ingram, would you have answered that question [on the 28th] June 2004 as you in fact did answer it?

INGRAM: It certainly wouldn't have been within my power to have remembered everything that I had been informed in writing or verbally. I would have been wholly dependent upon best advice from the Department on this.

CHAIRMAN: Mr Ingram, if we look at the date, 18 September 2003 – a reference there to tactical questioners, saying that a suspect was hooded, and it refers to the Baha Mousa incident, does it not?

INGRAM: It does, yes.

CHAIRMAN: It would appear to indicate that the tactical questioners had asked for Mr Baha Mousa to be hooded for the purposes of interrogation.
That would seem to be a fair reading of that?

INGRAM: With respect, Sir, I don't necessarily read it that way.

CHAIRMAN: Now if I could ask you just, please, to look at something again. You were asked about your answer [on the 28th June 2004] to a parliamentary question by Mr McNamara.
The background note we have is MOD050381, if you could put that up on the screen. What [your military assistant] really appears to be pointing out to you is that the question asks about interrogation and you do not need to answer about using hooding for security purposes.

INGRAM: Correct, yes. He is more or less saying don't elaborate –

CHAIRMAN: Because otherwise you may get into problems over hooding in transit or you may have to speak about that; is that right?

INGRAM: I don't think into problems –

CHAIRMAN: I say 'problems'. You may have to explain.

INGRAM: Why impart information that is not being sought would be the approach.

THE RIOTS

FROM SPOKEN EVIDENCE

The Riots was commissioned by the Tricycle Theatre from an idea by Nicolas Kent and first performed on 17 November 2011 at the Tricycle Theatre, London, with the following cast (in alphabetical order):

Barbara Cleaver / Sadie King / Karyn McCluskey Sarah Ball
Martin Sylvester Brown Kingsley Ben-Adir
Man 1 / Sergeant Paul Evans Grant Burgin
Diane Abbott MP / Camila Batmanghelidjh Dona Croll
Inspector Winter / Harry Fletcher Christopher Fox
**Michael Gove MP / Simon Hughes MP /
Sir Hugh Orde** Rupert Holliday Evans
Chelsea Ives Clementine Marlowe-Hunt
Man 2 / Jacob Sakil Okezie Morro
Pastor Nims Obunge / Leroy Logan Cyril Nri
Man 3 / Owen Jones / David Swarbrick Tom Padley
**Greg Powell / Judge Andrew Gilbart QC /
John McDonnell MP** Alan Parnaby
Mohamed Hammoudan / John Azah Selva Rasalingam
Stafford Scott Steve Toussaint
**Chief Inspector Graham Dean /
HH Judge Robert Atherton / Iain Duncan Smith MP** Tim Woodward

Director, Nicolas Kent
Designer, Polly Sullivan
Lighting Designer, Jack Knowles
Associate Lighting Designer, Charlie Hayday
Sound Designer, Sarah Weltman
Audio Visual Designer, Jasmine Robinson
Assistant Director, Ben Bennett
Literary Consultant, Jack Bradley
Casting Director, Marilyn Johnson
Researcher, Cressida Brown
Assistant to the Director, Tara Robinson
Associate Producer, Zoe Ingenhaag
Press Representative, Emma Holland
Production Manager, Shaz McGee
Company Stage Manager, Charlotte Padgham
Assistant Stage Manager, Helen Stone
Costume Supervisor, Anna Bliss Scully

Large and prominent: photographs and moving footage. The most dramatic that can be found of the riots in progress. Shops being looted, shopkeepers defending themselves. Anarchy on the streets of England. Loud surround sound coming at the audience from different directions. Noises of riot. Of sirens. Helicopters. Shouts.

All of this fading out into silence. Theatre is dark. A pause and then:

Two loud gun shots ricochet around the auditorium.

A long beat. Dark and silent.

MAN 1 and MAN 2 on stage but they cannot be clearly seen. It is almost as if they are disembodied voices. They are rioters and, like MAN 3, who comes later, they should be separated from the rest of the characters. They are Other. A world apart from the audience.

They speak throughout in matter-of-fact tones. No heat, no melodrama, just telling us how it is.

MAN 1: I was on Twitter at the time and my trend was on London so I seen everybody talkin' 'bout 'Mark Duggan got shot'. Everyone on Blackberry was like I got a lotta friends from Tottenham so they was all 'Rest in Peace Mark Duggan, Rest in Peace.' Coupla hours later an' I heard they were goin' to protest the next day.

MAN 2: Yeah I basically the same. I was at home an' I see it on Facebook that he'd been killed everyone was sayin' RIP an' that.

Now the stage lights up to reveal STAFFORD SCOTT.

The stage is bright but as the action moves on through this act, as the demonstration moves from the afternoon into dusk and then to dark, the lights gradually dim.

STAFFORD SCOTT: *(His name on screen.)* I was there [for the march on August 6th][1] I felt people needed to be there. What was happening at the time was quite outrageous. A young black male Mark Duggan, someone who was born and brought up on Broadwater Farm, somebody I, I could

---

1. [ ] are used throughout to indicate words added to the transcripts for clarification.

have held in one hand from the day I first met him, he'd been gun down on the streets.

There'd been this um misinformation put out that there'd been some kind of shootout that immediately um concerned the community because um we know that Mark wasn't of that ilk. And we know that um most young people, regardless of lifestyle, are not going to get themselves in a situation where they're involved in a shootout with trained, armed, heavily armed, police officers so we knew that that just didn't ring true. It just didn't make sense. And also the fact that the police hadn't had the decency to come to the parents' home to tell the parents what had happened to their son. That infuriated the community.

MARTIN SYLVESTER BROWN: What was released in the press immediately that evening [after Mark Duggan's death] was that he fired at the police. Nobody ever believed [that] for a second… It's not [about] knowing him. Even if you didn't know him, you know nobody shoots at the police in Tottenham. You know, we've got, we've got a history. There's been a history of, of gun offence and even more importantly a history of death by the police, you know, that go way back. You know, there, there's a furious relationship there. There's a long history. A long history and it's all there. It's all documented.

STAFFORD SCOTT: …All this nonsense about [Mark] being a gangster was extremely disrespectful to this family and we wanted to go the police. Um it was almost a tongue in cheek thing. It's been described as a march but it wasn't, there was about fifty or sixty of us. We had some really hastily prepared banners and we strolled to the police station. We didn't march and make noise or anything, and why I say it was tongue in cheek was because we agreed that the women of the group – that was Simone, who is Mark's baby's mother, um she and two other women, and one was her mother, the other a white woman called Jenny who grew up on the estate with Mark – were going to go into the police station and they were going to report that Mark had been killed. And the reason they were going to report that is because tongue in cheek, well, they were saying, well, maybe the police wasn't aware of what happened because the, because the police haven't fulfilled their duty in coming to inform the family.

MARTIN SYLVESTER BROWN: *(His name on screen.)* [Our group, Haringey Young People Empowered] were having a meeting in Bernie Grant's Arts Centre [tackling] issues affecting young people: violent crime, crime against young women, postal code violence mostly trying to create more of a unity because there was postal code rivalries. [The centre] is basically a few minutes from where the [Mark Duggan] protests were taking place. Planning to go, I said to everybody, 'OK, who's coming to the protest?' Everybody was like, 'Nah, nah. I'm not going to the protest. It's going to kick. It's going to kick off. You, you know, you know anger. You know anger.

CHIEF INSPECTOR GRAHAM DEAN: *(In uniform. His name on screen.)* First of all never volunteer for anything...

I'm a cadre trained chief inspector. That is just a flash word for list er a group of senior officers who are trained in public order. We have an on call system and because my girls were away I volunteered to do the weekend so I was on call. I knew that there was a vigil taking place at Tottenham. I'd phoned the senior management at Tottenham er during the day to say, look are there any issues do you want me in, um I'm more than happy to come in just let me know. Cos I was actually cutting my mum and dad's hedge in er West London so I would have to go and get my public order kit. So I said, look, do you need me in before I start cutting the hedge. [And] they said no no, was no issues at the time, everything was quite calm.

MARTIN SYLVESTER BROWN: And then, um, one was like, 'Nah. It's been cancelled because everybody knows it's going to kick off. So it's been cancelled'. I'm like, 'Oh really? OK.' So then I left to go to south London because a friend of mine was going to China for a year.

STAFFORD SCOTT: [The women] went inside the station. The police's response was 'This is a matter for the IPCC [the Independent Police Complaints Commission], we cannot speak to you now.' A very unfortunate response...

The family didn't go there to ask them specifically about the incidents that led up to Mark's killing. What they wanted was formal acknowledgement that it was Mark who had been killed. Because when some family members turned up at the scene on the day um they were told that, that wasn't Mark there. They were told that, that person who was on the floor was from another gang. [But the police told the women] they couldn't talk because of the IPCC.

When the women came out we discussed it. We basically said to the women, 'Look that's, that's not true, they can't be correct, tell them that we want the most senior officer to come here to explain to us why they can't say anything to us and let's see if the most senior officer can tell us something.'

We got there at five o'clock [and] we wanted to be away before 7.30 because Spurs was playing a friendly game about half a mile down the road and we didn't want those crowds converging on each other...

PASTOR NIMS OBUNGE: *(His name: Pastor Nims Obunge on screen.)* I got called by a friend who said 'The march is now on.' I ran...drove, up there to be with the family. So from about five, five-thirty-ish I was there till um the first cars got burned. The intention was to stand there. I, I, I got to meet with the Duggan family and um listen to the challenges they had been through. The, the upset that I heard from the family seemed justified, that they didn't feel they were supported. Um, and I felt that it was right that somebody gave them answers. And if they weren't getting it at home, they had a right to stand where they were

THE RIOTS

standing, with the community, and get the answers they requested.

STAFFORD SCOTT: We asked for this senior police officer about quarter past five, half past five.

Somewhere just before the end of the Spurs game a black police officer turned up. We didn't know at the time that he was reportedly the most senior officer. He got a lot of stick, a lot of cat calls. Not for being the most senior officer but for being a black police officer in that situation.

CHIEF INSPECTOR GRAHAM DEAN: [That]...gentleman, [is] an incredibly er conscientious good lad/er superb bloke. Um he had been there because he was in charge of the football. There was a Tottenham Hotspur home game... So he'd been there all day er and then got called down because [there'd] been problems at the vigil. [He's] a bona fide chief inspector, who actually works at Haringey.

STAFFORD SCOTT: [This policeman] went inside the station. He came out after quite a period of time maybe an hour, people weren't very happy.

PASTOR NIMS OBUNGE: I remember being called by my wife [while I was there] to come home, [and I said], 'There's something that I feel that's about to happen in Tottenham and I want to see whether I can help stop it.' I felt an unrest. There were too many tell-tale signs. Speaking to the community, walking around the community, um, on Friday af- after Mark's death and listening to people's commentary on the scenario there was a, there was just an annoyance. People were annoyed.

STAFFORD SCOTT: So the chief inspector eventually said OK there is a superintendent who's acting up as a chief superintendent and I'll get hold of him and his name is Gurdip Singh. He was out in, I think they said Redhill erm yeah or somewhere near Ilford. They said they was going to send a car for him, a police car blues and twos flashing. Gants Hill [was where] he was, and he'd be there in one hour. It was quarter to eight [when] he said [this]. I actually I pointed out to him at the time and it's the only time I actually spoke to him, and I said you know what, we wanted to be gone a long time ago. It's quarter to eight now it's going to be dusk soon we want to be out of here before night fall comes and if we're not out of here before night fall comes on your head be it.

The stage lights are dimmer now.

We said we'd wait for an hour.

Lights dimmer. Dusk has come.

We waited for the hour.

I should have said part of the reason the women was in the road was so traffic wasn't going up and down. We didn't want Tottenham to go about its normal business when our community was so affected so the road was in effect closed from about quarter past five that, that evening and that becomes significant later on.

It is now turning to dark.

At quarter [to] nine the women, and among the initial group there were lots of young women with children in pushchairs and in arms said look we've got to go, children need feeding, we've got to go. So Simone [Mark Duggan's] um his partner and mother of his children, she said she was going. So we left to go. At that point you could feel the change in, in, in atmosphere.

A map of Tottenham on screen with the police station at its centre.

As the leader of the Broadwater Farm Defence campaign I've led several *(Exhaling.)* oooof several, I must have set a record for marching on Tottenham police station…

OK and, and the way [the police] respond is always the same. They close a part of the High Road, divert traffic round the one-way and send it out via Wood Green. Now on this day, and I think this is down to officers who don't know the area, and it's down to ineptitude, [instead of diverting traffic to go round] they diverted it [so] they let traffic up [and then] there was no way out.

[So two or three officers were] getting the traffic to U-turn and go back these little roads um. They couldn't get them out onto the one-way so they have to send them back.

Sorry for being [so detailed] but it's really really really important.

So the traffic keeps on coming and these guys are there sending them away. Now all of a sudden, where did those officers go? Why did they leave and where did they go? Because as far as I saw nothing untoward happened towards those officers. This had been peaceful.

But [the] officers was gone [and] why they are important is [that] it was their cars on the corner of Forster Road. So they'd gone and these cars are just there. And there was an incident actually much earlier on when we was at the station where a police car obviously responding to some call came zooming through and it it almost looked as if it wasn't gonna stop, so some people took some of those things that were in the road and they they chucked them in front of it forcing the car to stop. It stopped. Officers rushed to the car. They obviously said, look you can't come through here, there's a dead end. Before it reversed some of the kids got some of the fruit from the veg stalls and started to pelt the car with tomatoes and things.

CHIEF INSPECTOR GRAHAM DEAN: If it's only fruit, we can wash that off later. There are high emotions here, members of the family...do we react to people throwing fruit? I wasn't there so I'm not going to say. [But] I can take that car in later and wash it.

STAFFORD SCOTT: [Now] when [the kids] saw these two [unguarded police] cars they did the same thing. There was some vegetable stalls. They took some tomatoes and things and started to pelt it. Pelted it and looked up the road. Where by now there's, there's, there's a much stronger line of police officers. There's forty or fifty officers standing in the road and there's vans behind them yeah? And I'm watching this and thinking well if there's all of you officers how comes you haven't sent a few to turn away the traffic.

The thing is had they done that from the off it would have meant that they would have had officers [in the right place when] we would have been leaving. I've never seen anything like that in my life. I've never seen them employ a policy of leave them to it and certainly not when it comes to my community. It's not about sensitive policing it's about effective policing. And even officers who wanted to be sensitive would of, would have been aware of the, the need to do some of these things.

[The] kids threw a few fruits and things. Nothing happened. They then got emboldened. They decided to get up to the car and start to smash the windows. They were frustrated and the police cars represented a symbol of their frustration so they just went to it. You could see it was in stages. You could see, 'Oh let's throw things at it'. They're not doing nothing. 'Let's smash it'. They're not doing nothing. 'Let's open the doors, let's see if we can get the CS gas canisters.' So that's what they did, they took out everything they could take out of it and they kept looking at the police and it's like, wow, they're not doing nothing. These kids have never ever seen this before in their life. They're used to getting stopped before they do something.

By now it is almost dark.

[So] they steal everything in the cars. Nothing happens. They get emboldened. They push the cars out into the road and it's almost as if the kids are saying, OK, well they must not be able to see us so let's push the car into the middle of the road and they can see us. The police did nothing so they decided to set the car on fire. Set one car on fire.

On stage a bright flare in the darkness.

The police did nothing. They rolled out the other car when they rolled out the other car mmm let me remember, was it on fire or not, no it wasn't on fire it went across the road into a shop, a Kurdish man's shop, a Turkish shop. The Turkish guys came out and started to call the police and say, look, man. Look at this car they've pushed into our thing, and even then the police just stood there. They just looked. The Kurdish guys pushed the car from their shop front back into the road and then the youth went and set fire to the car.

A second bright flare; the stage is now lit with flares which crescendo into the Carpetright fire.

CHIEF INSPECTOR GRAHAM DEAN: The first I heard was when someone, one of the Police Support Unit commanders [who have undergone training in public order policing], one of the inspectors who was actually there er facing some of the disorder phoned me to say are you the, on call er we got problems yeah there's, there's a police car on fire there's a barricade being built and we have we have serious issues [I was] incredibly [surprised]. So I asked the first question which is 'Is this a wind up?' to which he said, 'No this is legit it's happening.' So I said, right, in that case that's fine, I'm on my way.

MARTIN SYLVESTER BROWN: I'm in south London [and I] get a message that it's kicking off in Tottenham. I'm like, *(Claps his hands.)* 'I knew it!'

STAFFORD SCOTT: [We older people were telling them not to.] Absolutely, absolutely. I mean let me be absolutely clear a riot in those situations is the worse thing that can happen for justice. [Tottenham] is one of the last places in London that can afford something like that to happen...

MARTIN SYLVESTER BROWN: So then *(Laughs.)*, so then, um, I get on the train back to Tottenham. And I come down and then, you know, I've got my drum, you know when you go to a protest you bring a drum, and my umbrella. Because I take my umbrella everywhere. And I'm aware that, that day I'm wearing, like, Birkenstocks. You know? Can you imagine? *(Laughs.)* And I'm looking, I'm looking about, a bit too preppy to be honest, with you.

STAFFORD SCOTT: When we went out there, there was about fifty maybe sixty...by the time we left there there were probably 200 maybe a little bit more um but by then we had been there for about four hours and that's the way of demonstrations. They tend to attract people who may or may have not known it was going on [and who later come] along and join them.

PASTOR NIMS OBUNGE: I got the family, the Duggan family, supported them out of the area, because the idea was this was no longer what was intended. I walked with [them], tried to get them on to Bruce Grove and on their way out because, and I, I do remember a member of the family, who may not want to be named, just really upset and crying and just – really really really distressed, and saying, 'This is not why we came, this is not why we came,' um, and so that, that was rather distressing and I could – that was just such an upset – um, but by then Tottenham was ready to start burning.

There were no police officers from Tottenham High Street till Sainsbury's, so people have felt quite frustrated that Tottenham was left to burn. The police have said, no, they were under-resourced. Um, so my question is, could they have done more to resource it earlier on? To nip things in the bud? Those are questions that they will have to answer over their internal inquiries.

INSPECTOR WINTER: *(Plain clothes, name on screen. He is sitting with a cup of tea beside him.)* On – on the Saturday evening, when – when the disorder started, we were in the Tottenham area erm conducting an operation. Erm, and I work in a specialist area of policing to do with surveillance [and] then we were tasked to go to the Tottenham police station to assist them.

It was, it was very tense because... From the information we'd been given, people had been trying to break into the police station to sort of for, for, for whatever reason, to sack it o-or try to set fire to it or, or whatever. So everybody was very tense...nobody was allowed to leave. W-w-we had a small amount of difficulty getting into the backyard because we were – all turned up very scruffy looking – erm in a range of unmarked police cars, some of which didn't have lights or sirens. *(Laugh.)* It's a solid wooden gate and they just wouldn't open it until one of us managed to locate the right frequency on our radio and said, y'know 'Please let us in before they start throwing bricks at our cars!' *(Laugh.)* Ther-there were quite a lot of people milling round but I'm not sure if they were involved in the disorder.

MAN 2: I was at my mate's house in Tottenham so that we could see all the helicopters an' that goin' round. I was a bit worried cos um some-a my family live in Tottenham but like I was a bit excited at the same time.

MARTIN SYLVESTER BROWN: I get down there. And everybody's out. Everybody's out. Everybody, everybody – people I haven't seen in about ten years. Like, 'Woah, was that chap...? That chap looks big now'. I see all these people I haven't seen in a long time.

CHIEF INSPECTOR DEAN: At that stage you could get into the nick. There was [that] chief inspector who was there who'd been on right from the very beginning er for who was geographically based, er in fact he'd been doing the football. I grabbed hold of him, we went out of line of fire into one of the walkways er next to the police station, and said right what's the score what do we need to do. And we had a chat.

INSPECTOR WINTER: W-we literally borrowed equipment an-an-and some...trained officers and formed a serial to go out...erm and stand around the police station... Er – initially there were probably about seventeen of us. Probably two or three hundred at that point.

CHIEF INSPECTOR GRAHAM DEAN: There were two cordons, one with unprotected police officers and no disorder whatsoever to the south. There were people standing there looking. No disorder. No issues. Actually that's quite usual. You'll get, you'll get a nucleus of issues, a nucleus of problems and for any event, not necessarily a riot, you'll get people coming out to have a look at it.

Er and then [there was] a large barricade, people throwing things er petrol bombs being thrown and missiles being thrown to the north…

This was about, forgive me if I'm not specific, but this was about twenty to ten.

MOHAMED HAMMOUDAN: *(Name on screen. He should be separate from the rest of the cast.)* Was getting to about ten o'clock, it was Ramadan round er my er Mum's house. We broke fast, w-we visited family and then I said to the boys, 'Come let's go home'. Er [my two] boys stay with me over the weekends. As, as I's driving up I lived in the flats above what used to be called Allied Carpets but now is Carpetright, not far from Tottenham stadium, [and as I was driving] towards Tottenham the upper end of Tottenham is erm, is where the police station is I actually thought you know. 'There must be something going on,' yeah? There was a load of roadworks *(Breath.)* And the roadworks ki-kind of formed of a cage so it almost seemed like it was like people were caged in. An' 'en I, I, I, got a sense there was something was going. Something innate in me said 'Y'know what I should take the boys back to their Mum's tonight cos it doesn't feel safe. Erm. An' then – because the road was closed off, an' I says 'Ah no I' be fine, I' be fine' So I d- I just drove home as normal, parked up the car, went and picked up the post went upstairs.

CHIEF INSPECTOR GRAHAM DEAN: We've got disorder. But it's fairly big disorder in Tottenham High Road.

MAN 1: When I first actually heard about the riots, I was in my house, with my girl an' I've seen on, on the TV 'Oh riots in Tottenham' I thought 'What!' so I took my girl home an' I've got one of my friends an' I walk down to Tottenham an' I've just seen a good few thousand worth of people on

Tottenham High Road. An' I've never seen such people on any High Road in my life unless I was at carnival. The atmosphere were literally hot. There was so much body heat, there was two fires, everythin'. It looked like a movie, looked like Hollywood come down an' they set up everythin' to look like a mad war zone an' I thought 'Wow'. An' I've seen a good few hundred police tryina diffuse the situation. So I thought – I thought to myself 'Ra!'. There's police there. I'm hundred per cent sure all the police north London were there at the time.

CHIEF INSPECTOR GRAHAM DEAN: We've got a barricade being built, we've got fires being lit er and there's obviously the issue of vulnerable people, and people at risk.

The initial issue for me was let's create some space; let's distance from the police station which was the focus, let's see if we can arrest people er, and get the – get the fire brigade in behind us and we'll do that.

[We] split it three ways. [One] was protection and security of the station. Then, someone to push north, to alleviate the pressure, and to arrest people if possible. Er. And then someone to protect their backs because we could see fires being set. So we knew we were going to have to get the fire brigade in – possibly get the ambulance crews in. So it made sense that they kept the LFB and the LAS – sorry, fire brigade and the ambulance service, came from the south, er, and we would provide a sterile corridor for them to work in.

MARTIN SYLVESTER BROWN: We walk onto Bruce Grove and we're basically, on the front line. Which is strange because I just assumed they'd kettle it off and contain it. But they didn't. They kind of had a line protecting the police station. And after that, anyone – pretty much fair game – you know, anyone can get in and get out and do what they wanted to do. And that's how it was able to spread. I took out my drum and started playing. I just thought, 'Why not?' I just wanted to see what would happen. The police looked over curiously. But I think they just looked at me and thought, 'He's in Birkenstocks. He's not really a threat'... It's funny because since I changed my, my way of dress, I didn't really get stopped by the police.

MOHAMED HAMMOUDAN: I was gonna wake up erm to have something to eat erm because o' Ramadan so you normally wake up a-around three o'clock. An' at about ten to two Amir woke [me] up. I'm deaf in in in my right ear – uh no my left ear, sorry, so I always sleep on my right ear and I don't hear a thing [Amir said], 'Dad there's stuff – the th-th-the fire alarm's going off. Th-th-the smoke detector's going off. There's people knocking on the door'. I said 'Are you sure Amir?' And subconsciously I can hear all this stuff but I thought it was the TV, you know? I thought all this noise was coming from the TV. So I'd woked up and I was a bit dazed. Went and opened the door.

I could see my neighbour. I don't know her name. There's just a whole loada commotion, people knocking on the door, running up and down. And they were saying 'Get out! Get out! There's a fire!'

These strange people with hoods an', an' a lot of them had those kinda Palestinian-sty-style heads – erm masks on or w – scarves wrapped round their faces go up t – y'know, you could see their eyes. Erm... So a – f-first thing I thought I thought y'know phhhw 'I-i-is this real?' Are they really here?' Erm then I thought 'The-the-the-they're t-t-telling to people to leave your door open a's get out'. So that imme-immediately alerted me, thinking 'What, are they here to rob us? Y'ow? Is that – is this like a big ploy? Are they really here to rob us?' *(Sigh.)* So I shut the door.

An' as I shut the door erm I thought 'God this this is serious. This is really serious'. Erm I can see smoke coming through the skirting boards down from Carpetright. There is a fire. And there's so much commotion outside.

It felt like an eternity to wake [Karim] up. I wasn't in a panic. I was more thinking 'I need to get these two out,' yeah? An' I n- I need to do it quickly, yeah? So I was saying to [Karim] 'Listen Baba you need to get up because there's a fire and you need to get get outa here as quick as possible.' An' he was just like tryna put his socks on. I said 'Forget about your socks! Just forget about your socks! Just put your shoes on, yeah?' I said – An' he's tryn – he's tryna put on his – I didn't have any shoes on! I-I-I had a vest on – a-a-and a pair of tracksuit bottoms on and and it felt like an eternity and Amir he were just standing there waiting to leave and he was like his eyes *(Laugh.)* his big brown eyes just standing there and then a' then Karim was taking an eternity. I-i-it was – must have been three-four minutes at the most. It felt four or four five hours. *(Breath.)*

About ten minutes had passed since the time I woke up.

CHIEF INSPECTER GRAHAM DEAN: By this stage I have two stroke three PSUs who are in the front line, who have been there now at least three hours. Who have been taking flak. I obviously did not have enough protected officers, so that was the first thing I asked for. But of course it's Saturday night, it's school holiday period, so it's heavy annual leave – and it's we had the, we had the football earlier. And of course you had the FA Charity Shield the next day.

INSPECTOR WINTER: I know people have said 'Why didn't you go in there and arrest people?' but it was a case of… At one point there were thirty of us and probably about five-six hundred people causing disorder. If I send five of my officers in to arrest someone who's thrown a brick at us, then either they're going to be surrounded and overwhelmed and it's going to be a more resource-intensive operation to try and bring them back, or y'know, s-someone's gonna get very badly hurt so. F-foremost in my mind is what happened to PC Keith Blakelock [in the Broadwater Farm riots]. I, I don't want anybody to get killed.

MARTIN SYLVESTER BROWN: And at the bottom of Bruce Grove there's a McDonald's [and] there's like, like a Percy Ingle, Superdrug and so forth. That space there, just a bit further down was, I would say the first line where some of the people had built up a line of fire. So basically the police got to try charge that down into that, that box zone. Everyone kind of ran back. And some people were, like, made a volley of bottles and things like that.

We were like, 'Woah'. And some people ran back and some people ran forwards to follow the volley.

I thought [the police] was going to contain the situation. So I was to my friend, 'Yo, what we want to do is, what we want to do is basically move in and move out freely. We got to keep finding new holes to get in and out, to get in and out, so that we don't get kettled. Because I'm not looking to get batoned'.

So we went back. I saw a friend of mine from, from way back. And he was like, 'Madness! Madness!' Yeah, madness! And then we cut down to come back onto Bruce Grove. More people were out. More fires starting. Mostly young people. I know older people were there [but] they threw their bits and then they just went. Young people were just coming out, coming out, coming out. Streaming out into the streets. It felt like a carnival, it felt like carnival but without the aggression. I'm talking about Tottenham carnival now. You're seeing people that you haven't seen in ages. Everybody's out. It's packed like carnival. It was a really strange vibe. Because I'm, I'm here and there's a lot of people, a lot of people I know have got a lot of confidence in each other in the same space. But you don't, you don't get the sense that anything is about to kick off. Bear in mind, you know, there's no, there's nobody actually enforcing. And I know that a lot of time in riots what what you hear [about] is people start turning on each other. Wasn't any of that, not in Tottenham. I heard it was like that in Wood Green. So I'm out of there and I say to my friend, 'Bra, I've never felt Tottenham feel so peaceful!'

CHIEF INSPECTOR GRAHAM DEAN: We came past a supermarket – and I can see [the officers] are on their last legs. It was a hot night, they had hot kit on, body armour, all the other stuff that goes on – carrying heavy shields

THE RIOTS

I can see that they are suffering from heat exhaustion. I said, go into that store [and get water]. We will pay for that [later. The shopkeepers] were superb. We took some [water and] they grabbed hold [of more] and started running up and down the road, giving them out to officers. Absolutely fantastic to actually see members of the public [doing that] because it felt, not everyone dislikes us.

MAN 1: The riotin' an' lootin' was somethin' that you sit around talk with your friends 'Oh imagine all the shops in the High Road was open, you could go in there an' take whatever you want', thass somethin' you don't expect to happen. So when it's actually happenin' I thought 'Wow, I need to take advantage of the situation cos, this never goin'ta happen again, there's no police, the shopkeepers aren't there, so why not, just go an' take what you want an' come back home'.

I made like a good three trips, took clothes, jewellery, electrics. I even took a-a-a DVD box set of um *Harry Potter* an' I don't even like *Harry Potter*, never wanna see the movies in my life but cos it's there I know it's free so I'm takin' it. I even got a pair of socks, an' I don't even wore the socks yet.

MOHAMED HAMMOUDAN: Time I got out was two o'clock. My ironing board is in the lobby where I always leave my keys. That's all I picked up was my keys yeah? An' I even locked the door behind me, yeah? Cos instinctively I thought we were coming back. I actually thought that fire w-would be like a low-scale fire, be a few carpets burnt. Fire brigade would be here any minute. It'd be fine yeah?

MAN 2: I was just full of adrenaline really at the time. I was just runnin' round I just um thought I'd quickly make some money an' go back home really.

INSPECTOR WINTER: [We were holding the line for] probably about two and a half hours – before some assistance erm started to come. Level Two officers ac-across London – pan London ad hoc serials were formed *(Breath.)* and through the night we had people coming from Lewisham and Bromley and places like that we had people from Essex and Hertfordshire and Thames Valley Police turn up erm which was – which was welcome because obviously before we'd got to the disorder, my team had certainly worked probably about a seven or eight-hour day – so we were quite tired *(Laugh.)* by that point and wearing all the kit and and having to move around so much is shattering!

You've got people coming forwards within a couple of feet of you and they've thrown something at you and they're taunting you erm but you can see that they've got a group of friends and maybe it's a come-on, they're trying to lure you out. *(Pause – lifts cup.)* I think anybody who says they weren't scared *(Drinks from cup and then puts cup on saucer.)* is either lying or an idiot. Erm I mean I've – I've done quite a lot of public order policing. I went to the G8 erm protest in Scotland *(Breath.)* which is slightly different; climate change protest at the G20 in London, er the student protests as well *(Breath.)* erm and, and I've not seen violence on *that* scale, or that much hatred for the uniform – erm as, as seem to be exhibited there. F-foremost in my mind is what happened to PC Keith Blakelock [in the Broadwater Farm riots. [I was] making sure that actually all of my officers are there, sort of counting them every thirty seconds to make sure not one – one hadn't gone adrift, *(Laugh.)* ye-heah it was my biggest priority. It's heartbreaking t- having to watch people's homes and livelihoods being burnt. We don't know if there are people inside those buildings that are on fire or on that bus so actually having to restrain ourselves from rushing in is quite a difficult task cos… One of the key things we do is we-we preserve and save life and property and we weren't able to – w-we certainly abl- weren't able to execute the saving the property aspect of it.

MOHAMED HAMMOUDAN: An' a-a-as as I was walking down the corridor it became apparent to me that this was a bigger fire than I anticipated because the whole place was full of smoke, y'know? Th-the staircases they're quite steep – must be at least thirty steps – going down to the erm front door – or th-the the main door. *(Breath.)* So as as we were going down we couldn't see in front of us. We couldn't see who's in front of us. So it was whatever making the de-de-decision whether we would we would go through the smoke or we would g- run back an' go through the other entrance. We didn't know [whether] we were going to the fire. We were just going into like a load a smoke we didn't have a clue. There was people around us, and those other people was still running around, knocking on people's door, telling them to get out.

Those people with Palestinian scarves, they were actually ge- trying to get people out, they're – And – y'know, I quickly put two an' two together a' I thought they were, they were probably involved *(Breath.)* in the disturbances, in the riots, potentially involved in, in setting the fire downstairs to the carpet shop. Some of them got a bit of a conscience and thought 'This has gone too far,' yeah?

Twitter messages begin, slowly, to scroll around the theatre. At this stage they should be faint and fairly unobtrusive.

MARTIN SYLVESTER BROWN: [I was at my friend's house] and we were on Twitter and we got a memo that, basically, there were people in the house that was burning they need support. 'If you can help, come here'. So we left there to go down in the direction of Allied Carpets where we heard that people were being, being escorted out of their houses.

MOHAMED HAMMOUDAN: There were no police around. There was *no* policemen.

CHIEF INSPECTOR GRAHAM DEAN: It had been hard work to get [to Carpetright]. It's actually on a very busy junction. Wide junction – so – Last thing I want to do is get there and get past it. Wide road ahead, wide road behind. So we got there, and then I had to put my resources three ways.

MOHAMED HAMMOUDAN: As we got out the front door, I looked to my right and the place was ablaze. You could feel the heat coming through, yeah? You could feel the heat. I got my two boys over [the road] and as I was going across *(Breath.)* one of the neighbours said 'Could you take my son across as well?' Because they were tryna get some other people out of, of, of, of th-this stairwell you see? They were coughing, they couldn't get out. So I took him and waited and as I was waiting, I'm thinking the fire brigade are gonna come in a minute, yeah? The police are gonna be here in a minute. I was still thinking 'This is gonna be OK. Yeah, it's gonna be OK'. An' then it it kin- it kinda felt really unsafe because you've got your children there y- and you're y-y-you're f- you're kinda feeling really vulnerable, you haven't got your mobile phone, you haven't got – *(Breath.)* you haven't got your wallet, you haven't got *anything*. Everything you just left behind you an-an-and fled out. And erm an' then you've got, you've got, it kinda felt really weird because you've got these people who're just out of the building looking at their their their homes being burnt up and then other people with a sense of euphoria going on. It felt like, it felt like our building was like a trophy.

MARTIN SYLVESTER BROWN: We saw this huge blaze. Huge blaze! The building that everyone's taken notice of. The one that's no longer there. Huge building Allied Carpets – up in flames. The whole building. We were watching it. It was just *(Exhales.)*, it was just, er, an immense flame. Carpetright. But we all call it Allied Carpets. Because, um, it was Allied Carpets for about ten-twenty years. When we got there, we were just *(Exhales.)* in awe. The ash was being blown down on us. We had to cover our mouths. The wind's taking up the ash and the ash is raining down. It looked like boulders but they're not. They're just ash clouds.

MOHAMED HAMMOUDAN: I started talking to, to some of these young people. I said to 'em, 'This is not Aldis, this is not McDonald's, this is not JD Sports, this is a residential area where people live.' Cos at the time other young people, where there was a erm wher- was a tyre shop nearby, yeah? were throwing the tyres *into* the fire t-to make it fuel even more. And one of these th-th-this young woman who's sitting in, in un-underneath a bus stop was saying to me 'Well you're just trying to prang me up?' Wh-which means you know tryna make you feel guilty. And then there was thi-thi-this this smiling lad erm who said 'Are you you telling the truth? D-do people actually live in there?' I said 'Yes, people *are* living there above the shop. I'm gonna take you to other people who are just in the same situation as me and they're gonna say – tell you exactly the same thing' [and] he actually realised I am telling the truth. Yeah? And his immediate reaction was like 'This has gone too far. It weren't supposed to be like this.' *(Breath.)* An' I said to him 'What d'you mean? "It weren't supposed to be like this?"' He se- he se- he said 'It was supposed to be us and the police and the people who've been oppressing us'. So I said 'Who? Who's been oppressing you?' An' he said 'Well the government, y'ow? The government has been oppressing us'. And then, then, then he said, which is quite ironic, *(Laugh.)* 'e goes 'An' I've gotta get up and fast tomorrow as well'. And I couldn't make out whether he was just a part of the looting and rioting or he actually was a part of setting the whole building a-alight.

INSPECTOR WINTER: [My strongest memory] was in Tottenham and it was a shop owner and his shop was ablaze and all his stock was in there and he'd just purchased some new stock that was in there and um he wanted to go in there and get it out and we had to physically restrain him and tell him that there was no way he could go in there because it would be too dangerous and then he would just be bringing stuff out onto the streets where it would probably be further stolen from him because we weren't going to be able to stay there and protect it um and it's heartbreaking and, and, and when I walked down Tottenham High Road on the Sunday, speaking to someone who'd come here from Somalia, um um you know and he just couldn't comprehend what had happened because he thought he'd come here to safety and now he'd seen something that was akin to what would have happened in his own country in the mid Nineties.

MOHAMED HAMMOUDAN: [I took my children to their mother and then I was driving with my sister] back towards Tottenham an' I started I started looking at the destruction and and the amount of people on the streets and the amount of people carrying stuff, *(Laugh.)* not only young people but people well into their, their you know, their forties wi-wi-with trollies and people walking off with rolls and rolls of carpet they they've taken out of Carpetright, yeah? And I just had to start laughing.

The Twitter messages are now brighter and faster. Telling of spreading riots, the message stream gets faster and faster to the accompaniment of pinging...

MARTIN SYLVESTER BROWN: The road towards Edmonton and Enfield was completely free. And that's when a lot of young people started coming down from Edmonton. And we know they're from Edmonton because they spray graffiti: N9, N18. And this is where they start breaking into shops and taking out things like that.

I'd assume that they're anarchists and the ones that I saw, they were white. A lot of people had their face covered up. But you can, I can, I would say that I would assume the difference between people that I recognise from Tottenham, carrying a specific Tottenham persona, wearing a specific dress and people that, you know, were a bit different. They come with a different tip. So, um, it's a mix. Because you've got the legitimate, you've got the legitimate anger. And then you've got obviously people that jump on that anger.

Fire and mayhem. Carpetright going up. Woman jumping from building.

On the map Tottenham shrinks as the area covered by the maps expands to reveal more of London. New sites of unrest (if possible in order of their kicking off)[2] *are revealed, the riots spreading. Expand to map of England showing the spread.*

MAN 3: I was at my girl's house at the time yeah? An' I didn't even hear 'bout the shootin' for a good coupla days innit like. I see the riots an' I thought yeah straight I'm gonna get involved in the riots an' that, an' I done my fing an' then I was like 'Why we even riotin?' An' then someone just told me like 'Oh yeah some guy got shot innit' I didn't really care to be honest at the start I didn't know who it was innit, then I see it on the news an' that, an' he was buried in Wood Green innit. I looked at him an' it was like Mark Duggan an' I was like dunno why there's such a big deal about it. I just took advantage of the riots an' done whatever wanted to do innit, that was it.

I was just like 'Yeah man, once in a lifetime thing,' we see it on video games an' stuff like that yeah, might as well do it innit, iss down the road thought 'Why not?' innit, could get lucky or whatever. Shit. I wanted a new iPod an' shit an' I got one innit.

INSPECTOR WINTER: *(Who has his notebook with him which he consults.)* F-f-for the first three days of what was happening – the first day in Tottenham, the second day in Enfield and I think on the Monday we we went to Ealing, erm. O-on that – on the first Saturday, we did a – pretty much a twenty-four hour shift – Had two hours sleep – M-most of us in London don't live in London. We we commute in

---

2. 6th August 20.20: Tottenham police station, Haringey
   7th August 03.00: Wood Green, Haringey
   7th August 18.38: Enfield
   7th August 23.30: Brixton
   8th August 00.29: Walthamstow
   8th August 16.31: Hackney
   8th August 18.30: Peckham
   8th August, 20.07: Birmingham
   8th August 20.23: Croydon
   8th August 21.49: Clapham Junction
   8th August 22.45: Ealing
   8th August 23.42: Camden
   9th August 00.39: Eltham
   (Manchester, Nottingham, Liverpool, Bristol)

from Surrey or Hertfordshire so I ended up sleeping – I think it was Hackney police station – I slept in the corridor *(Breath.)* – I ended up using my body armour as a pillow – for two hours before we were redeployed to go to erm must have been to go to Enfield. We basically followed the level of the devastation. I think it was like twenty out of the thirty-two London boroughs *(Breath.)* had been affected by disorder.

BARBARA CLEAVER: *(Her name on screen plus 'Doctor')* I run the A&E Department [at the Chelsea and Westminster]. I arrived at work at ten o'clock [on Monday] night, and the nurse in charge was like 'Oh gosh, have you heard what is happening?' 'No, I haven't'. And she is like 'There's riots all over London, and it's horrendous, and we might be put on a major incident alert'. There was a lot of tension there, and I was like 'Really!' I couldn't quite believe it. And there was a very senior police officer in the department, and fairly often we have fairly low-ranking police officers, but this was a Sergeant. And I went up to him, and I said 'If you don't mind me asking, what's going on?' And his first words to me were 'Well, we've lost Clapham'. 'What do you mean, you've lost Clapham?' How can you lose Clapham? Well, he was like 'We are no longer policing Clapham… There aren't the resources, so Clapham is now being held by the rioters. The whole of Clapham High Street is on fire. There's looting happening, and we've got no police in there, we're just watching it from a distance.'

CHIEF INSPECTOR GRAHAM DEAN: My experience in Enfield was people weren't standing there to have a fight. People were trying to break into things, they were damaging things and then running away. It wasn't an urban riot, it was opportunist crime. I was in Hackney on I think the Tuesday night, but by then nothing was happening anywhere. And that was incredibly difficult because I've got all these police officers who are ready for anything, in kit, and of course by this stage there's no one to play with. There's no one that wishes to engage police.

THE RIOTS

PASTOR NIMS OBUNGE: I think there were two [things I saw] that were quite a bit crazy. One was a mother testing the shoes, um, for her child outside the JD Sports, saying, yeah, I would like to see whether this fits. The fact that you're you're, you're looting and you're testing shoes, for-for your child! The other one was, um, was in the McDonald's, I think where they, they went over and started making themselves food. And I just thought y'know, why would you do that? If you're nicking nick, but don't stop over and start cooking.

INSPECTOR WINTER: When you have a serial come from another county, another police force, normally when something like this occurs what-what should happen is you should have a local police officer who goes with them to give them some-some level of knowledge of where they are. Um because of the level of deployments this time that wasn't possible. *(Coughs.)* Excuse me. What happened this time was if they were lucky they got an A to Z which they had to sign for, and if they didn't give it back they were charged forty pounds. Some people do have satnav on their phones and things like that but with these vans, because they're you know, because the likelihood of them being destroyed is quite high, you don't want to put any valuable equipment in them.

I know one police force from up North which shall remain unnamed, when they got told they were deploying here, brought their three worst vans in the hope they would be petrol bombed and destroyed so the Met would have to buy them brand new ones. But the situation is now... Actually they drove all the way down here, those vans have maybe done three or four trips so now the vans are knackered so they're in rental vehicles, they're in Europcar rental vans with police logos stuck on the back and a stick-on blue light, and it's still got the Europcar livery on.

We were aware of what was happening in the rest of the country because we had several vans full of Manchester police officers down here who then had to go back because they'd sent their trained police officers down here to deal with our disorder when their disorder started kicking off there. There was a serial of police officers coming from Avon and Somerset um and then we got told a couple of hours later actually they've had to turn back because there's – something's kicked off in Bristol.

Fade up an audio of the rioters in a loop that gets louder and fades, gets louder and fades, to a background of sirens also getting louder and fading:

Mental bro

What happened last night yeah went mental yeah, went mental

Police got terrored, mate

Took 'em out, mate

An' lissen is gonna happen tonight yeh

Iss happenin' every night for a few days mate, London ain't got shit on us check this now yeah bruv, check this now yeah? Took three thousand police officers yeah just to rush for four hundred of us yeah? See what I-mean they haven't got a shot on Salford yeah, wait till it gets later on about twelve-twelve o'clock yeah – they gettin' fuckin' – Ah shit there's a police goin' past[3].

SERGEANT PAUL EVANS: *(His name, and rank, on screen.)* We came on duty [on the Tuesday]. Bear in mind you've just had three nights of rioting in London. We'd not really had anything in Manchester, at all. On the Monday night *(Coughs.)* in Birmingham it'd all kicked off there. [On the Tuesday] we came in and there was information that there was going to be disorder during the day. We got kitted up in our armour and we deployed into the city, where we all waited. There was three vans in the city, just waited for them, for something to happen. People were like y'know waving at us and saying stay safe tonight lads and y'know and good luck and all that, so you're thinking well you're representing them aren't you, ultimately that's what we're there to do, to protect the decent people of Manchester

---

3. This recording is by Shiv Malik.

THE RIOTS

and when they're all patting you on the back and saying I'm off home now to watch it on the telly and *(Chuckles.)* you're stuck here but thanks anyway for what you're doing.

Probably about half three [in the afternoon] we started to hear that they were looting the Salford shopping precinct.

SIR HUGH ORDE: *(His name on screen alongside 'Head of the Association of Chief Police Officers'.)* Salford was one of the places where the intensity was probably the worst. And that was within the community. What was the motivator behind that? Part of it was they have some very bad gangs up there who are being dealt with.

SERGEANT PAUL EVANS: There was mass groups of a hundred plus youths who were all covered up in broad daylight. So we then had the drive, under blue lights from Manchester city centre to Salford precinct, which probably took us about fifteen minutes. There was probably twenty-four of us, about two hundred of them initially. We're thinking we can't possibly arrest two hundred people. We had people in the shops, and then we had to get this mob away from there. We went into the estate where we're getting bricked. You don't engage the crowd. [There were so] many of them against twenty-four of us. But they're not all highly trained, they're not all fit, strong, they're not all – we're aggressive as well, you've got to be.

They've not got any organisation. It's a mob mentality, and the mob mentality is [that] they will descend on one person and kill them if they can and that's no doubt what they would have done if they'd surrounded a cop, that's what they did to Keith Blakelock.

MAN 3: I didn't really see any sort of police activity, I just saw police runnin' around like dickheads doin' nothin' innit like. I see on the news in Birmingham an' that like people gettin' nicks an' that if I got hit by the police obviously I would – I would like try an' hit 'em back.

PAUL EVANS: It was horrendous, it was absolutely horrendous, because you've got children chucking bricks at you and

and bits of debris, and then on, if you like stood against the building lines and in the gardens you've got another two hundred people, holding babies in arms, can you believe.

Three words [to describe the rioters?][4] Errrm, hate is one. I know it's a strong word and I don't hate many people but I do feel hate towards them erm, greed. That's what I thought, when they were looting the shops, I just thought, none of you are starving, y'know like they are in third-world countries, no one's starving in this country. So yeah, greed was another thing, and *(Pause.)* cowards, yeah cowards probably was the last one.

INSPECTOR WINTER: [Three words?] That's a difficult one. I would say they were a pack, which I appreciate is more than three words, but um, yeah...out of control, and...scary.

SIR HUGH ORDE: Crikey. Opportunist would be one. Unthinking would be another. Three *(Long pause.)* and frustrated. But [those words] are not joined up.

PASTOR NIMS OBUNGE: *(Sighs.)* Hm. Frustrated. Opportunist. *(Pause.)* And Criminal.

JACOB SAKIL: *(His name on LED and 'Former Young Mayor of Lewisham'.)*[5]

[Three words?] The walking dead.

Interval.

---

4. Note that on these three words, and the ones that follow, there should be pauses between each word. This pause should be particularly long between the second and third word, save for Jacob Sakil, Michael Gove and Iain Duncan Smith who all issued theirs out smoothly.
5. Jacob has a tinge of an American accent.

Throughout this second half MOHAMED HAMMOUDAN sits and watches. He is separate from the rest of the cast. He is listening to these thinkers, these politicians, community activists and rioters, who are all on stage trying to explain what happened.

MARTIN SYLVESTER BROWN: [To describe the rioters] I would use the word, maybe united. Umm that is a word I would use. *(Pause.)* Dissatisfied. And I would say hurt.

DIANE ABBOTT: *(Her name on screen and 'MP for Hackney North and Stoke Newington'.)* I [see what happened in Tottenham] as a classic race riot just like the race riots of the Eighties. Starts with a black person dying at the hands of the police, Cherry Groce, Mrs Jarrett. The police showing insensitivity, obduracy. The community feelings starting to run high. Rumours, heightened rumours about how and why the black person died. A demonstration which tips into a riot. That's a classic race riot. It's the profile [of] the Brixton Riots, it was the profile right up to the Broadwater Farm [riots]. A classic race riot is superficially an anti-police riot, but is actually a confrontation between the black community and the state, the police being the armoured state which they are confronted with most immediately. But a classic race riot actually speaks to a wider and more extensive set of tensions between people and the state, whether it is what's happening in the education system, whether it's what's happening in relation to immigration. [It] speaks to the relationship between black people and the state generally. The police just provide the flashpoint.

CHIEF INSPECTOR GRAHAM DEAN: Er, did I think it was a race riot? D'you know, I'm not convinced it was. Er, I don't know what the catalyst is and because it didn't have the same feel as the Eighties. When I was at Brixton in 1981, when I was at Peckham in 1985, when I was at Broadwater Farm it was clear it was youth, and it was clear that it was predominantly black. I, I, I think a lot of the difference in feel, for me was Broadwater Farm was closed, it was contained, it was locking horns and no one moving. With the disorder we had in Tottenham High Road on the

6th August, there was always an escape route for people. [Going back to your question] I have the luxury of not having to think why – I have the luxury of it's happening here – Graham clear that street. Graham sort it.

LEROY LOGAN: *('Superintendent Leroy Logan' on screen.)* I'm a superintendent in the Met but I'm also part of the Black Police Association executive, so it's from that standpoint um I'll speak about my views.

It's the arena of the Black Police Association to be aware of any sort of critical incident that involves race. So we were monitoring it, um, we were detecting a certain amount of community tension, but nothing to suggest it would develop in the way that it did.

DIANE ABBOTT: Obviously with a race riot you always have criminality. The thing that struck me as slightly different was that because there was this riot on the streets of Tottenham, people saw it and people went up to Wood Green and people went to Tottenham Hale to loot, and what struck me was I switched on my television the following morning, the people were still there looting. People had been allowed to loot for five hours straight in Wood Green and Tottenham Hale. Now, I've said since 'Do you think people would be allowed to loot for five minutes in South Kensington?' No, but they were allowed to loot for five hours in Wood Green.

My view is had the police called in, I don't know, people from Thames Valley or whatever, the police could have closed down the looting and they could have arrested people, they could have stopped it, and I think you wouldn't have had the looting that followed. That's my view.

LEROY LOGAN: I don't think I'll comment on Diane's view cos I've no evidence to that effect. All I would say is um there seemed to be a holding back in terms of the officers seeing criminality, erm the smashing of the cars, the burning of the bus and then obviously that spreading to buildings and looting and so forth but I think the initial damage, the criminal damage to buildings, I think there was hanging back. And it may be just the historical baggage as it were. It may have been a factor for them to hold back, um, not to be seen to be too heavy handed in a very sensitive area.

STAFFORD SCOTT: A lot of people are saying that you can't compare what happened [in August] with what happened in the Eighties. What I really want people to understand is you absolutely can make comparisons, cos the lives of those young people hasn't changed. If you look at all the base line stats – the amount of stop and search that happens are the the the same.

LEROY LOGAN: As a youngster I was quite resentful of the police because of the way I'd been stopped and searched.

I was applying to join the organisation in '82, my father was badly beaten up by officers after a stop and search, and he was fifty-seven, he wasn't the stereotypical person who might be a troublemaker, he was just driving his lorry along and got stopped, they laid into him. He sued them eventually – but, at that time, I was not pleased that had happened to my father. And at that time I was applying to join that organisation, and that had a lot um it was either I continue my application, join the organisation or I become a very bitter person.

You know [today] you're eight times more likely to be stopped and searched if you're black than you're white, um more likely to be strip-searched, and detained for that fact. And of course there is the way in which it's handled, the lack of respect and dignity, we hear about, you know, inappropriate language being used, ugh excessive force.

JACOB SAKIL: *(His name on screen.)* I've been stopped and searched on many occasions. A lot of police officers believe they are the law [and can] do what the hell they wanna do. [They get] away with murder and the young people fester up that anger and they rebel. It's like a never ending circle. [One time] when the police um stopped me they was using cuss words. I understand they tryina speak the lingo but I can speak as intelligent as them. They arrested me, and they treated me as if I'd done something wrong already. And the guys sayin' 'Don't fuckin' play with me, don't fuckin' play with me, I know that you're der der der', I'm like 'What? What you talkin' about?' and at the time I was the Young Mayor [of Lewisham]. When they find out who I were, then they apologised and by them apologisin' they was like 'Would you like a drop home?' I said 'No I don't want anything to do with you guys.'

GREG POWELL: *(Name on screen and, beside it, 'Solicitor'.)* There is a legacy for the police at any one moment in time, of how they treat youth generally in the inner-city: the endless stopping and searching; the endless grabbing up and, um, exercise of power. The police would say that very positive, pro-active policing is necessary because of knife crime or gun crime.

STAFFORD SCOTT: If [stop and search is supposed to combat crime in the community], it's the most unsuccessful tactic ever developed. And [now the police] are no longer required to give receipts when they do stop [you]. So that means that they are freer to do what they're doing to these kids before. The issue about stop and search isn't just about the stop and search. The issue is that most arrests that come out of stop and search are what we call knock-on charges. They're not what the person was stopped for.

GREG POWELL: What it creates is a deep reservoir of ill-will and a huge antipathy every client that gets mishandled or mistreated by police, that's their family, that's their friends, um, who then adopt, to some degree, their story and their antipathy. And at any moment, if the social conditions are right, that antipathy can explode into the kind of confrontation, which we saw.

JOHN AZAH: *(His name on screen plus 'Director of Kingston Race and Equality Council'.)* When I talk to my son about being stopped what he says to me is 'Dad it's OK to show me respect once a week, once a month when I get stopped in my, my, my nice car. If three times, four times a week, six times a month I get stopped purely because of my ethnicity, it doesn't, er, it doesn't matter how much respect they show me, I get frustrated. I feel here we go again.' And, therefore, there's a disconnect between what police are saying that 'oh we do our stop and searches very well, we give young people a receipt for stopping them' and [what the youth] are saying [which is] 'hold on a minute I walk the streets like everybody [but] my lived experience is there is a possibility that eight times out of ten, eight times out of ten, I will be stopped because of my heritage and my ethnicity. In 2010, 2011, that wasn't going to be good enough.

PASTOR NIMS OBUNGE: I had a young person say y'know I've just been totally manhandled by police so this is my time to get back, I've heard that.

DIANE ABBOTT: I think with the rioting that cascaded over the next few days starting with the riot in Wood Green, there was that kind of hyper-materialism, that kind of me-tooism. Remember this is twenty-four hour news, you saw these pictures over and over again. People looting in Wood Green. People trying on shoes, people queuing up. You think yeah why not? But also, there was also a mix of [people] because remember as the looting cascaded on over days, by the time it reached Salford the looters were all white.

SIMON HUGHES: *(His name on screen along with 'MP for Bermondsey and Southwark and Deputy Leader of the Liberal Democrats in the House of Commons'.)* On the day the riots came south of the river, Monday the 8th, I was in my office in parliament when I got a phone call from the borough commander of our local police who was literally holed up in Peckham police station unable to get out because quote there were many rioters around the police station. His call to me was to ask if I could do a public call to people to get off the streets, to go home, for parents to find out where youngsters were and so on, because things were not under control. Even though there had been events in north London over a couple of days, the speed and the frequency and the method of what happened meant that effectively the police were on the back foot. And most of them retreated into the major police stations in Southwark, Walworth and Peckham. I learned later that they were told to do that because most Metropolitan police were not trained to deal with public order events. They weren't allowed to go out with batons and shields and headgear only the [trained] people were allowed out on the streets.

I went literally straight away to the studios which are in Millbank and I did the rounds of the studios, I did all the major news channels, [and then] went into where the action was happening. At about the time that the police were beginning to regroup and pull things under control. [When] we arrived in the Walworth Road, uh, a lot of the people who had been there had clearly retreated. So we followed in the wake, literally behind as it were, where the shops that had been broken into…

JUDGE: Stephen Carter. You are 26 years old. You saw bags containing shirts and shoes taken from a store and still in their wrapping, and decided to make off with them. They were worth about £500.

Umang Patel. You are 21 years of age. On Monday 8th August you stole from JD Sports. You were one of those responsible for an overall loss of £170,000 worth of stock. You personally took £220-odd worth of sports clothing.

SIMON HUGHES: Having talked to my colleagues who were there [the rioters were mixed] mainly uh, male, [but] it wasn't all youngsters. There were many over 18 – people in their twenties and thirties, [and] women. I think it's fair to say, given our part of south London, that it was a mix of the community. I actually think that many people would define themselves as mixed-heritage or mixed-race so it wasn't all black.

ANON JUDGE: Ade Alagago. You have pleaded guilty to one charge of handling stolen goods: five mobile phones, two sets of headphones, batteries, chargers and a USB cable valued together at more than £300 clearly looted goods.

You were stopped and arrested just after midnight on Tuesday morning leaving the scene of the civil disorder in Woolwich.

DIANE ABBOTT: The Hackney riot kicked off in broad daylight and [of] the young people that came on the streets, numbers of them swarmed from an estate called the Pembury. The point about the Pembury is that it has got endemic gangs and there had been a police raid on the gangs a few weeks earlier.

SADIE KING: *(Her name on screen.)* I live on Pembury Estate.

DIANE ABBOTT: The Pembury has almost always been a no-go area for the police.

SADIE KING: Nobody has the dream of living in a council flat, but the thing about, the great thing about living on Pembury is it's a really genuinely diverse and tight community. It's got different elements to it. There are people who will say 'It's not like the old days when we used to you know make each other cups of tea' but the bit that I live in anyway, my neighbours are great, you can give them the keys, it is quite an old-fashioned community and that's with, that's young people as well.

DIANE ABBOTT: So there was a confrontation on the streets of Hackney in broad daylight with these young people, and they kind of circled each other. But what happened was, it got dark and all the other people came out, but it was all in and around the Pembury. But that is not coincidence, because the Pembury has gangs and the gangs were at war with the police. But what the police said to me was that as the night wore on you had older people, grown-ups coming out and nicking this and nicking that. So it started off as a young persons' interaction, but older people were also involved.

SADIE KING: It was an outburst. One or two community shops got in the way. But most of it was you know JD Sports. And all the banks were smashed, all the banks along here were smashed, that's not – surely they didn't think they were gonna go in there and take gold bars. [The banks are] not part of the community, they're symbols of things people can't have and things that are making people angry.

DIANE ABBOTT: The funny thing was that it was all kind of co-ordinated and done with texts and instant messenger, and one thing that [was] flying around in Hackney on Monday afternoon was 'Don't touch the Empire, don't touch the Empire'. Because the Hackney Empire, even though it has been partially closed and has had its problems as a theatre venue, it has done years and years of programmes with young people – music programmes, theatre programmes, drama programmes – with young black people. So although they were outside of the Hackney Empire for many hours in the afternoon, because there was a JD Sports two doors up and a betting shop almost across the road they didn't touch the Empire. Which shows that if you can give these young people some sort of ownership and some sort of point of engagement with society, you will begin to find a solution.

SADIE KING: There was no damage to [the] Pembury estate whatsoever.

I went out on the Mon- on the Tuesday to do shopping and when I was coming back from Tescos here and going up Clarence Road, there was loads of people walking up there with brooms. I've never seen so many people, particularly white people walking up Clarence Road. Older black men hang out on the corner and drink cans of beer and stuff and I asked them what [the people with brooms] were doing and they said 'There's some kind of clean-up campaign'. That really kind of jolted me – I thought what you doing? The council have already cleaned up the cars and they – they've just – brand new brooms, they just started sweeping the street for no reason cos it's already been cleaned up. It felt like an invasion like people not from our community have come into our community to clean up. It was patronising.

The brooms was funny it was really funny seeing all these I dunno, yeah, kind of do-gooders coming up Clarence Road with their brand new brooms and I – I remember thinking 'Who's cleaning your house, you know? Maybe some illegal immigrants that you're getting to do it for two quid an hour'.

INTER-LAPPING JUDGES VOICES: Michael Gillespie-Doyle. You are only 18. You went into Manchester knowing that the disturbances were under way. When you saw that the store had been broken into by others, you took your chance with your accomplice and went in and took goods.

Mohima Khanom. You are 23 years of age. You went voluntarily to the scene of civil disorder. You say you followed the example of others. You helped yourself to almost £9,500 worth of stock from Carphone Warehouse. Your naked greed is breathtaking.

Mary Boyd. You are 31. You were in the city centre doing what you usually do there – that is go drinking with friends in the street. You saw lots of people running past, and when you came across an abandoned bag containing alcohol, cigarettes and a mobile phone.

CAMILA BATMANGHELIDJH: *(Her name on screen, plus 'Founder of Kids Company'.)*

I actually wrote three weeks before the riots to Downing Street saying that I felt things were going to blow up at street level because I could feel it and it was coming from the kids. They felt this sense of wanting to take revenge.

Central government was presenting large chunks of these inner city environments as spaces where lazy, benefit acquiring er population were letting the rest of the nation down. The minute you start describing the poor as the lazy you split off a large section of society by er humiliating them. The underclass was described as 'amoral'. And this is very important in terms of how people ended up behaving. If your membership to mainstream society doesn't produce a reward in your eyes, then why have it?

It felt like government was constantly saying
'You're benefit scroungers, we're gonna cut your er
accommodation situation', [the Education Maintenance
Allowance] got cut and so on [and this] in the context of
unemployment that was running at one million for young
people.

SADIE KING: The thing that I really object to is the way young
people are treated in Hackney generally by...the police...
They have very fast quick-fix policies that are quite brutal,
um the main one on Pembury being dispersal zones.
Dispersal zones have been going for about five years.
They put notices up they have them for particular fixed
periods and what it does is it gives the police extra powers
to stop and search if you're under sixteen, if you're out
after a certain hour which isn't very late, about nine o'clock
or something, they can ask you to go home, can escort
you home or take you to a place of safety. Sometimes
they decide to do it in the summer which is awful. If you
see the flats [on the Pembury] there um you know, they
are nice flats but they're tiny. If you've got a couple of
teenagers living with you how can you possibly keep them
in from nine o'clock on a summer's evening. And they do
not have back gardens there's no facilities. So the street
and [the] communal areas is their space. The kids are so
used to [dispersal zones] now they'll separate. They'll go,
'OK we're not allowed to stop if there's two of us so we'll
separate when we see you'. It creates [in] kids of like 10 this
kind of anti-state, you know, anti-police culture, and they
see themselves as labelled and they see the police as there
to interrupt them.

STAFFORD SCOTT: They talk about a feral underclass. I think
it's a mindset. It's a mindset that says that we are treated
unjustly, we are never gonna get respect, we're never
gonna get the dignity that we want, so let's go and just take
the things that we want. And there are people out there
who have their own anger and frustration at the police, and
at these institutions that completely fail to deal with them.
And the truth of the matter is it wasn't a race thing. We

saw when the Turkish community came out to protect their things, we saw when the Sikhs came out to protect their things – it was the haves against the have nots.

CAMILA BATMANGHELIDJH: [The disrespect is] insidious. It's drip drip drip and then I think [Mark Duggan's] death was the tipping point.

STAFFORD SCOTT: In a three-mile radius four people have died at the hands or whilst in the custody of police officers. None of those four people were ever found guilty of committing any crime. The nearest they got was Joy Gardner who was an overstayer and they wrapped thirty feet of masking tape around her face. Nobody ever got charged for that. Nobody was ever held to account for that. We're a community that doesn't expect justice.

MICHAEL GOVE: *(His name on screen plus 'MP for Surrey and Secretary of State for Education'.)* The first thing my wife said [was] that the riots were like one of those Rorschach blot tests in that everyone sees that – what they want to in them. So that um, um one person who's got a particular view of society, and who believes that the principle sort of um thing that's wrong with society is the unequal distribution of opportunities of wealth, will see the riots as a reaction against that. Someone else, who's a stern old-fashioned Victorian moralist who thinks that it was a mistake to get rid of the cane in schools will say see what happens now you've got rid of corporal punishment and so on. So they were in that sense um er an opportunity for everyone to rehearse positions that they already had.

I think the rioters were a vicious, lawless and immoral minority. By definition, if you're um, if you're prepared to destroy people's property, if you're prepared to engage in violence like that, that's by definition without wanting to sort of engage in exercising tautology, vicious and lawless.

STAFFORD SCOTT: [We saw] what's happening with those politicians who just took and took and took and took. And we saw that only a few of them got charged even though loads of them broke the rules and then broke the laws and of those who got charged, they get silly sentences and come out after a quarter of their sentence.

GREG POWELL: *(His name on screen plus 'Solicitor'.)* Some of our regular clients, if I can describe them in that way, got arrested. But also because we're in north-west London and the south London cells became full, they migrated a number of prisoners from south London to the local Wembley-Kilburn police stations. And one of my colleagues was a duty solicitor on that particular day and so we picked up a – a group of clients, who really belong in south London.

I anticipated straight away that it would not be normal, because I remember acting for people in the 1980s – in the riots then. Experience tells us that what happens almost by reflex, is that the criminal justice system reacts in a very punitive way to send out a very clear message that you shouldn't be engaged in rioting because you get locked up.

STAFFORD SCOTT: What people need to understand is that the behaviours that we saw out there are the same behaviours or the same kind of mindset that helped to create some of those British suicide bombers. It's borne out of that same frustration, that same sense of being dispossessed and marginalised – and that was what makes them feel compelled to do something about it. Those kids were, to all intents and purposes, they were suicide bombers. And in our community they have been imploding as opposed to exploding. And on that Saturday, they exploded. So telling these kids stop what you're doing or we're gonna give you longer, more draconian sentences is like saying to someone strapped with a bomb, stop or I'll shoot – it doesn't mean anything. It reinforces their belief, it reinforces their cynicism.

LEROY LOGAN: I'm really concerned about the disproportionality of the convictions but unfortunately the Court of Public Opinion was so devastatingly bad. People were angry. Areas right across London and the UK or England anyway, were being torched.

I think the Justice System has to review what has taken place. I was being interviewed by some French TV [and when] they asked, 'Why have you gone so excessively long on the punishment?' they were actually um [citing] Ed Milliband's [hard line]. They couldn't believe he's seen as a socialist, left-winger and he's falling in line with the right wing.

I think you have to judge every case on its merits. Um, you know as a – as a superintendent authorising further detention for someone, I look at that individual case, I look at papers, I look at what investigation is carried out and I judge according to that. If it's a group of people, I'm still judging each one individually I don't judge it collectively.

HH JUDGE ROBERT ATHERTON: *(His name on screen followed by 'Sentencing remarks in Manchester on 18th August 2011'.)* David Swarbrick. You pleaded guilty at the first available opportunity to an offence of burglary of Quality Save, a shop on Oldham Street. You were arrested at 9.40 p.m. and were found to have stolen a number of items of cosmetics. The value was low. You had seen the incidents in the city and took advantage of the situation. You are almost 26 years of age.

DAVID SWARBRICK: *(His name on screen. In prison, he must be visibly set apart from the rest.)* Thursday 6th October 2011. HMP Manchester.

Dear [Tricycle Theatre],

My name is David Swarbrick, I am 26 years old. I was caught up in the Manchester riots, on my way through the city centre.

I ended up blocked in by police barricades + everywhere I looked or turned there was pure pandemonium + chaos. I witnessed a whole, broad range of members of society kettled in, corralled together – old people with shopping, students, all ethicities [sic], man, woman, kids, some with ski mask, some just with drinks, from pubs. While locked in Piccadilly Gardens, I saw dozens of shops of varying size and expense just open, doors gone, windows smashed, shutters peeled off fronts, like giant sardine cans. I entered a branch of a well-known brand. Subsequently, I was caught red-handed inside + apprehended, charged as entering as a trespasser + stealing 'things'.

JUDGE ATHERTON: I have read the letter which you have sent me and the Pre-Sentence Report. Your attitude towards your offending is to feel regret for the embarrassment which you have caused your family and the citizens of Manchester, yet on the other hand have described your general offending as being 'an occupational hazard', your comment to the police was that 'It's no big deal, it's only a bit of moisturizer'.

DAVID SWARBRICK: I was told under normal circumstances that I would have expected to receive a six-month sentence for a commercial burglary of a value £2,000 or less. At Crown, I was with eight other defendants in the dock. We were each sentenced one by one.

JUDGE ATHERTON: In my judgment the appropriate sentence after a trial would have been thirty months imprisonment. I reduce it by one third to twenty months and the suspended sentence will take effect consecutively making twenty-four months in all.

DAVID SWARBRICK: Twenty-four month = two years.

DIANE ABBOTT: I know that the sentences are very controversial, but I would think that the public would expect the sentences to be exemplary. I generally think it is not for politicians to second guess the sentencing by the judiciary in the context of an urban riot [I would expect] the Courts to seek to impose exemplary sentences. I think the public would expect them and excesses are dealt with under the Appeal system. That's my view, but I know that is not the view of many people on the Left.

PASTOR NIMS OBUNGE: [When people say that the British public demanded punitive sentences], I'd like to know when they spoke to the British public. Are we talking about journalists, the *Daily Mail*, or some of the other newspapers, say [is] the word of the British public. Y'know what is, who is, the British public? The media has had no social conscience or moral conscience because there is a a commercial responsibility. And so, the definition of the British public always leaves me wondering who defines the view of the public. I, I think that maybe we should have some community based punishments, rather than incarceration, um, in some cases.

JUDGE ANDREW GILBART QC: *(Name on screen plus 'The Honorary Recorder of Manchester on the 16th August 2011 at Manchester Crown Court'.)* David Beswick. You are 31 years old and in work. You took your car into Salford to go and watch the disturbances at something like 7.00 p.m. You were still there at 00.40 a.m. You knew that several stores had been attacked and looted. In your car was found a 37-inch television taken from one of the stores.

OWEN JONES: *(His name on screen.)* Many of the MPs who, er, stood up to demand the, um, demand tough action themselves three years ago had pillaged public finances to, um, to buy the same sorts of widescreen TVs that were being carted out of shops by looters, in an, admittedly, more disorderly fashion. Gerald Kaufman, an MP, stood up and demanded action was taken. And he claimed for £8,500 for buying himself a television set.

JUDGE GILBART: You told the police that you were looking after [the television] for another for payment of £20. In other words you were the means by which that stolen TV would be taken out of there. I regard it as a cynical offence by someone who knew exactly what he was doing.

You do not have a bad criminal record, and no previous offences for dishonesty. True it is that you have recently lost your mother. [But] you stood and watched crime going on for some hours, and then played your part. There must be a custodial sentence. As you admitted your guilt at the first opportunity, the sentence is one of eighteen months imprisonment.

CHELSEA IVES: *(Her name on screen plus 'HMP/YOI Holloway'.)* 10th October 2011

Hi my name is Chelsea Ives and I have recently just turned 18. I'm the girl that got shopped by her mum due to the riots. I read your article in the prison newspaper so I thought I'd share my veiws [sic] on the things that have involved me for your theatre and because the whole country knows who I am. I think it's terrible what the news have said about me, they have made it look like I'm a disruptive low-life teenager from a council estate. The public seem to automatically place me in an unnamed catorgory [sic] for thick, low-lifed individuals which is not me at all. I havn't [sic] even had the chance to speak for myself. It just feels like I shouldn't even have legal advice, because it seems the Judge has already made up his mind about my sentence due to the help and support of the media. The public just need to know I'm only accountable for my actions and not everyone else's and that I am sorry. Chelsea Ives.

HARRY FLETCHER: *(His name on screen plus 'Assistant General Secretary of NAPO'.)* I received phone calls from people during the period, I suppose we're talking 14th August onwards when they started court sitting at night and at weekends, that there were insufficient staff to provide information for the courts about the background and motivation of individual offenders.

My view has always been that the court sentence each individual based on the individual circumstances of that case. And they clearly couldn't have had sufficient information to determine whether the motivation was socio-economic, whether it was purely opportunistic and greed. The courts were also under tremendous political pressure to deliver swift justice.

MICHAEL GOVE: I can't know quite what the motivations were of all the people who became involved. It's undeniably the case that er there is a um somewhere in the human soul there's um a – the capacity for enjoyment in violence and destruction, wantonness. It's undeniably the case that there are people who, um if they have the opportunity to um engage in consequence-free violence and destruction will do so. So if – if you feel that the bonds of restraint aren't there, you'll do so. Some people will do so believing that they're animated by a – a higher cause, a higher purpose, but in fact they're just slipping from the rational into the emotional.

[My three words to describe the rioters?] Tragic lost souls.

MAN 3: Everyone was there man like it was black people, white people, everyone – everyone was there man, there was no, there was no – you can't blame anyone, everyone was there innit like. If something there for free you take it innit. I dunno why people try to lie about it man. If somethin' there for free you take it. Everyone was there man, dunno why – everyone was there man – everyone took part in it.

GREG POWELL: I think [the courts and the government] don't necessarily think through to cost benefit. If you want to look at it in purely managerial terms it would probably be better at the lower end of criminality to give people suspended sentences in order to deter them from future offending. And couple that to curfews, if you want to keep them in at night. And/or community payback, if you want them to do something on behalf of the community. A much more expensive solution is to give people immediate, fairly lengthy custody.

There are very strict limits to how much their individual identities matter. And that in its own way is a bit of a shock because you're being told, really, that you don't matter as a person. You're going to get a sentence which is much greater for your particular criminal act, than you would have got if you'd done it individually. And you're also being told that your personal identity is of no account. So that's liable to make you a bit bitter.

MAN 1: Like I said I knew I could make myself a good few hundred pound. I been applyin' for jobs the past year an' I ent got nothin'. An' it's not come, it's not come to the point where like I've got rent to pay or whatever but my Mum is not on no big money paying job, she can only give me – she can only buy me a certain amount things. An' my Dad's not here to help. It's just me an' my Mum by ourselves an' there's only so much she can give me so everythin' else I've gotta go out an' get myself. So if I know I can make myself extra money then why not?

HARRY FLETCHER: I do think that there is evidence that some people who had not been in trouble before, uh, got carried away. But I remember one kid shouting at a reporter 'We're getting our own back'. And I think that was related to the fact that a lot of the people who were rioting came from relatively deprived backgrounds where obtaining a 32-inch plasma screen or trainers that cost a hundred and fifty quid weren't possible unless they stole them. Yet the idols that they were supposed to look up to like footballers on a hundred thousand pounds a week and popstars had all these things. That's why I feel the courts had to have the information about individuals, because the motivations are very, very complex and different. Certainly some kids purely exploited the situation to get things for nothing, but others, er, were quite, er, definitely from deprived backgrounds, were excluded from mainstream society and saw it as a way of getting, to get goods they couldn't get in any other way.

IAIN DUNCAN SMITH: *(His name on screen plus 'MP for Chingford and Wood Green and Secretary of State for Work and Pensions'.)* The police do have a role to play and the criminal justice system has a role to play. They have to leave a very strong signal that first and foremost the criminal justice system will be there should [you] make that conscious decision to transgress it. [But] sentencing like that only ever has a short term effect. Er, it's like applying electrodes to somebody for a short period of time. It causes you immediately to recognize something has happened for the short period of time you will remember that that was painful [it] works at the moment of contact to get back control and to send a very swift signal that actually the justice system will work and you will I'm afraid pay a penalty for what you chose to do. [But this] will work only so far as there's something else happening behind it.

MAN 1: The way I see it – London in particular, north-east and south London, are majority workin'-class people. Middle-class and upper-class people will not be materialistic because they've got money, they work decent jobs, or they was born into a wealthy family whatever.

When I was young, having a pair of trainers in school was the 'in thing', or a nice jacket, cos like I said, we're all from – we're in a working-class area so if you turn around in your I dunno hundred pound trainers an' say 'Oh look at these what I got yesterday' people gonna think 'Ra this guy's top guy in the school cos he got the best trainers'. So that can in a way put you in a different – different calibre or class whatever in your school area. Think yeah that's the guy with the expensive trainers, then you got this guy over here with some no-name trainers from Shoe Zone or somethin' so yeah, havin' a good pair of trainers around here is a way to bein' different calibre compared to everyone else.

If I had money to myself put away in a bank or wherever from workin', then why do I need to go out risk myself gettin' nicked for lootin'? If I'm earnin' from workin' I don't need to go out an' do it again. If I had a job I wouldn't have wanted to do nothin' cos I'm not gonna spoil my chances for the future cos I know that if I get arrested an' I get, an' I get a criminal record, me tryina find a job again is gonna be even harder than it is now. So that was exactly why – why I went an' done it.

JOHN MCDONNELL: *(His name plus 'MP for Hayes and Harlington' on screen.)* Society has created a society of looters at every level: MPs fiddling expenses, bankers with their bonuses, corporations not paying their taxes, and all this was, was kids with the same moral values that have been inculcated in society motivated by the same level of consumerism, um coming out and seizing their opportunity. [And how] are those moral values transmitted to the kids? By example. I think [they're] a-absolutely indoctrinated with consumerist values. Under the Welfare State at least there was some feeling of solidarity and sharing and, yes, to use that expr- phrase 'being all in this together' but that's gone now.

IAIN DUNCAN SMITH: It is difficult to get jobs but there's no magic wand to say 'I'll tell you what let's make jobs easier to get and let's have more jobs'. The fact that lots of people have to commute longer distances in these cities for the very simple reason which is there are no jobs near them that they can do, they have to go somewhere else. So one of the things about restoring balance in these um areas, is that you also restore the likelihood that jobs will return to those areas that are viable and doable by local people.

OWEN JONES: In places like Tottenham today there's thiry-four unemployed people for every vacancy. Erm, and what's on offer often is low-paid work in the service sector – supermarkets, for example. Um, and that's not work people necessarily aspire to. People don't feel that same sense of pride working in a supermarket they might have felt in the work which used to exist. They call it 'The Hourglass Economy', where middle-income, skilled jobs, not just in manufacturing but in a whole range of different industries, all disappeared, um, in the 1980s at a very dramatic speed. And low-paid, service-sector jobs expanded at the bottom as well as professional jobs at the top, which most working-class kids have no access to.

There used to be a structure [for working-class youth]. You could leave school at 16 and go into an apprenticeship, which was respectably paid and [it] was a gateway to a life where you could be sustained by work. And that disappeared [and it] left a vacuum. More broadly what happened was [an] explosion in inequality. I mean,

Britain was one of the most equal Western societies in 1979; it's one of the least equal now. There are people in communities, like Hackney one of the poorest boroughs in the country, in which the poorest live alongside the richest. It's almost like being taunted: these are lives you will never have.

SIMON HUGHES: Don't give up hope that actually paradoxically, we might end up at the end of this government with a smaller gap between the rich and the poor than we did at the end of the last government.

[My three words for the rioters?] Impulsive. Reckless. This is not a word it's a phrase, there probably is a word but, um, uh, responding to the excitement of the opportunity.

IAIN DUNCAN SMITH: [My words?] Dysfunctional, criminal and lost.

OWEN JONES: One in five young people [are] out of work, um, with a sense that there's no future to put at risk. And if you only have a tiny fraction of young people who feel they have nothing to risk responding in this way – that's enough to bring chaos and violence to the streets of our cities.

JOHN MCDONNELL: I think the riots were an inchoate response to people's anger in society. There's a feeling of anxiety. All. All ages. Young people [are] just as much victims as the older ones. [And] where do those kids go when they come home? Well they go on the street. And who are the other people on the street? Other kids. So do they form gangs? Yeah maybe, but informal associations because they're out there. Where do you go when you've seven, nine of you in a two-bedroom property?

STAFFORD SCOTT: They are young people that live on the margins of society, and are now being told that they have to pay for the fat cat bankers who are still paying themselves crazy bonuses here is is an absolute awareness [of this amongst them.] They're not going to sit down and and watch *Channel 4 News* and get into all the detail for that, but they have an awareness – there is an absolute awareness that they lost their EMA.

JOHN MCDONNELL: The the EMA cuts are significant. There's a feeling of the ladder's kicked from underneath [young people]. One of our campaigns was to get people to aspire to go to university, and this just undermines that whole campaign. The second thing, the EMA was critical for them staying on in some form having that undermined is a real kick in the teeth.

[As for our youth services and youth facilities,] gone.

In the last Tory government, Tory councils, they cut the park wardens and they cut the youth services at the same time and they closed the youth centres so the kids streamed into the parks, there was no control erm lots of vandalism, we even had a murder in one of our parks. We rebuilt that, reopened the youth centres, and had some youth workers back on the streets again. [And now] they've even cut the park wardens so we're back to square one where areas have become no-go zones.

DIANE ABBOTT: [If I was the government] I would make youth provision statutory; the point is that youth provision is non-statutory, so whenever the government has to make cuts, that is the first thing that goes.

IAIN DUNCAN SMITH: Do you think that certain things that are important should be ring-fenced and sent down to councils without any opportunity for them to change it? There's no magic wand that says this is the right way or the other way, I mean the last government did a lot of ring-fencing of stuff and that leads to quite a lot of inefficiency. My sense about this is much more important is to get councils to recognise the importance and the seamlessness of certain things that have to happen, so things like youth services that helping kids are important because they help councils and they help the area in due course and that benefits the council.

LEROY LOGAN: We always have that summer madness in August, we always have that peak where young people invariably get restless, they get bored, you know and you've gotta give them something to do. And unfortunately through the recession and the cuts one of the biggest victims of that is the youth services. I know that a lot of boroughs have cut intensive supervision for those who are vulnerable, or at risk or even dangerous, and if you don't have those resources keeping those people engaged in activities and you know watched it, just develops this sort of powder keg and it just takes one spark and it explodes, you've seen that.

MICHAEL GOVE: I haven't seen anyone arh, um, erm, er produce evidence to suggest that um the lack of um local authority or other youth services has played a significant role here. I think it's easy to say the answer is more state spending on x or y, the question is why aren't there other er why aren't young people joining or involved in other organizations that can give um er purpose and enjoyment to their lives. In other words, whether it's the um scouts or the cadet force or other activities, one of the questions that we need to ask is to what extent are there cultural or other barriers that prevent people from becoming involved in other activities.

GREG POWELL: The Labour Party remains the single largest party which would, um, pretend, at least, towards some wider social engagement amongst many of its individual members. But I don't see it at a local level successfully reaching out and engaging and drawing people in. I mean, what struck me about the massacre in Norway, was that it seemed to me unthinkable – that comparable numbers of young Labour Party supporters [would] gather in a social setting to discuss the future of politics. There seemed to be something happening in Norway, amongst Norwegian youth, which does not have a parallel here. You wouldn't find a hall full of people to massacre who were future potential leaders of Labour...because they don't, I think, exist.

I don't think [the riots] was an 'accident' [waiting to happen]. Um, is it a, is it something which we can expect to happen again? I think 'yes'.

IAIN DUNCAN SMITH: [The inner city] came knocking.

I don't [blame] the last government particularly, I blame a whole series of governments who have failed to recognise that what was going on underneath our nose was the creation of a subculture and that what we were trying to do without realising, perhaps even intellectualising it, but what we were doing was ringfencing it saying as long as that doesn't break out anywhere else then we're sort of OK.

That's why I think the um, um violence and sort of criminality that took place on those few nights that exploded onto the streets is, whilst bad and desperate and terrible, is also in a strange way quite good. Er because, and I don't mean that glibly I simply mean because it is a strong reminder er that we er have to get this right and we have had a wakeup call to tell us you know we've got to a point now where this is gonna happen again unless we start to deal with it.

SADIE KING: [Do I think anything good came from the riots?] Yeah I think it's raised the issues. It's, it's opened up… the conversation about politics and it's opened up the conversation for once about the police um locally. I think that lots of people who wouldn't have said anything about the police are starting to say these young people feel intimidated, they are being um harassed, they feel like they're labelled. It's [as] if living here you're labelled as a gang member, even if you're a child.

Lost, angry…um… *(Pause.)* confused would be [my three words to describe the rioters].

OWEN JONES: [Mine would be] Faceless. Dehumanised. Unexplained.

If you want to make sure [the riots] never happen again then we need to understand them.

HARRY FLETCHER: [If I was the government, knowing what I know, fearing what I do, what would I do?] It would be, kind of not wanting to sound too pompous, it would be to adopt a Keynesian model, instead of cutting everything to pieces, you basically invest in public works, you create employment for people.

STAFFORD SCOTT: If I was in government I would recognise that we have a lot to learn, and the first thing we needed to learn is we've got a lot to learn. I would go around and I would identify authentic voices of those communities, because part of the problem is that government listens to who it chooses to listen to.

KARYN MCCLUSKEY: *(Her name on screen plus 'Co-director of the Scottish Violence Reduction Police Unit'.)* What happened in the riots was absolutely criminal, but I tell you what would be more criminal, if we missed this opportunity to really change, to set a really brave path, so that other countries are coming back to us in ten years' time and saying look what England and Wales did in response to this, look how they've changed.

It was fatal, fatal to take away the ring-fencing [around Sure Start]. We literally spend a huge amount of money on public services and a whole range of other things, in the UK. We need to need t-t-to talk about where actually we should invest to get the better return on our money. [A Nobel Prize-winning economist] said, for every pound you spend [in the] early years, between nought and three, you will have to spend fifty or sixty pounds at the age of sixteen to get the same effect. Makes perfect sense to me.

[In the 1970s] Denmark realized that they were falling off the cliffs and [they] fundamentally changed the way they did childcare. They developed what they called pedagogues who go into families and support children under the age of seven. Their outcomes are spectacular, y'know, and they support every family. Wouldn't it be a great strapline for the UK if the UK was the best place in the world to bring up your kids?

STAFFORD SCOTT: I don't think anything good ever comes out of riots. Ever. I think in some situations we had public inquiries and something good came out of those public inquiries. The only time we make any stride with race relations is on the back of an inquiry. Every inquiry always comes back saying yeah what they said is true, always does so it's the, the only thing that we find helpful.

[My three words for the rioters?] Frustrated, angry, and British.

The reason I say [British is because], this was a really British thing. In the Eighties [riots] there was lots of Caribbean involvement, lots of Jamaican involvement. [For these recent riots] the Turkish kids [who] were out there either came here really young, or were born here. The black kids who were out there – the majority were actually born here. [These kids were] giving voice to their disaffection and dissatisfaction with life in this country. [Their] riots weren't imported, they were bred here. It was a quintessentially English riot.

MOHAMED HAMMOUDAN is alone on the stage which is dark save for a spot on him. A reprise of some the riot noises but much softer, fading into nothingness.

MOHAMED HAMMOUDAN: The thing that really kind of got to me when I got back to to, to the fire [was] all these people taking photographs. My house has been burnt down and [they're treating it as a] a marker in his – in history. Was almost as if they just *need* to be there. They needed to catch the moment.

It's er – it's unbearable to think that you live relatively speaking, in a really affluent country where you've got y'know a huge amount of resources in public services shrinking but still y'know, relatively speaking to other countries huge – and the system just broke down. The system failed us, yeah? I'm all for people protesting, I'm all for people giving their views across, and holding people to t-to to account. But I just feel like y'know, the whole emergency services were just caught on the back foot, y'know. It's just like they had, they had no plan.

I feel, I feel empty yeah. *(Laugh.)* You have to start a new chapter without having erm the the seeds there from the past. You, you can't show people things any more. I can't show 'em photographs. I can't say to 'em 'Well y'know when I was twenty-two this this is what happened.'

I can remember sitting with my grandmother on the end, end of her bed and she was just covered with m-m-memorabilia. All that kind of stuff is just gone.

Erm. So – So – you almost. Almost it's like y' have to recreate y-y-y-your own history.

[My three words for the rioters?] Just angry people.

Spot out. The stage in darkness.

WWW.OBERONBOOKS.COM

Follow us on www.twitter.com/@oberonbooks
& www.facebook.com/OberonBooksLondon